Developments in Data Extraction, Management, and Analysis

Nhung Do
La Trobe University, Australia

Wenny Rahayu
La Trobe University, Australia

Torab Torabi
La Trobe University, Australia

Information Science
REFERENCE

Managing Director:	Lindsay Johnston
Editorial Director:	Joel Gamon
Book Production Manager:	Jennifer Romanchak
Publishing Systems Analyst:	Adrienne Freeland
Development Editor:	Heather Probst
Assistant Acquisitions Editor:	Kayla Wolfe
Typesetter:	Travis Gundrum
Cover Design:	Nick Newcomer

Published in the United States of America by
Information Science Reference (an imprint of IGI Global)
701 E. Chocolate Avenue
Hershey PA 17033
Tel: 717-533-8845
Fax: 717-533-8661
E-mail: cust@igi-global.com
Web site: http://www.igi-global.com

Library of Congress Cataloging-in-Publication Data

Developments in data extraction, management, and analysis / Nhung Do, J. Wenny Rahayu, and Torab Torabi, editors.
   p. cm.
 Includes bibliographical references and index.
 Summary: "This book is an essential collection of research on the area of data mining and analytics, presenting the most recent perspectives on data mining subjects and current issues"--Provided by publisher.
 ISBN 978-1-4666-2148-0 (hardcover) -- ISBN 978-1-4666-2149-7 (ebook) -- ISBN 978-1-4666-2150-3 (print & perpetual access) 1. Data mining. 2. Web usage mining. 3. Internet searching--Statistical services. I. Do, Nhung. II. Rahayu, Johanna Wenny. III. Torabi, Torab.
 QA76.9.D343D48 2012
 006.3'12--dc23
                                  2012019566

British Cataloguing in Publication Data
A Cataloguing in Publication record for this book is available from the British Library.

The views expressed in this book are those of the authors, but not necessarily of the publisher.

Table of Contents

    A. Raffaetà, Università Ca' Foscari Venezia, Italy
    L. Leonardi, Università Ca' Foscari Venezia, Italy
    G. Marketos, University of Piraeus, Greece
    G. Andrienko, Fraunhofer Institute for Intelligent Analysis and Information Systems, Germany
    N. Andrienko, Fraunhofer Institute for Intelligent Analysis and Information Systems, Germany
    E. Frentzos, University of Piraeus, Greece
    N. Giatrakos, University of Piraeus, Greece
    S. Orlando, Università Ca' Foscari Venezia, Italy
    N. Pelekis, University of Piraeus, Greece
    A. Roncato, Università Ca' Foscari Venezia, Italy
    C. Silvestri, Università Ca' Foscari Venezia, Italy

    Roberto Trasarti, ISTI-CNR, Italy
    Fosca Giannotti, ISTI-CNR Italy, and Northeastern University, USA
    Mirco Nanni, ISTI-CNR, Italy
    Dino Pedreschi, University of Pisa, Italy, & Northeastern University, USA
    Chiara Renso, ISTI-CNR, Italy

    Can Yildizli, Sabanci University, Turkey
    Thomas Brochmann Pedersen, Sabanci University, Turkey
    Yucel Saygin, Sabanci University, Turkey
    Erkay Savas, Sabanci University, Turkey
    Albert Levi, Sabanci University, Turkey

Detailed Table of Contents

  A. Raffaetà, Università Ca' Foscari Venezia, Italy

  L. Leonardi, Università Ca' Foscari Venezia, Italy

  G. Marketos, University of Piraeus, Greece

  G. Andrienko, Fraunhofer Institute for Intelligent Analysis and Information Systems, Germany

  N. Andrienko, Fraunhofer Institute for Intelligent Analysis and Information Systems, Germany

  E. Frentzos, University of Piraeus, Greece

  N. Giatrakos, University of Piraeus, Greece

  S. Orlando, Università Ca' Foscari Venezia, Italy

  N. Pelekis, University of Piraeus, Greece

  A. Roncato, Università Ca' Foscari Venezia, Italy

  C. Silvestri, Università Ca' Foscari Venezia, Italy

Technological advances in sensing technologies and wireless telecommunication devices enable research fields related to the management of trajectory data. The challenge after storing the data is the implementation of appropriate analytics for extracting useful knowledge. However, traditional data warehousing systems and techniques were not designed for analyzing trajectory data. In this paper, the authors demonstrate a framework that transforms the traditional data cube model into a trajectory warehouse. As a proof-of-concept, the authors implement T-Warehouse, a system that incorporates all the required steps for Visual Trajectory Data Warehousing, from trajectory reconstruction and ETL processing to Visual OLAP analysis on mobility data.

Roberto Trasarti, ISTI-CNR, Italy

Fosca Giannotti, ISTI-CNR Italy, and Northeastern University, USA

Mirco Nanni, ISTI-CNR, Italy

Dino Pedreschi, University of Pisa, Italy, & Northeastern University, USA

Chiara Renso, ISTI-CNR, Italy

The technologies of mobile communications and ubiquitous computing pervade society. Wireless networks sense the movement of people and vehicles, generating large volumes of mobility data, such as mobile phone call records and GPS tracks. This data can produce useful knowledge, supporting sustainable mobility and intelligent transportation systems, provided that a suitable knowledge discovery process is enacted for mining this mobility data. In this paper, the authors examine a formal framework, and the associated implementation, for a data mining query language for mobility data, created as a result of a European-wide research project called GeoPKDD (Geographic Privacy-Aware Knowledge Discovery and Delivery). The authors discuss how the system provides comprehensive support for the Mobility Knowledge Discovery process and illustrate its analytical power in unveiling the complexity of urban mobility in a large metropolitan area, based on a massive real life GPS dataset.

Can Yildizli, Sabanci University, Turkey

Thomas Brochmann Pedersen, Sabanci University, Turkey

Yucel Saygin, Sabanci University, Turkey

Erkay Savas, Sabanci University, Turkey

Albert Levi, Sabanci University, Turkey

Recent concerns about privacy issues have motivated data mining researchers to develop methods for performing data mining while preserving the privacy of individuals. One approach to develop privacy preserving data mining algorithms is secure multiparty computation, which allows for privacy preserving data mining algorithms that do not trade accuracy for privacy. However, earlier methods suffer from very high communication and computational costs, making them infeasible to use in any real world scenario. Moreover, these algorithms have strict assumptions on the involved parties, assuming involved parties will not collude with each other. In this paper, the authors propose a new secure multiparty computation based k-means clustering algorithm that is both secure and efficient enough to be used in a real world scenario. Experiments based on realistic scenarios reveal that this protocol has lower communication costs and significantly lower computational costs.

Chapter 4

Recommending database queries is an emerging and promising field of research and is of particular interest in the domain of OLAP systems, where the user is left with the tedious process of navigating large datacubes. In this paper, the authors present a framework for a recommender system for OLAP users that leverages former users' investigations to enhance discovery-driven analysis. This framework recommends the discoveries detected in former sessions that investigated the same unexpected data as the current session. This task is accomplished by (1) analysing the query log to discover pairs of cells at various levels of detail for which the measure values differ significantly, and (2) analysing a current query to detect if a particular pair of cells for which the measure values differ significantly can be related to what is discovered in the log. This framework is implemented in a system that uses the open source Mondrian server and recommends MDX queries. Preliminary experiments were conducted to assess the quality of the recommendations in terms of precision and recall, as well as the efficiency of their on-line computation.

Chapter 5

Testing is an essential part of the design life-cycle of a software product. Although most phases of data warehouse design have received considerable attention in the literature, not much research has been conducted concerning data warehouse testing. In this paper, the authors introduce a number of data mart-specific testing activities, classify them in terms of what is tested and how it is tested, and show how they can be framed within a reference design method to devise a comprehensive and scalable approach. Finally, the authors discuss some practical evidences emerging from a real case study.

In this paper, the authors present an empirical evaluation of similarity coefficients for binary valued data. Similarity coefficients provide a means to measure the similarity or distance between two binary valued objects in a dataset such that the attributes qualifying each object have a 0-1 value. This is useful in several domains, such as similarity of feature vectors in sensor networks, document search, router network mining, and web mining. The authors survey 35 similarity coefficients used in various domains and present conclusions about the efficacy of the similarity computed in (1) labeled data to quantify the accuracy of the similarity coefficients, (2) varying density of the data to evaluate the effect of sparsity of the values, and (3) varying number of attributes to see the effect of high dimensionality in the data on the similarity computed.

Negin Daneshpour, Amirkabir University of Technology, Iran

Ahmad Abdollahzadeh Barfourosh, Amirkabir University of Technology, Iran

On-Line Analytical Processing (OLAP) systems based on data warehouses are the main systems for managerial decision making and must have a quick response time. Several algorithms have been presented to select the proper set of data and elicit suitable structured environments to handle the queries submitted to OLAP systems, which are called view selection algorithms to materialize. As users' requirements may change during run time, materialization must be viewed dynamically. In this work, the authors propose and operate a dynamic view management system to select and materialize views with new and improved architecture, which predicts incoming queries through association rule mining and three probabilistic reasoning approaches: Conditional probability, Bayes' rule, and Naïve Bayes' rule. The proposed system is compared with DynaMat system and Hybrid system through two standard measures. Experimental results show that the proposed dynamic view selection system improves these measures. This system outperforms DynaMat and Hybrid for each type of query and each sequence of incoming queries.

M. Sulaiman Khan, University of Liverpool, UK

Maybin Muyeba, Manchester Metropolitan University, UK

Frans Coenen, University of Liverpool, UK

David Reid, Liverpool Hope University, UK

Hissam Tawfik, Liverpool Hope University, UK

In this paper, a composite fuzzy association rule mining mechanism (CFARM), directed at identifying patterns in datasets comprised of composite attributes, is described. Composite attributes are defined as attributes that can take simultaneously two or more values that subscribe to a common schema. The objective is to generate fuzzy association rules using "properties" associated with these composite attributes. The exemplar application is the analysis of the nutrients contained in items found in grocery data sets. The paper commences with a review of the back ground and related work, and a formal definition of the CFARM concepts. The CFARM algorithm is then fully described and evaluated using both real and synthetic data sets.

Yun Sing Koh, The University of Auckland, New Zealand

Russel Pears, Auckland University of Technology, New Zealand

Gillian Dobbie, The University of Auckland, New Zealand

Association rule mining discovers relationships among items in a transactional database. Most approaches assume that all items within a dataset have a uniform distribution with respect to support. However, this is not always the case, and weighted association rule mining (WARM) was introduced to provide importance to individual items. Previous approaches to the weighted association rule mining problem require users to assign weights to items. In certain cases, it is difficult to provide weights to all items within a dataset. In this paper, the authors propose a method that is based on a novel Valency model that automatically infers item weights based on interactions between items. The authors experiment shows that the weighting scheme results in rules that better capture the natural variation that occurs in a dataset when compared with a miner that does not employ a weighting scheme. The authors applied the model in a real world application to mine text from a given collection of documents. The use of item weighting enabled the authors to attach more importance to terms that are distinctive. The results demonstrate that keyword discrimination via item weighting leads to informative rules.

Baoqing Jiang, Henan University, China
Xiaohua Hu, Henan University China, & Drexel Univeristy, USA
Qing Wei, Henan University of Economics and Law, China
Jingjing Song, Qingyuan Polytechnic, China
Chong Han, Henan University, China
Meng Liang, Henan University, China

This paper examines the problem of weak ratio rules between nonnegative real-valued data in a transactional database. The weak ratio rule is a weaker form than Flip Korn's ratio rule. After analyzing the mathematical model of weak ratio rules problem, the authors conclude that it is a generalization of Boolean association rules problem and every weak ratio rule is supported by a Boolean association rule. Following the properties of weak ratio rules, the authors propose an algorithm for mining an important subset of weak ratio rules and construct a weak ratio rule uncertainty reasoning method. An example is given to show how to apply weak ratio rules to reconstruct lost data, and forecast and detect outliers.

DongHong Sun, Tsinghua University, China
Li Liu, University of Technology, Sydney, Australia
Peng Zhang, Chinese Academy of Sciences, China
Xingquan Zhu, University of Technology, Sydney, Australia
Yong Shi, Chinese Academy of Sciences, China & University of Nebraska at Omaha, USA

Due to the flexibility of multi-criteria optimization, Regularized Multiple Criteria Linear Programming (RMCLP) has received attention in decision support systems. Numerous theoretical and empirical studies have demonstrated that RMCLP is effective and efficient in classifying large scale data sets. However, a possible limitation of RMCLP is poor interpretability and low comprehensibility for end users and experts. This deficiency has limited RMCLP's use in many real-world applications where both accuracy and transparency of decision making are required, such as in Customer Relationship Management (CRM) and Credit Card Portfolio Management. In this paper, the authors present a clustering based rule extraction method to extract explainable and understandable rules from the RMCLP model. Experiments on both synthetic and real world data sets demonstrate that this rule extraction method can effectively extract explicit decision rules from RMCLP with only a small compromise in performance.

Chapter 12

In recent years, new applications emerged that produce data streams, such as stock data and sensor networks. Therefore, finding frequent subsequences, or clusters of subsequences, in data streams is an essential task in data mining. Data streams are continuous in nature, unbounded in size and have a high arrival rate. Due to these characteristics, traditional clustering algorithms fail to effectively find clusters in data streams. Thus, an efficient incremental algorithm is proposed to find frequent subsequences in multiple data streams. The described approach for finding frequent subsequences is by clustering subsequences of a data stream. The proposed algorithm uses a window model to buffer the continuous data streams. Further, it does not recompute the clustering results for the whole data stream at every window, but rather it builds on clustering results of previous windows. The proposed approach also employs a decay value for each discovered cluster to determine when to remove old clusters and retain recent ones. In addition, the proposed algorithm is efficient as it scans the data streams once and it is considered an Any-time algorithm since the frequent subsequences are ready at the end of every window.

Chapter 13

An important component of near-real-time data warehouses is the near-real-time integration layer. One important element in near-real-time data integration is the join of a continuous input data stream with a disk-based relation. For high-throughput streams, stream-based algorithms, such as Mesh Join (MESH-JOIN), can be used. However, in MESHJOIN the performance of the algorithm is inversely proportional to the size of disk-based relation. The Index Nested Loop Join (INLJ) can be set up so that it processes stream input, and can deal with intermittences in the update stream but it has low throughput. This paper introduces a robust stream-based join algorithm called Hybrid Join (HYBRIDJOIN), which combines the two approaches. A theoretical result shows that HYBRIDJOIN is asymptotically as fast as the fastest of both algorithms. The authors present performance measurements of the implementation. In experiments using synthetic data based on a Zipfian distribution, HYBRIDJOIN performs significantly better for typical parameters of the Zipfian distribution, and in general performs in accordance with the theoretical model while the other two algorithms are unacceptably slow under different settings.

Chapter 14

In this paper, data field is proposed to group data objects via simulating their mutual interactions and opposite movements for hierarchical clustering. Enlightened by the field in physical space, data field to simulate nuclear field is presented to illuminate the interaction between objects in data space. In the data field, the self-organized process of equipotential lines on many data objects discovers their hierarchical clustering-characteristics. During the clustering process, a random sample is first generated to optimize the impact factor. The masses of data objects are then estimated to select core data object with nonzero masses. Taking the core data objects as the initial clusters, the clusters are iteratively merged hierarchy by hierarchy with good performance. The results of a case study show that the data field is capable of hierarchical clustering on objects varying size, shape or granularity without user-specified parameters, as well as considering the object features inside the clusters and removing the outliers from noisy data. The comparisons illustrate that the data field clustering performs better than K-means, BIRCH, CURE, and CHAMELEON.

Chapter 15

Ye Zhu, Cleveland State University, USA
Yongjian Fu, Cleveland State University, USA
Huirong Fu, Oakland University, USA

Time series data mining poses new challenges to privacy. Through extensive experiments, the authors find that existing privacy-preserving techniques such as aggregation and adding random noise are insufficient due to privacy attacks such as data flow separation attack. This paper also presents a general model for publishing and mining time series data and its privacy issues. Based on the model, a spectrum of privacy preserving methods is proposed. For each method, effects on classification accuracy, aggregation error, and privacy leak are studied. Experiments are conducted to evaluate the performance of the methods. The results show that the methods can effectively preserve privacy without losing much classification accuracy and within a specified limit of aggregation error.

Preface

INTRODUCTION

The size of data produced in the world has recently exploded and the trend is accelerating significantly. According to IBM (2012), around 2.5 quintillion bytes of data are created every day and 90 percent of the data in the world today has been created within the past 2 years. Not only is the source of data diverse, there are diverse kinds of data. Data comes from different sources such as sensors used to gather climate information, posts to social media sites, digital pictures, videos posted online, transaction records of online purchases and cell phone GPS signals. One important factor that contributes to "big data" is repeated observations over time and space. For example, cellphone databases store time and location information every 15 seconds for each of a few million phones. In fact, most large datasets are likely to inherent temporal and spatial dimensions which are critical and result in performance problems.

The term "big data" has been used to refer to the increasing amount of data. The most interesting aspect of big data is its ability to derive useful information in order to provide deep knowledge about data in a manner of time. Indeed, it is necessary for organizations to adopt big data to explore customer data, predict market directions, understand patterns and develop predictive models. However, the challenge behind the issue of big data is how to optimize the systems to handle different workloads. In particular, the integration of big data processing places a strain on storage, networks, infrastructure, and accessing and analyzing methodologies. Consequently, big data management is an important step in exploiting this opportunity. Several approaches in big data have recently been developed. Nevertheless, they tend to look at different aspects of big data and to date, one comprehensive big data management solution has not been designed. This chapter will investigate and discuss the limitations of previous approaches in the field of big data management. It will explain the limitations and propose future research to address these absences.

The rest of this chapter is organized as follows. The first section gives an overview of big data and discusses its characteristics in providing an understanding of the nature of big data, followed by a discussion about the state-of-the-art research in this area. The following sections then examine the latest technologies and techniques in the big data management domain, such as physical management, data service provision, business intelligence support and visualization (Figure 1). Firstly, the layer of physical management for big data, such as distributed computing, parallel database systems and cloud computing, provides a strategy to access, store and secure enormous and highly differentiated data sources that are now available to companies. Secondly, the layer of data service provision represents the day-to-day operations of big data. For instance, the NoSQL database and Apache Hadoop/MapReduce paradigm are discussed as techniques to process big data to derive meaningful information. An additional layer of big data business intelligence support which covers wider data mining tasks is investigated to provide

Figure 1. Layers of big data management

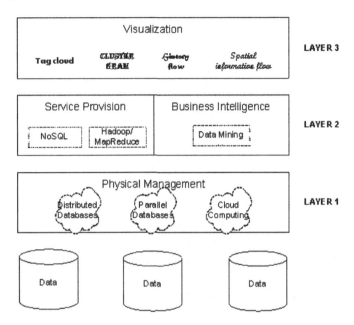

smarter and faster decision making. The last section demonstrates the big data visualization layer which is important for business stakeholders to foresee data overload, share big data internally and with external partners, and recognize actionable insights.

BIG DATA: AN OVERVIEW

The concept of big data has been widely defined as data which consists of datasets that grow too large for typical database tools to capture, manage and process. Another meta-definition was given by Jacobs (2009) regarding the period of time as follows:

- **1980s:** Data whose size forced us to look beyond the tried-and-true methods which were prevalent at that time.
- **1990s:** Any data that transcended the bounds of Microsoft Excel and a desktop PC, requiring serious software on UNIX workstations to analyze.
- **Nowadays:** Data that is too large to be placed in a relational database and analyzed with the help of a desktop statistics/visualization package; data whose analysis requires massively parallel software, running on tens, hundreds, even thousands of servers.

It should be noted that big data is not just about data volume. Most definitions of big data tend to focus on the size of the data in storage. However, there are other important characteristics of big data, namely data velocity and variety. Derived from Russom (2011), figure 2 demonstrates the overlap of the three characteristics of big data. Other terminologies have been used to describe these, such as the terms "aspects" by Russom (2011) and Saugatuck (2011) or "dimensions" by Dumbill (2012).

Figure 2. Three characteristics of big data

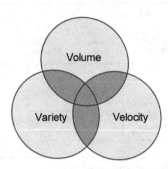

Volume: According to Russom (2011), data volume is the primary attribute of big data. Nowadays, data tends to be increasingly larger in which the current limits are in the order of terabytes, exabytes and zettabytes. This characteristic leads to the benefit of processing huge amounts of data to extract useful information. For example, it would be predicted much better if customer demands were taken into account of 300 factors rather than 6 factors. On the other hand, the challenge behind this increasingly large data is how to develop scalable storages and propose a distributed approach to query (Dumbill, 2012).

In the context of data mining applications for large datasets, the scalability of the clustering algorithm has become a very important issue. It is very likely that it is impossible for a single processor computer to store the whole dataset in the main memory for processing. In fact, parallel clustering algorithms have been significantly implemented to provide scalable and high performance for large datasets. As proposed by Kwok, Smith, Lozano and Taniar (2002), a parallel version of the fuzzy c-means algorithm for clustering large datasets has been implemented. It has been shown that the algorithm enables the processing of huge datasets more robustly than existing parallel k-means algorithms.

Variety: Data is rarely presented in a form which is perfectly ordered and ready for processing, for instance, text from social networks, image data and raw feeds directly from sensor sources. Being diverse in terms of sources, data types and entities represented such as structured data, unstructured data (text and human language) and semi-structured data (XML, RSS feeds) result in the challenge of taking the time to clean up the data before processing (Russom, 2011). As noted by Dumbill (2012), big data practitioners report that 80 percent of effort involved in dealing with data is cleaning it up in first place which is very high cost in terms of data acquisition and cleaning.

In our previous work (Do, Rahayu and Torabi, 2011), we proposed a conflict detection method in adopting global XML standard for database systems. This approach might be used to define conflicts before the stage of cleaning up big data. In our approach, a comprehensive taxonomy of all possible conflicts in adopting an XML standard has been created in order to provide the background information for the proposed conflict detection methodology (Figure 3). The key issue in finding commonality at an appropriate functional level has been addressed by the query approach proposed in the research. We have shown that it is possible to identify all possible conflicts by using the query mechanism along with the detection flow and the algorithms.

In respect to the variety of data, our earlier work focuses mostly on the management of XML data updates and proposes a framework and optimization technique for XML data warehousing as follows:

Figure 3. Overview of conflict detection (Do et al. 2011)

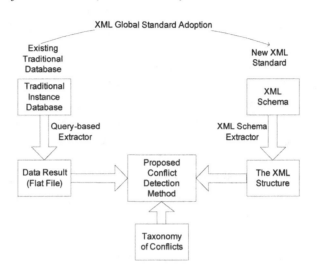

- **XML Data Update:** Pardede, Rahayu and Taniar (2005) introduced a methodology to preserve semantic constraints during an XML update. The update operations are divided into deletion, insertion, and replacement. Each operation considers a different type of target node such as key, key reference and simple data content whether it is an element or an attribute. Since the update requires a document structure validation, the transformation of the document conceptual constraints into a schema language also needs to be implemented. The constraints captured are classified based on the XML structural relationship. Another better approach is to maintain the semantics of the documents after some update operations (Pardede et al., 2008). Ideally, different XML conceptual constraints are identified and then transformed into the logical model constraints. These generic methods are the basic functions that need to be followed by any XML storage, regardless of the underlying data model.
- **XML Data Warehousing:** a framework for warehousing multi-version XML documents was suggested by Rusu, Rahayu and Taniar (2005). There are three main stages involved in the dynamic XML warehousing process. In the first stage, the changes between the incoming successive versions of the dynamic XML documents are identified. The output of this stage is a collection of historical data and changes. In the second stage, the data is cleaned and integrated. The final XML data warehouse is built by constructing the fact that the XML documents and the required dimensions are in the last stage. Furthermore, we continued to investigate the partitioning methods for multi-version XML data warehouses in our following work (Rusu et al., 2009). In this approach, optimization techniques for the XML data warehouse are investigated when documents are multi-versioned, and data volume and temporal changes are large. It has been shown that partitioning can be used successfully to fragment the XML data warehouse, using one of the XML-oriented partitioning techniques such as document, schema-based and cascaded partitioning.

Velocity: Data has recently been time-sensitive and fast-moving (Dumbill, 2012). For example, online retailers tend to compile large histories of customers' every click and interactions, not just final sales, which provides fast information by which to recommend additional purchases. This allows retailers to seize a competitive advantage and is a decision-making-driven approach.

In general, big data is a term applied to datasets that grow so large that it goes beyond the ability of current technologies to capture, manage and process the data within a reasonable elapsed time. Following are two types of big data as raised by Agrawal, Das and Abbadi (2010):

- **Single Large Applications:** The application usually starts small and increases its popularity and data footprints so that it cannot be served by single nodes. It requires system architectures such as expensive commercial solutions and moves beyond relation database technologies. The climate, oceanography and weather agency with petabytes of data to be managed and volumes are only going to accelerate as an example of the single large applications.
- **Large Multitenant Databases:** A large number of applications, each of which has a small data footprint. A representative example is Facebook being a social networking website launched in February 2004. As of February 2012, Facebook has more than million active users and handles 40 billion photos from its user base.

Big data creates value in several ways. In particular, it falls into one of the two value categories: (i) analytical use; (ii) enable new products. A few examples of big data advantages are as follows:

- **Real Time Data Analyses:** Traffic patterns and weather trends can be integrated and generate useful information such as travel times and alternative routes.
- **New Insights and Yield Better Patient Care:** Patient's information from medical monitors with millions of readings can be used to extract emerging problems.
- **Retailers:** Demands for a specific product at a specific location at a specific time can be integrated to make forecasts more accurate and increase inventory management.
- **Web Services Providers:** Hidden patterns of customers using services can be used to develop new features and customers accomplish their goals more directly.

Nevertheless, big data management is still a young research area, where variety and velocity characters of big data are yet to be determined and implemented. The reason why this area is a step behind the business domain is because big data is extremely huge, unstructured and time-sensitive and big data management technology has only recently reached maturity. The next section will discuss current approaches in the area of big data management in order to take advantage of this opportunity.

CURRENT APPROACHES IN BIG DATA MANAGEMENT

Working with large datasets has increasingly become common in many domains. Database sizes have been expanding significantly from gigabytes, to terabytes, to petabytes, and now exabytes. Consider two common sources of big data such as the logs of web hits which record millions of visits a day to a handful of pages or retail transactions which log billions and billions of individual transactions a year. For many years, it was easy to store data by loading it into a relational database. Finding patterns and extracting useful information from these databases was possible using data analytic techniques. However, in some areas, data growth has reached the point where a single relational database is not sufficient to handle this. Significantly, genuine relational data elements constitute less than 10 percent of the big data world and that share is falling rapidly. In brief, this has been a challenge for meaningful data integration in the real, messy, often schema-less, and complex big data world of databases using multi-disciplinary, multi-technology methods (Bizer, Boncz, Brodie and Erling, 2011). New visions for big data management are therefore required. Over the last few years, as a result of the increase of data size, we have witnessed a growing amount of research which needs to be stored and integrated, and the complex tools needed to query it. This section discusses some of the current approaches in the area.

Layer of Physical Management for Big Data

One of the fundamental questions for processing huge datasets effectively is how to access, store and secure enormous and highly differentiated data sources. In recent years, much work has been conducted in the area of physical management for big data. This subsection will discuss some of the latest trends in the area of big data physical management such as distributed computing, parallel database systems and cloud computing. Please refer to layer 1 in Figure 1.

Distributed Computing as a Strategy for Very Large Datasets

Attempts to address the data growth problems have revolved around scaling up and adding more storage and processing power in a single machine. However, it is difficult for current computer architectures to keep up with the growth of storage and processing needs. As a result of this, distributed computing was proposed as the most successful strategy for very large datasets, aiming to scale out to more computers and create a distributed infrastructure of hundreds or even thousands of computers (Figure 4a). It is clear (Jacobs, 2009) that purchasing 8 commodity servers with 8 processing cores and 128GB RAM each is cheaper than one single system with a total of 64 processors and 1 terabyte RAM. Regarding the performance cost of storing and retrieving data on other nodes in a network, Jacobs (2009) indicated that this is comparable to the cost of using disks.

In a distributed system, the hugely increasing amount of data is stored locally. It is impossible to adopt centralized data mining to extract hidden patterns due to the enormous network communication costs of integrating datasets from different sites into a centralized site. Accordingly, distributed data mining has been an active area of data mining research and association rule mining is a significant issue. Ashrafi, Taniar and Smith (2004) have developed an optimized distributed association mining algorithm for geographically distributed datasets. Support counts of candidate item sets are generated more rapidly than by other algorithms and the size of average transactions, datasets and message exchanges are equally reduced. This algorithm also provides an efficient method for generating association rules from different datasets which are distributed among various sites.

Figure 4. Physical management for big data: (a) Distributed computing; (b) Parallel computing; (c) Cloud computing

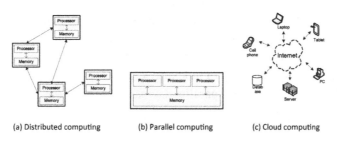

(a) Distributed computing   (b) Parallel computing   (c) Cloud computing

Although distributed computing shows great promise for handling large datasets, there have been significant issues with distributed computing for big data. One of the major problems is having no uniform distribution of work across nodes (Jacobs, 2009). It is yet to be determined how data is distributed across nodes. Also, Jacobs (2009) pointed out that another important issue in distributed computing is reliability. For instance, it is more likely for a four-engine airplane to experience an engine failure in a given period than a craft with two equivalent engines. It has been argued that data replicated to improve the efficiency of different kinds of analyses can provide redundancy against inevitable node failure. However, it is more difficult to maintain multiple copies of the larger datasets. Additionally, distributed computing tends to lack the toolsets with which we are familiar on a single machine (Prekopcsk, Makrai, Henk and Gspr-Papanek, 2011). It requires new programming paradigms and new tools for data analytics. Many projects have been developed to resolve efficient data access and provide different data analytics functions in a distributed environment. However, complex command-line mechanisms and programming tasks are usually required to make them work.

Parallel Database Systems for Big Data

Due to the limitations of distributed computing, parallel database systems have been developed as an adequate tool to manage and process heavy workloads. The most recent research on parallel computing to large scale data analysis includes (Pavlo, Paulson, Rasin, Abadi, DeWitt, Madden and Stonebraker, 2009) and (Stonebraker, Abadi, Dewitt, Madden, Paulson, Pavlo and Rasin, 2010). Indeed, parallel computing and distributed computing have been seen as a tightly-coupled form and it is transparent to the end-user that the data is stored on multiple machines. Agrawal, Das and Abbadi (2011) urged that parallel computing grow beyond prototype systems to large commercial systems in order to facilitate ad-hoc approaches to scaling.

Parallel database systems have existed since the late 1980s. They are based on a cluster of commodity computers, called "shared nothing nodes", connected through a high-speed interconnect (Figure 4b). They use the techniques of horizontal partitioning of relational tables along with the partitioned execution of SQL queries such as select, aggregation, join, projection and update (Stonebraker et al., 2010). In particular, horizontal partitioning distributes the rows of a relational table across cluster nodes to be executed in parallel. In order to understand how data partitioning is used in parallel database systems, consider the following SQL query:

Select logId, count From Logs Where created_time < "25/1/2012"

Resulting from *Logs* table horizontally partitioned across cluster nodes, a *Select* operator against *Logs* records with a specified date predicate on each cluster node is executed, providing the query to be processed in parallel. Intermediate results from each node are then sent to a single node that performs a merge operation and returns the final results of the query.

A key benefit of parallel databases is automatically managing various alternative partitioning strategies for tables involved in the query. It is not necessary for programmers to specify the underlying storage details, such as indexing options and join strategies. They only need to determine their goal in a high level language. For instance, if *Logs* and *Users* are hash partitioned on *logId* attribute, the query optimizer will recognize and omit the shuffle operator from the compiled query plan.

Our previous work presented a taxonomy of indexing schemes and sorting for parallel databases, and addressed the issue of high performance for parallel database processing as follows:

- **Indexing schemes for parallel database systems**: Taniar and Rahayu (2002) introduced a taxonomy of indexing schemes in parallel database systems including the Non-Replicated Indexing scheme (NRI), the Partially-Replicated Indexing scheme (PRI), and the Fully-Replicated Indexing scheme (FRI). Both NRI and PRI schemes have three different variations. Particularly, the index attribute is also the record partitioning attribute, the local index is built from its local data, and the indexed partitioning attribute is different from the record partitioning attribute. For the FRI scheme, there are only two variations, which are the first and the third variations of the above. Following Taniar et al. (2004), a global indexing tree structure for parallel database systems was proposed. A global indexing tree is a tree structure used for indexing where the complete index tree is partially partitioned into multi-processors but the overall structure of the global index is still maintained.
- **Parallel database sorting:** Taniar and Rahayu (2002) suggested a taxonomy for parallel external sorting in high performance database systems such as parallel merge-all sort, parallel binary-merge sort, parallel redistribution binary-merge sort, parallel redistribution merge-all sort and parallel partitioned sort.
- **High performance parallel database processing**: This makes use of parallelism techniques applied to an underlying parallel computing platform in order to achieve high performance (Taniar, Leung, Rahayu and Goel, 2008). There are four different forms of parallelism available for database processing: (i) interquery parallelism; (ii) intraquery parallelism; (iii) intraoperation parallelism; and (iv) interoperation parallelism. These may be combined in the parallel processing of a database job in order to achieve a better performance result.

Some of the available commercial parallel databases are Teradata, Netezza, DataAllegro (Microsoft) ParAccel, Greenplum, Aster, Vertica, DB2.

Future work and trends identified in parallel databases for big data should be extensibility in order to facilitate analytics over big data. The demand for improved parallelization of user-defined types and functions in both commercial and open source systems should be considered.

Cloud Facilitation of Big Data

In conjunction with distributed and parallel databases systems, cloud computing is a successful computational paradigm for managing and processing big data repositories because of its innovative metaphors such as Database as a Service (DaaS) and Infrastructure as a Service (IaaS) (Cuzzocrea, Song and Davis, 2011). DaaS provides a set of tools for end users to create, store, access and manage their databases seamlessly on remote data servers. In addition, IaaS houses, runs and maintains these services to ensure elasticity, pay-per-use, transfer of risk and low time to market. It is the most appropriate computational service framework to implement big data applications because application requirements are to run over big data repositories. Furthermore, cloud architecture provides many features such as scalability, elasticity, fault-tolerance, self-manageability, and ability to run on commodity hardware, compared to current traditional databases where it does not meet these goals (Agrawal et al., 2011).

Integrating public data and private corporate data in the cloud has been particularly critical. It is highly dependent on the local storage capability for processing multi-petabyte data sets with processing inside rather than requiring large scale data movement. We can see that the cloud provides a point of access as well as a mechanism for integration between private corporate data warehouses and the processing of public data (Figure 4c). Its virtualized architecture enables the parallel processing needed to solve these problems and there will be an increasing demand for Software as a Service (SaaS) solutions to provide processing and data integration tasks (Saugatuck, 2011).

For a long time, relational database systems with ACID (atomicity, consistency, isolation and durability) properties have been the default home for computational data. However, it is not suitable for handling the exponential growth in data (Shim, 2012). Much research has discussed the CAP theorem for storing extremely huge amounts of data in the cloud. Particularly, the CAP theorem represents three properties of a system including consistency (C), availability (A) and partitions (P). The CAP theorem asserts that there are at most two of these three properties for any shared-data system. The tradeoff between consistency and availability/performance has become a key factor in designing large scale data management systems (Ramakrishnan, 2012). As Brewer (2012) stated, when it is necessary to choose between C and A, during network partitioning, the designer usually chooses A. By choosing availability over consistency, the complexity of distributed systems is increasingly built by a highly available system. Nonetheless, data inconsistency results in a dimension of design complexity in application development. Thus, it is necessary for programmers to decide whether to use fast inconsistent accesses or slow consistent accesses to secure both high performance and correctness. Additionally, conflict resolution rules should be defined to meet the application's needs.

As a consequence of the increased accessibility of people to various resources, future work in cloud data management will very likely continue to be around effective techniques for dealing with the elasticity of cloud infrastructures; designing scalable, elastic, autonomous multitenant database systems; security and privacy of data outsourced to the cloud, etc.

Layer of Big Data Service Provision

Even though storing data is an important part of building a data platform, data is only useful if we can do something with it and enormous datasets present computational problems. Big data analytics has recently seen increased research interest due to its ability to extract useful knowledge for decision making from these data which is impossible for actual database-inspired analysis tools (Cuzzocrea et al., 2011). Generally, in an enterprise environment, the information might live in structured, unstructured and semi-structured sources. In order to integrate data from structured systems with the structured or unstructured data, current approaches use MapReduce paradigms. Other approaches propose to use Apache Hadoop/MapReduce and NoSQL database implementations of MapReduce. We will present some of the research work which uses these approaches. Please refer to layer 2 in Figure 1.

MapReduce Paradigm

The MapReduce paradigm was first popularized by Google in 2004 and has been a successful strategy for processing extremely large datasets. Much work has been conducted, based on this approach. Naturally, MapReduce has moved past testing and development to become a viable extension and an alternative to a relational database system for managing and analyzing huge datasets (Sheppard, 2011) (Loukides, 2011). An attractive quality of the MapReduce model is simplicity. It consists of only two functions including Map and Reduce which are written by users to process key/value data pairs. In particular, the input dataset is stored in a collection of partitions in a distributed file system deployed on each node in the cluster (Stonebraker et al., 2010).

The MapReduce approach (Figure 5a) is a programming model with an associated computational framework, inspired by the map and reduce primitives in many functional languages. The Map partitions computational tasks into smaller tasks and assigns them to appropriate <Key, Value> pairs. The tasks are executed efficiently by exploiting parallelism. The final result of the overall computational task is obtained via the Reduce operation, by combining all values sharing the same Key value.

Stonebraker et al. (2010) suggested that it would be beneficial to map parallel database systems onto MapReduce systems. In fact, the MapReduce system is an Extract-Load-Transform (ELT) system which is complementary to database systems, and is not a complete technology, since a database is not designed to be good at ELT tasks. Parallel database systems excel at efficiently querying large datasets while MapReduce systems excel at complex analytics and ELT tasks. Accordingly, MapReduce systems should learn from parallel databases such as technologies and techniques for efficient query parallel executions due to the fact that writing SQL code for each task is easier than writing MapReduce code. Another reason for the mapping is MapReduce can perform queries in parallel. In contrast, it is not easy to fit these queries into the MapReduce paradigm or group-by aggregation.

An open issue in relation to the MapReduce paradigm that needs to be addressed is that without a schema, each MapReduce user must write a custom parser, complicating the sharing of data among multiple applications. In addition, a schema is needed to maintain information, which is critical for optimizing declarative queries including what indices exist, how tables are partitioned, table cardinalities and histograms that capture the distribution of values within a column.

Apache Hadoop/ MapReduce

Numerous open source and commercial technologies, based on the MapReduce paradigm, have been developed as a tool for big data analytics. The most popular is Apache Hadoop which is an open source project under development by Yahoo! and Apache (Stonebraker et al., 2010). In particular, Apache Hadoop has a number of advantages over other forms of processing, including open source availability, standardization, usability over a fairly wide range of problems, recent evolution, and suitability to current IT infrastructure (Saugatuck, 2011). In general, Apache Hadoop contains two elements:

Figure 5. (a) MapReduce paradigm (b) Hadoop distributed file system

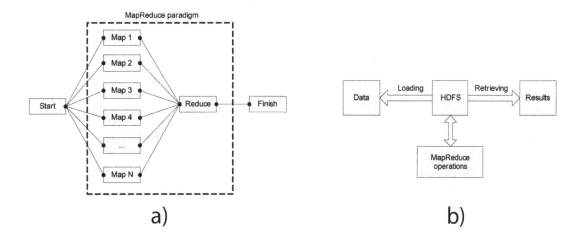

- **Hadoop Distributed File System (HDFS):** Fault-tolerant, scalable, simply expandable, highly configurable distributed storage system.
- **Hadoop MapReduce:** Software framework which enables easily writing applications for processing huge amount of data in parallel on large clusters of a commodity hardware in a reliable, fault-tolerant manner.

Apache Hadoop runs MapReduce tasks over big data and makes available HDFS to support file-oriented, distributed data management operations (Cuzzocrea et al., 2011; Pavlo et al., 2009; Saugatuck, 2011) (Refer to Figure 5b for a demonstration.). Noticeably, Facebook is the most well-known example of an Apache Hadoop user (Dumbill, 2012). By using the Hadoop/MapReduce, Facebook can process the large user data and use patterns of friendships in order to provide alternative functions such as "suggest other people you might know". This leads to a new era of creative data. Importantly, companies not only use their own data but also data distributed by their users. According to Cohen, Dolan, Dunlap, Hellerstein and Welton (2009), Apache Hadoop is a kind of MAD system which facilitates Magnetism, Agility and Depth features that users expect from a system of big data analysis. It is an evolution of next-generation data warehousing systems in regard to the ELT phase of such systems. Apache Hadoop is capable of attracting all data sources, adapting its engines to evolutions that may occur in big data sources, supporting depth analysis over big data sources much more which is beyond the possibilities of traditional SQL-based analysis tools.

The Apache Hadoop project includes a number of related open source Apache products such as Pig, Hive, Cassandra, HBase, Avro, Chukwa, Mahout and Zookeeper. Of these projects, Hive and Pig are most familiar, as they are frequently used in Hadoop projects. The NoSQL databases HBase and Cassandra are used as the database grounding for a significant number of Hadoop projects (Saugatuck, 2011). Hive is a BI tool to query and manage structured data built on top of Hadoop's HDFS. It allows the final analytics components to be obtained from big data processed, materialized and stored via Hadoop. HiveQL is a SQL-like query language running MapReduce jobs immersed into SQL statements (Cuzzocrea et al., 2011).Many of the key Hadoop developers have found a home at Cloudera, which provides commercial support. Amazon's Elastic MapReduce makes it much easier to put Hadoop to work without investing in racks of Linux machines, by providing preconfigured Hadoop images for its EC2 clusters (Loukides, 2011).

In response to the wide use of Apache Hadoop, Saugatuck (2011) suggested that although it resolves the volume issue of the three big data characteristics, it needs help to resolve velocity and variety. Future research should address real time processing and the integration of different object types on big data.

NoSQL Database Implementations of MapReduce

NoSQL stands for Not Only SQL. It is a class of non-relational data storage systems which usually do not require a fixed table schema and never use the concept of joins. All NoSQL offerings relax one or more of the ACID properties. It is designed to handle extremely huge datasets effectively and is now more acceptable to clients. This results from the explosion of social media sites with large data needs, the rise of cloud-based solutions, moving to dynamically-typed languages which are a shift to dynamically-typed data with frequent schema changes, such as Ruby/Groovy and the open source community.

There are different types of NoSQL (Saugatuck, 2011) as follows:

- **Key-Value Systems:** Based on Amazon's Dynamo (2007). It uses a hash table with a unique key and pointer to a data item. Some examples are Memcached, Dynamo and Voldemort. Amazon's S3 uses Dynamo as its storage mechanism.
- **Columnar Systems:** Used to store and process very large amounts of data distributed over many machines. Keys point to multiple columns. The most important example is Google's BigTable, where rows are identified by a row key with the data is sorted and stored by this key. BigTable has served as the basis of a number of NoSQL systems, including Hadoop's Cassandra (open sourced by Facebook) and HBase, and Hypertable. Column-based systems also include AsterData and Greenplum.
- **Document Databases:** Based on Lotus Notes. These are similar to key-value, however, they are based on versioned documents that are collections of other key-value collections. The best known of these are MongoDB and CouchDB.
- **Graph Database Systems:** Built with nodes, relationships between nodes and the properties of nodes. Instead of tables of rows and columns, a flexible graph model is used which can scale across multiple machines. An example is the open source Neo4J.

Each of these has advantages and disadvantages that are tied to particular types of problems. No single solution has been found for big data problems. Rather, it is necessary to combine a variety of different database models which are more specialized and suitable for handling specific types of problems. There are two types of NoSQL databases: key/value and schema-less which come in multiple flavors, column-based, document-based or graph-based.

Loukides (2011) noted the following two NoSQL databases as leaders in the field:

- **Cassandra:** Developed by Facebook and has been used at Twitter, Rackspace, Reddit, and other large sites. Cassandra, which has a very flexible data model, is designed for high performance, reliability, and automatic replication.
- **HBase:** A part of the Apache Hadoop project and modeled on Google's BigTable. HBase is suitable for extremely huge datasets which are distributed across thousands of nodes.

As stated by Saugatuck (2011) and Loukides (2011), several limitations have prevented the wide use of NoSQL databases. Although key/value systems are very simple, fast, scalable and can be distributed horizontally, many data structures cannot be easily modeled as key/value pairs. Furthermore, schema-less data models are superior to key/value pair models such as the consistency, excellent performance and scalability. However, a disadvantage with schema-less databases is that there are typically no ACID transactions or joins. Other important issues are integration backup and recovery, their suitability to particular types of querying and their ability to handle distributed storage, all of which are still to be solved.

Layer of Business Intelligence Support Using Big Data

In respect to business intelligence support using big data, it should provide historical, current and predictive views of business operations. Common functions of business intelligence technologies are reporting, online analytical processing, predictive analytics, data mining, process mining, complex event processing, business performance management and benchmarking. As business intelligence using big data aims to support better business decision making, several studies on data mining for big data have maximized this attraction. Data mining which has successfully developed over decades is a combination of techniques, methods and algorithms utilized in order to extract knowledge hidden in the large amount of data. One of the major issues of data mining for big data is due to the additional algorithmic constraints created by the large volume of data. In addition, the problem of temporal locality leads to a number of unique mining challenges.

Bar-Yossef (2002) proposed three models for computing over large datasets (Figure 6 is derived from [Bar-Yossef, 2002]) as follows:

- **Sampling Computation:** This is a randomized algorithm that queries its input at random locations and, based on the query results, decides the outputs (Figure 6a). This output is typically an approximation of the function's value on the input. The main measure of cost for the sampling algorithm is the number of queries performed being independent of the input size and depending on the approximation accuracy and the error probability. While sampling computations would be ultra-efficient such as being independent of dataset size, sampling may require random access and it tends to be hard to sample from disorganized datasets.
- **Data Stream Computation:** This processes data streams in which the input is presented as a sequence of items and can be examined in only a few passes (Figure 6b). The algorithm has only one-way and forward access to the items in the stream. Particularly, it cannot go backwards on the stream nor have random access to the data. Also, the input data stream is usually much larger than the storage capabilities of the algorithm. Consequently, the algorithm cannot store the stream and use standard random access to it. These algorithms have limited memory available to them and also limited processing time per item.
- **Sketch Computation:** This compresses each data segment into a small "sketch" and computes over the sketches (Figure 6c). A sketch is a compact representation of the data that encapsulates their properties that are necessary for computing some functions of the data. The goal is to design a sketching scheme that compresses the data as much as possible, yet still enables the algorithm to output an approximation of the function with low probability of error. Sketching is likely to appropriate for distributed datasets and is useful for "dimension reduction". Nonetheless, its limitations are too restricted for some problems and it usually has linear running time.

Since sampling is the oldest and most pervasive model of computation over massive data sets, it is very useful to study a sampling algorithm. Cohen et al. (2009) investigated the random sampling algorithm in more detail, to repeatedly take samples of a dataset in a controlled fashion, compute a summary statistic over each sample, and carefully combine the samples to estimate of a property of the entire dataset more robustly. Intuitively, rare outliers will appear in a few or no samples, and hence will not perturb the estimator used. There are two standard random sampling techniques as follows:

Figure 6. (a) Sampling computation; (b) Data stream computation; (c) Sketch computation

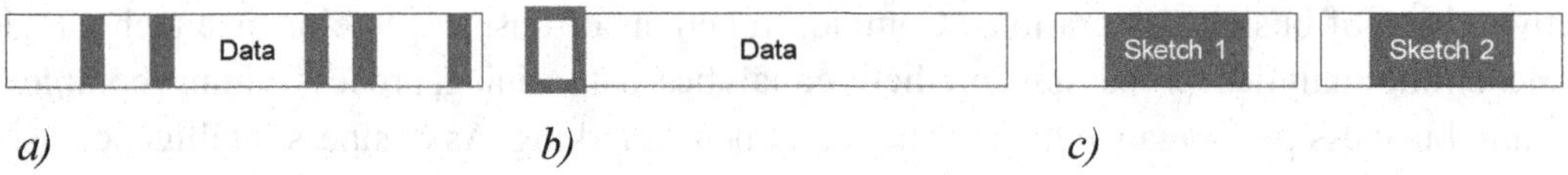

a)   *b)*   *c)*

- **Bootstrap method** is straightforward. From a population of size N, pick k members from the population and compute the desired θ. Next, replace the subsample and pick another random k numbers. The new θ will be different from the previous one. Repeat this "sampling" process tens of thousands of times. The distribution of the resulting θ is called the "sampling distribution". The larger the sampling distribution, the more accurate the measure.
- **Jackknife method** which repeatedly re-computes a summary statistic θ by leaving out one or more data items from the full dataset to measure the influence of certain sub-populations.

From the above, we can see that business intelligence support using big data is a new research area which has not received much attention as yet. Future work will continue the research trends in discovering patterns and frequently changing structures from dynamic data. Certainly, there is a growing demand to develop advanced sampling techniques on real time and complex data which raises the issue of selecting small targeted datasets logically and physically from different sources. In addition, it requires a technique to link different business intelligence applications in order to obtain useful information. Furthermore, it is necessary to look at mining tasks which have not been extensively researched so far, such as big data cleaning.

Layer of Big Data Visualization

In conjunction with the second layer of service provision for big data, the third layer of big data visualization should be implemented in order to synthesize the results of big data analysis. Please refer to layer 3 of figure 1. As can be seen, visualization for large datasets has been developed and studied for several years. The purpose of visualization is not only to illustrate the image of a picture but also its insight. Visualization should allow business users to identify patterns in order to take actionable steps. The key challenge that needs to be met is how to present information in a way that people can consume it effectively. Obviously, it is difficult to evaluate visualization techniques without considering their support for decision making in multi-paradigm, multi-domain problems that deal with complex spatio-temporal multi-dimensional data (Khan and Hornbak, 2011).

In recent years, there has been a tremendous amount of research and innovation in the field of visualization such as techniques and technologies used for creating images, diagrams, or animations to communicate, understand and improve the results of big data analyses. The following examples provide a glimpse into this important field that supports big data analytics (Manyika et al., 2011).

- **Tag cloud** is a visualization technique that presents the text in the form of a tag cloud. Typically, tags are usually single words and the font size or color is used to show the importance of each tag. This format helps the reader to quickly perceive the most prominent concepts in a large body of text, for instance, a weighted visual list, in which words that appear most frequently are larger and words that appear less frequently are smaller (Figure 7).
- **History flow** is used to chart the evolution of a document as it is edited by multiple contributing authors. In general, the horizontal axis presents the time, while the vertical axis demonstrates the text. There are different color codes for different authors and the vertical length of a bar indicates the amount of text written by each author. It tends to be various insights merged easily by visualizing the history of a document in this manner.

Figure 7. Tag cloud

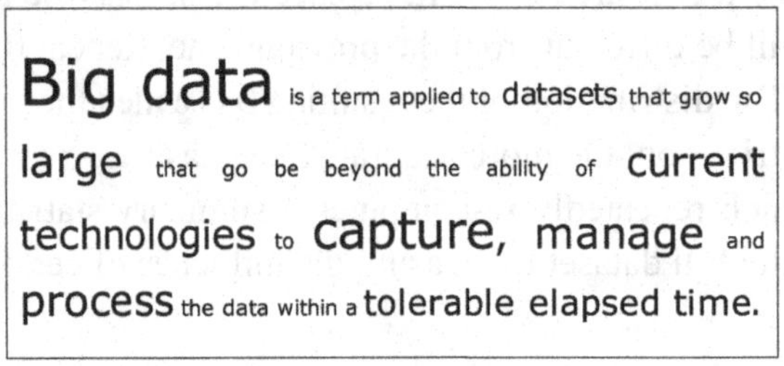

Big data is a term applied to datasets that grow so
large that go be beyond the ability of current
technologies to capture, manage and
process the data within a tolerable elapsed time.

- **Spatial information** flow is a visualization technique that is used to present spatial information flows. Figure 8 shows the progress of Bonnie hurricane hitting Florida in July 2010. The lines and colors are used to depict the hurricane's movement and the maximum sustained winds. The size of the lines on a particular location depicts the severity of the hurricane crossing that place. The greater the lines, the larger the flow. This visualization allows us to determine quickly which locations are most closely affected by Bonnie in terms of hurricane volume.

In our earlier work, a region-based filter for moving object datasets was proposed to extract meaningful information in real time (Thompson, Rahayu and Torabi, 2012). Ideally, a filter is constructed in real time by drawing and manipulating regions on a visualization of a dataset. The partitions are then visualized to identify meaningful subsets of the data.

Over the last few years, it has become clear that, due to the specific characteristics of big data such as large volume, the complexity of different sources and temporality, alternative visualization solutions should be further investigated. It is necessary to address the issues of real time and data streaming visualization. In addition, integrating different data sources from different data formats to be visualized in a single framework is still a significant challenge in the big data area.

Figure 8. Spatial information flow from (NOAA, 2012)

NORTH AMERICA
EUROPE
AFRICA
SOUTH AMERICA

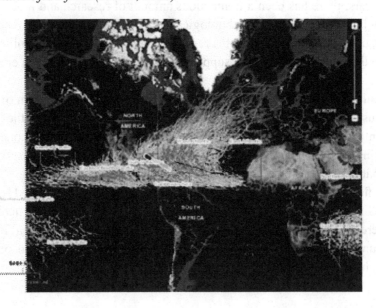

CONCLUSION AND FUTURE WORK

In this chapter, we highlighted some of the trends and advancements made by the research work in big data management. We have shown that these trends are not limited to one area, but they are spread across multiple domains. There is an extensive research work in physical management for storing big data including distributed computing, parallel databases and cloud computing. Big data service provision investigated MapReduce paradigm, Apache Hadoop/MapReduce paradigm, and NoSQL databases in order to provide deep knowledge analysis over big data. Random sampling, data stream and sketching algorithms were proposed for computing over large datasets in the business intelligence layer. Big data visualization such as tag clouds, history flows and spatial information flows were discussed as tools to synthesize the results of big data analysis. In general, big data management provides a snapshot of the growing infrastructure needs of emerging data management and analytics solutions. It points to the areas that need to be strengthened and the solutions that need to be put into place to meet the next generation of integrated data management and analytics solutions.

The future work is summarized as follows:

- In the physical management layer, there is a demand for effective techniques for dealing with the elasticity of big data infrastructures, designing scalable multitenant database systems, security and privacy of big data. Other important issues of the integration backup and recovery, the suitability to particular types of querying, and the ability to handle distributed storages remain to be investigated.
- New solutions need to provide adequate access and easily distributed workloads across multiple machines in the data provision service for big data. In order to provide analysis for big data and avoid performance failures, it is necessary to find a way to process the huge data from different sources with different data formats in real time without integrating them into a centralized database.
- Business intelligence support, using big data, should address the issue of selecting small targeted datasets logically and physically from different sources in real time. In addition, it requires techniques to link different business intelligence in order to extract useful knowledge for decision making.
- Alternative visualization solutions should be further investigated to address the issues of real time and data streaming visualization. In addition, the integration of different data types has been critical in the big data visualization area.

Nhung Do
La Trobe University, Australia

Wenny Rahayu
La Trobe University, Australia

Torab Torabi
La Trobe University, Australia

REFERENCES

Agrawal, D., Das, S., & Abbadi, A. E. (2010). Big data and cloud computing: New wine or just new bottles? *Proceedings of the VLDB Endowment, 3*(2).

Agrawal, D., Das, S., & Abbadi, A. E. (2011). Big data and cloud computing: Current state and future opportunities. *Proceedings of the 14th International Conference on Extending Database Technology (EDBT/ICDT '11)*, (pp. 530-533).

Ashrafi, M. Z., Taniar, D., & Smith, K. A. (2004). ODAM: An optimized distributed association rule mining algorithm. *IEEE Distributed Systems Online, 5*(3).

Bar-Yossef, Z. (2002). *The complexity of massive data set computations. Dissertations and Theses.* Berkeley: University of California.

Bizer, C., Boncz, P., Brodie, M. L., & Erling, O. (2011). The meaningful use of big data: Four perspectives - Four challenges. *SIGMOD Record, 40*(4).

Brewer, E. (2012). *CAP twelve years later: How the rules have changed. The Growing Impact of the CAP Theorem.* IEEE Computer Society.

Cohen, J., Dolan, B., & Dunlap, M. (2009). MAD skills: New analysis practices for big data. *Proceedings of the VLDB Endowment, 2*(2).

Cuzzocrea, A., II, Song, Y., & Davis, K. C. (2011). Analytics over Large-scale multidimensional data: The big data revolution! *Proceedings of the ACM 14th International Workshop on Data Warehousing and OLAP (DOLAP '11)*, (pp. 101-104). ACM.

Do, N., Rahayu, W., & Torabi, T. (2011). Conflict detection method in adopting global XML standard for database systems. In *Proceedings of the 5ᵗʰ International Conference on Ubiquitous Information Management and Communication* (ICUIMC '11). New York, NY: ACM.

Dumbill, E. (2011). *The SMAQ stack for big data: Storage, MapReduce and query are ushering in data-driven products and services.* O'Reilly Media.

Dumbill, E. (2012). *What is big data? An introduction to the big data landscape.* Retrieved from radar.oreilly.com/print/2012/01/what-is-big-data.html

IBM. (2012). *Bringing big data to the enterprise.* Retrieved from www-01.ibm.com/software/au/data/bigdata/

Jacobs, A. (2009). The pathologies of big data. *Communications of the ACM, 52*(8). doi:10.1145/1536616.1536632

Khan, A., & Hornbak, K. (2011). Big data from the built environment. *Proceedings of the 2nd International Workshop on Research in the large (LARGE '11)*, (pp. 29-32). ACM.

Kwok, T., Smith, K. A., Lozano, S., & Taniar, D. (2002). Parallel fuzzy c-means clustering for large data sets. *Proceedings of the 8th International Euro-Par Conference (Euro-Par 2002), Lecture Notes in Computer Science, Vol. 2400*, (pp. 365-374). Springer.

Loukides, M. (2011). *What is data science? Analysis: The future belongs to the companies and people that turn data into products.* O'Reilly Media.

Manyika, J., Chui, M., Brown, B., Bughin, J., Dobbs, R., Roxburgh, C., & Byers, A. H. (2011). *Big data: The next frontier for innovation, competition, and productivity*. McKinsey Global Institute.

NOAA. (2012). *Historical hurricane tracks*. Retrieved from www.csc.noaa.gov/hurricanes/

Pardede, E., Rahayu, W., & Taniar, D. (2005). Preserving conceptual constraints during XML updates. *International Journal of Web Information Systems, 1*(2), 65–82. doi:10.1108/17440080580000084

Pardede, E., Rahayu, W., & Taniar, D. (2008). XML data update management in XML-enabled database. *Journal of Computer and System Sciences, 74*(2), 170–195. doi:10.1016/j.jcss.2007.04.008

Pavlo, A., Paulson, E., Rasin, A., Abadi, D. J., DeWitt, D. J., Madden, S., & Stonebraker, M. (2009). A comparison of approaches to large-scale data analysis. *Proceedings of the 35th SIGMOD International Conference on Management of Data (Sigmod '09)*, (pp. 165-178).

Prekopcsk, Z., Makrai, G., Henk, T., & Gspr-Papanek, C. (2011). Radoop: Analyzing big data with RapidMiner and Hadoop. *Proceedings of the 2nd RapidMiner Community Meeting and Conference (RCOMM 2011)*, 2011.

Ramakrishnan, R. (2012). *CAP and cloud data management. The growing impact of the CAP theorem*. IEEE Computer Society.

Russom, P. (2011). Big data analytics. *TDWI Research*, Fourth Quarter 2011.

Rusu, L. I., Rahayu, W., & Taniar, D. (2005). A methodology for building xml data warehouses. *International Journal of Data Warehousing and Mining, 1*(2), 23–48. doi:10.4018/jdwm.2005040102

Rusu, L. I., Rahayu, W., & Taniar, D. (2009). Partitioning methods for multi-version XML data warehouses. *Distributed and Parallel Databases, 25*(1-2), 47–69. doi:10.1007/s10619-009-7034-y

Saugatuck Technology. (2011). *Understanding big data: Management study*. Technical Report, Sep 2011.

Sheppard, B. (2011). *Putting big data to work: Opportunities for enterprise*. GigaOM Pro.

Shim, S. S. Y. (2012). *The CAP theorem's growing impact. The Growing Impact of the CAP Theorem*. IEEE Computer Society. doi:10.1109/MC.2012.54

Stonebraker, M., Abadi, D., Dewitt, D. J., Madden, S., Paulson, E., Pavlo, A., & Rasin, A. (2010). MapReduce and parallel DBMSs: Friends or foes? *Communications of the ACM, 53*(1). doi:10.1145/1629175.1629197

Taniar, D., Leung, C. H. C., Rahayu, W., & Goel, S. (2008). *High performance parallel database processing and grid databases*. John Wiley & Sons, 2008.doi:10.1002/9780470391365

Taniar, D., & Rahayu, W. (2002). A taxonomy of indexing schemes for parallel database systems. *Distributed and Parallel Databases, 12*(1), 73–106. doi:10.1023/A:1015682215394

Taniar, D., & Rahayu, W. (2002). Parallel database sorting. *Information Sciences, 146*(1-4), 171–219. doi:10.1016/S0020-0255(02)00196-2

Taniar, D., & Rahayu, W. (2004). Global parallel index for multi-processors database systems. *Information Sciences, 165*(1-2), 103–127. doi:10.1016/j.ins.2003.09.019

Thompson, J., Rahayu, W., & Torabi, T. (2012). An interactive region-based filter for moving objects datasets: Making sense of chaos. *The 26th IEEE International Conference on Advanced Information Networking and Applications*.

Chapter 1
Visual Mobility Analysis Using T-Warehouse

A. Raffaetà
Università Ca' Foscari Venezia, Italy

E. Frentzos
University of Piraeus, Greece

L. Leonardi
Università Ca' Foscari Venezia, Italy

N. Giatrakos
University of Piraeus, Greece

G. Marketos
University of Piraeus, Greece

S. Orlando
Università Ca' Foscari Venezia, Italy

G. Andrienko
Fraunhofer Institute for Intelligent Analysis and Information Systems, Germany

N. Pelekis
University of Piraeus, Greece

N. Andrienko
Fraunhofer Institute for Intelligent Analysis and Information Systems, Germany

A. Roncato
Università Ca' Foscari Venezia, Italy

C. Silvestri
Università Ca' Foscari Venezia, Italy

ABSTRACT

Technological advances in sensing technologies and wireless telecommunication devices enable research fields related to the management of trajectory data. The challenge after storing the data is the implementation of appropriate analytics for extracting useful knowledge. However, traditional data warehousing systems and techniques were not designed for analyzing trajectory data. In this paper, the authors demonstrate a framework that transforms the traditional data cube model into a trajectory warehouse. As a proof-of-concept, the authors implement T-Warehouse, a system that incorporates all the required steps for Visual Trajectory Data Warehousing, from trajectory reconstruction and ETL processing to Visual OLAP analysis on mobility data.

DOI: 10.4018/978-1-4666-2148-0.ch001

INTRODUCTION

The usage of location aware devices, such as mobile phones and GPS-enabled devices, is widely spread nowadays, allowing access to vast volumes of trajectory datasets. Effective analysis of such trajectory data on the one hand imposes new challenges for their efficient management, while on the other hand it raises opportunities for discovering behavioral patterns that can be exploited in applications like traffic management and service accessibility.

Data Warehousing and Online Analytical Processing (OLAP) techniques can be employed in order to convert this vast amount of raw data into useful knowledge. Specifically, the variable number of moving objects in different urban areas, the average speed of vehicles, the ups and downs of vehicles' speed can be analyzed in a Trajectory Data Warehouse (TDW) and provide us with useful insights, like discovering popular movements. DWs are optimized for OLAP operations that include the aggregation or de-aggregation of information (called roll-up and drill-down, respectively) along a dimension of analysis, the selection of specific parts of a cube (slicing and dicing) and the reorientation of the multidimensional view of the data on the screen (pivoting) (Kimball et al., 2008).

The motivation behind a TDW is to transform raw trajectories into valuable knowledge that can be used for decision making purposes in ubiquitous applications, such as Location-Based Services (LBS), traffic control management. Intuitively, the high volume of raw data produced by sensing and positioning technologies, the complex nature of data stored in trajectory databases and the specialized query processing demands make extracting valuable information from such spatio-temporal data a hard task. For this reason, the idea is to develop specific traditional aggregation techniques to produce summarized trajectory information and provide visual OLAP style analyses.

It is worth noticing that visual representations of data are essential for enabling a human analyst to understand the data, extract relevant information, and derive knowledge. One of the objectives of visualization is to aid abstraction and generalization (Thomas & Cook, 2005). With relatively small and simple data, this can be achieved by appropriate positioning and/or appearance of visual elements representing individual data items. When the data are large and complex, a common approach is to apply computational techniques for data abstraction and generalization, in particular, aggregation. The visualization is then applied to the resulting aggregates. Trajectory Data Warehouse offers a powerful technological support to visual analysis of movement data by efficiently aggregating the data in various ways and at different spatial and temporal scales.

One could mention an abundance of applications that would benefit from the aforementioned approach. As an example, let us consider an advertising company which is interested in analyzing mobility data in different areas of a city in order to decide upon road advertisements (placed on panels on the roads). More specifically, the analysis concerns the demographical profiles of the people visiting different urban areas of the city at different times of the day so as to decide about the proper sequence of advertisements that will be shown on the panels at different time periods. This knowledge will enable the company to execute more focused marketing campaigns and apply a more effective strategy.

The above analysis can be efficiently offered by a TDW. However, various issues and challenges have to be considered to develop such a system:

- The presence of a preprocessing phase dealing with the explicit construction of the trajectories, which are then stored into a Moving Object Database (MOD) that offers powerful and efficient operations for their manipulation.

- The implementation of an efficient trajectory-oriented Extract-Transform-Load (ETL) process.
- The incorporation of appropriate aggregation mechanisms suitable for the trajectory oriented cube model.
- The design of a Visual OLAP interface that allows for multidimensional and interactive analysis.

Based on our recent results in the field (Orlando et al., 2007; Marketos et al., 2008) which to the best of our knowledge are the only works that cope with the problem in all its aspects, as a proof-of-concept, we propose T-Warehouse, a system for Visual Trajectory Data Warehousing. Our contribution can be summarized as follows:

- We describe the architectural aspects of our framework as well as various research challenges that are tackled.
- We suggest the appropriate spatial and temporal visualisation techniques supporting OLAP analysis of movement data. Among these there is a novel technique called cross visualisation that we have designed to represent specific measures of trajectory warehouse, namely numbers of trajectories traversing borders of grid cells.
- We investigate the power, flexibility and efficiency of our framework for applying OLAP analysis on real world mobility data.

The rest of the paper is organized as follows. Initially, we present the architecture of T-Warehouse and its various components. Then we illustrate the functionalities offered by T-Warehouse, by focusing on the visualization tools. Next we describe the case study concerning GPS-equipped cars moving in the urban area of Milan (Italy). By using this large dataset we provide an experimental evaluation of the accuracy of our method for computing spatio-temporal aggregates and we demonstrate how different kinds of analysis can be implemented by using T-Warehouse. Finally, we discuss some related work and we draw some conclusions.

SYSTEM ARCHITECTURE

The overall architecture of T-Warehouse is illustrated in Figure 1. More specifically, mobile devices are transmitting periodically the latest part of their trajectory, according to some user-defined parameters. This vast amount of data collected by all subscribed users is forwarded to a stream-based module (trajectory reconstruction software), whose purpose is to perform some basic trajectory preprocessing. This may include parameterized trajectory compression (so as to discard unnecessary details and concurrently keep informative abstractions of the portions of the trajectories transmitted so far), as well as techniques to handle missing/erroneous values. These trajectories are stored to Hermes MOD (Pelekis et al., 2008) which addresses the need for representing movements of objects (i.e., trajectories) in databases in order to perform querying and analysis on them and for providing efficient indexing, query processing. On Hermes MOD, appropriate querying and ETL processes are applied (possibly taking into account various types of infrastructural geodata) so as to derive information about trajectories (e.g. trajectory content in different granularities, aggregations, motional metadata) to feed in the TDW. Finally, incorporating GIS layers (e.g. geographic, topographic or demographic layers) and combining them with trajectory data results in a conceptually richer framework providing thus more advanced analysis capabilities. Below, we thoroughly illustrate the main components accompanied by our contributions.

Figure 1. T-Warehouse architecture

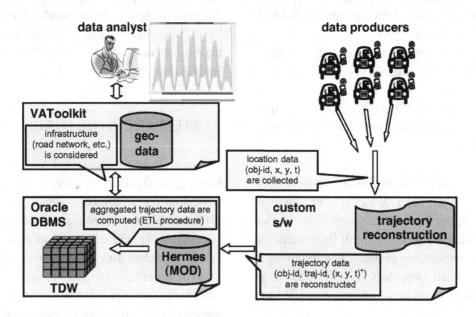

Trajectory Reconstruction

In real-world applications the movement of a spatio-temporal object is often given by means of a finite set of observations, i.e., time-stamped positions along with object-ids. The finite set of observations taken from the actual continuous movement is called a sampling. A first important task consists in grouping and filtering these raw points arriving in streaming in order to generate several meaningful trajectories, which are portions of the whole movement of an object (Marketos et al., 2008). In many situations an (approximate) reconstruction of each trajectory from its sampling is needed. Among the several possible solutions, in this paper we use linear local interpolation, i.e., objects are assumed to move straight between two observed points with constant speed. The linear (local) interpolation seems to be a quite standard approach to the problem (see Pfoser et al., 2000), and yields a good trade-off between flexibility and simplicity.

The trajectory reconstruction module in Figure 1 accomplishes this task by employing an appro-

priate algorithm (Marketos et al., 2008). Due to the fact that the notion of trajectory cannot be the same in every application, we define the following generic trajectory reconstruction parameters:

- **Temporal gap between trajectories (gap_{time}):** The maximum allowed time interval between two consecutive time-stamped positions of the same trajectory for a single moving object. As such, any time-stamped position of object o_i, received after more than gap_{time} units from its last recorded position, will cause a new trajectory of the same object to be created (case *a* in Figure 2).
- **Spatial gap between trajectories (gap_{space}):** The maximum allowed Euclidean distance in 2D plane between two consecutive time-stamped positions of the same trajectory. As such, any time-stamped position of object o_i, with distance from the last recorded position of this object greater than gap_{space}, will cause a new trajectory to be created for o_i (case *b* in Figure 2).

- **Maximum speed (V_{max}):** The maximum allowed speed of a moving object. It is used in order to determine whether a reported time-stamped position must be considered as noise and consequently discarded from the output trajectory. When a new time-stamped location of object o_i is received, it is checked with respect to the last known position of that object, and the corresponding speed is calculated. If it exceeds V_{max}, this location is considered as noise and (temporarily) it is not considered in the trajectory reconstruction process (however, it is kept separately as it may turn out to be useful again - see the parameter that follows) (case c in Figure 2).

- **Maximum noise duration ($noise_{max}$):** The maximum duration of a noisy part of a trajectory. Any sequence of noisy time-stamped positions of the same object will result in a new trajectory given that its duration exceeds $noise_{max}$. For example, consider an application recording positions of pedestrians where the maximum speed set for a pedestrian is $V_{max} = 3\ m\ /\ sec$. When he/she picks up a transportation mean (e.g., a bus), the recorded instant speed will exceed V_{max}, flagging the positions on the bus as noise. The maximum noise length parameter stands for supporting this scenario: when the duration of this sequence of "noise" exceeds $noise_{max}$, a new trajectory containing all these positions is created (case d in Figure 2).

- **Tolerance distance (D_{tol}):** The tolerance of the transmitted time-stamped positions. In other words, it is the maximum distance between two consecutive time-stamped positions of the same object in order for the object to be considered as stationary. When a new time-stamped location of object o_i is received, it is checked with respect to the last known position of that object, and if the distance of the two locations is smaller than D_{tol}, it is considered redundant and consequently discarded (case e in Figure 2).

The algorithm that utilizes the aforementioned parameters is thoroughly presented and evaluated in Marketos et al. (2008). It expects as input a set of observations, and a list containing the partial trajectories processed so far by the trajectory reconstruction manager; these partial trajectories are composed by several of the most recent trajectory points, depending on the values of the algorithm parameters.

As a first step, from each observation the algorithm extracts the object identifier and checks whether the object has been processed so far. If so, it retrieves its partial trajectory from the corresponding list, while, in the opposite case, creates a new trajectory and adds it to the list. Then, it compares the incoming point with the tail of the partial trajectory by applying the above mentioned trajectory reconstruction parameters. In this way, the algorithm decides if the incoming point can be considered as part of an existing trajectory or a new one has to be created.

TDW Schema and Loading

Let us assume a MOD that stores raw locations of moving objects (e.g. humans); a typical schema, to be considered as a minimum requirement, for such a MOD is illustrated in Figure 3.

OBJECTS includes a unique object identifier (*object-id*), demographic information (e.g. description, gender, birth-date, profession) as well as device-related technographic information (e.g. GPS type). RAW_LOCATIONS stores object locations at various time stamps (i.e., observations), while MOD_TRAJECTORIES maintains the trajectories of the objects, after the application of the trajectory reconstruction process. Formally, let $D = \{T_1, T_2, \dots, T_N\}$ be a collection of trajectories of a set of moving objects stored in the MOD.

Figure 2. Raw locations and reconstructed trajectories

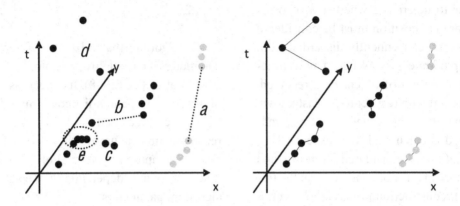

Assuming linear interpolation between consecutive observations, the trajectory $T_i = \langle (x_{i_1}, y_{i_1}, t_{i_1}), \ldots, (x_{i_{n_i}}, y_{i_{n_i}}, t_{i_{n_i}}) \rangle$ consists of a sequence of n_i line segments in a $3D$ space, where each segment represents the continuous "development" of the corresponding moving object between consecutive locations (x_{i_j}, y_{i_j}) sampled at time t_{i_j} (see the right picture of Figure 2). Projecting T_i on the spatial $2D$ plane (temporal $1D$ line), we get the *route* r_i (the *lifespan* l_i, respectively) of the trajectory. Additional motion parameters can be derived, including the traversed length *len* of route r_i, average speed, acceleration, etc.

As we mentioned before, our aim is to feed the TDW with aggregate data so as to offer OLAP analysis. Therefore, we need an appropriate TDW schema that can handle trajectory data. Following the multidimensional model (Agarwal et al., 1996), a data cube for trajectories consists of a fact table containing keys to dimension tables and a number of measures. The dimensions of analysis include a spatial (SPACE_DIM) and a temporal (TIME_DIM) dimension describing geography and time, respectively. Non spatio-temporal dimensions can be also considered. For example, the schema in Figure 4 contains the dimension OBJECT_PRO-

Figure 3. An example of a MOD

OBJECTS (object-id: *identifier*, description: *text*, gender: {M | F}, birth-date: *date*, profession: *text*, device-type: *text*)

RAW_LOCATIONS (object-id: *identifier*, timestamp: *datetime*, eastings-x: *numeric*, northings-y: *numeric*, altitude-z: *numeric*)

MOD_TRAJECTORIES (trajectory-id: *identifier*, object-id: *identifier*, trajectory: *3D geometry*)

Figure 4. An example of TDW

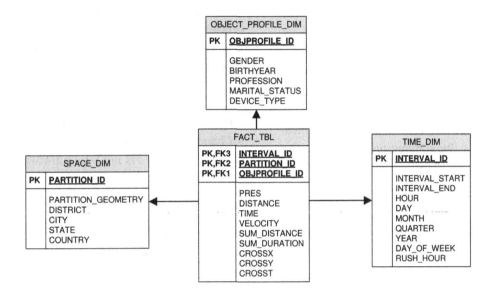

FILE_DIM which collects demographical information, such as gender, age, job, of moving objects.

Dimensions are organized in hierarchies that favor the data aggregation process. In Figure 4 the spatial hierarchy is rooted in *Partition_Geometry*, which represents the smallest spatial unit we consider (i.e., a rectangle belonging to a grid which partitions the spatial domain). Further every *Partition_Geometry* is contained in exactly one *district* and the remaining levels of the spatial hierarchy are city, state and country. Similarly, we consider an interval of minutes as the minimal temporal unit. Such intervals belong to a hour, that can be flagged as a typical one or a *rush_hour*, and is included in one day. A day is contained in both a month and it is also a day_ of_week. Finally, the temporal hierarchy is composed by quarter, year.

Let us now describe the measures of interest for our T-warehouse. We recall that measures represent aggregated information about trajectories of certain profiles that intersect the spatio-temporal cells.

The measure Pres for a base cell $bc=(R,T,P)$ represents the number of trajectories having profile P lying in the spatial region R in the time interval T. It is calculated by counting all the distinct trajectory ids belonging to P that pass through the spatio-temporal cell (R,T).

The measure Distance, i.e. the average traveled distance of a trajectory in a cell, for a base cell $bc=(R,T,P)$ is computed by introducing an auxiliary measure, called *sum_distance*, defined as follows:

$$sum\_distance(bc) = \Sigma_{i \in P, TP_i \in (R,T)} len(TP_i)$$

where TP_i is the portion of the trajectory i which lies within the region R during the time interval T and $len(TP_i)$ is its length. *sum_distance* represents the total distance travelled by trajectories having profile P in R during T. Then, the measure Distance can be computed as:

$$Distance(bc) = \frac{sum\_distance(bc)}{Pres(bc)}$$

The average travel duration of a trajectory in $bc=(R,T,P)$, represented by the measure Time, is computed in an analogous way:

$$Time(bc) = \frac{sum\_duration(bc)}{Pres(bc)}$$

where, *sum_duration* is also an auxiliary measure defined as the summation of the duration *lifespan(TP)* of each portion *TP* of the trajectories having profile *P* inside (R,T).

$$sum\_duration(bc) = \Sigma_{i \in P, TP_i \in (R,T)} lifespan(TP_i)$$

The measure Velocity is calculated by dividing the auxiliary measure *sum_distance* with *sum_duration*:

$$Velocity(bc) = \frac{sum\_distance(bc)}{sum\_duration(bc)}$$

In a likewise fashion, we could compute and store acceleration by utilizing speed and duration.

The remaining measures ($CrossX, CrossY, CrossT$) are auxiliary measures that will be defined in the following subsection.

It is worth remarking that for base cells all these measures are computed in an exact way by using the MOD. This is possible thanks to the fact that our MOD Hermes (Pelekis et al., 2006) provides a rich palette of spatial and temporal operators for handling trajectories. Unfortunately, rolling-up these measures is not straightforward due to the count distinct problem (Tao et al., 2004) as it will be discussed in detail in the next subsection.

In order to calculate the measures of the data cube, we have to extract the portions of the trajectories that fit into the base cells of the cube. In Marketos et al. (2008), we proposed and evaluated two alternative strategies for computing the measures: a cell-oriented (COA) and a trajectory-oriented (TOA) one. Figure 5 illustrates the application of the COA approach on the two trajectories that lie within three spatio-temporal cells. First, the procedure searches for the portions of trajectories under the constraint that they reside inside each spatio-temporal cell (R,T) (the start/end of each portion has been marked with a circle

Figure 5. Applying the cell oriented algorithm

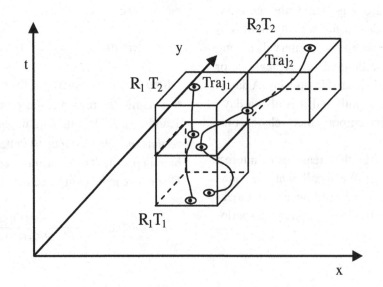

containing a dot). Then, the algorithm proceeds to the decomposition of the portions with respect to the user profiles they belong to. The efficiency of the above described COA solution depends on the effective computation of the parts of the moving object trajectories that reside in the spatio-temporal cells. This step is actually a spatio-temporal range query that returns not only the identifiers but also the portions of trajectories that satisfy the range constraints. To efficiently support this trajectory-based query processing requirement, we employ the TB-tree (Pfoser et al., 2000), a state-of-the-art index for trajectories that can efficiently support trajectory query processing. On the other hand, the TOA approach discovers the spatio-temporal cells where each trajectory resides in. The main challenge here is to avoid checking all cells. This becomes possible by utilizing Minimum Bounding Rectangles of trajectories as rough approximations of them and by exploiting the fact that the granularity of cells is fixed in order to detect (possibly) involved cells in constant time. Further details about the two approaches as well as a comparison study can be found in Marketos et al. (2008).

Aggregation

In order to allow for OLAP processing, T-Warehouse offers aggregation capabilities over measures, i.e., operations for computing measures at some higher level of the hierarchy starting from those at lower level. The aggregate functions computing the super-aggregates of the measures are categorized by Gray et al. (1997) into three classes according to the complexity required for this computation:

- Distributive, the super-aggregates can be computed from the sub-aggregates.
- Algebraic, the super-aggregates can be computed from the sub-aggregates with a finite set of auxiliary measures. and

- Holistic, the super-aggregates cannot be computed from sub-aggregates, even if we employ auxiliary measures.

According to this classification, *sum_distance* and *sum_duration* are distributive since we can aggregate such measures by using the function sum whereas Velocity is algebraic: we need the auxiliary measures $\langle sum\_distance, sum\_duration \rangle$. For a cell C arising as the union of adjacent cells, the aggregate function performs a component-wise addition, thus producing a pair $\langle sum\_distance_f, sum\_duration_f \rangle$. Then the average speed in C is given by $sum\_distance_f / sum\_duration_f$.

The most complex measures are Pres, Distance and Time which are holistic. In fact, since a trajectory might span multiple base cells, in the aggregation phase we have to cope with the so called distinct count problem (Tao et al., 2004): if an object remains in the query region for several timestamps during the query interval, one should avoid to count it multiple times in the result. This is problematic since, once loaded in the TDW, the identifiers of the trajectories are lost. This problem causes aggregation hindrances in OLAP operations for the above measures.

Notice that once a technique for rolling-up the measure Pres is devised, it is straightforward to define a roll-up operation for Distance and Time. In fact the latter can be implemented as the sum of the corresponding auxiliary measures (*sum_distance* and *sum_duration*) divided by the result of the roll-up of Pres. Hence, we will focus only on the measure Pres.

In order to implement a roll-up operation over Pres, a first solution is to define a distributive aggregate function, denoted by $Pres_{Distr}$, which simply obtains the super-aggregate of a cell C by summing up the measures Pres in the base cells composing C. In the literature, this is a common approach to aggregate spatio-temporal data but, as we will show in accuracy of spatio-temporal aggregates subsection, it produces a very rough approximation.

Following the proposal in Orlando et al. (2007), an alternative solution is to define an algebraic aggregate function, denoted by $Pres_{Alg}$. More formally, let $C_{(x,y),t,p}$ be a base cell, which contains, among the others, the following measures:

- $\mathbf{C_{(x,y),t,p}}$**.Pres:** The number of distinct trajectories of profile p intersecting the cell.

- $\mathbf{C_{(x,y),t,p}}$**.CrossX:** The number of distinct trajectories of profile p crossing the spatial border between $C_{(x-1,y),t,p}$ and $C_{(x,y),t,p}$, where $C_{(x-1,y),t,p}$ is the adjacent cell (on the left) along with x-axis.

- $\mathbf{C_{(x,y),t,p}}$**.CrossY:** The number of distinct trajectories of profile p crossing the spatial border between $C_{(x,y-1),t,p}$ and $C_{(x,y),t,p}$, where $C_{(x,y-1),t,p}$ is the adjacent cell (below) along with y-axis.

- $\mathbf{C_{(x,y),t,p}}$**.CrossT:** The number of distinct trajectories of profile p crossing the temporal border between $C_{(x,y),t-1,p}$ and $C_{(x,y),t,p}$, where $C_{(x,y),t-1,p}$ is the adjacent cell (below) along with t-axis.

Let $C_{(x',y'),t',p'}$ be a cell consisting of the union of two adjacent cells with respect to a spatial/temporal dimension, for example $C_{(x',y'),t',p'} = C_{(x,y),t,p} \cup C_{(x+1,y),t,p}$ (when aggregating along x-axis). In order to compute the super-aggregate corresponding to $C_{(x',y'),t',p'}$, we proceed as follows:

$$C_{(x',y'),t',p'}.Pres = C_{(x,y),t,p}.Pres + C_{(x+1,y),t,p}.Pres - C_{(x+1,y),t,p}.CrossX$$

The other measures associated with $C_{(x',y'),t',p'}$ can be computed as follows:

$$C_{(x',y'),t',p'}.CrossX = C_{(x,y),t,p}.CrossX$$
$$C_{(x',y'),t',p'}.CrossY = C_{(x,y),t,p}.CrossY + C_{(x+1,y),t,p}.CrossY$$
$$C_{(x',y'),t',p'}.CrossT = C_{(x,y),t,p}.CrossT + C_{(x+1,y),t,p}.CrossT$$

The computation of $C_{(x',y'),t',p'}.Pres$ can be thought of as an application of the well-known Inclusion/Exclusion principle for sets: $|A \cup B| = |A| + |B| - |A \cap B|$. Note that in some cases $C_{(x+1,y),t,p}.CrossX$ is not equal to $|A \cap B|$, and this may introduce errors in the values returned by this algebraic function. In fact, if a trajectory is fast and agile, it can be found in both $C_{(x,y),t,p}$ and $C_{(x+1,y),t,p}$ without crossing the X border (since it can reach $C_{(x+1,y),t,p}$ by crossing the Y borders of $C_{(x,y),t,p}$ and $C_{(x+1,y),t,p}$ as shown in Figure 6(a)). In the following figures we illustrate the two main kinds of error that the algebraic aggregate function can introduce in the roll-up phase due to the agility of trajectories. In Figure 6(a), if we group together the cells C_1 and C_2, we obtain that the number of distinct trajectories is $C_1.Pres + C_2.Pres - C_2.CrossX = 1 + 1 - 0 = 2$. This is an overestimate of the number of distinct trajectories. On the other hand, in Figure 6(b), if we group together C_1 and C_2 we correctly obtain $C_1.Pres + C_2.Pres - C_2.CrossX = 1 + 1 - 1 = 1$, similarly by aggregating C_3 and C_4. However, if we group $C_1 \cup C_2$ with $C_3 \cup C_4$ we obtain $C_1 \cup C_2.Press + C_3 \cup C_4.Pres - C_1 \cup C_2.CrossY = 1 + 1 - 2 = 0$. This is an underestimate of the number of distinct trajectories.

Note that in order to face the distinct count problem when aggregating cells with different

Figure 6. (a) Overestimate of Pres, and (b) underestimate of Pres during the roll-up

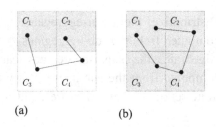

(a)　　　　　　　　(b)

profiles, analogously to what we did for the spatial and temporal dimensions, it could be helpful to consider a measure *crossP*, specifying the number of distinct trajectories changing their profile from one cell to an adjacent one. However, since profile changes are rather rare in real-world scenarios and only appear in long term situations, we omit computing *crossP* and we simply use the distributive aggregate function *sum* for this kind of aggregations. (In any case, when needed, *crossP* can be added in our framework without additional difficulty.)

OLAP AND VISUALISATION

A TDW serves two core needs: to provide the appropriate infrastructure for advanced reporting capabilities and to facilitate the application of trajectory mining algorithms on the aggregated data. According to their needs, end users could have access either to basic reports or OLAP-style analysis. What-if scenarios and multidimensional analysis are typical examples of analytics that can be supported by a TDW. Some interesting questions in the context of traffic monitoring, that an analyst may want to answer via the functionalities offered by TDW, are "When and in which area of the town does the most intense traffic appear?", if we consider the road network, "which are the most trafficated roads?", "Is there any difference in traffic between the working days and the weekend?", "How does the movement propagate from place to place? ".

Even if standard, table based OLAP operations could be used to answer this kind of queries, the interpretation of results, and the consequent refinement of queries and exploration of results, is not immediate. Integrating OLAP tools with Geographical Information Systems (GISs) provides advanced analysis capabilities. For instance, trajectory data can be georeferenced in a map, combined with several layers (such as topographic,

demographic, thematic). Finally, performing OLAP operations on TDW specialised measures in a visual way makes the exploration of the data cube more rapid and intuitive.

We developed OLAP visual operations, by using the Visual Analytics Toolkit (Andrienko et al., 2007), an interactive Java™ based geographical information system. This toolkit permits a user to view georeferenced data over a map. It also offers functionalities to handle temporal data, by using graphs or animations, according to the type of data to analyse.

By using our system, it is simple to handle and visualise the spatio-temporal grids of the TDW at various levels of granularities. If the roll-up operation involves the spatial dimension, visually this affects the granularity of the grid which becomes larger. The inverse operation is the drill-down which increases the level of detail of data; it allows the user to descend into the hierarchies. In this case, we can select the spatial area we are interested in and if we reduce the spatial dimension of the cells, a smaller grid is visualised as shown in Figure 7.

Starting from this visualisation of the space, one can then decide to highlight some measures, which can be visualised according to several methods. The unclassified choropleth map technique fills the grid cells with colour shades so that the degree of darkness is proportional to the value of a selected measure. For building a classified choropleth map, the value range of the selected measure is divided into intervals, also called classes. Each class is assigned a particular color. These colors are then used for filling the grid cells on the map. In the Triangle visualisation technique, a triangle is drawn in each grid cell at a chosen level of the TDW hierarchy. The base and the height of such a triangle correspond to the values of two selected measures that the user wants to analyze. The Line thickness visualisation style draws linear symbols whose thickness is proportional to the value of a given TDW measure.

Figure 7. Drill-down

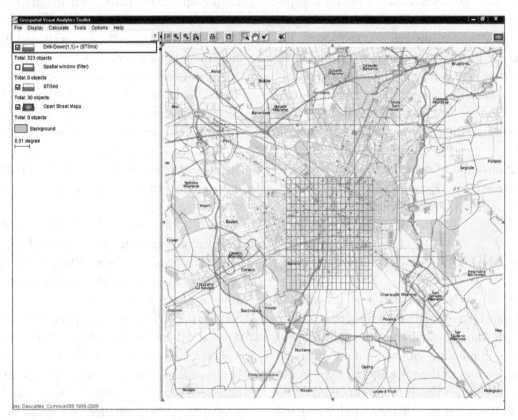

These visualisation methods can be used in animated displays, where each frame represents the selected measure(s) in one time interval from the period of interest.

Cartographic visualization techniques offer limited opportunities for the examination of the temporal variation of the data. This weakness needs to be compensated by using additional visualisations appropriately representing the temporal aspect, such as the composite time series display demonstrated in Figures 9 and 10. The display consists of two parts with a common horizontal axis representing the time period under study divided into intervals. The upper part is a generalized time graph. The vertical axis represents the value range of the selected measure. Instead of the lines showing the variation of the measure in each grid cell at a given granularity over time, there is a polygon enclosing all the lines. The

lower and upper boundaries of the polygon show the ranges of the values in each time interval. Additional details are provided by dividing the polygon area into 10 parts. The division is done as follows. For each time interval, the range of values of the measure is divided into deciles, i.e. 10 parts containing approximately equal number of values. The positions of the corresponding deciles in consecutive time intervals are connected by lines and the areas between the lines are filled in two different shades of grey. On top of this, a thick black line represents the temporal variation of the mean value from all grid cells, which is computed for each interval.

The lower part of the display is a temporal histogram. The vertical dimension represents the number of cells. Each segmented bar shows the statistical distribution of the values of the measure in one time interval. For this purpose, the overall

Figure 9. The evolution of Pres during the week

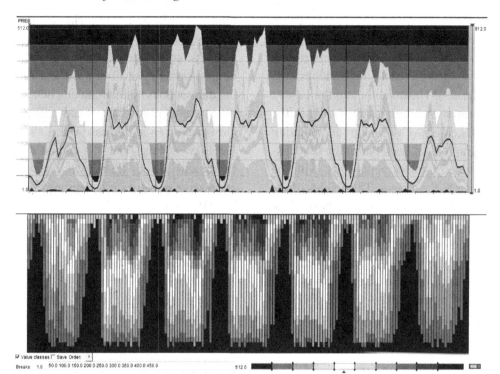

Figure 10. The evolution of Velocity during the week

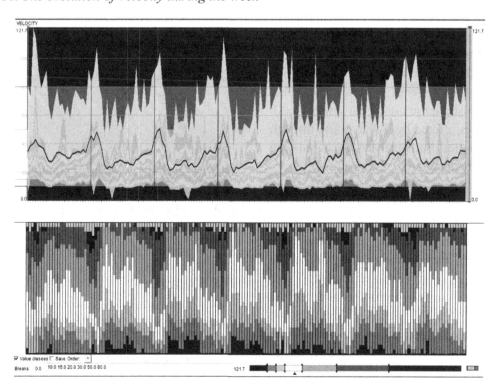

range of the values is divided into intervals, or classes, and each class is given a particular color. According to the chosen color scale, shades of blue correspond to low values (the lower, the darker) and shades of red to high values (the higher, the darker). The division into the classes and the corresponding colors are shown in the upper part of the display by background painting of the time graph area. Each bar in the time histogram is divided into segments filled with the colors assigned to the classes. The heights of the segments are proportional to the numbers of the grid cells whose values belong to the respective classes. Grey-colored segments stand for the cells where the aggregate values are not defined. The upper and lower parts of the display provide two complementary overall views of the temporal variation of the data.

APPLYING T-WAREHOUSE TO TRAFFIC DATA

In this section, first, we quantitatively evaluate the roll-up accuracy of our T-Warehouse. In particular, we show the error in computing Pres since, as discussed in aggregation subsection, it is an approximation of the exact value and this affects also the measures Distance and Time. Then, we illustrate the use of the visual OLAP functionalities offered by T-Warehouse through several examples. Both analyses are based on a large mobility dataset described below.

Dataset

We used a real world dataset containing the observations of GPS-equipped cars moving in the urban area of Milan (Italy). The dataset consists of two millions of raw location records that represent the movement of 17,000 objects (i.e. about 200,000 trajectories) moving during a week period from Sunday to Saturday. As base granularity, we set

a grid of rectangles, of size 330m × 440m, and time intervals of 1 hour. The spatial hierarchy aggregates groups of 10-20-40-80 spatially adjacent base cells, whereas the temporal hierarchy is hour- 3-hours interval-day-week. Unfortunately, the dataset does not contain any details about the demographical profiles of the different objects. However, even in this case where the schema of the TDW consists just of a spatial and a temporal dimension, our framework does not loose in expressive power as it is demonstrated in Visual OLAP Analysis subsection.

Accuracy of Spatio-Temporal Aggregates

Before presenting the results of our experiments, we first define the metric that we use to quantify the overall error for the measure Pres, generated by an aggregation operation. Then we describe the sketches based algorithm adopted in Tao et al. (2004) and used in our experiments.

In order to compare the errors we chose to adopt as an aggregation accuracy metric the normalized absolute error defined as follows:

$$Error = \frac{\sum_C Error(C)}{\sum_C C.Pres} = \frac{\sum_C |\widehat{C.Pres} - C.Pres|}{\sum_C C.Pres}$$

(1)

where C are cells at a coarser granularity than the base one, $C.Pres$ is the exact value of Pres in the cell C whereas $\widehat{C.Pres}$ is the approximated value obtained using one of the discussed methods, i.e. $Pres_{FM}$(sketches), $Pres_{Distr}$ or $Pres_{Alg}$.

FM Sketches

The FM algorithm is a bitmap-based algorithm devised by Flajolet and Martin (1985) that can be used to estimate the number of distinct items in a set using a limited amount of memory. Each entry in the sketch used by FM is a bitmap of length $r = \log UB$, where UB is an upper bound on the number of distinct items. A hash function h maps every object ID i (trajectory identifiers in our case) to a pseudo-random integer $h(i)$ corresponding to a position in the r-bit sketch that will be set (the whole bitmap is initially unset). The values are mapped by h according to a geometric distribution, that is, the probability that a generic ID i will be mapped to a position v is $Prob[h(i)=v]=2^{-v}$ for $v^3 1$

After processing all objects, the most simple version of FM approximates the overall object count with $1.29'2^k$, where k is the position of the leftmost bit of the sketch that is still unset. Unfortunately, this approach may entail large errors in the count approximation. For this reason, Flajolet and Martin (1985) propose the adoption of m sketches that use different and independent hash functions. Only one randomly selected sketch is modified on update, thus each sketch becomes responsible for approximately n/m (distinct) objects. Then, the count is computed by using all sketches.

Interestingly, FM sketches can be merged in a distributive way. Suppose that a pair of sketches are updated according to the IDs of the objects contained in a different set, and that the intersection of those sets is possibly not empty. The sketch obtained as the *bitwise-OR* of the corresponding bitmaps in the original sketches will be identical to the one directly updated using the union of the sets of items.

Quantitative Evaluation

In Figure 8 we compare the accuracy of these different approximate aggregation methods. The graphs show the normalised absolute errors as functions of cell granularities. Cell granularities are reported as values relative to the base one. For example, $g-2$ indicates that we are considering cells having double size w.r.t. the base cells along all dimensions.

Figure 8. Cumulative errors of roll-up phase

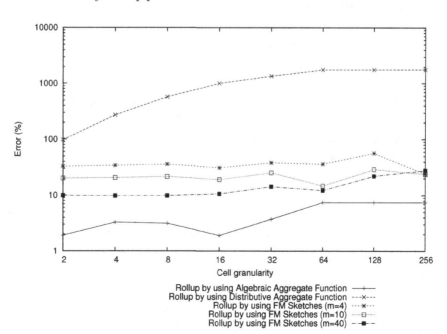

Notice that we avoid plotting the error for $g=1$, corresponding to base cells, because here we are interested in the aggregation error ($g>1$). Further, we recall that at the base granularity the measure Pres is exact because by using the spatio-temporal operators offered by the MOD the base cells are loaded with the correct values.

As shown by the corresponding curves, the distributive aggregate function (the top curve) quickly reaches very large errors as the roll-up granularity increases. This is due to the fact that we simply sum the sub-aggregates and as a consequence trajectories crossing different cells are counted many times: the number of duplicates becomes higher and higher at coarser granularities. Conversely, we obtained very accurate results with our algebraic method, especially at small granularities where the error is less than 3%. One can observe that the cumulative error starts increasing when larger granularities g are considered, since the number of trajectories that visit the various cells several times gets larger but the error remains always smaller than 10%. Finally, we can remark that for all granularities the aggregate function $Pres_{Alg}$ outperforms sketches and we also save memory. We highlight that in order to obtain an accuracy around 10% 40 sketches have to be used, each $32-bit$ long, that is ten times the memory allocated by the four counters used by our algebraic aggregation method.

Visual OLAP Analysis

In this subsection we present the functionalities and the flexibility of T-Warehouse for the visual analysis of the Milan dataset.

First of all we want to study how the traffic varies along the week and answer the query: "When does the most intense traffic appear? " The time series display in Figure 9 summarizes the temporal variation of the measure Pres over the whole territory (i.e. all grid cells). The time period of the data (one week from Sunday to Saturday) has been divided into hourly intervals.

The territory has been divided into cells of the size $3.3km \times 4.4km$, i.e. 10 base cells are aggregated together along the x and y axes. The appearance of the display shows a clear subdivision of the whole time period into days. We can observe that the presence is much higher in the day hours than in the night and noticeably higher on the working days than on Sunday and Saturday. On each of the working days, there are two peaks of the number of cells with high presence, signified by the shades of red. These peaks correspond to the morning and afternoon rush hours, which occur in the intervals $6-9am$ and $3-6pm$. Interesting is the increase of traffic intensity on the Sunday afternoon. It is also visible that the traffic on Friday was less intense than on the previous working days: there were no cells with the values lying in the upper two classes of the values of presence.

Comparing the display of the presence with the display of the speed of the objects at the same granularity, shown in Figure 10, one can immediately realise that presence and average speed are inversely proportional. During the early and late hours of the day the speed is high whereas from 6am up to 6pm the speed decreases significantly, exhibiting a dual behaviour with respect to the presence.

The composite time series displays representing the temporal evolution of the measures need to be combined with cartographic visualisations showing the data in the spatial context. For example, Figure 11 is a screen-shot of the animation representing the values of the speed and the presence by triangular symbols. The height of the triangle is proportional to the speed and the base to the presence. One animation frame corresponds to one hourly interval and the whole animation shows the variation of the presence and speed over the week. This reveals additional information with respect to the time series displays. Thus, the image in Figure 11 shows that the presence is higher in the centre and this has a strong impact on the speed of cars, which is very low. On the other hand, it highlights that along the ring roads, the speed is higher except in the north-east zone where the larger number of cars slows down the traffic.

Next, we compare the data of our DW at two different spatial granularities. We roll-up the data illustrated in Figure 11 by aggregating two adjacent rectangles and 3 consecutive hours. Figure 12(a) and Figure 12(b) show the 8 screenshots of the data at 0-3am, 3-6am, and so forth taken on Tuesday and on Saturday, as representative of the situation on a working day and on the week-end. We chose an unclassified choropleth map, that gives us an overall view of the data: the denser is the traffic in a cell, the darker is its colour. During the working days, we can see that the traffic is concentrated in the centre and in the north-east areas of Milan and the rush hours are from 6am to 9am and from 3pm to 6pm, even though the centre is crowded also from 6pm up to 9pm. On the week-end, the densest area remains the centre but the peak of the traffic is reached in a different time interval starting later, around 9am instead of 6am but remaining more sensibly intense for the whole night.

Now we apply to these data a drill-down operation in order to obtain the data at the base granularity for the spatial dimension. The result is visualised in Figure 12(c) and Figure 12(d) using the technique of classified choropleth map. Like in Figure 9, the shades of red represent high values of the presence and the shades of blue low values. At this level of detail, the information about the presence is strictly connected to the main roads. We can distinguish several rings around the centre and some radial streets that are used to enter/exit to/from the centre. This allows us to answer queries about the traffic conditions at the road network level and their evolution over time. It is interesting to notice that from 0am to 3am on Tuesday there are few cars moving around, and there is no dense area. Then the outer ring of the town becomes denser and later the inner rings and the radial roads. It may be concluded that in the morning there is a flow from the outside to

the centre. An opposite pattern can be observed in the second part of the day (not illustrated in the figure). On Saturday (Figure 12(d)) the situation is different. From 0am to 3am (the night from Friday to Saturday) there is traffic in some radial roads which reveals movement closer to the centre. From 3am to 9am, however, the traffic is not as intense as on Tuesday. Later it becomes denser, and there is traffic up to midnight also in the radial roads.

In order to understand how the traffic flows from one cell to the other ones, we can use the Cross Visualisation operation which is intended to illustrate the cross measures, i.e. the number of trajectories traversing the x border and y border of a cell. The idea is that the thickness of the lines of the grid is proportional to the values of the cross, thus providing a qualitative representation of these measures. In Figure 13 the measure *CrossX* (crossing of x border) is represented by vertical lines, whereas the measure *CrossY* (crossing of y border) by the horizontal lines.

Finally, T-Warehouse provides the user with an operation called *Cyclic Time analysis* which allows for a kind of cyclic aggregation. For instance, it is possible to capture what happens on Mondays, on Tuesdays and so on for the whole period of analysis, thus aggregating data concerning the same days of the week.

RELATED WORK

The research in TDW has intersections with two research fields extensively studied over the last decade, namely spatial data warehouses and moving object databases. In Gómez et al. (2009) the authors present a complete survey of both fields, as well as a description of the emerging works on Spatio-Temporal Data Warehouses (STDW).

The pioneering work by Han et al. (1998) introduces the concept of spatial data warehousing (SDW). The authors extend the idea of cube

Figure 11. Relationship between Pres (widths of the triangles) and Velocity (heights of the triangles)

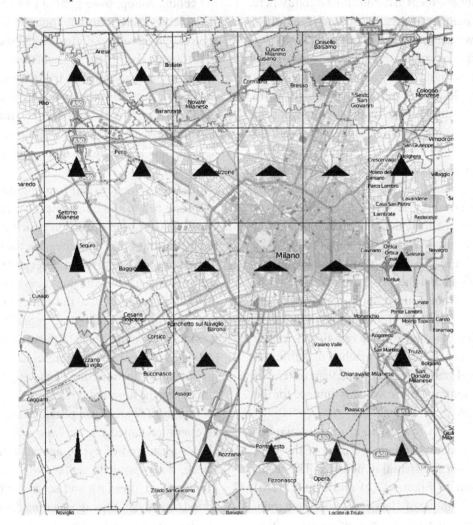

dimensions so as to include spatial and non-spatial ones, and of cube measures so as to represent space regions and/or calculate numerical data. One step further from modeling a SDW is modeling a STDW. As stated in Vaisman and Zimányi (2009) there is no commonly agreed definition of what a STDW is and what functionality such a data warehouse should support. In Vaisman and Zimányi (2009) the authors propose a conceptual framework for defining STDWs and a taxonomy for spatio-temporal OLAP queries through which they classify the approaches in literature. According to this classification, T-Warehouse is very

expressive as it succeeds in supporting Spatio-Temporal OLAP queries.

Another major research direction concerns the efficient implementation of aggregate queries. Tao and Papadias (2005) propose a technique based on the combined use of specialised indexes and materialisation of aggregate measures. Choi et al. (2006) try to overcome the limitations of multi-tree structures by introducing a new index structure that combines the benefits of Quadtrees and Grid files. However, the above frameworks focus on calculating simple measures (e.g. count customers) and they do not cope with trajectories.

Figure 12. Pres at different granularities

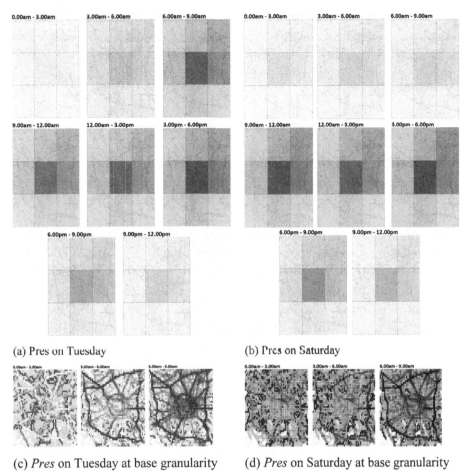

(a) Pres on Tuesday

(b) Pres on Saturday

(c) *Pres* on Tuesday at base granularity

(d) *Pres* on Saturday at base granularity

Traffic analysis is a topic that has been largely studied in the past, even if nowadays the large availability of trajectory data makes it possible to perform innovative and accurate analyses. To the best of our knowledge, however, this is the first work that leverages the depth of analyses allowed by a TDW, and the intuitive interaction obtained thanks to the visual spatio-temporal OLAP interface to support the decision making of traffic analysts.

Visual analysis of large collections of movement data is one of the research topics in the area of geographic visualisation. Starting from the work by Fredrikson et al. (1999), spatial, temporal, and attributive aggregations have been applied to movement data. Temporally aggregated data are represented, for instance, by means of a temporal histogram where the bars correspond to time intervals and their heights are proportional e.g. to the number of locations visited or the distance traveled (Dykes & Mountain, 2003). Spatial aggregation produces a statistical surface, which is visualized on a map. Spatio-temporal aggregation produces a series of surfaces (one surface per time interval) visualized by means of an animated map display (Dykes & Mountain, 2003; Forer & Huisman, 2000). In these works, movement data are treated as a set of independent points in space and time.

Figure 13. Visualisation of CrossX and CrossY

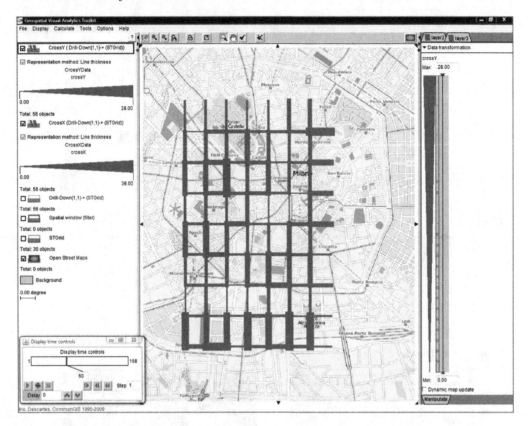

Another way of aggregating movement data is based on considering the data as a set of moves between predefined places (spatial compartments). Each move is treated as a vector characterized by its origin and destination places, start and end times, and, possibly, additional attributes such as duration and travelled distance. Moves with coinciding origins and destinations are united into aggregate moves, which are characterized by the count of the original moves and other statistics. The results may be visualized as a transition matrix where the rows and columns correspond to the places and symbols in the cells or cell coloring or shading encode the derived attribute values (Guo, 2007). An obvious disadvantage is the lack of spatial context. Another technique is flow map, where aggregated moves are represented by bands or arrows connecting pairs of locations (Tobler,

1987). When this kind of spatial aggregation is combined with temporal aggregation, the result can be visualized by an animated matrix or flow map display or by a juxtaposed sequence of such displays. Drecki and Forer (2000) use a three-dimensional representation to show aggregate moves corresponding to several consecutive time intervals (reproduced in Andrienko & Andrienko, 2007).

The work (Andrienko & Andrienko, 2008) surveys the methods that are used for aggregation of movement data and visualization of the resulting aggregates and proposes some novel techniques designed specifically for this kind of data. By this moment, there were no published works concerning visual analysis of movement data with the use of trajectory data warehouses.

CONCLUSION

This paper discussed the main design issues concerning a DW which stores aggregate measures computed over trajectories and allows performing OLAP analyses over both the temporal and spatial dimensions. In particular, we focused on issues related to storing and aggregating (rolling-up) the holistic measure Pres, which, along with other measures (speed, distance covered, etc.), is very useful to convey actionable knowledge to a traffic analyst. Moreover, we demonstrated how T-Warehouse can be used within a visual analytics environment for enabling interactive analysis and interpretation of the data.

Finally, we discussed the usage of T-Warehouse in the context of traffic analysis. In particular we presented a set of OLAP visual operations that permit answering interesting questions in the context of traffic monitoring. We showed a real use case which regards a large real dataset storing the trajectories of a fleet of cars moving in the metropolitan area of Milan (Italy).

REFERENCES

Agarwal, S., Agrawal, R., Deshpande, P., Gupta, A., Naughton, J., Ramakrishnan, R., et al. (1996). On the computation of multidimensional aggregates. In *Proceedings of VLDB* (pp. 506–521).

Andrienko, G., & Andrienko, N. (2008). Spatio-temporal aggregation for visual analysis of movements. In *Proceedings of IEEE Symposium on Visual Analytics Science and Technology* (pp. 51–58). Washington, DC: IEEE Computer Society Press.

Andrienko, G., Andrienko, N., & Wrobel, S. (2007). Visual analytics tools for analysis of movement data. *ACM SIGKDD Explorations, 9*(2), 28–46. doi:10.1145/1345448.1345455

Andrienko, N., & Andrienko, G. (2007). Designing visual analytics methods for massive collections of movement data. *Cartographica, 42*(2), 117–138.

Choi, W., Kwon, D., & Lee, S. (2006). Spatio-temporal data warehouses using an adaptive cell-based approach. *DKE, 59*(1), 189–207. doi:10.1016/j.datak.2005.08.001

Drecki, I., & Forer, P. (2000). *Tourism in New Zealand - international visitors on the move (a1 cartographic plate)*. Lincoln, NE: Tourism, Recreation Research and Education Centre, Lincoln University.

Dykes, J. A., & Mountain, D. M. (2003). Seeking structure in records of spatio-temporal behavior: visualization issues. *Computational Statistics & Data Analysis, 43*(4), 581–603. doi:10.1016/S0167-9473(02)00294-3

Flajolet, P., & Martin, G. (1985). Probabilistic counting algorithms for data base applications. *Journal of Computer and System Sciences, 31*(2), 182–209. doi:10.1016/0022-0000(85)90041-8

Forer, P., & Huisman, O. (2000). Information, place and cyberspace: Issues in accessibility. In *Time and sequencing: Substitution at the physical/virtual interface* (pp. 73–90). Berlin: Springer Verlag.

Fredrikson, A., North, C., Plaisant, C., & Shneiderman, B. (1999). Temporal, geographical and categorical aggregations viewed through coordinated displays: A case study with highway incident data. In *Proceedings of the Workshop on New Paradigms in Information Visualization and Manipulation* (pp. 26–34).

Gómez, L., Kuijpers, B., Moelans, B., & Vaisman, A. (2009). A survey on spatio-temporal data warehousing. *International Journal of Data Warehousing and Mining, 5*(3), 28–55.

Gray, J., Chaudhuri, S., Bosworth, A., Layman, A., Reichart, D., & Venkatrao, M. (1997). Data cube: A relational aggregation operator generalizing group-by, cross-tab and sub-totals. *Data Mining and Knowledge Discovery*, *1*(1), 29–54. doi:10.1023/A:1009726021843

Guo, D. (2007). Visual analytics of spatial interaction patterns for pandemic decision support. *International Journal of Geographical Information Science*, *21*(8), 859–877. doi:10.1080/13658810701349037

Han, J., Stefanovic, N., & Kopersky, K. (1998). Selective materialization: An efficient method for spatial data cube construction. In *Proceedings of PAKDD* (pp. 144–158).

Kimball, R., Ross, M., Thornthwaite, W., Mundy, J., & Becker, B. (2008). *The Data Warehouse Lifecycle Toolkit, 2nd Edition: Practical Techniques for Building Data Warehouse and Intellingent Business Systems*. New York: John Wiley & Sons.

Marketos, G., Frentzos, E., Ntoutsi, I., Pelekis, N., Raffaetà, A., & Theodoridis, Y. (2008). Building real world trajectory warehouses. In *Proceedings of 7th International ACM Workshop on Data Engineering for Wireless and Mobile Access* (pp. 8–15).

Orlando, S., Orsini, R., Raffaetà, A., Roncato, A., & Silvestri, C. (2007). Trajectory Data Warehouses: Design and Implementation Issues. *Journal of Computing Science and Engineering*, *1*(2), 240–261.

Pelekis, N., Frentzos, E., Giatrakos, N., & Theodoridis, Y. (2008). HERMES: aggregative LBS via a trajectory DB engine. In *Proceedings of the ACM SIGMOD International Conference on Management of Data* (pp. 1255–1258). New York: ACM.

Pelekis, N., Theodoridis, Y., Vosinakis, S., & Panayiotopoulos, T. (2006). Hermes – a framework for location-based data management. In *Proceedings of EDBT* (pp. 1130–1134).

Pfoser, D., Jensen, C. S., & Theodoridis, Y. (2000). Novel Approaches in Query Processing for Moving Object Trajectories. In *Proceedings of VLDB* (pp. 395–406).

Tao, Y., Kollios, G., Considine, J., Li, F., & Papadias, D. (2004). Spatio-temporal aggregation using sketches. In *Proceedings of ICDE* (pp. 214–225).

Tao, Y., & Papadias, D. (2005). Historical spatiotemporal aggregation. *Proceedings of ACM TOIS*, *23*, 61–102.

Thomas, J., & Cook, K. (2005). *Illuminating the Path: The Research and development Agenda for Visual Analytics*. Washington, DC: IEEE Computer Society.

Tobler, W. (1987). Experiments in migration mapping by computer. *The American Cartographer*, *14*(2), 155–163. doi:10.1559/152304087783875273

Vaisman, A., & Zimányi, E. (2009). What is spatiotemporal data warehousing? In *Proceedings of the 11th International Conference on Data Warehousing and Knowledge Discovery* (pp. 9–23). Berlin: Springer-Verlag.

This work was previously published in the International Journal of Data Warehousing and Mining, Volume 7, Issue 1, edited by David Taniar, pp.1-23, copyright 2011 by IGI Publishing (an imprint of IGI Global).

Chapter 2
A Query Language for Mobility Data Mining

Roberto Trasarti
ISTI-CNR, Italy

Mirco Nanni
ISTI-CNR, Italy

Fosca Giannotti
ISTI-CNR Italy, & Northeastern University, USA

Dino Pedreschi
University of Pisa, Italy, & Northeastern University, USA

Chiara Renso
ISTI-CNR, Italy

ABSTRACT

The technologies of mobile communications and ubiquitous computing pervade society. Wireless networks sense the movement of people and vehicles, generating large volumes of mobility data, such as mobile phone call records and GPS tracks. This data can produce useful knowledge, supporting sustainable mobility and intelligent transportation systems, provided that a suitable knowledge discovery process is enacted for mining this mobility data. In this paper, the authors examine a formal framework, and the associated implementation, for a data mining query language for mobility data, created as a result of a European-wide research project called GeoPKDD (Geographic Privacy-Aware Knowledge Discovery and Delivery). The authors discuss how the system provides comprehensive support for the Mobility Knowledge Discovery process and illustrate its analytical power in unveiling the complexity of urban mobility in a large metropolitan area, based on a massive real life GPS dataset.

INTRODUCTION

Research on mobility data analysis has been recently fostered by the widespread diffusion of new techniques and systems for monitoring, collecting and storing location-aware data, generated by a wealth of wireless and mobile technologies, such as GPS positioning, mobile phones and sensor networks, tracking devices (Giannotti et al., 2008). These continuously feed massive repositories of spatio-temporally referenced data of moving objects, which call for suitable analytical methods for understanding mobile behavior. So far, research efforts have been largely aimed towards either

DOI: 10.4018/978-1-4666-2148-0.ch002

the definition of new movement model, or the development of solutions to algorithmic issues, to improve existing model-mining schemes in terms of effectiveness and/or efficiency. Unfortunately, discovering useful knowledge from these new forms of mobility data cannot be achieved by simply invoking an automated tool: as data miners know, successful analytics is the fruit of an overall knowledge discovery process, from raw data to knowledge. Figure 1 depicts the steps of the knowledge discovery process on movement data. Here, raw positioning data are collected from mobile devices and stored in the data repository. Trajectory data are then built, stored and analyzed by data mining algorithms to discover models hidden in the data. This process is typically iterative, since the composition of subsequent data mining methods is needed, both on data and model themselves, to obtain useful results. Finally, the extracted models have to be interpreted in order to be deployed by the final users.

The need of mastering the overall complexity of the knowledge discovery process led past re-search in the direction of inductive databases and data mining query languages (DMQL). Here, approaches provided various instances of querying and mining systems, all supporting the idea that discovering useful knowledge is a human-driven, and iterative and exploratory query process. Two main principles underlie this vision:

- **Persistence of data and models:** not only data, but also extracted models should be stored, in order to be further queried or mined (closure principle).
- **Expressiveness of the query language:** a high-level vision over data and models should be provided to the analyst.

The various DMQL proposals, described in the next section, refer to relational or transactional data and associated models; therefore, they are not directly exploitable for mobility knowledge discovery, given the very nature of movement of data and models. To bridge this gap, we designed and realized a comprehensive querying and mining

Figure 1. The Mobility Knowledge Discovery process

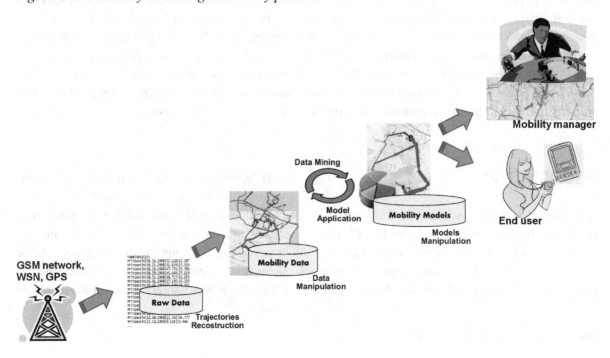

system, centred on movement data – the trajectories of the moving objects – and their analytical abstractions. This paper is devoted to introduce both a conceptual framework for a spatio-temporal DMQL and an associated implementation, designed to support the following functionalities:

1. The construction of trajectory data out of raw location data, as well as their storage and querying through spatio-temporal primitives.
2. The extraction of trajectory models representing collective behaviour using trajectory mining algorithms.
3. The compositionality of models, which are suitably represented and stored in order to be re-used.
4. The extensibility with new mining models and algorithms.

We firstly introduce the formal framework that defines the foundations of the proposed data mining query language for spatio-temporal data. Secondly, we sketch the language implementation in the GeoPKDD system, showing how the above functionalities are supported. Thirdly, we show the expressiveness of the proposed DMQL in a complex mobility data analysis task, aimed at discovering common behavioural models of group of vehicles in an urban setting.

RELATED WORK

Our work has been inspired by the literature on inductive databases (Imielinski et al., 1996). Here, the task of extracting useful and interesting knowledge from data is viewed as an exploratory human-driven, iterative querying process. The analyst, exploiting an expressive query language, drives the discovery process through a sequence of complex mining queries, extracts models, refines the queries, materializes the extracted models in

the database, combines the models to produce more complex knowledge, and cross-over the data and the models.

The inductive database vision inspired several Data Mining Query Languages (DMQL). Some approaches provide an interface between data sources and data mining tasks, adopting an SQL-based style for creating and manipulating data mining models, thus abstracting away from the algorithmic details. Among the most recent DMQL's, the Mining Views approach (Fromonnd et al., 2008) supports different kinds of data mining models, represented as relational tables. The user interacts with the database using SQL queries, and when a table of models is accessed by a query the system executes a data mining algorithm to materialize the table. An alternative work is the IQL language (De Raedt et al., 2006), which introduces a relational calculus extended with functions for data mining.

A thoroughly different approach is followed in various popular data mining suites, such as SPSS Clementine (Clementine, 2010) and Weka (Holmes et al., 2009), which support the design of procedural workflows for composing the different tools and obtaining the desired analytical results. A recent survey of DMQL's is in Manco et al. (2008). The main motivation of our work is that any systems can be easily adapted to deal with spatio-temporal data and models.

The conceptual framework underlying our DMQL is inspired by the abstract model proposed in Johnson et al. (2000) and subsequently refined by Calders et al. (2006), known as the 3W-Model, or the *Three World model* for data mining, where the three conceptual entities introduced are the D(ata)-world, the I(ntensional)-world, and the E(xtensional)-world. The 3W-Model provides a view of data mining in algebraic terms: a knowledge discovery process is the application of a sequence of operators in order to transform a set of tables. The model provides a methodology for defining a DMQL: the object representation of

3W entities and the implementation of a suitable set of operators are key elements in the design of a knowledge discovery process. However, some major limitations affect the 3W model: (i) in the *D-World* there is no possibility to express complex relations (e.g., cyclic relations), because the nesting of this data model has a fixed depth; (ii) in the *I-World*, regions are expressed by linear inequality sets, which prevents the expressibility of certain mining models requiring more complex mathematic structures (e.g., SVM, clustering, time series, surrounding regions). The framework that we propose, the Two-worlds model introduced in the next section, overcomes these drawbacks simplifying the definition of Data World, introducing new relations and collapsing the I-World and E-World into the definition of Model World. This allows the expression of complex relations as well as complex mining models in the Model World avoiding the limitation of the linear inequality sets.

The GeoPKDD system presented here is an extension of a query language system briefly presented in Ortale et al. (2008), called Daedalus. GeoPKDD improves Daedalus respect to several aspects, including a better optimized architecture and an extension of the query language. Furthermore, we have to point out in the present paper we firstly introduce the Two-worlds conceptual framework and a specific case study where the system has been tested.

THE TWO-WORLDS MODEL

In this section we introduce the Two-worlds model, which provides the conceptual and formal framework for our Data Mining Query Language for movement data.

Due to the complexity of spatio-temporal data, we believe that the proposed framework should be based on a rich formalism, capable to representing the specificity of movement data. We choose the object-relational data model, which combines the simplicity of the relational data model and SQL with the basic object oriented capabilities. The main feature of the object-oriented database model is that objects and classes are directly supported in database schemas supporting the extension of the original types with custom types representing complex structures.

In an object-relational formalism, each entity is denoted as an object and each object may have a number of attributes of different type: descriptive, numerical, categorical, but also attributes of object type. An object is a cohesive package that consists of a set of attributes, methods. The object type can contain also data structures such as lists which are not a standard type in a relational database.

A database is defined as $\mathcal{D} = \{\mathcal{S}_1, \ldots, \mathcal{S}_n\}$ where each schema is a set of tables $\mathcal{S} = \{\mathcal{T}_1, \ldots, \mathcal{T}_m\}$ and each table is defined by an ordered set of attributes $\mathcal{T}_j = (A_1 \ldots A_k)$ where $0 \leq j \leq m$. As mentioned above, the types of the attributes are:

- Numerical.
- Categorical.
- Descriptive (string of characters).
- **Object**: a complex type containing other attributes and methods.

We call this set of attributes A^{global}. The content of a table is a set of tuples $r(T_j) = \{t_1 \ldots t_r\}$ where $0 \leq j \leq m$, t is an ordered set of values $< v_1 \ldots v_k >| \forall i, v_i \in dom(A_i) \cup NULL$. Based on the concept of inheritance in object-relational model, we define two subsets of type attributes, the Data attributes A^d and the Model attributes A^m, which inherit directly from the Object. Furthermore, we call A^s the set of standard data types, which are neither in A^d or A^m; therefore, the global set of type attributes is partitioned into three subsets: $A^{global} = A^m \cup A^d \cup A^s$ where $A^d \cap A^m = \varnothing$.

The Data World

The D-World represents the entities to be analyzed, as well as their properties and mutual relationships. The types of attributes A^d that characterize the D-World are:

- **Spatial Objects**: A spatial object is an object which has a geometric shape and a position in space. Example geometric shapes are points, lines, polygons, where the spatial position is denoted by spatial coordinates X, Y. Therefore this kind of objects are represented as $So = \{type, P\}$ where $type \in \{point, line, polygon\}$ define the typology of geometry used to give semantic to the list of spatial points $P = \{p_1 \dots p_m\}$ as described in Oracle Spatial (2010). When the coordinates of the points P are expressed in a geographical coordinate system we denote the spatial object as a geographical object.

- **Temporal Objects**: A temporal object is represented as $To = \{t, d\}$ where t is an absolute temporal reference (w.r.t. a time reference system) and d is a duration expressed in seconds. The temporal reference t can also be set to a special value called null, which means that the temporal object represents a relative time period.

- **Moving Objects**: A moving object is an object that changes in time and space. We denote as Moving object the spatio-temporal evolution of the position of a spatial object. Hereafter, we concentrate on Moving points defined as $Mo = <p_1, t_1> \dots <p_n, t_n>$ where p_j is a spatial object representing a point, t_j is an absolute timepoint representing an absolute timepoint and $t_i < t_j$ for

$0 \geq i < j \leq n$. In this paper we use the terms trajectory and moving point as synonyms.

Then we can formally define the D-World as a filtered set of tables from a database $\mathcal{D}$ containing the above mentioned types:

- **Definition:** D-World.

Given a database D, the Data World DW is a subset of the database which contains tables defined only by attributes in A^s and A^d.

Intuitively, the D-World is the set of tables in the database which describe the trajectory dataset and/or a set of spatial and temporal objects (e.g., regions and/or hours, days, etc.).

The Model World

The M-World contains the movement models extracted from the data, together with their properties and relationships. The M-World is a collection of models, unveiled at the different stages of the knowledge discovery process. In the proposed framework, we present three kinds of attribute types A^m describing the basic trajectory mining models.

- **T-Pattern:** This type of attribute is represented as $tp = \{R, T, s\}$ where $R = \{So_0 \dots So_k\}$ is a set of spatial objects representing polygons, $Ti = \{p_1 \dots p_{k-1}\}$ is a set of pair of temporal objects $p_j = [To_{min}, To_{max}]$ representing the minimum and maximum time period between two consecutive polygons and s is the number of trajectories from which it is supported. Alternatively, a T-Pattern can be represented as $r_0 \xrightarrow{p_1} r_1 \cdots \xrightarrow{p_k} r_k$. Originally presented in Giannotti (2007), a T-Pattern is a concise description of frequent behaviours, in terms of both space (i.e., the regions of space visited during movements) and time (i.e., the duration of movements). As an example, consider the following T-Pattern over regions of interest in the center of a town:

$$RailwayStation \xrightarrow{10\,min,15\,min} CastleSquare \xrightarrow{30\,min,50\,min} Museum$$

This model describes a group of people that move between railway station to Castle Square in 15 minutes and then to Museum in 50 minutes.

- **Cluster:** It is defined as $Cl = \{Mo_1 \ldots Mo_k\}$ is a set of moving objects with a spatio-temporal affinity between them.
- **Flock:** A flock $f = \{To, r, Mo\}$ in a time interval defined by To consists of at least m entities such that for every discrete period of time d in To, there is a disk of radius r from a discovered representative moving point b of which contains all the m entities. The representative moving point is the medoid segment of discovered during the mining process. This type describes

(parts of) trajectories which move in group within a given time period.

With reference to the above types, the M-World is defined as:

- **Definition:** M-World

Given a database D, the M-World MW is a subset of the database which contains tables defined only by attributes in A^s and A^m.

THE TWO-WORLDS OPERATORS

According to Figure 2, operators are either intra-world or inter-world. In Table 1, we summarize the classes of operators in the Two-worlds framework.

- **Data Constructor Operators:** The aim of this class of operators is to build objects in D-World starting from the raw data, thus realizing the data acquisition step of the knowledge discovery process. Though conceptually simple, the constructor operators can involve complex tasks, such as the trajectory reconstruction operator, where a moving point is built from a set of

Figure 2. The proposed two-worlds framework

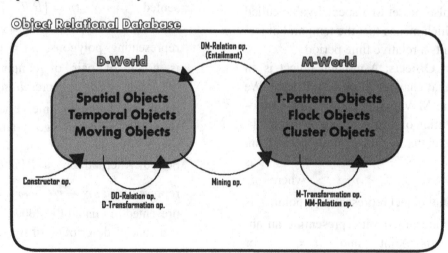

Table 1. Summary of definitions for operators in the two-worlds model

Operator name	Definition
Data Constructor operator	$OP_{constructor}(T, p) \rightarrow (T_d)$
Model Constructor operator	$OP_{mining}(T_d, p) \rightarrow (T_m)$
D-Transformation operator	$OP_{D-Transformation}(T_d, p) \rightarrow (T_d')$
M-Transformation operator	$OP_{M-Transformation}(T_m, p) \rightarrow (T_m')$
DD-Relation operator	$OP_{DD-Relation}(T_{dd}, f) \rightarrow (T_{dd}^R)$
MM-Relation operator	$OP_{MM-Relation}(T_{mm}, f) \rightarrow (T_{mm}^R)$
DM-Relation operator	$OP_{DM-Relation}(T_{dm}, f) \rightarrow (T_{dm}^R)$
Notation: T = database table containing standard data types. T_d = a table in D-World. T_m = a table in M-World. f = a relation predicate	$T_{dd}^R \subseteq T_{dd} \subseteq T_d \times T_d$ $T_{mm}^R \subseteq T_{mm} \subseteq T_m \times T_m$ $T_{dm}^R \subseteq T_{dm} \subseteq T_d \times T_m$ p = a set of parameters

sample points by applying several heuristics for filtering noise and splitting different trajectories of the same moving object. Formally, a general constructor operator is defined as a function $OP_{constructor}(T, p) \rightarrow (T_d)$ that builds a single-attribute table of data values (i.e, of type in A^d), given a table of objects with type in A^s and a set of parameters.

- **Model Constructor Operators:** Each mining operator populates the M-World starting from objects in the D-World. Therefore, it is generically defined as a function $OP_{mining}(T_d, p) \rightarrow (T_m)$ that builds a single-attribute table of model objects (i.e., attribute in A^m), given a table of data objects (attributes in A^d) and a proper set of parameters.

The operator realizes the extraction of models from the D-World through a data

mining algorithm. For this reason, one specific operator is defined for each model in M-World, and the parameters given are used by the specific operator to perform the analysis task.

- **Transformation Operators:** Transformation operators are intra-world tasks aimed to manipulating data and models. These operations are the means for expressing data pre-processing and post-processing tasks. Depending on which world the transformation is defined on, we can have two kinds of operators, respectively one for D-World and one for M-World:
  - **Data Transformation Operators:** transform a table of the data world into a table containing a single data attribute, based on a proper set of input parameters. Formally defined as a

function $OP_{D-Transformation}(T_d, p) \rightarrow (T'_d)$.

○ **Model Transformation Operators:** transform a table of the model world into a table containing a single model attribute, based on a proper set of input parameters. Formally defined as $OP_{M-Transformation}(T_m, p) \rightarrow (T'_m)$.

• **Relation Operators:** The Relation Operators include both intra-world and inter-world operations and have the objective of creating relations between data, models, and the combination of the two. Given a pair of sets of data and/or models, these operators create a new table representing the relation between the two sets. We defined three generic relation operators: data-to-data, model-to-model and data-to-model (and vice-versa) representing the three possible combinations of the two worlds. Therefore, the Relation Operators have three classes:

○ **DD-Relation Operators:** they realize a join operation between two tables in the D-World. Both tables are required to contain exactly one attribute in A^d, i.e., each record contains one data object. The record selection condition is formalized as a Boolean function evaluated on each pair of data objects, and the final result of the operator contains only the pairs that passed the selection.

○ **MM-Relation Operators:** similarly to DD-Relation, these operators realize a join between two tables in the M-World. Both tables are required to contain only one attribute in A^m. As in the previous case, the selection condition is formalized as a Boolean function evaluated on each pair of model objects, and the final result of

the operator contains the pairs that passed the selection.

○ **DM-Relation Operators:** these operators realize a join between a table in the D-World and a table in M-World. The former is required to contain exactly one attribute in A^d, while the latter must contain one attribute in A^m. The selection condition is formalized as a Boolean function evaluated on each pair of objects (one for A^d and one for A^m), and the final result of the operator contains the pairs that passed the selection.

In the case of the DD-Relations and MM-Relations, the function f can assume three types of predicates: intersects, contains and equals. The semantics of these predicates depends on the type of the data (resp. model) objects to which they are applied, and not all combinations of data (resp. model) types are defined. Table 2 summarizes the data-to-data, model-to-model, model-to-data (and vice-versa) relations.

We can notice that some of the cells are empty and these correspond to combinations that either make no sense (such as temporal object in relation with spatial object) or they are not yet implemented in the system. The semantics of the predicates Intersect, Contains and Equals is inherited from the classical spatio-temporal relations well known in the literature. Whenever a model object is involved, the relations are evaluated on its corresponding spatio-temporal representation, which is assigned in the following way:

• A T-Pattern is represented as a sequence of regions;
• A Cluster is represented by the moving point which is the medoid of the cluster, i.e., the object that minimizes the sum of distances from other objects in the cluster;

Table 2. The relation predicates defined by pair of data and models

	Spatial Object	Temporal Object	Moving Object	T-Pattern	Cluster	Flock
Spatial Object	Intersects Contains Equals		Intersects Contains	Intersects Contains		
Temporal Object		Intersects Contains Equals	Intersects Contains			Intersects Contains
Moving Object	Intersects Contains	Intersects Contains	Intersects Contains Equals	Intersects Contains Entails	Intersects Contains Entails	Intersects Contains Entails
T-Pattern	Intersects Contains		Intersects Contains Entails	Intersects Contains Equals		
Cluster			Intersects Contains Entails		Intersects Contains Equals	
Flock		Intersects Contains	Intersects Contains Entails			Intersects Contains Equals

- A Flock is represented by the representative moving point obtained by the mining process.

By adopting this representation of models, the Intersect and Contains predicates can be evaluated by a simple composition of classical predicates. Since some predicates do not apply to some pairs of data/model types, whenever an invalid combination of predicates and object types are used in a query, the predicate simply evaluates to false.

The last class of relation operators are the DM-Relations. In this case, a specific predicate called Entail is defined between the models and the original data type from which they are extracted. As in the previous cases, its semantics depends on the types involved:

- **T-Pattern Entailment:** Given a T-Pattern $tp = \{R, T, s\}$ and a Moving Object mo, the function $entails(mo, tp)$ is true iff mo intersects all the regions R and the time gap between the intersections with two

consequential regions $r_k, r_{k+1} \in R$ is contained in the (relative) time interval $i_k \in T$.

- **Cluster Entailment:** Given a Cluster $c = \{T, dist\}$ and a Moving Object mo, the function $entails(mo, c)$ is true iff mo is included in the set of moving points T.

- **Flock Entailment:** Given a Flock $f = \{I, r, b\}$ and a Moving Object mo, the function $entails(mo, f)$ is true iff within the time interval I, mo lies within a circular neighbourhood of radius r around the flock base, i.e., moving point b.

The entailment operators realize one of the most important relations in our framework, since they allow to apply/combine the models to the data, creating an iterative knowledge discovery process.

THE DATA MINING QUERY LANGUAGE

Based on the previously introduced Two-worlds framework, we defined a data mining query language to support the user specifying the knowledge discovery tasks. There are several advantages from having such language:

- The compositionality of the operators allows the user to create their own knowledge discovery process combining the different operators;
- The iterative querying capability makes easier for the user to apply the data mining algorithms on the data to extract the models, but also to apply such models to data. This is an iterative process which allows the user to use the models, not only as static knowledge to be presented as a result, but also as an active element of the process used to go deeper in the data understanding.
- The repeatability of the process, having a language that supports the steps of the discovery process allows to materialize the executed process as a language script. Thus, the output is not only the set of mined models, but also the script storing the process, thus making the process immediately repeatable on different datasets.

In the following, we present portions of the formal grammar to describe how the operators are mapped on the query language statements:

```
DMQL:= ConstructionOperator | Rela-
tionOperator | TransformationOpera-
tor| MiningOperator | SQL Standard
```

The language is an extension of the standard SQL adding the four classes of operators as four new statements:

```
DataConstructionOperator:=
'CREATE DATA' TableName 'USING' Data-
ConstructorName
'FROM (' SqlCall ')'
['WHERE' Parameters]
```

```
ModelConstructionOperator:=
'CREATE MODELS' TableName 'USING'
ModelConstructorName
'FROM (' SqlCall ')'
['WHERE ' Parameters]
TransformationOperator:=
'CREATE TRANSFORMATION TableName 'US-
ING' TransformationName
'FROM (' SqlCall ')
['WHERE' Parameters]
RelationOperator:=
'CREATE RELATION' TableName 'USING'
RelationPredicate
'FROM (' SqlCall ')'
```

The structure of these new statements is similar: *TableName* is the name of the table in the database that will be used to store the respective type of information according to the class of operator described in previous section. The internal *SqlCall* is the input data used to by the operators and should follow the format requested by it. As an example, consider this *ModelConstructionOperator* query which is an instantiation of the Model:

```
CREATE MODELS ClusteringTable USING
Optics
FROM (Select t.id, t.trajobj from
Trajectories t)
WHERE OPTICS.eps = .02 AND
OPTICS.Npoints = 120
```

In this example the system will store a table of models objects called *ClusteringTable* resulting from the execution of an algorithm called *Optics* using the trajectories in the table *Trajectories* selected by the inner query. The WHERE clause of the query specifies some parameters for the algorithm. According to the particular algorithm used, the extracted model objects are Clusters.

In the next section we show the implementation of the framework where each class of operators, and therefore statements of the language, has its relative library.

Figure 3. The architecture of the GeoPKDD system

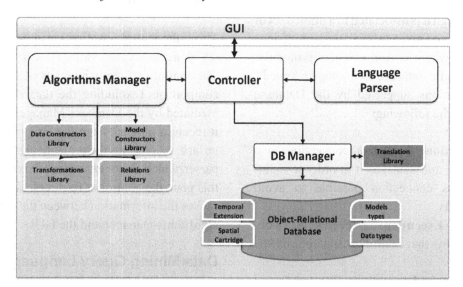

THE GEOPKDD SYSTEM

The first preliminary choice for implementing the Two-worlds model and the associated query language, has been to demand the storing and management of trajectories to an existing Moving Object Database (MOD). This provides storage and querying support for spatio-temporal data. However, since a requirement is that also models have to be represented and stored, the chosen MOD must provide mechanisms to extend the supported data types and functions.

The second choice that drove the development of the systems was observing that adopting the Weka (Holmes et al., 2009) vision of library of algorithms may permit to have a system that might grow during time adding new mining methods.

These two main pillar, lead to the introduction of the architecture of the GeoPKDD system, depicted in Figure 3, that assembles together four main components, namely: (i) the Controller, (ii) the Language parser, (iii) the Database Manager, (iv) the Algorithms Manager with its Libraries. In the following we briefly describe each part of the system.

The Object-Relational Database

The technological solution adopted for data storage of the GeoPKDD system is based on Oracle 11g extended with components for moving object data storage and manipulation, spatial objects representation, mining models storage and semantic technology (Oracle Semantic Technologies, 2010). The moving object support is provided by an Oracle data cartridge, named Hermes (Pelekis et al., 2006), which defines a collection of moving object data types, each accompanied with a palette of specialized operations. It is based on Oracle Spatial (Oracle Spatial, 2010), and therefore is able to natively represent spatial objects. For the purpose of the present work, Oracle 11g has been further extended with a set of new data types representing the data mining models that can be extracted during the analysis process thus supporting the storage of M-World objects, such as T-Pattern, Cluster or Flock data type.

The Database Manager

This component acts as a mediator between the database and the rest of the system, and provides a uniform access interface to the database functionalities. Although it is associated to a limited set of operations, this component is very important since it makes the whole system essentially modular w.r.t. the specific database technology adopted.

The operations supported by the Database Manager are the following:

- **Connection:** Creates a connection to a database and manages it in order to maintain less connection possible to avoid overloads.
- **Query Execution:** Executes a query passed by the controller and returns the results.
- **Creation and Insertion:** The component can automatically create tables and insert information in the database if it receives a command from the controller, which is very useful when the controller does not have a query to execute but only the data or model object to insert. This avoids the explicit generation of a query by the controller which might be dependent from the database technology.
- **Translation:** Translates a specified object in the database to an internal representation, and vice-versa. The main use of this function is to keep the system detached from the database, in fact different databases might represent data and model objects in different ways, possibly with different syntaxes.

The importance of having a system able to change easily the underlying database technology is important to make it portable to different real application contexts, where different policies or technological choices might lead to adopt different database systems.

The Controller

This is the central coordination unit of the system, which manages the overall flow of information. The controller directly interacts with all the main components (excluding the database, which is mediated by the Database Manager). Whenever it receives a query from the Graphical User Interface, it delegates the syntactical analysis to the parser, which elaborates a plan of execution. From this plan, the controller retrieves, elaborates and moves the information between the database, the algorithms manager and the GUI.

Data Mining Query Language Parser

This component supports the processing of queries expressed by the data mining query language, briefly presented in later sections. The queries issued by the user through the graphical interface are caught by the Controller, which is responsible for processing query statements and for coordinating the computations required. Each statement is converted into a sequence of the following tasks:

- **Information Retrieval (R):** The parser produces a query the controller will use to retrieve information from the database.
- **Information Preparation (P):** The data or models are prepared in order to be used in the system. When specific algorithms of the Algorithms Library are involved by the query, this step can be used to prepare the information to adhere to possible particular requirements or formats.
- **Algorithm Execution (E):** The data or models are used to execute an algorithm (data mining or others), possibly together with algorithm-specific parameters.
- **Information Storing (S):** After each manipulation operation, the results are stored again in the database. In order to perform this task, the resulting information is con-

verted into a object relational form to be inserted into the database.

- **Information Visualization (V):** Using the graphical user interface, the system can redirect the flow of information not only towards the database, but also use it to visualize the results.

Any sequence of these tasks is called a plan of execution, and is used by the controller to execute the query. As an example, consider the following mining query:

```
CREATE MODELS PatternsTable USING T-
PATTERN
FROM (Select t.id, t.trajobj from
Trajectories t)
WHERE T-PATTERN.support = .02 AND
T-PATTERN.time = 120
```

where the table Trajectories contains two columns, namely id and trajobj, the first one being a number that identifies the trajectory, and trajobj being the moving point column that contains the real trajectory. The plan for this query will be the following:

1. R[Select t.id, t.trajobj from Trajectories t].
2. P[Data type: Moving point].
3. E[Mining algorithm: T-Pattern, Parameters: support=.02, time threshold =20].
4. P[Model type: T-Pattern].
5. S[Create/Replace table: PatternsTable, converting the results in insert queries].

where, between the steps 3 and 4, the system uses the Model constructor library to get the appropriate algorithm to execute. After the last step the DBManager takes the control in order to execute the query generated in the step 5.

Algorithms Manager

This component is a plug-in module able to manage different set of libraries:

- **Data Constructors Library:** Used to construct the basic data objects in the data world.
- **Model Constructors Library:** The set of data mining algorithms used to extract models from data.
- **Transformations Library:** Algorithms which manipulate the data and model objects.
- **Relations Library:** Primitives used to create relations between tables of data and/or models.

The Algorithms manager receives commands from the controller to execute one of the algorithms, and it manages the flow of information and the passage of the parameters to the algorithms.

In the following section, an exhaustive presentation of the libraries is provided together with an example of query for each of them. Due to the lack of space, the full list of parameters for each algorithm is omitted.

The Data Constructor Algorithms Library

This component collects a set of methods used to implement the Constructor Operators. The aim of these algorithms is to build a set of objects starting from a set of plain relational data defined only by attributes in A^s. This section describes the predefined constructors associated to the three (complex) data types handled by the system. Three operators have been defined: the moving object builder, the geometry builder and the period builder to construct the trajectory objects, the spatial objects and the temporal objects respectively. We omit here the spatial and temporal builders for the lack of space and we show, as an example, the moving point builder.

- **Moving Point Builder:** This algorithm builds a trajectory from a table of observations in the form: $< id, x, y, t >$ where *id* is the identifier of the trajectory, *x* and *y* are the coordinates of an observation and *t* the time when the observation is taken. In literature it is well know that raw data coming from typical localization devices may contain errors, therefore this algorithm cleans the data using several thresholds to identify outlier observations. Then, the trajectory object is built on the clean data.

The parameters required in the definition of the generic construction operator are used to specify a set of constraints to clean and prepare the data. Examples of these parameters are the *Maximum Space/Time Gap*, representing the maximum space/temporal interval allowed between two consecutive observations, and the *Maximum Speed* allowed between two observations.

The resulting *Moving point* objects are stored in the database with their corresponding *identifier (id)*. The process can cause a cut of an original trajectory into several shorter ones (for instance, the observations collected along a month can generate several daily trajectories). In this case, the new *id* associated to the cut trajectories is composed by the original one and a progressive number separated by a special character. An example of a constructor query for moving points is the following:

```
CREATE DATA MobilityData BUILDING
MOVING_POINTS
FROM (SELECT userid,lon,lat,datetime
FROM MobilityRawData
ORDER BY userid,datetime)
WHERE MOVING_POINT.MAX_SPACE_GAP =
0.2 AND
MOVING_POINT.MAX_TIME_GAP = 1800
```

This query is used to build a table of data objects called *MobilityData*, retrieving the basic information from the inner query and specifying two constraints for pre-processing the data, namely the maximum space and time gap between the observations.

The Model Constructor Library

This library contains the trajectory data mining algorithms plugged into the data mining query language through the Algorithms Manager interface. Each mining algorithm implements a mining operator of the language. Below, we describe the mining algorithms integrated into the system, namely the T-Pattern, the Flock, and two clustering algorithms, Optics and H-Clustering.

- **T-Pattern:** The trajectory patterns discovery algorithm (Giannotti et al., 2007), processes a set of trajectories following four steps.

  ○ **Popular Regions Detection:** The starting set of trajectories $T = \{t_1 \dots t_n\}$ is intersected with a NxN spatial grid and the number of trajectories traversing each cell are counted. If the count of a cell is greater than a frequency threshold *support* the cell is considered *dense*.

  ○ **Region of Interest Construction:** Dense cells represent an extremely fine-grained information that is difficult to handle properly, due to their (typically) large number, but they are a useful basic information for computing larger regions, easier to handle and more meaningful for a models extraction task. These large regions are obtained aggregating neighboring dense cells and are called Regions of interest.

○ **Trajectories Translation:** Once the regions of interest $R = \{r_1 \dots r_k\}$ are computed, the original set of trajectories $T = \{t_1 \dots t_n\}$ are translated into a set of temporal annotated sequences $S = \{s_1 \dots s_n\}$ where s_j is the ordered sequence of regions intersected by t_j and the corresponding time point in which the trajectory enters in the region.

○ **Patterns Discovery:** Based on a time tolerance *time* the algorithm extracts from S the common sequences of regions with their typical transition times. This result represents the Trajectory patterns.

The two thresholds are parameters of the algorithm. There are several other parameters to guide the algorithm in the discovery process and are omitted for readability reasons. An example of query is the following:

```
CREATE MODELS PatternsTable USING T-
PATTERN
FROM (Select t.id, t.trajobj from
Trajectories t)
WHERE T-PATTERN.support = .02 AND
T-PATTERN.time = 120
```

• **Moving Flocks:** The algorithm extracts the flocks from a set of trajectories following three steps:

○ **Trajectories Synchronization:** This step generates a set of trajectories whose points are synchronised based on the user-specified granularity,

○ **Spatial Neighbour Computation:** Performed in order to calculate the location proximity between points co-occurring in time. Two moving objects are referred to as spatial neighbours for a specific time instance if their locations for this time instance are close.

○ **Bases Discovery:** A portion of trajectory (in a time slice) is considered base with its corresponding disks of radius *r* one at a time. Disks in adjacent time slices are merged if the number of common members in both disks is at least equal to the user-defined *min_points* threshold. This merging process is performed in a recursive manner.

The bases discovered become models if their temporal duration is greater than or equals the user-defined threshold *min_time_slices*.

• **Optics**: The Algorithm presented in Nanni et al. (2006) uses a distance function $dist(l_i, l_j)$ defined between trajectories and a distance threshold *eps* which cuts the obtained reachability plot in a subset $C_1 \dots C_k$ of clusters and a threshold *MinPts* which filters the small clusters. Each cluster is composed of connected dense objects (i.e., objects that are closer than *eps*) plus the other objects that fall in their neighbourhood (w.r.t. *eps*). It provides three different function distances: *CommonEnd*, *CommonStart*, *RouteSimilarity* which respectively compare the ends, the starts or the complete path of trajectories.

• **H-Clustering**: This method is used in Nanni et al. (2010) and defines a hierarchical clustering method. As with *Optics*, the user must specify the distance function *dist*, which is used to build a hierarchy of clusters, plus the desired number of clusters *k*, which is used to cut the hierarchy at that level. The approach followed by this algorithm is specular to *Optics*: while in the former the users have more control on the process, but not on the size of the results, in this case the users can simply specify a distance method and then cut the result in order to obtain a specified number of clusters. An example of query which uses this algorithm is the following:

```
CREATE MODELS HClusteringTable USING
H-CLUSTERING
FROM (Select t.id, t.trajobj from
Trajectories t)
WHERE H-CLUSTERING.METHOD = Spatial
AND
H-CLUSTERING.K = 5
```

It is important to notice that the last two algorithms extract the same kind of model (cluster) from the same type of data (moving object).

The Transformation Library

This set of algorithms implement the transformation operators, which can be used to apply manipulations on the data and the models. In the following, the methods currently integrated in the system are described.

- **Filtering:** The filtering methods are used to obtain part of the moving point or to apply some spatio-temporal primitives on the data objects. Examples of filtering methods are begin, end, and middle point, which create a new trajectory formed by a single point which is, respectively, the beginning, ending or middle point of the original trajectory.

There are three Trajectory Anonymity methods integrated in the system at the moment: *Never Walk Alone* (Abul et al., 2008), *Wait For Me* (Nanni et al., 2010) and *Always Walk with Other* (Nergiz et al., 2006). All of them are based on the idea of k-anonymous trajectory datasets, where the itinerary of each person is indistinguishable from that of

other k-*1* persons. Here, anonymity is viewed as hiding the behaviour of individuals in the crowd. The T-anonymity methods transform a trajectory dataset into a k-anonymous dataset, such that the key analytical properties are preserved. An example of this kind of query follows:

```
CREATE TRANSFORMATION ResampeData US-
ING NEVER_WALK_ALONE
FROM (SELECT t.id, t.trajobj FROM
Trajectories t)
WHERE ANONYMIZATION.K = 10 AND
ANONYMIZATION.TIME_SLOT = 600
```

where the K parameter is used by the method as constraint for the minimum anonymity level to be guaranteed.

The Relation Library

The implementation of the relation operators consists in the implementation of the predicates which characterize them. Although there are several types of relations, in the system they are implemented by adopting the same, standardized interface. In the implementation, in order to avoid the replication of the source data, an *id* representing the real object is used, hence the input is a set of rows in the form $< id_{set1}, obj_{set1}, id_{set2}, obj_{set2} >$, and the output is a subset of rows formed by the same pair of ids. If the pair $< id_{set1}, id_{set2} >$ is in the output it means that the two object obj_{set1} and obj_{set2} satisfy the predicate used. An example of relation query is the following:

```
CREATE RELATION TrajectoriesCluster-
ing USING ENTAILS
FROM (Select t.id, t.traj, c.id,
c.cluster
FROM Trajectories t, ClustersTable c)
```

If the pair $< t.id, c.id >$ exists it means that the data identified by *t.traj*, corresponding to the *t.id*, entails the model *c.cluster* corresponding to the *c.id*.

Models Interpretation

The GeoPKDD system aims at supporting the whole knowledge discovery process on movement data. Previous sections introduce a number of language constructs and operators that supports some of the steps of the knowledge discovery process, such as data pre-processing, iterative data mining, data and model manipulation.

We have enriched the GeoPKDD system with a new component (Baglioni et al., 2009) with the objective of interpreting the movement data and the discovered models. This component exploits application domain knowledge encoded in an ontology to infer a semantic interpretation of the movement data and models. The reasoning capabilities provided by the ontology permit the classification of both trajectory data and extracted models as belonging to a specific domain concept. This is possible thanks to the choice of a unique repository for data, mined models and ontology, namely Oracle 11g with Semantic Technologies (Oracle Semantic Technologies, 2010). This Oracle cartridge provides support for the inter-

nal representation of ontologies, together with a reasoning engine to perform inferences on data and models through the ontology representation. The specific reasoning task used here is the classification of the models and data respect to the concepts represented in the ontology. For example, the concept of Commuter can be defined in the ontology as a trajectory travelling from outside the city to the city centre with a high frequency. Therefore, the reasoning engine computes a classification of each trajectory into the appropriate ontology concept based on its definition. Thus, a tracked person having high frequency of movements from outside the city to the central area is classified, by the ontology reasoner, as a commuter. As a consequence, trajectories and models may be classified as a specific "behaviour" according to the ontology definitions.

Figure 4 illustrates how the semantic component is integrated into the GeoPKDD system. A textual file encoding the ontology is imported into the system through the ontology importer that, contextually, maps database tables representing data and models into the corresponding ontology concepts. Then, data and models objects are imported into the repository as ontology instances. Once both data, models and the ontology are

Figure 4. The extension of the GeoPKDD architecture with the semantic component

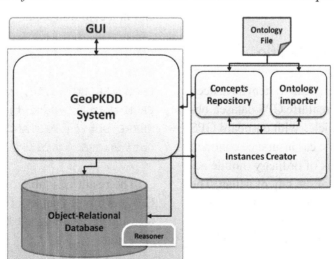

imported into the object relational database, the reasoning engine is run in order to infer which instances belong to which domain concept. For example, we may discover that some models behave as a commuter, or that some trajectories are typical home-work routinary movements.

Extending the System

The system is built as a plug-in environment which allows extending it with new data types, model types and new algorithms.

A new data or model type can be introduced by (i) adding a corresponding new type on the database to represent the new object, and (ii) to extend the translation Library of the database manager to allow the system to read and store it. The new data type will be accessible from the system as a generic data or model, and only the algorithms which use this kind of data or model need to be updated or created.

Another way to extend the system is to add a new algorithm. The plug-in interface to be used for this purpose depends on the library in which the algorithm will be used (Data Construction, Model Constructor, Transformation or Relation) and the type of data and/or models it will use. The language needs not to be manually extended to accommodate the new functionality, since the parser and the algorithm manager automatically adapt to the new operator.

A Real Application Scenario

The analysis capabilities of our system have been applied onto a massive real life GPS dataset, obtained from 17,000 vehicles with on-board GPS receivers under a specific car insurance contract, tracked during one week of ordinary mobile activity in the urban area of the city of Milan. The dataset, which has been donated by Octotelematics (Octotelematics, 2010) for research purposes, contains more than 2 million observations.

The aim of the analysis for this example is to find common behaviours of group of people which have the same destination. This can be useful to understand how the people move in the city and can give to a mobility manager some hints on how to organize new public transportation services or how to modify the pre-existing ones.

The first step of the analysis is to build the moving points specifying some strategies of data cleaning:

```
CREATE DATA MobilityData BUILDING
MOVING_POINTS
FROM (SELECT userid,lon,lat,datetime
FROM MobilityRawData
ORDER BY userid,datetime)
WHERE MOVING_POINT.MAX_TIME_GAP =
1800 (Seconds) AND
MOVING_POINT.MAX_SPEED = 200 (Km/h)
```

In this case we want to cut the moving points if between two consecutive observations there are more than 30 minutes (because we consider them two different trips) and remove observations which lead to a speed greater than 200 Km/h. The result is a set of more than 200,000 trajectories (Figure 5).

Having the dataset of trajectories and applying the Optics clustering algorithm we can discover the different groups of similar trajectories which end in a common area:

```
CREATE MODEL ClustersTable USING Op-
tics
FROM (SELECT t.id, t.object
FROM MobilityData t)
WHERE Optics.DISTANCE = CommonEnd AND
Optics.EPS = 0.035
```

The result is a table of clusters stored in the ClustersTable. The set of trajectories belonging to a cluster is obtained by applying a relation statement.

Figure 5. The trajectories obtained from the data constructor query

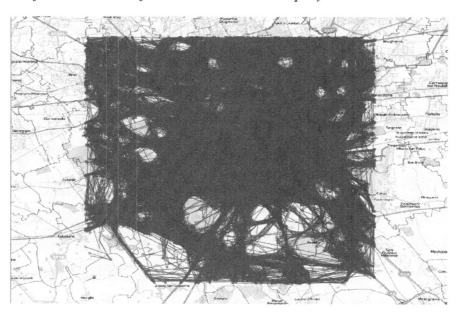

```
CREATE RELATION TrajectoriesCluster-
ing USING ENTAILS
FROM (Select t.id, t.object, c.id,
t.object
FROM MobilityData t, ClustersTable c)
```

A standard SQL query can count the number of trajectories which entails the cluster from the resulting table *TrajectoriesClustering*, selecting the most populated (in this case the one with id = 3):

```
SELECT t.id, t.object
FROM MobilityData t, Trajectories-
Clustering r
WHERE r.id1 = t.id AND r.id2 = 3
```

The resulting trajectories are shown in Figure 6 and represent the trajectories which entail the cluster with *id = 3*. Comparing them with some point of interest of the city, we discover that this cluster represents people moving towards the *Linate* airport. Thus, having this well defined set of trajectories, we can apply the T-Pattern algorithm in order to find the common behaviours of this particular group of people. The query:

```
CREATE MODELS PatternsTable USING T-
PATTERN
FROM (SELECT t.id, t.object
FROM MobilityData t, Trajectories-
Clustering r
WHERE r.id1 = t.id AND r.id2 = 3)
WHERE T-PATTERN.support = .02 AND
T-PATTERN.time = 120
```

These results suggest that the most frequent routes to the Linate Airport follow the eastern side of the tangenziale highway. That is even clearer on Figure 7, where four most significant models are selected and shown in detail, together with the corresponding timings.

The starting region of each T-pattern has a dark border, and consecutive regions in a T-pattern are connected through a line. Beside the visualization of each T-pattern, the list of typical transition times between consecutive regions is reported in the format *step_number min_time max_time*. For instance, the lower left picture of Figure 7 describes a T-pattern composed of four regions, and therefore three transitions. The first block of transition times is composed of interval [37.45, 37.89]

Figure 6. The set of trajectories which entail a cluster extracted

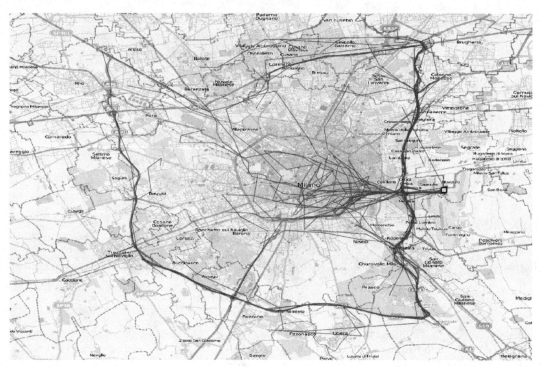

Figure 7. Selected T-Patterns to Linate airport

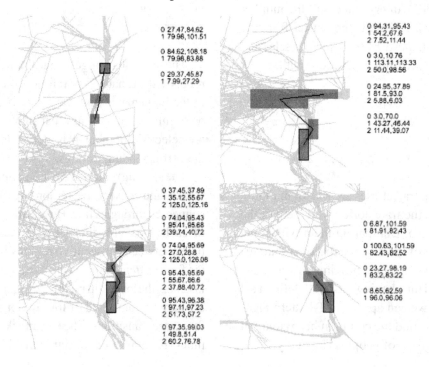

0 27.47,84.62
1 79.96,101.51

0 84.62,108.18
1 79.96,83.88

0 29.37,45.87
1 7.99,27.29

0 94.31,95.43
1 54.2,67.6
2 7.52,11.44

0 3.0,10.76
1 113.11,113.33
2 50.0,98.56

0 24.95,37.89
1 81.5,93.0
2 5.88,6.03

0 3.0,70.0
1 43.27,46.44
2 11.44,39.07

0 37.45,37.89
1 35.12,55.67
2 125.0,125.16

0 74.04,95.43
1 95.41,95.68
2 39.74,40.72

0 74.04,95.69
1 27.0,28.8
2 125.0,126.08

0 95.43,95.69
1 55.67,86.6
2 37.88,40.72

0 95.43,96.38
1 97.11,97.23
2 51.73,57.2

0 97.35,99.03
1 49.8,51.4
2 60.2,76.78

0 6.87,101.59
1 81.91,82.43

0 100.63,101.59
1 82.43,82.52

0 23.27,98.19
1 83.2,83.22

0 8.65,62.59
1 96.0,96.06

(around half a minute) for the first transition (*step_number* equal to 0), [35.12, 55.67] (from half to one minute) for the second one, and [125,125.16] (around two minutes) for the last one.

CONCLUSION

In this paper we proposed a spatio-temporal data analysis theoretical framework called Two-worlds model. This model incorporates a data mining query language, as an extension of the classic SQL, to support the entire knowledge discovery process allowing progressive mining and querying. Furthermore, the framework has been realized into a running system called GeoPKDD, offering primitive functionalities to handle pre-processing, mining and post-processing tasks over movement data. Moreover, the flexibility of the system allows an easy integration of new kind of data, model and algorithms. A case of study on urban mobility was presented in order to validate the capabilities of the proposed system.

REFERENCES

Abul, O., Bonchi, F., & Nanni, M. (2008). Never walk alone: Uncertainty for anonymity in moving objects databases. In *Proceedings of the IEEE International Conference on Data Engineering* (pp. 376-385). Washington, DC: IEEE Computer Society.

Baglioni, M., de Macedo, J., Renso, C., Trasarti, R., & Wachowicz, M. (2009). Towards semantic interpretation of movement behaviour. In *Proceedings of the 12th AGILE International Conference on Geographic Information Science*. Berlin: Springer.

Calders, T., Lakshmanan, L. V. S., & Paredaens, J. (2006). Expressive power of an algebra for data mining. *ACM Transactions on Database Systems, 31*(4), 1169–1214. doi:10.1145/1189769.1189770

Clementine. (2010). *Statistical analysis software SPSS Clementine*. Retrieved April 20, 2010, from http://www.spss.com/clementine/

De Raedt, L., & Nijssen, S. (2006). IQL: A proposal for an inductive query language. In *Proceedings of the 5th International Workshop Knowledge Discovery in Inductive Databases (KDID 2006)* (pp. 189-207).

Fromonnd, E., Goethals, B., Prado, A., Blockeel, H., & Calders, T. (2008). Mining views: Database views for data mining. In *Proceedings of the 24th IEEE International Conference on Data Engineering* (pp.1608-1611). Washington, DC: IEEE Computer Society.

Giannotti, F., Nanni, M., Pinelli, F., & Pedreschi, D. (2007). Trajectory pattern mining. In *Proceedings of ACM SIGKDD* (pp. 330-339). New York: ACM.

Giannotti, F., & Pedreschi, D. (2008). *Mobility, data mining, and privacy*. Berlin, Germany: Springer-Verlag. doi:10.1007/978-3-540-75177-9

Holmes, G., Pfahringer, B., Reutemann, P., Witten, I. H., Hall, M., & Frank, E. (2009). The Weka data mining software. *SIGKDD Explorations, 11*(1).

Imielinski, T., & Mannila, H. (1996). A data base perspective on knowledge discovery. *Communications of the ACM, 39*, 58–64. doi:10.1145/240455.240472

Johnson, T., Lakshmanan, L. V. S., & Ng, R. T. (2000). The 3W Model and Algebra for Unified Data Mining. In *Proceedings of the Very Large Data Base Conference* (pp. 21-32). San Francisco, CA: Morgan Kaufmann Publishers.

Manco, G., Giannotti, F., Kujpers, B., Raffaeta, A., Baglioni, M., & Renso, C. (2008). Querying and reasoning for spatio-temporal data mining. In *Mobility, Data Mining, and Privacy: Geographic Knowledge Discovery*. Berlin, Germany: Springer-Verlag. doi:10.1007/978-3-540-75177-9_13

Nanni, M., Abul, O., & Bonchi, F. (2010). *Anonymization of moving objects data bases by clustering and perturbation.*

Nanni, M., & Pedreschi, D. (2006). Time-focused clustering of trajectories of moving objects. *Journal of Intelligent Information Systems, 27*(3), 267–289. doi:10.1007/s10844-006-9953-7

Nergiz, N. E., Atzori, M., & Saygin, Y. (2008). Towards trajectory anonymization: a generalization-based approach. In *Proceedings of the Workshop on Security and Privacy in GIS and LBS - SPRINGL 2008* (pp. 52-61). New York: ACM.

Octotelematics. (2010). *Octo Telematics Italia.* Retrieved April 20, 2010, from http://www.octotelematics.it/

Oracle Semantic Technologies. (2010). *Oracle Database Semantic Technologies.* Retrieved April 20, 2010, from http://www.oracle.com/technology/tech/semantic_technologies

Oracle Spatial. (2010). *Oracle Spatial e Oracle Locator.* Retrieved April 20, 2010, from http://www.oracle.com/lang/it/database/spatial.html

Ortale, R., Ritacco, E., Pelekis, N., Trasarti, R., Costa, G., Giannotti, F., et al. (2008). The DAEDALUS Framework: Progressive Querying and Mining of Movement Data. In *Proceedings of the ACM SIGSPATIAL International Conference on Advances in Geographic Information Systems (ACM GIS 2008).*

Pelekis, N., & Theodoridis, Y. (2006). Boosting location-based services with a moving object database engine. In *Proceedings of the Fifth ACM International Workshop on Data Engineering for Wireless and Mobile Access, MOBIDE 2006* (pp. 3-10). New York: ACM.

This work was previously published in the International Journal of Data Warehousing and Mining, Volume 7, Issue 1, edited by David Taniar, pp. 24-45, copyright 2011 by IGI Publishing (an imprint of IGI Global).

Chapter 3
Distributed Privacy Preserving Clustering via Homomorphic Secret Sharing and its Application to (Vertically) Partitioned Spatio-Temporal Data

Can Yildizli
Sabanci University, Turkey

Yucel Saygin
Sabanci University, Turkey

Thomas Brochmann Pedersen
Sabanci University, Turkey

Erkay Savas
Sabanci University, Turkey

Albert Levi
Sabanci University, Turkey

ABSTRACT

Recent concerns about privacy issues have motivated data mining researchers to develop methods for performing data mining while preserving the privacy of individuals. One approach to develop privacy preserving data mining algorithms is secure multiparty computation, which allows for privacy preserving data mining algorithms that do not trade accuracy for privacy. However, earlier methods suffer from very high communication and computational costs, making them infeasible to use in any real world scenario. Moreover, these algorithms have strict assumptions on the involved parties, assuming involved parties will not collude with each other. In this paper, the authors propose a new secure multiparty computation based k-means clustering algorithm that is both secure and efficient enough to be used in a real world scenario. Experiments based on realistic scenarios reveal that this protocol has lower communication costs and significantly lower computational costs.

DOI: 10.4018/978-1-4666-2148-0.ch003

INTRODUCTION

Massive amounts of data are collected for various reasons by many organizations with the hope that data mining technology will extract useful knowledge from the collected data and turn it into something beneficial for the organization. In fact, data mining technology proved its success in numerous areas such as business intelligence, life-sciences, and security. On the other hand, the popularity of data mining was about to pave the way to its demise. Part of the reason for that is the launch of large scale projects related to homeland security. Some projects were actually stopped since they failed to meet privacy concerns. According to a recent article in Computer World by Vijayan (2007) "The chairman of the House Committee on Homeland Security, has asked Department of Homeland Security Secretary Michael Chertoff to provide a detailed listing of all IT programs that have been canceled, discontinued or modified because of privacy concerns". In addition to that, the Chairman also asked for information about the measures being taken to address privacy issues (Vijayan, 2007). As a result of increased privacy concerns, data mining researchers focused on developing techniques that would enable data mining while preserving the privacy of individuals and started a popular branch of research named "privacy preserving data mining" (Agrawal & Srikant, 2000). Protocols based on statistics and cryptography were proposed for privacy preserving classification, clustering, and pattern mining in centralized and distributed environments. However, privacy preserving data management, in general, is still an ongoing research topic, and efficient, as well as provably secure, methods without strong assumptions are yet to be proposed.

In this work, we propose a new secure multi-party computation algorithm for distributed privacy preserving k-means clustering. Our algorithm is both more efficient and more secure than the current state of the art secure k-means clustering algorithm of Vaidya and Clifton (2003). In this protocol we avoid the computationally heavy public key encryption. Instead we use secret sharing as the underlying cryptographic primitive. The main contributions of this work can be listed as:

- We show that our protocol outperforms the state of the art protocol by Vaidya and Clifton (2003). Backed by experiments we show that our protocol has a much lower computational overhead due to the fact that we replace computationally expensive public key encryption operations with additive secret sharing.
- As a case study we apply our technique on a trajectory data set obtained in the context of the GeoPKDD project (http://www.geopkdd.eu/).
- To the best of our knowledge, this is the first work which implements and tests privacy preserving clustering in a realistic setting. We run the protocols on a real dataset of trajectories in a novel testing platform. The test platform is a combination of simulation and real execution, which enables a detailed comparison of the protocols in a controlled environment.
- We take full advantage of the security model, which we share with (Vaidya & Clifton, 2003).

The work presented in this paper extends the work done by Kaya et al. (2007) and Doganay et al. (2008). In Kaya et al. (2007), a privacy preserving distributed clustering protocol for horizontally partitioned data is proposed. The clustering protocol relies on two third parties to perform comparisons when needed. In Doganay et al. (2008) a protocol for k-means clustering over vertically partitioned data is presented. The protocol uses the same comparison protocol as in Kaya et al. (2007), but modified in a way that the third parties are not needed (the comparison is done by some of the data holders). The major claim of Doganay et al. (2008) is that the proposed algorithm performs better than the privacy preserving k-means clustering protocol by Vaidya and Clifton (2003); however, the performance was only analyzed theoretically in terms of the amount of data send and received. In this work, we improve the performance of the protocol of Doganay et al. (2008) by reducing the amount of communication. We also present thorough tests of the protocol in real world scenarios to compare the performance with the protocol by Vaidya and Clifton (2003). The comparison shows that the protocol proposed in this work has a performance which is orders of magnitude better than that of Vaidya and Clifton (2003) in most real world settings.

The rest of this paper is organized as follows: First, we outline the related work. Second, we explain the central tools used in our scheme and in Vaidya and Clifton (2003). Third, we state the problem and present our algorithm. Fourth, we discuss how our method preserves the privacy of the data records of individuals. Fifth, we analyze the computation and communication overhead of our algorithm and compare to Vaidya and Clifton (2003). Sixth, simulation results that support the analysis are given. Finally, we give our conclusions in the last section.

RELATED WORK

Privacy preserving data mining algorithms fall in two categories: (1) Random perturbation-based and (2) secure multi-party computation based.

Perturbation techniques mix additive or multiplicative noise with the data so that actual values in the data set are not learned, yet the data mining results gathered from the perturbed data will not deviate significantly from the results gathered from the original data. The work of Agrawal and Srikant (2000) falls into this category. One recent significant work by Liu et al. (2006) shows that random projection based multiplicative data perturbation is a very efficient way to perform privacy preserving distributed data mining. The

results obtained from perturbed data have below 5% error rate (Liu et al., 2006) as compared to the results obtained from the original data. Algorithms in that category present a very practical and efficient way of performing privacy preserving data mining; however, they are based on trading accuracy of the data mining results with privacy of individuals. Furthermore, algorithms in this category do not preserve privacy in any formal cryptological sense, i.e. one cannot easily calculate how much effort and resources are needed to filter out the noise and breach privacy. Indeed, the very nature of data perturbation ensures that statistical information about the original data is preserved. A survey on attacks on privacy preserving data perturbation techniques can be read in Aggarwal and Yu (2008, ch. 5).

Algorithms based on secure multiparty computation (SMC) do not have to trade accuracy with privacy and they preserve the security and privacy of the data of individuals in a formal way. In the SMC literature a number of generalized SMC protocols have been presented. These generalized SMC protocols can compute any "reasonable" function among distributed parties without revealing the private inputs (Yao, 1982; Ben-Or et al., 1988). Therefore, theoretically, it is possible to perform distributed data mining without revealing the data of the individual data holders.

However, generalized SMC protocols suffer from high levels of communication and computation costs. Therefore, these solutions should be used with caution in data mining problems where the size of the data is measured in gigabytes. Clifton et al. (2002) proposed that data mining algorithms should make use of a relatively small set of primitive functions. Optimized SMC protocols for these primitive functions can then be used to solve data mining problems at a reasonable cost. A very central primitive function which is at the core of almost any data mining application is comparison. A data mining protocol which uses SMC comparison as a primitive function for privacy preserving k-means clustering over vertically partitioned data is proposed by Vaidya and Clifton (2003).

Another protocol based on SMC is proposed by Kantarcioglu and Clifton (2004) for association rule mining. They make use of the commutative encryption property of RSA encryption.

Protocols which rely on public key cryptography (Kantarcioglu & Clifton, 2004; Vaidya & Clifton, 2003) suffer from two drawbacks: Evaluation of public key functions is computationally heavy, and ciphertexts in public key encryptions are large. The size of ciphertexts becomes a severe problem when using homomorphic properties of the encryption, which is the case in both Kantarcioglu and Clifton (2004) and Vaidya and Clifton (2003). To take advantage of the homomorphic property, each integer value (typically 32 or 64 bits) has to be encrypted in a ciphertext of at least 1024 bits, thus potentially leading to large communication overheads.

Another class of SMC protocols relies on secret sharing instead of public key encryption (Ben-Or et al., 1988). Secret sharing has the advantage that it requires very little computation. The use of secret sharing to perform privacy preserving data mining gained some momentum in recent years. One of the most notable examples is the work of Laur et al. (2006) in which they use secret sharing for private support vector classification. One other notable use of secret sharing in a privacy preserving data mining algorithm is the work of Wright and Yang (2004) to compute Bayesian networks over vertically partitioned data.

Even though secret sharing requires less computation, it often leads to a larger number of message transfers. The classical secret sharing technique by Shamir (1979), for instance, needs a number of messages which is quadratic in the number of participants. The use of encryption versus secret sharing presents a tradeoff between computational cost and communication cost. However, in certain scenarios the drawbacks of secret sharing can be limited, and its power fully harnessed. As we demonstrate in this paper, one

such scenario is the one use in Vaidya and Clifton (2003), who assumes the existence of a few non-colluding parties.

Like the work of Vaidya and Clifton (2003), we address privacy preserving k-means clustering over vertically partitioned data, where each party involved has a subset of attributes of all the entities in the dataset. In Doganay et al. (2008), it was proposed to substitute the expensive public key encryption used in Vaidya and Clifton (2003) with secret sharing to increase the performance of k-means clustering. However, the protocol of Doganay et al. (2008) suffers from the quadratic communication overhead which often comes with secret sharing. Furthermore, Doganay et al. (2008) only gave a theoretical analysis of the performance gain. In this paper, we extend the work of Doganay et al. (2008). We modify the protocol in two aspects: (i) by taking full advantage of the non-colluding assumption, which is made in both Vaidya and Clifton (2003) and Doganay et al. (2008), and (ii) the initial secret sharing step now only brings a linear amount of communication. Furthermore we improve the "permutation" step of the protocol, and give full test results demonstrating a large performance gain over Vaidya and Clifton (2003) in a real-world setting.

PRELIMINARIES

As Vaidya and Clifton (2003), we assume that some of the parties in the protocol are non-colluding. Non-colluding parties are assumed not to reveal their private inputs to each other (or to any other parties) and they do not collaborate to compute anything that is not supposed to be computed in a given protocol. They may have their own incentives for non-colluding behavior (e.g. parties do not want to reveal their private data) or they may be designed this way. It is one of the most common assumptions in many cryptographic protocols and privacy preserving data mining applications. Vaidya and Clifton (2003) assume the existence of 3 parties who are pairwise non-colluding. In this paper we assume the existence of 4 such pairwise non-colluding parties. Since the security of our protocol relies on secret sharing, our protocol is secure even if the parties have unlimited computing power. In contrast, Vaidya and Clifton (2003) assume that all parties are computationally bounded. As always in an information theoretical scenario, we assume the existence of authentic and confidential channels. Such channels can always be implemented with a combination of symmetric and public key cryptography. We will not address this issue further.

Both our scheme and the scheme of Vaidya and Clifton (2003) are based on homomorphic cryptographic methods. The improvement of our scheme over that of Vaidya and Clifton (2003) comes from the use of homomorphic secret sharing instead of homomorphic encryption. Another common element is secure comparison. Vaidya and Clifton (2003) leave it up to the implementer to choose any secure comparison algorithm he finds suitable. However, they mention the secure circuit evaluation of Yao (1982) as a possibility. They also suggest a simplified version of their protocol where a secret offset is added to the values which are to be compared, and a third party then performs the comparison. The simplified version is less secure, but considerably more efficient than the full version. While it is not secure enough in all cases, it may be reasonable in some applications. In this paper, we compare the performance of our work with the simplified version of the protocol by Vaidya and Clifton (2003). In the two following subsections we will discuss the homomorphic primitives, and secure comparison protocols used in this paper.

Homomorphic Cryptographic Primitives

A public key encryption scheme is a set of three functions G, E, and D. The function G is a key generation function and when G is called with a random argument it generates a key-pair: *(pk, sk)* $= G(r)$, where *pk* is called the public key, and *sk* is called the secret key. The two keys satisfy the following decryption condition: when $c = E(pk, m, r)$, $D(sk, c) = m$, where c is called the ciphertext, m is called the *message* or *plaintext*, and r is a random number. Furthermore it is computationally infeasible to compute the message m when given only *pk* and $E(pk, m, r)$. An encryption scheme is said to be additively homomorphic if $E(pk, m_0, r)E(pk, m_1, r') = E(pk, m_0 + m_1, r'')$, for some value r''. Additively homomorphic encryption schemes are the central tool of Vaidya and Clifton (2003). The well-known Paillier homomorphic encryption scheme takes plaintext values of size at most n bits, and creates $2n$-bit ciphertexts. Typically n is either 1024 or 2048. In order to use the homomorphic property of Paillier encryption each integer (typically 32 or 64 bits) will be encrypted in at least 2048 bit ciphertexts, thus giving a communication overhead of 64 times. Other homomorphic encryption schemes suffer similar blowup in message size. Practical applications of Vaidya and Clifton (2003) will suffer from this overhead.

A *(t, n)* secret sharing scheme is a set of two functions S and R. The function S is a sharing function and takes a secret s, and a random number r as inputs and creates n secret shares: $S(s, r) = (s_1, \ldots, s_n)$. The two functions satisfy that for any set $I \subseteq \{1, \ldots, n\}$ of t indices $R(I, s_{I_1}, \ldots, s_{I_t}) = s$. Furthermore we require that it is impossible to recover any information about s from a set of t - 1 secret shares. A secret sharing scheme is additively homomorphic if $R(I, s_{I_1} + s'_{I_1}, \ldots, s_{I_t} + s'_{I_t}) = s + s'$. The most widely used secret sharing scheme is that of Shamir (1979).

A very simple *(n, n)* secret sharing scheme which is additively homomorphic is $S(s) = (r_1, \ldots, r_{n-1}, r)$, where $r_i \in \mathbb{Z}_m$ is random for $i \in \{1, \ldots, n-1\}$, and $r = s - \sum_{i=1}^{n-1} r_i \mod m$.

To recover s all secret shares are added: $s = r + \sum_{i=1}^{n-1} r_i \mod m$. If even one secret share is missing nothing is known about s. We use this simple additive secret sharing scheme in this paper.

Notice that an (n, n) additive secret sharing scheme requires that $(n-1)$ messages are sent. If all n parties have to share a secret input, each party has to send one share to each other party, giving a number of exchanged messages which is quadratic in the number of parties. However, n parties only share their secret inputs between two 2 non-colluding parties, the secret can be kept with a $(2, 2)$ secret sharing, reducing the number of messages to $2n$. In this paper we take advantage of the existence of non-colluding parties to reduce the number of messages from quadratic to linear, thus improving (Doganay et al., 2008).

The two homomorphic schemes described in this section are useful tools in computing simple functions over distributed data. As a simple example, suppose we want to compute the sum of n numbers $a_1, \ldots, a_n$, where each number is a secret known to only one party. With homomorphic encryption, the first party can compute $(pk, sk) = G(r)(pk, sk) = G(r)$, and send pk to all the other $n - 1$ parties. He then sends $E(pk, a_1, r_1)$ to the second party, who computes $E(pk, a_1 + a_2, r_2) = E(pk, a_1, r_1)E(pk, a_2, r'_2)$. The second party forwards this ciphertext to the third party, and so on, until the last party sends $E(pk, \sum_i a_i, r_n)$ back to the first party, who can then decrypt the result. Since it is computationally infeasible for any party, except for the first, to compute the intermediate results, no one will be able to learn anything else than the final sum. A similar procedure can be implemented with homomorphic secret sharing.

Secure Comparison

Vaidya and Clifton (2003) suggest using Yao's circuit evaluation for the comparisons. They argue that even though Yao's protocol is very inefficient, it may be plausible to use it for the comparison, since they only perform $(k - 1)n$ comparisons in each iteration of the k-means algorithm. They also give a variant of their protocol, which does not rely on secure comparison, but which compares the distances in a way which does not release too much private information (see "Secure Closest Cluster Computation" subsection).

In our protocol, we use a comparison protocol proposed by Kaya et al. (2007) and Kaya (2007), which is based on a protocol by Fischlin (2001). The comparison protocol of Fischlin (2001) uses homomorphic encryption and a trick of by Sander et al (1999) to implement secure comparison. The idea was generalized to secret sharing in Kaya et al. (2007) and Kaya (2007). In the comparison protocol of Kaya et al. (2007) and Kaya (2007), two parties, who wish to compare two integers, each create bitwise secret shares of their own inputs and send these shares to two semi-honest non-colluding third parties. The protocol utilizes the fact that additive secret sharing is homomorphic with respect to addition, thus bitwise additive secret sharing is homomorphic with respect to bitwise XOR. The protocol of Kaya (2007), like the protocol of Fischlin (2001), uses the trick by Sander et al. (1999) to convert XOR homomorphic encryption (secret sharing in our case) into AND homomorphic encryption (or secret sharing) without disclosing the secret. The AND homomorphic representation, however, has a small probability of giving the wrong result when computing the conjunction of two secret bits. The probability is controlled with the parameter λ, where the probability of error is $2^{-\lambda}$. When comparing two n bit integers, the errors in the conjunctions translate to an error in the comparison with a probability of at most $n2^{-\lambda}$. The error in the comparison is one-sided: if the result of the comparison is true, the protocol always returns true. The parameter λ also affects the size of the secret shares of each bit, which becomes λ bits long. For large values of λ this has a negative effect on the performance. In our implementation we have used a value of λ = 32. For the proofs of correctness and security, the reader is referred to Kaya (2007).

We have modified the protocol of Kaya (2007) slightly, by observing that the two semi-honest third parties are actually not needed in the protocol. In the original protocol, the parties involved in secure comparison secret-share their inputs between 2 semi-honest third parties, sending one share to each of the two third parties. This is equivalent to each party secret-sharing their inputs among themselves; each party sends a secret share of its input to the other party while keeping the remaining secret share to itself. Therefore, in our protocol, the parties who perform the secure comparison apply the protocol of Kaya (2007) by secret-sharing their inputs among themselves. In the original protocol (Kaya, 2007), two third parties end up with secret shares of a binary vector. The vector is as long as the inputs that are compared. If the statement is false (the first input is not greater than the second), the vector is the zero vector. If the first input to the comparison is greater than the other, then the vector has exactly one 1-bit at the first bit position where the first input is greater than the second input. Since the position of the 1-bit gives information about the relative difference between these two inputs, the two parties performing the comparison agree on a permutation and permute the vector before it is sent to the party who will learn the result of the comparison. In our protocol, the two parties who perform the comparison are supposed to know the result but not the position of the 1 bit, so they send the permuted vector to a third party (another data holder), who open the shares, finds the result, and sends the result back to the two parties performing the comparison.

OUR ALGORITHM

Our privacy-preserving clustering algorithm is an improvement of the one proposed by Vaidya and Clifton (2003). The central difference between our algorithm and the algorithm of Vaidya and Clifton (2003) is the search for the cluster which is closest to a given entity. In Vaidya and Clifton (2003) homomorphic encryption is used to do a secure computation of the closest cluster, whereas we use secret sharing. The power of secret sharing in this setting is that the computation overhead is lower and the size of messages smaller (however, at the cost of an increase in the number messages sent). As we demonstrate in "Experiments" section, the decrease in computation and message size overshadows the increase in the number of messages. To make our presentation clear, we simplify some parts of the algorithms, but apply the same simplifications to Vaidya and Clifton (2003) when we compare the efficiency of the two algorithms in "Experiments" section.

Our algorithm performs distributed k-means clustering with r parties. The data is vertically partitioned such that each of the r parties has some of the attributes of the dataset. The number of entities in the dataset is n. The goal of the r parties is to perform k-means clustering on their aggregated data without revealing the values of the attributes they own to the other parties. The algorithm will divide the entries into k clusters and each party learns the cluster means corresponding to their own attributes, and the index of the cluster into which each entity is assigned. Ideally, no party should learn anything else than this.

Let μ_c, $c \in \{1,...,k\}$, represent the cluster means of the result. Let μ_{ci} be the projection of cluster mean c onto the attributes of party i $\left(\mu_c = (\mu_{c1},...,\mu_{cr})\right)$. As output of privacy preserving k-means clustering party i gets:

- The final mean μ_{ci} for each cluster $c \in \{1,...,k\}$.
- The cluster index for each entity $j \in \{1,...n\}$.

Privacy preserving k-means clustering over vertically partitioned data is studied by Vaidya & Clifton (2003). In our work we follow the same approach. However, Vaidya & Clifton (2003) make use of additive homomorphic encryption, which is their bottleneck. In contrast, we use additive secret sharing to achieve privacy, which gives us lower computation and communication overhead than Vaidya and Clifton (2003).

Like the work of Vaidya and Clifton (2003), our algorithm follows the standard k-means clustering method. Firstly, initial cluster means are selected, and all entities in the dataset are assigned to the closest initial clusters. After the initial assignment of clusters, the cluster means are recalculated and each entity is reassigned to the cluster with the closest cluster mean. The process continues until a termination criterion is met. Algorithm 1 shows the pseudo code of the privacy preserving k-means clustering algorithm, which is common to our work and Vaidya and Clifton (2003).

The final clustering result depends on how we choose the initial cluster means. It is, however, a standard approach to choose the initial cluster means randomly, which is the case in Vaidya and Clifton (2003) as well.

The algorithm presented by Vaidya and Clifton (2003) terminates when the change in cluster means between two iterations is less than a given threshold. In the tests presented in "Experiments" section, we run the algorithm for a fixed number of rounds. Besides eliminating the influence of the random initial clusters, it also guarantees a fair and clear comparison between the algorithm proposed by Vaidya and Clifton (2003) and our algorithm (which has a small probability of error in each round due to the comparison protocol).

Another factor to be considered is the distance measure used. For simplicity we use Euclidean distance. Whenever we compare our work to the work of Vaidya and Clifton (2003), we use Euclidean distance in their algorithm as well. Both protocols, however, can be used with any distance measure which can be expressed as a monotone function of the sub-distances computed on the attributes of the individual parties.

Since the data is vertically partitioned, each party can compute part of the distances between each of the n entities in the dataset and the cluster

Algorithm 1. Privacy preserving k-means algorithm

```
do in parallel for each party i ∈ {1,...,r}
        for each cluster c←1,...,k do
                initialize μ_{ci} randomly
        end for
end parallel
repeat
        for each entity j←1,...,n do
                Cluster[j] ← SecurelyComputeClosestCluster(j)
        end for
        do in parallel for each party i ∈ {1,...,r}
                for each cluster c←1,...,k do
                        μ_{ci}← mean of party i's attributes in cluster c
                end for
        end parallel
until termination criteria met
```

means. Since we use Euclidean distance the square of the total distance between an entity and a cluster mean is the sum of the squares of the sub-distances computed at the subspaces of each party:

$$\| x_i - \mu_c \|^2 = \sum_{p=1}^{r} \| x_{ip} - \mu_{cp} \|^2 \, . \tag{1}$$

However, the parties cannot reveal their sub-distances in order to compute the sum of them, since the local sub-distances may contain private information. We therefore need to compute and compare the distances securely without revealing the individual sub-distances. This is done in the "SecurelyComputeClosestCluster" algorithm, which we will describe in the next subsection. It is in the secure computation of closest clusters that our algorithm varies from that of Vaidya and Clifton (2003).

Secure Closest Cluster Computation

To find the cluster mean which is closest to a given entity in the database we have to securely sum the sub-distances computed by each party and compare the results in a way that nothing other than the comparison result is learned. With n entities, the closest cluster algorithm has to be invoked nt times, where t is the number of iterations in the standard k-means algorithm.

Similar to Vaidya and Clifton (2003), the security of our closest cluster algorithm relies on three ideas:

- The n secret sub-distance of each party is secret shared, so that no one will see it (where Vaidya & Clifton (2003) adds random blinding values in a protocol which applies encryption).
- The comparison of distances is performed on secret shares so that only the comparison result is learned. The actual values of the distances are not learned.

- Since the minimum distance is found by comparing the distances pair-wise, the ordering of distances is permuted before the search for the minimum. Once the permuted index of the minimum distance is found, the inverse permutation is computed on the permuted index to find the actual identity of the minimum distance. In Vaidya and Clifton (2003) this is the step that requires the highest amount of communication and computation since they rely heavily on public key encryptions.

The most important difference between our work and the work of Vaidya and Clifton (2003) is the secure computation of the closest cluster.

In Vaidya and Clifton (2003) all parties encrypt their sub-distances and send them to a "blinding party". The blinding party uses the homomorphic property of the encryption to add random blinding factors to the sub-distances in a way that the blinding factors cancel out once the sub-distances are added up to form the real distances. The blinding party also permutes the distances. It then sends the permuted and blinded ciphertexts back to the original senders, who decrypt the ciphertexts. Because of the random blinding factors, the original senders cannot recognize their own sub-distances, and thus do not learn the permutation. The index of the minimum (permuted) distance is sent back to the blinding party, who can invert the permutation and inform all parties about the index of the minimum distance (the cluster which is closest to the current element). In the original proposal by Vaidya and Clifton (2003), the parties now have to enter a secure comparison algorithm to find the minimum element. This, however, can be very expensive, so a less secure, but a more efficient alternative is also suggested by Vaidya and Clifton (2003): In the alternative protocol, the blinding party adds the random blinding factors in a way that they do not cancel out, but so that the same random offset is added to each real distance. The blinded and permuted distances, once decrypted,

Algorithm 2. Secure closest cluster computation

Require: entity e, cluster means $\mu_1,\ldots,\mu_k$
Ensure: Closest cluster to e
    Phase 1: **Sharing the secrets**
    do in parallel for each party $i \in \{3,\ldots,r\}$ # Not party 1 and 2
        for each cluster $c \leftarrow 1,\ldots,k$ **do**
            $X_{ic} \leftarrow$ local component of the distance from e to cluster mean μ_c
            $s_{ic1} \leftarrow$ random 32-bit number
            $s_{ic2} \leftarrow X_{ic} - s_{ic1}$ mod 2^{32}
            $\alpha_{ic1} \leftarrow$ random 32-bit number
            $\alpha_{ic2} \leftarrow 1+\alpha_{ic1}$ if $X_{ic} < s_{ic1}$, else α_{ic1} # Multi-precision int
            Send (s_{ic1},α_{ic1}) to party 1, and $(s_{ic2},-\alpha_{ic2})$ to party 2
        end for   # $(X_{ic} = s_{ic1} + s_{ic2} + (\alpha_{ic1} + \alpha_{ic2})2^{32})$
    end parallel
    Phase 2: **Permute distances**
    do in parallel for parties $i \in \{1,2\}$ # Only parties 1,2
        $D_{ci} = X_{ic} + \sum_{j=3}^{r} s_{jci} + 2^{32} \alpha_{jci}$ #$D = D_{c1} + D_{c2}$ (multi-precision)
        $(D_{1i}',\ldots,D_{ki}') \leftarrow$ SecurePermute$(D_{1i},\ldots,D_{ki})$
        Send $(D_{1i}',\ldots,D_{ki}')$ to party $i + 2$
    end parallel
    Phase 3: **Find minimum distance**
    index $\leftarrow$ SecureFindMinimum$(D_{1i}',\ldots,D_{ik}')$ # Only parties 3 and 4
    Send *index* to party 1
    Party 1: *result* $\leftarrow$ InversePermutation(*index*)
    return *result*

---

are then sent to a "search party" who adds up the sub-distances. Once added up, the real distances plus the offset can be readily compared. Due to the offset, however, the search party does not learn the actual distances, but only their relative sizes. The blinding and search parties do not need to be extra parties, but can be two of the data holders.

In contrast to Vaidya and Clifton (2003), we use additive secret sharing, which require less computation, and less communication. Our algorithm for securely computing the closest cluster mean for each entity has three phases. Pseudo code outlining these three phases is given in Algorithm 2.

Throughout the paper, we assume that we are working with 32-bit integers. If larger (or smaller) values are needed, the protocol can easily be adapted.

- **Phase 1:** In the first phase of the secure closest cluster computation algorithm non-colluding parties 1 and 2 receive additive secret shares of all sub-distances between the current entity and all the cluster means. Let X_{ic} be the ith sub-distance between the entity that is being evaluated and the cluster mean c. Party i creates a random number s_{ic1} (secret share 1), and sets secret share 2 to $s_{ic2} = X_{ic} - s_{ic2} \mod 2^{32}$. Furthermore, party i creates an additive secret share of a bit, which is 1 if the creation of s_{ic2} caused overflow: $\alpha_{ic2} - \alpha_{ic1} = -1$. The secret sharing of the overflow bit is done with multi-precision integers so that another overflow will not occur (this can cause a small leak of information, which will be discussed in the next section). Note that $s_{ic1} + s_{ic2} + (\alpha_{ic2} + \alpha_{ic1})2^{32}$ $= s_{ic1} + s_{ic2} \mod 2^{32} = X_{ic}$. The overflow secret shares are also sent to nodes 1 and 2.

- **Phase 2:** After the completion of Phase 1, for every cluster c, parties 1 and 2 sum up the received shares with their own sub-distance to form the two additive secret shares

$$D_{c1} = X_{1c} + \sum_{i=3}^{r}(s_{ic1} + 2^{32}\alpha_{ic1}), \quad \text{a n d}$$

$$D_{c2} = X_{1c} + \sum_{i=3}^{r}(s_{ic1} + 2^{32}\alpha_{ic1}).$$ The summations should be done with multi precision to prevent any overflow. The sum of the two shares $D_{c1} + D_{c2}$ is exactly the distance between the current entity and cluster mean c. Parties 1 and 2 could now perform a series of secure comparisons to find the minimum distance. However, this would not only reveal the minimum distance, but the ordering of several of the distances. To prevent anyone from learning the ordering of the distances, parties 1 and 2 agree on a permutation, and permute there vectors of shares: $(D_{11}, D_{21}, ..., D_{k1})$ and $(D_{12}, D_{22}, ..., D_{k2})$, and send the permuted vectors to parties 3 and 4.

- **Phase 3:** The task of parties 3 and 4 is now to find the minimum element from the permuted list $(D_1, ..., D_k)$, where party 3 knows D_{c1}, and party 4 knows D_{c2} of each element, c. This is done by comparing each of the elements with the current smallest element one by one. The comparison presents the following problem: We have protocols for comparing known natural numbers, but we have additive integer shares of the two values. The problem is solved by observing that $D_c < D_{c'}$ if and only if $D_{c1} - D_{c'1} < D_{c'2} - D_{c2}$. Party 3 knows the left hand side, and party 4 knows the right

hand side. To make sure that the numbers are positive, they need to add a value which is larger than the largest possible value of the shares D_{c1} and D_{c2}: i.e. $2^{32} + 2^{32}(r-2) + 2^{64}(r-2)$, a conservative estimate of all the terms of the sum of D_{c1} and D_{c2}. They can now compute the result of the comparison by applying any secure comparison algorithm. We use the secure comparison described in "Secure Comparison" subsection above.

Once Phase 3 is completed parties 3 and 4 need the help of parties 1 and 2 to invert the permutation and obtain the real index of the minimum number: party 3 sends the permuted index to party 1, who broadcasts the result.

There are two major differences between this protocol and the protocol of Doganay et al. (2008), which are given below:

- Phase 1 is changed so that the number of messages is linear in the number of parties. In Doganay et al. (2008) the number of messages was quadratic, and the size of the messages linear in the number of parties. We discuss this difference further in "Handling Collusions" subsection below.

In Doganay et al. (2008), Phase 2 required two rounds: first the shares are send to parties 3 and 4. After parties 3 and 4 have permuted the vectors, they send the permuted vectors back. In our proposal parties 1 and 2 perform the permutation before sending the vectors to parties 3 and 4, who then performs the comparison in Phase 2.

PRIVACY DISCUSSION

Before going into the discussion about privacy, we have to define what we mean by private information in the algorithm. Above we set as our goal that the only information party i will learn after the algorithm is:

- The final mean μ_{ci} for each cluster $c \in \{1, \ldots, k\}$.
- The cluster index for each entity $j \in \{1, \ldots, n\}$.

No other information other than these two should be learned from the algorithm. The actual values of data attributes belonging to the data holders are obviously private information. The sub-distances calculated by each party according to their set of attributes are also private information since one may recover the actual values of the entities by knowing the distances of the entities to the cluster means.

In both our protocol and the protocol by Vaidya and Clifton (2003), everyone learns how entities switch between the clusters in each iteration. This information should, ideally speaking, be kept secret. However, solution to this problem seems likely to bring considerable overhead, since we would need to add secure computation of the new cluster means, and secure computation of local sub-distances. We therefore allow this information to leak, and leave it as future work to find a solution.

Privacy in our Protocol

In order to examine how our method protects privacy, we focus on the "Securely Computing the Closest Cluster" algorithm which is the only part of the algorithm in which there are interactions between the parties. In Phase 1 of the algorithm, all parties secret-share their local sub-distances between parties 1 and 2. Since s_{ic1} is a random number, it clearly does not give away any information. The subtraction of s_{ic1} (a uniformly random number) and the secret X_{ic} is also a uniformly random number, since we compute it using modulo arithmetic (i.e. we work in an algebraic ring). Without both secret shares, no in-

formation what so ever can be obtained about X_{ic}. Since parties 1 and 2 are assumed to be non-colluding, the secret sharing keeps the privacy of the local sub-distances. The parties also secret share the overflow bits. But since α_{ic2} is either 0 or 1 minus α_{ic1} (without taking modulo) that is a potential leak of information. If, for instance $\alpha_{ic2} = 2^{32} + 1$ (or $\alpha_{ic2} = 0$), party 2 knows that the overflow bit was 1 (or 0, respectively), however, the only thing he learns from this information is that $X_{ic} < s_{ic1}$. Putting this information together with $s_{ic2} = X_{ic} - \alpha_{ic1}$, will release a small amount of probabilistic information about X_{ic}. The probability that α_{ic2} is an extreme value (which is the only case which releases information) is 2^{-31}. and can be made smaller by increasing the interval from which α_{ic1} is chosen.

The only information transmitted in Phase 2 when players 1 and 2 agree on a random permutation, and when they send the permuted secret shares to parties 3 and 4. Now parties 3 and 4 are in the same position as players 1 and 2 were before: the secret sharing protects all sub-distances, as long as nodes 1, 2, 3, and 4 do not collude pairwise. The ordering of distances is protected as long as neither of parties 1 and 2 collude with any of parties 3 and 4.

In Phase 3, the secure comparison is privacy-preserving under the assumption that parties 3 and 4 are non-colluding; detailed proof is explained in Kaya (2007).

Finally the "Securely Computing the Closest Cluster" algorithm returns the closest cluster to the given entity. Clearly this is exactly what the parties are supposed to learn in the last round. However, all parties will see how entities change cluster in each iteration of the k-means clustering algorithm. An entity, which fluctuates between two clusters, can be assumed to be approximately halfway between the two cluster means. This is more information than is strictly allowed. However, the original algorithm by Vaidya and Clifton (2003) suffers from the same problem as well.

Security Comparison

In both our protocol and the protocol by Vaidya and Clifton (2003), privacy breaches may occur when two or more parties collude. Therefore, in both protocols, some non-collusion assumptions have to be made for some specific parties. In the protocol by Vaidya and Clifton (2003), each party, upon computing local distances X_{ic}, sends X_{ic} to party 1. Party 1 adds random values α_{ic} to X_{ic} of each party. After this phase, each party sends $X_{ic} + \alpha_{ic}$ to party r. Here, collusion between parties 1 and r allows them to learn the value of X_{ic} of all other parties, which is no doubt a severe privacy breach.

In our protocol, if two of the parties 1,2,3, and 4 collude, they may be able to open the additive secret shares, and obtain all the local sub-distances (if they have one of each share). This is the same situation as a collusion between parties 1 and r in the protocol by Vaidya and Clifton (2003).

As a solution to this problem, Vaidya and Clifton (2003) propose an extension to their protocol that increases the number of colluding parties needed to reveal X_{ic} of each party. In essence, they apply their permutation steps more than once according to a chosen anti-collusion parameter. If this parameter is denoted as p, they repeat the permutation algorithm $p - 1$ times by choosing a different party at each time to play the role of party 1. This method increases security of the protocol; however, it also increases computation and communication cost considerably. The protocol by Doganay et al. (2008) overcame this problem by using (n, n) secret sharing instead of $(2, 2)$ secret sharing. This brings back a quadratic amount of messages in Phase 1 of the "find closest cluster" protocol. The approach in Doganay et al. (2008) is further discussed in the next subsection.

In the simplified version of the protocol by Vaidya and Clifton (2003), party r performs all the comparisons in clear text, where a random

offset has been added to all distances. While this makes it unlikely that party r can compute the distances, it can certainly sort them, and learn the total ordering of distances.

In our protocol, if one of parties 1 and 2 collude with one of parties 3 and 4, they can invert the permutation, and link the comparison results to the clusters.

The repeated permutation method of Vaidya and Clifton (2003) described above, will also fix the ordering problem. This repeated permutation can also be applied to our protocol to increase the non-collusion threshold. Since our permutation algorithm does not contain any encryption or similar expensive operations, it can be applied more than once without bringing too much computation and communication overhead.

Finally, if node 5 colludes with one of the nodes 3 or 4, they will be able to learn the magnitude of the difference between the two distances of each comparison; however, they will not be able to link this to a specific cluster, unless they collude with one of the parties 1 or 2. This information will indicate how "dense" the clusters are. In the simplified version of the protocol of Vaidya and Clifton (2003), party r can always compute the exact pairwise difference of the distances.

In this section we compared the security of the simplified (and less secure) version of the protocol of Vaidya and Clifton (2003) with our protocol. However, the full protocol of Vaidya and Clifton (2003) requires secure comparison. Whatever secure comparison is chosen in Vaidya and Clifton (2003), a similar method can be applied to our comparison step, thus giving the same increase in security (and decrease in efficiency) to the two protocols. The comparison between our protocol and the simplified protocol of Vaidya and Clifton (2003) is thus fair.

The comparison of the security of the two protocols reveals that collusion between 2 specific parties leads to some privacy breach in both protocols.

Handling Collusions

In our protocol the local sub-distances are secret shared among two parties. If these parties collude, they will learn the sub-distances. In the paper by Doganay et al. (2008), this leak is prevented by extending Phase 1 of the "find closest cluster" protocol: The sub-distances (and overflow bits) are secret shared among all parties. After receiving shares from all the other $(r-1)$ parties, the shares are added up, and sent to either party 1 or party 2 (parties with odd identity send the sum to party 1, and parties with even identity send to party 2). When parties 1 and 2 add up the shares they receive, they have additive secret shares of the overall distances, just as in the original protocol. The drawback of this protocol is that the (multi-precision) secret shares become very large, slowing down the subsequent secure comparison, and a quadratic number of these large secret shares need to be sent. However, since each party keeps a share of his own sub-distance until he adds it with all the random shares received from other parties, no one can recover it.

The protocol presented in this paper does not prevent the leak of local sub-distances when the secret sharing parties collude. However, given the non-colluding model, which is also necessary for the security of the protocol of Doganay et al. (2008), this leak will never occur. We thus argue that if there is any concern over the possible collusion of two parties, a different approach than those of Vaidya and Clifton (2003), Doganay et al. (2008) and the one presented in this paper, is needed all together.

COST ANALYSIS

A privacy preserving distributed data mining algorithm aiming to be used in real life applications should not bring too much communication and computation overhead. In the following two subsections we analyze the communication and

computation overheads of our algorithm. The overheads mainly occur in the "Securely Finding the Closest Cluster" part of the algorithm. Thus, we only analyze this portion of the two algorithms. It should be noted that both communication and computation overheads of the k-means clustering algorithm depend on the dataset. The number of iterations required before the termination criteria is met depends on the data and the initial cluster means. Therefore, in the communication and computation cost analysis, we only consider one iteration of the k-means algorithm. We let r be the number of parties, n the number of entities in the database and k the number of clusters. We assume that the values in the dataset are 32 bit integers.

The performance of any distributed algorithm primarily relies on how it uses the following three resources:

- The amount of computation done.
- The amount of data sent.
- The number of rounds (in one round, a party can send at most one message to any other party).

These three factors add to the total time of the protocol through the parameters: computation speed, network bandwidth, and network latency, respectively. Depending on how a protocol uses the three resources, it will be more or less sensitive to the three parameters.

The protocol of Vaidya and Clifton (2003) relies on computationally expensive public key encryption, causing a large amount of data to be sent. Each 32-bit sub-distance is encrypted in a ciphertext of several thousands of bits. If Paillier encryption is used, it is recommended to use at least 2048 bit ciphertexts to provide the minimum acceptable security level of 80 bits (Note that our protocol provides utmost security under the non-collusion assumption since the secret sharing provides information theoretic security). In the first phase of the "Securely Finding the Closest Cluster" every party sends k ciphertexts to party 1. Party one has to encrypt the r random blinding factors, and multiply with the k ciphertexts, the resulting k ciphertexts are sent back. The computational power of party 1 becomes a bottleneck in the protocol, since he has to perform $(r - 1)k$ encryptions and ciphertext multiplications in every instance of the "Securely Finding the Closest Cluster" part. The bandwidth of the first party may also become a concern, since he has to send and receive a total of $2048*(r - 1)k$ bits in the first round. The remaining parts of the protocol of Vaidya and Clifton (2003) are less of a concern, since everything else is done on 32-bit integers. The number of rounds in the protocol is 2 in the first phase (send and receive from party 1), 1 in the second phase (send to party r), and 2 in the final round (send permuted answer to node 1, broadcast result). In total the "Securely Finding the Closest Cluster" protocol of Vaidya and Clifton (2003) has 5 rounds, so the delay due to rounds is 5 times the network latency.

Our protocol does not rely on any difficult computation, so computing speed is not a big issue. Most of the time parties only send secret shares, which are 32 bit integers (even the multi precision overflow shares are at most 33 bits). The bottleneck is in the secure comparison adapted from Kaya et al. (2007). Parties 3 and 4 first need to create secret shares of each bit in the secret shares D_{c1} and D_{c2} which are now more than 32 bits (since they are multi-precision). The number of bits in these secret shares is $\ell = 66 + log2(r - 1)$, so ℓ shares need to be created (this can be done in one round). During the comparison, the XOR-homomorphic secret shares are turned into AND-homomorphic secret share (non-interactively), and the result consists of a vector of ℓ AND-homomorphic secret shares, each of λ bits, where λ is an error parameter with a typical value between 30 and 50. When the result is opened by party 5 the two nodes each have to send $\ell*\lambda$ (easily close to 2000 bits: still less than Vaidya and Clifton (2003) where k ciphertexts are sent in two rounds). However, a large message is only sent in one round, instead of two. Our protocol also requires more rounds: in the first phase, 1 round is needed (everyone sends their shares to parties 1 and 2). In the second phase, 1 round is needed (parties 1 and 2 send the permutes secret shares), and in the last phase each of the $k - 1$ comparisons needs 3 rounds (first secret shares of the bits are exchanged, the result vectors are sent to party 5, and the answer is sent back), finally the result has to be sent to party 1 to invert the permutation, and the result is broadcast: in total our protocol needs $4 + 3(k-1)$ rounds. This makes our protocol more sensitive to network latency. However, as we demonstrate in "Results" subsection below, the extra encryptions needed in Vaidya and Clifton (2003) when k increases outweigh the benefits of a constant number of rounds.

If latency is high, our protocol suffers, whereas the protocol of Vaidya and Clifton (2003) suffers under low bandwidth or slow CPU speed. In the next section, we show the results of experiments in two real-world scenarios, which shows that our protocol outperforms that of Vaidya and Clifton (2003).

EXPERIMENTS

We implemented our protocol and the protocol of Vaidya and Clifton (2003) and performed simulations on them in order to compare their performance in real-world scenarios. In the implementation, we use the same software code for the k-means-clustering algorithm and only change the function "find closest cluster" described in "Our Algorithm" section.

For testing purposes in our simulations we used a spatio-temporal dataset consisting of trajectories of private cars in Milan obtained in the context of the GeoPKDD project (http://www.geopkdd.eu/). The dataset consists of 100 trajectories (a subset of the full dataset) with sample points at irregular intervals over a period of time of one week. The number of sample points for each trajectory is 500. Since each sample point consists of one x and one y coordinate, each item in the dataset has 1000 attributes. In the tests, the sample points are partitioned evenly among the parties; that is, every party has equal or near equal number of sample points. However, the distribution of sample points does not affect neither of the two algorithms considerably (since the first step of each iteration is to compute local distances).

It is important to note that the initial cluster assignments of entities greatly affect the execution time of the k-means clustering algorithm. In order to make a fair comparison, we run the cluster algorithm for a fixed number of rounds regardless of any termination criteria.

In the implementation of our protocol, we have used a value of 32 for the error parameter λ, giving a probability of approximately $\log k 2^{-27}$ of returning the wrong cluster in the "find closest cluster" function. The relatively large error probability can be justified by the nature of the k-means clustering algorithm: even though an element is assigned to the wrong cluster in one round, it is likely to be assigned to the right cluster in a future round. However, the number of rounds before a termination criteria is met can differ. This is another reason for choosing a fixed number of rounds for the k-means clustering algorithm in our tests.

We have implemented the simplified version with offset of the protocol of Vaidya and Clifton (2003) discussed in "Secure Closest Cluster Computation" subsection above. Furthermore, we assume that all parties know the public keys of all other parties before the protocol starts (typically this is done with an existing public key infrastructure). This assumption gives an advantage to the protocol, which guarantees a fair comparison. As homomorphic encryption, we use the Paillier public key encryption, which is the most efficient additively homomorphic encryption scheme known to the authors. We use a key size of 1024

bits, which gives ciphertexts of 2048 bits. This key size is the absolute minimum recommended.

The implementations are done in C++ using the gmp library (http://gmplib.org/) for multi-precision integer operations, and a freely available Paillier encryption library (Bethencourt, 2010), which relies on gmp.

The tests are done on a 3.0 GHz Intel Core2 Quad PC (the programs do not take advantage of the multi-cores) with 2GB's of RAM.

As argued in "Cost Analysis" section, there are four factors which influence the relative performance of the two protocols:

- CPU speed.
  ◦ Number of clusters (k).
  ◦ Number of parties (r).
- Network bandwidth.
- Network latency.

In our experiments we compare the influence of the four last factors. In order to test the two protocols in an environment with full control over network properties we have designed a simulator which is capable of simulating the behavior of networked applications. The simulator is described in the next subsection, and the results of our simulations are given in the subsequent subsection.

Network Application Simulator

When comparing the performance of distributed applications it is necessary to create an environment with full control over the network properties while not influencing the computation of the application itself. A wide variety of network simulation tools exist, however the emphasis of most of these tools is on the simulation of the network behavior, and not the overall distributed application. ns-2, for instance, requires that the application is rewritten in the scripting language TCL. Moreover, many network simulation tools do not consider processing times, but only the operation of the network.

Figure 1. Sensitivity to number of parties (k - 8, bandwidth 5000 kbps, and latency 12ms)

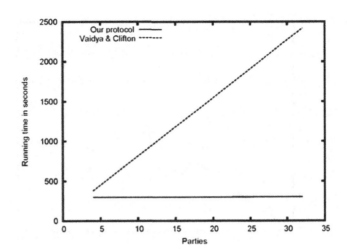

In our tests, we are only interested in controlling the point to point network properties in a naïve scenario where bandwidth and latency follow simple random distributions. We also require that the simulator reports accurate measurements of running time.

To satisfy our simulation needs, we have created a network application simulator (NAS), which can simulate an arbitrary number of networked computers (only RAM memory sets an upper limit). NAS is a discrete event simulator in which

the entities are the processes and the network. The state transitions (events) happen when a process starts, connects with another process, sends a message, receives a message, or terminates. In a normal simulator the transition times (message transfer time and process computing time) are sampled from random distributions. In NAS, however, only the network properties are sampled: the process computing time is accurately measured by running the actual process until the next event occurs. NAS achieves this by intercepting all

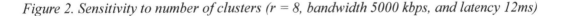

Figure 2. Sensitivity to number of clusters (r = 8, bandwidth 5000 kbps, and latency 12ms)

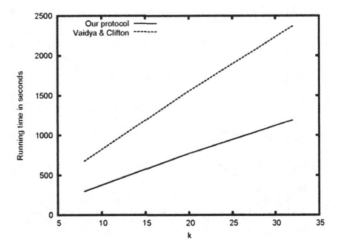

Figure 3. Sensitivity to latency (k = 8, r = 8, and bandwidth 5000 kbps)

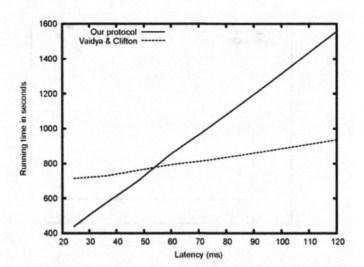

network system calls which the process performs. When NAS intercepts a system call of the process, the computation time is recorded, and the process is suspended until the next event occurs at that process. NAS is capable of simulating the behavior of any distributed application without having to rewrite, or even recompile, the program. This allows us to do black-box comparisons of distributed applications (though, in this paper, we have written both applications from scratch).

Results

We have designed the following tests to fully demonstrate the tradeoffs between computational overhead (through the size of the data, and the number of clusters), communication overhead (through network bandwidth), and number of rounds (through network latency).

In the following tests we vary one of the parameters: number of parties, value of k, network

Figure 4. Sensitivity to latency (k = 8, r = 8, and bandwidth 400 kbps)

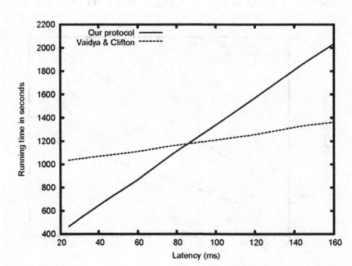

Figure 5. Sensitivity to bandwidth (k = 8, r = 8, and latency 12ms)

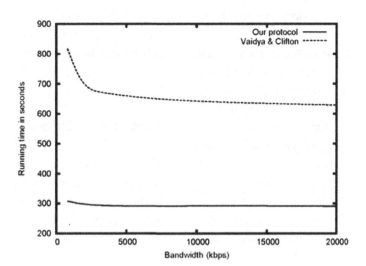

bandwidth, or network latency. To set the starting point of the tests, we have chosen a setting which gives as much benefit to the protocol of Vaidya and Clifton (2003) as possible, while still representing a realistic scenario: the default values of the network parameters is a latency of 12 ms (measured between Istanbul and London), and a bandwidth of 5000 kbps (which is very high in a setting where the parties are geographically separated). The default number of parties is set to 8, which seems reasonable for a distributed clustering, and the value of k is set to 8.

In the protocol of Vaidya and Clifton (2003), party 1 needs to create a vector of encrypted blinding factors for each other node. The protocol therefore has a computational bottleneck at the first party, which increases linearly with the number of parties. In the protocol presented in this paper, most of the work is done by the two comparison parties (parties 3 and 4). The initial creation of secret shares is done by each party in parallel, and the only dependency on the number of parties is when parties 1 and 2 have to sum up the multi-precision integers. Figure 1 clearly shows the linear relationship between the number of parties, and the computational time in Vaidya and Clifton (2003).

The number of rounds in our comparison step depends on k since we do interactive comparison. For this reason the performance of our protocol has a linear dependency on k. In the protocol by Vaidya and Clifton (2003) all the comparisons are done by party r (non-interactively). However, the number of encryptions done, and the amount of data sent by party 1, depends linearly on k. So the overall performances of both protocols are linear in k. Figure 2 shows that the impact of the extra rounds in our protocol is smaller than the impact of the extra computation in the protocol of Vaidya and Clifton (2003) in our experimental setting.

The major drawback of our protocol is the extra number of rounds, which is linear in the number of clusters $(4 + 3(k - 1))$. This dependency makes our protocol very sensitive to network latency. The protocol of Vaidya and Clifton (2003), on the other hand, uses 5 rounds in each iteration of the clustering algorithm, so the influence of latency is low. However, as Figure 3 shows, with a bandwidth of 5000 kbps, our protocol is still faster up to a latency of approximately 54 ms. If the number of participants increases or the bandwidth decreases the performance of the two protocols intersect at a higher latency. Figure 4 shows that with a latency of 400 kbps our protocol is faster than that of Vaidya and Clifton (2003) up to a latency of approximately 85 ms.

No message sent in our protocol is very large compared to the vectors of ciphertexts sent in the protocol of Vaidya and Clifton (2003). For this reason our protocol is less sensitive to the impact of bandwidth. However, for a fixed network latency, there is a point beyond which an increase in the bandwidth does not affect the protocol (when a message can be sent in a time close to 0 ms). Figure 5 shows that the protocol of Vaidya and Clifton (2003) is more sensitive to bandwidth. With low bandwidth their protocol suffers. Figure 5 also justifies our choice of a default bandwidth of 5000kbps: the protocol of Vaidya and Clifton (2003) does not get much extra benefit from a higher bandwidth (since, after that point, the impact of latency is now larger than the impact of the bandwidth).

The tests performed in this section show that, for most realistic scenarios, our protocol performs considerably better than the protocol presented by Vaidya and Clifton (2003).

CONCLUSION

In this paper, we proposed an improvement of the protocols by Doganay et al. (2008) for applying k-means clustering to vertically partitioned data without compromising the privacy of individuals. We reduced the number of rounds in the protocol. We also reduced the number of messages send from being quadratic in the number of parties to linear. We implemented and tested privacy preserving clustering in a realistic setting and on a real dataset of trajectories in a novel testing platform. The detailed tests on real trajectory data sets show that the new version of the protocol performs considerably better than the original protocol by Vaidya and Clifton (2003). They use the additive homomorphic property of certain public key encryptions, but we based our protocol on additive secret sharing which is also homomorphic with respect to addition. Due to the fact that we use secret sharing rather than encryption, we do not suffer from the heavy computation and bit expansion drawbacks of public key encryption schemes.

ACKNOWLEDGMENT

This work was partially funded by the Information Society Technologies Programme of the European Commission, Future and Emerging Technologies under IST-014915 GeoPKDD project.

REFERENCES

Aggarwal, C. C., & Yu, P. S. (Eds.). (2008). *Privacy-Preserving Data Mining*. New York: Springer.

Agrawal, R., & Srikant, R. (2000). Privacy-preserving data mining. *SIGMOD Record, 29*(2), 439–450. doi:10.1145/335191.335438

Ben-Or, M., Goldwasser, S., & Wigderson, A. (1998). Completeness theorems for non-cryptographic fault-tolerant distributed computation. In *STOC '88: Proceedings of the Twentieth Annual ACM Symposium on Theory of Computing* (pp. 1–10). New York: ACM.

Bethencourt, J. (2010). *Paillier library.* Retrieved from http://acsc.cs.utexas.edu/libpaillier/

Clifton, C., Kantarcioglu, M., Vaidya, J., Lin, X., & Zhu, M. Y. (2002). Tools for privacy preserving distributed data mining. *SIGKDD Explorations, 4*(2), 28–34. doi:10.1145/772862.772867

Doganay, M. C., Pedersen, T. B., Saygin, Y., Savas, E., & Levi, A. (2008). Distributed privacy preserving k-means clustering with additive secret sharing. In F. Fotouhi, L. Xiong, & T. M. Truta (Eds.), *PAIS '08: Proceedings of the 2008 International Workshop on Privacy and Anonymity in Information Society* (pp. 3–11). New York: ACM.

Fischlin, M. (2001). A cost-effective pay-per-multiplication comparison method for millionaires. In D. Naccache (Ed.), *CT-RSA 2001: Topics in Cryptology -The Cryptographers' Track at RSA Conference* (LNCS 2010, pp. 457–471).

Kantarcioglu, M., & Clifton, C. (2004). Privacy-preserving distributed mining of association rules on horizontally partitioned data. *IEEE Transactions on Knowledge and Data Engineering, 16*(9), 1026–1037. doi:10.1109/TKDE.2004.45

Kaya, S. V. (2007). *Toolbox for Privacy Preserving Data Mining.* Unpublished master's thesis, Sabanci University, Istanbul, Turkey.

Kaya, S. V., Pedersen, T. B., Savas, E., & Saygin, Y. (2007). Efficient privacy preserving distributed clustering based on secret sharing. In *PAKDD 2007 International Workshops: Emerging Technologies in Knowledge Discovery and Data Mining* (LNCS 4819, pp. 280–291).

Laur, S., Lipmaa, H., & Mielikäinen, T. (2006). Cryptographically private support vector machines. In *KDD '06: Proceedings of the 12th ACM SIGKDD International Conference on Knowledge Discovery and Data Mining* (pp. 618–624). New York: ACM.

Liu, K., Kargupta, H., & Ryan, J. (2006). Random projection-based multiplicative data perturbation for privacy preserving distributed data mining. *IEEE Transactions on Knowledge and Data Engineering, 18*(1), 92–106. doi:10.1109/TKDE.2006.14

Sander, T., Young, A., & Yung, M. (1999). Non-interactive cryptocomputing for NC[1]. In *FOCS '99: Proceedings of the 40th Annual Symposium on Foundations of Computer Science* (pp. 554). Washington, DC: IEEE Computer Society.

Shamir, A. (1979). How to share a secret. *Communications of the ACM, 22*(11), 612–613. doi:10.1145/359168.359176

Vaidya, J., & Clifton, C. (2003). Privacy-preserving k-means clustering over vertically partitioned data. In *KDD '03: Proceedings of the ninth ACM SIGKDD International Conference on Knowledge Discovery and Data Mining* (pp. 206–215). New York: ACM.

Vijayan, J. (2007, September 18). House committee chair wants info on cancelled DHS data-mining programs. *Computer World.*

Wright, R., & Yang, Z. (2004). Privacy-preserving bayesian network structure computation on distributed heterogeneous data. In *KDD '04: Proceedings of the tenth ACM SIGKDD International Conference on Knowledge Discovery and Data Mining* (pp. 713–718). New York: ACM.

Yao, A. C. (1982). Protocols for secure computations. In *Proceedings of the 23rd Annual IEEE Symposium on Foundations of Computer Science* (pp. 160–164). Washington, DC: IEEE Computer Society.

This work was previously published in the International Journal of Data Warehousing and Mining, Volume 7, Issue 1, edited by David Taniar, pp. 46-66, copyright 2011 by IGI Publishing (an imprint of IGI Global).

Chapter 4
Query Recommendations for OLAP Discovery–Driven Analysis

Arnaud Giacometti
Université François Rabelais Tours, Laboratoire d'Informatique, France

Elsa Negre
Université François Rabelais Tours, Laboratoire d'Informatique, France

Patrick Marcel
Université François Rabelais Tours, Laboratoire d'Informatique, France

Arnaud Soulet
Université François Rabelais Tours, Laboratoire d'Informatique, France

ABSTRACT

Recommending database queries is an emerging and promising field of research and is of particular interest in the domain of OLAP systems, where the user is left with the tedious process of navigating large datacubes. In this paper, the authors present a framework for a recommender system for OLAP users that leverages former users' investigations to enhance discovery-driven analysis. This framework recommends the discoveries detected in former sessions that investigated the same unexpected data as the current session. This task is accomplished by (1) analysing the query log to discover pairs of cells at various levels of detail for which the measure values differ significantly, and (2) analysing a current query to detect if a particular pair of cells for which the measure values differ significantly can be related to what is discovered in the log. This framework is implemented in a system that uses the open source Mondrian server and recommends MDX queries. Preliminary experiments were conducted to assess the quality of the recommendations in terms of precision and recall, as well as the efficiency of their on-line computation.

INTRODUCTION

One of the goals of recommender systems is to help users navigating large amounts of data. Existing recommender systems are usually categorized into content-based methods and collaborative filtering methods (Adomavicius et al., 2005). Content-based methods recommend to the user items similar to the ones that interested him in the past, whereas collaborative filtering methods recommend to the user items that interested similar users.

DOI: 10.4018/978-1-4666-2148-0.ch004

Applying recommendation technology to database, especially for recommending queries, is an emerging and promising topic (Khoussainova et al., 2009; Chatzopoulou et al., 2009; Stefanidis et al., 2009). It is of particular relevance to the domain of multidimensional databases, where OLAP analysis is inherently tedious since the user has to navigate large datacubes to find valuable information, often having no idea on what her forthcoming queries should be. This is often the case in discovery-driven analysis (Sarawagi et al., 1998) where the user investigates a particular surprising drop or increase in the data.

In our earlier works (Giacometti et al., 2008, 2009a) we proposed to adapt techniques stemming from collaborative filtering to recommend OLAP queries to the user. The basic idea is to compute a similarity between the current user's sequence of queries (a session) and the former sequences of queries logged by the server. In these works, similarity between sessions is only based on the query text, irrespective of the query results. In this present article, to take into consideration what the users were looking for, we leverage query results to compute recommendations. Our approach is inspired by what is done in web search and e-commerce applications (Parikh et al., 2008) where inferred properties of former sessions are used to support the current session.

The present work improves on Giacometti et al. (2009b), where we proposed a framework tailored for recommending queries in the context of discovery driven analysis of OLAP cubes. The basic idea is to infer, for every former session on the OLAP system, what the user was investigating. As it is the case in discovery-driven analysis, this has the form of a pair of cells showing a significant unexpected difference in the data. We proposed a framework for detecting in the log of an OLAP server such pairs, arranging them into a specialisation relation, and recording per session the queries at various levels of detail that contain the pairs detected. During subsequent analyses, if a difference is found that was investigated in a former session, then the discoveries of this former session are suggested to the current user.

The goal of the present paper is to demonstrate the validity of this approach for recommending query in the particular context of discovery-driven analysis of OLAP cubes. To this end, we extend the work of Giacometti et al. (2009b) in the following ways: First the framework has been slightly changed to better take into account sessions investigating the same difference pair. This means that discoveries are no more recorded only for a particular session but can span across sessions. Second, the framework has been implemented and we undertook a few experiments to assess the effectiveness and the efficiency of our approach. Finally, we propose a dedicated architecture for implementing the approach beyond a prototypical setting.

This paper is organized as follows. The section discusses our approach with a simple yet realistic example. The third section reviews related work. Preliminary definitions on OLAP data model and query model are recalled in the fourth section. The framework of our recommender system is formally presented in the fifth section, and the algorithms are presented in the sixth section. In these sections, the example given in the second section is used as a running example to illustrate the framework. The seventh section introduces our prototypical implementation of the framework, and the eighth section presents some preliminary experiments. Finally, before concluding, we briefly discuss the feasibility of our approach in a real context and propose an architecture thereof.

MOTIVATING EXAMPLE

In this section we illustrate our approach with an artificial yet realistic motivating example that will be used as a running example throughout this paper. This example uses typical discovery-driven analysis sessions of a simple datacube containing sale results of various products in various locations

Figure 1. Example of a log and a current session

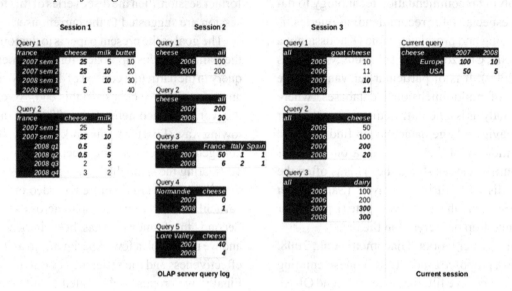

at different times. These sessions are sequences of queries, the result of which are depicted in Figure 1. On the left are three sessions from the log of the OLAP server and on the right is a current session. This current session consists of only one query (q) that asks for the aggregated sales of cheese in 2007 and 2008 in Europe and USA. The current user may wonder where to navigate the cube further. We will now show how the information in the log can be exploited to provide her with some suggestions.

Let us first describe the sessions contained in the log of the OLAP server. In what follows, query q_i^j denotes the ith query of the jth session. Session 1 first asked for the sales for various dairy products (cheese, milk, and butter) in France for each semester of 2007 and 2008 (query q_1^1), and then for the sales of cheese and milk in France for each quarter of 2008 and each semester of 2007 $\left(q_2^1\right)$.

The second session first asked for the sales of cheese in 2006-2007 $\left(q_1^2\right)$ and then the sales of cheese in 2007-2008 $\left(q_2^2\right)$. Next it asked for the sales of cheese for 2007-2008 in France, Italy and Spain $\left(q_3^2\right)$. Then for the sales of cheese for 2007-

2008 in two french regions, namely Normandie q_4^2, and finally the Loire Valley $\left(q_5^2\right)$.

The third session asked for the sales of goat cheese for 2005-2008 $\left(q_1^3\right)$. Then the user rolled up and asked for the sales of cheese for 2005-2008 $\left(q_2^3\right)$. Finally, she rolled up again to obtain the sales of all dairy products for 2005-2008 $\left(q_3^3\right)$.

By observing these sessions one can notice that each of them is concerned with a general difference that is a drop of the sales of cheese from 2007 to 2008. It appears for instance for query q_2^3 of session 3 and for query q_2^2 of session 2. In the log, there is no difference that can be said to be more general than this one (note for instance that the sales of dairy products are stable from 2007 compared to 2008). Hence this particular difference, the drop of sales for cheese from 2007 to 2008, is said to be the most general difference pair (*mgdp* for short). The queries whose result displays this difference are called most general difference queries (*mgdq* for short). This difference also appears for queries q of the current session, q_1^1, q_3^2, q_5^2 and q_1^3, at lower levels of detail. These queries can be said to confirm this difference and are called drill-down differences

Figure 2. Example of a log and a current session, with some computed recommendations

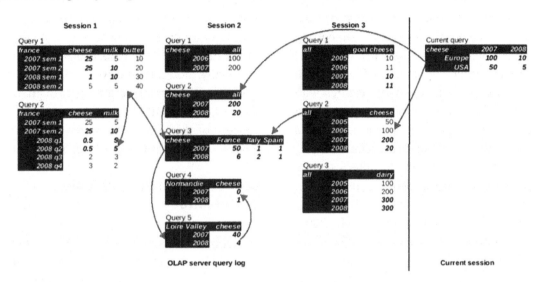

in what follows. On the other hand, query q_4^2 shows that the sales of cheese in a particular region increased from 2007 to 2008. This query is said to be an exception to the general difference in what follows.

Suppose now that the log is processed to find the most general difference queries it contains, as well as their drill-down differences and exceptions. Note that this processing uses the cube schema, more precisely the dimension tables, to detect roll-ups and drill-downs. A recommender system for OLAP analysts should detect that the current user's query is a drill-down difference of one of the mgdq of the log (namely the drop of the sales of cheese). It would then suggest to the user to navigate the cube to see the mgdq, its drill-down differences and exceptions. In our framework, such a suggestion has the form of a graph whose vertices are queries. This graph allows the user to navigate the relevant queries of the log, starting from the current query. Figure 2 illustrates this principle, by depicting two paths in such a graph, computed from what is detected in the log presented in Figure 1. Each arrow can be interpreted as "if you have evaluated this query then you might be interested by that next query". For instance, it is recommended to the user to evaluate

query q_2^3, whose result displays the mgdp, then the drill-down queries that detail the location hierarchy (France first with query q_3^2, then Loire Valley with query q_5^2) and finally query q_4^2 whose result displays an exception to the general difference in a particular French region. Note that the graph's vertices are the recommended query texts that the user simply has to evaluate if she is interested in the recommendation. For instance, for query q_2^2, the MDX text would be SELECT {[2007], [2008]} ON ROWS, {[Country.All]} ON COLUMNS FROM [SalesCube] WHERE ([cheese]).

Our framework can be used as a basis for such a recommender system. It is composed of two parts: The processing of the log, and the computation of recommendations. It is detailed after the sections "Related work" and "OLAP data model and query model."

RELATED WORK

Anticipating Database Queries

In a recent paper, Khoussainova et al. (2009) point out the need for systems leveraging former sessions to support database users analyzing large amount of data. The only works we know that proposes to recommend queries for supporting database exploration is those of Chatzopoulou et al. (2009) and Stefanidis et al. (2009). Although these works share some common features with ours, they differ on two important aspects: First they do not assume a particular database schema and hence the roll-up/drill-down relationship is not exploited, and second, the fact that a session is a sequence of queries is not taken into account.

In the context of multidimensional databases, our previous works (Giacometti et al., 2008, 2009a) propose a framework and a system for recommending OLAP queries to a current user by taking advantage of former analytical sessions. This framework is based on the proposal of methods for evaluating the distance between multidimensional queries on the one hand, and the distance between sessions on the other hand. Following a classical collaborative filtering approach, the current session is compared to the sessions found in the log and the sessions close to the current session are used for computing recommendations.

In the present paper our goal is to complement this approach by taking users' discoveries into consideration. The idea is no more to recommend queries of sessions that are close to the current session. Instead, our framework recommends queries based on sessions that investigated the same general difference as the one investigated by the current user.

In the same context, the recent work of Jerbi et al. (2009) recommends OLAP queries to the current user by transforming the current query with user preferences. They suppose that a user profile exists from which the preferences that are the most relevant to the current query are used to transform it into a recommended query. This work is more of a content-based method as it does not take former sessions into account. Note that this is closed to that of personalizing OLAP queries with a user profile (Bellatreche et al., 2005), the

main difference being that a personalized query is included in the current query, whereas it is not necessary for the recommended query computed by the method of Jerbi et al. (2009).

Finally, note that the work of Sapia (1999, 2000) shares with our work the goal of predicting the forthcoming OLAP query. However the main concern of this work is to prefetch data, not to guide the user towards interesting parts of the cube.

Discovery-Driven Analysis of Datacubes

To support interactive analysis of multidimensional data, Sarawagi et al. (1998) introduced discovery-driven analysis of OLAP cubes. This and subsequent work resulted in the definition of advanced OLAP operators to guide the user towards unexpected data in the cube or to propose to explain an unexpected result. We now present two of these operators that can be thought of as implementations of some of the operators of our framework, and that are indeed used for implementing it (see "Implementing the framework").

The DIFF operator proposed in Sarawagi (1999) explores the reasons why an aggregate is lower (or higher) in one cell compared to another. It takes as parameter two cells c and c', and looks into the two isomorphic subcubes C and C' that detail the two cells (i.e., the subcubes that are aggregated to form the observed c and c'). As a result, it summarizes the differences in these two subcubes by providing the pairs of cells (one in C and one in C') that contribute the most to the difference between c and c'.

For instance, on the example given in the second section, a DIFF computed on the two cells in the result of query q_2^2 would include in its answer the two cells in the result of query q_5^2 and the first two cells in the result of query q_3^2 (since in both cases the difference is important), but it will not include the two cells of query q_4^2 (since in this case the difference is not important).

In Sathe et al. (2001) a RELAX operator has been proposed that can be thought of as the opposite to the DIFF operator. Indeed RELAX tries to confirm at a lesser level of details a particular significant difference, and summarizes the exceptions to this confirmation. In its basic form, the RELAX operator takes as parameter two cells c and c', and rolls up to less detailed levels to check if the difference between c and c' also occurs at these levels. For each of these roll-ups, the most relevant exceptions (i.e., pairs of cells for which the difference does not hold) to this difference are computed.

For instance, on the example given in the second section, a RELAX computed on the two cells in the result of query q_5^2. would include in its answer both the two cells in the result of query q_2^2 (as a general difference that confirms the initial difference at a lesser level of details) and the two cells in the result of query q_4^2 (that are exception to this general difference since the sign of the difference in this case is the opposite).

For both DIFF and RELAX, various optimizations were proposed to guarantee that these operators can be launched on-line. Both operators perform a single pass over the data. DIFF relies on dynamic programming and RELAX uses an Apriori-like trick. Their efficiency justifies the fact that they are used in our implementation of our framework.

We next discuss briefly how these operators relate to our approach.

Discussion

First, note that both DIFF and RELAX are slightly different from the other classical OLAP operators (roll-up, slice, etc.), in the sense that they do not produce a cube nor a cross-tab as a result, but a list of cells in the navigated cube. This list can be large. The main difference with our present work is that these operators are applied only on query results and they do not take into consideration what other

users have discovered. Taking the queries of the log into account can be viewed as a way of filtering the result of these operators, and to propose to the current users only those query results that the former users did find relevant. Indeed, consider the example given in the previous section. Suppose the current user applies the RELAX operator on the result of her/his current query to search for differences that generalize the difference of sales of cheese in USA for 2007-2008. The answer can contain general differences for the sales result at higher levels of dimension products (dairy, food, consumable, etc.), combined with higher levels of dimension location (North-America, America, Outside Europe, etc.), combined with higher levels of dimension time (21st century, etc.). Obviously this answer can be very large. However, in the log there are only three sessions that focused on the drop of the sales of cheese, and thus our framework will propose to the current user to search in this direction first.

Finally, note that discovery-driven analysis is still attracting attention. Indeed, two recent works use a data mining approach to inform the user of potentially interesting regions of a cube by either automatically detecting interesting cells (Cariou et al., 2007) or proposing interesting drill paths (Cariou et al., 2008). In the former case, the goal is simply to highlight in a given query result the cells whose measure deviates the most from a theoretical value computed under independence model hypothesis. In the latter case however, the goal can be seen as recommending drill-down queries to the user. This approach does not take into account former explorations and thus it is very close to the DIFF operator described above.

Session Properties Used in Information Retrieval

The idea of using former sessions to improve current search is very popular in Information Retrieval (Adomavicius et al., 2005) and Web Usage Mining (Spiliopoulou et al., 2000).

In recent works, properties of the session are inferred to support subsequent searches. For instance, in (Downey et al., 2008), the information goal of a session is defined as the last URL visited during the session or alternatively the last click on a search engine result page.

In Parikh et al. (2008) in the domain of e-commerce, the session goal is a particular event occurring in the session. In this case of the EBay site, the goal of a session is a buy event. This allows enriching all the sessions (and especially the queries of the sessions) with the description of the item bought, which is called the context of the session. The authors show how defining the context of a session helps recovering from null result in subsequent searches, provides a better understanding of the queries in the session, or helps generating recommendations.

These works have influenced our approach. Indeed, the mgdq detected in an OLAP session can be viewed as the session context and the drill-down differences and exceptions, if any, can be viewed as the session goals.

OLAP DATA MODEL AND QUERY MODEL

In this section, we define formally the data model and the query model that we use throughout the paper for presenting our framework. The model is a classical star schema queried with MDX queries. We now give the formal definitions. Basic knowledge is assumed on the relational model and query language (relation instance and schema, primary and foreign key, etc.) (Abiteboul et al., 1995).

Dimension, Level, Roll-Up/Drill-Down, Member

A dimension D is a relation name with schema $\{L_0, ..., L_d\}$ such that L_0 is the primary key of D.

Given a dimension D with schema $S = \{L_0, ..., L_d\}$, Roll-up and Drill-down are two partial map-

pings from S to S, defined by: Given an attribute L_j in S, Roll-up(L_j)=L_k if there exists a functional dependency $L_j \rightarrow L_k$ or undefined otherwise, and Drill-down(L_j)=L_l if there exists a functional dependency $L_l \rightarrow L_j$ or undefined otherwise. The attributes of the schema of a dimension are called aggregation levels (or levels for short).

A dimension table for D is an instance of D. For a dimension table D with schema $S = \{L_0, ..., L_d\}$, a member is an element of $\bigcup_j adom(L_j)$ for j in [0,d] ($adom(L_j)$ denotes the active domain of L_j). Given two levels L_j, L_k of a dimension D such that L_k=Roll-up(L_j), we use $m_j < m_k$ to denote that $(m_j, m_k) \in \pi_{\{L_j, L_k\}}(D)$. $<$ is transitive and defines a hierarchy for D.

Fact and Fact Table, Measure

An n-dimensional fact table F is a relation instance with schema $\{L_1^0, ..., L_n^0, m\}$ where $\{L_1^0, ..., L_n^0\}$ is the primary key of F, L_i^0 is the primary key of some dimension table D_i. Elements of *dom(m)* are called measures. Given a Fact table F, a fact is a tuple of F.

Note that we consider that, without loss of generality, a fact is associated with only one measure value.

Cube and Cells, Cell References

An n-dimensional cube $C = \langle D_1, ..., D_n, F \rangle$ is defined as the classical n + 1 relation instances of a star schema, i.e., $D_1, ..., D_n$ are dimension tables and F is a fact table. Given an n-dimensional cube $C = \langle D_1, ..., D_n, F \rangle$, a cell reference (or reference for short) over schema $\{L_1, ..., L_n\}$ is an n-tuple $\langle m_1, ..., m_n \rangle$ where $m_i \in dom(L_i)$ is a member of dimension D_i for all $i \in [1, n]$. A cell c is a tuple $c = \langle m_1, ..., m_n, mes \rangle$ where $\langle m_1, ..., m_n \rangle$ is a reference over $\{L_1, ..., L_n\}$ and *mes* is a value of *dom(m)*. Given a cube C, a cell whose reference is $\langle\, m_1, \,...,\, m_N \,\rangle$, is the result of the relational query:

$$\{\langle m_1,\ldots,m_N \rangle\} \bowtie \pi_m\big(\sigma_{(L_1\,=\,m_1)\,and\,\ldots\,and(L_N\,=\,m_N)} $$
$$(\pi_{L_1,\,\ldots,\,L_N\,;\,m}((F \bowtie D_1\,\ldots\,\bowtie D_N)))\big)$$

mes is called the measure of the cell. In what follows we will use measure(c) to denote the measure of the cell c.

Specialisation Relation Over Reference and Cells

Given a cube C and two cells r and r', we consider the classical relation over cell references defined by: $r <_{cells} r'$ if for all dimensions D_i with hierarchy $<_i$, either $r(i) = r'(i)$ or $r(i) <_i r'(i)$. This relation is extended to cells as follows: For two cells c, c' of an n-dimensional cube C, $c <_{cells} c'$ if $r <_{cells} r'$ where r is the reference of c and r' is the reference of c'. Note that this relation corresponds to the one used in the cube lattice (see e.g., Lakshmanan et al. 2003).

- **Example 1:** Consider the motivating example. The cell $\langle$ cheese, 2007, Europe, 100 $\rangle$ has reference $\langle$ cheese, 2007, Europe $\rangle$ and is part of the result of query q. The cell $\langle$ Cheese, 2007, All, 200 $\rangle$ has reference $\langle$ cheese, 2007, All $\rangle$ and is part of the result of query q_2^2. We have $\langle$ cheese, 2007, Europe, 100 $\rangle <_i \langle$ cheese, 2007, All, 200 $\rangle$.

Multidimensional Query and Query Result

In this article, the multidimensional queries considered, i.e., logged or recommended, are the ones expressed with MDX, the de facto standard. As in our previous work (Giacometti et al., 2008,

2009), we define multidimensional queries as sets of references in the following way: Given an n-dimensional cube C = $\langle$ $D_1, \ldots, D_n, F$ $\rangle$, let R_i be a set of members of dimension D_i for all $i \in$ [1, n], a query over C is the set of references $R_1 \times \ldots \times R_n$. This definition complies with the MDX standard. Indeed, given an MDX query: SELECT s_1 ON ROWS, s_2 ON COLUMNS, ... FROM f WHERE w, each of s_1, s_2,... and w respectively defines a relational query over dimension tables, the Cartesian product of which corresponds to our definition of query. Given a cube C, the result of a query q on C is the set of cells whose references are in q.

In what follows, we note $r \in q$ to denote that r is a reference of a query q and $c \in q$ to denote that c is a cell of the result of a query q. r(i) denotes the ith member of a reference r. When the context is clear, a query q will be confounded with its result, and we note cells(q) the set of cells of a query q.

- **Example 2:** Consider the motivating example. The current query q is the set of references {cheese} × {2007, 2008} × {Europe, USA}. Its result is the set of cells {$\langle$ cheese, 2007, Europe, 100 $\rangle$, $\langle$ cheese, 2008, Europe, 10 $\rangle$, $\langle$ cheese, 2007, USA, 50 $\rangle$, $\langle$ cheese, 2008, USA, 5 $\rangle$}. This query can be expressed in MDX over a cube called SalesCube as:
  - SELECT {[Europe], [USA]} ON ROWS, {[2007], [2008]} ON COLUMNS
  - FROM [SalesCube]
  - WHERE ([cheese])

Session, Log

A session is a sequence of queries, and a log is a set of sessions. We denote the set of queries of a session s by queries(s) and the set of queries of a log L by queries (L). For instance, the log illustrated Figure 1 is the set $\left\{ \left\langle q_1^1, q_1^2 \right\rangle, \left\langle q_1^2, q_2^2, q_3^2, q_4^2, q_5^2 \right\rangle, \left\langle q_3^1, q_3^2, q_3^3 \right\rangle \right\}$.

THE RECOMMENDER SYSTEM FRAMEWORK

Overview of the Approach

Recommendations are computed on the basis of the differences discovered in the log. The key idea is to detect the difference that the current query is investigating and to recommend the queries in the log that investigated the same difference.

More precisely, the log is preprocessed offline in the following way: (1) The log is examined to discover the pairs of cells whose measure differ significantly, to retain the most general ones (the most general difference pairs, mgdp) as well as the queries that contains them (the most general difference queries, mgdq). (2) For such pairs, a structure called investigation is created that records the set of mgdq and, at a lower level of detail, the queries that confirm the difference (their drill-down differences), and the queries that contradicts the difference (their exceptions).

Recommendations are computed online each time a current query is added to the current session by the current user. The current query is analyzed to detect to which investigations it corresponds (this query may be itself a mgdq, a drill-down difference, or an exception of what is detected in the log). Then a navigation plan (a set of queries arranged in a graph) is proposed for the current user to see drill-down differences or exceptions to the mgdq, by using the queries of the investigations.

In what follows, we detail the framework, starting with explaining how the log is processed and then how recommendations are computed.

Difference Pairs

We now define the pairs of cells that will be considered during the processing of the log. First note that the specialization relation over cells can be extended to pairs of cells in the following way.

- **Definition 1, Specialization over pairs:** Let C be a cube and c, c', c'', c''' be four cells in C. The pair $\langle c, c' \rangle$ is a generalization of $\langle c'', c''' \rangle$, noted $\langle c, c' \rangle <_{cells} \langle c'', c''' \rangle$ if both
  ○ c $<_{cells}$ c'' and c' $<_{cells}$ c'''.
- **Example 3:** Let c $= \langle$ cheese, 2007, all, 200 $\rangle$, c' $= \langle$ cheese, 2008, all, 20 $\rangle$, c'' $= \langle$ cheese, 2007, France, 50 $\rangle$, and c''' $= \langle$ cheese, 2008, France, 6 $\rangle$ be four cells in the cube analyzed, that appear in the results of query q_2^2 and q_3^2. We have $\langle c, c' \rangle <_{cells} \langle c'', c''' \rangle$.

If we have $\langle c, c' \rangle <_{cells} \langle c'', c''' \rangle$, we will say that $\langle c, c' \rangle$ is a roll-up pair of $\langle c'', c''' \rangle$ and $\langle c'', c''' \rangle$ is a drill-down pair of $\langle c, c' \rangle$. Moreover, if $\langle c'', c''' \rangle$ is a drill-down pair of $\langle c, c' \rangle$ and sign(measure(c'') − measure(c''')) ≠ sign(measure(c) − measure(c')) we will say that $\langle c'', c''' \rangle$ is an exception pair of $\langle c, c' \rangle$. Given a set S of pairs of cells, the most general pairs are the pairs of S that have no roll-up pairs in S.

- **Definition 2, Most general pairs:** Let S be a set of pairs of cells. The most general pairs of S is denoted by the set max $<_{cells}$ (S). For a given pair of cells $\langle c, c' \rangle$ of S, the set of the most general pairs for $\langle c, c' \rangle$ in S is the set:

$$\max \ <_{\text{cells}} \left(\left| \left\{ \begin{array}{l} \langle c'', c''' \rangle \in S \, | \, \langle c'', c''' \rangle \ is \ a \ roll - \\ up \ pair \ of \ \langle c, c' \rangle \end{array} \right\} \right| \right).$$

In what follows we will call a significant difference pair (or difference pair for short) a pair of cells such that their measures differ significantly. This significance is computed in two steps. First, a user-defined function *fdp* on which we do not impose particular requirements is used to detect base difference pair (examples of such functions are given in the section "Implementing the framework").

- **Definition 3, Base difference pair:** Let C be a cube, *fdp* be a Boolean function over the pairs of cells in C and c', c be two cells in C. The pair $\langle c, c' \rangle$ is a difference pair for C with regards to *fdp* if *fdp(c,c')=true*.

- **Example 4:** If the function *fdp* outputs true if the measures differ at least by a factor of 10, then the pair of cells $\langle c, c' \rangle$ of Example 3 is a base difference pair.

The operator difference outputs the pairs of cells in a query q that are base difference pairs, i.e., difference(*fdp*, q) = $\{\langle c, c' \rangle \in q \, | \, \text{fdp}(c, c')$ is true$\}$ for some Boolean function *fdp* over pairs of cells. For a given base difference pair $\langle c, c' \rangle$, we define its roll-up (resp. drill-down) difference pairs as its roll-up (resp. drill-down) pairs that show a significant difference w.r.t. $\langle c, c' \rangle$. This significance is computed with another user-defined Boolean function, example of which is given in the section "Implementing the framework."

- **Definition 4, Roll-up/drill-down difference pairs:** Let $\langle c, c' \rangle$ be a difference pair, $\langle c'', c''' \rangle$ be one of its roll-up (resp. drill-down) pairs and r be Boolean function over couples of pairs of cells. We say that

$\langle c'', c''' \rangle$ is a roll-up difference pair (resp. q' is a drill-down difference pair) for $\langle c, c' \rangle$ if *r(c,c',c'',c''')=true*.

The next operators detect, for a pair $\langle c, c' \rangle$, a set of queries Q and a Boolean function *r*, which are the pairs of Q that are roll-up (resp. drill-down, resp. exception) difference pairs for $\langle c, c' \rangle$. Formally, rollupDifferencePairs (c, c', Q, r) = $\{\langle c'', c''' \rangle \, | \, \exists q \in Q$ with $\langle c'', c''' \rangle \in q$ and $\langle c'', c''' \rangle <_{\text{cells}} \langle c, c' \rangle$ Ù $r(c,c',c'',c''')=true\}$, drilldownDifferencePairs (c, c', Q, r) = $\{\langle c'', c''' \rangle \, | \, \exists q \in Q$ with $\langle c'', c''' \rangle \in q$ and $\langle c'', c''' \rangle >_{\text{cells}} \langle c, c' \rangle$ Ù $r(c,c',c'',c''')=true\}$, exceptionPairs (c, c', Q) = $\{\langle c'', c''' \rangle \, | \, \exists q \in Q$ with $\langle c'', c''' \rangle \in q$ and $\langle c'', c''' \rangle$ is an exception pair for $\langle c, c' \rangle\}$.

In what follows, base difference pairs, roll-up difference pairs and drill-down difference pairs will be called simply difference pairs. A most general difference pair (mgdp) of a set S of pairs of cells is a most general pair of S that is also a difference pair.

- **Example 5:** Recall Examples 3 and 4. In Figure 1 every cell that is part of a difference pair has its measure in bold face. Base difference pairs are detected with the Boolean function used in example 4, and their roll-up and drill-down difference pairs are detected with a function outputting true if, for two difference pairs of cells $\langle c, c' \rangle$ and $\langle c'', c''' \rangle$, $\dfrac{measure(c'') - measure(c''')}{measure(c) - measure(c')} > \beta$ for some threshold $\beta > 0$.

If $\langle c, c' \rangle$ and $\langle c'', c''' \rangle$ are the pairs given in Examples 3 and 4, then $\langle c, c' \rangle$ is a roll-up difference pair of $\langle c'', c''' \rangle$. If S is the set of all pairs of cells in the queries in session 2, then $\langle c, c' \rangle$ is the most general difference pair of $\langle c'', c''' \rangle$ in S.

Difference Queries

We define a difference query to be a query whose result displays one or more difference pairs. A query is a roll-up (resp. drill-down) difference query of a difference query if its result confirms the difference at a higher (resp. lower) level of detail. An exception is a query that contradicts a difference at a lower level of detail. The following definitions formalize these notions.

- **Definition 5, Difference query:** Let C be a cube, *fdp* be a Boolean function over the pairs of cells in C. A query q over C is a difference query if there exist two cells c, c' $\in$ q such that the pair $\langle c, c' \rangle$ is a difference pair for C and *fdp*.

- **Definition 6, Roll-up/drill-down/exception difference query:** Let q and q' be two queries, and let $\langle c, c' \rangle$ be a difference pair in q. We say that q' is a roll-up (resp. drill-down, resp. exception) difference query for q if there exists a difference pair $\langle c'', c''' \rangle$ in q' that is a roll-up (resp. drill-down, resp. exception) difference pair $\langle c, c' \rangle$. q' is said to be a roll-up (resp. drill-down, resp. exception) difference query for q w.r.t. the pair $\langle c, c' \rangle$.

The next operators detect, for a pair $\langle c, c' \rangle$ and a set of queries Q, which are the queries of Q that are roll-up (resp. drill-down, resp. exception) difference queries w.r.t. $\langle c, c' \rangle$. Formally, rollupDifference(c, c', Q) = {q $\in$ Q | q is a roll-up difference query w.r.t. $\langle c, c' \rangle$}, drilldownDifference(c, c', Q) = {q $\in$ Q | q is a drill-down difference query w.r.t. $\langle c, c' \rangle$}, and

exception(c, c', Q) = {q $\in$ Q | q is an exception difference query w.r.t. $\langle c, c' \rangle$}.

- **Example 6:** Continuing Example 4, q_2^2 is a difference query, as is the current query q. Thus q_2^2 is a roll-up difference query for q, and a roll-up difference query for the difference pair $\langle\langle$ cheese, 2007, Europe, 100 $\rangle$, $\langle$ cheese, 2008, Europe, 10 $\rangle\rangle$.

A most general difference query (mgdq) is a query that contains a most general difference pair.

- **Definition 7, mgdq:** Let q be a query, S be a set of pairs of cells and $\langle c, c' \rangle$ be a pair in S. q is a mgdq if it contains a pair of S that is a most general difference pair of S.
- **Example 7:** Consider the set of queries of session 2 Q = { $q_1^2, \ldots, q_5^2$ }, and the difference pair $\langle\langle$ cheese, 2007, Europe, 100 $\rangle,\langle$ cheese, 2008, Europe, 10 $\rangle\rangle$. q_2^2 is the mgdq of Q. Query q_4^2 is an exception difference query of q_2^2.

ALGORITHMS FOR THE RECOMMENDER SYSTEM

This section introduces the algorithms underlying our approach.

Processing the Log

We begin with the algorithm used to discover the various kinds of difference pairs from a log file and relate them together.

First, Algorithm 1 processes the log to discover the mgdq, their drill-down differences and exceptions. This algorithm outputs a set of what we call investigations, i.e., the various queries that investigated a particular difference pair. Note that one investigation is created per mgdp discovered in the log, provided this mgdp comes with some drill-down difference pairs or exception pairs.

- **Definition 8, Investigation:** An investigation i for a log L is a tuple $\langle c, c', M, D, E \rangle$ where $\langle c,c' \rangle$ is a most general difference pair appearing in L, M, D and E are subsets of queries(L), M is the set of queries that contains $\langle c,c' \rangle$, D is the set of drill-down difference queries w.r.t. $\langle c,c' \rangle$, E is the set of exception difference queries w.r.t. $\langle c,c' \rangle$, and at-least one of D, E is non-empty.

To express the time complexity of this algorithm, we consider the number n_c of cells in the log file. Then $C_{n_c}^2$ is the number of pairs in the log and $(C_{n_c}^2)^2$ is the number of couples of pairs in the log. To simplify, we use $n = C_{n_c}^2 = \dfrac{n_c \times (n_c - 1)}{2}$. The time complexity is: n (for detecting base difference pairs) + n² (for detecting the roll-up difference pairs) + n² (for computing the mgdp) + 2n² (for detecting drill-down difference queries and exception queries), and thus in O(n²).

Note that for a given investigation i, a query can be at the same time mgdq or drill-down difference or exception. Thus the queries in i are labeled with their type (mgdq, drill-down difference or exception) and are associated with their pair of cells that is the drill-down or exception pair w.r.t. the mgdp. In an investigation i =<m, M, D, E>, m is called the difference pair of the investigation. For a set of investigations I, mgdq(I) is the set of mgdq of every investigation in I.

Algorithm 1. Discovering investigations

```
Input: A log L, a Boolean function fdp, a Boolean function r
Output: A set I of investigations
I, DP, RDP, MP ← Ø
// detect base difference pairs
foreach query q ∈ queries(L) do
    DP = DP ∪ difference(fdp,q)

// detect all their roll-up difference pairs
foreach pair p ∈ DP do
    RDP = RDP ∪ rollup DifferencePairs (p,queries(L),r)
// retain only the most general
MDP = max <_cells (RDP)
// detect drill-down difference queries and exception queries
foreach m ∈ MDP do
    M = {q ∈ queries(L) | m ∈ q }
    D = drilldown Difference(m,queries(L))
    E = exception (m,queries(L))
    // update the set of investigations
    if D ≠ Ø or E ≠ Ø then
        I = I ∪ <m,M,D,E>
```

- **Example 8:** Consider the log of Figure 1. Suppose the pair of cells $t_1 = \langle$ cheese, 2007sem1, France, 25 $\rangle$, $\langle$ cheese, 2008sem1, France, 1 $\rangle$ is detected as a base difference pair for query q_1^1. The pair $t_2 = \langle$ cheese, 2007, all, 200 $\rangle$, $\langle$ cheese, 2008, all, 20 $\rangle$ is detected as a roll-up difference pair of t_1. It is also an mgdp of this log. Thus query q_2^2 is a mgdq of the log, as well as query q_2^3 since both queries contain t_2. For these mgdq, queries $q_1^1, q_2^1, q_3^2, q_5^2$ are drill-down difference queries and queries q_3^2, q_4^2, q_1^3 are exception queries. The following investigation is created: $< t_2, \{q_2^2, q_2^3\}, \{q_1^1, q_2^1, q_3^2, q_5^2\}, \{q_3^2, q_4^2, q_1^3\} >$. Similarly, Algorithm 1 produces two other investigations corresponding to the mgdp $\langle$ milk, 2007sem2, France, 10 $\rangle$, $\langle$ cheese, 2008sem1, France, 1 $\rangle$ and $\langle$ milk, 2008sem1, France, 10 $\rangle$, $\langle$ cheese, 2008sem1, France, 1 $\rangle$ (see Figure 3).

Computing Recommendations

The algorithms for computing recommendations are given. In their simplest form, recommendations are sets of queries extracted from investigations. A more sophisticated form for presentation to the user is to arrange these queries into a graph for the user to navigate.

Given a current session cs, a current query q and a set of investigations I, the recommender system first identifies in I the set of mgdp to which q can be related. For such an mgdp m, q can be either a drill-down difference query w.r.t. m, a roll-up difference query w.r.t. m, or an exception w.r.t. m. In each case a specific function is used to construct the recommendation from the investigation whose difference pair is m.

Algorithm 2. Recommendations for a current query

```
Input: A current query q, a set I of investigations, a Boolean function fdp
Output: A graph G of recommended queries
G tp⟨∅,∅⟩
M ← mgdq(I)
foreach difference pair ⟨c,c'⟩ of difference(q,fdp) do
    // first check if q is a drill-down difference
    C ← rollup Difference(c,c',M)
    if C ≠ ∅ then
        G C ≠∪ recommend Drilldown(c,c',q,C)

    // then check if q is a roll-up difference
    C ← drilldown Difference(c,c',M)
    if C ≠ ∅ then
        G C ≠∪ recommend Rollup(c,c',q,C)
    // finally check if q is an exception to a difference
    foreach difference pair ⟨x,x'⟩ of m ∈ M do
        C ← exceptions(x,x',{q})
        if C ≠ ∅ then
            G C ≠∪ recommend Exception(c,c',q,C)
```

Figure 3. Result of the processing of the log

difference pair	mgdq	drill-down queries	exceptions
$\langle$ *cheese, 2007, all, 200* $\rangle$ $\langle$ *cheese, 2008, all, 20* $\rangle$	$\{q_2^2, q_2^3\}$	$\{q_1^1, q_2^1, q_3^2, q_5^2\}$	$\{q_3^2, q_4^2, q_1^3\}$
$\langle$ *milk, 2007sem2, France, 10* $\rangle$ $\langle$ *cheese,2008sem1,France,1* $\rangle$	$\{q_1^1\}$	$\{q_2^1\}$	$\varnothing$
$\langle$ *milk, 2008sem1, France, 10* $\rangle$ $\langle$ *cheese,2008sem1,France,1* $\rangle$	$\{q_1^1\}$	$\{q_2^1\}$	$\varnothing$

Function *recommendDrilldown* is given in Table 1. The idea is to recommend the queries of the investigations which mgdq is a roll-up difference query of the current query, with the queries of the session arranged in a given order (first the mgdq, then the drill-down differences of the current query, etc.). The recommendation is a navigation plan, i.e., a graph of queries rooted in the current query q. The other functions used in Algorithm 2 for computing recommendations follow the same general principle. For instance, if the current query q is detected as an exception of the mgdq of an investigation, then it makes sense to present first the exceptions of the mgdq that are the roll-up difference queries of q, and then the exceptions of the mgdq that are drill-down difference queries of q.

- **Example 9:** Consider the log of Figure 1. The pair of cells t_1 = $\langle$ cheese, 2007, Europe, 100 $\rangle$,$\langle$ cheese, 2008, Europe, 10 $\rangle$ is detected as a difference pair for the current query. It is a drill-down pair of pair t_2 = $\langle$ cheese, 2007, all, 200 $\rangle$,$\langle$ cheese, 2008, all, 20 $\rangle$ that is one of the most general difference pair detected in the log. Thus a recommendation for the current query will use the investigation $< t_2, \{q_2^2, q_2^3\}, \{q_1^1, q_2^1, q_3^2, q_5^2\}, \{q_3^2, q_4^2, q_1^3\} >$ whose queries will be arranged into a graph as depicted by Figure 4. Note that few links

between queries inside S_1 and S_2 are missing to alleviate the schema. In this example, there is no recommendation corresponding to the sets S_3 and S_4.

IMPLEMENTING THE FRAMEWORK

In this section we describe our implementation of Algorithms 1 and 2 that are at the core of our framework. We used Java and the Mondrian OLAP

Figure 4. Navigation plan of Figure 1 resulting from recommender system Table 1. Function recommendDrilldown

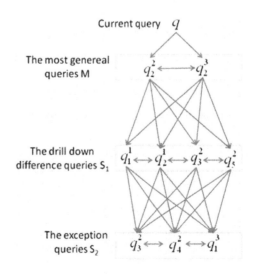

Table 1. Function recommendDrilldown

Function recommendDrilldown(c,c',q,C)
Input: A difference pair $\langle c,c' \rangle$, a current query q, a set C of difference pairs
$\langle$ Output: A graph G = $\langle$ V,E $\rangle$ of queries

$\langle$ E $\leftarrow \emptyset$

V $\leftarrow \emptyset$

foreach pair m $\in$ C do

> // get the investigation having m as mgdp
>
> i d $\langle$ m,M,D,X $\rangle$
>
> //create vertices
>
> V /cre $\bigcup$ M $\bigcup$ D $\bigcup$ X
>
> //create edges
>
> // arrange the queries of i into a graph
>
> let S_1 = drilldownDifference(c,c',D) // the drill-down differences of q
>
> let S_2 = exceptions(c,c',M) // the exceptions to q in M
>
> let S_3 = D-S_1 // the drill-down diff. to m which are not drill-down diff. of q
>
> let S_4 = E-S_2 // the exceptions to m which are not exceptions of q
>
> // 1. Link q to the most general queries M
>
> E 1. L× M) $\bigcup$ (M × M)
>
> // 2. Link the most general queries to the drill-down diff. of q
>
> E 2. $\bigcup$ (M × S_1) $\bigcup$ (S_1 × S_1)
>
> // 3. Link the drill-down diff. of q to the exceptions to q
>
> E 3. $\bigcup$ (S_1 × S_2) $\bigcup$ (S_2 × S_2)
>
> // 4. Link the exceptions of q to the drill-down diff. to m
>
> E 4. $\bigcup$ (S_2 × S_3) $\bigcup$ (S_3 × S_3)
>
> // 5. Link the drill-down diff. of m to the exceptions to m
>
> E 5. $\bigcup$ (S_3 × S_4) $\bigcup$ (S_4 × S_4)

engine (Pentaho, 2009) to process and recommend MDX (Microsoft, 2008) queries.

In our implementation, the detection and construction of investigations is an offline process that reads a log file and resubmits the queries to detect difference pairs in their result. In the framework, the detection of base difference pairs relies on a function *fdp* used as a parameter of Algorithm 1. Our implementation proposes basic functions for this test relying on the comparison of the difference $measure(c) - measure(c') > \alpha$ or ratio $\frac{measure(c)}{measure(c')} > \alpha$ of two cells' measures with a given threshold α. Comparisons can be done for all pairs $\langle c, c' \rangle$ of cells in a query result or only for all pairs $\langle c, c' \rangle$ along a particular dimension.

The implementation of the operators rollup-DifferencePairs, drilldownDifferencePairs and exceptionPairs for detecting the various types of difference pairs relies on the RELAX and DIFF operators proposed by Sarawagi (Sarawagi, 1999; Sathe et al., 2001). We use the Java implementation named iCube that is freely available for download (Sarawagi, 2009). These operators have a built-in function *r* to detect if a pair's difference is significant w.r.t. another given pair. It is to be noticed that, due to the lack of a standard Java API for OLAP, part of the implementation effort has been spent on the interoperability between Mondrian and iCube.

To implement the operators rollupDifference, drilldownDifference and exception from the RELAX and DIFF operators, a function is needed that detects if the results of these operators appears in a given set of queries. In our implementation, we use the function *detect* that, given a difference pair for a query *q* detects in a set *Q* if there are roll-up differences, drill-down differences or exceptions to the pair, with the operator *op* (Table 2).

Table 2. Function detect

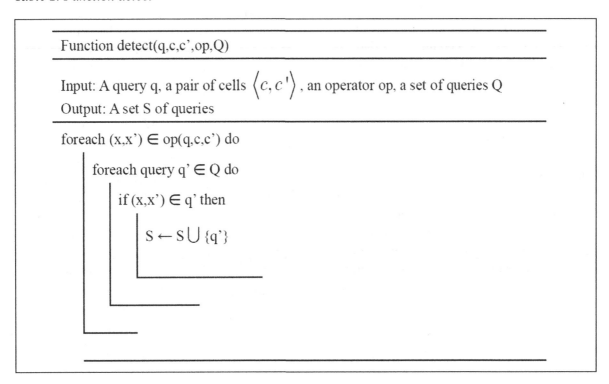

In a call to function *detect*, the *op* operator can be either DIFF or RELAX. For instance, if DIFF is used and Q is the server log, the call *detect(q, c, c', DIFF, Q)* detects the queries of the log that are drill-down difference queries of *q* w.r.t. $\langle c, c' \rangle$.

As the result of the RELAX operator contains both generalizations and exceptions to generalizations for a given pair of cells, it is used to detect both roll-up differences and exceptions. Thus the detection of exceptions to a pair $\langle c'', c''' \rangle$ is done by calling *detect(q, c, c', RELAX, Q)* where $\langle c, c' \rangle$ is a drill-down pair of $\langle c'', c''' \rangle$ and by checking that the exception pairs obtained are indeed drill-down pairs of $\langle c'', c''' \rangle$.

EXPERIMENTS

In this section, we describe the experiments we conducted to illustrate the effectiveness of our approach. These tests consist essentially in a precision/recall analysis of the recommendations computed from a query log composed of several sessions. The sessions are synthetically generated sequences of MDX queries, produced with our log generator, over the Foodmart test database supplied with the Mondrian OLAP engine. We first describe the generator and then present the experiments.

The Log Generator

Our log generator is implemented in Java (Algorithm 3). It produces a log of X sessions, each of them consisting of at-most Y queries. To fit the context of discovery-driven analysis, each session simulates a discovery-driven analysis session by using whenever possible the *icube* operators DIFF or RELAX.

The Z parameter is a number that is used to play with the density of the log. It represents the number of dimensions (the Z first dimensions out of the total number of dimensions of the considered cube) that can be manipulated in a session to explore the cube. The higher this number, the higher the probability of exploring different parts of the cube, and hence the sparser the log.

Finally, the function *fdp* is used to detect difference pairs.

The Experiments

The experiments were conducted on a Xeon E5430 with 32 GB RAM, running Linux CentOS5. We used 5 generated log files of quite high density (5 dimensions out of the 13 dimensions available for the FoodMart cube). Four of them were processed for computing investigations. They contained 25 sessions (119 queries), 50 sessions (242 queries), 100 sessions (437 queries) and 200 sessions (936 queries) respectively.

The processing was done with Algorithm 1 and took from less than 1 hour to 24 hours depending on the size of the log file and the value used for detecting the difference pairs. The fifth log file contained 25 sessions and was only used for choosing the current queries for which recommendations were to be computed. For each session of size s, a random n in [1,s] is chosen, the final n queries of the session were removed and played the role of the expected queries. The (s-n)th query of the session played the role of a current query.

Our first experiments tested the parameter α used in the function that detects difference pairs by computing the ratio between two cells' measures. This value should be small enough to be able to propose at-least one recommendation but also big enough not to overwhelm the user with recommendations. Ideally it should be such that the ratio $\frac{(number\ of\ investigations)}{(number\ of\ sessions)}$ is close to

Algorithm 3. Log generator

```
Input: a number (X) of sessions, a maximal number (Y) of queries per session,
a number (Z) of dimensions in the pool, a function fdp for detecting difference pair
Output: a log L
// create X sessions as follows:
Repeat X times
    // create the first query
    Randomly select two dimensions d₁, d₂ among the Z dimensions
    Create the first MDX query as:
        SELECT d₁.all.Children ON ROWS,
               d₂.all.Children ON COLUMNS
        FROM Sales;
    // create subsequent queries
    Let y be a random integer in [2,Y]
    Repeat y times
        Let q be the query created previously
        Randomly select a difference pair p in the result of q
        Randomly select op in {DIFF, RELAX}
        Apply op on the pair p and get a set S of one member per dimension
        // generate one query that contains one difference pair of the result of op
        If S ≠ Ø
            For each member m of dimension d of S
                Randomly choose M={m} or M={m.Parent.Children}
                Modify q by substituting in q the members in dimension d by the members in M
        If S = Ø
            Randomly select among the Z dimensions a dimension d whose displayed level is all
            Modify q by adding d.all.Children
```

1 if each session indeed investigates one particular mgdp. For each log file, four values of α were tested: 2, 3, 5 and 7. For the log containing 25 sessions, 8 values were tested: 0.5, 2, 3, 5, 7, 10, 15 and 25. The results of these tests are depicted in Figure 5.

As expected, Figure 5 (a) shows that α directly influences the number of investigations detected in the log. More interestingly, Figure 5 (b) shows how α relates to the number of investigations per session. Note that the evolution is similar whatever the size of the log. Thus in what follows, unless otherwise stated, a mean is computed over all log files. Figure 5 (c) shows that the mean number of recommended queries for

various α is quite stable with a maximum for $\alpha = 3$. Figure 5 (d) shows as expected, for the log of 25 sessions, that the less investigations, the more absences of recommendations. These tests suggest that for this dataset, a value for α in [3,5] would be a good candidate, which was confirmed by our precision test (see below).

We next evaluated the time taken to compute recommendations, focusing on the on-line phase. In this test, the time used to arrange the recommended queries into a graph is not taken into account. It means that we evaluated the time taken by Algorithm 2 but with functions recommendDrilldown, recommendRollup and recommendException simply delivering lists of recom-

Figure 5. Assessing the value of α

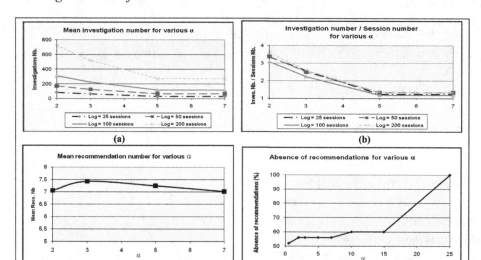

(a) (b)

(c) (d)

mended queries. Figures 6 and 7 show that whatever the value for α and the number of investigations or the log size (in terms of number of queries), this time does not exceed 72 ms, and seems to grow linearly with the number of investigations (resp., the log size). Note that, as expected, the higher α, the more efficient the computation, since α directly impacts the number of investigations to be searched to compute recommendations.

Our final tests consisted in evaluating, for a set of 25 current queries, to what extent the recommended queries were relevant by a precision/recall analysis. Regular precision and recall would assess the fraction of the n removed queries found in the set of recommended queries. In our case, given that it is very unlikely to have in the log files the same query twice, precision and recall were computed w.r.t. the members found in the queries. Thus precision gives the number of members both expected and recommended di-

Figure 6. Mean recommendation time by number of investigations for various α

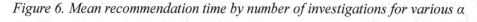

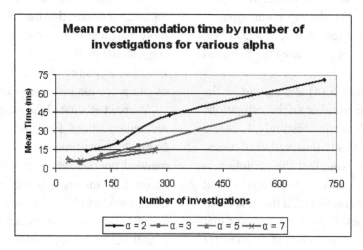

Figure 7. Mean recommendation time by log size for various α

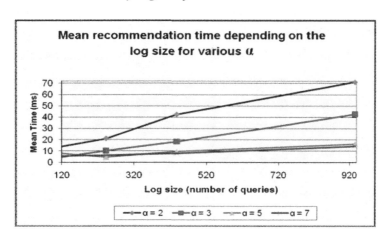

vided by the number of members that are recommended, and recall gives the number of members both expected and recommended divided by the number of members that are expected. Figure 8 displays the results of these tests. Figure 8 (a) shows the mean precision which is very high, for the best mean recall which is very low. The low recall is easily explained by the fact that the set of expected members (from the n removed queries of the chosen session) can be very large and can very seldom appear in the set of recommended members. Nevertheless, in these cases, the achieved precision is very satisfactory, showing that recommendations indeed focus on what is expected. Precision alone is given in Figure 8 (b) and (c) for various values of α. Figure 8 (b) takes into account the cases when no recommendation can be issued, with a precision only above average. However, when recommendations can be issued (Figure 8 (c)), the achieved precision is very high, demonstrating the effectiveness of the approach for logs of a rather high density.

Figure 8. Precision / Recall analysis

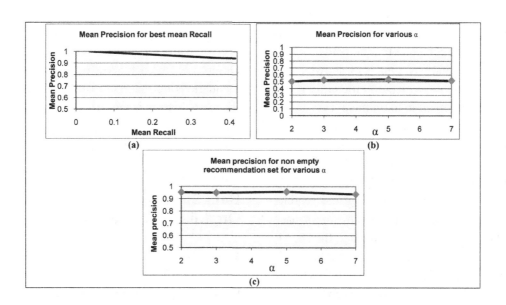

Figure 9. Architecture of a recommender system for discovery-driven analysis

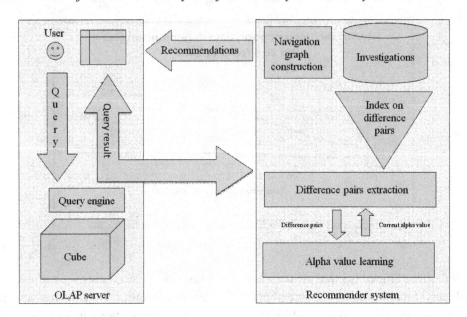

ON THE FEASABILITY OF THE APPROACH

In this section, we briefly comment the feasibility of our approach, beyond the prototypical implementation, to adapt it to real OLAP systems. Recall that in what we have presented so far, the approach is a two-step process. The first phase processes the log off-line to discover investigations. This phase is very time consuming since it has to resubmit the queries of the log and to pair cells of all the answers (Ordonez et al., 2009). The second phase computes recommendations by accessing investigations. Our tests showed that this phase can be implemented efficiently if the list of investigations is in main memory.

In a real setting, as illustrated in Figure 9, the off-line phase is purely suppressed. Instead, investigations are created and maintained on the fly during the current user analysis. To this end, a dedicated server for maintaining and searching investigations is needed. Each time a user (current) query arrives, it is passed to the OLAP query engine to be executed and once the result is known, it is passed to the recommender system to be analysed and to give rise to recommenda-

tions. The recommender system maintains a list of investigations indexed by their difference pairs. The list includes the investigations created for the current analysis session.

The recommender system analyses the current query result q using the following architecture (data structures needed are discussed in the next subsection). For each difference pair detected d in q, an index to access investigations is used to find the investigations to which d is either a rollup, a drilldown, or an exception. If no investigation is found, a new investigation with d as mgdp is created and the index is modified accordingly. Otherwise, for each investigation found, recommendations are generated using Algorithm 2. Then the investigation is modified (q is added w.r.t. its relation with the difference pair of the investigation), and so is the index, if d is the new difference pair of the investigation.

Data Structure and Organisation Needed

With this setting, it is easy to see that the most time consuming phase is the first one, that raises the following problem: Given a pair of cells p,

Figure 10. Detail of the index mechanism

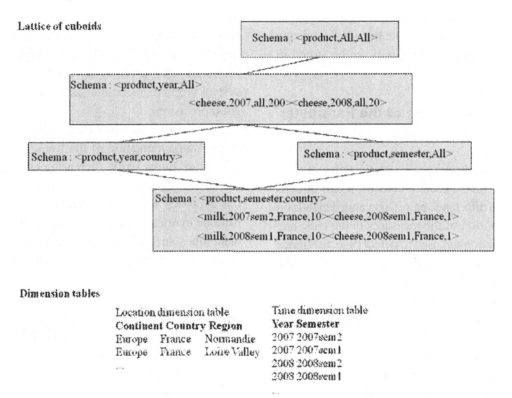

find the roll-up or drill-down pairs of cells of p. That is, given a cell reference, find all its ancestors or descendants.

To the best of our knowledge, no index mechanism exists in the literature that can help solving this particular problem efficiently (even though some storage techniques could be adapted) (Lakshmanan et al., 2003). We propose the following indexing mechanism that is basically a set of pairs, together with the dimension tables. Our index relies on the lattice of cuboids to store pairs of cells. It means that all the pairs having a given schema are stored altogether. For instance, consider the 2 pairs of cells: $\langle$ cheese, 2007, all, 200 $\rangle$, $\langle$ cheese, 2008, all, 20 $\rangle$ and $\langle$ milk, 2008sem1, France, 10 $\rangle$, $\langle$ cheese, 2008sem1, France, 1 $\rangle$. These two pairs have the same schema and thus are stored together. Note that, by definition of investigation, we have to store

only the most general difference pairs in the index. Each cuboid points to its direct ancestors and descendants.

To find all the ancestors or descendent of a pair *p*, the lattice of cuboids is used as a search structure. The schema of *p* is used to locate the cuboid it belongs to. If the pair already exists in the cuboid, corresponding investigations are accessed and recommendation can be computed. Otherwise, if the pair does not exist in the cuboid, all cuboids that are ancestors or descendants of the current cuboid are searched recursively for correspondence with *p*.

In addition to the dimension tables, in a given cuboid, an efficient data structure, like for instance a trie, is needed to search for an ancestor/descendant of a given cell. Once a difference pair is found that is an ancestor or a descendant of a given pair, a pointer is used to access its investigation.

This index is illustrated Figure 10, that partly displays the index for the investigations given Figure 3. Empty cuboids like the one for schema ⟨ product, year, country ⟩ will not be stored in practice.

Adjusting the Value of the Parameter α

Our approach heavily relies on the value of the α parameter that is used to detect if a pair of cells is indeed a difference pair. This value depends on the distribution of the measures in the cube and on the function *fdp* used to detect base difference pair. In the new setting that we are describing, the value for α could be learned by the system on the fly. Assume the recommender system maintains a value guessed from the analysis of the query result. Each time a current query is processed (i.e., the result is scanned for difference pairs), this result is used as a sample of the data of the cube. The recommender system then updates the value for α based on this sample of the data of the cube and on the *fdp* function. For instance, suppose that *fdp* compares the ratio of two cell measures with the value of α. To learn the value of α, the recommender systems records the mean μ and the standard deviation σ of these ratios, with no processing overhead since the ratios are computed to detect difference pairs. A naïve estimation for α can be for instance $\mu + \sigma$. Note that the fact that a recommendation suggested by the system has been followed by the user can also be taken into account for adjusting the value of α.

CONCLUSION

In this paper we propose a framework for recommending queries to support OLAP discovery-driven analysis. The key idea is to infer from the log of the OLAP server what former users were investigating, and to use this information as a basis for helping the current user to navigate the cube. This framework is implemented with Java and the Mondrian OLAP engine to recommend MDX queries. Our preliminary tests show that our system proposes recommendations of promising good precision.

Achieving a scalable, more efficient and effective implementation of the framework is the first of our future work. Increasing effectiveness can be done by recommending queries even when our approach fails in computing any. This can be done by incorporating other recommendation techniques such as the ones we have proposed in our earlier works. As for efficiency and scalability, the processing of the log can be replaced by an incremental approach, as presented in the previous section.

Our long-term goal is to provide OLAP users and administrators with a platform for computing various types of recommendations. This platform will integrate the present framework with our earlier work (Giacometti et al., 2008, 2009), and should also not be limited to discovery-driven analysis. It should include content-based techniques (Chatzopoulou et al., 2009) as well as context-aware methods combined with user profiles (Jerbi et al., 2009; Bellatreche et al., 2005; Golfarelli et al., 2009) to compute personalized recommendations, i.e., w.r.t. the user, in a multiple-user scenario. We are working in that direction.

In addition to this, we will conduct experimentations on real data sets with feedback from users. This will allow not only to improve the overall quality of the recommended queries but also to determine to which context a particular approach for computing recommendations is adapted. To this end we are currently working with IRSA (a French social security health examination centre) to analyze over 500.000 health care examination questionnaires.

REFERENCES

Abiteboul, S., Hull, R., & Vianu, V. (1995). *Foundations of Databases*. Reading, MA: Addison-Wesley.

Adomavicius, G., & Tuzhilin, A. (2005). Toward the next generation of recommender systems: A survey of the state-of-the-art and possible extensions. *IEEE Transactions on Knowledge and Data Engineering, 17*(6), 734–749. doi:10.1109/TKDE.2005.99

Bellatreche, L., Giacometti, A., Marcel, P., Mouloudi, H., & Laurent, D. (2005). A personalization framework for OLAP queries. In *Proceedings of the 8th ACM International Workshop on Data Warehousing and OLAP* (pp. 9–18). New York, NY: ACM.

Cariou, V., Cubillé, J., Derquenne, C., Goutier, S., Guisnel, F., & Klajnmic, H. (2007). Built-in indicators to automatically detect interesting cells in a cube. In *Proceedings of the 9th International Conference on Data Warehousing and Knowledge Discovery* (LNCS 4654, pp. 123–134).

Cariou, V., Cubillé, J., Derquenne, C., Goutier, S., Guisnel, F., & Klajnmic, H. (2008). Built-in indicators to discover interesting drill paths in a cube. In *Proceedings of the 10th International Conference on Data Warehousing and Knowledge Discovery* (LNCS 5182, pp. 33–44).

Chatzopoulou, G., Eirinaki, M., & Polyzotis, N. (2009). Query recommendations for interactive database exploration. In *Proceedings of the 21st International Conference on Scientific and Statistical Database Management* (LNCS 5566, pp. 3–18).

Downey, D., Dumais, S. T., Liebling, D. J., & Horvitz, E. (2008). Understanding the relationship between searchers' queries and information goals. In *Proceedings of the 17th ACM Conference on Information and Knowledge Management* (pp. 449–458). New York, NY: ACM.

Giacometti, A., Marcel, P., & Negre, E. (2008). A framework for recommending OLAP queries. In *Proceedings of the 11th ACM International Workshop on Data Warehousing and OLAP* (pp. 73–80). New York, NY: ACM.

Giacometti, A., Marcel, P., & Negre, E. (2009a). Recommending multidimensional queries. In *Proceedings of the 11th International Conference on Data Warehousing and Knowledge Discovery* (LNCS 5691, pp. 453–466).

Giacometti, A., Marcel, P., & Negre, E. (2009b). Query recommendation for OLAP discovery driven analysis. In *Proceedings of the 12th ACM International Workshop on Data Warehousing and OLAP* (pp. 81–88). New York, NY: ACM.

Golfarelli, M., & Rizzi, S. (2009). Expressing OLAP preferences. In *Proceedings of the 22th International Conference on Scientific and Statistical Database Management* (LNCS 5566, pp. 83–91).

Gray, J., Chaudhuri, S., Bosworth, A., Layman, A., Reichart, D., & Venkatrao, M. (1997). Data cube: A relational aggregation operator generalizing group-by, cross-tab, and sub totals. *Data Mining and Knowledge Discovery, 1*(1), 29–53. doi:10.1023/A:1009726021843

Jerbi, H., Ravat, F., Teste, O., & Zurfluh, G. (2009). Preference-based recommendations for olap analysis. In *Proceedings of the 11th International Conference on Data Warehousing and Knowledge Discovery* (LNCS 5691, pp. 467–478).

Khoussainova, N., Balazinska, M., Gatterbauer, W., Kwon, Y., & Suciu, D. (2009). A case for a collaborative query management system. In *Proceedings of 4th Biennial Conference on Innovative Data Systems Research*. Retrieved from http://www.cidrdb.org

Lakshmanan, L., Pei, J., & Zhao, Y. (2003). QC-Trees: An efficient summary structure for semantic OLAP. In *Proceedings of the 2003 ACM International Conference on Management of Data* (pp. 64–75). New York, NY: ACM.

Microsoft. (2008). *Multidimensional expressions (MDX) reference*. Retrieved September 23, 2010, from http://msdn.microsoft.com/en-us/library/ms145506.aspx

Ordonez, C., & Chen, Z. (2009). Evaluating statistical tests on OLAP cubes to compare degree of disease. *IEEE Transactions on Information Technology in Biomedicine, 13*(5), 756–765. doi:10.1109/TITB.2008.926989

Parikh, N., & Sundaresan, N. (2008). Inferring semantic query relations from collective user behavior. In *Proceedings of the 17th ACM Conference on Information and Knowledge Management* (pp. 349–358). New York, NY: ACM.

Pentaho. (2009). *Mondrian open source OLAP engine*. Retrieved September 23, 2010, from http://mondrian.pentaho.org/

Sapia, C. (1999). On modeling and predicting query behaviour in OLAP systems. In *Proceedings of the International Workshop on Design and Management of Data Warehouses* (pp. 2.1–2.10). CEUR-WS.org.

Sapia, C. (2000). Promise: Predicting query behavior to enable predictive caching strategies for OLAP systems. In *Proceedings of the International Conference on Data Warehousing and Knowledge Discovery* (LNCS 1874, pp. 224–233).

Sarawagi, S. (1999). Explaining differences in multidimensional aggregates. In *Proceedings of the 25th International Conference on Very Large Data Bases* (pp. 42–53). San Francisco, CA: Morgan Kaufmann.

Sarawagi, S. (2009). *I3: Intelligent, interactive inspection of cubes*. Retrieved September 23, 2010, from http://www.cse.iitb.ac.in/~sunita/icube/

Sarawagi, S., Agrawal, R., & Megiddo, N. (1998). Discovery-driven exploration of OLAP data cubes. In *Proceedings of the 6th International Conference on Extending Database Technology* (LNCS 1377, pp. 168–182).

Sathe, G., & Sarawagi, S. (2001). Intelligent rollups in multidimensional OLAP data. In *Proceedings of the 27th International Conference on Very Large Data Bases* (pp. 531–540). San Francisco, CA: Morgan Kaufmann.

Spiliopoulou, M., Srivastava, J., Kohavi, R., & Masand, B. M. (2000). Web mining for e-commerce. *SIGKDD Explorations, 2*(2), 106–107.

Stefanidis, K., Drosou, M., & Pitoura, E. (2009). "You may also like ": Results in relational databases. In *Proceedings of the 3rd International Workshop on Personalized Access, Profile Management and Context Awareness in Databases* (pp. 37–42). New York, NY: ACM.

This work was previously published in the International Journal of Data Warehousing and Mining, Volume 7, Issue 2, edited by David Taniar, pp. 1-25, copyright 2011 by IGI Publishing (an imprint of IGI Global).

Chapter 5
Data Warehouse Testing

Matteo Golfarelli
University of Bologna, Italy

Stefano Rizzi
University of Bologna, Italy

ABSTRACT

Testing is an essential part of the design life-cycle of a software product. Although most phases of data warehouse design have received considerable attention in the literature, not much research has been conducted concerning data warehouse testing. In this paper, the authors introduce a number of data mart-specific testing activities, classify them in terms of what is tested and how it is tested, and show how they can be framed within a reference design method to devise a comprehensive and scalable approach. Finally, the authors discuss some practical evidences emerging from a real case study.

INTRODUCTION

Testing is an essential part of the design life-cycle of any software product. Needless to say, testing is especially critical to success in data warehousing projects because users need to trust the quality of the information they access. Nevertheless, while most phases of data warehouse design have received considerable attention in the literature, not much has been written about data warehouse testing.

As agreed by most authors, the difference between testing data warehouse systems and generic software systems or even transactional systems depends on several aspects (BiPM, 2009; Mookerjea & Malisetty, 2008):

- Software testing is predominantly focused on program code, while data warehouse testing is directed at data and information. The key to data warehouse testing is to know the data and what the answers to user queries are supposed to be.

DOI: 10.4018/978-1-4666-2148-0.ch005

- Differently from generic software systems, data warehouse testing involves a huge data volume, which significantly impacts performance and productivity.
- Data warehouse testing has a broader scope than software testing because it focuses on the correctness and usefulness of the information delivered to users. In fact, data validation is one of the main goals of data warehouse testing.
- Though a generic software system may have a large number of different use scenarios, the valid combinations of those scenarios are generally limited. Data warehouse systems are aimed at supporting any views of data, so the possible combinations are virtually unlimited and cannot be fully tested.
- While most testing activities are carried out before deployment in generic software systems, data warehouse testing activities still go on after system release.
- Typical software development projects are self-contained. Data warehousing projects never really come to an end; it is very difficult to anticipate future requirements for the decision-making process, so only a few requirements can be stated from the beginning. Besides, it is almost impossible to predict all the possible types of errors that will be encountered in real operational data. For this reason, regression testing is inherently involved.

Like for most generic software systems, different types of tests can be devised for data warehouse systems. For instance, it is very useful to distinguish between unit test, a white-box test performed on each individual component considered in isolation from the others, and integration test, a black-box test where the system is tested in its entirety. Also regression test, that checks that the system still functions correctly after a change has occurred, is considered to be very

important for data warehouse systems because of their ever-evolving nature. However, the peculiar characteristics of data warehouse testing and the complexity of data warehouse projects ask for a deep revision and contextualization of these test types, aimed in particular at emphasizing the relationships between testing activities on the one side, design phases and project documentation on the other.

From the methodological point of view we mention that, while testing issues are often considered only during the very last phases of data warehouse projects, all authors agree that advancing an accurate test planning to the early projects phases is one of the keys to success. The main reason for this is that, as software engineers know very well, the earlier an error is detected in the software design cycle, the cheapest correcting that error is. Besides, planning early testing activities to be carried out during design and before implementation gives project managers an effective way to regularly measure and document the project progress state.

Since the correctness of a system can only be measured with reference to a set of requirements, a successful testing begins with the gathering and documentation of end-user requirements (Haertzen, 2009). Since most end-users requirements are about data analysis and data quality, it is inevitable that data warehouse testing primarily focuses on the ETL process on the one hand (this is sometimes called back-end testing) (BiPM, 2009), on reporting and OLAP on the other (front-end testing) (BiPM, 2009). While back-end testing aims at ensuring that data loaded into the data warehouse are consistent with the source data, front-end testing aims at verifying that data are correctly navigated and aggregated in the available reports.

From the organizational point of view, several roles are involved with testing (Haertzen, 2009). Designers draw conceptual schemata that represent the users' requirements to be used as a reference for testing. Designers are also responsible for logical schemata of data repositories and for data staging flows, which should be tested for efficiency and robustness. Testers develop and execute test plans and scripts. Developers perform white box unit tests. Database administrators test for performance and stress, and set up test environments. Finally, end-users perform functional tests on reporting and OLAP front-end tools.

In this paper we propose a comprehensive approach to testing data warehouse systems. More precisely, considering that data warehouse systems are commonly built in a bottom-up fashion, by iteratively designing and implementing one data mart at a time, we will focus on the test of a single data mart. The main features of our approach are:

- **Earliness:** A consistent portion of the testing effort is advanced to the design phase to reduce the impact of error correction.
- **Modularity:** A number of data mart-specific testing activities are identified and classified in terms of what is tested and how it is tested.
- **Tight Coupling:** A close relationship is established between testing activities and design phases within the framework of a reference methodological approach to design.
- **Scalability:** Some testing activities can be smoothly removed to cut the testing effort when facing small projects.
- **Measurability:** When possible, testing activities are related to quality metrics to allow their quantitative assessment.

This paper is organized as follows. After briefly reviewing the related literature, we propose the reference methodological framework. Then, we classify and describe the data mart-specific testing activities we devised, and we briefly discuss some issues related to test coverage. We propose a modular timeline for testing in the framework of the reference design method, and finally we discuss some practical evidences emerged from a case study.

RELATED WORKS

The literature on software engineering is huge, and it includes a detailed discussion of different approaches to the testing of software systems (Pressman, 2005; Sommerville, 2004). However, only a few works discuss the issues raised by testing in the data warehousing context.

Mookerjea and Malisetty (2008) summarize the main challenges of data warehouse and ETL testing, and discuss their phases and goals distinguishing between retrospective and prospective testing. They also propose to base part of the testing activities (those related to incremental load) on mock data.

Tanuska, Verschelde, and Kopcek (2008) propose a basic set of attributes for a data warehouse test scenario based on the IEEE 829 standard. These attributes include the test purpose, its performance requirements, its acceptance criteria, and the activities for its completion.

Brahmkshatriya (2007) proposes a process for data warehouse testing centered on a unit test phase, an integration test phase, and a user acceptance test phase.

Van Bergenhenegouwen (2008) reports eight classical mistakes in data warehouse testing; among these: not closely involving end users, testing reports rather than data, skipping the comparison between data warehouse data and source data, and using only mock data. Besides, unit testing, system testing, acceptance testing, and performance testing are proposed as the main testing steps.

BiPM (2009) explains the differences between testing OLTP and OLAP systems and proposes a detailed list of testing categories. They also enumerate possible test scenarios and different types of data to be used for testing.

Haertzen (2009) discusses the main aspects in data warehouse testing. In particular, he distinguishes the different roles required in the testing team, and the different types of testing each role should carry out.

Cooper and Arbuckle (2002) present some lessons learnt on data warehouse testing, emphasizing the role played by constraint testing, source-to-target testing, and validation of error processing procedures.

All papers mentioned above provide useful hints and list some key testing activities. On the other hand, our paper is the first attempt to define a comprehensive framework for data mart testing.

METHODOLOGICAL FRAMEWORK

To discuss how testing relates to the different phases of data mart design, we adopt as a methodological framework the one described by Golfarelli and Rizzi (2009). As sketched in the UML activity diagram reproduced in Figure 1, this framework includes the following phases:

- **Requirement Analysis:** Requirements and a preliminary workload are elicited from users and represented either informally by means of proper glossaries or formally, for example, by means of goal-oriented diagrams as proposed by Giorgini, Rizzi, and Garzetti (2008).
- **Analysis and Reconciliation:** Data sources are inspected, normalized, and integrated to obtain a reconciled schema, and source data quality is assessed.
- **Conceptual Design:** A conceptual schema for the data mart, for example, in the form of a set of fact schemata as proposed by Golfarelli, Maio, and Rizzi (1998), is designed considering both user requirements and data available in the reconciled schema, and the preliminary workload is refined.
- **Logical Design:** A logical schema for the data mart (e.g., in the form of a set of star schemata) is obtained by properly translating the conceptual schema.

- **Data Staging Design:** ETL procedures are designed considering the source schemata, the reconciled schema, and the data mart logical schema.
- **Physical Design:** Includes index selection, schema fragmentation, and all other issues related to physical allocation.
- **Implementation:** Includes implementation of ETL procedures and creation of front-end reports.

Note that this methodological framework is general enough to host both supply-driven, demand-driven, and mixed approaches to design. While conceptual design in a supply-driven approach is mainly based on an analysis of the available source schemata (Golfarelli, Maio, & Rizzi, 1998), in a demand-driven approach user requirements are the driving force of conceptual design (Bruckner, List, & Schiefer, 2001). Finally, in a mixed approach requirement analysis and

Figure 1. Reference design method

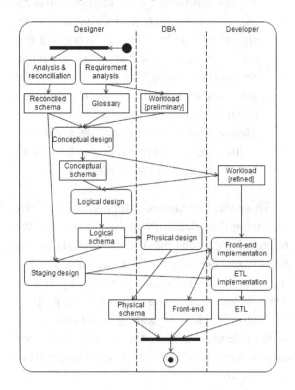

source schema analysis are carried out in parallel, and requirements are used to simplify source schema analysis (Bonifati et al., 2001).

Noticeably, the framework adopted is well-suited to support an incremental approach to design by introducing some prototyping steps and by properly iterating the design phases.

TESTING ACTIVITIES

In order to better frame the different testing activities and to promote modularity and scalability, we identify two distinct, though not independent, classification coordinates: what is tested and how it is tested.

As concerns the first coordinate, what, we already mentioned that testing data quality is undoubtedly at the core of data warehouse testing. Testing data quality mainly entails an accurate check on the correctness of the data loaded by ETL procedures and accessed by front-end tools. However, in the light of the complexity of data warehouse projects and of the close relationship between good design and good performance, we argue that testing the design quality is almost equally important. Testing design quality mainly implies verifying that user requirements are well expressed by the conceptual schema of the data mart and that the conceptual and logical schemata are well-built. Overall, the items to be tested can then be summarized as follows:

- **Conceptual Schema:** It describes the data mart from an implementation-independent point of view, specifying the facts to be monitored, their measures, and the hierarchies to be used for aggregation. Our methodological framework adopts the Dimensional Fact Model to this end (Golfarelli, Maio, & Rizzi, 1998).
- **Logical Schema:** It describes the structure of the data repository at the core of the

data mart. If the implementation target is a ROLAP platform, the logical schema is actually a relational schema (typically, a star schema or one of its variants).
- **ETL Procedures:** The complex procedures that are in charge of feeding the data repository starting from data sources.
- **Physical Schema:** The physical repository storing data, including the indexes created to improve performance.
- **Front-End:** The applications accessed by end-users to analyze data; typically, these are either static reporting tools or more flexible OLAP tools.

As concerns the second coordinate, how, the eight types of test that, in our experience, best fit the characteristics of data warehouse systems are summarized below:

- **Functional Test:** It verifies that an item is compliant with its specified business requirements.
- **Usability Test:** It evaluates an item by letting users interact with it, in order to verify that the item is easy to use and comprehensible.
- **Performance Test:** It checks that an item performance is satisfactory under typical workload conditions.
- **Stress Test:** It shows how well an item performs with peak loads of data and very heavy workloads.
- **Recovery Test:** It checks how well an item is able to recover from crashes, hardware failures and other similar problems.
- **Security Test:** It checks that an item protects data and maintains functionality as intended.
- **Maintainability Test:** It checks that an item can be easily modified to correct faults, improve performance, or adapt to a changed environment.

- **Regression Test:** It checks that an item still functions correctly after a change has occurred.

Remarkably, these types of test are tightly related to seven of the software quality factors described by McCall, Richards, and Walters (1977): correctness, usability, efficiency, reliability, integrity, flexibility, maintainability.

The relationship between what and how is summarized in Table 1, where each check mark points out that a given type of test should be applied to a given item.

√Starting from this table, in the following subsections we discuss the main testing activities and how they are related to the methodological framework outlined in the previous section.

ΩWe preliminarily remark that a requirement for an effective test is the early definition, for each testing activity, of the necessary conditions for passing the test. These conditions should be verifiable and quantifiable. This means that proper metrics should be introduced, together with their acceptance thresholds, so as to get rid of subjectivity and ambiguity issues. Using quantifiable metrics is also necessary for automating testing activities.

While for some types of tests, such as performance tests, the metrics devised for generic software systems (such as the maximum query response time) can be reused and acceptance thresholds can be set intuitively, for other types of tests data mart-specific metrics are needed. Unfortunately, very few such metrics have been defined in the literature. Besides, the criteria for setting their acceptance thresholds often depend on the specific features of the project being considered. So, in most cases, ad hoc metrics will have to be defined together with their thresholds.

Testing the Conceptual Schema

Software engineers know very well that the earlier an error is detected in the software design cycle, the cheapest correcting that error is. One of the advantages of adopting a data warehouse method that entails a conceptual design phase is that the conceptual schema produced can be thoroughly tested for user requirements to be effectively supported.

Functional Test

We propose three types of test on the data mart conceptual schema in the scope of functional testing.

The first, that we call fact test, verifies that the workload preliminarily expressed by users during

Table 1. What vs. how in testing

	Conceptual schema	Logical schema	ETL pro-cedures	Physical schema	Front-end
Functional	√	√	√		√
Usability	√	√	√		√
Performance		√	√	√	√
Stress			√	√	√
Recovery			√	√	
Security	√		√	√	√
Maintainability		√	√		√
Regression	√	√	√	√	√
	Analysis & Design		Implementation		

requirement analysis is actually supported by the conceptual schema. This can be easily achieved by checking, for each workload query, that the required measures have been included in the fact schema and that the required aggregation level can be expressed as a valid grouping set on the fact schema.

The second test (hierarchy test) measures to what extent the functional dependencies represented by hierarchies in the conceptual schema are actually verified on source data. While in supply-driven approaches this type of test may have little utility since hierarchies are mainly designed starting from the source schema, in demand-driven approaches it is very useful to check if the requirements have been correctly understood and modeled. Besides, this test can lead designers to discover denormalization issues they were not aware of in source data, which has a significant impact on ETL design. Hierarchies should also be checked to be in multidimensional normal form that ensures summarizability (Lehner, Albrecht, & Wedekind, 1998; Lechtenbörger & Vossen, 2003).

We call the third type of test a conformity test, because it is aimed at assessing how well conformed hierarchies have been designed. This test can be carried out by measuring the sparseness of the bus matrix (Golfarelli & Rizzi, 2009), which associates each fact with its dimensions, thus pointing out the existence of conformed hierarchies. Intuitively, if the bus matrix is very sparse, the designer probably failed to recognize the semantic and structural similarities between apparently different hierarchies. Conversely, if the bus matrix is very dense, the designer probably failed to recognize the semantic and structural similarities between apparently different facts.

Usability Test

Other types of test that can be executed on the conceptual schema are related to its understandability, thus falling in the scope of usability test-ing. An example of a quantitative approach to this test is the one described by Serrano et al. (2007), where a set of metrics for measuring the quality of a conceptual schema from the point of view of its understandability are proposed and validated. Examples of these metrics are the average number of levels per hierarchy and the number of measures per fact. To better characterize usability, we introduce two more metrics. The first computes the number of advanced (and more difficultly understood by users) constructs appearing in the conceptual schema; for the Dimensional Fact Model, advanced constructs are dynamic hierarchies, cross-dimensional attributes, multiple arcs, irregular hierarchies, optional arcs, and non-additivities (Golfarelli & Rizzi, 2009). The second metric aims at evaluating the information content of hierarchies in terms of the functional dependencies they express and is computed as a function of the ratio between the width and the depth of hierarchies (roll-up factor).

The usability test is not completed unless a nomenclature check is made. This requires verifying that the names chosen for attributes, measures, and domain values are appropriate, consistent, and well interpretable by users. Preparing a comprehensive glossary of terms during conceptual design and leaning on that glossary for this type of test is strongly recommended.

Security Test

Considering the strategic nature of the information managed by data warehouses and the strong impact of security on design, it is essential to specify security requirements during the very early stages of the design life-cycle. In this context, we area specifically interested in confidentiality, i.e., the protection of information from unauthorized disclosure either by direct access or by indirect inference. Ensuring confidentiality requires defining which subjects (users, groups, roles) can or cannot access each object (fact, measure, attribute, etc.). These type of requirements should be discussed with users during requirement analysis, and they can be represented during conceptual design by preparing a security schema based on some ad hoc formalism, like the UML extension proposed by Fernández-Medina et al. (2007), that classifies subjects and objects by their clearance level, compartment, and role, or the MDSCL constraint language for OLAP security by Priebe and Pernul (2001), that uses a set of HIDE statements to express negative authorization constraints. Assuming that each query in the workload is associated with one or more subjects that are allowed to execute it, the security schema can then be tested by checking that it is consistent with the workload.

Another useful test in this stage can be carried out by a small pool of users who are in charge of defining and enforcing the confidentiality policies for their company, and consists in checking the security schema against possible unauthorized accesses.

Testing the Logical Schema

Testing the logical schema before it is implemented and before ETL design dramatically reduces the impact of errors due to bad logical design.

Functional Test

An effective approach to functional testing consists in executing some sample loadings of the data mart starting from source data (early loading test). This practice has several benefits: it allows an indirect check on the correctness of the logical schema, it gives a precious feedback on the most common types of errors the ETL will have to handle, and it enables an early functional test of the front-end. Note that early loading tests are based on a draft prototype of ETL procedures, where most issues that will be addressed by ETL design (such as data cleaning, incremental extraction, loading of dynamic hierarchies, and performance optimization) are not considered. Some sections of this

prototype can then be reused, after ETL design, to produce the final ETL implementation.

Another useful type of functional test aims at verifying that a sample of queries in the preliminary workload can correctly be formulated in SQL on the logical schema. In putting the sample together, priority should be given to the queries involving irregular portions of hierarchies (e.g., those including many-to-many associations or cross-dimensional attributes), those based on complex aggregation schemes (e.g., queries that require measures aggregated through different operators along the different hierarchies), and those leaning on non-standard temporal scenarios (such as yesterday-for-today).

Usability Test

In the scope of usability testing, Serrano, Calero, and Piattini (2003) propose some simple metrics based on the number of fact tables and dimension tables in a logical schema. These metrics can be adopted to effectively capture schema understandability.

Performance Test

Finally, a performance test can be carried out on the logical schema by checking to what extent it is compliant with the multidimensional normal forms that support an efficient database design (Lehner, Albrecht, & Wedekind, 1998; Lechtenbörger & Vossen, 2003).

Testing the ETL Procedures

ETL testing is probably the most complex and critical testing phase, because it directly affects the quality of data mart data. Since ETL is heavily code-based, most standard techniques for generic software system testing can be reused here.

Note that the quality of data mart data obviously depends on the quality of source data. Assessing source data quality beforehand—rather than, indirectly, during ETL and front-end testing—is useful for better estimating the effort of ETL design and for an earlier planning of forced-error tests. This assessment is normally done during the analysis and reconciliation design phase.

Functional Test

A functional test of ETL is aimed at checking that ETL procedures correctly extract, clean, transform, and load data into the data mart. The best approach here is to set up unit tests and integration tests.

Unit tests are white-box test that each developer carries out on the units (s)he developed. They allow for breaking down the testing complexity, and they also enable more detailed reports on the project progress to be produced. Units for ETL testing can be either vertical (one test unit for each conformed dimension, plus one test unit for each group of correlated facts) or horizontal (separate tests for static extraction, incremental extraction, cleaning, transformation, static loading, incremental loading, view update); the most effective choice mainly depends on the number of facts in the data marts, on how complex cleaning and transformation are, and on how the implementation plan was allotted to the developers. In particular, crucial aspects to be considered during the loading test are related to both dimension tables (correctness of roll-up functions, effective management of dynamic hierarchies and irregular hierarchies), fact tables (effective management of late updates), and materialized views (use of correct aggregation functions).

In the scope of ETL unit test it is useful to distinguish between an integrity test (that operates on the data flow) and a code test (that operates on the control flow). A common way to perform an integrity test consists in including some debugging code to check for simple consistency rules (such as *number of input rows = number of output rows + number of rejected rows*) to be verified at different points in the unit data flow. On the other

hand, a code test can be done by generating a set of input data to force the unit to execute each arc in its control graph at least once (Beizer, 1990).

After unit tests have been completed, an integration test allows the correctness of data flows in ETL procedures to be checked. Different quality dimensions, such as data coherence (the respect of integrity constraints), completeness (the percentage of data found), and freshness (the age of data) should be considered. Some metrics for quantifying these quality dimensions have been proposed by Vassiliadis, Bouzeghoub, and Quix (1999). In particular, Ordonez and García-García (2008) have proposed metrics for evaluating completeness and consistency with respect to referential integrity; these metrics were specifically devised to work in presence of denormalized tables and materialized views, so they are effectively applicable to data warehouses.

During requirement analysis the designer, together with users and database administrators, should have singled out and ranked by their gravity the most common causes of faulty data, aimed at planning a proper strategy for dealing with ETL errors. Common strategies for dealing with errors of a given kind are "automatically clean faulty data", "reject faulty data", "hand faulty data to data mart administrator", etc. So, not surprisingly, a distinctive feature of ETL functional testing is that it should be carried out with at least three different databases, including respectively (i) correct and complete data, (ii) data simulating the presence of faulty data of different kinds, and (iii) real data. In particular, tests using dirty simulated data are sometimes called forced-error tests: they are designed to force ETL procedures into error conditions aimed at verifying that the system can deal with faulty data as planned during requirement analysis.

Usability Test

Considering that running ETL procedures is in charge of the data warehouse administrators, a usability test of ETL should be focused on assessing the amount of human intervention necessary to complete the periodic loading of the data mart. Some simple but effective metrics to quantify this feature compute the percentages of successfully loaded records, of faulty records that were automatically corrected, of faulty records that were either rejected or flagged, over the total number of processed records.

Performance and Stress Test

Performance and stress tests are complementary in assessing the efficiency of ETL procedures. Performance tests evaluate the behavior of ETL with reference to a routine workload, i.e., when a domain-typical amount of data has to be extracted and loaded; in particular, they check that the processing time is compatible with the time frames expected for data-staging processes. On the other hand, stress tests simulate an extraordinary workload due to a significantly larger amount of data.

Recovery Test

The recovery test of ETL checks for robustness by simulating faults in one or more components and evaluating the system response. For example, the power supply can be cut off while an ETL process is in progress or a database can be set offline while an OLAP session is in progress to check for effectiveness of the restore policies.

Security Test

Each stage of the data movement process involves a certain security risk. As concerns ETL, the most critical security requirement concerns integrity, which requires information to be protected from malicious or accidental modification. Integrity should be tested by mainly verifying that the database used to temporarily store the data being processed (the so-called data staging area) cannot be violated, and that the network infrastructure hosting the data flows that connect the data sources to the data mart is secure.

A common approach to test for network security is penetration testing, a method that simulates an attack from the point of view of a malicious attacker aimed at determining the feasibility of an attack and the amount of business impact of a successful exploit. Other approaches can be found in the Open Source Security Testing Methodology Manual, a peer-reviewed methodology for security tests and metrics (Herzog, 2010).

Testing the Physical Schema

Performance and Stress Test

We assume that the logical schema quality has already been verified during the logical schema tests, and that all issues related to data quality are in charge of ETL tests. Then, physical schema testing is mainly aimed at checking the database performances using either standard (performance test) or heavy (stress test) workloads. Like for ETL, the size of the tested databases and their data distribution must be discussed with the designers and the database administrator. Performance tests can be carried out either on a database including real data or on a mock database, but the database size should be compatible with the average expected data volume. On the other hand, stress tests are typically carried out on mock databases whose size is significantly larger than what expected. Standard database metrics—such as average and maximum query response time—can be used to quantify the test results, with reference to both the standard report workload and an extemporary OLAP workload. To advance these testing activities as much as possible and to make their results independent of front-end applications, we suggest using SQL to code the workloads.

Recovery Test

Recovery tests enable testers to verify the DBMS behavior after critical errors such as power leaks during update, network fault, and hard disk failures, considering the specific back-up policies adopted and the possible use of RAID configurations.

Security Test

Access grants in relational DBMS are expressed at table/view level, which is insufficient to effectively deal with the complexity of data mart authorization patterns. For this reason, access control in data marts is normally enforced at either the front-end or OLAP server level. However, in cases where access control is achieved using SQL views, security tests should check for confidentiality and availability by verifying that the security schema defined during conceptual design has been correctly translated to the database level.

As concerns integrity, a penetration test can be carried out to check the robustness of the cryptography technique adopted to protect data.

Testing the Front-End

Functional Test

Functional testing of the analysis front-ends must necessarily involve a large number of end-users, who generally are so familiar with application domains that they can detect even the slightest abnormality in data. Nevertheless, wrong results in OLAP analyses may be difficult to recognize. They can be caused not only by faulty ETL procedures, but even by incorrect data aggregations or selections in front-end tools. Some errors are not due to the data mart; instead, they result from the overly poor data quality of the source database. In order to allow this situation to be recognized, a common approach to front-end functional testing in real projects consists in comparing the results of OLAP analyses with those obtained by directly querying the source databases. Of course, though this approach can be effective on a sample basis, it cannot be extensively adopted due to the huge number of possible aggregations that characterize multidimensional queries.

A significant sample of queries to be tested can be selected in mainly two ways. In the "black-box way", the workload specification obtained in output by the workload refinement phase (typically, a use case diagram where actors stand for user profiles and use cases represent the most frequent analysis queries) is used to determine the test cases, much like use case diagrams are profitably employed for testing-in-the-large in generic software systems. In the "white-box way", instead, the subset of data aggregations to be tested can be determined by applying proper coverage criteria to the multidimensional lattice of each fact, much like decision, statement, and path coverage criteria are applied to the control graph of a generic software procedure during testing-in-the-small. (The multidimensional lattice of a fact is the lattice whose nodes and arcs correspond, respectively, to the group-by sets supported by that fact and to the roll-up relationships that relate those group-by sets.) While this "white-box way" may be trivial for additive measures, it becomes crucial for non-additive measures, that are more easily subject to aggregation errors.

Also in front-end testing it may be useful to distinguish between unit and integration tests. While unit tests should be aimed at checking the correctness of the reports involving single facts, integration tests entail analysis sessions that either correlate multiple facts (the so-called drill-across queries) or take advantage of different application components. For example, this is the case when dashboard data are "drilled through" an OLAP application.

Note that, in order to better separate different error causes, the functional test of the front-end should be carried out after the ETL has been implemented and tested. However, in some cases it may be useful to execute a preliminary, more superficial functional test as soon as the front-end has been prototyped, using data loaded on a sample basis during the early loading test of the logical schema.

Usability Test

An integral part of front-end tests are usability tests, that check for OLAP reports to be suitably represented and commented to avoid any misunderstanding about the real meaning of data. This type of test includes a set of user activities such as accessing the system, launching reports, navigating data via OLAP operators, and interpreting the results.

Performance and Stress Test

A performance test submits a group of concurrent queries to the front-end and checks for the time needed to process those queries. Performance tests imply a preliminary specification of the standard workload in terms of number of concurrent users, types of queries, and data volume. On the other hand, stress tests entail applying progressively heavier workloads than the standard loads to evaluate the system stability. Note that performance and stress tests should be focused on the front-end, which includes the client interface but also the reporting and OLAP server-side engines. This means that the access times due to the DBMS should be subtracted from the overall response times measured. Finally, we remark that a critical evaluation of the results of this kind of tests is made much easier by the existence of a SLA (Service Level Agreement) that defines the target performances for the data mart.

Security Test

A client/server connection is typically used for data exchange between the front-end and the data server. Though the information transmitted is aggregated, it may be highly security-critical

(Priebe & Pernul, 2001). The guidelines for network testing from the integrity point of view are the same seen for ETL.

In the scope of security test, it is also fundamental to check for user profiles to be properly set up. The availability requirement, ensuring that data are available to authorized users when they need them, is indirectly checked by users during functional test of the front-end. As to confidentiality, it can be tested by verifying, on a sample basis, that users cannot access forbidden information according to what stated in the security schema.

Maintainability Test

Maintenance and evolution are fundamental parts of the life-cycle of all data warehouses. This is especially true for data warehouses built up in a bottom-up fashion, i.e., by iteratively designing one data mart at a time. So, it is not surprising that maintainability, meant as the ease with which a system can be maintained, is among the most desired qualities for this kind of systems.

Maintainability cannot be measured directly. Thus, it is commonly assessed by measuring maintenance process attributes, such as the time required to make a change. However, since testing takes place during design and development, i.e., well before maintenance begins, this type of measure is not useful for testing. So, there is a need for a maintainability prediction model that allows maintenance process measures to be predicted from software measures like cohesion, coupling and complexity. An example of a model well-suited for assessing ETL maintainability is the one by Frappier, Matwin, and Mili (1994), which proposes a set of metrics based, for instance, on the strength of the inter-module relationships or on the intra-module complexity of information flows.

While most maintainability metrics are meant to be used on pieces of software, like ETL procedures, the literature also proposes some metrics specifically devised for database schemata, and relates them to abstract quality factors. For instance, Papastefanatos et al. (2008) introduce a set of metrics aimed at evaluating the quality of a data mart logical schema with respect to its ability to sustain changes during an evolution process.

Besides specific metrics for software or schemata, other general metrics that should be applied to assess maintainability of the different items involved in data mart testing are related to the depth and precision of the project documentation, to the meeting of guidelines for good design, and to the existence of a comprehensive glossary of terms.

Regression Test

A very relevant problem for frequently updated systems, such as data warehouses, concerns checking for new components and new add-on features to be compatible with the operation of the whole system. In this case, the term regression test is used to define the testing activities carried out to make sure that any change applied to the system does not jeopardize the quality of preexisting, already tested features and does not corrupt the system performances.

Testing the whole system many times from scratch has huge costs. Three main directions can be followed to reduce these costs:

- An expensive part of each test is the validation of the test results. In regression testing, it is often possible to skip this phase by just checking that the test results are consistent with those obtained at the previous iteration.
- Test automation allows the efficiency of testing activities to be increased, so that reproducing previous tests becomes less expensive.
- Impact analysis can be used to significantly restrict the scope of testing. In general, impact analysis is aimed at determining what other application objects are affected by a change in a single application object (Kimball & Caserta, 2004). Remarkably, some ETL tool vendors already provide some impact analysis functionalities. An approach to impact analysis for changes in the source data schemata is proposed by Papastefanatos et al. (2007).

Table 2. Coverage criteria for some testing activities; the expected coverage is expressed with reference to the coverage criterion

Testing activity	Coverage criterion	Measurement	Expected coverage
fact test	each information need expressed by users during requirement analysis must be tested	percentage of queries in the preliminary workload that are supported by the conceptual schema	partial, depending on the extent of the preliminary workload
conformity test	all data mart dimensions must be tested	bus matrix sparseness	total
usability test of the conceptual schema	all facts, dimensions, and measures must be tested	conceptual metrics	total
ETL unit test	all decision points must be tested	correct loading of the test data sets	total
ETL forced-error test	all error types specified by users must be tested	correct loading of the faulty data sets	total
front-end unit test	at least one group-by set for each attribute in the multidimensional lattice of each fact must be tested	correct analysis result of a real data set	total

TEST COVERAGE

Testing can reduce the probability of a system fault but cannot set it to zero, so measuring the coverage of tests is necessary to assess the overall system reliability. Measuring test coverage requires first of all the definition of a suitable coverage criterion. Different coverage criteria, such as statement coverage, decision coverage, and path coverage, were devised in the scope of code testing. The choice of one or another criterion deeply affects the test length and cost, as well as the achievable coverage. So, coverage criteria are chosen by trading off test effectiveness and efficiency. Examples of coverage criteria that we propose for some of the testing activities described above are reported in Table 2.

A MODULAR TIMELINE FOR TESTING

From a methodological point of view, the three main phases of testing are (Mookerjea & Malisetty, 2008):

- **Create a Test Plan:** The test plan describes the tests that must be performed and their expected coverage of the system requirements.
- **Prepare Test Cases:** Test cases enable the implementation of the test plan by detailing the testing steps together with their expected results. The reference databases for testing should be prepared during this phase, and a wide, comprehensive set of representative workloads should be defined.
- **Execute Tests:** A test execution log tracks each test along and its results.

Figure 2 shows a UML activity diagram that enriches the one in Figure 1 by framing the different testing activities within the design method. The diagram also shows the main artifacts produced

during the data mart life-cycle as object nodes, emphasizing how their state (in brackets) changes in response to testing activities. Iterations due to unsatisfactory test outcomes are not shown to keep the diagram readable.

The diagram in Figure 2 can be used in a project for preparing the test plan. However, though adopting a comprehensive testing method can lead to a consistent saving in post-deployment error correction activities and to a considerable gain in terms of better data and design quality, this may not be worth the extra-effort for testing in some small or medium projects. This is the reason why our approach has been conceived to be modular—thanks to the fragmentation into small testing activities introduced by distinguishing the what and how coordinates—and largely scalable without losing its effectiveness. The basic customization suggestions we provide are:

- The prototype implemented during early loading test of the logical schema allows functional test of the front-end to be advanced, thus making end-users more involved in the project and possibly leading to an early discovery of serious misunderstandings about requirements. However, this prototyping phase can be removed for small projects or when designers and users share a large confidence in the requirements expressed.
- Usability metrics on the conceptual and logical schemata can give useful suggestions, but their effectiveness is limited. While they can be easily computed if a CASE tool is used, when schemata are manually managed they can safely be abandoned.
- It may not be possible to create a testing environment that is identical to the one where the data warehouse is actually going to be deployed. This makes performance testing harder and may make stress testing impossible.

Figure 2. UML activity diagram for design and testing

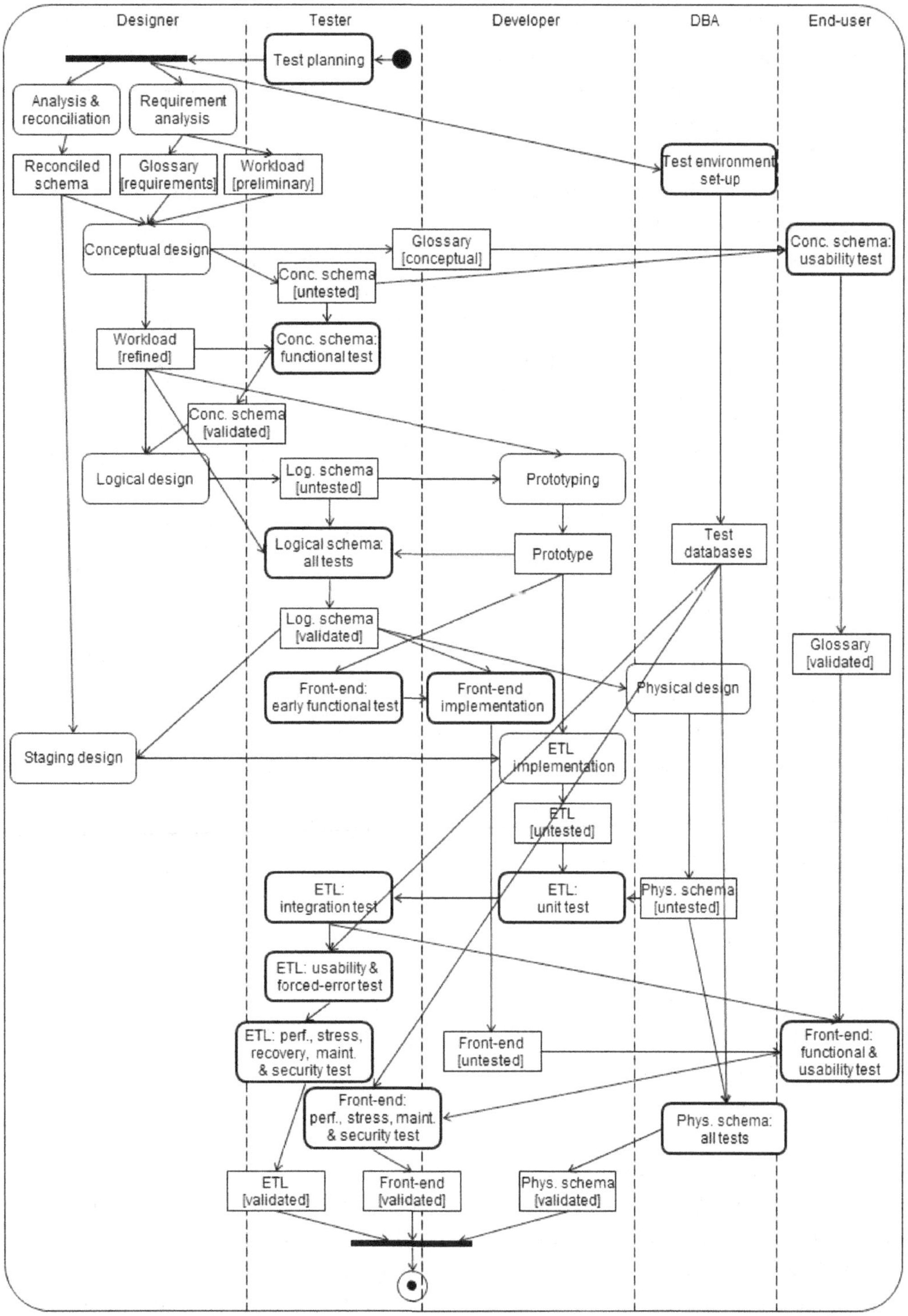

- Checking the core workload should always be done. However, if the workload has already been checked against the conceptual schema, checking it also against the logical schema can be skipped to reduce the overall testing cost. Besides, if an early front-end functional test is carried out on a prototype, such test can be used instead of the conceptual/logical schema functional test to check that the requirements have correctly been represented.

It is worth mentioning here that test automation plays a basic role in reducing the costs of testing activities (especially regression tests) on the one hand, on increasing test coverage on the other (Cooper & Arbuckle, 2002). Remarkably, commercial tools (such as QACenter by Computerware) can be used for implementation-related testing activities to simulate specific workloads and analysis sessions, or to measure a process outcome. As to design-related testing activities, the metrics proposed in the previous sections can be measured by writing ad hoc procedures that access the meta-data repository and the DBMS catalog.

PRACTICAL EVIDENCES

In order to validate our approach on a case study, in the last six months we supported a professional design team engaged in a large data warehouse project. Due to space limitations, the case study cannot be reported in detail; here we summarize its most relevant outcomes:

- The chance to perform an effective test depends on the documentation completeness and accuracy in terms of collected requirements and project description.
- The test phase is part of the data warehouse life-cycle, and it acts in synergy with design. For this reason, the test phase should be planned and arranged at the beginning of the project, by specifying the goals of testing, which types of tests must be performed, which data sets need to be tested, and which quality level is expected.
- Different approaches to test are required for differently skilled design teams and differently sized projects. A testing method should be smoothly customizable and still preserve most of its effectiveness.
- Testing is not a one-man activity. The testing team should include testers, developers, designers, database administrators, and end-users, and it should be set up during the project planning phase.
- Testing of data warehouse systems is largely based on data. A successful testing must rely on real data, but it also must include mock data to reproduce the most common error situations that can be encountered in ETL. Accurately preparing the right data sets is one of the most critical activities to be carried out during test planning.
- No matter how deeply the system has been tested: it is almost sure that, sooner or later, an unexpected data fault, which cannot be properly handled by ETL, will occur. So keep in mind that, while testing must come to an end someday, data quality certification is an everlasting process. The borderline between testing and certification clearly depends on how precisely requirement were stated and on the contract that regulates the project.

CONCLUSION

In this paper we have proposed a comprehensive approach which adapts and extends the testing methods proposed for general-purpose software to the peculiarities of data warehouse projects. Our proposal builds on a set of tips and suggestions coming from our direct experience on real projects, as well as from some interviews we made to data warehouse practitioners. As a result, a set of relevant testing activities have been identified, classified, and framed within a reference design method.

A further feedback from practitioners has been collected through a questionnaire we sent to a set of Italian software houses specialized in designing data warehouse systems and to a sample of their customers. The customer sample includes both private companies and public bodies; project sizes range from 60-80 (medium-size private companies) to 500-750 (state Ministries) man-days. From the filled questionnaires, it clearly emerges that all the interviewees firmly believe that an engineered approach to testing can effectively reduce the overall cost and duration of projects. However, most interviewees acknowledge that: (1) testing activities are usually carried out informally and often by the same team in charge of design and development; (2) passing a final inspection is not always necessary to honor the contract; and (3) only a few of the contracts that mandatorily require a final inspection also specify in detail a testing procedure to be followed. Motivations for this gap between theory and practice comes from the lack of a clear testing method as well as, as stated by the interviewees, by the resources and time necessary for testing. We believe our method can bridge this gap because not only it delivers 360-degree coverage for testing, but it also frames testing activities within a modular method that can be shaped according to project specificities, size, and constraints.

REFERENCES

Beizer, B. (1990). *Software Testing Techniques*. New York, NY: Van Nostrand Reinhold.

BiPM. (2009). *Data warehouse testing and implementation*. Retrieved from http://www.bipminstitute.com/data-warehouse

Bonifati, A., Cattaneo, F., Ceri, S., Fuggetta, A., & Paraboschi, S. (2001). Designing data marts for data warehouses. *ACM Transactions on Software Engineering and Methodology*, *10*(4), 452–483. doi:10.1145/384189.384190

Brahmkshatriya, K. (2007). *Data warehouse testing*. Retrieved from http://www.stickyminds.com

Bruckner, R., List, B., & Schiefer, J. (2001). Developing requirements for data warehouse systems with use cases. In *Proceedings of the Americas Conference on Information Systems* (pp. 329–335).

Cooper, R., & Arbuckle, S. (2002). *How to thoroughly test a data warehouse*. Paper presented at the STAREAST Conference, Orlando, FL.

Fernández-Medina, E., Trujillo, J., Villarroel, R., & Piattini, M. (2007). Developing secure data warehouses with a UML extension. *Information Systems*, *32*(6), 826–856. doi:10.1016/j.is.2006.07.003

Frappier, M., Matwin, S., & Mili, A. (1994). *Software metrics for predicting maintainability*. Longueuil, QC, Canada: Canadian Space Agency.

Giorgini, P., Rizzi, S., & Garzetti, M. (2008). GRAnD: A goal-oriented approach to requirement analysis in data warehouses. *Decision Support Systems*, *5*(1), 4–21. doi:10.1016/j.dss.2006.12.001

Golfarelli, M., Maio, D., & Rizzi, S. (1998). The dimensional fact model: A conceptual model for data warehouses. *International Journal of Cooperative Information Systems*, *7*(2-3), 215–247. doi:10.1142/S0218843098000118

Golfarelli, M., & Rizzi, S. (2009). *Data warehouse design: Modern principles and methodologies*. New York, NY: McGraw-Hill.

Haertzen, D. (2009). *Testing the data warehouse*. Retrieved from http://www.infogoal.com

Herzog, P. (2010). *Open Source Security Testing Methodology Manual.* Retrieved from http://www.isecom.org/osstmm/

Katic, N., Quirchmayr, G., Schiefer, J., Stolba, M., & Tjoa, A. M. (1998). A prototype model for data warehouse security based on metadata. In *Proceedings of the DEXA Workshop* (pp. 300–308).

Kimball, R., & Caserta, J. (2004). *The Data Warehouse ETL Toolkit.* New York, NY: John Wiley & Sons.

Lechtenbörger, J., & Vossen, G. (2003). Multidimensional normal forms for data warehouse design. *Information Systems, 28*(5), 415–434. doi:10.1016/S0306-4379(02)00024-8

Lehner, W., Albrecht, J., & Wedekind, H. (1998). Normal forms for multidimensional databases. In *Proceedings of the Scientific and Statistical Database Management Conference,* Capri, Italy (pp. 63–72).

McCall, J., Richards, P., & Walters, G. (1977). *Factors in software quality* (Tech. Rep. No. AD-A049-014, 015, 055). Springfield, VA: NTIS.

Mookerjea, A., & Malisetty, P. (2008). *Best practices in data warehouse testing.* Paper presented at the Test 2008 Conference, New Delhi, India.

Ordonez, C., & García-García, J. (2008). Referential integrity quality metrics. *Decision Support Systems, 44*(2), 495–508. doi:10.1016/j.dss.2007.06.004

Papastefanatos, G., Vassiliadis, P., Simitsis, A., & Vassiliou, Y. (2007). What-if analysis for data warehouse evolution. In *Proceedings of the DaWaK Conference,* Regensburg, Germany (pp. 23–33).

Papastefanatos, G., Vassiliadis, P., Simitsis, A., & Vassiliou, Y. (2008). Design metrics for data warehouse evolution. In *Proceedings of the ER Conference* (pp. 440–454).

Pressman, R. (2005). *Software Engineering: A practitioner's approach.* New York, NY: McGraw-Hill.

Priebe, T., & Pernul, G. (2001). A pragmatic approach to conceptual modeling of OLAP security. In *Proceedings of the ER Conference* (pp. 311–324).

Serrano, M., Calero, C., & Piattini, M. (2003). Experimental validation of multidimensional data models metrics. In *Proceedings of the HICSS Conference* (p. 327).

Serrano, M., Trujillo, J., Calero, C., & Piattini, M. (2007). Metrics for data warehouse conceptual models understandability. *Information and Software Technology, 49*(8), 851–870. doi:10.1016/j.infsof.2006.09.008

Sommerville, I. (2004). *Software Engineering.* Upper Saddle River, NJ: Pearson Education.

Tanuska, P., Verschelde, W., & Kopcek, M. (2008). The proposal of data warehouse test scenario. In *Proceedings of the ECUMICT Conference,* Gent, Belgium.

Van Bergenhenegouwen, A. (2008). *Data warehouse testing.* Retrieved from http://www.ti.kviv.be

Vassiliadis, P., Bouzeghoub, M., & Quix, C. (1999). Towards quality-oriented data warehouse usage and evolution. In *Proceedings of the CAiSE Conference,* Heidelberg, Germany.

This work was previously published in the International Journal of Data Warehousing and Mining, Volume 7, Issue 2, edited by David Taniar, pp. 26-43, copyright 2011 by IGI Publishing (an imprint of IGI Global).

Chapter 6
An Empirical Evaluation of Similarity Coefficients for Binary Valued Data

David M. Lewis
Carnegie Mellon University, USA

Vandana P. Janeja
University of Maryland, Baltimore County, USA

ABSTRACT

In this paper, the authors present an empirical evaluation of similarity coefficients for binary valued data. Similarity coefficients provide a means to measure the similarity or distance between two binary valued objects in a dataset such that the attributes qualifying each object have a 0-1 value. This is useful in several domains, such as similarity of feature vectors in sensor networks, document search, router network mining, and web mining. The authors survey 35 similarity coefficients used in various domains and present conclusions about the efficacy of the similarity computed in (1) labeled data to quantify the accuracy of the similarity coefficients, (2) varying density of the data to evaluate the effect of sparsity of the values, and (3) varying number of attributes to see the effect of high dimensionality in the data on the similarity computed.

INTRODUCTION

Similarity coefficients can be an effective tool for measuring the similarity among objects in a dataset. While coefficients exist for both binary data and non-binary data, this paper focuses only on those for binary data. In a binary dataset, each attribute must have a value such as 1-0 or Y-N. These attribute sets are called feature vectors. Computing the similarity among feature vectors is an important component of many data mining tasks (Yang, Claramunt, Aufaure, & Zhang,

DOI: 10.4018/978-1-4666-2148-0.ch006

2010; Zhang, Jing, Hu, Ng, Jiangxi, & Zhou, 2008). Examples include data clustering (Ahmad & Day, 2007; Guha, Rastogi, & Shim, 2000), spatial neighborhood discovery (Janeja, Adam, Atluri, & Vaidya, 2010), similarity based search (Karabatis, Chen, Janeja, Lobo, Advani, Lindvall, & Feldmann, 2009), and router network mining (Lewis, 2008). These examples are explained in the following section.

A number of different similarity coefficients have been proposed, but few studies compare their performance. As such, it is not always clear which will produce the best results. Approaches often default to those coefficients which are most convenient or well known- Jaccard's coefficient being a common choice. However, this strategy may not always be best, as different coefficients can lead to different conclusions.

We collected 35 different coefficients through a survey of publications across venues (such as ACM, IEEE, PubMed, etc.). Each coefficient was applied to a labeled dataset as well as 15 synthetically generated datasets. We assessed the quality of the results and ranked the top performers. The objective was to recommend the similarity coefficients, from this set of 35, to be used with binary (presence / absence) datasets of certain characteristics including varying density and varying number of attributes.

The remainder of paper is divided into five sections: "Motivating Examples", "Background on Similarity Coefficients", "Methodology", "Experimental Results", and "Conclusions".

MOTIVATING EXAMPLES

Spatial Neighborhood Discovery

Let us consider an example in the domain of water monitoring using sensors placed in a river stream (Adam et al., 2004; Janeja et al., 2010). The sensor network comprises of sensors placed in the various parts of the stream, with the goal of detecting anomalous levels of toxicity in a water body. In order to find outliers in the form of anomalous readings in sensors or sensors that may be malfunctioning, it is first required to discover a spatial neighborhood comprising of the relevant sensors with a similar behavior. Each sensor is characterized by a set of attributes or features in proximity such as a factory, bridge, railroad, stream, certain type of vegetation, etc. Such information can be accumulated with the help of domain experts. Indeed, in many cases such studies precede sensor placement.

In addition to spatial proximity, this feature information is used to identify relationships between the sensors to place them in similarly behaving spatial neighborhoods. The study (Adam et al., 2004; Janeja et al., 2010) measures similarities, across the sensors, between feature vectors using the Jaccard coefficient. This facilitates the quantification of the heterogeneity in the neighborhood resulting from the impact of the various features. The study shows the impact of refining the neighborhood, using such similarity coefficients, on the outliers discovered.

Similarity Based Searching

The discovery of software artifacts (files, documents, and datasets) relevant to a software change request can increase software reuse and reduce the cost of software development and maintenance (Karabatis et al., 2009; Lindvall, Feldmann, Karabatis, Chen, & Janej, 2009). However, traditional search techniques often fail to provide the relevant documents because they do not consider relationships between software artifacts. When a software project is modified, numerous supporting files, design documents, and datasets need to be updated or deleted. For someone unfamiliar with the project and its evolution, finding these artifacts can be extremely difficult.

The paper (Karabatis et al., 2009; Lindvall et al., 2009) proposes the creation of Semantic Networks which convey relationships between artifacts and assist in automatically discovering not only the requested artifacts based on a user query, but additional relevant ones that the user may not be aware of. The approach first derives a universal feature vector which has all the potential attributes across the set of artifacts. Based on the vector a binary valued feature vector for each artifact is generated. The similarities between these feature vectors is utilized to generate a similarity based network which is used as a basis of creating a semantic network for searching relevant documents.

Router Mining

Configuring routers can be a tricky task, especially on large networks (Lewis & Janeja, 2009). Not surprisingly, misconfigurations occur frequently, resulting in a layer-3 topology that differs considerably from what was originally planned. Such misconfigurations might lead to bottlenecks (a router that fulfills a very unique role and will therefore cripple the network if it fails) or redundancies (a router that is very similar in function to a number of other routers and can therefore be reallocated with little consequence).

When applied to a 0-1 dataset depicting the internal link structure among routers, similarity coefficients can readily identify these bottlenecks and redundancies. Bottleneck routers will have a low degree of similarity to all other routers as determined by the similarity coefficient, while redundant routers will have a high degree of similarity to one or more routers as determined by the similarity coefficient.

Ultimately, an administrator will need to interpret the findings, but similarity coefficients can act as a useful flagging mechanism for identifying such bottleneck or redundant routers.

BACKGROUND ON SIMILARITY COEFFICIENTS

Component Variables

The coefficients assessed in this paper are all composed of four variables: a, b, c, and d. Let us consider objects o_i and o_j where each object is qualified by features $f_1,...,f_n$ having values 0 or 1. Here, a equals the number of positive matches such that o_i and o_j both have a value of 1, b equals the number of mismatches such that o_i has a value of 1 and o_j has a value of 0, c equals the number of mismatches such that o_i has a value of 0 and o_j has a value of 1, and d equals the number of negative matches such that o_i and o_j both have a value of 0. The concept is illustrated with this sample matrix.

	f_1	f_2	f_3	f_4	f_5
o_i	1	1	1	0	0
o_j	1	1	0	1	0

- Column f_1 represents a 1-1 positive match (a).
- Column f_2 represents another 1-1 positive match (a).
- Column f_3 represents a 1-0 mismatch (b).
- Column f_4 represents a 0-1 mismatch (c).
- Column f_5 represents a 0-0 negative match (d).

So, with respect to this sample matrix, a is 2, b is 1, c is 1, and d is 1. Once these variables have been derived, the similarity between two objects can be computed. Generally (but not always), a and d will contribute to similarity, while b and c will diminish it.

Coefficient Categories

Similarity coefficients can be broken into three distinct categories: asymmetric, symmetric, and hybrid.

Asymmetric coefficients ignore negative matches (d), and should therefore be applied to data where absences (0s) are thought to carry no information. An example is *Jaccard's Coefficient*, which is defined as:

$$\frac{a}{a+b+c}$$

Symmetric coefficients acknowledge negative matches, and should therefore be applied to data where absences are thought to carry information. An example is the *Simple Matching Coefficient*, which is defined as:

$$\frac{a+d}{a+b+c}$$

Hybrid coefficients acknowledge negative matches either in the numerator or in the denominator, but not in both. Their usefulness is somewhat ambiguous. An example is *Russell & Rao's Coefficient*, which is defined as:

$$\frac{a}{a+b+c+d}$$

METHODOLOGY

Identifying and Classifying the Coefficients

Thirty-five binary similarity coefficients were identified through a survey of publications across venues, such as ACM, IEEE, and PubMed. The coefficients were broken into three major categories as outlined in the previous section—those for use with asymmetric datasets (where absences do not carry information), those for use with symmetric datasets (where absences do carry information), and hybrids (which can potentially apply to either). Ten coefficients fall into the first category, 22 into the second, and 3 into the third.

Then, the coefficients were further divided based on the range between their minimum and maximum possible output values. Most of the coefficients have a range of 0 to 1 or -1 to 1, and four have unbounded ranges (where values can go infinitely high or low). It is important to recognize these distinctions so that the values can be appropriately scaled prior to comparison. A full listing of the coefficients and their properties can be found in Table 2 in Appendix A.

Acquiring the Data Matrices

We ran tests on 16 binary valued datasets. One was provided by the authors of a previous study in software artifacts (as described under Motivating Examples) (Karabatis et al., 2009; Lindvall et al., 2009), and 15 were generated synthetically.

The Software Artifacts dataset consists of 20 Java files (rows) and 202 features (columns). The features were derived by parsing the Java files, and consist of classes, methods, import statements, keywords, parameters, etc. A value of 1 indicates that the feature is related to the Java file, and a value of 0 indicates that the feature is not related. Because there are 20 files, 190 one-to-one file pairs exist. The dataset is partially labeled, as domain experts had identified 10 file pairs as perfectly similar. It contains approximately 14% 1s and 86% 0s, and can thus be considered relatively sparse in terms of data density.

The 15 synthetic datasets were generated to test the performance of the similarity coefficients across a range of densities and a range of differently sized feature vectors. These datasets are described below.

Feature Vector Length	Data Densities
40	15% 30% 50% 70% 90%
120	15% 30% 50% 70% 90%
202	15% 30% 50% 70% 90%

The synthetic datasets were populated with binary values using the random function in Microsoft Excel. Due to probability, the random function can be expected to produce an approximately even distribution of 1s and 0s. To attain specific densities, we used the random function a second time on each dataset. For the 15% dataset, 7 out of 10 1s were randomly turned to 0s. For the 30% dataset, 4 out of 10 1s were randomly turned to 0s, and so on.

Generating the Similarity Matrices

We created a Java program to compute the similarity matrices. The program is available for download at http://userpages.umbc.edu/~lewisd1/simcoef/ and a brief demo appears in Appendix B (Figures 7 through 9).

When computing a similarity matrix, the first step is to determine the values of a, b, c, and d for each object pair in the data matrix. Given n objects, the number of one-to-one object pairs is:

$$\frac{n!}{2!(n-2)!}$$

Once these values are computed, they can be plugged into the similarity equations for the index computations. The output is a $n \times n$ triangular matrix showing the computed similarity between each file pair. We evaluated a total of 560 similarity matrices (16 datasets x 35 similarity coefficients).

Data Matrix

	f_1	f_2	f_3	f_4
o_1	1	1	0	0
o_2	1	0	1	0
o_3	0	0	0	1

Variable Matrix

	a	b	c	d
o_1 / o_2	1	1	1	1
o_1 / o_3	0	2	1	1
o_2 / o_3	0	2	2	0

Index Computation

$$o_1 / o_2 \quad \frac{1+1}{1+1+1+1} = .5$$

$$o_1 / o_3 \quad \frac{0+1}{0+2+1+1} = .25$$

$$o_2 / o_3 \quad \frac{0+0}{0+2+2+0} = 0$$

Similarity Coefficient Matrix

	o_1	o_2	o_3
o_1		.5	.25
o_2			0
o_3			

Evaluating the Coefficients

We consider two ways to measure the similarity namely (a) Actual similarity indices values and (b) similarity percentiles. We next describe these two evaluation methods. The first is a more obvious way to compare coefficient indices directly with each other, such that those with a higher value (typically closer to 1) produce a "better similarity." However, if we have labeled data we can use a more robust method of measuring similarity by looking at percentile similarities. This will give us a more normalized level of comparison across different types of coefficients. For example, let us say that Coefficient1 produces an index of .1 between file1 and file2, and an index of .9 between file1 and file3. Let us then say that Coefficient2 produces an index of .4 between file1 and file2, and an index of .6 between file1 and file3. When compared to each other, it could be said that Coefficient1 does a better job of identifying similar and dissimilar files than Coefficient2 because the resulting values fall closer to 1 and 0. However, when taken independently, Coefficient1 and Coefficient2 indicate the same thing-that file1 and file3 are more similar than file1 and file2. To account for this issue, we used percentiles as thresholds rather than fixed values in the labeled data.

To assess the performance of the coefficients, we first computed their accuracy with respect to the Software Artifacts dataset. We began by scanning each similarity matrix for file pairs with similarity indices in the upper 95th percentile. These file pairs were considered to be perfectly similar. We then generated confusion matrices by comparing the set of files ranked most similar by each coefficient to the set of files ranked most similar by the group of domain experts. We repeated the process using the similarity indices in the 90th percentile and 85th percentile as thresholds for perfect similarity.

The confusion matrices were also used to calculate precision and recall for each coefficient. The measures of accuracy, precision, and recall are defined as follows, where tp is the number of true positives, fn is the number of false negatives, fp is the number of false negatives, and tn is the number of true negatives.

- Accuracy $\dfrac{tp + tn}{tp + fn + fp + tn}$

- Precision $\dfrac{tp}{tp + fp}$

- Recall $\dfrac{tp}{tp + fn}$

The aforementioned steps apply only to labeled data. Because the synthetic datasets are not labeled, it was necessary to implement alternative analysis techniques. These techniques focused primarily on the qualitative analysis of various graphs plotting the similarity indices produced by each coefficient. One set of graphs depicts the similarity indices produced by each coefficient for every object pair (see Figures 1 through 6). These graphs show the sometimes subtle and sometimes extreme differences between the indices produced by the different coefficients. Certain trends emerge when comparing the graphs of different datasets.

EXPERIMENTAL RESULTS

Software Artifacts Dataset

The results of the accuracy, precision, and recall calculations are expressed in Table 1. We decided to average the values computed across the 95th, 90th, and 85th percentile thresholds. It is worth noting that accuracy and precision values generally decreased as the threshold was lowered, while recall values increased. Thus, the highest accuracy and precision values were achieved using the 95th percentile and the highest recall values were achieved using the 85th percentile.

Accuracy is the ratio of file pairs correctly identified as perfectly similar or dissimilar to the total number of file pairs. The maximum accuracy values were 94.39% within the asymmetric category, 94.74% within the symmetric category, and 94.39% within the hybrid category as shown in Table 1. We were somewhat surprised that a symmetric coefficient achieved the highest overall accuracy, as we consider the Software Artifacts dataset to be asymmetric (we care about the features a file does have than those it does not have).

Precision is the ratio of file pairs correctly identified as perfectly similar to the total number of file pairs correctly or incorrectly identified as perfectly similar. The maximum precision values were 55.70% within the asymmetric category, 59.04% within the symmetric category, and 55.70% within the hybrid category. Again, the highest overall value was achieved by a symmetric coefficient.

Recall is the ratio of file pairs correctly identified as perfectly similar to the total number of file pairs that were expected to be perfectly similar.

Figure 1. Similarity indices for synthetic dataset of 15% density and 40 attributes (asymmetric coefficients shown)

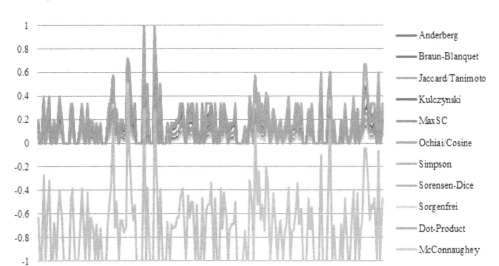

The maximum recall values were 73.33% within the asymmetric category, 86.67% within the symmetric category, and 86.67% within the hybrid category. Here, a symmetric coefficient and a hybrid coefficient tied for the highest overall value.

The coefficients performed with surprising consistency, regardless of category. The standard deviation among all accuracy values was only 0.007. The standard deviation for precision was .049, and the standard deviation for recall was .069. By comparison, the standard deviation among the actual coefficient indices (excluding those with an unbounded range) was .432. This shows that while the coefficients generate widely different indices, they still point to similar conclusions. That said many data mining algorithms are sensitive to distance thresholds. In such algorithms these minor differences will be a factor in deciding the most robust similarity coefficient which shows the highest accuracy. Accuracy is arguably the most important measure, as coefficients with the highest accuracy ratings can be said to do the best job of replicating human knowledge. With this dataset, all accuracy values were fairly high because only 10 of the

190 file pairs were expected to be perfectly similar.

Precision and recall values were lower, which means that a good number of file pairs were both incorrectly excluded and incorrectly included from the group of highly similar file pairs. Overall, each coefficient incorrectly included more file pairs than it incorrectly excluded. On average, the asymmetric coefficients found 69.69% of the file pairs that were expected to be perfectly similar. The symmetric coefficients found 71.11% of the file pairs, and the hybrid coefficients found 70.00%. The resultant sets also consisted of 45.76% false positives within the asymmetric category, 50.09% false positives within the symmetric category, and 52.92% false positives within the hybrid category. The top performing coefficients in each category are shown in Table 1. Overall, we found that:

- In terms of both accuracy and precision the top performer was Baulieu, a symmetric coefficient.
- Yule 1, also a symmetric coefficient, and Fossum, a hybrid coefficient, tied for best recall.

Table 1. Accuracy, precision, and recall of all coefficients (maximal values underlined)

	Coefficient Name	Accuracy	Precision	Recall
Asymmetric	Anderberg	.9421	.5483	.6333
	Braun-Blanquet	.9421	.5483	.6333
	Jaccard/Tanimoto	.9421	.5483	.6333
	Kulczynski	.9439	.5570	.7333
	MaxSC	.9351	.4983	.7333
	Ochiai/Cosine	.9439	.5570	.7333
	Simpson	.9351	.4983	.7333
	Sorensen-Dice	.9421	.5483	.7333
	Sorgenfrei	.9439	.5570	.6333
	Dot-Product	.9421	.5483	.7333
	McConnaughey	.9439	.5570	.7333
Symmetric	Baroni-Urbani & Buser	.9351	.4816	.7000
	Faith	.9421	.5483	.6000
	Ochiai 2	.9204	.5237	.6667
	Relative Matching	.9421	.5532	.6000
	Rogers & Tanimoto	.9228	.4227	.7000
	Simple Matching	.9228	.4227	.7000
	Sokal & Sneath	.9228	.4227	.8000
	Sokal & Sneath 4	.9404	.5237	.7333
	Baulieu	.9474	.5904	.6333
	Fleiss	.9404	.5237	.7333
	Goodman & Kruskal	.9421	.5483	.7333
	Hamann	.9228	.4227	.7000
	Kappa	.9404	.5237	.7333
	Loevinger	.9351	.4983	.7667
	Maxwell & Pilliner	.9404	.5237	.7333
	Michael	.9386	.5149	.5667
	Phi	.9404	.5237	.7333
	Scott	.9386	.5149	.7333
	Yule 1	.9333	.4728	.8667
	Yule 2	.9333	.4728	.7000
	Dennis	.9386	.4904	.7333
	Stiles	.9347	.4613	.7778
Hybrid	Russell & Rao	.9333	.4786	.5667
	Forbes	.9158	.3786	.6667
	Fossum	.9439	.5570	.8667

Figure 2. Similarity indices for synthetic dataset of 50% density and 120 attributes (asymmetric coefficients shown)

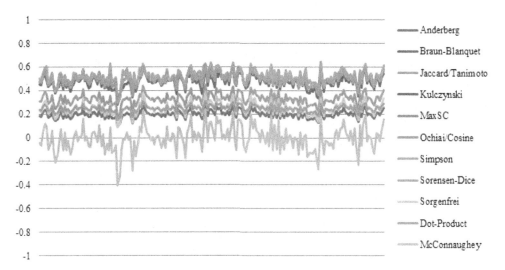

Overall, the coefficients did a fair job of finding the file pairs that the domain experts had identified as perfectly similar. However, for just about every file pair that was correctly identified, another file pair was incorrectly identified. This shows that similarity coefficients cannot always reflect the knowledge of human experts. As such, they may best be used as a supplementary tool in situations where intuition is important, or where data alone does not paint the full picture. The decision for selecting a coefficient also relies on the need whether the 1-1 match is more important than also considering a 0-0 match. This will be dependent on the domain.

Figure 3. Similarity indices for synthetic dataset of 90% density and 202 attributes (asymmetric coefficients shown)

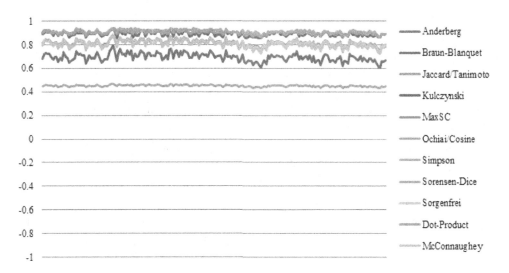

Figure 4. Similarity indices for synthetic dataset of 15% density and 40 attributes (symmetric coefficients shown)

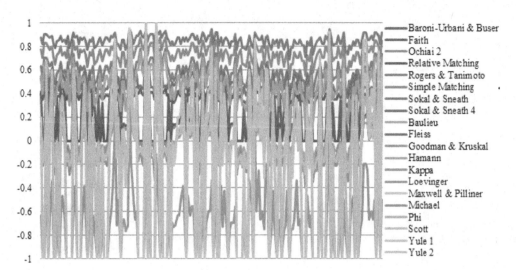

Synthetic Datasets

The values produced by each coefficient for the synthetic datasets of 15% density and 40 attributes, 50% density and 120 attributes, and 90% density and 202 attributes are depicted in Figures 2, 3 and 4 for asymmetric coefficients and in Figures 5 and 6 for symmetric coefficients. These graphs are shown because they represent the best overall cross section. Looking at the graphs, we are able to observe the following:

- The lines produced by each coefficient generally follow the same trend. Where one line has a positive slope, most other lines have a positive slope. Where one line has a negative slope, most other lines have a negative slope. Rarely do any two coefficients disagree entirely, with one indicating that a pair of objects is very dissimilar and another indicating that it is very similar. This reaffirms our earlier finding that, despite different equations, the coefficients typically agree on which pairs are similar and which are not.

- The coefficients differ, however, in how they rank the similar and dissimilar pairs. For example, looking at Figure 2, we see that Simpson ranks the F4/F9 and F4/F15 pairs as most similar. Sorensen-Dice, on the other hand, ranks F3/F16 as most similar. These differences are the main source of the accuracy, precision, and recall variations found in the prior section.

- Looking at Figure 2 again, we can clearly see that the values produced by McConnaughey differ considerably from the values produced by all other asymmetric coefficients. This highlights the need to use percentiles as thresholds rather than fixed values when identifying similar pairs. For example, if we used 0.6 as a threshold for high similarity, McConnaughey and a number of other coefficients would come up with nothing.

- By comparing the graphs of the symmetric coefficients (Figures 2, 3, and 4), it is clear that the lines become flatter and more elevated as data density and number of attributes increase. Because symmetric coef-

Figure 5. Similarity indices for synthetic dataset of 50% density and 120 attributes (symmetric coefficients shown)

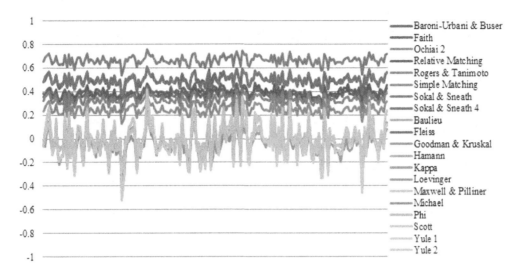

ficients interpret matching 1's as a similarity, the overall similarity among all items is higher when more 1's are in the dataset. This is why the lines become elevated. The lines grow flatter as the number of attributes increases because it becomes more likely that two items will have at least one attribute in common, and less likely that they will have all attributes in common.

• Comparing the graphs of asymmetric coefficients (Figures 5 and 6), we can see that most of the lines (with some exceptions) become flatter as the number of attributes increases. This occurs for the reason described in the previous bullet point. However, unlike the asymmetric coefficients, which produce their highest average values when there are many 1's, the symmetric coefficients produce their highest average values when there are an equal number of 1's and 0's.

We highlight some key findings using only the similarity indices values. This is an important analysis as many data mining algorithms are de-

pendent on distance thresholds. In such threshold sensitive algorithms the actual values of the coefficients play an important role.

Symmetric coefficients (those which include 0s): Sokal & Sneath consistently produces the highest similarity indices. However, Sokal & Sneath rarely generates 1s. Loevinger, Yule 1, and Yule 2 are tied for generating 1s most often. Although Yule 1 and Yule 2 produce some of the lowest similarity indices. Goodman and Kruskal produces the lowest indices in symmetric coefficients.

In general it was observed that the results fluctuated based on the density and the number of attributes in equal measure. For instance for density 15% all attribute sizes in the data from 40 to 202 consistently shows Sokal and Sneath as producing high similarity followed by Simple matching and Roger and Tanimoto. However as density increases to say 90% for all attribute sizes in the data from 40 to 202 again shows Sokal and Sneath as producing high similarity. However other coefficients also show up as high similarity indices namely Simple Matching, Relative

Figure 6. Similarity indices for synthetic dataset of 90% density and 202 attributes (symmetric coefficients shown)

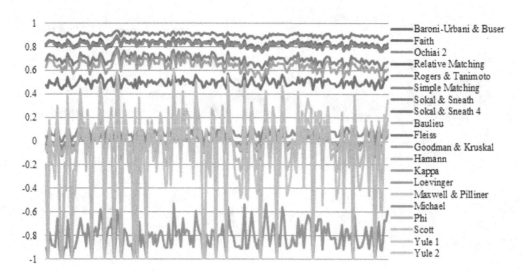

Matching, Baroni Urbani User, Faith and Rogers & Tanimoto coefficients.

Asymmetric coefficients (those which exclude 0s): These coefficients are equally affected by density more than the number of attributes in the data. We found that Sorgenfrei, Anderberg and Dot-Product produce low similarity values starting with a low density of 15%. However as density increases to

30% or 90% at varying attribute ranges then McConnaughey, Anderberg and Sorgenfrei perform better and produce somewhat higher similarity values. However in high similarity values we found that regardless of density or number of attributes Simpson and MaxSC produce highest similarity values and dot-product produces the lowest similarity values. In asymmetric coefficients the fluctuations are quite visible across varying density of the data.

Coefficients that produce results in an unbounded range are difficult to compare, as they operate on different scales. For sparse datasets Sokal & Sneath produced the highest similarity indices across all categories of coefficients. For the denser dataset, MaxSC/Simpson produced the

highest similarity indices across all categories of coefficients.

Although different coefficients may produce vastly different similarity indices for a file pair, the total similarity of each file remains remarkably consistent across different coefficients. This suggests that the core mechanics of most of the coefficients are, in fact, rather similar. Where they seem to primarily differ is in the intervals between indices.

CONCLUSION

Several similarity coefficients for binary valued data have been used in the literature, however there is no exhaustive study showing an empirical evaluation of such coefficients. In this paper we have presented such an empirical evaluation of similarity coefficients for binary valued data. We surveyed 35 similarity coefficients in various categories of symmetric, asymmetric and hybrid coefficients, used in various domains and present results about the efficacy of the similarity computed in (1) Labeled data to quantify the accuracy of the similarity coefficients, (2) varying density of the data to evaluate the effect of sparsity of the values, and (3) Varying number of attributes to see the effect of high dimensionality in the data on the similarity computed. Our findings in the labeled and synthetic data found conclusive results for the best and worst similarity coefficients. Some of the commonly used coefficients were not found in the top most similarity coefficients.

A key takeaway of this study is that the most intuitive and commonly used coefficients such as Jaccard and Simple Matching may not produce the best results. Jaccard, which is arguably the most widely used asymmetric coefficient, and Simple Matching, which is arguably the most widely used symmetric coefficient, performed low or midpack in tests of accuracy, precision, and recall (see Table 1). Many lesser known and more complex coefficients such as Baulieu, Yule 1, and Fossum achieved better results.

The study also indicates that coefficient categories may be unimportant, meaning that an asymmetric coefficient could potentially be applied to a symmetric dataset and vice-versa. The Software Artifacts dataset is decidedly asymmetric, but asymmetric coefficients were often outperformed by symmetric and hybrid coefficients.

Our experiments with varying density and number of attributes also showed measurable impact on both symmetric and asymmetric coefficients.

REFERENCES

Adam, N. R., Janeja, V. P., & Atluri, V. (2004). Neighborhood based detection of anomalies in high dimensional spatio-temporal sensor datasets. In *Proceedings of the 2004 ACM Symposium on Applied Computing*.

Ahmad, A., & Dey, L. (2007). A k-mean clustering algorithm for mixed numeric and categorical data. *Data & Knowledge Engineering, 63*(2), 503–527. doi:10.1016/j.datak.2007.03.016

Balestre, M., Von Pinho, R. G., Souza, J. C., & Lima, J. L. (2008). Comparison of maize similarity and dissimilarity genetic coefficients based on microsatellite markers. *Genetics and Molecular Research, 7*(3), 695–705. doi:10.4238/vol7-3gmr458

Baroni-Urbani, C., & Buser, M. W. (1976). Similarity of binary data. *Systematic Zoology, 25*(3), 251–259. doi:10.2307/2412493

Boyce, R. L., & Ellison, P. C. (2001). Choosing the best similarity index when performing fuzzy set ordination on binary data. *Journal of Vegetation Science, 12*, 711–720. doi:10.2307/3236912

Carrio, J. A., Pinto, F. R., Simas, C., Nunes, S., Sousa, N. G., & Frazão, N. (2005). Assessment of band-based similarity coefficients for automatic type and subtype classification of microbial isolates analyzed by pulsed-field gel electrophoresis. *Journal of Clinical Microbiology, 43*(11), 5483–5490. doi:10.1128/JCM.43.11.5483-5490.2005

Cha, S-H., Tappert, C., & Yoon, S. (2006). Enhancing binary feature vector similarity measures. *Journal of Pattern Recognition Research*, 63-77.

da Silva Meyer, A., Franco Garcia, A. A., Pereira de Souza, A., & Lopes de Souza, C. Jr. (2004). Comparison of similarity coefficients used for cluster analysis with dominant markers in maize (zea mays l). *Genetics and Molecular Biology, 27*(1), 83–91.

Dalirsefat, S., da Silva Meyer, A., & Mirhosein, S. Z. (2009). Comparison of similarity coefficients used for cluster analysis with amplified fragment length polymorphism markers in the silkworm, bombyx mori. *Journal of Insect Science, 9*, Retrieved from http://www.insectscience.org/9.71/. doi:10.1673/031.009.7101

Guha, S., Rastogi, R., & Shim, K. (2000). Rock: A robust clustering algorithm for categorical attributes. In *Proceedings of the 15th International Conference on Data Engineering*.

Haranczyk, M., & Holliday, J. (2008). Comparison of similarity coefficients for clustering and compound selection. *Journal of Chemical Information and Modeling, 48*(3), 498–508. doi:10.1021/ci700413a

Jackson, D. A., Somers, K. M., & Harvey, H. H. (1989). Similarity coefficients: Measures of co-occurrence and association or simply measures of occurrence? *American Naturalist, 133*(3), 436–453. doi:10.1086/284927

Janeja, V. P., Adam, N., Atluri, V., & Vaidya, J. (2010). Spatial neighborhood based anomaly detection in sensor datasets. *Data Mining and Knowledge Discovery, 20*(2), 221–258. doi:10.1007/s10618-009-0147-0

Karabatis, G., Chen, Z., Janeja, V. P., Lobo, T., Advani, M., Lindvall, M., & Feldmann, R. L. (2009). Using semantic networks and context in search for relevant software engineering artifacts. *Journal of Data Semantics.*

Kosman, E., & Leonard, K. J. (2005). Similarity coefficients for molecular markers in studies of genetic relationships between individuals for haploid, diploid, and polyploid species. *Molecular Ecology, 14*, 415–424. doi:10.1111/j.1365-294X.2005.02416.x

Lewis, D. M. (2008). *Using similarity coefficients to identify synonymous routers.*

Lewis, D. M., & Janeja, V. P. (2009). An evaluative comparison of similarity coefficients for binary valued data. In *Proceedings of ACM SIGMOD: Undergraduate Research Competition.*

Lindvall, M., Feldmann, R. L., Karabatis, G., Chen, Z., & Janeja, V. P. (2009). Searching for relevant software change artifacts using semantic networks. In *Proceedings of the Symposium on Applied Computing* (pp. 496-500).

Moura Duarte, J., Bosco dos Santos, J., & Cunha Melo, L. (1999). Comparison of similarity coefficients based on rapd markers in the common bean. *Genetics and Molecular Biology, 22*(3), 427–432.

Murguia, M., & Villasenor, J. L. (2003). Estimating the effect of the similarity coefficient and the cluster algorithm on biogeographic classifications. *Annales Botanici Fennici, 40*, 415–421.

Warrens, M. J. (2008). Bounds of resemblance measures for binary (presence/absence) variables. *Journal of Classification, 25*, 195–208. doi:10.1007/s00357-008-9024-6

Yang, Y., Claramunt, C., Aufaure, M., & Zhang, W. (2010). User-Centric Similarity and Proximity Measures for Spatial Personalization. *International Journal of Data Warehousing and Mining, 6*(2), 59–78. doi:10.4018/jdwm.2010040104

Yin, Y., & Yasuda, K. (2005). Similarity coefficient methods applied to the cell formation problem: a comparative investigation. *Computers & Industrial Engineering, 48*, 471–489. doi:10.1016/j.cie.2003.01.001

Zhang, X., Jing, L., Hu, X., Ng, M. K., Jiangxi, J., & Zhou, X. (2008). Medical Document Clustering Using Ontology-Based Term Similarity Measures. *International Journal of Data Warehousing and Mining, 4*(1), 62–73. doi:10.4018/jdwm.2008010104

APPENDIX A

Table 2. All coefficients and their properties

Asymmetric, 0 to 1 range

Anderberg

Expression:
$$\frac{a}{a + 2(b + c)}$$

Prior Uses: Biochemistry & Molecular Biology; Genetics & Heredity

References: da Silva Meyer, Franco Garcia, Pereira de Souza, & Lopes de Souza, 2004; Moura Duarte, Bosco dos Santos, & Cunha Melo, 1999; Yin & Yasuda, 2005; Yin & Yasuda, 2005

Braun-Blanquet

Expression:
$$\frac{a}{\max(a + b, a + c)}$$

Prior Uses: Ecology; Plant Sciences; Forestry; Biology; Environmental Sciences

References: Jackson, Somers, & Harvey, 1989; Warrens, 2008

Jaccard/Tanimoto

Expression:
$$\frac{a}{a + b + c}$$

Prior Uses: Plant Sciences; Agronomy; Horticulture; Genetics & Heredity; Ecology

References: Balestre, Von Pinho, Souza, & Lima, 2008; Boyce & Ellison, 2001; Carrio et al., 2005; Cha, Tappert, & Yoon, 2006; da Silva Meyer et al., 2004; Dalirsefat, da Silva Meyer, & Mirhosein, 2009; Haranczyk & Holliday, 2008; Jackson et al., 1989; Kosman & Leonard, 2005; Moura Duarte et al., 1999; Murguia & Villasenor, 2003; Warrens, 2008; Yin & Yasuda, 2005

Kulczynski

Expression:
$$.5\left(\frac{a}{a + b} + \frac{a}{a + c}\right)$$

Prior Uses: Marine & Freshwater Biology; Ecology; Agriculture; Chemistry; Forestry

References: Boyce & Ellison, 2001; Haranczyk & Holliday, 2008; Murguia & Villasenor, 2003; Warrens, 2008; Yin & Yasuda, 2005

continued on following page

Table 2. Continued

Ochiai/Cosine

Expression:
$$\frac{a}{\sqrt{(a+b)(a+c)}}$$

Prior Uses: Computer Science; Analytical Chemistry; Information Science & Library Science; Biochemical Research Methods; Chemistry

References: Balestre et al., 2008; Boyce & Ellison, 2001; da Silva Meyer et al., 2004; Haranczyk & Holliday, 2008; Jackson et al., 1989; Moura Duarte et al., 1999; Warrens, 2008; Yin & Yasuda, 2005

Simpson

Expression:
$$\frac{a}{\min(a+b, a+c)}$$

Prior Uses: Ecology; Microbiology; Paleontology; Biodiversity Conservation; Biotechnology & Applied Microbiology

References: Carrio et al., 2005; Dalirsefat et al., 2009; Haranczyk & Holliday, 2008; Jackson et al., 1989; Kosman & Leonard, 2005; Murguia & Villasenor, 2003; Warrens, 2008

Sorensen-Dice

Expression:
$$\frac{2a}{2a+b+c}$$

Prior Uses: Biochemistry & Molecular Biology; Genetics & Heredity; Agriculture; Biology; Plant Sciences

References: Balestre et al., 2008; Boyce & Ellison, 2001; Cha et al., 2006; da Silva Meyer et al., 2004; Jackson et al., 1989; Kosman & Leonard, 2005; Moura Duarte et al., 1999; Warrens, 2008; Yin & Yasuda, 2005

Sorgenfrei

Expression:
$$\frac{a^2}{(a+b)(a+c)}$$

Prior Uses: Industrial Engineering; Manufacturing Engineering; Operations Research & Management Science

References: Warrens, 2008; Yin & Yasuda, 2005

Asymmetric, 0 to .5 range

Dot-Product

Expression:
$$\frac{a}{2a+b+c}$$

Prior Uses: Analytical Chemistry, Artificial Intelligence, Computer Science, Biochemistry & Molecular Biology, Biotechnology & Applied Microbiology

References: Yin & Yasuda, 2005

continued on following page

Table 2. Continued

Asymmetric, -1 to 1 range

McConnaughey

Expression:
$$\frac{a^2 - bc}{(a + b)(a + c)}$$

Prior Uses: Mathematics; Mathematical Psychology

References: Warrens, 2008

Symmetric, 0 to 1 range

Baroni-Urbani & Buser

Expression:
$$\frac{a + \sqrt{ad}}{a + b + c + \sqrt{ad}}$$

Prior Uses: Ecology; Chemistry; Physical Geography; Biodiversity Conservation; Information Systems

References: Baroni-Urbani & Buser, 1976; Boyce & Ellison, 2001; Haranczyk & Holliday, 2008; Yin & Yasuda, 2005

Faith

Expression:
$$\frac{a + .5d}{a + b + c + d}$$

Prior Uses: Plant Sciences; Ecology; Forestry

References: Boyce & Ellison, 2001

Ochiai 2

Expression:
$$\frac{ad}{\sqrt{(a + b)(a + c)(d + b)(d + c)}}$$

Prior Uses: Biochemistry & Molecular Biology; Genetics & Heredity

References: da Silva Meyer et al., 2004; Moura Duarte et al., 1999;

Relative Matching

Expression:
$$\frac{a + \sqrt{ad}}{a + b + c + d \sqrt{ad}}$$

Prior Uses: Zoology

References: Jackson et al., 1989

continued on following page

Table 2. Continued

Rogers & Tanimoto

Expression: $$\frac{a+d}{a+d+2(b+c)}$$

Prior Uses: Biochemistry & Molecular Biology; Genetics & Heredity; Agriculture; Ecology; Forestry

References: Balestre et al., 2008; Baroni-Urbani & Buser, 1976; Boyce & Ellison, 2001; da Silva Meyer et al., 2004; Haranczyk & Holliday, 2008; Jackson et al., 1989; Moura Duarte et al., 1999; Yin & Yasuda, 2005

Simple Matching

Expression: $$\frac{a+d}{a+b+c+d}$$

Prior Uses: Plant Sciences; Biotechnology & Applied Microbiology; Electrical & Electronic Engineering; Agronomy; Microbiology

References: Balestre et al., 2008; Boyce & Ellison, 2001; da Silva Meyer et al., 2004; Dalirsefat et al., 2009; Haranczyk & Holliday, 2008; Jackson et al., 1989; Moura Duarte et al., 1999; Yin & Yasuda, 2005

Sokal & Sneath

Expression: $$\frac{2(a+d)}{2(a+d)+b+c}$$

Prior Uses: Plant Sciences; Agronomy; Genetics & Heredity; Immunology; Soil Science

References: Baroni-Urbani & Buser, 1976; Yin & Yasuda, 2005

Sokal & Sneath 4

Expression: $$.25\left(\frac{a}{a+b}+\frac{a}{a+c}+\frac{a}{b+d}+\frac{a}{c+d}\right)$$

Prior Uses: Industrial Engineering; Manufacturing Engineering; Operations Research & Management Science

References: Yin & Yasuda, 2005

Symmetric, -1 to 1 range

Baulieu

Expression: $$\frac{4(ad-bc)}{(a+b+c+d)^2}$$

Prior Uses: Mathematics; Mathematical Psychology

References: Warrens, 2008

continued on following page

Table 2. Continued

Fleiss

Expression:
$$\frac{(ad - bc)[(a + b)(c + d) + (a + c)(b + d)]}{2(a + b)(a + c)(d + b)(d + c)}$$

Prior Uses: Statistics & Probability; Health Sciences & Services; Mathematical & Computational Biology; Biology; Clinical Neurology

References: Warrens, 2008

Goodman & Kruskal

Expression:
$$\frac{2\min(a, d) - b - c}{2\min(a, d) + b + c}$$

Prior Uses: Statistics & Probability; Public, Environmental, & Occupational Health; Infectious Diseases; Mathematical Psychology; Mathematics

References: Warrens, 2008

Hamann

Expression:
$$\frac{(a + d) - (b + c)}{a + b + c + d}$$

Prior Uses: Agriculture; Biochemistry & Molecular Biology; Genetics & Heredity; Mathematics

References: Balestre et al., 2008; Yin & Yasuda, 2005

Kappa

Expression:
$$\frac{(ad - bc)}{(b + a)(b + d) + (c + a)(c + d)}$$

Prior Uses: Radiology, Nuclear Medicine, & Medical Imaging; Public, Environmental, & Occupational Health; Clinical Neurology; Orthopedics; Surgery

References: Warrens, 2008

Loevinger

Expression:
$$\frac{ad - bc}{\min[(b + a)(b + d), (c + a)(c + d)]}$$

Prior Uses: Mathematics; Mathematical Psychology; Social Sciences; Experimental Statistics & Probability; Neurosciences

References: Warrens, 2008

continued on following page

Table 2. Continued

Maxwell & Pilliner

Expression:

$$\frac{2(ad - bc)}{(a + b)(c + d) + (a + c)(b + d)}$$

Prior Uses: Mathematics; Mathematical Psychology

References: Warrens, 2008

Michael

Expression:

$$\frac{4(ad - bc)}{(a + d)^2 + (b + c)^2}$$

Prior Uses: Mathematics; Mathematical Psychology

References: Warrens, 2008

Phi

Expression:

$$\frac{ad - bc}{\sqrt{(a + b)(a + c)(d + b)(d + c)}}$$

Prior Uses: Mathematics; Social Sciences; Mathematical Psychology; Thermodynamics; Physical Chemistry

References: Haranczyk & Holliday, 2008; Jackson et al., 1989; Warrens, 2008; Yin & Yasuda, 2005

Scott

Expression:

$$\frac{4ad - (b + c)^2}{(2a + b + c)(2d + b + c)}$$

Prior Uses: Mathematics; Social Sciences; Mathematical Psychology

References: Warrens, 2008

Yule 1

Expression:

$$\frac{ad - bc}{ad + bc}$$

Prior Uses: Information Systems; Imaging Science & Photographic Technology; Information Science & Library Science; Statistics & Probability; Agriculture

References: Haranczyk & Holliday, 2008; Jackson et al., 1989; Warrens, 2008; Yin & Yasuda, 2005

continued on following page

Table 2. Continued

Yule 2

Expression:

$$\frac{\sqrt{ad} - \sqrt{bc}}{\sqrt{ad} + \sqrt{bc}}$$

Prior Uses: Mathematics; Social Sciences; Mathematical Psychology

References: Warrens, 2008

Symmetric, -∞ to ∞ range

Dennis

Expression:

$$\frac{ad - bc}{\sqrt{(a + b + c + d)(a + b)(a + c)}}$$

Prior Uses: Chemistry; Information Systems; Computer Science

References: Haranczyk & Holliday, 2008

Stiles

Expression:

$$\log_{10} \frac{(a + b + c + d)\left[|ad - bc| - .5(a + b + c + d)\right]^2}{(a + b)(a + c)(b + c)(c + d)}$$

Prior Uses: Chemistry; Information Systems; Computer Science

References: Haranczyk & Holliday, 2008

Hybrid, 0 to 1 range

Russell & Rao

Expression:

$$\frac{a}{a + b + c + d}$$

Prior Uses: Chemistry; Information Systems; Computer Science; Ecology; Forestry

References: Balestre et al., 2008; Boyce & Ellison, 2001; da Silva Meyer et al., 2004; Haranczyk & Holliday, 2008; Jackson et al., 1989; Moura Duarte et al., 1999; Yin & Yasuda, 2005

Hybrid, 0 to ∞ range

Forbes

Expression:

$$\frac{a(a + b + c + d)}{(a + b)(a + c)}$$

Prior Uses: Chemistry; Information Systems; Computer Science

References: Haranczyk & Holliday, 2008

continued on following page

Table 2. Continued

Fossum

Expression: $\dfrac{(a+b+c+d)(a-.5)^2}{(a+b)(a+c)}$

Prior Uses: Chemistry; Computer Science; Information Systems

References: Haranczyk & Holliday, 2008; Warrens, 2008

APPENDIX B

Figure 7. Press "Browse" and select the file with the binary matrix that you want to analyze (files should be plaintext with undelimited or comma-separated values). Then press "Open".

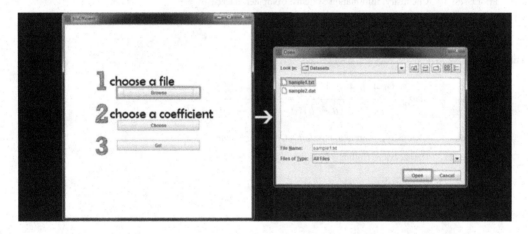

Figure 8. Press "Choose" to see a list of all 35 coefficients. Further information on each coefficient is available by pressing the "i" button next to the coefficient's name. One, some, or all of the coefficients may be selected.

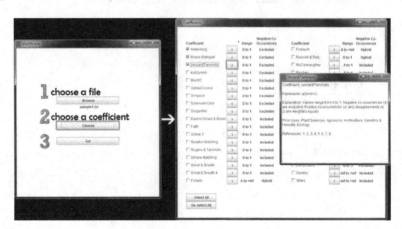

Figure 9. Press "Go" to generate the coefficient matrices. Output files are saved in the same directory as the input file. The output filename is the name of the input file followed by the coefficient name (such as "sample1-Anderberg").

Chapter 7
Dynamic View Management System for Query Prediction to View Materialization

Negin Daneshpour
Amirkabir University of Technology, Iran

Ahmad Abdollahzadeh Barfourosh
Amirkabir University of Technology, Iran

ABSTRACT

On-Line Analytical Processing (OLAP) systems based on data warehouses are the main systems for managerial decision making and must have a quick response time. Several algorithms have been presented to select the proper set of data and elicit suitable structured environments to handle the queries submitted to OLAP systems, which are called view selection algorithms to materialize. As users' requirements may change during run time, materialization must be viewed dynamically. In this work, the authors propose and operate a dynamic view management system to select and materialize views with new and improved architecture, which predicts incoming queries through association rule mining and three probabilistic reasoning approaches: Conditional probability, Bayes' rule, and Naïve Bayes' rule. The proposed system is compared with DynaMat system and Hybrid system through two standard measures. Experimental results show that the proposed dynamic view selection system improves these measures. This system outperforms DynaMat and Hybrid for each type of query and each sequence of incoming queries.

INTRODUCTION

OLAP is defined as online analytical processing system to answer the multidimensional queries (Dehne et al., 2008; Lawrence & Rau-Chaplin, 2008; Ravat et al., 2008). Multidimensional queries are complex and operate on huge amount of data, furthermore; these queries are used to managerial decisions in decision support systems (DSS) and data mining.

Multidimensional structures are used to decrease query response time. Multidimensional

DOI: 10.4018/978-1-4666-2148-0.ch007

structures, data cube, are the structures of the Data warehouses to represent data sources.

To achieve analytical process of queries, data cubes store data in different summarization degree related to the aggregation function type. When we have multidimensional data, we can construct a lattice of cuboids which contains data in different level of summarization. The cuboid which stores data in the minimum level of summarization is called "base cuboid" and another cuboid which stores data in the maximum level of summarization is called "apex cuboid".

Data cubes are pre-computed and stored in data warehouses in the form of materialized views to improve query response time. Data cube computation is time and money consuming and various researches have been done to improve query response time based on parallel processing, index selection and view selection (Agrawal, Chaudhuri, & Narasayya, 2000, Agrawal, Chaudhuri, Kollar, Marathe, Narasayya, & Syamala, 2004; Agrawal, Narasayya, & Yang, 2004; Asgharzadeh Talebi et al., 2008; Chaudhuri, 1997; Le et al., 2007; Taniar et al., 2008; Taniar & Wenny Rahayu, 2002a, 2002b, 2002c, 2002d, 2004).

We focus on view selection techniques which are the main issue to construct data warehouses (Ahmed et al., 2007; Aouiche et al., 2006; Aouiche & Darmont, 2009; Choi et al., 2003; Gong & Zhao, 2008; Gupta, 1997; Gupta & Mumick, 2005; Harinarayan et al., 1996; Hung et al., 2007; Kalnis et al., 2002; Kotidis & Roussopoulos, 1999, 2001; Lawrence & Rau-Chaplin, 2008; Mahboudi et al., 2006; Nadeau & Teorey, 2002; Phan & Li, 2008; Ramachandran et al., 2005; Shah et al., 2006; Shukla et al., 1998; Valluri et al., 2002; Xu et al., 2007; Zhang et al., 2003).

Other important issues in data warehousing are: multidimensional design methodologies, partitioning methods, refreshment mechanisms, building XML data warehouses, and warehousing XML documents (Bellatreche et al., 2009; Chen et al., 2010; Maurer et al. 2009; Romero & Abello, 2009; Rusu et al., 2005, 2006, 2009).

Three choices for view materialization are reported (Han & Kamber, 2006):

1. **Base Cuboid Materialization:** In this choice, only base cuboid, which can be used to answer all multidimensional aggregated queries, is pre-calculated and materialized.
2. **Full Materialization:** In this choice, all of the cuboids, which are answers to all multidimensional aggregated queries, are pre-calculated and materialized.
3. **Partial Materialization:** In this choice, the proper subset of the whole set of possible cuboids which is the answers to some multidimensional aggregated queries, is selected, pre-calculated and materialized.

The first choice requires minimum amount of memory to materialize a view which is sufficient to calculate the answers of all multidimensional aggregated queries; but it could be slow and leads to expensive process of computing multidimensional aggregates on the fly.

The second choice has quick response time; but it requires huge amounts of memory space in order to store all of the pre-computed cuboids and it will be time consuming processes to maintain all of them.

The third choice, which could be more efficient, presents an interesting trade-off between storage space and response time.

There are several works that present techniques for partial materialization which we call view selection techniques (Ahmed et al., 2007; Aouiche et al., 2006; Aouiche & Darmont, 2009; Asgharzadeh Talebi et al., 2008; Choi et al., 2003; El-Helw et al., 2009; Gong & Zhao, 2008; Gou et al., 2006; Gupta, 1997; Gupta & Mumick, 2005; Hanusse, 2009; Harinarayan et al., 1996; Hung et al., 2007; Kalnis et al., 2002; Kotidis & Roussopoulos, 1999, 2001; Lawrence & Rau-Chaplin, 2008; Lin & Kuo, 2004; Liu et al., 2008; Mahboudi et al., 2006; Nadeau & Teorey, 2002; Phan & Li, 2008; Ramachandran et al., 2005; Sapia, 1999;

Shah et al., 2006; Shukla et al., 1998; Valluri et al., 2002; Xu et al., 2007; Zhang et al., 2003). We investigated and analyzed them in our previous works (Daneshpour & Abdollahzadeh Barfourosh, 2008, in press).

Space limitation to store views and view maintenance cost are two constraining factors for choosing views to be materialized. Because of limitation in resources, space is a constraining factor.

Views are maintained when systems are off-line. When the maintenance time is bigger than offline time of the system, we should reduce this time by discarding some materialized views.

We divided view selection techniques into two main groups:

- **Static Techniques:** Which views are selected and materialized before processing the first query. These views are maintained until the processing of the last query.
- **Dynamic Techniques:** Which views are selected and materialized during query processing and they can be changed and removed during run time based on change in users' requirements.

Dynamic view materialization techniques will change the set of the materialized views during run time. Changes are based on users' requirements which we assume to change frequently and make the queries unknown to the system. To improve dynamic view materialization techniques, it is necessary to analyze queries' changes and in order to do this, based on the parts of the queries which are going to be affected, we categorize three types:

1. Queries' dimensions may change.
2. Queries' aggregate functions may change.
3. Queries' measure may change.

In all three types, static techniques decide to materialize views once considering all possible queries and limited space, but dynamic techniques decide to materialize views periodically considering incoming queries at that time and limited space. These techniques are more flexible and efficient on time and space than static techniques.

Dynamic techniques are more complex than static ones, because in these techniques it is important to find the suitable time to materialize predicted views and moreover we should identify insignificant old materialized views to be deleted.

Dynamic techniques use algorithms based on query prediction which is going to be done in two directions: indirectly (Choi et al., 2003; Gong & Zhao, 2008; Kalnis et al., 2002; Kotidis & Roussopoulos, 1999, 2001; Lawrence & Rau-Chaplin, 2008; Phan & Li, 2008; Xu et al., 2007; Zhang et al., 2003), directly (Ramachandran et al., 2005; Shah et al., 2006).

Hybrid algorithm (Ramachandran et al., 2005; Shah et al., 2006) is the only algorithm which directly uses query prediction, and is based on probabilistic reasoning and uses Markov chain models to predict the next queries.

The results of Hybrid algorithm is promising and make intend to investigate prediction techniques and the other techniques introduced in probabilistic reasoning such as: Conditional probability, Bayes' rule, Naïve Bayes' rule, Monte Carlo algorithms, Dempster-Shafer theory, Fuzzy logic, Rule-based approaches, and so on (Russell & Norvig, 2003).

To predict future data trends, classification techniques and regression analysis are two forms of data analysis that can be used. Classification predicts categorical (discrete, unordered) labels, while regression models continuous-valued functions. Whereas we want to predict the next query definition which is a categorical label, classification techniques are suitable.

Many classification techniques have been proposed by researchers, and some of the most operational of them are: Decision tree classifiers, Bayesian classifier, Naïve Bayesian Classifier, Rule based classifiers, Backpropagation, Support Vector Machines, Classification based on association rule mining, K-nearest-neighbor classifiers, Case-Based Reasoning, Genetic Algorithms, Rough Set Approach, and Fuzzy logic techniques.

Whereas we want to predict the next query, while queries are entered sequentially, sequential pattern mining which is a sequential version of association rule mining is the suitable choice.

This work presents a new dynamic view selection system (PR_Q_Predictor system) using association rule mining and probabilistic reasoning approaches to predict the next query. PR_Q_Predictor system first classifies past queries by association rule analysis which is a two-step process consisting of frequent item-set mining, followed by rule generation (Han & Kamber, 2006), and then predicts the next query using generated rules.

PR_Q_Predictor system classifies past queries in two-step process. The first step searches for patterns of queries that occur repeatedly in incoming queries, where each query is considered an item and the resulting queries form frequent item-sets. The second step analyzes the frequent item-sets in order to generate association rules. These rules are represented in the form of the sequential queries and their last query occurrence probability which is calculated through three probabilistic reasoning approaches which are: Conditional probability, Bayes' rule, and Naïve Bayes' rule.

The architecture of PR_Q_Predictor system which will take probabilistic reasoning approaches to predict the next query will be introduced. PR_Q_Predictor system comparing with Hybrid system which uses Markov chain models to predict a sequence of incoming drill-down queries, predicts the next query through the other techniques of probabilistic reasoning approaches without the assumption that queries are drill-down. Therefore, it can be used to predict each type of queries (drill-down queries, roll-up queries, slice or dice queries).

Moreover, this work presents an experimental environment to compare the proposed system with other systems. We surveyed important systems

and categorized them based on their techniques, and then analyzed the systems with different techniques. Among these systems, due to difference on assumptions we choose Dynamat system (Kotidis & Roussopoulos, 1999, 2001) and Hybrid system (Ramachandran et al., 2005; Shah et al., 2006) for comparisons. The other well known systems such as (Choi et al., 2003; Gong & Zhao, 2008; Kalnis et al., 2002; Phan & Li, 2008; Xu et al., 2007; Zhang et al., 2003) are not justified to be compared because of their inputs and assumptions.

DynaMat system was selected to compare with PR_Q_Predictor system, because it is a well-known dynamic view management system and can be used for each type of queries.

We also selected Hybrid system to compare with the proposed system, because it uses probabilistic reasoning approaches to predict incoming sequence of queries and outperforms DynaMat for drill-down queries and corresponds with the assumption of PR_Q_Predictor system.

We use two evaluation parameters to evaluate the proposed approaches and compare them with other systems. These are the Detailed Cost Saving Ratio (DCSR) and the total number of view replacements in the pool with new selections which are the standard parameters and have been used in the previous works (Kotidis & Roussopoulos, 1999; Shah et al., 2006).

DCSR captures the different levels of effectiveness of the materialized data with regard to the incoming queries. The total number of view replacements in the pool helps in assessing the frequency with which a replacement routine is involved.

Experimental results show that our approaches outperform DynaMat approaches and Hybrid system.

Execution time can be measured and calculated as an evaluation parameter in this regard too, but it has the same effect as DCSR because DCSR uses the size of tuples in the views used to answer incoming queries, to measure the effectiveness. When this size increases, the execution time of incoming queries increases too. Then this measure has direct effect to execution time and we don't measure execution time as another evaluation parameter.

The remainder of this work is organized as follows: in the next section some well-known view selection algorithms are described. The justification of the technique used in the proposed system is presented. The architecture of the proposed dynamic view selection system and the algorithm of the approaches are then discussed. We define our experimental environment, and evaluation parameters, and then present the experimental results compared with DynaMat and Hybrid. Conclusions of this work are also presented.

RELATED WORKS

There are algorithms for view materialization (Aouiche et al., 2006; Aouiche & Darmont, 2009; Choi et al., 2003; Gong & Zhao, 2008; Gupta, 1997; Gupta & Mumick, 2005; Harinarayan et al., 1996; Hung et al., 2007; Kalnis et al., 2002; Kotidis & Roussopoulos, 1999, 2001; Lawrence & Rau-Chaplin, 2008; Mahboudi et al., 2006; Nadeau & Teorey, 2002; Phan & Li, 2008; Ramachandran et al., 2005; Shah et al., 2006; Shukla et al., 1998; Valluri et al., 2002; Xu et al., 2007; Zhang et al., 2003) which we investigated and analyzed them in our previous works (Daneshpour & Abdollahzadeh Barfourosh, 2008, in press).

Some of the view materialization algorithms are static (Aouiche et al., 2006; Aouiche & Darmont, 2009; Asgharzadeh Talebi et al., 2008; El-Helw et al., 2009; Gou et al., 2006; Gupta, 1997; Gupta & Mumick, 2005; Hanusse, 2009; Harinarayan et al., 1996; Hung et al., 2007; Kalnis et al., 2002; Lawrence & Rau-Chaplin, 2008; Lin & Kuo, 2004; Mahboudi et al., 2006; Nadeau & Teorey, 2002; Shukla et al., 1998; Valluri et al., 2002) and the others are dynamic (Choi et al., 2003; Gong & Zhao, 2008; Kalnis et al., 2002; Kotidis & Roussopoulos, 1999; Kotidis & Roussopoulos,

2001; Lawrence & Rau-Chaplin, 2008; Phan & Li, 2008; Ramachandran et al., 2005; Shah et al., 2006; Xu et al., 2007; Zhang et al., 2003).

Static algorithms select and materialize views before processing the first query and these views are maintained firm until processing the last query. In these algorithms some cuboids of a cube are selected and materialized as views in an allocated pool based on the benefit functions. These functions frequently depend on the query processing cost and the cost of updating materialized views.

Since users' requirements may change during the time, static algorithms cannot work efficiently and it is better to have a dynamic technique to select views. Therefore, we consider some dynamic algorithms and finally present a system which dynamically selects views.

We surveyed dynamic algorithms and divided them into two categories based on their incoming workloads:

1.   Algorithms with a predefined workload.
2.   Algorithms with an unknown workload.

In case one, authors assume that the incoming workload is predefined. This workload is a sequence of queries and updates statements. They proposed algorithms (XTZ and PL algorithms) which materialize views dynamically assuming predefined workloads (Phan & Li, 2008; Xu et al., 2007).

In case two the workload is not predefined (Choi et al., 2003; Gong & Zhao, 2008; Kalnis et al., 2002; Kotidis & Roussopoulos, 1999, 2001; Lawrence & Rau-Chaplin, 2008; Ramachandran et al., 2005; Shah et al., 2006; Zhang et al., 2003). Whereas users' requirements are unknown, we focus on these algorithms.

As we compare our work with (Kotidis & Roussopoulos, 1999; Shah et al., 2006), we present the techniques of these two works in more detail. At the end of this section, we present a table containing the comparisons and analysis of the techniques used in the algorithms with an unknown workload and their limitations.

DynaMat system is presented in (Kotidis & Roussopoulos, 1999, 2001). The architecture of the system consists of these components: View Pool, Fragment Locator, Directory Index, and Admission Control Entity, which will be described below.

- View Pool is the information repository that is used for storing materialized results.
- Fragment Locator is used to determine whether or not already materialized results can be efficiently used to answer the query.
- A Directory Index is maintained in order to support sub-linear search in View Pool for finding candidate materialized results. If the search fails to reveal an efficient way to use data stored in View Pool for answering the query, the system follows the conventional approach where the warehouse infrastructure (fact table + indices) is queried.
- Admission Control Entity decides whether or not it is beneficial to store the result of the query in the Pool.

DynaMat system has two constraining factors: Time constraint to update materialized results, and Space constraint to store views. Each time DynaMat reaches the space or time bounds it uses a benefit measure for replacing materialized views.

DynaMat uses four different benefit measures which are:

1. **Least Recently Used (LRU):** Least Recently Used materialized views are selected to replace.
2. **Least Frequently Used (LFU):** Least Frequently Used materialized views are selected to replace.
3. **Smaller-Fragment-First (SFF):** Smaller materialized views are selected to replace.
4. **Smaller-Penalty-First (SPF):** Materialized views with smaller SPF are selected to re-

place. This measure is computed through the product of the frequency of using the materialized view and the cost of re-computing it from its father, divided to its size.

As long as there is enough space in the pool, results from incoming queries are always stored in it. In cases where DynaMat hits the space constraint, it has to enforce a replacement policy. This decision is made using the benefit measure of the materialized views.

When the base relations are updated, the materialized views have to be updated. In cases where DynaMat has the time constraint, it has to enforce a maintenance policy.

DynaMat system was experimented and compared with a system that is given all queries in advance and the pre-computed optimal static view selection. The comparison is made based on the average cost saving to answer input queries for quantifying the benefits of view materialization against incoming queries. These experiments showed that DynaMat's dynamic view selection outperforms the optimal static view selection and consequently, any sub-optimal static algorithm that has appeared in the literature (Baralis et al., 1997; Gupta, 1997; Gupta et al., 1997; Harinarayan et al., 1996).

We compare our system with DynaMat which is a well known system and the most similar one to it.

Applications of randomized search heuristics (Kalnis et al., 2002), namely Iterative Improvement and Simulated Annealing select a suboptimal set of views in a short time. The search space of this system is an undirected graph, consisting of nodes and edges.

Each node (also called state) corresponds to a candidate solution that is a set of views which meets the space or time constraint. Each node has a querying cost assigned to it and the aim of this system is to find the query with the minimum cost. An edge defines a move (or transition) from one state to another after applying a simple transformation.

Randomized algorithms start from a random initial state and apply sequences of transformations trying to detect the global minimum (minimum cost) which is the best state and has the best set of views to materialize. In this algorithm some parts of the space are not extensively searched and good local minimal may be missed.

In Choi et al. (2003), a dynamic predicate-based partitioning system is proposed (DMP algorithm). It partitions views/tables based on user predicates dynamically. Each partition is stored in a table in a commercial multidimensional database. It assumes that allocated pool to store materialized views is large enough to store the base cuboid.

In order to eliminate the overhead, DMP system attempts to select one partition to answer a given query. When there is not any single partition that can answer the query, there are two ways to solve it: 1) Use a whole materialized view to answer the query; 2) Use the base tables to answer the query.

When there is a materialized view available for answering the query, the system considers whether it needs to repartition the materialized view after processing the query.

When a user query is issued, and it cannot be answered using a partition but a materialized view, V, the system calculates the predicate benefits to see whether there is any change in the m top predicates associated with V, by taking both of the predicates used in q and V into account. If there is any change in the m top predicates, the system repartitions V using the new m predicates.

DMP system was experimented in various conditions, but it was not compared with other dynamic systems. Its algorithm is simple, but it materializes a small number of views that suffers from low variety, because it starts from base cuboid as a first partition and after each query arrival partitions existing partitions. For this reason we don't compare our system with it.

In Zhang et al. (2003), a genetic algorithm is presented to select a set of nodes in a DAG (Directed Acyclic Graph) of incoming queries to materialize. In this work, first a DAG of incom-

ing queries is generated. Then some of the nodes of this DAG are selected to materialize through a genetic algorithm. These nodes are selected to materialize so that the total cost of query processing, view maintenance, and reorganization cost is minimal.

Materialized view reorganization cost is a cost of generating new materialized views from the old materialized views and the base relations.

This algorithm against the others selects the parts of queries to materialize and join them to respond queries. Therefore, it requires extra time to join materialized views to process some queries and we don't compare our system with it.

The main consideration of (Lawrence & Rau-Chaplin, 2008) is an OLAP system (LC algorithm) with two phases of operation: Startup and Online. In the Startup Phase an initial set of views are selected based on some estimated query probabilities. This is the classical (static) view selection problem. In the Online Phase an "in use" OLAP system is considered, for which a set of views M has already been selected and materialized.

LC algorithm develops online adaptations of the greedy heuristic introduced by Harinarayan et al. (1996) and three randomized techniques (iterative improvement, simulated annealing and two-phase optimization) initially proposed for static view selection by Kalnis et al. (2002)

For the static phase, the randomized methods must be adapted so as to take into account maintenance cost in addition to the space constraint while for the online phase all of the methods must be adapted to take into account the existing pool of previously materialized views.

Experiments show that the greedy heuristic-online adaptation outperforms the three randomized methods. However, as the number of dimensions grows the computational cost of greedy heuristic-online may become impractically large and in this case the randomized methods offer an attractive alternative.

LC system was experimented for the above mentioned two types of algorithms, but it was not compared with other dynamic systems. Moreover it uses randomized algorithm which has its limitations. For these reasons we don't compare our system with it.

The proposed idea of hybrid approach (Ramachandran et al., 2005; Shah et al., 2006) is to divide the set of all views into a static set and a dynamic set such that the views selected for materialization from the dynamic set can be queried and/or replaced on the fly whereas the views selected for materialization from the static set are persistent over multiple query (and maintenance) windows.

Hybrid approach proposes pre-fetching algorithm for dynamic materialization which dynamically selects the highly aggregated views to be materialized based on the query access pattern of users.

At query time, the hybrid approach utilizes View Pool which is a dedicated (allocated) disk space. The allocated disk space corresponding to the materialized (or to be materialized) static views is called the Static View Pool whereas the allocated disk space corresponding to the materialized dynamic views is called the Dynamic View Pool.

Static views are selected to materialize using a greedy algorithm that provides a sub-optimal solution. The purposes of the materialized static views are: efficient maintenance of dynamic views, and pre materialization of the static views due to very large size of them and hence it is not feasible to compute them on the run time.

The hybrid approach extends the Markov chain model in developing a formal framework for modeling user interaction and navigation in an OLAP scenario. Each of the views visited (accessed) by the user maps to the states of the Markov chain. The access pattern information determines the probability that a user follows a particular navigation path and can be mapped to the state transition probabilities associated with a Markov chain.

A user query access pattern is defined as an ordered sequence of queries q_1, q_2, ..., q_n, addressed to views v_1, v_2, ..., v_n, respectively, such that $v_1 \cdot v_2$, $v_2 \cdot v_3$, ..., $v_{n-1} \cdot v_n$ where '$\cdot$' is either '$<$' or '$>$' i.e. given a query, a user drills-down and/or rolls-up the results for analytical processing. The probability that a user will drill-down to a particular view v_2 given that user is currently querying another view v_1 could be found by computing the transition probability between the two nodes in the nth *degree* probability matrix where n equals the number of hops (length of path) to reach state (view) v_2 from state (view) v_1.

Hybrid algorithm uses *startNode* to define the current context. A change in the *startNode* of a pattern indicates a context change. As long as a user navigates within the same context, no (or minimal) fetching is required after the initial fetch. The materialized dynamic views are used to answer aggregated user queries as long as the user stays in the same context. The context is defined by the past access patterns of users.

The algorithm begins with the first user query (the start query) and carries out a breadth first search to compute the benefit (weight) of each of the ancestor dynamic views. The benefit of a view depends on the following factors:

- The number of descendant (all descendants including children) queries it can answer, if materialized.
- The probability that the user takes a path from the initial query (*startNode*) to the current view which is computed based on the information about the user past query access patterns.

This algorithm works with the assumption that we have only drill-down queries. Experimental results show that Hybrid approach outperforms DynaMat.

We compare our system for drill-down queries with hybrid system which outperforms DynaMat for these types of queries and uses one of the probabilistic reasoning approaches (Markov chain model) to predict incoming queries.

A clustering based algorithm (CDA algorithm) is presented in (Gong & Zhao, 2008). In this algorithm incoming queries are SPJ (Select-Project-Join) queries without aggregate functions. It firstly materializes views statically through PBS algorithm (Shukla et al., 1998). Then clusters materialized views based on some similarity parameters.

In this algorithm, queries are entered, if their results have not been materialized, and there are materialized views with the same cluster of them, the algorithm selects some of them to replace the results of incoming queries based on benefit function. If there are not any materialized views in the same cluster of the incoming query, the algorithm selects some of the old materialized views to replace the results of the incoming query based on the benefit function.

CDA algorithm has two limitations: 1) The type of incoming queries is not aggregate query; moreover, 2) clusters are created in a static algorithm and they aren't updated. Whereas the input queries of our proposed system are the aggregate multidimensional query which is an input query to data warehouses, we don't compare our system with this algorithm.

Most of these dynamic algorithms decide to materialize the results of a query upon the query arrival. In some of them, the incoming workload is pre-determined. The results of comparisons and analysis of the techniques used in these algorithms and their limitations are presented in Table 1.

Table 1 consists of 5 columns. Columns 1 and 2 present the name and the presentation year of each algorithm respectively. In column 3 the type of incoming workload is presented. There are two types of incoming workloads: predefined incoming workload, and unknown incoming workload.

Table 1. The comparison and analysis of the previous works

Name	Year	Type of incoming workload	Technique	Limitations
XTZ	2007	Predefined	Finding shortest path in a DAG	Using predefined sequence of queries
PL	2008	Predefined	Genetic algorithm	Using predefined sequence of queries
DynaMat	1999	Unknown	Materializing the results of the last queries based on some benefit functions	Using some benefit functions to predict incoming queries which should be improved
Randomized	2002	Unknown	Randomized search	some parts of the space are not extensively searched and good local minima which is the best state and have the best set of views to materialize may be missed
DMP	2003	Unknown	Partitioning views based on query's predicates	materializing a small number of views that suffers from low variety
ZYK	2003	Unknown	Genetic algorithm	it requires extra time to join materialized views to process some queries
Hybrid	2006	Unknown	Extended Markov chain Model for modeling user interactions and navigations in an OLAP scenario	It is a good algorithm only for drill-down queries.
LC	2008	Unknown	Randomized search & greedy heuristic	good local minima which is the best state and have the best set of views to materialize may be missed
CDA	2008	Unknown	clustering	The type of incoming queries is not aggregate query; moreover, clusters are created in a static algorithm and they don't be updated

The technique of each algorithm is presented in column 4, and in column 5 the limitations of the algorithms are presented.

Our proposed system has unknown workload and uses two techniques to view selection which are: probabilistic reasoning, and the classification technique. Table 1 shows that none of the previous algorithms uses classification technique, and hybrid system is the only system which uses the probabilistic reasoning approach (Markov Chain Model).

In this work we present a new system (PR_Q_Predictor system) with different and improved architecture which uses three probabilistic reasoning approaches to predict and materialize the next query based on the previous sequence of queries. These approaches are: Conditional probability, Bayes' rule, and Naïve Bayes' rule.

PR_Q_Predictor system firstly classifies past queries by association rule analysis (Han & Kamber, 2006) and extracts patterns of queries that occur repeatedly in incoming queries through this classification. Then it predicts the next query using these rules through probabilistic reasoning approaches.

The proposed system compares with DynaMat which is a well known system and the most similar one to it, and with Hybrid system which outperforms DynaMat for drill-down queries and uses a probabilistic reasoning approach to predict incoming sequence of queries.

JUSTIFICATION OF THE TECHNIQUE USED IN THE PROPOSED SYSTEM

In this work, PR_Q_Predictor system is presented to materialize views dynamically. This system predicts the next query and materializes its results. To predict future data trends, classification techniques and regression analysis are two methodologies of data analysis that can be used (Han & Kamber, 2006).

Regression analysis is a statistical methodology that is used for numeric prediction and predicts continuous-valued data. For example, if a marketing manager would like to predict how much a customer with a given profile will spend during a sale, it will be possible by regression methodology.

Classification techniques predict categorical (discrete, unordered) labels. For example, if the marketing manager needs data analysis to find out the possibility of a given customer buys a new computer, it should be used classification techniques.

Whereas PR_Q_Predictor system aims to predict the next query content with its definition, to choose a prediction technique, it should be specified the type of the data elements which should be predicted. The type of the data elements is categorical (discrete) or numeric (continuous-valued). OLAP queries are multidimensional aggregated queries which can be presented in a structure as follow:

$$\begin{aligned}&\text{select field\_list, aggregate\_list,}\\&\text{from Fact\_Table, Dimension\_Table\_list,}\\&\text{where condition\_list,}\\&\text{group by field\_list.}\end{aligned} \quad (1)$$

The following parameters should be predicted to define query content for incoming queries:

- The list of selected fields which should be grouped by.
- The list of measures which aggregates and their aggregate function.
- The list of Dimension tables which should be joined with Fact table.
- The list of conditions on fields.

All of these data elements are categorical (Han & Kamber, 2006); therefore a suitable classification technique should be used to predict the next query (Han & Kamber, 2006).

Many classification techniques have been proposed by researchers, and some of the most operational of them are: Decision tree classifiers, Bayesian classifier, Naïve Bayesian Classifier, Rule based classifiers, Backpropagation, Support Vector Machines, Classification based on association rule mining, K-nearest-neighbor classifiers, Case-Based Reasoning, Genetic Algorithms, Rough Set Approach, and Fuzzy logic techniques. In these techniques X considers as a tuple with $x1, x2, \ldots, xn$ fields (attributes) in databases. Each tuple, X, is assumed to belong to a predefined class as determined by another database attribute called the class label attribute. A class label attribute will be added to the tuple and in result of that we have a tuple with $(n+1)$ fields.

Classification techniques are used to classify data to predict a value of the class label attribute. In previous example (the marketing manager needs data analysis to find out the possibility of a given customer buys a new computer), each tuple X is a profile of a customer with three attributes: age $(x1)$, credit_rating $(x2)$, job $(x3)$. Classification technique predicts the possibility of a given customer buys a new computer and assigns a categorical value (yes /no) to the class label attribute $(x4)$.

PR_Q_Predictor system wants to predict the next query content with its definition. In this system, each tuple X is a definition of a query with following attributes: the list of selected fields which should be grouped by(x1), the list of measures which aggregates and their aggregate function (x2), the list of Dimension tables which should be joined with Fact table (x3), and the list of conditions on fields (x4).

Classification techniques are suitable to predict the value of the one of attributes. OLAP queries have some additional features such as being sequential and ordered which should be considered in time of the analyzing. Therefore classification techniques have to be extended to mine sequential patterns to be able to predict the next query content with its definition.

The sequential pattern mining problem was first introduced by Agrawal and Srikant (1995). In order to do sequential pattern mining, different solutions have been proposed (Han et al., 2000; Pei et al., 2001, 2004; Srikant et al., 1996; Zaki, 2001). All of these solutions are based on association rule mining (frequent item-set mining).

The next section describes the proposed system to predict the next query through sequential pattern mining based on frequent item-set mining.

PROPOSED SYSTEM OVERVIEW AND ARCHITECTURE

PR_Q_Predictor (Probabilistic Reasoning Query Predictor) system is designed to operate as a complete view management system that can predict the next query and materialize the suitable view for it.

This system uses two techniques to view selection: classification technique, and probabilistic reasoning. It firstly classifies past queries by association rule analysis, and then predicts the next query using extracted rules.

Association rules are mined in a two-step process consisting of frequent item-set mining, followed by rule generation. The first step searches for patterns of queries that occur repeatedly in the input queries, where each query is considered an item and the resulting queries form frequent item-sets. The second step analyzes the frequent item-sets in order to generate association rules.

We represent association rules in the repository, in the form of the serial queries and their last query occurrence probability which is calculated through three probabilistic reasoning approaches: Conditional probability, Bayes' rule, and Naïve Bayes' rule.

This system has two constraining factors: space limitation, and view maintenance cost limitation.

Figure 1 depicts the architecture of PR_Q_Predictor system. This architecture has 6 data units and 5 process units. Data units are: 1) Data Warehouse infrastructure, and 2) Log File, which comprise

Figure1. Architecture of PR_Q_Predictor System

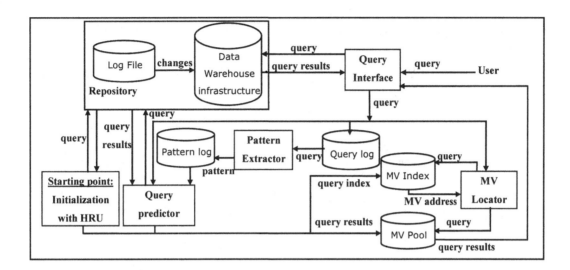

Repository unit, and 3) Query Log, 4) Pattern Log, 5) MV Pool, and 6) MV Index. Process units are: 1) MV Locator, 2) Pattern Extractor, 3) Query Predictor, 4) Query Interface, and 5) Initialization with HRU. The tasks of each unit are explained in the following paragraphs.

- **Data Warehouse infrastructure:** It contains fact tables and dimensions. If the system does not have any materialized view answerable to the entered query, it follows the conventional approach for answering the query, where the data warehouse infrastructure is queried.
- **Log File:** It contains updated data received from the data sources which should be stored in the Data Warehouse infrastructure and the materialized views.
- **Query Log:** When a query enters to the system, the system assigns to it a unique identifier, then its description and its identifier are stored in Query Log.
- **Pattern log:** It contains extracted patterns of queries that occur repeatedly in the input queries. These patterns are extracted from

Query Log, and stored in the form of the serial queries and their last query occurrence probability.

- **MV Pool:** MV Pool is the information repository that is used for storing materialized results.
- **MV Index:** An MV Index contains the list of the materialized views in MV Pool. It is maintained in order to support sub-linear search in MV Pool for finding candidate materialized results.
- **MV Locator:** This unit determines whether or not already materialized results in MV Pool can be efficiently used to answer the query through MV Index. If the search fails to reveal an efficient way to use data stored in MV Pool for answering the query, the system follows the conventional approach, where the warehouse infrastructure is queried.
- **Pattern Extractor:** It classifies queries by association rule analysis in two-step process:
  ○ It first searches for frequent item-sets which are patterns of queries that oc-

cur repeatedly in the input queries and extracts them from logged queries upon ThQ queries arrival through Apriori algorithm (Agrawal & Srikant, 1994) which is a well-known and the easiest algorithm for pattern extraction. ThQ is a definite threshold number of queries.

   ○ Secondly it stores extracted patterns in Pattern Log in the form of the serial queries and their last query occurrence probability.

System transfers queries' identifiers (Query Log's information) into the main memory, to speed up Apriori algorithm.

- **Query Predictor:** Upon each query arrival, *Query Predictor* predicts the next query and stores its description and results in *MV Index* and *MV Pool* respectively, if there is enough free space in the pool. We use three probabilistic reasoning approaches for query prediction. The first one is based on Conditional probability and is presented in 2:

$$
\begin{aligned}
&P\left(q_n = a_n \mid q_1 = a_1, q_2 = a_2, \ldots, q_{n-1} = a_{n-1}\right) = \\
&P\left(q_1 = a_1, q_2 = a_2, \ldots, q_n = a_n\right) / \\
&P\left(q_1 = a_1, q_2 = a_2, \ldots, q_{n-1} = a_{n-1}\right) = \\
&n\left(q_1 = a_1, q_2 = a_2, \ldots, q_n = a_n\right) / \\
&n\left(q_1 = a_1, q_2 = a_2, \ldots, q_{n-1} = a_{n-1}\right)
\end{aligned}
$$

$$(2)$$

The second approach for query prediction is based on Bayes' rule and presented in 3:

$$
\begin{aligned}
&P\left(q_n = a_n \mid q_1 = a_1, q_2 = a_2, \ldots, q_{n-1} = a_{n-1}\right) = \\
&P\left(q_n = a_n\right) * P\left(q_1 = a_1 \mid q_n = a_n\right) * \\
&P\left(q_2 = a_2 \mid q_n = a_n, q_1 = a_1\right) * \ldots * \\
&P\left(q_{n-1} = a_{n-1} \mid q_n = a_n, q_1 = a_1, \ldots, q_{n-2} = a_{n-2}\right) / \\
&P\left(q_1 = a_1, q_2 = a_2, \ldots, q_{n-1} = a_{n-1}\right)
\end{aligned}
$$

$$(3)$$

The third approach for query prediction is based on Naïve Bayes' rule and presented in 4:

$$
\begin{aligned}
&P\left(q_n = a_n \mid q_1 = a_1, q_2 = a_2, \ldots, q_{n-1} = a_{n-1}\right) = \\
&P\left(q_n = a_n\right) * P\left(q_1 = a_1 \mid q_n = a_n\right) * \\
&P\left(q_2 = a_2 \mid q_n = a_n\right) * \ldots * P\left(q_{n-1} = a_{n-1} \mid q_n = a_n\right) / \\
&P\left(q_1 = a_1, q_2 = a_2, \ldots, q_{n-1} = a_{n-1}\right)
\end{aligned}
$$

$$(4)$$

In these formulas, $q_1 q_2 q_3 \ldots q_{n-1}$ is the stream of previous entered queries. We calculate the probability of entering q_n when $q_1 q_2 q_3 \ldots q_{n-1}$ is the stream of queries entered before.

The maximum length of query stream depends on the maximum length of recurrent patterns of queries, $max\left(l_p\right)$. We select queries with maximum probability and their probabilities considering the stream of previous queries with length between 1 and $\left(max\left(l_p\right) - 1\right)$; and then select the one with the maximum probability and materialize it.

If there is not enough free space in the pool to materialize the predicted query, the system will select the old materialized views to remove from the pool based on some parameters, such as the time that the views were last accessed by the system to handle queries, or the frequency of access for the views, or the size of the views. Therefore, the least recently used materialized views, or the least frequently used materialized views, or materialized views based on their size can be selected to remove from the pool.

- **Query Interface:** Queries arrive to this unit. Upon each query arrival, this unit sends it to *MV Locator* unit (to determine whether or not already materialized results in *MV Pool* can be efficiently used to answer the query), *Query Log* unit (to store its description), and *Query Predictor* unit (to predict the next query and stores its description and results in *MV Index* and *MV Pool* respectively).

If *MV Locator* finds a materialized view to answer the query, query results are sent from the *MV Pool* to *Query Interface*. If it doesn't find a materialized view to answer the query, *Query Interface* sends the query to the Repository, and receives the results from it.

- **Initialization with HRU:** In this system, before query arrival, initialization phase is executed and some cuboids are materialized based on HRU algorithm (Harinarayan et al., 1996).

HRU algorithm works as follow: the input of this algorithm is a lattice of cuboids with space costs associated with each cuboid. It firstly materializes the base cuboid and after that while there are enough space to materialize views, it selects the cuboid with a maximum value for the benefit function as a view to materialize. The benefit function of this algorithm is executed from 5:

$$B(v, M) = D*N_C \qquad (5)$$

where *B(v,M)* is the benefit of choosing a view *v* to materialize, when the set *M* of views has been materialized before. N_C is the number of cuboids that can be computed using *v*, and

$$D = \text{Size}(A) - \text{Size}(v) \qquad (6)$$

where *Size(v)* is the space required materializing view *v*, and *A* is the smallest ancestor of view *v* from set *M* of selected views.

PR_Q_Predictor system has two operational phases which are:

1. **On-line phase:** This is the run time phase of the system. During on-line phase, PR_Q_Predictor system answers queries posed to the warehouse,

2. **Off-line phase:** This is the update phase of the system. During off-line phase, logged updates received from the data sources are stored in the warehouse and the materialized results in the pool, are refreshed. We assume that the update phase is off-line and the queries are not permitted during this phase. The maximum time to update is specified by the administrator and would probably lead us to evict some of the data stored in the pool as they are not updateable within this time constraint. We update the recently used views.

In this section, we presented the architecture of PR_Q_Predictor system and described each unit of it. In the following section we present an algorithm for this architecture.

ALGORITHM OF PR_Q_ PREDICTOR SYSTEM

Algorithm of PR_Q_Predictor system is presented in Figure 2. This algorithm has 4 inputs as follows:

1. **Q:** A stream of queries which arrives.
2. **S:** A size of *MV Pool*.
3. **C:** A lattice of cuboids of the data warehouse.
4. **recur_pattern_threshold:** A specified threshold to determine a pattern is recurrent.
5. **ThQ:** A specified threshold to extract recurrent patterns of queries.

The output is a set of materialized views, *M*. In this algorithm q_i is an entered query, v_i is a view corresponded to this query, S_M is a space required to materialize *M*, and S_v is a space required to materialize *v*. This algorithm has 2 parts which are as below:

1. View materialization statistically.
2. View materialization dynamically during query arrival.

Figure 2. Algorithm of PR_Q_Predictor System

Input: Q, S, C, recur_pattern_threshold, ThQ

Otput: M

PR_Q_Predictor()

1: { //M = HRU(C);

2:    M = {base cuboid};

3:    S=S-S$_M$;

4: while (S>0)

5:    {select v ∈ C and v ∉ M and B(v,M) is maximized;

6:        M = M U {v};}

7: while (q$_i$ is entering)

8:      {Answer query(q$_i$, M);

9:        pattern extaction(Q,recur_pattern_threshold);

10:      predict next query(recur_patterns);

11:      //view materialization

12:      If ((v$_i$ ∉ M) and $\left(\left(S_{v_i} + S_M \right) < S \right)$)   M = M U {vi};

13:      else if (v$_i$ ∉ M)

14:      {   While $\left(\left(S_{v_i} + S_M \right) > S \right)$

15:                {   select v$_{LRU}$ ∈ M

16:                        M = M − {v$_{LRU}$}; }

17:                M = M U {v$_i$};

18:      }}

19:}

In part 1, before query arrival, HRU algorithm is executed to select the cuboids to materialize based on its benefit function. This part is presented in lines 1- 6.

The first line of part 2 is Line 7. While queries arrive this part is executed. In this part, first an arrived query is answered (line 8). There is a definite threshold (*ThQ*) to determine after how many query arrivals we should extract the recurrent patterns which will be assigned by the analyst. When the algorithm meets the threshold, recurrent patterns of queries are extracted (line 9). After that, the algorithm predicts the next query (line 10) and materializes it (line 11-17).

The procedure of answering arrived queries is presented in Figure 3. This procedure selects a materialized view with the minimum size that can answer the query if it exists. If there is not a suitable materialized view, query is executed on fact and dimension tables. In this procedure, $F(v_i)$ is an ancestor of v_i that can be used to answer q_i.

The procedure of extracting recurrent patterns is presented in Figure 4. Given a threshold "*ThQ*", the algorithm of PR_Q_Predictor system (presented in Figure 2) calls the pattern extraction procedure (Figure 4). This procedure extracts the recurrent patterns and calculate the conditional probability of their last query occurrence through Formula 3 (Conditional probability), or Formula 4 (Bayes' rule), or Formula 5 (Naïve Bayes' rule).

The procedure for the next query prediction is presented in Figure 5. In this procedure, first,

Figure 3. Answering query procedure (line 8 of Figure 2)

Input: q_i, M

Output: results of q_i

Answer query()

1: {search q_i definition in MV Index;

2:   if (q_i definition is in MV Index)

3:     {rewrite q_i to answer through v_i;

4:       answer q_i through v_i;}

5:   else if $F(v_i) \in M$

6:     {find smallest $F(v_i)$ to answer q_i;

7:       rewrite q_i to answer through smallest $F(v_i)$;

8:       answer q_i through smallest $F(v_i)$;}

9:   else

10:     { rewrite q_i to answer through Fact and Dimension Tables;

11:       answer q_i through Fact and Dimension Tables;}

12: }

we should extract maximum length of recurrent patterns from pattern log (*max_len_of_pattern*). Then we find the next query with maximum Conditional/Bayes'/Naïve Bayes' probability from recurrent patterns with lengths between 2 and *max_len_of_pattern*.

Example 1 shows how the presented algorithm works. Whereas lines 1-6 of the PR_Q_Predictor

Figure 4. Pattern extraction procedure (line 9 of Figure 2)

Input: Q, recur_pattern_threshold

Output: recur_patterns//recurrent patterns with their conditional probability of the last query occurrence

pattern extraction ()

1: {recur_patterns = recurrent binary patterns in Q and their conditional probability of the
    last query occurrence calculated with Conditional probability or Bayes' theorem or
    Naïve Bayes' theorem;

2:   n=2;

3:   while (nary patterns are recurrent)

4:     {recur_patterns = recur_patterns U recurrent (n+1)ary patterns from nary patterns and
        their conditional probability of the last query occurrence calculated with Conditional
        probability or Bayes' theorem or Naïve bayes' theorem;

5:     n=n+1;}

6: }

Figure 5. Query prediction procedure (line 10 of Figure 2)

Input: recur_patterns

Output: predicted query

predict next query ()

1: {max_len_of_pattern = maximum length of patterns in recur_patterns;

2: n=2;

3: while (n <= max_len_of_pattern)

4: {find nary recurrent pattern with maximum Conditional probability or

     Bayes' probability or Naïve Bayes' probability to predict next query;

5: n = n+1;

6: }

7: predicted query = last query with maximum Conditional probability or

    Bayes' probability or Naïve Bayes' probability from founded recurrent patterns;

8: }

procedure correspond with HRU algorithm (Harinarayan et al., 1996), in this example working of these lines are not explained.

Example 1: As we explained in the previous section, when a query enters to the system for the first time, the system assigns to it a unique identifier (in the form of q_i), and if it enters again, the previous identifier assigns to it again. Assume the administrator of the system assigns 2 and 30 to *recur_pattern_threshold* and *ThQ* respectively, and Q is a stream of arrived queries to the system:

$Q: q_{11}q_5q_9q_7q_8q_4q_{11}q_2q_5q_9q_9q_3q_1q_{11}q_5q_9q_{12}q_4q_1q_3q_{11}$
$q_5q_7q_8q_3q_1q_9q_9q_7q_8q_4$

Now, if q_{11} is entered to the system (line 7 of PR_Q_Predictor algorithm), *Answer query(q_{11}, M)* is called (line 8 of PR_Q_Predictor algorithm) and q_{11} is answered through this procedure.

Whereas the number of entered queries to the system is 30, *pattern extraction(Q, 2)* is called (line 9 of PR_Q_Predictor algorithm) and recurrent patterns are extracted through this procedure. Suppose this procedure uses conditional probability to calculate last query occurrence probability. In

this procedure first recurrent binary patterns are extracted and their last query occurrence probabilities are calculated, which are presented below:

- $q_{11}q_5$, **last query occurrence probability:** 3/4.

- q_5q_9, **last query occurrence probability:** 3/4.

- q_9q_7, **last query occurrence probability:** 1/2.

- q_7q_8, **last query occurrence probability:** 1.

- q_8q_4, **last query occurrence probability:** 2/3.

- q_4q_{11}, **last query occurrence probability:** 2/3.

- q_3q_1, **last query occurrence probability:** 2/3.

After that, recurrent triplicate patterns are extracted through incoming queries and recurrent binary patterns, and their last query occurrence probabilities are calculated, which are presented below:

- $q_{11}q_5q_9$, **last query occurrence probability: 2/3.**
- $q_9q_7q_8$, **last query occurrence probability: 1.**
- $q_7q_8q_4$, **last query occurrence probability: 2/3.**
- $q_8q_4q_{11}$, **last query occurrence probability: 1.**

Then, recurrent quadruple patterns are extracted through incoming queries and recurrent triplicate patterns, and their last query occurrence probabilities are calculated, which are presented below:

- $q_9q_7q_8q_4$, **last query occurrence probability: 1.**
- $q_7q_8q_4q_{11}$, **last query occurrence probability: 1.**

After that recurrent quintuple patterns are extracted through incoming queries and recurrent quadruple patterns, and their last query occurrence probabilities are calculated, which are presented below:

- $q_9q_7q_8q_4q_{11}$, **last query occurrence probability: 1.**

Whereas there is only one recurrent quintuple pattern, we cannot extract any recurrent sextet pattern and pattern extraction procedure terminates.

Now *predict next query()* is called (line 10 of PR_Q_Predictor algorithm) and next query is predicted through this procedure. In this procedure, first max_len_of_pattern is extracted. Whereas maximum length of recurrent extracted patterns is 5 (equals to the length of pattern: $q_9q_7q_8q_4q_{11}$) and the stream $Q+q_{11}$ is the steam of incoming queries, we should search below recurrent patterns (if there exist) with maximum probabilities for the last queries:

- $q_{11}q_?$
- $q_4q_{11}q_?$
- $q_8q_4q_{11}q_?$
- $q_7q_8q_4q_{11}q_?$

Then we should select the pattern from them with maximum probability for its last query and return its last query as a predicted query. While there exists only $q_{11}q_5$ with the last query occurrence probability: 3/4, q_5 is returned as a predicted query.

Now if the answer to q_5 was not materialized before, and there exists enough space to materialize it, it is materialized (line 12 of PR_Q_Predictor algorithm).

If the answer to q_5 was not materialized before, and there does not exist enough space to materialize it (line 13 of PR_Q_Predictor algorithm), least recently used views are deleted until enough free space is created (lines 14-16 of PR_Q_Predictor algorithm) and then the answer to q_5 (v_5) is materialized (line 17 of PR_Q_Predictor algorithm).

Now if q_5 is entered as the next query, v_5 is used to answer it through *Answer query()* procedure (lines 1-4 of *Answer query()* procedure), and the next query is predicted and materialized as explained, and these activities are continued while the query is entered.

In this section we presented our algorithm to predict and materialize the next query and explained it through an example. In the next section we show the results of experiments executed on this algorithm.

EXPERIMENTS

The comparison and analysis of the different aspects of the proposed approaches are based on a simulator that we developed in this research. The simulation prototype consists of the implementations of algorithms and techniques required for the experiments including each of the components of the proposed system.

The simulator also includes a Query Access Pattern Generator that simulates a typical user interaction with an OLAP system. It generates random sequence of drill-down, roll-up, and slice or dice queries for a synthetic data warehouse.

We compare our system with well-known dynamic view management system, DynaMat (Kotidis & Roussopoulos, 1999) and Hybrid system (Shah et al., 2006) which uses Markov chain models to predict a sequence of incoming queries and outperforms DynaMat for drill-down queries.

In order to evaluate and analyze the effectiveness of the proposed system, a number of experiments were carried out to achieve the following specific goals:

1. Measure the effect of varying the threshold number to extract recurrent patterns of queries on the average cost savings and cumulative replacement count,
2. Measure the effect of varying the number of distinct random sequence of queries on the average cost savings under MV Pool size constraint,
3. Compare the average cost savings for queries of the proposed approaches with that of DynaMat and Hybrid,
4. Compare the total number of view replacements in the MV Pool of the proposed approaches with that of DynaMat and Hybrid.

The following subsections present our data set, evaluation parameters, system setup, and the results of experiments.

Data Set

In this section the data sets which are used to evaluate the performance of the proposed approaches are introduced. We investigated all possible solutions to compare the data sets which they used. They mostly generate data set randomly and oc-

casionally (Agrawal, Narasayya, & Yang, 2004; Aouiche & Darmont, 2009; Choi et al., 2003; Gong & Zhao, 2008; Nadeau & Teorey, 2002; Harinarayan et al., 1996; Phan & Li, 2008) used other kind of data sets.

We have used random data sets and headcount dataset to cover all these varieties of data sets. Headcount data set contains 33 million actual population records. Whereas the proposed approaches are compared with DynaMat system and Hybrid system, we generate random datasets similar to datasets which they used.

For a multidimensional lattice with n dimensions, $d_1, d_2 \ldots d_n$, and no hierarchies, there are 2^n different views. If the n dimensions, $d_1, d_2 \ldots d_n$, contain hierarchies of length $h_1, h_2 \ldots h_n$, respectively, then there are $\Pi_{i=1}^{n} (h_i + 1)$ different views. Thus, the total number of views for a multidimensional lattice with dimension hierarchies is much higher than the number of views for a multidimensional lattice with no dimension hierarchies.

In order to evaluate the proposed approaches on a large data set without dimension hierarchies, we generated two synthetic data sets, which are described as follows:

1. Synthetic schema1 (Table 2) has 10 dimensions and no dimension hierarchies. The numbers represent the distinct values of each of the dimensions. The total number of views is $2^{10} = 1024$.

In schema1, the maximum size of the base fact table is 1000*1000*100*10*10*2*2*2*2*2 = 320 billion tuples. For experimental purposes a small data density (approximately 5 million tuples) is selected.

2. Synthetic schema2 (Table 3) has 6 dimensions and no dimension hierarchies. The numbers represent the distinct values of each of the dimensions. The total number of views is $2^6 = 64$.

Table 2. Description of a schema1

Dimension Number	1	2	3	4	5	6	7	8	9	10
Dimension Size	1000	1000	100	10	10	2	2	2	2	2

In schema2, the maximum size of the base fact table is 500*250*80*50*10*2 = 10 billion tuples. For experimental purposes a data density of 0.1% (approximately 10 million tuples) is selected.

Schema1 has more dimensions than schema2 and then has more total number of views. The proposed system compares with DynaMat using this schema.

Schema2 is identical to the schema that Hybrid has been experimented on it. This schema is generated to compare PR_Q_Predictor system's experimental results with Hybrid results.

We can generate a synthetic data set with dimension hierarchies and experiment PR_Q_Predictor system through it. Since data sets with dimension hierarchies have more total number of views than data sets without dimension hierarchies, in the worst case it will be reached to the same results as data sets without dimension hierarchies. Therefore, we relinquish to do our experiments on a dataset with dimension hierarchies.

Evaluation Parameters

To compare the three approaches, the following evaluation parameters which are the standard parameters and have been used in the previous works (Kotidis & Roussopoulos, 1999; Shah et al., 2006) are measured:

Table 3. Description of a schema2

Dimension Number	1	2	3	4	5	6
Dimension Size	500	250	80	50	10	2

1. **The cost of answering the query q from the best matching view:** This cost is assumed to be equal to the size of tuples in the view, and it is measured using the Detailed Cost Saving Ratio, DCSR (Kotidis & Roussopoulos, 1999).

Let M denote the set of materialized views in the MV Pool. If c_i is the cost of answering query q_i from the base fact table, and c_v is the cost of answering q_i from the best matching view v from M then,

$$\text{DCSR} = \frac{\sum_i s_i}{\sum_i c_i} \qquad (7)$$

In this formula, $s_i = 0$ if q_i cannot be answered through M, and $s_i = c_i - c_v$ if v in M is used to answer q_i.

Thus, to maximize the overall performance, DCSR values should be as high as possible.

2. **The total number of view replacements in the MV Pool:** This measure is referred to as Cumulative Replacement Count, CRC (Kotidis & Roussopoulos, 1999).

Since dynamic approaches are based on principles similar to cache management in memories, a replacement strategy is often used to identify the candidate views, from the set of materialized views, to be replaced with new selections. Hence this measure is essential since it helps in assessing the frequency with which a replacement routine is involved. To maximize the overall performance, CRC values should be as low as possible.

These two evaluation parameters are measured for the proposed approaches, DynaMat approaches, and Hybrid system; and then the results are compared.

Setup

An OLAP system consists of a number of iterations of the alternating query and maintenance phases. However, for experimental evaluation purposes, we assume a single query phase, which is followed by an update phase.

Two categories of query access patterns are generated to do experiments. Category1 is generated under schema1 to compare with DynaMat and category2 is generated under schema2 to compare with the results of Hybrid system.

Category1 contains three sets of query access patterns which are representative of OLAP queries. These access patterns were generated using the Query Access Pattern Generator module of our simulator.

Each access pattern has 5 queries and starts querying a cuboid. Then it randomly selects a dimension from two definite dimensions to drill-down or roll-up. The probability to select one of them is assumed 10% and the other is assumed 90%. After selecting a dimension, the probability to slice is assumed 10%. These assumptions are done to reach a query set with less variety.

For each set, we generated 600 access patterns. They have 3000 queries with different number of distinct queries as follows:

1. The first set is generated based on 6 different types of access patterns, three of them are drill-down and the other three are roll-up. It has 606 different queries.
2. The second set is generated based on 8 different types of access patterns, four of them are drill-down and the other four are roll-up. It has 723 different queries.

3. The third set is generated based on 10 different types of access patterns, five of them are drill-down and the other five are roll-up. It has 776 different queries.

If the difference of probabilities to select from two dimensions decreases or the probability to slice increases, it should be generated more number of access patterns to show the results of PR_Q_Predictor system and DynaMat system.

Category2 contains 100 query access patterns with the length of seven. Each query access pattern starts by querying randomly a cuboid and continues with a 70% chance that the user will drill-down and a 20% chance that the user will roll-up from a given query node. The remaining 10% corresponds to the chance that the user will send a slice or a dice query to the same node. These probabilities are assumed to reach a query set with high probability to drill-down and suitable for Hybrid system.

Performance was measured for these two categories of queries. In fact, we computed the DCSR per view and CRC for these groups.

Results

PR_Q_Predictor system was experimented with various thresholds to extract recurrent patterns of queries. The results show that the increase in the threshold value results in the decrease in DCSR and CRC. Increase in the threshold causes extracting a less number of patterns which decreases DCSR. Moreover the increase in the threshold causes the decrease in the total number of view replacements in MV Pool.

We show the results of the experiments on schema1 when the threshold to extract recurrent patterns of queries is defined as 3 numbers; and the results of the experiments on schema2 when the threshold to extract recurrent patterns of queries is defined as 2 numbers.

Figure 6. Average DCSR for three proposed approaches with thresholds to extract recurrent patterns=3

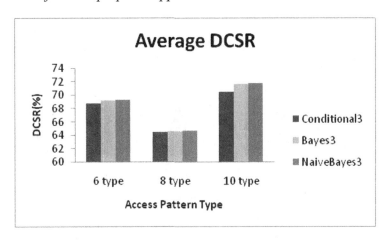

Figure 7. CRC for three proposed approaches with thresholds to extract recurrent patterns=3

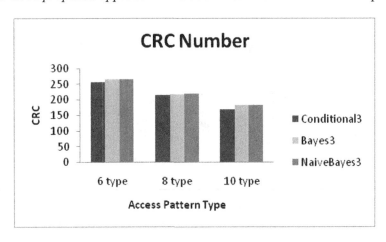

Figure 8. Average DCSR for 4 DynaMat approaches

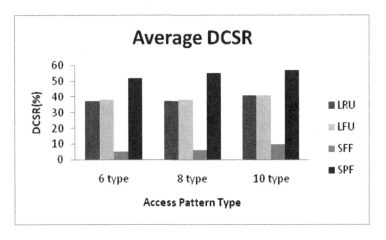

Figure 9. CRC for 3 DynaMat approaches

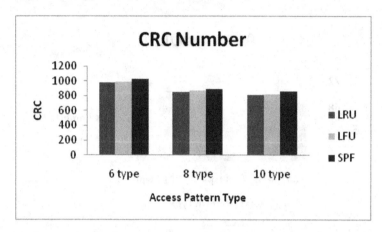

Figure 10. Average DCSR for PR_Q_Predictor system compare with average DCSR for the best Dy-naMat approaches

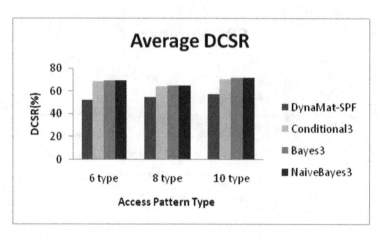

Figure 11. CRC for PR_Q_Predictor system compare with it for the best DynaMat approaches

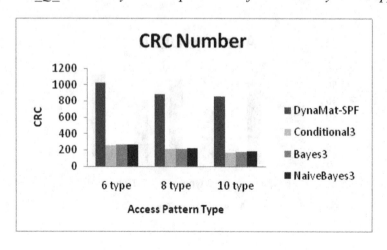

Figure 12. Average DCSR for PR_Q_Predictor system compare with average DCSR for the best DynaMat approaches and Hybrid

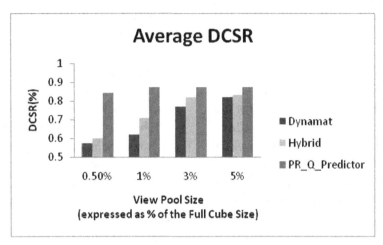

Before evaluating the results against DynaMat, we first compare the three proposed approaches on the average cost savings and cumulative replacement count. Figure 6 depicts the cost savings (average DCSR) and Figure 7 depicts the cumulative replacement count for a space constraint of 0.5% for the schema1 and 3 sets of queries in category1 for all three approaches of the proposed system. The results show that the three approaches have similar results with insignificant variance.

Now 4 different approaches in DynaMat are compared on the average cost savings and the cumulative replacement count. Figure 8 shows DCSR per view for the schema1 and 3 sets of queries in category1 with a space constraint of 0.5% for 4 approaches of DynaMat.

DCSR results (Figure 8) show SPF approach outperforms the other approaches in DynaMat and SFF approach has low DCSR for the generated access patterns. Whereas, SFF approach is

Figure 13. Comparing average DCSR for PR_Q_Predictor system with 100 access patterns and 200 access patterns

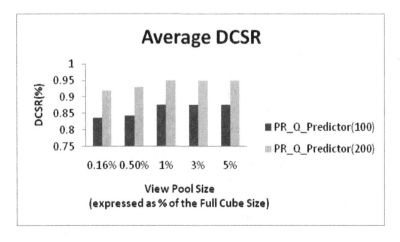

not suitable for the generated queries, we ignore it for CRC measuring.

The corresponding CRC results for the schema1 are shown in Figure 9. These results are much similar.

Now the approaches of PR_Q_Predictor system are compared with SPF approach of DynaMat system. Figure 10 shows DCSR per view for the schema1 with a space constraint of 0.5% and three sets of queries in category1 for SPF approach of DynaMat and all three proposed approaches.

DCSR results (Figure 10) show that the approaches of PR_Q_Predictor system clearly outperform SPF approach and consequently all DynaMat approaches, because the proposed Query Predictor which uses the Pattern Log information provides an extra layer of optimization for the selection of views.

The corresponding CRC results for the schema1 are shown in Figure 11. The results show that PR_Q_Predictor system's approaches require a fewer number of replacements; therefore, the reusability of their already materialized views for answering the incoming queries increases.

Now PR_Q_Predictor system is compared with Hybrid system for schema2. As Hybrid has been compared with DynaMat in schema2, to make comparisons meaningful, we also present the results of this schema for DynaMat.

Figure 12 shows DCSR per view for 100 access patterns in category2 with four various space constraints: 0.5%, 1%, 3%, and 5% for Hybrid system, SPF approach of DynaMat, and the average of three approaches in PR_Q_Predictor system. The proposed system outperforms these two systems. The difference in the results of PR_Q_Predictor system in comparison with DynaMat system and Hybrid system is more obvious when we have a smaller space to view materialization. These results show the effectiveness of PR_Q_Predictor system's prediction in comparison with the others by restriction in the space.

The proposed system was experimented for restricted space: 20% of the cube with 10 million

tuples which is equal to the 0.16% of the full cube size; the results of PR_Q_Predictor system are better than the results of Hybrid when it has more space (0.5% space of the full cube size).

In Figure 13 the results have been shown via five various space constraints: 0.16%, 0.5%, 1%, 3%, and 5% when we have 2 different numbers of access patterns for category2: 100, and 200.

Table 4 compares CRC results for all proposed three approaches of PR_Q_Predictor system in average with Hybrid system. When the space decreases, CRC result increases. Whereas the space constraints enforced to Hybrid experimentations are too large for PR_Q_Predictor system, the average CRC results for all proposed three approaches of the proposed system is zero for four various space constraints (0.5%, 1%, 3%, and 5%), while these averages are 480, 450, 440, and 420 in Hybrid system for 0.5%, 1%, 3%, and 5% space constraints respectively.

The last row in Table 4 shows the results of the experiments for these two systems in the more limited space (0.16% of the full cube size) which view replacement occurs for PR_QPredictor system. In this case, the average CRC results for all proposed three approaches of PR_Q_Predictor system in average is 15 while this result for Hybrid system is more than 480.

Table 4 shows that the average CRC results for PR_Q_Predictor system in the worst case, when we have the most limited space (0.16% of the

Table 4. CRC for PR_Q_Predictor system compared with it for Hybrid system

View management system Space	Hybrid	PR_Q_Predictor
10% of the full cube size	410	0
5% of the full cube size	420	0
3% of the full cube size	440	0
1% of the full cube size	450	0
0.5% of the full cube size	480	0
0.16% of the full cube size	>480	15

full cube size), is 15 while this result for Hybrid in the best case, when it has the largest space to materialize views (10% of the full cube size), is 410. As a result, in our system the replacement routine is called with lower frequency and it requires a fewer number of replacements.

Additionally, Figures 10, 11, and 12 show that PR_Q_Predictor system outperforms DynaMat and Hybrid systems. PR_Q_Predictor system was also experimented for 33 million actual population records (headcount data set) and compared with DynaMat and Hybrid systems. The results of these experiments corresponded with the results of experiments on schema 2 presented in Figures 12 and 13 and Table 4.

CONCLUSION

In this work, we proposed and implemented a new dynamic view materialization system with different and improved architecture, based on three probabilistic reasoning approaches which are: Conditional probability, Bayes' rule, and Naïve Bayes' rule. In this system, the input queries were logged to extract the recurrent patterns of queries periodically upon a definite threshold number of query arrivals, and then the incoming query was predicted using the recurrent patterns based on these three probabilistic reasoning approaches.

The proposed system was implemented and experimented in an experimental environment and compared with DynaMat system which is a well-known dynamic view management system without any limitations on the type of the input queries.

The comparisons were done through two evaluation parameters: DCSR (the average cost saving per query execution), and CRC (the total number of view replacements in MV pool).

Experimental results showed that all three approaches of the proposed system present the same results which increase the efficiency of the

system and outperform DynaMat approaches. The average cost savings of our approaches were about 15% more than the best approach of DynaMat (SPF approach). Moreover, the CRC of the proposed system was much less than DynaMat approaches' CRC.

The proposed system was also compared with Hybrid system which is the only dynamic view management system based on probabilistic reasoning approaches and outperforms DynaMat for drill-down queries.

Experiments showed that PR_Q_Predictor system outperforms Hybrid system to view materialization especially when there is a less space to view materialization. The average cost saving of PR_Q_Predictor system was about 13% more than Hybrid system's average cost saving; and the CRC of the proposed approaches were much less than Hybrid system's CRC. Moreover this system outperforms DynaMat system and Hybrid system for each type of queries and each sequence of incoming queries.

PR_Q_Predictor system uses LRU approach for view replacement. As a future work, we intend to improve the proposed system by changing the replacement technique (LRU) to predict less appropriate views to remove from the pool which may improve the performance of the system.

ACKNOWLEDGMENT

This research has been supported partially by Education & Research Institute for ICT (ERICT).

REFERENCES

Agrawal, R., & Srikant, R. (1994). Fast Algorithms for Mining Association Rules. In *Proceedings of the 20th VLDB Conference,* Santiago, Chile (pp. 487-499).

Agrawal, R., & Srikant, R. (1995). Mining Sequential Patterns. In *Proceedings of the 11ᵗʰ International Conference on Data Engineering,* Taipei, Taiwan (pp. 3-14).

Agrawal, S., Chaudhuri, S., Kollar, L., Marathe, A., Narasayya, V., & Syamala, M. (2004). Database Tuning Advisor for Microsoft SQL Server 2005. In *Proceedings of the 30th VLDB Conference,* Toronto, ON, Canada (pp. 1110- 1121).

Agrawal, S., Chaudhuri, S., & Narasayya, V. (2000). Automated Selection of Materialized Views and Indexes for SQL Databases. In *Proceedings of the 26th International Conference on Very Large Databases,* Cairo, Egypt (pp. 496-505).

Agrawal, S., Narasayya, V., & Yang, B. (2004). Integrating Vertical and Horizontal Partitioning into Automated Physical Database Design. In *Proceedings of the SIGMOD 2004 Conference,* Paris, France (pp. 359-370).

Ahmed, M., Agrawal, V., & Sundararaghavan, P. (2007). Statistical Sampling to Instantiate Materialized View Selection Problems in Data Warehouses. *International Journal of Data Warehousing and Mining, 3*(1), 1–28. doi:10.4018/jdwm.2007010101

Aouiche, K., & Darmont, J. (2009). Data mining-based materialized view and index selection in data warehouses. *Journal of Intelligent Information Systems, 32*(1), 65–93. doi:10.1007/s10844-009-0080-0

Aouiche, K., Jouve, P. E., & Darmont, J. (2006). Clustering-Based Materialized View Selection in Data Warehouses. In *Proceedings of the ADBIS'06 Conference* (LNCS 4152, pp. 81-95).

Asgharzadeh Talebi, Z., Chirkova, R., Fathi, Y., & Stallmann, M. (2008). Exact and Inexact Methods for Selecting Views and Indexes for OLAP Performance Improvement. In *Proceedings of the EDBT '08 Conference* (pp. 311-322).

Baralis, E., Paraboschi, S., & Teniente, E. (1997). Materialized View Selection in a Multidimensional Database. In *Proceedings of the 23rd VLDB Conference,* Athens, Greece (pp. 156-165).

Bellatreche, L., Boukhalfa, K., Richard, P., & Woameno, K. Y. (2009). Referential Horizontal Partitioning Selection Problem in Data Warehouses: Hardness Study and Selection Algorithms. *International Journal of Data Warehousing and Mining, 5*(4), 1–23. doi:10.4018/jdwm.2009080701

Chaudhuri, S., & Narasayya, V. (1997). An Efficient, Cost-Driven Index Selection Tool for Microsoft SQL Server. In *Proceedings of the 23rd VLDB Conference,* Athens, Greece (pp. 146-155).

Chen, L., Wenny Rahayu, J., & Taniar, D. (2010). Towards Near Real-Time Data Warehousing. In *Proceedings of the AINA 2010 Conference* (pp. 1150-1157).

Choi, C. H., Xu Yu, J., & Lu, H. (2003). Dynamic Materialized View Management Based on Predicates. In *Proceedings of the APWeb 2003 Conference* (LNCS 2642, pp. 583-594).

Daneshpour, N., & Abdollahzadeh Barfourosh, A. (2008). *View Selection Algorithms to Build Data Warehouse* (Tech. Rep. No. CE/ TR.DS/ 86/ 01). Tehran, Iran: AIS Lab, IT & Computer Engineering Department, Amirkabir University of Technology. Retrieved from http://ceit.aut.ac.ir/~daneshpour/Publications.htm

Daneshpour, N., & Abdollahzadeh Barfourosh, A. (in press). A Solution to View Management to Build a Data Warehouse. *Amirkabir Journal of Science and Technology.*

Dehne, F., Eavis, T., & Rau-Chaplin, A. (2008). RCUBE: Parallel Multi-Dimensional ROLAP Indexing. *International Journal of Data Warehousing and Mining, 4*(3), 1–14. doi:10.4018/jdwm.2008070101

El-Helw, A., Ilyas, I. F., & Zuzarte, C. (2009). StatAdvisor: Recommending Statistical Views. In *Proceedings of the VLDB '09 Conference* (pp. 1306-1317).

Gong, A., & Zhao, W. (2008). Clustering-based Dynamic Materialized View Selection Algorithm. In *Proceedings of the 5th IEEE International Conference on Fuzzy Systems & Knowledge Discovery* (pp. 391-395).

Gou, G., Xu Yu, J., & Lu, H. (2006). A* Search: An Efficient and Flexible Approach to Materialized View Selection. *IEEE Transactions on Systems, Man and Cybernetics. Part C, Applications and Reviews, 36*(3), 411–425. doi:10.1109/TSMCC.2004.843248

Gupta, H. (1997). Selection of Views to Materialize in a Data Warehouse. In *Proceedings of the International Conference on Database Theory,* Delphi, Greece (pp. 98-112).

Gupta, H., Harinarayan, V., Rajaraman, A., & Ullman, J. (1997). Index Selection for OLAP. In *Proceedings of the ICDE Conference,* Birmingham, UK (pp. 208-219).

Gupta, H., & Mumick, I. S. (2005). Selection of Views to Materialize in a Data Warehouse. *IEEE Transactions on Knowledge and Data Engineering, 17*(1), 24–43. doi:10.1109/TKDE.2005.16

Han, J., & Kamber, M. (2006). *Data mining Concepts and Techniques.* San Francisco, CA: Morgan Kaufmann.

Han, J., Pei, J., Mortazavi-Asl, B., Chen, Q., Dayal, U., & Hsu, M.-C. (2000). FreeSpan: Frequent pattern-projected sequential pattern mining. In *Proceedings of the 2000 ACM SIGKDD International Conference on Knowledge Discovery in Databases (KDD '00),* Boston, MA (pp. 355-359).

Hanusse, N., Maabout, S., & Tofan, R. (2009). A view selection algorithm with performance guarantee. In *Proceedings of the EDBT 2009 Conference* (pp. 946-957).

Harinarayan, V., Rajaraman, A., & Ullman, J. D. (1996). Implementing Data Cubes Efficiently. In *Proceedings of the SIGMOD '96 Conference,* Montreal, QC, Canada (pp. 205-216).

Hung, M. C., Huang, M. L., Yang, D. L., & Hsueh, N. L. (2007). Efficient approaches for materialized views selection in a data warehouse. *Information Sciences, 177,* 1333–1348. doi:10.1016/j.ins.2006.09.007

Kalnis, P., Mamoulis, N., & Papadias, D. (2002). View Selection Using Randomized Search. *Data & Knowledge Engineering, 42,* 89–111. doi:10.1016/S0169-023X(02)00045-9

Kotidis, Y., & Roussopoulos, N. (1999). DynaMat: A Dynamic View Management System for Data Warehouses. In *Proceedings of the SIGMOD '99 Conference,* Philadelphia, PA (pp. 371-382).

Kotidis, Y., & Roussopoulos, N. (2001). A Case for Dynamic View Management. *ACM Transactions on Database Systems, 26*(4), 388–423. doi:10.1145/503099.503100

Lawrence, M., & Rau-Chaplin, A. (2008). Dynamic View Selection for OLAP. *International Journal of Data Warehousing and Mining, 4*(1), 47–61. doi:10.4018/jdwm.2008010103

Le, D. X. T., Wenny Rahayu, J., & Taniar, D. (2007). A high performance integrated web data warehousing. *Cluster Computing, 10*(1), 95–109. doi:10.1007/s10586-007-0008-9

Lin, W. Y., & Kuo, I. C. (2004). A Genetic Selection Algorithm for OLAP Data Cubes. *Knowledge and Information Systems, 6,* 83–102. doi:10.1007/s10115-003-0093-x

Liu, Y. C., Hsu, P. Y., Sheen, G. J., Ku, S., & Chang, K. W. (2008). Simultaneous determination of view selection and update policy with stochastic query and response time constraints. *Information Sciences, 178*, 3491–3509. doi:10.1016/j.ins.2008.05.021

Mahboudi, H., Aouiche, K., & Darmon, J. (2006). Materialized View Selection by Query Clustering in XML Data Warehouses. In *Proceedings of the 4th International Multi-Conference on Computer Science and Information Technology (CSIT 2006)*, Amman, Jordan (Vol. 2, pp. 68-77).

Maurer, D., Wenny Rahayu, J., Rusu, L. I., & Taniar, D. (2009). A Right-Time Refresh for XML Data Warehouses. In *Proceedings of the DASFAA 2009 Conference* (pp. 745-749).

Nadeau, T. P., & Teorey, T. J. (2002). Achieving Scalability in OLAP Materialized View Selection. In *Proceedings of the DOLAP '02 Conference*, McLean, VA (pp. 28-34).

Pei, J., Han, J., Mortazavi-Asl, B., Pinto, H., Chen, Q., Dayal, U., & Hsu, M.-C. (2001). PrefixSpan: Mining sequential patterns efficiently by prefix-projected pattern growth. In *Proceedings of the International Conference on Data Engineering (ICDE'01)*, Heidelberg, Germany (pp. 215-224).

Pei, J., Han, J., Mortazavi-Asl, B., Wang, J., Pinto, H., & Chen, Q. (2004). Mining sequential patterns by pattern-growth: The prefixspan approach. *IEEE Transactions on Knowledge and Data Engineering, 16*, 1424–1440. doi:10.1109/TKDE.2004.77

Phan, T., & Li, W. S. (2008). Dynamic Materialization of Query Views for Data Warehouse Workloads. In *Proceedings of the ICDE 2008 Conference* (pp. 436-445). Washington, DC: IEEE Computer Society.

Ramachandran, K., Shah, B., & Raghavan, V. (2005). *Access Pattern-Based Dynamin Prefetching of Views in an OLAP System*. Paper presented at the International Conference on Enterprise Information Systems.

Ravat, F., Teste, O., Tournier, R., & Zurfluh, G. (2008). Algebraic and Graphic Languages for OLAP Manipulations. *International Journal of Data Warehousing and Mining, 4*(1), 17–46. doi:10.4018/jdwm.2008010102

Romero, O., & Abelló, A. (2009). A Survey of Multidimensional Modeling Methodologies. *International Journal of Data Warehousing and Mining, 5*(2), 1–23. doi:10.4018/jdwm.2009040101

Russell, S., & Norvig, P. (2003). *Artificial Intelligence: A Modern Approach* (2nd ed.). Upper Saddle River, NJ: Prentice Hall.

Rusu, L. I., Wenny Rahayu, J., & Taniar, D. (2005). A Methodology for Building XML Data Warehouses. *International Journal of Data Warehousing and Mining, 1*(2), 23–48. doi:10.4018/jdwm.2005040102

Rusu, L. I., Wenny Rahayu, J., & Taniar, D. (2006). Warehousing Dynamic XML Documents. In *Proceedings of the DaWaK 2006 Conference* (pp. 175-184).

Rusu, L. I., Wenny Rahayu, J., & Taniar, D. (2009). Partitioning methods for multi-version XML data warehouses. *Distributed and Parallel Databases, 25*(1-2), 47–69. doi:10.1007/s10619-009-7034-y

Sapia, C. (1999). *On Modeling and Predicting Query Behavior in OLAP Systems*. Paper presented at the DMDW'99 Conference.

Shah, B., Ramachandran, K., & Raghavan, V. (2006). A Hybrid Approach for Data Warehouse View Selection. *International Journal of Data Warehousing and Mining, 2*(2), 1–37. doi:10.4018/jdwm.2006040101

Shukla, A., Deshpande, P. M., & Naughton, J. F. (1998). Materialized View Selection for Multi-dimensional Datasets. In *Proceedings of the 24th VLDB Conference,* New York, NY (pp. 488-499).

Srikant, R., & Agrawal, R. (1996). Mining sequential patterns: Generalizations and performance improvements. In *Proceedings of the 5th International Conference on Extending Database Technology (EDBT'96),* Avignon, France (pp. 3-17).

Taniar, D., Leung, C. H. C., Wenny Rahayu, J., & Goel, S. (2008). *High Performance Parallel Database Processing and Grid Databases.* New York, NY: John Wiley & Sons. doi:10.1002/9780470391365

Taniar, D., & Wenny Rahayu, J. (2002a). A Taxonomy of Indexing Schemes for Parallel Database Systems. *Distributed and Parallel Databases, 12*(1), 73–106. doi:10.1023/A:1015682215394

Taniar, D., & Wenny Rahayu, J. (2002b). Parallel database sorting. *Information Science, 146*(1-4), 171–219. doi:10.1016/S0020-0255(02)00196-2

Taniar, D., & Wenny Rahayu, J. (2002c). Parallel group-by query processing in a cluster architecture. *International Journal of Computer Systems: Science and Engineering, 17*(1), 23–39.

Taniar, D., & Wenny Rahayu, J. (2002d). Parallel sort-merge object-oriented collection join algorithms. *International Journal of Computer Systems: Science and Engineering, 17*(3), 145–158.

Taniar, D., & Wenny Rahayu, J. (2004). Global parallel index for multi-processors database systems. *Information Science, 165*(1-2), 103–127. doi:10.1016/j.ins.2003.09.019

Valluri, S. R., Vadapalli, S., & Karlapalem, K. (2002). View Relevance Driven Materialized View Selection in Data Warehousing Environment. In *Proceedings of the ADC2002 Conference* (Vol. 5, pp. 187-196).

Xu, W., Theodoratos, D., & Zuzarte, C. (2007). A Dynamic View Materialization Scheme for Sequences of Query & Update Statements. In *Proceedings of the DaWaK 2007 Conference* (LNCS 4654, pp. 55-65).

Zaki, M. (2001). SPADE: An efficient algorithm for mining frequent sequences. *Machine Learning, 40,* 31–60. doi:10.1023/A:1007652502315

Zhang, C., Yang, J., & Kalapalem, K. (2003). Dynamic Materialized View Selection in Data Warehouse Environment. *Informatica, 27*(1), 451–460.

KEY TERMS AND DEFINITIONS

CRC: Cumulative Replacement Count.
DAG: Directed Acyclic Graph.
DCSR: Detailed Cost Saving Ratio.
DSS: Decision Support Systems.
LFU: Least Frequently Used.
LRU: Least Recently Used.
OLAP: On-Line Analytical Processing.
PR_Q_Predictor: Probabilistic Reasoning Query Predictor.
SFF: Smaller Fragment First.
SPF: Smaller Penalty First.

This work was previously published in the International Journal of Data Warehousing and Mining, Volume 7, Issue 2, edited by David Taniar, pp. 67-96, copyright 2011 by IGI Publishing (an imprint of IGI Global).

Chapter 8

Finding Associations in Composite Data Sets:
The CFARM Algorithm

M. Sulaiman Khan
University of Liverpool, UK

Frans Coenen
University of Liverpool, UK

Maybin Muyeba
Manchester Metropolitan University, UK

David Reid
Liverpool Hope University, UK

Hissam Tawfik
Liverpool Hope University, UK

ABSTRACT

In this paper, a composite fuzzy association rule mining mechanism (CFARM), directed at identifying patterns in datasets comprised of composite attributes, is described. Composite attributes are defined as attributes that can take simultaneously two or more values that subscribe to a common schema. The objective is to generate fuzzy association rules using "properties" associated with these composite attributes. The exemplar application is the analysis of the nutrients contained in items found in grocery data sets. The paper commences with a review of the back ground and related work, and a formal definition of the CFARM concepts. The CFARM algorithm is then fully described and evaluated using both real and synthetic data sets.

INTRODUCTION

Data mining is an important well established research area and Association Rule Mining (ARM) is a very popular topic in the data mining community. The objective of ARM is to identify patterns, expressed as Association Rules (ARs), usually from binary-valued transaction data sets (Fayyad et al., 1996; Bodon, 2003; Coenen et al., 2004a, 2004b; Agrawal et al., 1993). Work has been done on a variety of extensions of the standard (binary-valued) approach to ARM thus allowing for its applicability to quantitative and categorical (non-binary) data (Gyenesei, 2001; Dong & Tjortjis, 2003; Srikant & Agrawal, 1996; Au & Chan, 1999). To deal with quantitative data, values are divided into ranges such that each range represents a binary valued attribute

DOI: 10.4018/978-1-4666-2148-0.ch008

and then labelling the identified range attributes; for example "low", "medium", "high", etc. There are two possible ways for assigning ranges: using crisp boundaries or fuzzy boundaries. Fuzzy ARM uses the latter to identify fuzzy ARs. Some earlier works show that more expressive ARs can be obtained using fuzzy ARM than "crisp" methods (Gyenesei, 2001; Kuok et al., 1998; Dubois et al., 2006; Khan et al., 2006). ARM (both fuzzy and standard) algorithms typically use the support-confidence framework to identify "interesting" ARs during the rule generation process. However, this framework has a number of disadvantages, for example, generating a vast AR set many of which are either obvious, subsumed by other rules, or largely redundant. Consequently there are motivations in the data mining community for finding more expressive, succinct or significant and useful ARs. Earlier work (Kuok et al., 1998; Khan et al., 2006) demonstrates this using the certainty measure, which is of note in the context of the work described here.

In this paper we introduce a particular category of a fuzzy ARM application called Composite item Fuzzy ARM (CFARM). CFARM's objective is to generate fuzzy ARs from "properties" associated with composite attributes (Kim et al., 1989), i.e., attributes or items composed of sets of sub-attributes or sub-items that have a common schema. Image mining is a typical example where different areas of an image has groups of pixels such that each group can be represented by the normalized summation of the RGB values of the pixels in that group. In this case the set of composite attributes (I) is the set of groups, and the set of properties (P) shared by the groups is equivalent to the RGB summation values (i.e., $P=\{R,G,B\}$). We can then express fuzzy sets such as "light", "medium" and "dark" and find associations between such composite attribute attributes with their properties. Considering the familiar market basket scenario, we can have defined I as a set of groceries and P as a set of nutritional properties that these groceries may possess, for

example protein, iron, calcium and copper (i.e., P = {Pr, Fe, Ca, Cu...}). Of note is the difference in these two examples. In the shopping basket, I is constant, i.e., it only represents a categorical list of common properties. In the image mining example, I is a normalized summation of properties.

Further, a stock control database can have I as a collection of stock items where P a collection of stock item properties is common to all items, including for example cost price, sale price, re-order time, etc. Given that we have quantitative attributes that can be partitioned into intervals or ranges, we rename such partitions with linguistic values or in this case, introduce fuzzy sets for these attributes. We are motivated by the fact that the approach described in this paper is a new way of dealing with so-called composite attributes that may potentially have fuzzy features.

The main contributions of the paper are:

1. The concept of CFARM.
2. The potential of ARs from itemset properties.
3. A practical example of the use of CFARM.
4. Employment of certainty factor, a quality measure to produce strong rules.
5. New Fuzzy Apriori-T algorithm for better efficiency.

We also demonstrate that a more succinct set of property ARs (than that generated using a non-fuzzy method) can be produced using the proposed approach.

The paper is organised as follows. In Section 2 we present the background and related work to the proposed composite fuzzy ARM approach described. Section 3 presents a sequence of terms and concepts for the work and Section 4 introduces the CFARM algorithm. The motivation for the work is expanded upon in Section 5 where an example application is described. A complete analysis of the operation of the CFARM algorithm is given in Section 6, and Section 7 concludes the paper with a summary of the contribution of the work and directions for future work.

BACKGROUND AND RELATED WORK

The most familiar ARM approach is to first generate all the itemsets (attribute sets) and then derive sets of ARs (Agrawal et al., 1993). A frequent itemset is defined as one that appears most often in the given data set. To determine "frequency" of an item, there is a user supplied support threshold measure that checks item frequencies. Similarly, a confidence threshold is a conditional probability measure of the strength of ARs generated. The user must select support and confidence thresholds to influence the number and strength of ARs. Ensuring that itemsets with low support but from which high confidence rules may be generated depends on careful selection of support and confidence.

Some drawbacks on using only the support and confidence framework to assess association rules have been reported (Berzal et al., 2002; Silverstein et al., 1998; Sánchez, 1999). To avoid some of these and to ensure interesting discovered rules, the certainty factor and the new concept a very strong rule was proposed in Berzal et al. (2002) and Sánchez (1999). Implementations can be found in Gyenesei (2001), Kuok et al. (1998), and Khan et al. (2006, 2008).

From database literature, the term composite item has been used previously in the context of data mining. Wang et al. (2006) and Ye and Keane (1997) define a composite item as combining several items, e.g., if itemset {A, B} and {A, C} are not frequent then rules {B}→{A} and {C}→{A} will not be generated, but by combining B and C to make a new *composite* item {BC} which may be frequent, rules such as {BC}→{A} may be generated. The difference with the approach in this paper is that we define a composite item to be a structured attribute as indicated in the introduction to this paper and explained further in Section 3. The definition concurs with database literature (Kim et al., 1987, 1989), the earliest references to composite attributes that the authors are aware of, which also defines composite attributes (items)

in this manner, i.e., as attributes that comprise two or more sub-attributes. The difference with fuzzy ARM algorithms is their non-use of composite items.

ARM typically operates using binary valued attributes. Given quantitative attributes, these can be discretised into a number of interval partitions where each partition is regarded as a binary valued attribute. A major problem in discretising quantitative attributes using interval partitions (Gyenesei, 2001; Khan et al., 2006; Kuok et al., 1998) is the "sharp boundary problem". Fuzzy ARM (Kuok et al. 1998; Gyenesei, 2001; Chen & Wei, 2002; Au & Chan, 1999) is one approach to addressing this problem. Fuzzy ARM is used to discover frequent itemsets using fuzzy sets (with overlapping partitions) to handle the quantitative attributes. Fuzzy approaches deal with quantitative attributes by mapping numeric values to membership degrees from their partitions. The mapping is undertaken in such a way that individual item contributions to support counts remain at unity regardless of whether an item value belongs to one or more fuzzy sets (a similar approach was used in Gyenesei, 2001). The main benefit of using fuzzy ARs is that fuzzy sets can soften the effect of sharp boundaries and make the rules more understandable to the user. Detailed overviews for fuzzy association rules are given in Gyenesei (2001), Kuok et al. (1998), Delgado et al. (2003), and Au and Chan (1999).

More generally, fuzzy data mining algorithms have been utilized in many application domains, example include (i) fuzzy ARs for classifier in capturing correlations between genes (Khabbaz et al., 2008), (ii) parallel fuzzy c-Means clustering for large data sets (Kwok et al., 2002), and (iii) acquisition of fuzzy association rules from medical data (Delgado et al., 2001, 2002).

To the best of our knowledge there seems to be no work on composite association rule mining using fuzzy approaches.

To illustrate the work described here we consider super market basket analysis where the set

Table 1. Example composite attributes (groceries) with their associated properties (nutrients)

Items/Nutrients	Protein	Fibre	Carbohydrate	Fat	...
Yogurt	2.9	0.0	5.1	0.3	...
Pita Bread	9.5	3.6	39.9	1.6	...
Wafers	7.1	4.9	58.3	24.9	...
...	...	...	...	...	...

of groceries (*I*) have a shared set of nutritional quantitative properties (*P*). Some examples are given in Table 1. The objective is then to identify patterns linking the properties (nutrients in the case of the example).

Table 1 shows some items from market basket data that we can extract nutrients, presumably "edible items", all with common properties or nutrients. The context of our problem is illustrated in Figure 1. The figure shows edible composite items with common properties such as Protein, Fibre, Iron, etc. defined by the same five fuzzy sets {Very Low, Low, Ideal, High, Very High}.

In Figure 1, a composite item such as "yogurt" can have properties of nutrients (protein, iron, calcium, etc.) measured quantitatively as such and therefore can be expressed as fuzzy sets in the usual way. The amount of nutrients in an item can be measured by the degree of membership, for example membership of "fibre" in "yogurt" is zero. We define the problem of addressing composite item fuzzy association rules in the next section.

PROBLEM DEFINITION

In this section a sequence of terms and concepts is presented to: (i) define the term composite attributes, (ii) describe the concept of fuzzy association rule mining, and (iii) the fuzzy approach adopted by the authors. The normalization process for Fuzzy Transactions (*FT)* and rule interestingness measures will also be discussed later in this section. In this section, we look data, and fuzzy specific concepts, and finally quality measures for fuzzy association rules.

Data Specific Concepts

- **Raw Data:** A Raw Dataset (the input data) *D* consists of a set of transactions $T=\{t_1, t_2, t_3, \dots t_n\}$, a set of composite items $I = \{i_1, i_2, i_3, \cdots, i_{|I|}\}$ and a set of properties $P=\{p_1, p_2, p_3, \dots p_m\}$,. Each transaction t_i (the "i^{th}" transaction) is some subset of *I*, and each item $t_i[i_j]$ (the "j^{th}" item in the "j^{th}" transaction) is a subset of *P*. Thus each

Figure 1. Edible items, nutrients & fuzzy intervals

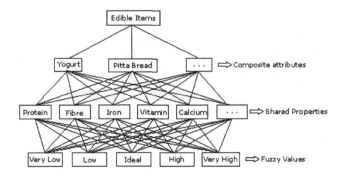

item i_j will have associated with it a set of values corresponding to the set P, i.e., $t_i[i_j] = \{v \mid v_1, v_2, v_3, \cdots, v_m\}$. The "$k^{th}$" property value for the "j^{th}" item in the "i^{th}" transaction is given by $t_i[i_j[v_k]]$. Note that a property attribute can take either a categorical or a quantitative value. An example is given in Table 2 where each composite item is represented using the notation <label,value>; thus record 1 comprises two items *a* and *b* which have (numeric) values {2,4,6} and {4,5,3} respectively. Note that in this example each distinct item has a common set of property values (in practice this is usually the case).

In the rest of this paper the term item is used to mean an *item* in an itemset in the manner associated with traditional ARM, and the term *attribute* is used to mean a property item (sub-item).

- **Property Dataset:** In the process described here the given raw dataset D is initially transformed into a property data set D^p. A property dataset D^p consists of property transactions $T^p = \{t_1^p, t_2^p, t_3^p, \ldots t_n^p\}$ and a set of property attributes P (instead of a set of composite items I). Each transaction t_i^p (the "i^{th}" transaction) is some subset of $P = \{p_1, p_2, p_3, \cdots, p_m\}$. The value for each property attribute $t_i^p[p_j]$ (the "j^{th}" property attribute in the "i^{th}" property

transaction) has a numeric value obtained by aggregating the numeric values for all p_j in t_i. Thus:

$$(t_i^p[p_j]) = \frac{\sum_{j=1}^{|t_i|} t_i[i_j[v_k]]}{|t_i|} \qquad (1)$$

An example is given in Table 3.

In Table 3 the values are calculated by first aggregating and then averaging the items' property values using Table 2, e.g., in Table 3 row 1 the value for property X is calculates by first aggregating the property values from Table 2 row 1 using item "a" and "b" as 1.0+3.0=4.0 and later averaging them 4.0/2.0=2.0. Same for the property value Y as 5.0+7.0=12.0, then 12.0/2.0=6.0.

- **Fuzzy Dataset:** With respect to the work described here, once a property data set D^p has been established this is further transformed into a fuzzy dataset D'. A fuzzy dataset D' consists of fuzzy transactions $T' = \{t_1', t_2', t_3', \ldots, t_n'\}$ and a set of fuzzy property attributes P' each of which in turn has a number of fuzzy sets associated with it identified by a set of linguistic labels $L = \{l_1, l_2, l_3, \ldots, l_{|L|}\}$ (for example

Table 2. Example raw dataset D

TID	Record
1	{<a,{1,5,4}>, <b,{3,7,2}>}
2	{<c,{6,2,4}>, <d,{2,5,1}>}
3	{<a,{1,5,4}>, <c,{6,2,4}>, <d,{2,5,1}>}
4	{<b,{3,7,2}>, <d,{2,5,1}>}

D = {T₁, T₂, T₃, T₄}
I = {a, b, c, d}
P = {x, y, z}

Table 3. Example property data set D^p generated from raw data set given in Table 2

TID	X	Y	Z
1	2.0	6.0	3.0
2	4.0	3.5	2.5
3	3.0	4.0	3.0
4	2.5	6.0	1.5

Table 4. Example fuzzy data set (L={small, medium, large}, μ unspecified)

TID	X			Y			Z		
	Small	Medium	Large	Small	Medium	Large	Small	Medium	Large
1	0.79	0.21	0.00	0.00	0.00	1.00	0.16	0.84	0.00
2	0.00	0.43	0.57	0.53	0.47	0.00	0.62	0.38	0.00
3	0.00	1.00	0.00	0.01	0.99	0.00	0.16	0.84	0.00
4	0.18	0.72	0.00	0.00	0.00	1.00	1.00	0.00	0.00

$L=\{$small, medium, large$\}$). The fuzzy sets describe a sequence of overlapping user defined ranges into which all possible values for property attributes may be mapped. Each property attribute $t_i^p[p_j]$ is associated (to some degree) with several fuzzy sets. The degree of association is given by a membership degree value, in the range $[0,1]$, which indicates the correspondence between the value of a given $t_i^p[p_j]$ and the set of fuzzy linguistic *labels*. The "kth" label for the "jth" property attribute for the "ith" fuzzy transaction is given by $t_i'[p_j[l_k]]$. The nature of the user defined fuzzy ranges is expressed in a properties table (see definition 6 below). The numeric values for each property attribute $t_i^p[p_j]$ are fuzzified (mapped) into the appropriate membership degree values using a membership function $\mu(t_i^p[p_j], l_k)$ that applies the value of $t_i^p[p_j]$ to the definition of a specified label $l_k \in L$, thus

$$t_i'[p_j] = \{\mu(t_i^p[p_j]], l_1), \mu(t_i^p[p_j]], l_2), \mu(t_i^p[p_j]], l_3), ..., \mu(t_i^p[p_j]], l_{|L|})\}$$

The nature of the function is discussed in more detail in Section 3.2. The complete set of fuzzy property attributes P' is then given by $P \times L$.

An example fuzzy data set is given in Table 4 based on the property data set given in Table 3. Note that the membership values have all been normalised so that the contribution to the support count for a single attribute in a single record remains in $[0,1]$.

- **Composite Itemset Value Table:** A Composite Itemset Value (CIV) table is a table that allows us to get property values for specific items. For completeness the CIV table for the example raw dataset given in Table 2 is given in Table 5.
- **Properties Table:** A Properties Table is a table that maps all possible values for each property attribute $t_i^p[p_j]$ onto user defined (overlapping) ranges, each associated with a linguistic label taken from the set of available linguistic labels L. Properties tables provide a mapping of property attribute values to membership values according to the correspondence between the given values to the given ranges (linguistic labels). An example is given in Table 6 for the raw data set given in Table 2.

Table 5. CIV Table

Item	Property attributes		
	X	Y	Z
A	2	4	6
B	4	5	3
C	1	2	5
D	4	1	3

Table 6. Property table for raw dataset given in Table 2

Property	Linguistic values		
	Low	Medium	High
X	$v_k \leq 2.6$	$1.9 < v_k \leq 4.2$	$3.7 < v_k$
Y	$v_k \leq 3.9$	$3.1 < v_k \leq 4.8$	$4.3 < v_k$
Z	$v_k \leq 3.0$	$2.3 < v_k \leq 4.1$	$3.6 < v_k$

Fuzzy Specific Concepts

- **Fuzzy Association Rules:** A Fuzzy Association Rule (Kuok et al., 1998) is an implication of the form: if $\langle A \ is \ X \rangle$ then $\langle B \ is \ Y \rangle$ where A and B are disjoint itemsets and X and Y are fuzzy sets. In our case the itemsets are made up of property attributes and the fuzzy sets are identified by linguistic labels (for example "small", "medium", "large").

- **Fuzzy Frequent Itemset:** A property attribute set X, where $A \subseteq P \times L$, is a fuzzy frequent attribute set if its fuzzy support *value* is greater than or equal to a user supplied minimum support threshold (the notion of fuzzy support values is discussed further in Section 3.3). The significance of fuzzy frequent attribute sets is that fuzzy association rules are generated from the set of discovered frequent attribute sets.

- **Fuzzy Normalisation:** Fuzzy normalisation is the process of finding the contribu-

tion to the fuzzy support value, m', for individual property attributes $t_i^p[p_j[l_k]]$ such that a partition of unity is guaranteed. This is given by the equation (where μ is the membership function):

$$t_i'[p_j[l_k]] = \frac{\mu(t_i^p[p_j[l_k]])}{\sum_{x=1}^{|L|} \mu(t_i^p[p_j[l_x]])} \qquad (2)$$

Without normalisation, the sum of the support contributions of individual fuzzy sets associated with an attribute in a single transaction may no longer be unity. This is illustrated in Tables 7 and 8 (both taken from the example application outlined in Section 5). In the tables, the possible values for the item "Proteins" have been organised into five fuzzy sets labelled: "Very Low" (VL), "Low" (L), "Ideal", "High" (H) and "Very High" (VH). Table 7 shows a set of raw membership degree values, while Table 8 shows the normalised equivalents.

Table 7. Fragment of example data set without normalization

TID	Proteins					...
	VL	L	Ideal	H	VH	...
1	0.0	0.0	0.0	0.32	1.0	...
2	0.0	0.38	0.83	0.0	0.0	...
3	...	...	...	...	...	...

Table 8. Fragment of example data set with normalization

TID	Proteins					...
	VL	L	Ideal	H	VH	...
1	0.0	0.0	0.0	0.24	0.76	...
2	0.0	0.31	0.69	0.0	0.0	...
3	...	...	...	...	...	...

In Table 7, without normalisation, it would increase the support of protein by 0.32 in row 1 and 0.21 in row 2. That means, these transactions will be counted 0.32+1.0=1.32 and 0.38+0.83=1.21 times for protein. However, it is unreasonable for one transaction to contribute more than others, if the corresponding discrete sets are disjoint.

The normalisation process ensures fuzzy membership values for each property attribute are consistent and are not affected by boundary values.

- **Fuzzy Membership Function:** Contribution or membership degree to a particular fuzzy set (described by a linguistic label), $t_i[p_j[l_k]]$ is determined by a membership function. There are many different types of membership function and the type of representation of the membership function depends on the nature of the fuzzy set. The most common membership function is an isosceles trapezoidal function, others include triangular, rectangular and semi-circular functions. An example, using the market basket analysis application introduced in Section 1, is given in Figure 2. The figure demonstrates the membership functions for the Protein nutrient. With respect to the application, the trapezoidal shape was chosen as it best

captures the intuition (promoted by nutritionists) that nutrient values above or below the ideal is undesirable. Note that the ideal nutrient value equates to 1.

$$\mu(x, \alpha, \beta, \gamma, \delta) = \begin{cases} 0, \delta < x < \alpha \\ \dfrac{(x - \alpha)}{(\beta - \alpha)}, \alpha \leq x \leq \beta \\ \dfrac{(\delta - x)}{(\delta - \gamma)}, \gamma \leq x \leq \delta \\ 1, \beta < x < \gamma \end{cases} \quad (3)$$

Equation 3 (Paetz, 2002) is a function representing all the membership degrees of an input value "x". Other parameters α, β, γ and δ refer to the corners of the trapezium proceeding in a clockwise fashion starting with the bottom-left corner. The value x has an "ideal" value between the points β to γ along the "X" axis, with the lowest value α and the highest value δ. From the example in Figure 2, an "ideal" protein intake will have values in the range [40,60]. If there are missing properties (or trace elements) in an item, as shown in Figure 1 (e.g., Bread has no proteins, so called "trace" elements), the fuzzy function evaluates to zero degree membership.

Figure 2. Fuzzy membership functions

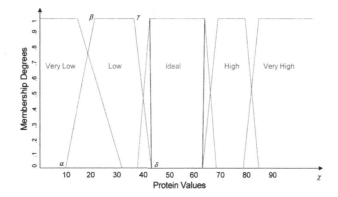

Quality Measures for Fuzzy Association Rules

A very important aspect in data mining is the discovery of interesting knowledge, where interestingness relates to unexpectedness (Fayyad et al., 1996). Extensive study in databases has been carried out recently in order to find out the most interesting rules with subjective and objective measures. Subjective measures (Silberschatz & Tuzhilin, 1995) take into account the user's goals and domain knowledge. Objective measures (Freitas, 1998) evaluate the interestingness of a rule in terms of rule structure and the underlying data in rule generation such as support, confidence, certainty and entropy.

However, the support-confidence framework remains the most popular approach in traditional ARM and identifies frequent itemsets and assesses the relevance of the generated ARs. The support-confidence framework, with some modifications, can also be applied to composite item fuzzy association rule mining.

- **Fuzzy Support:** Frequent fuzzy attribute sets are identified by calculating fuzzy support (significance) values. Fuzzy Support $(Supp_{Fuzzy})$ is typically calculated as follows:

$$Supp_{Fuzzy}(A) = \frac{\text{Sum of votes satisfying A}}{\text{Number of records in } T}$$

where $A = \{a_1, a_2, a_3, ..., a_{|A|}\}$ is a set of property attribute-fuzzy set (label) pairs such that $A \subseteq P \times L$. A record t_i' "satisfies" A if $A \subseteq t_i'$. The individual vote per record, t_i, is obtaining by multiplying the membership degree associated with each attribute-fuzzy set pair $[i[l]] \in A$:

vote for t_i satisfying $A = \prod_{\forall[i[l]]\in A} t_i'[i[l]]$ (4)

$$Supp_{Fuzzy}(A) = \frac{\sum_{i=1}^{i=n} \prod_{\forall[i[l]]\in A} t_i'[i[l]]}{n}$$ (5)

Note that by using the product operator (often referred to in fuzzy ARM literature as the *mul* operator) for fuzzy aggregation, the degree of contribution of all items is taken into account and thus provides for a more effective result (and also ensures that the overall contribution remains within the range [0,1]). Alternatives found in the literature include the *min* and *max* operators as:

$$Supp_{Fuzzy}(A) = \frac{\sum_{i=1}^{i=n} \min_{\forall[i[l]]\in A}(t_i'[i[l]])}{n}$$

$$Supp_{Fuzzy}(A) = \frac{\sum_{i=1}^{i=n} \max_{\forall[i[l]]\in A}(t_i'[i[l]])}{n}$$

However these do not include the contribution of all values. Table 9 demonstrates the effect of using mul, min and max fuzzy support calculation using $T' = \{t_1', t_2', t_3', t_4'\}$ and $A = \{a_1, a_2, a_3, a_4\}$. Note that the vote for t_3' is zero because t_3' is not a subset of A.

We use an example to illustrate the computation of the fuzzy support value. Let A={X, Z} and P={Small, Large} and a part of database shown in Table 4. The fuzzy support of {A, P} is calculated as follows: Support$_{Fuzzy}$ (A, P)=(0.5+0+0.5)/3=0.33

- **Fuzzy Confidence:** Frequent attribute sets with fuzzy support above the user specified threshold are used to generate all possible rules. A fuzzy AR derived from a fuzzy frequent attribute set C is of the form:

Table 9. Effect of fuzzy mul operator

T'	A					Vote for t_i satisfying A		
	a_1	a_2	a_3	a_4		Max	Min	Mul
t'_1	0.4	0.6	0.7	0.9	→	0.900	0.400	0.151
t'_2	0.9	0.8	0.5	0.6	→	0.900	0.500	0.216
t'_3	0.7	0.5	0.3	0.8	→	0.800	0.300	0.084
t'_4	0.8	0.9	0.7	0.2	→	0.900	0.200	0.101
					FS(A)	0.875	0.350	0.138

$A{\rightarrow}B$

where *A* and *B* are disjoint subsets of the set $P{\times}L$ such that $A{\cup}B{=}C$. Fuzzy Confidence $(Conf_{Fuzzy})$ is calculated in the same manner that confidence is calculated in traditional ARM:

$$Conf_{Fuzzy}(A \rightarrow B) = \frac{Supp_{Fuzzy}(A \cup B)}{Supp_{Fuzzy}(A)} \qquad (6)$$

- **Certainty Measure:** The Fuzzy Confidence measure $(Conf_{Fuzzy})$ described above is often criticised because it does not take into account the effect of $Supp_{Fuzzy}(B)$. The certainty measure (*Cert*) addresses this. The certainty measure is a statistical measure founded on the concepts of *covariance (Cov)* and *variance (Var)*. Certainty is calculated using Equation 7:

$$Cert(A \rightarrow B) = \frac{Cov(A, B)}{\sqrt{Var(A) \times Var(B)}} \qquad (7)$$

Certainty values range between -1 and +1, positive when the dependence between A and B is positive, 0 when there is independence and negative when the dependence is negative. We are only interested in rules that have a certainty value that is greater than 0. As the certainty value increases from 0 to 1, the more related the attributes are and consequently the more interesting the rule is. It is worth noting that the certainty of an association rule reaches its maximum possible value, 1, if and only if the rule is completely accurate (Delgado et al., 2003).

THE FUZZY APRIORI-T (CFARM) ALGORITHM

For fuzzy association rule mining standard ARM algorithms can be used or at least adopted after some modifications (Khan et al., 2006, 2008; Gyenesei, 2001). There is limited work addressing performance issues in fuzzy association rule mining but still there are some contributions in this area (Chen & Wei, 2002; Khan et al., 2006). An efficient algorithm is required because a significant amount of processing is undertaken to prepare the raw data prior to the application of fuzzy association rule mining. For example, filtration where data is filtered or extracted, specifically edible items from non-edible ones, conversion of quantitative properties into fuzzy sets and normalizing membership contributions of the properties.

Table 10. rawToPropertyDataSetConverter (T)

Input:
T= Raw data set
Output:
T^p = Property data set
1. $T^p = \varphi$ 2. *for each* $t_i \in T$ *do* 3. *for each* $\mathrm{p}_k \in P$ do 4. *for each* $\mathrm{i}_j \in t_1$ do 5. $value \Leftarrow value + t_i[i_j[p_k]]]$ 6. $t_i^p[p_j] \Leftarrow value\, /\, |t_i|$ 7. $T^p \Leftarrow T^p \cup t_i^p$

Table 11. propertToFuzzyDataSetConverter (Tᵖ)

Input:
T^p = property data set
Output:
T' = Fuzzy data set
1. $T' = \varphi$ 2. *for each* $t_i^p \in T^p$ *do* 3. *for each* $\mathrm{p}_j \in t_i^p$ *do* 4. *for each* $l_k \in L do$ 5. $t_i'[p_j[l_k]] \Leftarrow \mu([t_j^p[p_j]], l_k)$ 6. $T' \Leftarrow T' \cup t_i'[p_j]$

The proposed Composite Fuzzy Apriori-T ARM (CFARM) algorithm is developed using T-tree data structures (Coenen et al., 2004a) and works in a fashion similar to the Apriori algorithm (Bodon, 2003).

The CFARM algorithm consists of four major steps:

- **Data Preprocessing Steps:**
  - Transformation of ordinary transactional data set (T) into a property data set (T^p).
  - Transformation of property data set (T^p) into a fuzzy data set T'.
- **Association Rule Mining Steps:**
  - Apply Fuzzy Apriori-T association rule mining algorithm to T' using fuzzy support, confidence and certainty measures of the form described above to produce a set of frequent itemsets F.
  - Process F and generate a set of fuzzy ARs R such that $\forall r \in R$ the interestingness threshold (either confidence or certainty as desired by the end user) is above some user specified threshold.

The algorithms for steps 1and 2 are presented in Tables 10 and 11.

To illustrate steps 1 and 2 from Table 10, a fragment of a raw data set (T) is given in Table 2. This raw data is then cast into a properties data set (T^P). This is done, as described above; by averaging the property values for each transaction (Section 3.1 and Table 3). For example, assuming the CIV table given in Table 5 and considering transaction $t_1 = \{a, b\}$, from Table 2, a has property values $\{2,4,6\}$ and b has property values $\{4,5,3\}$.

Thus

$t_1^p = \{(2 + 4)\, /\, 2, (4 + 5)\, /\, 2, (6 + 3)\, /\, 2\}$

$= \{3.0, 4.5, 4.5\}$, assuming the properties table of the form presented in Table 6 where $L=\{$small, medium, large$\}$. The result is as shown in Table 3 which is then cast into a fuzzy data set T' as shown in Table 4.

The final part of the CFARM algorithm is given in Table 16. In the table, C_k is the set of candidate itemsets of cardinality k, F is the set of

Table 12. Frequent sets

1 (0.53)	1 2 (0.13)	
2 (0.23)	1 4 (0.21)	4 5 (0.13)
3 (0.43)	1 6 (0.26)	4 6 (0.19)
4 (0.40)	2 6 (0.12)	1 4 6 (0.11)
5 (0.30)	3 4 (0.19)	
6 (0.47)	3 5 (0.18)	

frequent itemsets, R is the set of potential rules and R' is the final set of generated fuzzy ARs.

The Fuzzy Apriori-T Algorithm

The Fuzzy Apriori-T algorithm (Apriori-Total) is founded on tree structure called the T-tree (Coenen et al., 2004b). This is a set enumeration tree structure in which to store frequent item set information. What distinguishes the T-tree from other set enumeration tree structures is:

1. Levels in each sub-branch of the tree are defined using arrays. This thus permits "indexing in" at all levels and consequently offers computational advantages.
2. To aid this indexing the tree is built in "reverse". Each branch is founded on the last element of the frequent sets to be stored. This allows direct indexing with attribute number rather than first applying some offset.

Thus given a data set of the form (ignoring any fuzzy membership issues):

Table 13. Apriori algorithm

```
K ← 1
nextlevelFlag=true;
generate candidate K-itemsets
Loop
count support values for candidate K-itemsets
prune unsupported K-itemsets
K ← 2
generate candidate K2 itemsets from previous level
if no K2 itemsets
break
end Loop
```

Table 14. The createTotalSupportTree method

```
Method: createTotalSupportTree
Arguments: none
Return: none
Fields: NA
-----------------------------
createTtreeTopLevel()
generateLevel2()
createTtreeLevelN()
-----------------------------
```

```
A=0.6, B=0.5, C=0.3, D=0.2, E=0.8,
F=0.3
{ 1 2 3 4 5 6 }
{0.6 0.3 0.2 0.4 0.1 0.9}
{0.5 0.2 0.8 0.5 0.6 0.4}
{0.5 0.2 0.3 0.3 0.2 0.1}
```

These can be presented in a T-tree of the form given in Figure 3 (note the reverse nature of the tree).

The internal representation of this "reverse" T-tree founded on arrays of T-tree nodes that can be conceptualised as shown in Figure 4. The storage required for each node (representing a frequent set) in the T-tree is then 12 Bytes:

1. Reference to T-tree node structure (4 Bytes).
2. Support count field in T-tree node structure (4 Bytes).

Table 15. The createTtreeTopLevel method

```
Method: createTtreeTopLevel
Arguments: none
Return: none
Fields: D: number of attributes
startTtreeRef: start of T-tree
dataArray 2D: array holding input sets
--------------------------------------
Dimension and initialise top level of T-tree(length=D)
Loop from i= 0 to i = number of records in dataArray
Loop j=0 to j=number of attributes in dataArray[i]
startTtreeRef[i][j]++
End loop
End Loop
pruneLevelN(startTtreeRef,1)
--------------------------------------
```

Table 16. The createTtreeLevelN method

```
Method: createTtreeLevelN
Arguments: none
Return: none
Fields: startTtreeRef: start of T-tree
nextlevelFlag: set true if next level exists
----------------------------------------
K <-- 2
while (nextlevelFlag)
addSupportToTtreeLevelN(K)
pruneLevelN(startTtreeRef,K)
nextlevelFlag ← false
generateLevelN(startTtreeRef,K,{})
K ← K+1
End loop
```

3. Reference to child array field in T-tree node structure (4 Bytes).

Thus housekeeping requirements are still 8 Bytes; however, storage gains are obtained because it is not necessary to explicitly store individual attribute labels (i.e., column numbers representing instantiated elements) as these are implied by the indexing. Of course this approach must also require storage for "stubs" (4 Bytes) where nodes are missing (unsupported). Overall the storage advantages for this technique is thus, in part, dependent on the number of missing combinations contained in the data set.

The T-tree described above is built in an Apriori manner, as first proposed in Bodon (2003), starting with one itemsets and continuing until no more candidate N-itemsets exist. Thus, at a high level, a standard Apriori algorithm is used (Table 13).

In more detail the Apriori-T algorithm commences with a method createTotalSupportTree

which is presented in Table 14. The method starts by generating the top level of the T-tree (createTtreeTopLevel) and then generating the next level (generateLevel2) from the supported sets in level 1. Remember that if a 1-itemset is not supported, none of its super sets will be supported according to downward closure property in ARM. Once we have generated level 2 further levels can be generated (createTtreeLevelN).

The method to generate the top level of a T-tree is as presented in Table 15. Note that the method includes a call to a general T-tree utility method pruneLevelN described later.

The generateLevel2 method loops through the top level of the T-tree creating new T-tree arrays where appropriate (i.e., where the immediate parent nodes is supported). The method is outlined in Table 16. Note that the method includes a call to a general T-tree utility method generateNextLevel (also described later).

Once we have a top level T-tree and a set of candidate second levels (arrays) we can proceed with generating the rest of the T-tree using an iterative process -- the createTtreeLevelN method presented in Table 16. The createTtreeLevelN method calls a number of other methods addSupportToTtreeLevelN, pruneLevelN (also called by the createTtreeTopLevel method) and generateLevelN which are presented in Tables 17, 18, and 19, respectively.

Figure 3. Conceptual example of the T-tree data structure

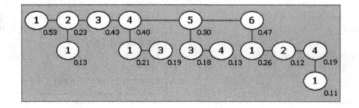

Table 17. addSupportToTtreeLevelN, addSupport-ToTtreeFindLevel methods

```
Method: addSupportToTtreeLevelN
Arguments: K the current level
Return: none
Fields: startTtreeRef: start of T-tree
dataArray 2D: array holding input sets
---------------------------------------
Loop i = 0 to i = number of records in dataArray
length ← number of attributes in dataArray[i]
addSupportToTtreeFindLevel(startTtreeRef,K,length,
dataArray[i]
End loop
---------------------------------------
Method: addSupportToTtreeFindLevel
Arguments:
linkref: refers to current array in T-tree
K: level marker
Length: array length at current branch in t-tree
record input data record under consideration
Return: none
Fields: None
---------------------------------------
if (K=1)
Loop from i = 0 to i = length
if (linkref[record[i]] != null)
increment linkref[record[i]].weightedsupport
End if
End Loop
else
Loop from i = K-1 to i = length
if (linkref[record[i]] != null &&
linkref[record[i]].childRef != null)
addSupportToTtreeFindLevel(linkref[record[i]].childRe,
K-1,i,record)
End if
End loop
end if else
---------------------------------------
```

Table 18. The pruneLevelN

```
Method: pruneLevelN
Arguments: linkref reference to current array in T-tree
K level marker
Return: true if entire array pruned
Fields: minSupport the minimum support threshold
---------------------------------------
if (K=1)
allUnsupported <-- true
Loop from i = 1 to i = length of array
if (linkref[i] != null)
if (linkref[i].support < minSupport)
linkref[i] <-- null
else allUnsupported <-- false
End if else
End if
return allUnsupported
End Loop
else
Loop from i = K to i = length of array
if (linkref[i] != null)
if (pruneLevelN(linkref[i].childRef,K-1)
linkref[i].childRef <-- null
End if
End if
End loop
End if else
---------------------------------------
```

AN EXAMPLE APPLICATION

To evaluate our approach we used a real market basket analysis data set (http://fimi.cs.helsinki.fi/), comprising 1600 composite edible items out of 16,469 total distinct products; the objective is to determine consumers' consumption patterns for different nutrients according to the government promoted Recommended Daily Allowance (RDA). The properties for each item comprised

Figure 4. Internal representation of T-tree presented in Figure 3

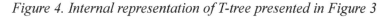
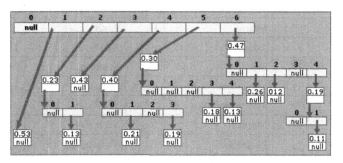

Table 19. The generateLevelN method and its related generateNextLevel method

```
Method: generateLevelN
Arguments: linkref reference to current array in T-tree
K level marker
I the item set represented by the parent node
Return: None, Fields: None
---------------------------------------
if (K=1)
Loop from i = 2 to i = length of array
if (linkref[i] != null)
generateNextLevel(linkref,i,I union i)
End if
End loop
else
Loop from i = K to i = length of array
if (linkref[i]!=null && linkref[i].childRef != null)
generateLevelN(linkref[i].childRef,K-1,I union i
---------------------------------------
Method: generateNextLevel
Arguments: linkref reference to current array in T-tree
I: index to parent node in vurrent array
I: the item set represented by the parent node
Return: None
Fields: nextLevelExists flafg set to true or false
---------------------------------------
linkref[i].childRef<--empty t-tree array nodes length i
Loop from j = 1 to j = i
if (linkRef[j] != null)
newI ← I union j
if (all newI true subsets all supported in the
T-tree sofar)
linkRef[i].childRef[j] <-- new T-tree Node
nextLevelExists <-- true
else linkRef[i].childRef[j] <-- null
End if else
End if
End loop
---------------------------------------
```

the 27 nutrients contained in the government sponsored RDA table (the complete list of nutrients is given in Table 20).

This RDA table is thus the CIV table used in the evaluation with actual nutrient values for individual items. The property data set will therefore comprise $1600 \times 27 = 43200$ attributes. The linguistic label set L was defined as follows L – {Very Low (VL), Low (L), Ideal (I), High (H), Very High (VH)}. Thus the set of fuzzy attributes $A = P \times L$ has $27 \times 5 = 135$ attributes. A fragment of this data set is given in Table 21.

For the example application we used Trapezoidal membership function shown in Figure 2. Core ($\beta - \gamma$) is the region where an attribute has a full membership degree, i.e., 1. Min ($\alpha - \beta$) is the region before core where the value approaches core and Max ($\gamma - \delta$) is the region after core region where an attribute membership value start decreasing until zero.

A representative fragment of a raw data set (T), comprising edible items, is given in Table 22 a. This raw data is then cast into a properties data set (T^P) using the given CIV/RDA table to give the properties data set in Table 22b.

At this point, two solutions may exist for the next mining step. One is to code fuzzy sets {very low, low, ideal, high, very high} as, for example, {1, 2, 3, 4, 5}, for the first nutrient (Biotin), {6, 7, 8, 9, 10} for the second nutrient (Calcium) and so on (Muyeba et al., 2006). The encoded data

Table 20. Nutrients listed in RDA table

#	Nutrient	#	Nutrient	#	Nutrient	#	Nutrient
1.	Biotin	8.	Folacin	15.	Protein	22.	VitaminB6
2.	Calcium	9.	Iodine	16.	Riboflavin	23.	Vitamin C
3.	Carbohydrate	10.	Iron	17.	Selenium	24.	Vitamin D
4.	Cholesterol	11.	Magnesium	18.	Sodium	25.	Vitamin E
5.	Copper	12.	Manganese	19.	Thiamin	26.	Vitamin K
6.	Fats	13.	Niacin	20.	Vitamin A	27.	Zinc
7.	Fiber	14.	Phosphorus	21.	Vitamin B12		

Table 21. Fragment of market basket composite item data set[1]

Nutrients / Fuzzy Ranges	Very Low				Low				Ideal				High				Very High		
	Min	Core		Max	Min	Core		Max	Min	Core		Max	Min	Core		Max	Min	Core	⋮
Fiber	0	1	10	15	10	15	20	25	20	25	30	35	30	33	38	39	35	40	⋮
Iron	0	.6	8	12	8	12	16	18	16	18	19	20	19	20	22	23	22	23	⋮
Protein	0	1	15	30	10	20	35	40	35	40	60	65	60	65	75	80	75	80	⋮
Vit.A	0	15	150	200	150	200	300	400	300	350	440	500	440	490	550	600	550	600	⋮
Zinc	0	.8	8	10	8	10	15	20	15	20	30	40	30	40	46	50	46	50	⋮
⋮	⋮	⋮	⋮	⋮	⋮	⋮	⋮	⋮	⋮	⋮	⋮	⋮	⋮	⋮	⋮	⋮	⋮	⋮	⋮

(Table 22c) can be mined by any binary association rule algorithm to find association rules. This approach only gives us, for instance, the total support of various fuzzy sets per nutrient and not the degree of (fuzzy) support. This directly affects the number and quality of rules (see Section 6 for further evidence). To overcome this, the fuzzy approach advocated in this paper has been adopted, where we convert RDA property data set (Table 22b) to linguistic values (Table 23) for each nutrient and corresponding degrees of membership for the fuzzy sets they represent. Each transaction then will have fuzzy values {very low, low, ideal, high, very high} for each nutrient present in every item of that transaction. Table 23 shows only two nutrients (i.e., a total of 10 fuzzy sets).

Note that Table 23 shows a normalised transaction file according to the calculation examples in previous sections and using Equation 2.

We have generated frequent sets using both discrete quantitative and fuzzy approaches. Discrete approach generated 76 frequent sets and fuzzy approach with un-normalised data and normalised data produced 43 and 39 frequent sets respectively. Rules generated using certainty factor with threshold 0.5 are shown in Table 24.

By comparing the itemsets supports with discrete and fuzzy approaches, it can be noted that for some rules (highlighted) using discrete method the support is slightly higher as compared to the same rules generated by fuzzy approach. This is due to the fact that in some cases discrete intervals allow more contribution of items near interval boundaries (sharp boundary problem), in result, higher the support and consequently more frequent sets. But in case of overlapped fuzzy intervals each item contribute its actual contribution in one or more intervals with overall maximum contribution=1 using normalisation. Table 24 gives formal proof.

Table 22. Example data fragment from example application

TID	Items
1	30, 31, 32
2	33, 34, 35
3	36, 37, 38, 39, 40, 41, 42, 43, 44, 45, 46
4	38, 39, 47, 48
5	38, 39, 48, 49, 50, 51, 52, 53, 54, 55, 56, 57, 58
6	32, 41, 59, 60, 61, 62
7	3, 39, 48
8	63, 64, 65, 66, 67, 68
9	32, 69
10	48, 70, 71, 72
A.) Fragment of retail data set (T)	

B.) Property data set (T^P)					**C.) Classical ARM data set**				
TID	Bio	Cal	Car	Chl	...	TID	Bio	Cal	Car	Chl	...
1	1	762	255	68	...	1	2	7	11	16	...
2	0	2	0	201	...	2	1	6	11	18	...
3	19	246	1240	1295	...	3	5	6	15	16	...
4	...	...	...	...	...	4	...	...	...	...	...

EXPERIMENTAL EVALUATION

In order to show the quality, performance and effectiveness of our approach, two sets of experiments were undertaken:

1. Comparison of CFARM, with and without normalisation, against standard (discrete) ARM to illustrate: (i) the difference of number of frequent sets generated, and (ii) the number of rules generated (using both the confidence and the certainty interestingness measures).

2. Comparison of execution times (performance) using Fuzzy Apriori ARM (Khan et al., 2006), Fuzzy Apriori-T (CFARM) with and without normalisation and Apriori-TFP (Coenen et al., 2004b) with discrete dataset (Boolean attributes).

All the experiments were performed on Mobile Intel(R) Pentium(R) 4 CPU 3.06 GHz machine with 1 GB ram and installed Microsoft Windows XP Professional with service pack 2 as operating system.

Table 23. Linguistic transaction file

TID	Calcium (Cal)					Carbohydrate (Car)					
	VL	L	Ideal	H	VH	VL	L	Ideal	H	VH	...
1	0.0	1.0	0.0	0.0	0.0	0.83	0.17	0.0	0.2	0.0	...
2	0.4	0.0	0.0	0.0	0.0	0.0	0.0	0.95	0.05	0.0	...
3	0.0	0.4	0.46	0.0	0.0	0.0	0.0	0.0	0.0	1.0	...
4	...	...	...	...	...	...	...	...	...	...	...

Table 24. Rules generated using discrete and fuzzy methods

Discrete Method with Crisp Intervals	Support	Fuzzy Approach with Normalised Data	Support	Certainty
5→25	0.500	5→25	0.500	0.500
25→35	0.600	25→35	0.600	0.612
25→35→62	0.400	25→35→62	0.400	0.667
25→35→110	0.400	25→35→110	0.400	0.667
25→40	0.600	25→40	0.600	0.612
25→40→95→115	0.400	25→40→95→115	0.496	0.816
25→40→115	**0.500**	**25→40→115**	**0.496**	**0.816**
25→115	**0.500**	**25→115**	**0.496**	**0.500**
35→62	0.400	35→62	0.400	0.667
35→110	0.400	35→110	0.400	0.667
40→95→115	**0.500**	**40→95→115**	**0.496**	**0.816**
40→115	**0.500**	**40→115**	**0.496**	**0.816**
85→95→135	**0.500**	**85→95→135**	**0.417**	**0.713**
85→135	**0.500**	**85→135**	**0.417**	**0.713**

Datasets

Both real and synthetic datasets are used in experiments. For real data we used Retail dataset, it is a real market basket data (http://fimi.cs.helsinki.fi/) and T10I4D100K synthetic data is obtained from the IBM dataset generator (http://www.almaden.ibm.com/software/quest/resources/index.html).

Table 25 characterises the two datasets in terms of the number of transactions, the number of distinct items, the average transaction size, and the maximum transaction size. It is worth mentioning that both datasets contains sparse data, since most association rules discovery algorithms were designed for these types of problems.

Table 25. Frequent itemsets comparison

Dataset	# of Transactions	Distinct Items	Avg. Trans. Size	Max. Trans. Size
Retail	88,162	16,469	10.3	76
T10I4D100K	100,000	1000	10.1	30

For the purpose of the experiments we mapped the item numbers onto products in a real RDA table.

Quality Measures

For experiment one both the real retail and synthetic datasets described above were used. Figures 5 and 6 show the results and demonstrates the difference between the numbers of frequent itemsets generated using:

1. Standard ARM using discrete intervals.
2. CFARM with fuzzy partitions without normalization (CFARM1).
3. CFARM with fuzzy partitions with normalization (CFARM2).

For the standard ARM the Apriori-TFP algorithm was used (Coenen et al., 2004b) and for CFARM-1 and CFARM-2 proposed Fuzzy Apriori-T was used with a range of support thresholds [0.15-0.6] for both algorithms.

Figure 5. Number of frequent itemsets

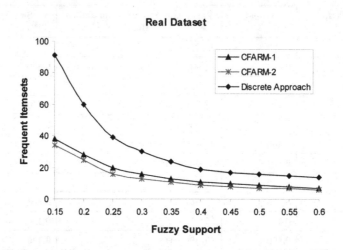

As expected the number of frequent itemsets increases as the minimum support decreases. From the results, it is clear that standard ARM produces more frequent itemsets (and consequently rules) than fizzy ARM. This is because the frequent itemsets generated more accurately reflect the true patterns in the data set than the numerous artificial patterns resulting from the use of crisp boundaries in standard ARM. At low support threshold level the approach with normalization (CFARM2) starts to produce less frequent itemsets than the approach without normalization (CFARM1). This is because the average contribution to support counts per transaction is greater without using normalization than with normalization.

Figures 7 and 8 show the comparison of number of interesting rules produced using specified fuzzy confidence and certainty thresholds [0.1-0.9] respectively with real and synthetic data. In both cases, the number of interesting rules is less as using CFARM2; this is a direct consequence of the fact that CFARM2 generates fewer frequent

Figure 6. Number of frequent itemsets

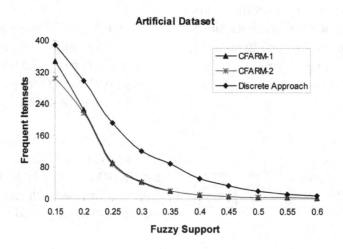

Figure 7. Number of interesting rules using confidence

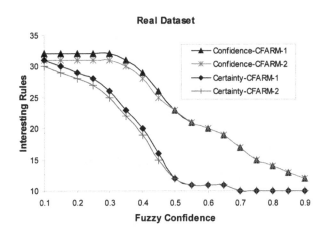

itemsets. Note that fewer, but arguably better, rules are generated using the certainty measure than the confidence measure (Figures 7 and 8) because the more related the attributes are and consequently the more interesting the rule is (Section 3.3).

The experiments show that using the proposed fuzzy normalization process less fuzzy ARs are generated. In addition, the novelty of the approach is its ability to analyse datasets comprised of composite items where each item has a number of property values such as the nutritional property values used in the application described here.

Some example fuzzy ARs produced by our approach are as follows:

IF *Protein* intake is *Ideal* THEN *Carbohydrate* intake is *low.*

IF *Protein* intake is *Low* THEN *Vitamin A* intake is *High.*

IF *Protein* intake is *High* AND *Vitamin A* intake is *Low* THEN *Fat* intake is *High.*

Figure 8. Number of interesting rules using certainty

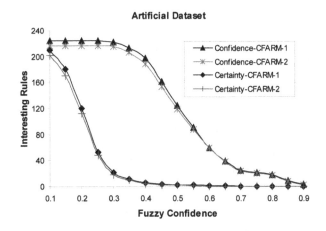

Figure 9. Performance measures: number of records

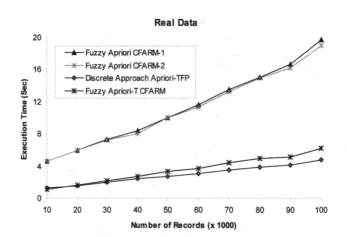

Note that, for the above rules we have replaced quantitative numeric data with real linguistic values for better understanding.

The rules above would first need defuzzifying (Roychowdhury & Pedrycz, 2001) each fuzzy value and then either aggregating them into real values or presenting them as a tabled list of nutritional values, whichever is appropriate to be interpreted by a domain expert. These rules would therefore be useful in analysing customer buying patterns concerning their nutrition.

Performance Measures

Experiment two investigated the effect on execution time caused by varying the size of data (number of records) and the number of attributes with and without normalization. For this experiment we have compared the execution time of proposed Fuzzy Apriori-T CFARM algorithm with Fuzzy Apriori ARM (Khan et al., 2006) using fuzzified datasets and Apriori-TFP (Coenen et al., 2004b) with discrete data (Boolean attributes). A support

Figure 10. Performance measures: number of records

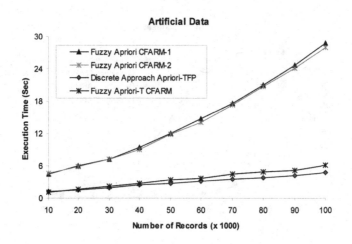

Figure 11. Performance measures: number of attributes

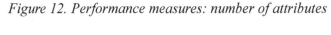

Real Data

threshold = 0.4, confidence = 0.5 and certainty value = 0.5 were used for all algorithms.

Figures 9 and 10 show the effect on execution time by increasing the number of records. To obtain different sizes both the datasets were partitioned into 10 equal partitions labelled 10K, 20K… 100K.. All 27 nutrients (properties) were used.

Note that the running time for candidate generation is independent of the number of records but run time for threshold count (support, confidence and certainty) is directly proportional to the number of records. Thus we would expect the CFARM algorithm to have near-linear scale up.

From the figures it can be seen that discrete method using Apriori-TFP algorithm and CFARM approach using Fuzzy Apriori-T algorithm have almost similar timings, the slight difference is due to the extra computational cost while generating fuzzy frequent sets. But a big difference of execution time can be noted between Fuzzy Apriori ARM and Fuzzy Apriori-T algorithms. This is due to the efficient frequent sets generation with Fuzzy Apriori-T algorithm using T-tree data struc-

Figure 12. Performance measures: number of attributes

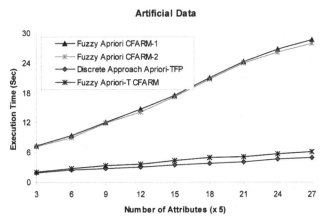

Artificial Data

tures. While the execution time increasing with the number of records. However the experiments also show that CFARM scales linearly with the number of records. Note that Fuzzy Apriori-T has the similar timings for dataset with and without normalisation, so only results with normalised data are shown in the figures.

Figures 11 and 12 show the effect on execution time by varying the numbers of attributes. Recall that each attribute has 5 fuzzy sets, therefore for (say) 27 attributes, we have 135 columns.

In this experiment, we give the experimental results based on the performance of the algorithm by varying the number of attributes. As expected, similar results are produced, i.e., as the number of attributes increases the execution time increases as well.

Further, the experiments show that proposed Fuzzy Apriori-T CFARM has better execution time, almost similar to Apriori-TFP, presently one of the efficient algorithm (Coenen et al., 2004a, 2004b) and the proposed Fuzzy Apriori-T scales linearly with the number of records and attributes.

CONCLUSION

In this paper, we have presented a novel approach for extracting hidden information from composite items. We defined composite items and developed a fuzzy framework for mining such items and measuring their interestingness using fuzzy measures. We showed that within such items, common properties can be defined as quantitative (sub)itemsets, transformed into fuzzy sets, mined and extracted rules measured using fuzzy support, confidence and certainty. Using the proposed CFARM algorithm a more succinct set of fuzzy association rules can be derived using fuzzy measures and certainty. The CFARM algorithm thus represents a new way of mining items efficiently with properties than standard quantitative ARM which does not use such properties, as described

in the literature. We also showed the application of our method with market basket data. As noted there is significant potential to apply CFARM to other applications than the daily recommended allowance analysis, used to illustrate the operation of CFARM in this paper, with composite items or attributes even with varying fuzzy sets between attributes. We feel that the approach presented here is novel in its use of composite items for fuzzy association rule mining. Further work will consider composite fuzzy association rule mining framework with weighted items and how the fuzzy approach can incorporate weights in generated composite fuzzy sets.

REFERENCES

Agrawal, R., Imielinski, T., & Swami, A. (1993). Mining association rules between sets of items in large databases. In *Proceedings of the ACM SIGMOD International Conference on Management of Data* (pp. 207-216).

Au, W. H., & Chan, K. C. C. (1999). FARM: A Data Mining System for Discovering Fuzzy Association Rules. In *Proceedings of the 8th IEEE International Conference on Fuzzy Systems,* Seoul, Korea (pp. 1217-1222).

Berzal, F., Blanco, I., Sánchez, D., & Vila, M. A. (2002). Measuring the accuracy and interest of association rules: A new framework. *Intelligent Data Analysis, 6*(3), 221–235.

Bodon, F. (2003). A Fast Apriori Implementation. In *Proceedings of the 1st IEEE ICDM Workshop on Frequent Itemset Mining Implementations (FIMI2003),* Melbourne, FL. Retrieved from http://www.ceur-ws.org/vol-90/

Chen, G., & Wei, Q. (2002). Fuzzy Association Rules and the Extended Mining Algorithms. *Information Sciences, 147*(1-4), 201–228. doi:10.1016/S0020-0255(02)00264-5

Coenen, F., Goulbourne, G., & Leng, P. (2004a). Tree structures for mining association rules. *Data Mining and Knowledge Discovery, 8*(1), 25–51. doi:10.1023/B:DAMI.0000005257.93780.3b

Coenen, F. P., Leng, P., & Ahmed, S. (2004b). Data Structures for Association Rule Mining: T-trees and P-trees. *IEEE Transactions on Data and Knowledge Engineering, 16*(6), 774–778. doi:10.1109/TKDE.2004.8

Delgado, M., Marin, M., Martín-Bautista, M. J., Sánchez, D., & Vila, M. A. (2003). Mining Fuzzy Association Rules: An Overview. In *Proceedings of the BISC International Workshop on Soft Computing for Internet and Bioinformatics* (pp. 351-373).

Delgado, M., Marin, N., Sánchez, D., & Vila, M. A. (2003). Fuzzy association rules: general model and applications. *IEEE Transactions on Fuzzy Systems, 11*(2), 214–225. doi:10.1109/TFUZZ.2003.809896

Delgado, M., Sánchez, D., Martín-Bautista, M. J., & Vila, M. A. (2001). Mining association rules with improved semantics in medical databases. *Artificial Intelligence in Medicine, 21*(1-3), 241–245. doi:10.1016/S0933-3657(00)00092-0

Delgado, M., Sánchez, D., & Vila, M. A. (2002). Acquisition of fuzzy association rules from medical data. In Barro, S., & Marin, R. (Eds.), *Fuzzy Logic in Medicine* (pp. 286–310).

Dong, L., & Tjortjis, C. (2003). Experiences of Using a Quantitative Approach for Mining Association Rules. In *Proceedings of the IDEAL 2003 Conference* (LNCS 2690, pp. 693-700).

Dubois, D., Hüllermeier, E., & Prade, H. (2006). A Systematic Approach to the Assessment of Fuzzy Association Rules. *Data Mining and Knowledge Discovery, 13*(2), 167–192. doi:10.1007/s10618-005-0032-4

Fayyad, U. M., Piatetsky-Shapiro, G., & Smyth, P. (1996). From Data Mining to Knowledge Discovery: An Overview. In *Advances in Knowledge Discovery & Data Mining* (pp. 1–34). Cambridge, MA: MIT Press.

Freitas, A. A. (1998). On Objective Measures of Rule Surprisingness. In *Proceedings of the 2nd European Symposium on Principle of Data Mining and Knowledge Discovery (PKDD-98)* (LNAI 1510, pp. 1-9).

Gyenesei, A. (2001). A Fuzzy Approach for Mining Quantitative Association Rules. *Acta Cybernetica, 15*(2), 305–320.

Khabbaz, M., Kianmehr, K., Al-Shalalfa, M., & Alhajj, R. (2008). Effectiveness of Fuzzy Classifier Rules in Capturing Correlations between Genes. *International Journal of Data Warehousing and Mining, 4*(4), 62–83. doi:10.4018/jdwm.2008100104

Khan, M. S., Muyeba, M., & Coenen, F. (2008). Mining Fuzzy Association Rules from Composite Items. In *Proceedings of the IFIP International Conference on Artificial Intelligence (IFIP-AI 2008),* Milan, Italy (pp. 67-76).

Khan, M. S., Muyeba, M., Tjortjis, C., & Coenen, F. (2006). An effective Fuzzy Healthy Association Rule Mining Algorithm (FHARM). In *Proceedings of the 7th Annual Workshop on Computational Intelligence* (p. 14).

Kim, W., Banerjee, J., Chou, H., Garza, J., & Woelk, D. (1987). Composite object support in an object-oriented database system. In *Proceedings of the OOPSLA '87 Conference,* Orlando, FL (pp. 118-125).

Kim, W., Bertino, E., & Garza, J. (1989). Composite objects revisited. *SIGMOD Record, 18*(2), 337–347. doi:10.1145/66926.66958

Kuok, C. M., Fu, A., & Wong, M. H. (1998). Mining fuzzy association rules in databases. *SIGMOD Record, 27*(1), 41–46. doi:10.1145/273244.273257

Kwok, T., Smith, K. A., Lozano, S., & Taniar, D. (2002). Parallel Fuzzy c-Means Clustering for Large Data Sets. In *Proceedings of the 8th International Euro-Par Conference* (LNCS 2400, pp. 365-374).

Muyeba, M., Sulaiman Khan, M., Malik, Z., & Tjortjis, C. (2006). Towards Healthy Association Rule Mining (HARM), A Fuzzy Quantitative Approach. In *Proceedings of the IDEAL '06 Conference* (LNCS 4224, pp. 1014-1022).

Paetz, J. (2002). A Note on Core Regions of Membership Functions. In *Proceedings of the EUNITE 2002 Conference,* Albufeira, Portugal (pp. 167-173).

Roychowdhury, S., & Pedrycz, W. (2001). A survey of defuzzification strategies. *International Journal of Intelligent Systems, 16*(6), 679–695. doi:10.1002/int.1030

Sánchez, D. (1999). *Acquisition of Relationships between Attributes in Relational Databases.* Unpublished doctoral dissertation, Department of Computer Science and Artificial Intelligence, University of Granada.

Silberschatz, A., & Tuzhilin, A. (1995). On subjective measures of interestingness in knowledge discovery. In U. Fayyad & R. Uthurusamy (Eds.), *Proceedings of the 1st ACM SIGKDD International Conference on Knowledge Discovery and Data Mining (KDD-1995)* (pp. 275-281). Cambridge, MA: AAAI/MIT Press.

Silverstein, C., Brin, S., & Motwani, R. (1998). Beyond market baskets: Generalizing association rules to dependence rules. *Data Mining and Knowledge Discovery, 2,* 39–68. doi:10.1023/A:1009713703947

Srikant, R., & Agrawal, R. (1996). Mining quantitative association rules in large relational tables. *SIGMOD Record, 25*(2), 1–12. doi:10.1145/235968.233311

Wang, K., Liu, J. N., & Ma, W. (2006). Mining the Most Reliable Association Rules with Composite Items. In *Proceedings of the 6th IEEE International Conference on Data Mining Workshops* (pp. 749-754).

Ye, X., & Keane, J. A. (1997). Mining composite items in association rules. In *Proceedings of the 1997 IEEE International Conference on Systems, Man, and Cybernetics (SMC 1997),* Orlando, FL (pp. 1367-1372).

ENDNOTES

1. Values could be in grams, milligrams, micrograms, International unit or any unit). Here Min is the minimum value, i.e., α, Core is the core region β, δ and Max is the maximum value γ in the fuzzy membership graph of Figure 2.

This work was previously published in the International Journal of Data Warehousing and Mining, Volume 7, Issue 3, edited by David Taniar, pp. 1-29, copyright 2011 by IGI Publishing (an imprint of IGI Global).

Chapter 9
Automatic Item Weight Generation for Pattern Mining and its Application

Yun Sing Koh
The University of Auckland, New Zealand

Russel Pears
Auckland University of Technology, New Zealand

Gillian Dobbie
The University of Auckland, New Zealand

ABSTRACT

Association rule mining discovers relationships among items in a transactional database. Most approaches assume that all items within a dataset have a uniform distribution with respect to support. However, this is not always the case, and weighted association rule mining (WARM) was introduced to provide importance to individual items. Previous approaches to the weighted association rule mining problem require users to assign weights to items. In certain cases, it is difficult to provide weights to all items within a dataset. In this paper, the authors propose a method that is based on a novel Valency model that automatically infers item weights based on interactions between items. The authors experiment shows that the weighting scheme results in rules that better capture the natural variation that occurs in a dataset when compared with a miner that does not employ a weighting scheme. The authors applied the model in a real world application to mine text from a given collection of documents. The use of item weighting enabled the authors to attach more importance to terms that are distinctive. The results demonstrate that keyword discrimination via item weighting leads to informative rules.

DOI: 10.4018/978-1-4666-2148-0.ch009

INTRODUCTION

Association rule mining (Agrawal et al., 1993) aims to extract interesting correlations, frequent patterns, associations or casual structures among sets of items in transactional databases. The relationships are not based on the inherent properties of the data themselves but rather based on the co-occurrence of the items within the database. There has been much work carried out in this area (Ashrafi et al., 2004; Daly & Taniar, 2004; Cokrowijoyo & Taniar, 2005; Koh et al., 2006; Ashrafi et al., 2007; Tzanis & Berberidis, 2007; Taniar et al., 2008; Giannikopoulos et al., 2010). The original motivation for seeking association rules came from the need to analyze supermarket transactional data also known as market basket analysis. An example of a common association rule is bread → butter. This indicates that a customer buying bread would also buy butter. Association rules have been widely used in a wide variety of domains, however, traditional rule mining techniques are vulnerable to the "rule explosion problem". Even modest sized datasets can produce thousands of rules, and as datasets get larger, the number of rules produced becomes unmanageable. This highlights a key problem in association rule mining; keeping the number of generated itemsets and rules in check, whilst identifying interesting rules amongst the plethora generated.

In the classical model of association rule mining, all items are treated with equal importance. In reality, most datasets are skewed with imbalanced data. By applying the classical model to these datasets, important but critical rules which occur infrequently may be missed. For example consider the rule: stiff neck, fever, aversion to light → meningitis. Meningitis occurs relatively infrequently in a medical dataset, however if it is not detected early the consequences can quickly become fatal. Recent research (Cai et al., 1998; Sun & Bai, 2008; Wang et al., 2000; Yan & Li, 2006) has used item weighting to emphasize such rules that rarely manifest but are nonetheless very important. For example, items in a market basket

dataset may be weighted based on the profit they generate. However, most datasets do not come with preassigned weights and so the weights must be manually assigned, which is time consuming and maybe error-prone. Research in the area of weighted association rule mining has concentrated on formulating efficient algorithms for exploiting pre-assigned weights rather than deducing item weights from a given transactional database. We believe that it is possible to deduce the relative importance of items based on their interactions with each other. In application domains where expert's input on item weights is either unavailable or impractical, an automated approach to assigning weights to items can contribute significantly to distinguishing high value rules from those with low value.

In this paper we discuss two major issues that are relevant to the field of weighted association rule mining. Firstly, we present a scheme that automates the process of assigning weights to items. The weights assignment process is underpinned by a "Valency model" that we propose. The model considers two factors: purity and connectivity. The purity of an item is determined by the number of items that it is associated with over the entire transactional database, whereas connectivity represents the strength of the interactions between items. We will elaborate on the Valency model later in the paper in Section 3. Secondly, association rules produced by the Valency model are evaluated through a scheme based on Principal Components Analysis. The formulation of this interest measure was motivated by the fact that none of the popularly used interest measures such as Confidence and Lift was able to capture differences between rules with highly weighted items from those with lowly weighted ones. We also apply the model to a real-world scenario, i.e., text mining. Text mining approaches typically extract keywords using measures of importance such as frequency of occurrence or measures such as TF-IDF (term frequency–inverse document frequency) to rank words in terms of their significance. While such measures are useful we are more interested in finding significant relationships between word occurrences. We apply association rules to identify significant correlations between keywords that occur across documents in a given corpus that relate to a specific topic, for example Swine Flu. We thus apply the Valency model which generates weights for the keywords depending on their patterns of interactions with other keywords in the corpus.

The rest of the paper is organized as follows. In the next section, we look at previous work in the area of weighted association rule mining. In Section 3 we give a formal definition of the weighted association rule mining problem. Section 4 describes our proposed Valency model while Section 5 presents the evaluation scheme used to assess the performance of the Valency model and our experimental results. We will be presenting the application of the Valency model in text mining in Section 6. Finally we summarize our research contributions in Section 7 and outline directions for future work.

RELATED WORK

The classical association rule mining scheme has thrived since its inception in (Agrawal et al., 1993) with application across a very wide range of domains. However, traditional Apriori like approaches were not designed to deal with the rare items problem (Liu et al., 1999; Koh & Rountree, 2005). Items which are rare but have high confidence levels are unlikely to reach the minimum support threshold and are therefore pruned out. For example, Cohen (Cohen et al., 2001) noted that in market basket analysis rules such as caviar → vodka will not be generated by traditional association rule mining algorithms. This is because both caviar and vodka are expensive items which are not purchased frequently, and will thus not meet the support threshold.

Numerous algorithms have been proposed to overcome this problem. Many of these algorithms follow the classical framework but substitute an

item's support with a weighted form of support. Each item is assigned a weight to represent the importance of individual items, with items that are considered interesting having a larger weight. This approach is called weighted association rule mining (WARM) (Cai et al., 1998; Wang et al., 2000; Yan & Li, 2006; Sanjay et al., 1997; Tao et al., 2003; Jiang et al., 2008; Zhao et al., 2009). Sanjay et al. (Sanjay et al., 1997) introduced weighted support to association rule mining by assigning weights to both items and transactions. In their approach rules whose weighted support is larger than a given threshold are kept for candidate generation, much like in traditional Apriori (Agrawal et al., 1993).

A similar approach was adopted by (Cai et al., 1998), but they applied weights to items and did not weigh transactions. They also proposed two different ways to calculate the weight of an itemset, either as the sum of all the constituent items' weights or as the average of the weights. However, both of these approaches invalidated the downward closure property (Agrawal & Srikant, 1994).

This led Tao et al. (2003) to propose a "weighted downward closure property". In their approach, two types of weights were assigned, item weight and itemset weight. The goal of using weighted support is to make use of the weight in the mining process and prioritize the selection of targeted itemsets according to their perceived significance in the dataset, rather than by their frequency alone.

Yan and Li (2006) working in the domain area of Web mining proposed that weights be assigned on the basis of the time taken by a user to view a web page. Unlike the previous approaches (Cai et al., 1998; Wang et al., 2000; Sanjay et al., 1997; Tao et al., 2003) that assumed a fixed weight for each item, Yan and Li (2006) allowed their weights to vary according to the dynamics of the system, as pages became more popular (or less popular) the weights would increase (or decrease), as the case may be.

Recently Jian and Ming (2008) introduced a system for incorporating weights for mining association rules in communication networks. They made use of a method based on a subjective judgements matrix to set weights for individual items. Inputs to the matrix were supplied by domain specialists in the area of communications networks.

Thus it can be seen in previous work that the weight assignment process relies on users' subjective judgments. The major issue with relying on subjective input is that rules generated only encapsulate known patterns, thus excluding the discovery of unexpected but nonetheless important rules. Another issue is that the reliance on domain specific information constrains the range of applicability to only those domains where such information is readily available. This motivated us to formulate a generic solution for the weight assignment problem that can be deployed across different application domains.

THE WEIGHTED ASSOCIATION RULE MINING (WARM) PROBLEM

Given a set of items, $I = i_1, i_2, ..., i_n$, a transaction may be defined as a subset of I and a dataset as a set D of transactions. A set X of items is called an itemset. The support of X, sup(X), is the proportion of transactions containing X in the dataset. An *association rule* is an implication of the form $X \rightarrow Y$, where $X \subseteq I$, $Y \subseteq I$, and $X \cap Y = \varnothing$. The rule $X \rightarrow Y$ has *support* of s in the transaction set D, if $s = $sup(XY). The rule $X \rightarrow Y$ holds in the transaction set D with *confidence c* where $c = $conf$(X \rightarrow Y) = sup(XY)/sup(X)$. Given a transactional database D, a support threshold *minsup* and a confidence threshold *minconf*, the task of association rule mining is to generate all association rules that have support and confidence above the user-specified thresholds.

In weighted association rule mining a weight w_i is assigned to each item i, where $-1 \leq w_i \leq$ 1, reflecting the relative importance of an item over other items that it is associated with. The weighted support of an item i is w_i sup(i). Similar to traditional association rule mining, a weighted support threshold and a confidence threshold is assigned to measure the strength of the association rules produced. The weight of a k-itemset, X, is given by:

$$\sum_{i \in X} w_i \text{sup}(X)$$

Here a k-itemset, X, is considered a frequent itemset if the weighted support of this itemset is greater than the user-defined minimum weighted support (wminsup) threshold.

$$\sum_{i \in X} w_i \text{sup}(X) \geq \text{wminsup}$$

The weighted support of a rule $X \rightarrow Y$ is:

$$\sum_{i \in X \cap Y} w_i \text{sup}(XY)$$

An association rule $X \rightarrow Y$ is called an interesting rule if $X \cap Y$ is a large itemset and the confidence of the rule is greater than or equal to a minimum confidence threshold. A general weighted association rule mining algorithm (Tao et al., 2003) is shown is Algorithm 1. The algorithm requires a weighted minimum support to be pro-

Algorithm 1. Weighted Association Rule Mining (WARM)

Input: Transaction database D, weighted minimum support *wminsup*, universe of items I
Output: Weighted Frequent itemsets
$L_k \rightarrow i \mid i \in I$, weight(c)*support(c) >wminsup
$k \rightarrow 1$
while ($|L_k| > 0$) do
    $k \rightarrow k + 1$
$C_k \rightarrow x \cup y \mid x, y \in L_{k-1}, |x \cap y| = $k-2
$L_k \rightarrow c \mid c \subset C_k$, weight(c)*support(c) > wminsup
$L_k \rightarrow \cup_k L_k$

---

vided. In this algorithm L_k represents the frequent itemsets also known as the large itemsets and C_k represents the candidate itemsets. Candidate itemsets whose weighted support exceeds the weighted minimum support are considered large itemsets and will be included in the rule generation phase.

Item weighting enables items with relatively low support to be considered interesting (large) and conversely, items which have relatively high support may turn out to be uninteresting (not large). This adds a new dimension to the classical association rule mining process and enables rules with high weights in their rule terms to be ranked ahead of others, thus reducing the burden on the end user in sifting through and identifying rules that are of the greatest value.

There are three very contrasting approaches to Weighted Association Rule Mining. At the one extreme we have the pure domain driven approach whereby all weights are supplied directly by the domain expert based on subjective knowledge or information supplied from the environment. Two examples of this type of weight assignment are item profit that is typically derived from sales transactional databases or page dwelling time derived from click stream data that is used to rank pages in order of importance. At the other extreme lies a purely automatic method where no knowledge whatsoever is assumed to be known apart from the patterns of interaction of items with each other. The third approach is applicable when the weights of only a subset of items are known. In these circumstances the purely automated approaches would not be appropriate. This is because these approaches would assign weights to items whose weights are already known and are supplied through domain knowledge.

Figure 1 presents our framework for Weighted Association Rule Mining that incorporates all three approaches to weight assignment. The framework accommodates all three forms of item weight models. The Domain Reliant model uses both the domain specific input and the transactional dataset to produce a set of weights for all candidate items and sets of items that are fed to the rule generation engine, as shown in pathway 1. The Automatic Weight Assignment model on the other hand only requires the transactional dataset as input and the model infers the weights of items and itemsets which are fed to the rule generator, as shown in pathway 3. Pathway 2 represents the hybrid situation where the Semi-Automatic model requires both the transactional dataset and domain specific input to generate the item and itemsets weights which are then fed to the rule generation engine.

Figure 1. Framework for Weighted Association Rule Mining

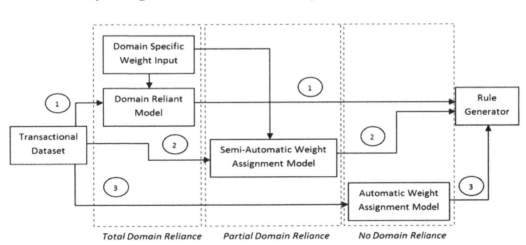

AUTOMATED WEIGHTING MECHANISM USING VALENCY MODEL

The Valency model is based on the intuitive notion that an item should be weighted based on the strength of its connections to other items as well as the number of items that it is connected with. We say that two items are connected if they have occurred together in at least one transaction. Items that appear often together when compared to their individual support have a high degree of connectivity and are thus weighted higher. At the same time, an item that is contained in a small clique of items is said to have a high degree of purity and is given a proportionally higher weight. We will formally define the notions of *connectivity* and *purity* with the help of the following example.

Table 1 shows an example transactional dataset. In Table 1a the left column represents the list of transaction IDs and the right column represent the items belonging to each particular transaction. In Table 1b the left column represents the list of items belonging to each particular transaction and the

right column represents the unique items which appear together with the item in the left column.

Figure 2 is an example transactional dataset based on Table 1 which can be represented as a graph whereby the nodes represent an item and the edges represent the support of the two items as an itemset. For example, the edge between node A and node B has a strength of 2, meaning that A and B occur together twice in the dataset.

The Valency model we developed for our research is inspired by the Inverse Distance Weighting function, which was proposed by Shepard (1968). Inverse distance weighting is an interpolation technique which generates values for unknown points as a function of the values of a set of known points scattered throughout the dataset. In defining purity we took into account the importance of an item being featured in a rule term. In general, we prefer rules that have items that are not merely associated with each other strongly but also are distinctive in the sense that they appear with relatively few items. Such distinctive items add value to rules as they are more likely to capture genuine affinities, and possibly causal effects than an item that is selected only on the basis of a strong statistical correlation (Tan et al., 2006).

A strong statistical correlation between two items does not always indicate that a natural affinity exists between them. Consider, for example an item X having very high support that ends

Table 1. Example of a transactional dataset

A.)	
tid	Itemset
100	A, B, C
200	A, C
300	A, B, D
400	A, E
500	E, F
600	E, F
B.)	
Item	Related Unique items
A	B, C, D, E
B	A, C, D
C	A, B
D	A, B
E	A, F
F	E

Figure 2. Example of graph representation

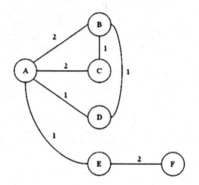

up being associated with many items Y, Z, etc., merely because of the fact that it occurs in a very large fraction of the transactions, thus making the associations between (X,Y) and (X,Z) spurious, even though the correlations between X and Y on the one hand and X and Z on the other hand are high. Keeping these facts in mind, we formally define the purity, p, for a given item k as:

$$p_k = 1 - \frac{log_2(|\ I_k\ |) + log_2(|\ I_k\ |)^2}{log_2(|\ U\ |)^3} \tag{1}$$

Where |U| represents the number of unique items in the dataset and $|I_k|$ represents the number of unique items which are co-occurring with item k. Purity as defined in Equation 1 ensures that the maximum purity value of 1 is obtained when the number of items linked with the given item is 1, whereas the purity converges to the minimum value of 0 as the number of linkages increases and become close to the number of items in the universal set of items. We chose to model purity with a non-linear logarithmic function as we wanted it to decrease sharply with the number of linkages. The log(|U|)³ term in the denominator ensures that the rate of decrease in purity is sensitive to the size of the universal set. For databases with a larger number of items (larger |U|) the gradient of descent is steeper when compared to databases with a smaller pool of items (smaller |U|) and so a smaller number of items will acquire high purity values. The second contribution to an item's Valency relies on how strongly it is connected to its neighboring items, or its *connectivity*. Given an item k which is connected to n items in its neighborhood, the connectivity, c_k is defined as:

$$c_k = \sum_{i \in \{N\}} \frac{count(i,k)}{count(k)} \tag{2}$$

N is the set of item in the neighborhood of k. We can now define the valency contained by an

item k, denoted by v_k as the combination of both the purity and the connectivity components:

$$v_k = \beta.p_k + (1 - \beta).\sum c_k.p_i \tag{3}$$

where β is a parameter that measures the relative contribution of the item k over the items that it is connected with in the database. The objective of the Valency model is to capture rules over small cliques of items such that items within a given clique have high purity and connectivity with other items contained within that clique. Since all items within a given clique are connected to each other, it follows from our definition of purity that all items within a clique have the same purity. Thus we can re-write the above equation as:

$$v_k = \beta.p_k + (1 - \beta).\sum_{i \in \{N\}} \frac{count(i,k)}{count(k)} \ .p_i =$$
$$\beta.p_k + (1 - \beta).p_k.\sum_{i \in \{N\}} \frac{count(i,k)}{count(k)} \tag{4}$$

Thus, for a given item k, the relative contribution made to the Valency by other items in the clique is dependent on both the value of the parameter β as well as the sum of the connectivity values from item k. We set the value of β as:

$$\beta = \frac{1}{n} \sum_{i \in \{N\}} \frac{count(i,k)}{count(k)} \tag{5}$$

With this setting of β we can re-write Equation 5 as:

$$v_k = \beta.p_k + n.\beta(1 - \beta).p_k \tag{6}$$

We can see from the above expression that the relative contribution of the neighboring items of k over itself is 1- β, which means that as the value of β increases the item k itself assumes more importance in relation to its neighbors. We use the Valency of an item as its weight. The weight calculation for an item is thus a computationally straightforward process as the weight for an item is independent of the weights of other items. Also, the weight assignment process for items can be accomplished in the first pass through the dataset as the local neighborhoods for each item can be computed on the fly together with the reading of the dataset. In the next section we discuss our evaluation criteria for determining the quality of the rules obtained by applying the Valency model.

RULE EVALUATION USING PRINCIPAL COMPONENTS ANALYSIS

A vast array of metrics for evaluating the quality of association rules have been proposed in the literature. Apart from the standard metrics of rule Support and Confidence, other measures such as Lift, Information Gain, Conviction, and Correlation have been used. The standard metrics are excellent at evaluating rules at the individual level in terms of the strength of correlation between terms and in assessing predictive accuracy. However, in the context of weighted association rule mining it is necessary that the contribution from each rule item is quantified and the contribution that it makes to the overall rule quality be assessed. Existing metrics tend to operate on the rule level rather than on the individual item level. This motivated us to investigate the use of Principal Components Analysis (PCA) to evaluate the quality of the rules output by our weighted association rule miner.

PCA is a mathematical technique that has been widely used in the data mining arena. Basically, PCA takes a set of variables and finds a set of independent axes (the Principal Components) which explain all or most of the variation that occurs within the dataset. Its main application is in the area of classification and clustering where it is used as a pre-processing technique for dimen-

sionality reduction. It has also been used before in association rule mining, but in a limited context where items are defined on a true numerical scale (Faloutsos et al., 1997). However, our use of PCA is quite different.

We concentrate solely on the right hand sides (RHSs) of rules as they encapsulate the actionable components of rules. Focusing on rule consequents allows us to test the degree of diversity amongst the actionable components discovered by the rule generator without the confounding effect of diversity amongst the left hand sides (LHSs) of rules. A set of rules with exactly the same RHS does not yield as much knowledge as rules that are diverse in their RHSs. For example, a set of rules egg, bread → milk; butter, bread → milk; and tuna, egg → milk, can be considered less interesting than rules with a greater diversity such as diaper → baby food; ham → cheese; and chips → soda. In a medical database containing information about a number of different diseases a rule generator that has poor coverage of the set of diseases (i.e., only identifies a small fraction of the diseases in the RHSs of the rules) is not as useful as one that has a better coverage with respect to the set of diseases.

To determine the value of the rules output by our miner, we first apply PCA to the transactional dataset and obtain the Eigen vectors for the first two principal components. These vectors will be a linear function of the form:

$$e_{k1} I_1 + e_{k2} I_2 + \ldots e_{kn} I_n \text{ where } e_{kp}$$

is the Eigen value for the pth item on the kth principal component (k is either 1 or 2). We process the rule set by removing LHS of each rule. This results in a collection of rule consequents (RHSs) containing duplicate entries as the LHS terms have been eliminated. After duplicate elimination we obtain a more compact representation of the rule set, R. We project the rule set R on its first two principal components and obtain a quantified version of the rule set, which we denote by S. The set

S contains a set of ordered pairs (X,Y) where X, Y are vectors representing principal components 1 and 2 respectively for each rule.

PCA enables us to capture the amount of variance that is explained by each rule term for each rule. The greater the amount of variance that is captured by a rule term, the higher the value of that term and the higher the contribution it makes to the rule as a whole. Thus PCA provides us with an independent method of evaluating the efficacy of our Valency model. If our Valency model is to outperform an unweighted association mining scheme such as Apriori then the delineation of the rules in PCA space produced by our Valency model should be better. In order to assess the quality of the delineation we applied the K-means clustering algorithm to the (X,Y) vectors and then visualized the clusters. We also quantified the degree of delineation by calculating a cluster purity measure along the axis that provided the better delineation, which happened to be the first principal axis (rather than the second) in most of the experiments that we carried out. In the next section we present the results of our experimentation with our Valency model.

Experimental Results

Our motivation in introducing the Valency model was to facilitate the automatic assignment of weights from a given transactional dataset without requiring additional information from users. As such we were interested in examining the impact of the weight assessment process in an environment where user input is not available, and this led us to compare our algorithm with the classical Apriori approach. Our experimentation was conducted in two steps, firstly a performance comparison with Apriori, and secondly an examination of the impact of key parameters of the Valency model.

We used seven UCI datasets (Asuncion & Newman, 2007). We also experimented with synthetic data for which we used the data generator proposed by Agrawal and Srikant (1994). Datasets, D, were created with the following parameters: number of transactions $|D|$, average size of transactions $|T|$, number of unique items $|I|$, and number of large itemsets $|L|$.

Table 2 shows the results of running both Apriori and our algorithm on the datasets mentioned above. Each row shows the dataset, the number of rules produced, the number of RHSs produced (bracketed), and the cluster purity obtained by clustering the resulting rule bases on the first two

Table 2. Clustering results for first two principal components

Datasets	Valency		Apriori	
	No. of Rules	**Cluster Purity**	**No. of Rules**	**Cluster Purity**
Bridges	505(15)	100	1875(15)	100
Flag	119948(121)	94.2	486500(719)	86.6
Flare	715(32)	100	244753(1052)	90.9
Hepatitis	45850(233)	96.6	720633(2065)	87.9
Mushroom	4005(134)	92.5	61515(1064)	92.5
Soybean	56753(1310)	99.7	188223(1211)	82.9
Synthetic (T25I200D1K)	266914(853)	98.4	618579(2195)	89.7
Zoo	5475(127)	99.2	644890(3128)	89.7

principal components. We see from the results that the effect of weighting is to produce a much more compact rule base as Valency's rule base is much smaller than Apriori's. In order to keep the comparison fair we ran the two algorithms at minimum support thresholds so that they produced rules bases which had approximately the same support distributions. The compact nature of Valency's rule base vis-a-vis Apriori is due to the influence of the purity component that reduces the weighted support of an item sharply as the number of items that it interacts with increases. We verified this by substituting the non linear purity function with a linear one. The linear function did not punish highly connected items as severely as its non linear counterpart, thus resulting in a rule base that exploded in size and became very similar to that of Apriori in both qualitative and quantitative terms. The effect of the linear function was to dilute the effect of purity and hence the weighting scheme was not as effective in discriminating between different items, thus resulting in a larger proportion of items assuming higher purity and higher weight values.

The second interesting aspect of the results is that Valency produced a better set of clusters when compared to Apriori. The cluster purity improvement measure for Valency ranges from 0% for the relatively sparse Bridges and Mushroom datasets to 20.3% for the denser Soybean dataset. This improvement is due to the fact that the items

that feature in Valency's rules capture a higher proportion of variance that occurs over the underlying dataset in relation to Apriori. This result confirms our hypothesis that it is possible to automatically deduce weights from the interactions that occur between items in a transactional database. The result for the experimentation with various types of synthetic datasets was broadly similar to that of the real-world datasets. As the density of the dataset increased so did the improvement in cluster purity value between Valency and Apriori.

Figure 3 shows the clusters generated in PCA space for the Apriori and Valency schemes on the Zoo dataset. For the Zoo dataset the 2nd principal component produced the cleaner demarcation between the clusters. The figure shows that Valency produces a visibly better separation of clusters around the point of intersection with the second principal axis.

The other visualizations were similar except that the axis of greater separation was the first principal component for both of the algorithms. Figures 4, 5, and 6 show the clusters generated in PCA space Apriori and Valency schemes on the hepatitis, Flag, and Synthetic dataset

In the next section we present the application of the Valency model to the text mining domain. We show how different terms are weighted based on their connection within a document.

Figure 3. PC1 and PC2 clusters for zoo dataset

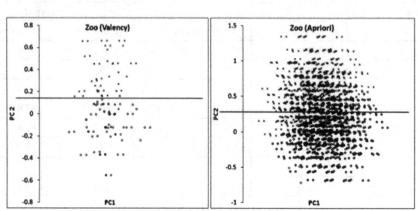

Figure 4. PC1 and PC2 clusters for hepatitis dataset

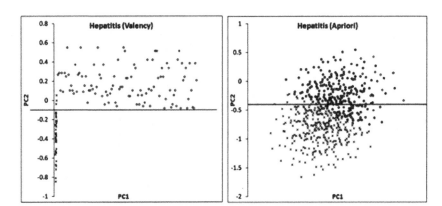

REAL WORLD APPLICATION: TEXT MINING USING THE VALENCY MODEL

Text mining (Antonie & Zaiane, 2002; Evans & Lefferts, 1995; Liu et al., 2003) is an increasingly important research field as the necessity of obtaining knowledge from enormous amounts of text documents grows with the accumulation and storage of new information. The main challenge in mining text is to adapt techniques that have been successfully used in traditional data mining so that they can be deployed across unstructured collections of textual data.

Text mining approaches typically extract keywords using measures of importance such as fre-

quency of occurrence or measures such as TF-IDF (term frequency–inverse document frequency) to rank words in terms of their significance. While such measures are useful we are more interested in finding significant relationships between word occurrences. As such, we employ association rule mining as the core data mining technique in this research. Association rules can be used to highlight correlations or causal relationships that occur between items in a dataset. In this research, association rules will be used to identify significant correlations between keywords that occur across documents in a given corpus that relate to a specific topic, for example Swine Flu.

In this proposed technique, weights are attached to keywords depending on their patterns

Figure 5. PC1 and PC2 clusters for flag dataset

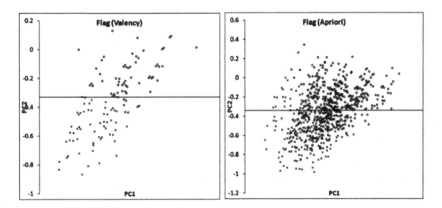

Figure 6. PC1 and PC2 clusters for synthetic dataset

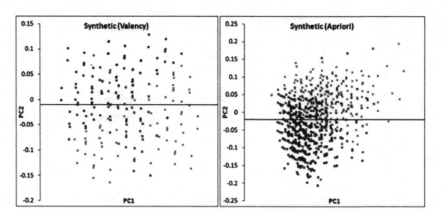

of interactions with other keywords in the corpus. We use the Valency model as the basis for constructing our weighted association rule miner. The main benefit of this technique is that the weight assignment process is automatic. The weights for each of the keyword are derived based on the distinctiveness (purity), and the co-occurrence of the keyword with other keywords (connectivity).

A word is selected as a keyword if it does not appear in a predefined stop-word list and is ranked highly on the TF-IDF measure. Association rules have been widely used across a number of domains and proved to be of use in the decision making process.

Prior Work in Text Mining using Association Rules

There has been prior work in using association rules to find interesting patterns within text documents. Association rule mining has been used for text mining and web text mining for the purpose of pattern, trend, event discovery and text classification (Feldman & Hirsh, 1996; Holt & Chung, 2001; Wu et al., 2004). In this line of research, the associations between terms and categories were described using association rules.

Earlier work on the application of association rules to text mining relied on the manual assignments of keywords. The assigned keywords were

then input to the association miner to generate rules that highlight the significant relationships between the supplied keywords. The drawbacks of such approaches that use manually assignment of keywords are that they are both tedious and static, in the sense that they cannot take into account trends that evolve over a period of time and require the extraction of new types of keywords.

Wong et al. (1999) also used association rule mining after filtering keywords based on the Bookstein's content-bearing measure (Bookstein et al., 1998) to identify interesting associations from a news corpus collected from news articles published in April 1995. Their main contribution was the design of a novel method for visualizing the association rules generated.

Chen and Wu (2006) used background knowledge about users to build rules that were personalized to the interests of the user. The target documents in the corpus were preprocessed into noun phrases which were ranked using the TF-IDF measure; all phrases that produced a value greater than a specified threshold were input to the Apriori algorithm. A set of user supplied keywords taken from the corpus were used to rank the novelty of the association rules produced.

More recent work by Lopes et al. (2007) used a modified form of the TF-IDF measure to filter words which were then passed to the classical Apriori association rule miner. The rules generated were restricted to those that contained at least one keyword that was manually selected from the set of keywords provided by the TF-IDF filter. Their research used two different corpora, one built from Journal articles in Information Sciences and the other a collection of news feed documents from major news wire services. In both cases Lopes et al showed that interesting and useful rules could be discovered. However the main drawback, as with earlier work was the use of a manually constructed set of keywords that were used to seed the association mining process.

All of the work done so far on discovering word associations has utilized the frequent pattern approach although different preprocessing techniques have been used to identify the initial set of keywords used for seeding. The main issue with the frequent pattern mining approach is that the associations discovered reflect patterns that are likely to be already known to the user, thus reducing the effectiveness of the knowledge generated (Yu et al., 2004). We show that the Valency model is able to reduce some of the problems affecting the frequent pattern mining approach.

Proposed Method

The proposed text mining algorithm is shown in Figure 7. The system will automatically extract interesting patterns based on the connections of keywords within a document corpus. The system

consists of two phases, the text preprocessing phase followed by the weighted association rule mining (WARM) phase.

The goal of the text preprocessing phase is to optimize the performance of the mining phase. Documents are filtered to remove irrelevant words by using a list of stop words (e.g., articles, determiners, prepositions and conjunctions). The Porter stemming algorithm is then applied to transform different forms of a word into its root by removing prefixes and suffixes. For example, the stemming process aims to unify the words "disease" and "diseases" to the word disease.

The filtered and stemmed documents are then indexed. In common with most research in text mining we use the TF-IDF method to identify a set of representative words that describe a given document succinctly. An index term for a given document can be thought of as a word whose semantics helps in identifying that document's main themes. Each document is thus represented by the set of words with the highest set of values returned by the TF-IDF scheme. The TF-IDF measure, while being useful in identifying the extent to which a word describes a document's theme does not take into account interactions of that word with other words occurring in the corpus. Thus for example, the keyword "federal" may occur frequently within a small fraction of documents in a corpus containing election results giving it a high TF-IDF score. However, "federal" may ap-

Figure 7. Text mining process

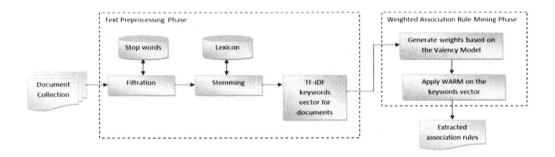

pear with many other high ranking TF-IDF words across the corpus thus reducing its distinctiveness and the extent to which it can contribute towards an interesting rule. In contrast the keyword "mining tax" may appear frequently in a few documents in the corpus but may be preferred to "federal" because it appears with a few other highly ranked TF-IDF keywords, thus making it a more attractive candidate for rule generation.

Thus it is desirable to rank the set of keywords produced by TF-IDF in terms of their interactions with each other. The Valency scheme models interactions between items (words) in the form of a graph and assigns a higher weight to items that interact strongly with a few other items. The Valency model has been used successfully in mining structured data and was shown to significantly outperform Apriori in terms of the quality of rules produced. However, this is the first known attempt at applying the model to unstructured collections of data.

The application of the Valency weight to each keyword before the identification of association rules distinguishes our work from previous research in this area. We believe that the application of the Valency weighting scheme will remove a large number of trivial rules involving keywords that merely co-occur together frequently and thus tend to represent already known knowledge. In the next section we describe the application of the Valency model in conjunction with the Weighted Association Rule Mining framework.

Document Collection Description

To evaluate the performance of the system in extracting interesting rules from text, we applied it on a selection of news articles from Google News. We used the top 100 pages which were ranked highest by Google News. We chose two central topics: Swine Flu and the Australian Election.

The documents for the "swine flu" study were collected on the 16 August 2010. The collection of 100 documents is 540KB in size. Each document contains on average 300 unique words. The articles for the "Australian election" were collected on the 21 August 2010. The collection of the 100 documents is 550KB in size. On average there were 320 unique words in each document. Figure 8 is an example of a typical news excerpt that is used.

Case Study Results

In this section we present a subjective evaluation of the rules produced based on the keywords that returned the highest weights. In each of the case studies we present the most interesting rules discovered.

Figure 8. An excerpt of a news article

> **Students hit hard as swine flu clobbers schools**
> **Daniel Simmons Ritchie | 5th August 2010**
>
> A swine flu outbreak across Wairarapa is knocking out students before lunchtime and stretching relief teachers to breaking point. Wairarapa is leading the Wellington region with nearly half of students at some schools staying home because of fever, chills, headaches, sneezing and in some cases diarrhoea and vomiting. Swabs taken from children's throats earlier this week have returned positive for H1N1, said Annette Neesdale, Medical Officer of Health. H1N1 was the predominant strain of flu in New Zealand this winter, so this result was not a surprise, Dr Neesdale said.

Case Study: Swine Flu

The 2009 flu pandemic was a global outbreak of a new strain of H1N1 influenza virus, often referred to as "swine flu". A total of 7444 rules were produced, out of which we picked 6 rules for discussion. These rules were selected as they highlight issues of importance.

- **Rule 1:** Pregnant swine flu women → health.
  - This rule emphasizes the health concerns for pregnant women who were infected with the virus. By referring back to the corpus we noticed the concerns that health authorities had for various patient groups such as pregnant women, diabetes patients, and so on. Such groups were identified as being of increased risk of developing complications from the virus. In particular with the pregnant patients group, the risks extended to the unborn child as well. This rule had a confidence of 0.91 and a lift value of 1.4.
- **Rule 2:** World health organization virus → pandemic.
  - This rule expresses the fears that the Swine Flu virus would give rise to a pandemic in its first wave of attacks that arose in early to mid 2009. The Director-General of the World Health Organization (WHO), gave a statement on 11 June 2009 confirming that the H1N1 strain was indeed a pandemic, having nearly 30,000 confirmed cases worldwide. This rule had a confidence of 1 and a lift value of 4.1
- **Rule 3:** Doses → swine flu vaccine.
  - This rule highlights the concerns in mid 2009 for the production of sufficient doses of the Swine Flu vaccine

in order to combat the rapid spread of the virus around this time. This rule had a confidence of 1 and a lift value of 5.
- **Rule 4:** New Zealand, public, swine flu, virus → influenza pandemic.
  - This rule highlights the New Zealand government concern on the spread of the swine flu virus turning into a second wave pandemic during winter (July - August 2010). This rule had a confidence of 1 and a lift value of 8.
- **Rule 5:** Health, school student, swine flu → school.
  - There was an outbreak early August in among schools in Wairarapa and Hawkes Bay, New Zealand whereby up to 50% of school students were sick with swine flu. This rule had a confidence of 1 and a lift value of 8.6.
- **Rule 6.:** Hospital India patients tested virus → died positive swine flu.
  - There were reports of patients in India dying from swine flu. From the 100 articles, 30 articles were related to swine flu occurrences in India. This rule had a confidence of 1 and a lift value of 5.

Case Study: Australian Election Corpus

The experiment was conducted with a minimum confidence of 0.90. We produced 5081 rules from the dataset. We found that numerous rules within the dataset were of interest. The average confidence value is at 0.98, and the average lift value is at 1.9. Here we pick at the 5 top rules produced based on diversity.

- **Rule 1:** June, labor party, poll, prime minister → julia gillard, kevin rudd.
  - On 24 June 2010, after Australian prime minister Kevin Rudd lost the support of his party and stood aside,

Gillard became federal leader of the Australian Labor Party and thus the Prime Minister. This was one of the issues during the election campiagn. This rule produced a confidence of 1.0 and a lift value of 11.4.

- **Rule 2:** Hung parliament, greens, independents, prime minister → parliment.
  - One member of the Australian Greens and three independent members were widely expected to hold the balance of power in the House of Representatives, which produced the first hung parliament, and would decide which party would be elected into parliament ("Voters leave", 2010). This rule has a confidence of 1.0, and a lift value of 2.7.

- **Rule 3:** Deal, greens → julia gillard, labor party.
  - It was believed that Labor was more likely to win Greens support for its policies in the Senate. This rule has a confidence of 1.0 and a lift value of 1.9.
- **Rule 4:** Asylum seeker, julia gillard → prime minister.
- **Rule 5:** Broadband network, poll → labor party.
  - These two rules relates to the cental issues that was proposed to be dealt with by Julia Gillard. Both the rules have a confidence of 1.0 with lift values of 1.6 and 1.3 respectively.

Table 3. Normalized weights for the case studies

Swine Flu			Australian Election		
Keywords	**Valency**	**TF-IDF**	**Keywords**	**Valency**	**TF-IDF**
strain	1	0.283	saturday	0.92	0.106
outbreak	0.888	0.19	chance	0.788	0.214
infect	0.748	0.332	afghanistan war	0.569	0.303
dose	0.637	0.734	carbon emissions	0.431	0.206
health	0.59	0.003	public tax	0.403	0.132
test	0.45	0.401	kevin rudd	0.307	0.209
student	0.4	0.862	broadband network	0.291	0.219
school	0.374	0.481	mp	0.283	0.6
mumbai	0.36	0.446	climate change	0.279	0.954
pregnant	0.293	0.346	deal	0.277	0.193
doctor	0.278	0.368	mining tax	0.276	0.308
tamiflu	0.278	0.363	asylum seekers	0.275	0.607
vaccine	0.275	0.549	greens	0.25	0.347
influenza	0.25	0.413	independents	0.224	0.243
positive	0.209	0.254	tony abbott	0.204	0.002
hospital	0.208	0.005	julia gillard	0.199	0.003
india	0.205	0.144	labor party	0.194	0.01
swine flu	0.2	0.006	hung parliment	0.186	0.198

Valency Weights vs. TF-IDF Score

To give some context of the normalized weights Table 3 is a subset of the weights that were generated based on the association of the keywords. We selected 18 keywords from top, middle, bottom ranked by Valency. We also provide the TF-IDF score for the keywords.

The max TF-IDF score is taken across all the TF-IDF scores for that keyword across the corpus. For example, if the keyword "mining tax" appears in documents 1 and 2 with scores 0.05 and 0.02 then the contribution made to document 1 should determine its contribution to the corpus. The reasoning behind this is that if it contributes strongly to at least one document then we are not concerned about its contribution to others.

We then ran the correlation between the Valency weights and max TF-IDF score. For the Australian Election case study it produced a weak correlation of value -0.10 and the Swine Flu case study produced a correlation of 0.06. Thus both cases illustrate that there is an absence of a strong correlation between both the Valency and TF-IDF, thus showing that the Valency is able to perform additional filtration of keywords after the application of the initial TF-IDF filter.

Performance Evaluation

Most current methods in text mining using association rule mining relies on the traditional Apriori algorithm to find interesting rules. In this section we present a comparison of results between our WARM algorithm and Apriori.

The performance comparison shows that the production of more interesting rules is not at the expense of efficiency. In order to make the comparison fair, the minimum support threshold for Apriori was set at a level such that the rules produced by both Apriori and WARM had the same support range. Table 4 gives the number of rules generated by Apriori versus WARM as well as the run time.

Table 4. Summary of results

Corpus	Valency		Apriori	
	Rules	**Time(s)**	**Rules**	**Time(s)**
Swine Flu	7444	15	213777	1240
Australian Elections	5081	14	319837	302

We notice that not only is there a vast difference in the execution time but also a significant difference in the number of rules produced. There were 29 times more rules produced by Apriori versus WARM in the Swine Flu case study, whereas there were 62 times more rules produced by Apriori versus WARM for the Australian election case study. Most of the rules can be considered to be trivial and are not of any interest. For example in the Apriori rule base generated for the Australian election we found rules which were well known or do not have much meaning.

The research area of text mining with association rules is still in its infancy and there is much to be done to extend the system. Current association rule mining techniques are not designed to cope with unstructured text data, thus the mining algorithm itself has to be structured to enable useful patterns to emerge. However, the critical point to this is that we should not constrain the structure of the rule to fit into a particular boxed format; otherwise the rules generated would be too rigid and not provide any additional value. With the overwhelming numbers of web articles, we believe that automatically finding the most useful rules (knowledge) without the need for manual interaction in the mining process would have a significant impact on how content would be delivered and consumed in the future.

CONCLUSION

In this paper, we propose a new item weighting scheme based on the Valency model. We fit the weights to items based on the notions of connectivity and purity. The Valency weighting function consists of two different parts: weights of an item based on its strength of connections and weights of its neighboring items. We used PCA to investigate the degree of variation captured by the rule bases. Overall, the Valency model produces better rules than traditional Apriori. In terms of future work we would like to investigate the effects of not just the immediate neighbors on an item's weight but to also capture the effects of non-neighboring items that are not directly connected to the given item under consideration. This paper also applied weighted association rule mining to automatically extract rules from text databases. We conducted a qualitative analysis of the rules produced from two different corpora, and carried out a comparison of the performance of our Valency based WARM technique versus Apriori. The results of that analysis showed that the use of item weighting via the Valency model produced a more interesting set of rules than the application of the traditional unweighted approach.

ACKNOWLEDGMENT

This paper is an expanded version of Koh et al. (2010).

REFERENCES

Agrawal, R., Imielinski, T., & Swami, A. N. (1993). Mining association rules between sets of items in large databases. In P. Buneman & S. Jajodia (Eds.), *Proceedings of the 1993 ACM SIGMOD International Conference on Management of Data* (pp. 207-216). New York, NY: ACM.

Agrawal, R., & Srikant, R. (1994). Fast algorithms for mining association rules in large databases. In J. B. Bocca, M. Jarke, & C. Zaniolo (Eds.), *Proceedings of the 20th International Conference on Very Large Data Bases* (pp. 487-499). San Francisco, CA: Morgan Kaufmann Publishers.

Antonie, M.-L., & Zaiane, O. R. (2002). Text document categorization by term association. In *Proceedings of the 2002 IEEE International Conference on Data Mining (ICDM '02)* (pp. 19-26). Washington, DC: IEEE Computer Society.

Ashrafi, M. Z., Taniar, D., & Smith, K. A. (2004). ODAM: An Optimized Distributed Association Rule Mining Algorithm. *IEEE Distributed Systems Online, 5*(3).

Ashrafi, M. Z., Taniar, D., & Smith, K. A. (2007). Redundant association rules reduction techniques. *International Journal of Business Intelligence and Data Mining, 2*(1), 29–63. doi:10.1504/IJBIDM.2007.012945

Asuncion, A., & Newman, D. (2007). *UCI machine learning repository.* Retrieved from http://www.ics.uci.edu/~mlearn/MLRepository.html

Bookstein, A., Klein, S. T., & Raita, T. (1998). Clumping properties of content-bearing words. *Journal of the American Society for Information Science American Society for Information Science, 49*(2), 102–114.

Cai, C. H., Fu, A. W. C., Cheng, C. H., & Kwong, W. W. (1998). Mining association rules with weighted items. In *Proceedings of the 1998 International Symposium on Database Engineering & Applications (IDEAS '98)* (pp. 6877). Washington, DC: IEEE Computer Society.

Chen, X., & Wu, Y.-F. (2006). Personalized knowledge discovery, mining novel association rules from text. In *Proceedings of the 6th SIAM International Conference on Data Mining* (pp. 589-597). Bethesda, MD: Society of Industrial and Applied Mathematics.

Cohen, E., Datar, M., Fujiwara, S., Gionis, A., Indyk, P., & Motwani, R. (2001). Finding interesting association rules without support pruning. *IEEE Transactions on Knowledge and Data Engineering, 13*, 64–78. doi:10.1109/69.908981

Daly, O., & Taniar, D. (2004). Exception Rules Mining Based on Negative Association Rules. In *Proceedings of the International Conference on Computational Science and Its Applications (ICCSA 2004)* (LNCS 3046, pp. 543-552).

Evans, D. A., & Lefferts, R. G. (1995). CLARIT-TREC experiments. In *Proceedings of the 2nd Text Retrieval Conference* (pp. 385-395). Elmsford, NY: Pergamon Press.

Faloutsos, C., Korn, F., Labrinidis, A., Labrinidis, R., Kotidis, Y., Perkovic, D., & Kaplunovich, A. (1997). *Quantifiable data mining using principal component analysis* (Tech. Rep. No. CS-TR-3754). College Park, MD: Institute for Systems Research, University of Maryland.

Feldman, R., & Hirsh, H. (1996). Mining associations in text in the presence of background knowledge. In *Proceedings of the 2nd International Conference on Knowledge Discovery and Data Mining (KDD-96)* (pp. 343-346). Menlo Park, CA: AAAI Press.

Giannikopoulos, P., Varlamis, I., & Eirinaki, M. (2010). Mining Frequent Generalized Patterns for Web Personalization in the Presence of Taxonomies. *International Journal of Data Warehousing and Mining, 6*(1), 58–76. doi:10.4018/jdwm.2010090804

Holt, J. D., & Chung, S. M. (2001). Multipass algorithms for mining association rules in text databases. *Knowledge and Information Systems, 3*(2), 168–183. doi:10.1007/PL00011664

Jian, W., & Ming, L. X. (2008). An effective mining algorithm for weighted association rules in communication networks. *Journal of Computers, 3*(4), 20–27.

Jiang, H., Zhao, Y., Yang, C., & Dong, X. (2008). Mining both positive and negative weighted association rules with multiple minimum supports. In *Proceedings of the International Conference on Computer Science and Software Engineering* (pp. 407-410). Washington, DC: IEEE Computer Society.

Jing, L.-P., Huang, H.-K., & Shi, H.-B. (2002). Improved feature selection approach TF-IDF in text mining. In *Proceedings of the 2002 Conference on Machine Learning and Cybernetics* (pp. 944-946). Washington, DC: IEEE Computer Society.

Koh, Y. S., Pears, R., & Yeap, W. (2010). Valency based weighted association rule mining. In M. Zaki, J. Yu, B. Ravindran, & V. Pudi (Eds.), *Advances in Knowledge Discovery and Data Mining* (LNCS 6118, pp. 274-285).

Koh, Y. S., & Rountree, N. (2005). Finding sporadic rules using apriori-inverse. In T. B. Ho, D. Cheung, & H. Liu (Eds.), *Advances in Knowledge Discovery and Data Mining* (LNCS 3518, pp. 97-106).

Koh, Y. S., Rountree, N., & O'Keefe, R. A. (2006). Finding Non-Coincidental Sporadic Rules Using Apriori-Inverse. *International Journal of Data Warehousing and Mining, 2*(2), 38–54. doi:10.4018/jdwm.2006040102

Liu, B., Dai, Y., Li, X., Lee, W. S., & Yu, P. S. (2003). Building text classifiers using positive and unlabeled examples. In *Proceedings of the 3rd IEEE International Conference on Data Mining (ICDM '03)* (pp. 179-186). Washington, DC: IEEE Computer Society.

Liu, B., Hsu, W., & Ma, Y. (1999). Mining association rules with multiple minimum supports. In *Proceedings of the 5th ACM SIGKDD International Conference on Knowledge Discovery and Data Mining* (pp. 337-341). New York, NY: ACM.

Lopes, A., Pinho, R., Paulovich, F., & Minghim, R. (2007). Visual text mining using association rules. *Computers & Graphics, 31*(3), 316–326. doi:10.1016/j.cag.2007.01.023

Qu, S., Wang, S., & Zou, Y. (2008). Improvement of text feature selection method based on TF-IDF. In *Proceedings of the 2008 International Seminar on Future Information Technology and Management Engineering (FITME '08)* (pp. 79-81). Washington, DC: IEEE Computer Society.

Ritchie, D. S. (2010). *Students hit hard as swine flu clobbers schools*. Retrieved October 20, 2010, from http://www.times-age.co.nz/local/news/students-hit-hard-as-swine-flu-clobbers-schools/3918707/

Sanjay, R., Ranka, S., & Tsur, S. (1997). *Weighted association rules, Model and algorithm*. Retrieved from http://citeseer.ist.psu.edu/185924.html

Shepard, D. (1968). A two-dimensional interpolation function for irregularly-spaced data. In *Proceedings of the 1968 23rd ACM National Conference* (pp. 517-524). New York, NY: ACM.

Sun, K., & Bai, F. (2008). Mining weighted association rules without preassigned weights. *IEEE Transactions on Knowledge and Data Engineering, 20*(4), 489–495. doi:10.1109/TKDE.2007.190723

Tan, P.-N., Steinbach, M., & Kumar, V. (2006). *Introduction to Data Mining*. Upper Saddle River, NJ: Pearson.

Taniar, D., Rahayu, W., Lee, V. C. S., & Daly, O. (2008). Exception rules in association rule mining. *Applied Mathematics and Computation, 205*(2), 735–750. doi:10.1016/j.amc.2008.05.020

Tao, F., Murtagh, F., & Farid, M. (2003). Weighted association rule mining using weighted support and significance framework. In *Proceedings of the 9th ACM SIGKDD International Conference on Knowledge Discovery and Data Mining* (pp. 661-666). New York, NY: ACM.

Tjioe, H. C., & Taniar, D. (2005). Mining Association Rules in Data Warehouses. *International Journal of Data Warehousing and Mining, 1*(3), 28–62. doi:10.4018/jdwm.2005070103

Tzanis, G., & Berberidis, C. (2007). Mining for Mutually Exclusive Items in Transaction Databases. *International Journal of Data Warehousing and Mining, 3*(3), 45–59. doi:10.4018/jdwm.2007070104

Voters leave Australia hanging. (2010). Retrieved October 20, 2010, from http://www.abc.net.au/news/stories/2010/08/21/2989767.htm

Wang, W., Yang, J., & Yu, P. S. (2000). Efficient mining of weighted association rules (WAR). In *Proceedings of the 6th ACM SIGKDD International Conference on Knowledge Discovery and Data Mining (KDD '00)* (pp. 270-274). New York, NY: ACM.

Wong, P. C., Whitney, P., & Thomas, J. (1999). Visualizing association rules for text mining. In *Proceedings of the IEEE Symposium on Information Visualization* (pp. 120-123). Washington, DC: IEEE Computer Society.

Wu, S.-T., Li, Y., Xu, Y., Pham, B., & Chen, P. (2004). Automatic pattern-taxonomy extraction for web mining. In *Proceedings of the 2004 IEEE/WIC/ACM International Conference on Web Intelligence (WI '04)* (pp. 242-248). Washington, DC: IEEE Computer Society.

Yan, L., & Li, C. (2006). Incorporating pageview weight into an association-rule-based web recommendation system. In A. Sattar & B. H. Kang (Eds.), *Proceedings of the Australian Conference on Artificial Intelligence* (LNCS 4304, pp. 577-586).

Yu, H., Han, J., & Chang, K. C.-C. (2004). PEBL Web page classification without negative examples. *IEEE Transactions on Knowledge and Data Engineering*, *16*(1), 70–81. doi:10.1109/TKDE.2004.1264823

Zhao, Y., Jiang, H., Geng, R., & Dong, X. (2009). Mining weighted negative association rules based on correlation from infrequent items. In *Proceedings of the International Conference on Advanced Computer Control* (pp. 270-273). Washington, DC: IEEE Computer Society.

This work was previously published in the International Journal of Data Warehousing and Mining, Volume 7, Issue 3, edited by David Taniar, pp. 30-49, copyright 2011 by IGI Publishing (an imprint of IGI Global).

Chapter 10
Weak Ratio Rules:
A Generalized Boolean Association Rules

Baoqing Jiang
Henan University, China

Jingjing Song
Qingyuan Polytechnic, China

Xiaohua Hu
*Henan University China, & Drexel Univeristy,
USA*

Chong Han
Henan University, China

Qing Wei
Henan University of Economics and Law, China

Meng Liang
Henan University, China

ABSTRACT

This paper examines the problem of weak ratio rules between nonnegative real-valued data in a transactional database. The weak ratio rule is a weaker form than Flip Korn's ratio rule. After analyzing the mathematical model of weak ratio rules problem, the authors conclude that it is a generalization of Boolean association rules problem and every weak ratio rule is supported by a Boolean association rule. Following the properties of weak ratio rules, the authors propose an algorithm for mining an important subset of weak ratio rules and construct a weak ratio rule uncertainty reasoning method. An example is given to show how to apply weak ratio rules to reconstruct lost data, and forecast and detect outliers.

INTRODUCTION

The problem of mining association rules from large databases has been subject of numerous studies. Some of them focus on developing faster algorithms for the classical method and/or adapting the algorithms to various situations, for example, distributed algorithm ODAM (Ashrafi, Taniar, & Smith, 2004), association rules mining in data warehouses (Tjioe & Taniar, 2005), multidimensional database mining (Yu et al., 2009; Casali et al., 2010), exception rules mining (Daly & Taniar, 2004; Taniar, Rahayu, Lee, & Daly, 2008) and redundant analysis (Ashrafi, Taniar, & Smith, 2007). Another direction is to define rules that modify some conditions of the classical rules to adapt to new applications (Marcus, Maletic, & Lin, 2001; Giannikopoulos, Varlamis, & Eirinaki,

DOI: 10.4018/978-1-4666-2148-0.ch010

2010). For instance, Srikant and Agrawal (1996) extended the categorical definition to include quantitative data and investigated the quantitative association rules problems.

For quantitative attributes, the general idea is partitioning the domain of a quantitative attribute into intervals, and applying Boolean algorithms to the intervals. But there is a conflict between the minimum support problem and the minimum confidence problem, while existing partitioning methods cannot avoid the conflict (Tong et al., 2005).

Fuzzy method had successfully been used in data mining (Kuok, Fu, & Wong, 1998; Kwok, Smith, Lozano, & Taniar, 2002). Fuzzy association rules solve interval partition problem in some extent. It needs to do fuzzy partition to the domain of quantitative attribute, i.e., to consider fuzzy set on the domain. However, in some actual problem, to some test data, we can not propose meaningful fuzzy sets.

Flip Korn et al. (1998) focused on real-valued data such as dollar amounts spent by customers on products in transactional database and proposed the following ratio rule:

bread : *butter* = 2:3

which means that the ratio of the dollar amounts spent by a customer on bread to butter is 2:3. Flip Korn also investigated the application of ratio rule on data cleaning, forecasting, "what-if" scenarios, outlier detection and visualization.

When quantitative attributes have no ratio relation, ratio rule can not better describe the quantitative association relation of quantitative attribute. At this time, there not exist real number a, b such that $x : y = a : b$ for attributes x, y, but there may exist real number a, b such that $x : y \leq a : b$.

In this paper, we focus on the relationship between nonnegative real-valued data in transactional database and investigate the influence of the values, of some attributes called antecedent, to the values of other attributes called consequent.

When antecedent and consequent only include one attribute, the quantitative relationship of antecedent and consequent can be expressed as $x : y \leq a : b$. For example, *bread : butter* $\leq$ 2:3 has such a reasoning meaning that if the dollar amount spent by a customer on bread is 2, then the dollar amounts spent by the customer on butter is at least 3. It is precisely this reason that the rules proposed by this paper are called weak ratio rules.

In order to establish the mathematical model of weak ratio rules problem, we investigate the Boolean association rules problem deeply and propose the equivalent description of it.

By the equivalent description of Boolean association rules problem, we can generalize it naturally to weak ratio rules as an implication of the form $A \Rightarrow B$, where A, B are nonnegative real-valued function defined on itemset I. An attribute is also called an item in this paper, I is the set of all items.

We use 2^I to denote the set of all subset of I, and $[0, +\infty)^I$ to denote the set of all nonnegative real-valued function on I. For any subset X of I, we consider X is the same as its characteristic function χ_X, a nonnegative real-valued function on I, whose value is 0 or 1. In this viewpoint, 2^I is a subset of $[0, +\infty)^I$.

By discussing the properties of weak ratio rule (simply as WRR in this paper sometimes), we come to that every WRR corresponds to a Boolean association rule (simply as BAR in this paper sometimes) as its support rule. The set of all WRRs can be classified by their support rules. In order to mine all WRRs, we need only mine all BARs, then for a single BAR $(X \Rightarrow Y)$ to mine the set of all WRRs $R_W(X \Rightarrow Y)$ supported by the BAR $(X \Rightarrow Y)$.

By analyzing the structure of $R_W(X \Rightarrow Y)$, we can find an important subset $Q_W(X \Rightarrow Y)$ of $R_W(X \Rightarrow Y)$. The subset can be expressed as an ideal of a chain-product. In this paper, we use a depth-first algorithm Boundary to mine the subset $Q_W(X \Rightarrow Y)$.

By Remark 5, we come to that if $(X \Rightarrow Y; ms, mc)$ is a BAR and a customer purchases all items in X, then there is mc possibility that the customer purchases all items in Y.

Similarly, if $(A \Rightarrow B; ms, mc)$ is a WRR and a customer purchases $F(x)$ (unit value) items $x(x \in \operatorname{supp} A)$, then how much unit value items $y(y \in \operatorname{supp} B)$ the customer purchases? In the section "Uncertainty reasoning method based on WRR", we propose an uncertainty reasoning method based on WRR by which we can solve the problem like "If a customer spends \$22 on bread and \$2.5 on beer, how much will s/he spend on chocolate?" easily.

Our paper consists of five main sections: problem statement, properties, mining algorithm, uncertainty reasoning and application.

PROBLEM STATEMENT

In this section, we propose the mathematical model of weak ratio rules problem. The model show that weak ratio rules problem is a generalization of Boolean association rules problem, and when antecedent and consequent only include one item, the quantitative relationship shown by weak ratio rules can be expressed as

$$bread : butter \leq 2:3,$$

a weaker form than Flip Korn's ratio rule.

Equivalent Description of Boolean Association Rules

In Boolean association rules problem (Agrawal & Srikant, 1994, 1996), the transactional database $\mathcal{D}$ can be thought as a 0-1 matrix, in which every row corresponds to a transaction and every column corresponds to an item. We use $\mathcal{D}(t, i)$ express the value at tth row and ith column of the matrix, then $\mathcal{D}(t, i) = 1$ means that customer purchases

item i in transaction t. The transactional database discussed in Boolean association rules problem is called in the paper Boolean transactional database which can be actually thought as a 0-1 matrix.

A transaction t can be thought as the item set D_t defined as $\{i \mid \mathcal{D}(t, i) = 1\}$.

So, the Boolean association rules problem can be described formally as the following definitions.

- **Definition 1:** *Let T, I be two nonempty finite sets,* $\mathcal{D}$ *a mapping from* $T \times I$ *to* $\{0,1\}$. *Then* $\mathcal{D}$ *is called a Boolean transactional database, and* I *is called the set of items of* $\mathcal{D}$, *and* T *is called the index set of transactions of* $\mathcal{D}$. $\forall t \in T$, *the subset*

$$D_t \triangleq \{i \mid \mathcal{D}(t, i) = 1\}$$

of I, is called a transaction of $\mathcal{D}$.

For the sake of convenience in this paper, a Boolean transactional database $\mathcal{D}$ is regarded as a set of transactions $\{D_t \mid t \in T\}$ or a matrix $(\mathcal{D}(t, i))_{T \times I}$. The transaction D_t is also called transaction t or customer t.

- **Definition 2:** Let $\mathcal{D} = \{D_t\}_{t \in T}$ be a Boolean transactional database, I the set of items of $\mathcal{D}$, and T the index set of transaction of $\mathcal{D}$ Let $X \in 2^I \setminus \{\varnothing\}$. If $X \subseteq D_t$, then we call transaction t supports X. We *use* $t(X, \mathcal{D})$, *simply* $t(X)$, to denote $\{t \mid X \subseteq D_t\}$, the set of all transactions supporting X.
- **Remark 3:** $t(X)$ has the same meaning as that in *(Zaki, 2000; Gouda & Zaki, 2005; Burdick et al., 2005)*, $\mid t(X) \mid$ is just support_*count(X)* in Han and Kamber (2006). It can be understood as the number of customers (or transactions) who purchase all items in X.
- **Definition 4:** Let $\mathcal{D} = \{D_t\}_{t \in T}$ be a Boolean transactional database, I the set of

items of $\mathcal{D}$, and T the index set of transaction of $\mathcal{D}$. Let $X, Y \in 2^I \setminus \{\phi\}$, $X \cap Y = \varnothing$, $ms, mc \in (0,1)$, $t(X, \mathcal{D}) \neq \varnothing$. Let

$$\sup(X \Rightarrow Y, \mathcal{D}) \triangleq \frac{|t(X \cup Y, \mathcal{D})|}{|T|}$$

$$\mathrm{conf}(X \Rightarrow Y, \mathcal{D}) \triangleq \frac{|t(X \cup Y, \mathcal{D})|}{|t(X, \mathcal{D})|}$$

then $\sup(X \Rightarrow Y, \mathcal{D})$ is called the support of $(X \Rightarrow Y)$ in $\mathcal{D}$, $\mathrm{conf}(X \Rightarrow Y, \mathcal{D})$ is called the confidence of $(X \Rightarrow Y)$ in $\mathcal{D}$. If $\sup(X \Rightarrow Y, \mathcal{D}) \geq ms$ and $\mathrm{conf}(X \Rightarrow Y, \mathcal{D}) \geq mc$, then $(X \Rightarrow Y)$ is called a Boolean association rule with minimum support threshold ms and minimum confidence threshold mc in $\mathcal{D}$. The set of all Boolean association rules with minimum support threshold ms and minimum confidence threshold mc in $\mathcal{D}$ is denoted by $R_b(\mathcal{D}; ms, mc)$.

- **Remark 5:** In Definition 4, $\sup(X \Rightarrow Y, \mathcal{D}), \mathrm{conf}(X \Rightarrow Y, \mathcal{D})$ can be simply denoted as $\sup(X \Rightarrow Y), \mathrm{conf}(X \Rightarrow Y)$ respectively. The inequality $\mathrm{conf}(X \Rightarrow Y) \geq mc$ means that the ratio of customers who purchase all items in $X \cup Y$ to customers who purchase all items in X is at least mc.

Weak Ratio Rules

In weak ratio rules problem, the transactional database $\mathcal{D}$ can be thought as a nonnegative real-valued matrix. The value $\mathcal{D}(t, i)$ at tth row and ith column means that customer purchases $\mathcal{D}(t, i)$ (unit value) item i in transaction t. The transactional database discussed in weak ratio rules problem is called in this paper pure quantitative transactional database, simply PQTD. Obviously, a Boolean transactional database is a special PQTD. If for any transaction t and item i, $\mathcal{D}(t, i) > 0$, then we say $\mathcal{D}$ is a positive PQTD. Table 1 and Table 2 show two PQTDs.

Let $\mathcal{D}$ denote a PQTD, I the set of all items, and T the set of all transactions. The value $\mathcal{D}(t, i)$, also denoted by $D_t(i)$, at tth row and ith column of $\mathcal{D}$ can be regarded as the dollar amounts spent by a customer on item i in transaction t. $D_t(i)$ can also be regarded as the quantity of item i bought by a customer in transaction t. For the sake of convenience, we also say transaction t as cus-

Table 1. A PQTD

	i_1	i_2	i_3	i_4	i_5
t_1	1	0	0	2	0
t_2	2	1	0	5	0
t_3	0	0	1	2	1
t_4	1	3	5	0	0
t_5	1	0	0	2	2
t_6	0	6	7	0	0

Table 2. A positive PQTD

	x_1	x_2	y_1
t_1	10	20	30
t_2	1	2	3
t_3	10	20	40
t_4	5	10	15
t_5	2	4	4

tomer t, and for the consistency, we explain $D_t(i)$ as the quantity of item i bought by customer t. For example, the first row in Table 2 expresses a transaction t_1 in which the customer purchases 10 units x_1, 20 units x_2 and 30 units y_1.

Weak ratio rules describe the "purchasing ratio" of transaction in a PQTD. In Table 2, the purchasing ratios of customers t_1, t_2, t_4 are all 1:2:3, and the purchasing ratio of customers t_3 is 1:2:4. When we investigate the influence of quantities of x_1, x_2 to quantity of y_1, the fact that 60% of transactions have purchasing ratio 1:2:3 indicates that if a customer purchases 1 unit of x_1 and 2 units of x_2 then there is 60% possibility that the customer purchases 3 units of y_1. Similarly, The fact that 20% of transactions have purchasing ratio 1:2:4 indicates that if a customer purchases 1 unit of x_1 and 2 units of x_2 then there is 20% possibility that the customer purchases 4 units of y_1. So as a whole, we can say that if a customer purchases 1 unit of x_1 and 2 units of x_2 then there is 80% (60%+20%) possibility that the customer purchases at least 3 units of y_1. The conclusion can be expressed as a rule

$$(1/x_1 + 2/x_2 \Rightarrow 3/y_1 ; 80\%)$$

where 80% is called the confidence of the rule, and $1/x_1 + 2/x_1$ antecedent, $3/y_1$ consequent.

In this paper, we propose a mathematical model to describe the above problem. The model takes Boolean association rules model (Definition 4) as a special case. The model can describe weaker quantitative relationship between attributes than that described by Ratio Rules (Korn et al., 1998).

Weak ratio rules problem can be described formally as the following definitions.

- **Definition 6:** Let T, I be a nonempty finite set, $\mathcal{D}$ a mapping from T×I to $[0, +\infty)$, then $\mathcal{D}$ is called a pure quantitative transactional database, and I is called the set of

items of $\mathcal{D}$, and T is called the index set of transactions of $\mathcal{D}$. $\forall t \in T$, the nonnegative real-valued function

$$
\begin{aligned}
D_t : \quad I \quad &\to \quad [0,+\infty) \\
i \quad &\mapsto \quad \mathcal{D}(t,i),
\end{aligned}
$$

on I, is called a transaction of $\mathcal{D}$.

A PQTD $\mathcal{D}$ can be expressed as a series of transactions $\{D_t\}_{t \in T}$ or a matrix $(D(t,i))_{T \times I}$, where the transaction D_t is a nonnegative real-valued function on I. The transaction D_t is also called transaction t or customer t.

- **Definition 7:** Let A be a nonnegative real-valued function on I. We use supp$A$ to denote the set $\{x \mid x \in I, A(x) > 0\}$ called the support of A. If $\text{supp}\, A = \{x_1, x_2, \cdots x_p\}$, then we express A as $A(x_1)/x_1 + A(x_2)/x_2 + \cdots + A(x_p)/x_p$ or $\dfrac{A(x_1)}{x_1} + \dfrac{A(x_2)}{x_2} + \cdots + \dfrac{A(x_p)}{x_p}$.

For any subset X, of I, the characteristic function χ_X is a nonnegative real-valued function on I, and the support of χ_X is just X. We do not distinguish between χ_X and X in this paper. We use $\varnothing$ to denote empty subset or zero function (the function A satisfying $A(x) = 0$ for any $x \in I$) on I. For any nonnegative real-valued function on I, we take it like a fuzzy set. For example, $\forall A, B \in [0, +\infty)^I$, we use $A \cap B$ to denote the nonnegative real-valued function whose value in i is $\min\{A(i), B(i)\}$, i.e., $(A \cap B)(i) = \min\{A(i), B(i)\}$; we use $A \cup B$ to denote the nonnegative real-valued function whose value in i is $\max\{A(i), B(i)\}$, i.e., $(A \cup B)(i) = \max\{A(i), B(i)\}$. And we use $A \subseteq B$ to express that "$A(i) \leq B(i)$ for any $i \in I$".

- **Definition 8:** Let $\mathcal{D} = \{D_t\}_{t \in T}$ be a PQTD, then $\{\operatorname{supp} D_t\}_{t \in T}$ is a Boolean transactional database, called support of $\mathcal{D}$, denoted by $\operatorname{supp}\mathcal{D}$.

The support transactional database $\operatorname{supp}\mathcal{D}$ (as a matrix) can be obtained by replacing the nonnegative elements of PQTD $\mathcal{D}$ with 1. When the transactions D_t in PQTD $\mathcal{D}$ degenerate to subset of I, the PQTD $\mathcal{D}$ degenerates to its support $\operatorname{supp}\mathcal{D}$.

- **Definition 9:** Let $\mathcal{D} = \{D_t\}_{t \in T}$ be a PQTD, I the set of items of $\mathcal{D}$, T the index set of transactions of $\mathcal{D}$. $A, B \in [0, +\infty)^I \setminus \{\varnothing\}$, $\operatorname{supp} A \cap \operatorname{supp} B = \varnothing$, $t \in T$.
  - **(1):** If $\operatorname{supp} A \subseteq \operatorname{supp} D_t$, i.e., $D_t(i) > 0$ for any $i \in \operatorname{supp} A$, then we say that transaction t supports A.
  - **(2):** If $\operatorname{supp} A \cup \operatorname{supp} B \subseteq \operatorname{supp} D_t$ and $\forall i \in \operatorname{supp} A$, $\forall j \in \operatorname{supp} B$, $\dfrac{B(j)}{A(i)} \leq \dfrac{D_t(j)}{D_t(i)}$ then we say that transaction t supports $(A \Rightarrow B)$.
- **Remark 10:**
  - **(1):** Obviously, when $\mathcal{D}$, A, B degenerate to their support, transaction t supports A has the same meaning as that in Definition 2, and t supports $(A \Rightarrow B)$ is equivalent to that t supports $(A \cup B)$.
  - **(2):** If t supports $(A \Rightarrow B)$ and $\forall i \in \operatorname{supp} A$, $D_t(i) = A(i)$, then $\forall j \in \operatorname{supp} B$, $D_t(j) \geq B(j)$.
- **Definition 11:** Let $\mathcal{D}$ be a PQTD, I the set of items of $\mathcal{D}$, T the index set of transaction of $\mathcal{D}$. $A, B \in [0, +\infty)^I \setminus \{\varnothing\}$, $A \cap B = \varnothing$, We use $t(A, \mathcal{D})$, simply $t(A)$, to denote the set of all transactions supporting A, and $t(A \Rightarrow B, \mathcal{D})$, simply $t(A \Rightarrow B)$, to de-

note the set of all transactions supporting $(A \Rightarrow B)$.

- **Definition 12:** Let $\mathcal{D}$ be a PQTD, I the set of items of $\mathcal{D}$, T the index set of transaction of $\mathcal{D}$. $A, B \in [0, +\infty)^I \setminus \{\varnothing\}$, $A \cap B = \varnothing$, $ms, mc \in (0,1)$, $t(A, \mathcal{D}) \neq \varnothing$. Let

$$\sup(A \Rightarrow B, \mathcal{D}) \triangleq \frac{|t(A \Rightarrow B, \mathcal{D})|}{|T|},$$

$$\operatorname{conf}(A \Rightarrow B, \mathcal{D}) \triangleq \frac{|t(A \Rightarrow B, \mathcal{D})|}{|t(A, \mathcal{D})|},$$

then $\sup(A \Rightarrow B, \mathcal{D})$ is called the support of $(A \Rightarrow B)$ in $\mathcal{D}$, $\operatorname{conf}(A \Rightarrow B, \mathcal{D})$ is called the confidence of $(A \Rightarrow B)$ in $\mathcal{D}$. If $\sup(A \Rightarrow B, \mathcal{D}) \geq ms$ and $\operatorname{conf}(A \Rightarrow B, \mathcal{D}) \geq mc$, then $(A \Rightarrow B)$ is called a weak ratio rule with minimum support threshold ms and minimum confidence threshold mc in $\mathcal{D}$. A, B are called antecedent and consequent of the rule respectively. The set of all weak ratio rules with minimum support threshold ms and minimum confidence threshold mc in $\mathcal{D}$ is denoted by $R_W(\mathcal{D}; ms, mc)$. If $(A \Rightarrow B) \in R_W(\mathcal{D}; ms, mc)$, then we also say that $(A \Rightarrow B; ms, mc)$ is a weak ratio rule in $\mathcal{D}$.

- **Remark 13:** To positive PQTD $\mathcal{D}$, for any $A, B \in [0, +\infty)^I \setminus \{\varnothing\}$, we can get that $t(A, \mathcal{D}) = T$, so $\operatorname{conf}(A \Rightarrow B, \mathcal{D}) = \sup(A \Rightarrow B, \mathcal{D})$. That is to say, we can use only one objective interestingness measure confidence and one threshold mc to describe the WRR model. Of course, we can consider that we still use two measures support and confidence, and the two thresholds ms and mc are equal.

In the following, no specification, $\mathcal{D}$, A, B, ms, mc, $(A \Rightarrow B)$ are the same as that in Definition 12. For the sake of convenience, the weak ratio rule $(A \Rightarrow B)$ is also denoted by $A \Rightarrow B$ sometimes. The symbols $\mathcal{D}$, $\text{supp}\mathcal{D}$ or ms, mc in notations $t(A, \mathcal{D})$, $t(A \Rightarrow B, \mathcal{D})$, $\sup(A, \mathcal{D})$, $\sup(A \Rightarrow B, \mathcal{D})$, $\text{conf}(A \Rightarrow B, \mathcal{D})$, $R_W(\mathcal{D}; ms, mc)$ and $R_b(\text{supp}\,\mathcal{D}; ms, mc)$ can be omitted sometimes.

- **Example 14:** For the PQTD in Table 1, it can be verified easily that: $t(2/i_4) = \{t_1, t_2, t_3, t_5\}$, $t(2/i_4 \Rightarrow 1/i_5) = \{t_3, t_5\}$, $\sup(2/i_4 \Rightarrow 1/i_5) = 1/3$, $\text{conf}(2/i_4 \Rightarrow 1/i_5) = 1/2$, therefore, $(2/i_4 \Rightarrow 1/i_5) \in R_W(ms, mc)$ as long as $ms \leq 1/3$ and $mc \leq 1/2$. Similarly, $(1/x_1 + 2/x_2 \Rightarrow 3/y_1; 0.8)$ is a WRR in the positive PQTD Table 2.

The following proposition is obvious by Remark 10, Definition 4 and Definition 12.

- **Proposition 15:** Let $\mathcal{D}$ be a Boolean transactional database, $X, Y \in 2^I \setminus \{\varnothing\}$, $X \cap Y = \varnothing$, then

$$(X \Rightarrow Y) \in R_W(\mathcal{D}; ms, mc) \Leftrightarrow$$
$$(X \Rightarrow Y) \in R_b(\mathcal{D}; ms, mc).$$

Proposition 15 shows that weak ratio rule problem is a generalization of Boolean association rule problem.

Now we discuss the relationship between Flip Korn's Ratio Rules (Korn et al., 1998) and the special weak ratio rule whose antecedent and consequent only include one item, and so reveal the significance of weak ratio rules.

Let $(a/x \Rightarrow b/y; ms, mc)$ be a weak ratio rule, then by Definition 9, transaction D_t supports a/x if and only if customer t purchases item x; transaction D_t supports $(a/x \Rightarrow b/y)$ if and only if customer t pur-

chases items x, y and the the ratio of quantity of item x to quantity of item y is less than or equal to $a : b$. Therefore, WRR $(a/x \Rightarrow b/y; ms, mc)$ has the following meaning:

- **(1):** In all customers, there are at least $(100 \times ms)\%$ customers who purchase item x, y and the ratio of the quantity of item x to the quantity of item y purchased by them is less than or equal to $a : b$;
- **(2):** In all customers who purchase item x, there are at least $(100 \times mc)\%$ customers who purchase item x, y and the ratio of the quantity of item x to the quantity of item y purchased by them is less than or equal to $a : b$.

Flip Korn's ratio rules reveal the association relation between items that the ratio of the quantity of item x to the quantity of item y purchased by customer is equal to $a : b$. But in actual transactional database, the quantity of item x may be not proportional to that of item y, and in this case, WRR may reveal partially the association relation between items.

To a general WRR $(A \Rightarrow B; ms, mc)$. If customer t purchases $A(i)$ unit quantity item $i (\forall i \in \text{supp}\,A)$, i.e., $\forall i \in \text{supp}\,A$, $D_t(i) = A(i)$, then by Definition 9, we know t supports A. By Definition 12, in all customers supporting A, there are at least $(100 \times mc)\%$ customers supporting $A \Rightarrow B$, and then by Remark 10(2), we have $\forall j \in \text{supp}\,B, D_t(j) \geq B(j)$, i.e., the $(100 \times mc)\%$ customers purchases at least $B(j)$ unit quantity item $j (\forall j \in \text{supp}\,B)$.

In a word, if $(A \Rightarrow B; ms, mc)$ is a WRR, then we can get the following affirmation: "If customer t purchases $A(i)$ unit quantity item i for any $i \in \text{supp}\,A$ then there is mc possibility that the customer purchases at least $B(j)$ unit quantity item j for any $j \in \text{supp}\,B$". We call the affirmation the reasoning meaning of $(A \Rightarrow B; ms, mc)$. The reasoning meaning of a WRR is a part of whole meaning of the WRR. The reasoning meaning of WRR can be used to construct WRR uncertainty reasoning methods in the section "Uncertainty reasoning method based on WRR", and the WRR uncertainty reasoning methods can be applied to reconstructing lost data, forecasting and outlier detection in the section "Application of WRR".

PROPERTIES OF WRR

For a given PQTD $\mathcal{D}$ and two thresholds $ms, mc \in (0,1)$, we discuss the overall structure of set $R_W(\mathcal{D}; ms, mc)$ and obtain that: Every WRR $(A \Rightarrow B)$ corresponds to a Boolean association rule $(\operatorname{supp} A \Rightarrow \operatorname{supp} B)$ as its support rule; The set of all WRRs can be classified by their support rules. In order to mine all WRRs, we need only mine all BARs, then for a single BAR $(X \Rightarrow Y)$ to mine the set of all WRRs $R_w(X \Rightarrow Y)$ supported by the BAR $(X \Rightarrow Y)$.

We introduce three binary relations $\leq, \leq_d, \sim_d$ on $R_w(X \Rightarrow Y)$, and then introduce two concepts basis rule and maximal rule. We discuss special subsets of $R_w(X \Rightarrow Y)$ consisting of basis rules or maximal rules.

Support Degree and Multiplying Operation

In Definition 9, the concept support can actually be rewritten as following definition.

- **Definition 16:** Let $A, B, D \in [0, +\infty)^I \setminus \{\varnothing\}$, $\operatorname{supp} A \cap \operatorname{supp} B = \varnothing$.
  - **(1):** If $\operatorname{supp} A \subseteq \operatorname{supp} D$, i.e., $D(i) > 0$ for any $i \in \operatorname{supp} A$, then we say that D supports A.
  - **(2):** If $\operatorname{supp} A \cup \operatorname{supp} B \subseteq \operatorname{supp} D$ and $\forall i \in \operatorname{supp} A$, $\forall j \in \operatorname{supp} B$,

$\dfrac{B(j)}{A(i)} \leq \dfrac{D(j)}{D(i)}$, then we say that D supports $(A \Rightarrow B)$.

- **Definition 17:** Let $A, D \in [0, +\infty)^I$, $A \neq \varnothing$, then

$$\operatorname{Inf}(D/A) \triangleq \bigwedge_{i \in \operatorname{supp} A} \frac{D(i)}{A(i)}$$

is called the support degree of D for A.

$$\operatorname{Sup}(D/A) \triangleq \bigvee_{i \in \operatorname{supp} A} \frac{D(i)}{A(i)}$$

is called the supremum support degree of D for A. Since suppA is a finite set, the infimum (supremum) notation $\wedge(\vee)$ can be replaced with min(max), that is to say, we have

$$\operatorname{Inf}(D/A) = \min\{\frac{D(i)}{A(i)} \mid i \in \operatorname{supp} A\},$$

$$\operatorname{Sup}(D/A) = \max\{\frac{D(i)}{A(i)} \mid i \in \operatorname{supp} A\}.$$

By the concept support degree, we have the following proposition:

When suppA, suppB all degenerate to singleton subset in Definition 16, we get the Proposition 18:

- **Proposition 18:** Let $D \in [0, +\infty)^I \setminus \{\varnothing\}$, $x, y \in I$, $x \neq y$, $a, b \in (0, +\infty)$, then
  - **(1):** D supports a/x if and only if $D(x) > 0$;
  - **(2):** D supports $(a/x \Rightarrow b/y)$ if and only if $D(x) > 0$, $D(y) > 0$, and $\dfrac{D(y)}{D(x)} \geq \dfrac{b}{a}$.
- **Proposition 19:** Let $A, D \in [0, +\infty)^I$, $A \neq \varnothing$, then

- **(1):** $\text{Inf}(D/A)$ is the maximal α in $[0,+\infty)$ satisfying $\alpha A \subseteq D$;

- **(2):** If $\text{supp}\,D \subseteq \text{supp}\,A$, then $\text{Sup}(D/A)$ is the minimal α in $[0,+\infty)$ satisfying $D \subseteq \alpha A$, where $\alpha A \in [0,+\infty)^{I}$, $\forall i \in I$,

$$(\alpha A)(i) \triangleq \alpha A(i)$$

- **Proof:** Only prove (1). Firstly, we prove $\text{Inf}(D/A) \in [0,+\infty)$ and $\text{Inf}(D/A)A \subseteq D$. The former is obvious. In order to prove the latter, we need only to prove $\forall i \in \text{supp}\,A$, $\text{Inf}(D/A)A(i) \le D(i)$ which can be obtained easily from the definition of support degree.

Secondly, we prove that $\alpha A \subseteq D$ implies $\alpha \le \text{Inf}(D/A)$. For any $i \in \text{supp}\,A$, $\alpha A(i) = (\alpha A)(i) \le D(i)$, $\alpha \le D(i)/A(i)$, $\alpha \le \max\{D(i)/A(i) \mid i \in \text{supp}\,A\} = \text{Inf}(D/A)$.

- **Proposition 20:** Let $A,B,D \in [0,+\infty)^{I} \setminus \{\varnothing\}$, $A \cap B = \varnothing$, then

  - **(1):** D supports A if and only if $0 < \text{Inf}(D/A)$;

  - **(2):** D supports $(A \Rightarrow B)$ if and only if $0 < \text{Inf}(D/A)$ and $\text{Sup}(D/A) \le \text{Inf}(D/B)$;

  - **(3):** D supports $(A \Rightarrow B)$ if and only if $\text{supp}\,A \cup \text{supp}\,B \subseteq \text{supp}\,D$ and there exists $\alpha \in (0,+\infty)$ such that $\forall i \in \text{supp}\,A$, $D(i) \le \alpha A(i)$, $\forall j \in \text{supp}\,B$, $\alpha B(j) \le D(j)$.

  - **Proof:** It is trivial.

Let $A \in [0,+\infty)^{I}$, $i_{0} \in I$, $\beta \in (0,+\infty)$ we use $A[i_{0},\beta]$ to denote the nonnegative real-valued function defined by replacing the value of A at i_{0} with $A(i_{0})$ multiplied by β, i.e.,

$$\forall i \in I, \ A[i_{0},\beta](i) = \begin{cases} A(i), i \ne i_{0}, \\ \beta A(i), i = i_{0}. \end{cases}$$

- **Proposition 21:** Let $A,B,D \in [0,+\infty)^{I}$, $A,B \ne \varnothing$, $A \cap B = \varnothing$, $i_{0} \in I$, $\beta \in (0,+\infty)$ $\beta \in (0,+\infty)$ then

  - **(1):** $D[i_{0},\beta]$ supports $A[i_{0},\beta]$ if and only if D supports A;

  - **(2):** $D[i_{0},\beta]$ supports $(A[i_{0},\beta] \Rightarrow B[i_{0},\beta])$ if and only if D supports $(A \Rightarrow B)$.

  - o **Proof:** The conclusions can be proved easily by $\text{Inf}(D[i_{0},\beta]/A[i_{0},\beta]) = \text{Inf}(D/A)$, $\text{Sup}(D[i_{0},\beta]/A[i_{0},\beta]) = \text{Sup}(D/A)$.

- **Proposition 22:** Let $A,B,D \in [0,+\infty)^{I}$, $A,B \ne \varnothing$, $A \cap B = \varnothing$, $\alpha \in (0,+\infty)$, then

  - **(1):** D supports αA if and only if D supports A;

  - **(2):** D supports $(\alpha A \Rightarrow \alpha B)$ if and only if D supports $(A \Rightarrow B)$;

  - **(3):** αD supports $(A \Rightarrow B)$ if and only if D supports $(A \Rightarrow B)$.

  - **Proof:** (1) and (2) can be proved from $\text{Inf}(D/\alpha A) = \dfrac{1}{\alpha}\text{Inf}(D/A)$ and $\text{Sup}(D/\alpha A) = \dfrac{1}{\alpha}\text{Sup}(D/A)$. (3) can be proved from $\text{Inf}(\alpha D/A) = \alpha\,\text{Inf}(D/A)$ and $\text{Sup}(\alpha D/A) = \alpha\,\text{Sup}(D/A)$.

Support Rule and Partition

Firstly, by Definition 12, we have the following proposition obviously.

- **Proposition 23:** If $ms_{1} \le ms$, $mc_{1} \le mc$, then $\text{R}_{\text{W}}(\mathcal{D};ms,mc) \subseteq \text{R}_{\text{W}}(\mathcal{D};ms_{1},mc_{1})$, i.e., If $(A \Rightarrow B; ms, mc)$ is a WRR, then $(A \Rightarrow B; ms_1, mc_1)$ is also a WRR.

The quantity unit of every attribute is determined before mining WRRs in a PQTD $\mathcal{D}$. The quantity unit may be 'kilogram' or 'gram'. The change of unit causes the change of value in $\mathcal{D}$. Is the association relation between attributes revealed by WRR affected by the change of quantity unit of attributes? The following Remark 25 give a negative answer.

Similar to natation $A[i_0, \beta]$, we use $\mathcal{D}[i_0, \beta]$ to denote the PQTD defined by replacing the value of PQTD $\mathcal{D}$ in column i_0 with $\mathcal{D}(t, i_0)$ multiplied by β, i.e., $\forall t \in T$, $i \in I$,

$$\mathcal{D}[i_0, \beta](t, i) = \begin{cases} \mathcal{D}(t, i), i \neq i_0, \\ \beta \mathcal{D}(t, i), i = i_0. \end{cases}$$

It is obvious that if $\mathcal{D} = \{D_t\}_{t \in T}$, then $\mathcal{D}[i_0, \beta] = \{D_t[i_0, \beta]\}_{t \in T}$.

- **Proposition 24:** Let $A, B \in [0, +\infty)^I \setminus \{\varnothing\}$, $A \cap B = \varnothing$, $i_0 \in I$, $\beta \in (0, +\infty)$, then

$$(A \Rightarrow B) \in R_W(\mathcal{D}; ms, mc)$$
$$\Leftrightarrow (A[i_0, \beta] \Rightarrow B[i_0, \beta])$$
$$\in R_W(\mathcal{D}[i_0, \beta]; ms, mc).$$

  - **Proof:** It can be verified easily by Definition 12, Definition 16 and Proposition 21.

- **Remark 25:** The Proposition 24 shows that the association relation between items revealed by weak ratio rules is not affected by the quantity unit change. For example, when the quantity unit 'kilogram', of item i_0, changes to 'gram', the value in column i_0 of PQTD changes 1000 times and by Proposition 24, the value at point i_0 of all weak ratio rules also change 1000 times.

The following Propositions 26 to 32 show the relationship between weak ratio rules and Boolean association rules: Every WRR corresponds a BAR as its support rule. We can classify WRRs by their support rules.

- **Proposition 26:** Let $\mathcal{D}$ be a PQTD, I the set of items of $\mathcal{D}$, T the index set of transaction of $\mathcal{D}$. $A, B \in [0, +\infty)^I \setminus \{\varnothing\}$, $A \cap B = \varnothing$, then
  - **(1):** $t(A, \mathcal{D}) = t(\operatorname{supp} A, \operatorname{supp} \mathcal{D})$;
  - **(2):** $t(A \Rightarrow B, \mathcal{D}) \subseteq t(\operatorname{supp} A \cup \operatorname{supp} B, \operatorname{supp} \mathcal{D})$;
  - **(3):** $\sup(A \Rightarrow B, \mathcal{D}) \leq \sup(\operatorname{supp} A \cup \operatorname{supp} B, \operatorname{supp} \mathcal{D})$;
  - **(4):** $\operatorname{conf}(A \Rightarrow B, \mathcal{D}) \leq \operatorname{conf}(\operatorname{supp} A \cup \operatorname{supp} B, \operatorname{supp} \mathcal{D})$ if $t(A, \mathcal{D}) \neq \varnothing$.
  - **Proof:** (1-2) are obvious by Definition 9 and Definition 2. (3-4) are obvious by Definition 12 and Definition 4.

- **Proposition 27:** Let $\mathcal{D}$ be a PQTD, $A, B, A_1, A_2 \in [0, +\infty)^I \setminus \{\varnothing\}$, $A \cap B = \varnothing$, $A_1 \subseteq A_2$, then:
  - **(1):** $t(A \Rightarrow B, \mathcal{D}) \subseteq t(A \cup B, \mathcal{D})$;
  - **(2):** $t(A_2, \mathcal{D}) \subseteq t(A_1, \mathcal{D})$.
  - **Proof:** It is trivial.

- **Proposition 28:** If $(A \Rightarrow B) \in R_W(\mathcal{D}; ms, mc)$, then $(\operatorname{supp} A \Rightarrow \operatorname{supp} B) \in R_b(\operatorname{supp} \mathcal{D}; ms, mc)$. The Boolean association rule $(\operatorname{supp} A \Rightarrow \operatorname{supp} B)$ is called support rule of weak ratio rule $(A \Rightarrow B)$.
  - **Proof:** It is trivial by Definition 4, Definition 12, and Proposition 26.

- **Proposition 29:** Suppose $(X \Rightarrow Y) \in R_b(\operatorname{supp} \mathcal{D}; ms, mc)$. $\forall i \in I$, Let

$$A(i) \triangleq \begin{cases} \bigvee\limits_{t \in t(X \cup Y, \operatorname{supp} D)} D_t(i), i \in X, \\ 0, \qquad\qquad\qquad i \notin X, \end{cases}$$

$$B(i) \triangleq \begin{cases} \bigwedge\limits_{t \in t(X \cup Y, \text{supp } D)} D_t(i), & i \in Y, \\ 0, & i \notin Y, \end{cases}$$

then $A, B \in [0, +\infty)^I \setminus \{\varnothing\}$, $A \cap B = \varnothing$, and

- **(1):** $\text{supp } A = X$, $\text{supp } B = Y$;
- **(2):** $t(A \Rightarrow B, \mathcal{D}) = t(X \cup Y, \text{supp } \mathcal{D})$;
- **(3):** $\sup(A \Rightarrow B, \mathcal{D}) = \sup(X \Rightarrow Y, \text{supp } \mathcal{D})$;
- **(4):** $\text{conf}(A \Rightarrow B, \mathcal{D}) = \text{conf}(X \Rightarrow Y, \text{supp } \mathcal{D})$;
- **(5):** $(A \Rightarrow B) \in R_W(\mathcal{D}; ms, mc)$.
- **Proof:**
  $(X \Rightarrow Y) \in R_b(\text{supp } \mathcal{D}; ms, mc)$ implies $t(X \cup Y, \text{supp } \mathcal{D}) \neq \varnothing$. $\forall t \in t(X \cup Y, \text{supp } \mathcal{D})$, $X \cup Y \subseteq \text{supp } D_t$, $\forall i \in X \cup Y$, $D_t(i) > 0$, therefore, $A, B \in [0, +\infty)^I \setminus \{\varnothing\}$, $A \cap B = \varnothing$, and (1) is true. To prove (2), by Proposition 26(2), we only need to prove $\forall t \in t(X \cup Y, \text{supp } \mathcal{D})$, t supports $(A \Rightarrow B)$. By the definitions of A, B, we know $\forall i \in X$, $A(i) \geq D_t(i)$, $\forall j \in Y$, $B(j) \leq D_t(j)$, hence $\frac{B(j)}{A(i)} \leq \frac{D_t(j)}{D_t(i)}$, by Definition 9, t supports $(A \Rightarrow B)$. (3-5) are obvious.

- **Remark 30:** The $\mathcal{D}$ in Proposition 15 can not be generalized to a PQTD. This is because $(X \Rightarrow Y) \in R_b(\text{supp } \mathcal{D}; ms, mc)$ can only imply $(A \Rightarrow B) \in R_W(\mathcal{D}; ms, mc)$ by Proposition 29, but not imply $(X \Rightarrow Y) \in R_W(\mathcal{D}; ms, mc)$ by the reasoning meaning of weak ratio rules.

- **Proposition 31:** The mapping

$$s: \quad R_W(\mathcal{D}; ms, mc) \quad \rightarrow \quad R_b(\text{supp } \mathcal{D}; ms, mc)$$
$$(A \Rightarrow B) \quad \mapsto \quad (\text{supp } A \Rightarrow \text{supp } B)$$

is surjective. $\forall (X \Rightarrow Y) \in R_b(\text{supp } \mathcal{D}; ms, mc)$, let

$$R_W(\mathcal{D}; ms, mc; X \Rightarrow Y)$$
$$\triangleq \{(A \Rightarrow B) \in R_W(\mathcal{D}; ms, mc) \mid s(A \Rightarrow B) = (X \Rightarrow Y)\},$$

then $\{R_W(\mathcal{D}; ms, mc; X \Rightarrow Y)\}_{(X \Rightarrow Y) \in R_b(\text{supp } \mathcal{D}; ms, mc)}$ is a partition of $R_W(\mathcal{D}; ms, mc)$.

- **Proof:** The conclusions are obvious from Proposition 28 and Proposition 29.

- **Proposition 32:** Let $(X \Rightarrow Y) \in R_b(\text{supp } \mathcal{D}; ms, mc)$, $A, B \in [0, +\infty)^I$ $\text{supp } A = X$, $\text{supp } B = Y$. Then $(A \Rightarrow B) \in R_W(\mathcal{D}; ms, mc; X \Rightarrow Y)$ if and only if $|t(A \Rightarrow B, \mathcal{D})| \geq (ms \times |T|) \vee (mc \times |t(X, \text{supp } \mathcal{D})|)$

- **Proof:** By Definition 12, we need only verify $\sup(A \Rightarrow B, \mathcal{D}) \geq ms$ and $\text{conf}(A \Rightarrow B, \mathcal{D}) \geq mc$.

$$\sup(A \Rightarrow B, \mathcal{D}) = \frac{|t(A \Rightarrow B, \mathcal{D})|}{|T|},$$

$$\text{conf}(A \Rightarrow B, \mathcal{D}) = \frac{|t(A \Rightarrow B, \mathcal{D})|}{|t(A, \mathcal{D})|}$$
$$= \frac{|t(A \Rightarrow B, \mathcal{D})|}{t(X, \text{supp } \mathcal{D})},$$

so

$$\sup(A \Rightarrow B, \mathcal{D}) \geq ms \Leftrightarrow |t(A \Rightarrow B, \mathcal{D})| \geq ms \times |T|,$$

$$\text{conf}(A \Rightarrow B, \mathcal{D}) \geq mc \Leftrightarrow |t(A \Rightarrow B, \mathcal{D})| \geq mc \times |t(X, \text{supp } \mathcal{D})|,$$

therefore
$(A \Rightarrow B) \in \mathrm{R}_{\mathrm{W}}(\mathcal{D}; ms, mc; X \Rightarrow Y)$ if and only if $|t(A \Rightarrow B, \mathcal{D})| \geq (ms \times |T|) \vee (mc \times |t(X, \operatorname{supp} \mathcal{D})|)$.

When we discuss WRRs, $\mathcal{D}$, *ms*, *mc* had all been determined, so $\mathrm{R}_{\mathrm{W}}(\mathcal{D}; ms, mc; X \Rightarrow Y)$ can be simply denoted as $\mathrm{R}_{\mathrm{W}}(X \Rightarrow Y)$ in the following.

Proposition 33 to Corollary 35 show a method by which a WRR can generate some other WRRs.

- **Proposition33:** Let $A, B \in [0, +\infty)^I \setminus \{\varnothing\}$, $A \cap B = \varnothing$, $\alpha \in (0, +\infty)$, then
  ○ **(1):** $t(\alpha A) = t(A)$;
  ○ **(2):** $t(\alpha A \Rightarrow \alpha B) = t(A \Rightarrow B)$;
  ○ **(3):** $\sup(\alpha A \Rightarrow \alpha B) = \sup(A \Rightarrow B)$
  ○ **(4):**
     $\operatorname{conf}(\alpha A \Rightarrow \alpha B) = \operatorname{conf}(A \Rightarrow B)$ if $t(A) \neq \varnothing$;
  ○ **(5):**
     $(A \Rightarrow B) \in \mathrm{R}_{\mathrm{W}}$
     $\Leftrightarrow (\alpha A \Rightarrow \alpha B) \in \mathrm{R}_{\mathrm{W}}$.
  ○ **Proof:** (1) and (2) can be proved from Definition 11, Definition 9, Definition 16 and Proposition 22. (3-5) is obvious.

For convenience, in the following, if we denote WRR $(A \Rightarrow B)$ in R_{W} as *r*, then the WRR $(\alpha A \Rightarrow \alpha B)$ in R_{W} as *αr*, and *αr* is called the scalar multiplication of *α* and *r*. Proposition 33 (5) show that *r* is a WRR if and only if its scalar multiplication *αr* is a WRR.

- **Proposition 34:** If $(A_1 \Rightarrow B_1) \in \mathrm{R}_{\mathrm{W}}$, $A_2, B_2 \in [0, +\infty)^I$, $A_2 \supseteq A_1$, $\varnothing \neq B_2 \subseteq B_1$, $\operatorname{supp} A_2 = \operatorname{supp} A_1$, then $(A_2 \Rightarrow B_2) \in \mathrm{R}_{\mathrm{W}}$.

  Proof:
  $t(A_2, \mathcal{D}) = t(\operatorname{supp} A_2, \operatorname{supp} \mathcal{D})$
  $= t(\operatorname{supp} A_1, \operatorname{supp} \mathcal{D}) =$
  $t(A_1, \mathcal{D}) \neq \varnothing$, so we need
  only prove

$t(A_2 \Rightarrow B_2, \mathcal{D}) \supseteq t(A_1 \Rightarrow B_1, \mathcal{D})$,

then we have $(A_2 \Rightarrow B_2) \in \mathrm{R}_{\mathrm{W}}$.

$\forall t \in t(A_1 \Rightarrow B_1, \mathcal{D})$, By Definition 9, $\operatorname{supp} A_1 \cup \operatorname{supp} B_1 \subseteq \operatorname{supp} D_t$ and $\forall i \in \operatorname{supp} A_1$, $\forall j \in \operatorname{supp} B_1$,

$$\frac{B_1(j)}{A_1(i)} \leq \frac{D_t(j)}{D_t(i)}.$$

To prove $t \in t(A_2 \Rightarrow B_2, \mathcal{D})$, we only need to prove $\operatorname{supp} A_2 \cup \operatorname{supp} B_2 \subseteq \operatorname{supp} D_t$ and $\forall i \in \operatorname{supp} A_2$, $\forall j \in \operatorname{supp} B_2$.

$$\frac{B_2(j)}{A_2(i)} \leq \frac{D_t(j)}{D_t(i)}.$$

By given information we have $\operatorname{supp} B_2 \subseteq \operatorname{supp} B_1$, so $\operatorname{supp} A_2 \cup \operatorname{supp} B_2 = \operatorname{supp} A_1 \cup \operatorname{supp} B_2 \subseteq \operatorname{supp} A_1 \cup \operatorname{supp} B_1 \subseteq \operatorname{supp} D_t$ Now that $A_2 \supseteq A_1$, $\operatorname{supp} A_2 \supseteq \operatorname{supp} A_1$, $B_2 \subseteq B_1$, therefore, $\forall i \in \operatorname{supp} A_2$, $\forall j \in \operatorname{supp} B_2$, $B_2(j) \leq B_1(j)$, $A_2(i) \geq A_1(i)$, hence

$$\frac{B_2(j)}{A_2(i)} \leq \frac{B_1(j)}{A_1(i)} \leq \frac{D_t(j)}{D_t(i)}.$$

- **Corollary 35:**
  Let $(A_1 \Rightarrow B_1) \in \mathrm{R}_{\mathrm{W}}(X \Rightarrow Y)$. If $A_2, B_2 \in [0, +\infty)^I$, $\operatorname{supp} A_2 = X$, $\operatorname{supp} B_2 = Y$, $A_2 \supseteq A_1$, $B_2 \subseteq B_1$, then $(A_2 \Rightarrow B_2) \in \mathrm{R}_W(X \Rightarrow Y)$.

Binary Relations between WRRs

By Proposition 31, in order to study the structure of R_{W}, we need only, for any $(X \Rightarrow Y) \in \mathrm{R}_{\mathrm{b}}$, study the structure of $\mathrm{R}_{\mathrm{W}}(X \Rightarrow Y)$. In the following, we propose three binary relations on $\mathrm{R}_{\mathrm{W}}(X \Rightarrow Y)$ and study two special subset of

$R_W(X \Rightarrow Y)$. Without special specification, X, Y satisfy $(X \Rightarrow Y) \in R_b$. By Definition 12, the WRR $(A \Rightarrow B)$ is actually an ordered pair $\langle A, B \rangle$ where A, B are nonnegative real-valued functions satisfying some properties. In this viewpoint, $R_W(X \Rightarrow Y)$ is a nonempty subset of

$$F(X \Rightarrow Y) \triangleq \{\langle A, B \rangle \mid A, B \in [0, +\infty)^I,$$
$$\operatorname{supp} A = X, \operatorname{supp} B = Y\}.$$

On $F(X \Rightarrow Y)$, we define partial order $\leq$:

$\langle A_2, B_2 \rangle \leq \langle A_1, B_1 \rangle$ if and only if

$A_2 \supseteq A_1$, $B_2 \subseteq B_1$,

then $F(X \Rightarrow Y)$ with $\leq$ forms a lattice, and

$$\langle A_1, B_1 \rangle \vee \langle A_2, B_2 \rangle = \langle A_1 \cap A_2, B_1 \cup B_2 \rangle,$$
$$\langle A_1, B_1 \rangle \wedge \langle A_2, B_2 \rangle = \langle A_1 \cup A_2, B_1 \cap B_2 \rangle.$$

By Corollary 35, $R_W(X \Rightarrow Y)$ is an ideal (Rosen, 2000) of lattice $F(X \Rightarrow Y)$. In the following, we take $\leq$ as the default partial order on $R_W(X \Rightarrow Y)$, i.e., for any $r_1 : (A_1 \Rightarrow B_1)$, $r_2 : (A_2 \Rightarrow B_2) \in R_W(X \Rightarrow Y)$,

$r_2 \leq r_1$ if and only if $A_2 \supseteq A_1$, $B_2 \subseteq B_1$.

We use $r_2 < r_1$ to express $r_2 \leq r_1$ but $r_2 \neq r_1$

- **Proposition 36:** Let $r_1, r_2 \in R_W(X \Rightarrow Y)$, $\alpha \in (0, +\infty)$, then
  ○ **(1):** $r_2 \leq r_1 \Leftrightarrow \alpha r_2 \leq \alpha r_1$;
  ○ **(2):** $r_2 < r_1 \Leftrightarrow \alpha r_2 < \alpha r_1$;
  ○ **(3):** $r_1 \leq \alpha r_1 \Leftrightarrow \alpha = 1$.
  ○ **Proof:** Only prove "$\Rightarrow$" in (3). Let $r_1 : (A_1 \Rightarrow B_1)$, then $\alpha r_1 : (\alpha A_1 \Rightarrow \alpha B_1)$. $r_1 \leq \alpha r_1$ means $A_1 \supseteq \alpha A_1$ and $B_1 \subseteq \alpha B_1$. $\forall i \in X$,

$A_1(i) > 0$ and $A_1(i) \geq \alpha A_1(i)$, so $\alpha \leq 1$. Similarly, $\alpha \geq 1$ can be obtained from $B_1 \subseteq \alpha B_1$.

- **Remark 37:** By Proposition 36(3), we know that αr_1 and r_1 are incomparable if $\alpha \neq 1$. For any positive real number α, inequalities $r_1 < \alpha r_1$ and $\alpha r_1 < r_1$ are impossible. For any positive real numbers β, α, inequality $\beta r_1 < \alpha r_1$ is impossible.

- **Definition 38:** Let $r_1 : (A_1 \Rightarrow B_1)$, $r_2 : (A_2 \Rightarrow B_2) \in R_W(X \Rightarrow Y)$. If there exists $\alpha \in (0, +\infty)$ such that $r_2 = \alpha r_1$, i.e., $A_2 = \alpha A_1$, $B_2 = \alpha B_1$, then r_1 and r_2 are called collinear, denoted by $r_2 \sim_d r_1$.

Obviously, the collinear relation $\sim_d$ is an equivalence relation. The equivalence class containing r is denoted by $[r]_{\sim_d}$ or simply $[r]$.

- **Definition 39:** Let $r_1 : (A_1 \Rightarrow B_1)$, $r_2 : (A_2 \Rightarrow B_2) \in R_W(X \Rightarrow Y)$. If there exists $\alpha \in (0, +\infty)$ such that $r_2 \leq \alpha r_1$, i.e., $A_2 \supseteq \alpha A_1$, $B_2 \subseteq \alpha B_1$, then we say r_1 can deduce r_2, denoted by $r_2 \lesssim_d r_1$.

Obviously, the deducible relation $\lesssim_d$ is reflexive and transitive, and is not antisymmetric (so $\lesssim_d$ is not a partial order). But we have the following result:

- **Proposition 40:** For any two WRRs $r_1, r_2 \in R_W(X \Rightarrow Y)$, r_1 and r_2 are collinear, if and only if r_1 and r_2 can deduce each other, i.e.,

$$r_2 \sim_d r_1 \Leftrightarrow r_2 \lesssim_d r_1 \text{ and } r_1 \lesssim_d r_2.$$

  ○ **Proof:** We only prove the sufficiency. If $r_2 \lesssim_d r_1$ and $r_1 \lesssim_d r_2$, then there exist $\alpha, \beta \in (0, +\infty)$ such that $r_2 \leq \alpha r_1$ and $r_1 \leq \beta r_2$. Therefore,

$r_2 \leq \alpha r_1 \leq (\alpha\beta)r_2$. By Proposition 36(3) we know $\alpha\beta = 1$, hence $r_2 \leq \alpha r_1 \leq (\alpha\beta)r_2 = r_2$, and so $r_2 = \alpha r_1$, i.e., r_1 and r_2 are collinear.

- **Lemma 41:** Let $r_1 : (A_1 \Rightarrow B_1)$, $r_2 : (A_2 \Rightarrow B_2) \in \mathrm{R_W}(X \Rightarrow Y)$, $\alpha \in (0, +\infty)$, then

$$A_2 \supseteq \alpha A_1 \Leftrightarrow \alpha \leq \mathrm{Inf}(A_2/A_1),$$
$$B_2 \subseteq \alpha B_1 \Leftrightarrow \mathrm{Sup}(B_2/B_1) \leq \alpha.$$

  - **Proof:** The conclusion is obvious from Proposition 19.

- **Proposition 42:** Let $r_1 : (A_1 \Rightarrow B_1)$, $r_2 : (A_2 \Rightarrow B_2) \in \mathrm{R_W}(X \Rightarrow Y)$, then the following conditions are equivalent:
  - **(1):** $r_2 \lesssim_d r_1$;
  - **(2):** $\mathrm{Sup}(B_2/B_1) \leq \mathrm{Inf}(A_2/A_1)$;
  - **(3):** $B_2 \subseteq \mathrm{Inf}(A_2/A_1)B_1$;
  - **(4):** $A_2 \supseteq \mathrm{Sup}(B_2/B_1)A_1$;
  - **(5):** There exists $r_3 \in \mathrm{R_W}(X \Rightarrow Y)$ such that $r_2 \leq r_3$ and $r_3 \sim_d r_1$;
  - **(6):** There exists $r_4 \in \mathrm{R_W}(X \Rightarrow Y)$ such that $r_2 \sim_d r_4$ and $r_4 \leq r_1$.
  - **Proof:** These conclusions are obvious from Lemma 41 and the definitions of $\lesssim_d$, $\sim_d$.

- **Corollary 43:** $\lesssim_d$ is the composition of $\leq$ and $\sim_d$, and the composition is commutative, i.e.,

$$\lesssim_d = \leq \circ \sim_d = \sim_d \circ \leq.$$

Between equivalence classes of collinear relation $\sim_d$, we can define a partial order $\leq_d$:

$$[r_2] \leq_d [r_1] \text{ if and only if } r_2 \lesssim_d r_1.$$

Obviously, $\leq_d$ is reflexive, antisymmetric, and transitive. We use $[r_2] <_d [r_1]$ to express that $[r_2] \leq_d [r_1]$ but $[r_2] \neq [r_1]$, i.e., r_1 can deduce r_2, but r_1 and r_2 is not collinear.

- **Proposition 44:** Let $r_1, r_2 \in \mathrm{R_W}(X \Rightarrow Y)$, then
  - **(1):** $[r_2] = [r_1] \Leftrightarrow$ there exists $\alpha \in (0, +\infty)$ such that $r_2 = \alpha r_1$;
  - **(2):** $[r_2] \leq_d [r_1] \Leftrightarrow$ there exists $\alpha \in (0, +\infty)$ such that $r_2 \leq \alpha r_1$;
  - **(3):** $[r_2] <_d [r_1] \Leftrightarrow$ there exists $\alpha \in (0, +\infty)$ such that $r_2 < \alpha r_1$.
  - **Proof:** We only prove (3). "$\Rightarrow$": By the definition of $<_d$, r_1 can deduce r_2, so there exists $\alpha \in (0, +\infty)$ such that $r_2 \leq \alpha r_1$. If $r_2 = \alpha r_1$ then r_1 and r_2 is collinear, this is a contradiction. Hence $r_2 < \alpha r_1$.

"Ü": If there exists $\alpha \in (0, +\infty)$ such that $r_2 < \alpha r_1$, then $r_2 \leq \alpha r_1$, i.e., r_1 can deduce r_2. If r_1 and r_2 is collinear, then there exists $\beta \in (0, +\infty)$ such that $r_2 = \beta r_1$, therefore $\beta r_1 < \alpha r_1$, which is impossible, so r_1 and r_2 is not collinear.

Basis Rules, Maximal Rules and Standard Rules

- **Definition 45:** Let E, M be nonempty subsets of $\mathrm{R_W}(X \Rightarrow Y)$, $E \subseteq M$. If for any $r_m \in M$, there exists $r_e \in E$ such that $r_m \leq_d r_e$, then we say E can deduce M. If E can deduce M, and for any two different rules in E one can not deduce another, then we say E is a basis of M. When E is a basis of M, the elements in E are called basis rules of M.

Obviously, if E is a basis of $R_W(X \Rightarrow Y)$, then any two different rules in E is not collinear. If we replace some rules in E with their collinear rules, then we can get a new basis of $R_W(X \Rightarrow Y)$. That is to say, If there exists a basis of $R_W(X \Rightarrow Y)$, then the basis of $R_W(X \Rightarrow Y)$ is not unique.

- **Definition 46:** Let $r_m \in R_W(X \Rightarrow Y)$ and r_m satisfies: $\forall r \in R_W(X \Rightarrow Y)$,

$$r_m \leq r \Rightarrow r_m = r$$

Then r_m is called maximal element of $R_W(X \Rightarrow Y)$. We use $M_W(X \Rightarrow Y)$ to denote the set of all maximal elements of $R_W(X \Rightarrow Y)$. Elements in $M_W(X \Rightarrow Y)$ are also called maximal rules.

- **Remark 47:** $R_W(X \Rightarrow Y)$ is an abbreviation of $R_W(\mathcal{D}; ms, mc; X \Rightarrow Y)$, so $M_W(X \Rightarrow Y)$ is also an abbreviation of $M_W(\mathcal{D}; ms, mc; X \Rightarrow Y)$.
- **Proposition 48:** If $r \in M_W(X \Rightarrow Y)$, then $\forall \alpha \in (0, +\infty)$, $\alpha r \in M_W(X \Rightarrow Y)$.
  - **Proof:** If $\alpha r \leq r_1 \in R_W(X \Rightarrow Y)$, then $r \leq \frac{1}{\alpha} r_1 \in R_W(X \Rightarrow Y)$. r is a maximal element of $R_W(X \Rightarrow Y)$, so $r = \frac{1}{\alpha} r_1$, therefore, $\alpha r = r_1$. This shows that αr is a maximal element of $R_W(X \Rightarrow Y)$.
- **Remark 49:** By Proposition 36(3), we know if $\alpha \neq 1$, then $\alpha r \neq r$. So, Proposition 48 show that $M_W(X \Rightarrow Y)$ is empty or infinite.
- **Remark 50:** By Proposition 48, in one same equivalence class, either the elements are all maximal elements or the elements are all not maximal elements. If

$r_m \in M_W(X \Rightarrow Y)$ then
$\{r \in M_W(X \Rightarrow Y) \mid r \sim_d r_m\}$
$= \{r \in R_W(X \Rightarrow Y) \mid r \sim_d r_m\}$, i.e., the equivalence class of $M_W(X \Rightarrow Y)$ equals equivalence class of $R_W(X \Rightarrow Y)$.

- **Proposition 51:** Let $r_1, r_2 \in R_W(X \Rightarrow Y)$. If r_1 can deduce r_2, but r_1 and r_2 is not collinear, then $r_2 \notin M_W(X \Rightarrow Y)$.
  - **Proof:** This is a Corollary of Proposition 44.
- **Proposition 52:** The set of maximal elements of $\{[r] \mid r \in R_W(X \Rightarrow Y)\}$ (the set of equivalence classes of $R_W(X \Rightarrow Y)$ with regard to $\sim_d$) with regard to $\leq_d$ is just the set of equivalence classes of $M_W(X \Rightarrow Y)$ with regard to $\sim_d$.
  - **Proof:** Let $[r]$ be a maximal element of $\{[r] \mid r \in R_W(X \Rightarrow Y)\}$ with regard to $\leq_d$. We will prove $[r]$ is an equivalence classes of $M_W(X \Rightarrow Y)$ with regard to $\sim_d$. Firstly, we prove $r \in M_W(X \Rightarrow Y)$. Suppose $r_1 \in R_W(X \Rightarrow Y)$ such that $r \leq r_1$, we will prove that $r = r_1$. On the contrary, if $r < r_1$, then by Proposition 44(3), we have $[r] <_d [r_1]$, which is contradictory to that $[r]$ is a maximal element of $\{[r] \mid r \in R_W(X \Rightarrow Y)\}$ with regard to $\leq_d$. So $r \in M_W(X \Rightarrow Y)$. By Remark 50, $[r]$ is the equivalence class of $M_W(X \Rightarrow Y)$ with regard to $\sim_d$ containing r.

On the other hand, let $[r_2]$ be an equivalence class of $M_W(X \Rightarrow Y)$ with regard to $\sim_d$. By Remark 50, $[r_2]$ is an equivalence class of $R_W(X \Rightarrow Y)$ with regard to $\sim_d$. If $[r_2]$ is not a maximal element of $\{[r] \mid r \in R_W(X \Rightarrow Y)\}$ with regard to $\leq_d$, then by Proposition 44(3) we knowthereexists $r_1 \in R_W(X \Rightarrow Y), \alpha \in (0, +\infty)$ such that $r_2 < \alpha r_1$, which is contradictory to $r_2 \in M_W(X \Rightarrow Y)$. Therefore, $[r_2]$ is a maximal element of $\{[r] \mid r \in R_W(X \Rightarrow Y)\}$ with regard to $\leq_d$.

- **Corollary 53:** Let $[r_1]$, $[r_2]$ be two different equivalence classes of $M_W(X \Rightarrow Y)$ with regard to $\sim_d$, $r_3 \in [r_1]$, $r_4 \in [r_2]$, then one of r_3, r_4 can not deduce another.
  - **Proof:** By Proposition 52, $[r_1]$, $[r_2]$ are two maximal elements of $\{[r] \mid r \in R_W(X \Rightarrow Y)\}$ with regard to $\leq_d$. If r_3 can deduce r_4, i.e., $r_4 \leq_d r_3$, then $[r_2] = [r_4] \leq_d [r_3] = [r_1]$, which contradicts to $[r_2]$ is maximal. So r_3 can not deduce r_4. Similarly, r_4 can not deduce r_3.

In the following, we discuss the relationship between $M_W(X \Rightarrow Y)$ and basis of $R_W(X \Rightarrow Y)$

- **Proposition 54:** Let E be a basis of $R_W(X \Rightarrow Y)$, then $E \subseteq M_W(X \Rightarrow Y)$.
  - **Proof:** For any $r_e \in E$, we prove r_e is a maximal element of $R_W(X \Rightarrow Y)$. If $r_e \leq r \in R_W(X \Rightarrow Y)$, we need only prove $r_e = r$. Since E can deduce $R_W(X \Rightarrow Y)$, there exist $r_2 \in E$, $\alpha \in (0, +\infty)$ such that $r \leq \alpha r_2$. Therefore $r_e \leq r \leq \alpha r_2$, this shows that r_2 can deduce r_e. Because one of different elements in E can not deduce another, we have $r_e = r_2$, $\alpha = 1$, hence $r_e \leq r \leq \alpha r_2 = r_e$, so $r_e = r$.

Proposition 54 shows that only maximal rules can be basis rules.

- **Corollary 55:** If there exists basis of $R_W(X \Rightarrow Y)$, then $M_W(X \Rightarrow Y)$ is non-empty and can deduce $R_W(X \Rightarrow Y)$.

- **Proposition 56:** If there exists basis of $R_W(X \Rightarrow Y)$, then the set E is a basis of $R_W(X \Rightarrow Y)$ if and only if E consists of the following rules obtained by selecting just one rule in every equivalence class of $M_W(X \Rightarrow Y)$ with regard to $\sim_d$.
  - **Proof:** (sufficiency): An equivalence class can be deduced by any element in it, so E can deduce $M_W(X \Rightarrow Y)$. By Corollary 55, $M_W(X \Rightarrow Y)$ can deduce $R_W(X \Rightarrow Y)$, therefore, E can deduce $R_W(X \Rightarrow Y)$. By Corollary 53, E is a basis.
  - **(necessity):** Let E be a basis of $R_W(X \Rightarrow Y)$. By Proposition 54, any element r in E is an element of $M_W(X \Rightarrow Y)$. So by the definition of basis, we obtain obviously that different elements of E belongs to different equivalence class of $M_W(X \Rightarrow Y)$ with regard to $\sim_d$. In the following, we need only prove that there must be an element belonging to E in every equivalence class of $M_W(X \Rightarrow Y)$ with regard to $\sim_d$. On the contrary, there must exist an equivalence class $[r_2]$ such that $[r_2] \cap E = \varnothing$. Suppose r_2 can be deduced by r_1 in E. If r_1 and r_2 are collinear, then $[r_1] = [r_2]$ which contradicts to $[r_2] \cap E = \varnothing$. Therefore, r_1 and r_2 are not collinear, by Proposition 51, $r_2 \notin M_W(X \Rightarrow Y)$ which is a contradiction.

By Proposition, if E is a basis of $R_W(X \Rightarrow Y)$ then when every rule in E deduces its equivalence class, the set E deduces $M_W(X \Rightarrow Y)$.

- **Definition 57:**
  L e t $r : (A \Rightarrow B) \in R_W(X \Rightarrow Y)$, $\alpha \in (0, +\infty)$. $X = \{x_1, x_2 \cdots, x_p\}$ and the order of elements is determined. If $A(x_1) = \alpha$, then r is called an α-rule. If all rules in basis E of $R_W(X \Rightarrow Y)$ are α-rules, then E is called an α-basis of $R_W(X \Rightarrow Y)$. A 1-rule is called a standard rule. A 1-basis is called a standard basis.

Obviously, r is a standard rule if and only if αr is an α-rule. If there exists a basis of $R_W(X \Rightarrow Y)$, then for any $\alpha \in (0, +\infty)$, in every equivalence class of $M_W(X \Rightarrow Y)$ with regard to $\sim_d$ there exists one and only one α-rule which is called α-maximal rule. Especially, in every equivalence class of $M_W(X \Rightarrow Y)$ with regard to $\sim_d$ there exists one and only one 1-rule which is called standard maximal rule. By Proposition 56, we have the following proposition:

- **Proposition 58:** If there exists a basis of $R_W(X \Rightarrow Y)$, then $\forall \alpha \in (0, +\infty)$, there exists unique α-basis of $R_W(X \Rightarrow Y)$, which consists of all α-maximal rules. Especially, there exists unique standard basis which consists of all standard maximal rules.

In the subsection "Mining standard basis", we prove that when X has only one element, there exists standard basis of $R_W(X \Rightarrow Y)$ and propose an algorithm for miming standard basis.

MINING WRR

By Proposition 31, for given $\mathcal{D}$, *ms*, and *mc*, in order to find set R_W of all WRRs, we only need to find every subset $R_W(X \Rightarrow Y)$ supported by $BAR(X \Rightarrow Y)$ in R_b. We can take advantage of the current Boolean association rule mining algorithms to find R_b, and so in the following, we

need only to solve the following problem: for a given $BAR(X \Rightarrow Y)$, how to find the set $R_W(X \Rightarrow Y)$.

In this section, we suppose $(X \Rightarrow Y) \in R_b(\operatorname{supp}\mathcal{D}; ms, mc)$, and $X = \{x_1, x_2 \cdots, x_p\}$, $Y = \{y_1, y_2 \cdots, y_p\}$. In the subsection "Mining quasi-maximal WRR", we define an important subset $Q_W(X \Rightarrow Y)$ of $R_W(X \Rightarrow Y)$, and propose an algorithm for finding $Q_W(X \Rightarrow Y)$. In the subsection "Mining standard basis", we propose an algorithm for finding standard basis of $R_W(X \Rightarrow Y)$ when X has only one element.

Preliminaries

- **Definition 59:** (Rosen, 2000; Habib & Nourine, 1997; Pitteloud, 2002; Bezrukov & Leck, 2005) Let P be a poset, and I be a subset of P. If every element x in I such that

$$"y \leq x \Rightarrow y \in I", \forall y \in P,$$

then I is called an ideal of P.

- **Remark 60:** The concept ideal is also called downset (Bezrukov & Leck, 2005; Loof et al., 2007), lower set (Gierz et al., 1980), lower segment (Burris & Sankappanavar, 1981).

By the Definition 59, an ideal is equivalent to an ideal property that if one element has the property then all the elements which are less than or equal to the element also have the property. We do not distinguish the two names in this paper, i.e., we say *I* is an ideal of *P*, and also sometimes say *I* is an ideal property on *P*. We say *x* in *I*, and also say *x* has ideal property *I*.

- **Definition 61:** (Stanat & McAllister, 1977) Let B be a subset of a poset P. $b \in B$, If there is no element c in B such that $b < c$, then b is called a maximal element of B. We use M(B) to denote the set of all maximal elements of B.

- **Definition 62:** (Rosen, 2000) The Cartesian product $P_1 \times P_2 \times \cdots \times P_m$ of posets $P_1, P_2, \cdots, P_m$ is a poset with the partial order $\leq$ defined as:

$\langle x_1, x_2, \cdots, x_m \rangle \leq \langle y_1, y_2, \cdots, y_m \rangle$ if $x_i \leq y_i$ for any $i = 1, 2, \cdots, m$.

The Cartesian product of chains is called chain-product.

The following paragraphes from Definition 63 to Algorithm 1 can be found completely in Jiang (2005).

- **Definition 63:** Let V be the chain-product of chains $C_1, C_2, \cdots, C_m$. $C_i = \{ v_{i0}, v_{i1}, \cdots, v_{in_i} \}$, $v_{i0} \prec v_{i1} \prec \cdots \prec v_{in_i}$, $i = 1, 2, \cdots, m$. For any element $\langle v_{1s_1}, v_{2s_2}, \cdots, v_{ms_m} \rangle$ of V, the m-dimensional vector $\langle s_1, s_2, \cdots, s_m \rangle$ is called the position of $\langle v_{1s_1}, v_{2s_2}, \cdots, v_{ms_m} \rangle$. And $\langle v_{1s_1}, v_{2s_2}, \cdots, v_{ms_m} \rangle$ is called the value at position $\langle s_1, s_2, \cdots, s_m \rangle$ The position of v, an element of V, is denoted by pos(v). The value at position p is denoted by value(p). For any element v of V, it is obvious that $v = value(pos(v))$. If for any $i = 1, 2, \cdots, m$, finite chain $C_i = \{ 0, 1, \cdots, n_i \}$, then the chain-product $C_1 \times C_2 \times \cdots \times C_m$ is called position lattice, denoted by $\mathrm{P}(n_1, n_2, \cdots, n_m)$.

Obviously, the mapping

$$pos: \quad V \quad \rightarrow \quad \mathrm{P}(n_1, n_2, \cdots, n_m)$$
$$v \quad \mapsto \quad pos(v)$$

and the mapping

$$value: \quad \mathrm{P}(n_1, n_2, \cdots, n_m) \quad \rightarrow \quad V$$
$$p \quad \mapsto \quad value(p)$$

are reciprocal lattice isomorphisms. $\mathrm{P}(n_1, n_2, \cdots, n_m)$ is called position lattice of V, denoted by *pos*(V). By the isomorphism *pos*, the discussion about V can be translated into the discussion about its position lattice *pos*(V), and the operations on v, the element of V, can be translated into the operations on their position *pos*(v).

- **Definition 64:**
  Let $p(c_1, c_2, \cdots, c_m) \in \mathrm{P}(n_1, n_2, \cdots, n_m)$, $1 \leq d \leq m - 1$, then $h = (c_1, c_2, \cdots, c_d)$ is called d-prefix of p. 0-prefix of p defined as the empty vector $\langle \rangle$. The d-prefix of p is denoted by $\mathrm{pref}(p, d)$ for any $0 \leq d \leq m - 1$ We use H to express the set of all prefixes of all vectors belonging to $\mathrm{P}(n_1, n_2, \cdots, n_m)$ i.e.,

$$H \triangleq \{ h \mid h = \langle \rangle \, or \, \exists d \in$$
$$\{ 1, 2, \cdots, m - 1 \} \, such \, that$$
$$h \in \mathrm{P}(n_1, n_2, \cdots, n_d) \}.$$

Obviously, $H = \{ \langle \rangle \} \cup (\bigcup_{d=1}^{m-1} \mathrm{P}(n_1, n_2, \cdots, n_d))$.

If we imagine a *m*-dimensional vector p as a string which length is m, then the d-prefix of p is just the prefix of string p. Like the concatenation of two strings, we can concatenate two vectors and form a new vector.

- **Definition 65:** Let $h_1 = (a_1, a_2, \cdots, a_s)$, $h_2 = (b_1, b_2, \cdots, b_t)$, then the vector $\langle h_1, h_2 \rangle$ $\triangleq \langle a_1, a_2, \cdots, a_s, b_1, b_2, \cdots, b_t \rangle$ is called the concatenation of vector h_1 with vector h_2.

Obviously, $d(\langle h_1, h_2 \rangle) = d(h_1) + d(h_2)$, where $d(h)$ expresses the dimension of vector h which may be empty vector. Let the dimension of empty vector $\langle\rangle$ be zero, i.e., $d(\langle\rangle) = 0$.

- **Definition 66:** Suppose X is a subset of $P(n_1, n_2, \cdots, n_m)$, $h \in H$. $E(h, X)$, called h-section of X, denotes the set of all vectors in X, whose d(h)-prefixe are equal to h, i.e.,

$$E(h, X) \triangleq \{x \in X \mid \text{pref}(x, d(h)) = h\}.$$

- **Lemma 67:** Let I be an ideal property on chain-product $C_1 \times C_2 \times \cdots \times C_m$, then $M(I) = value(M(pos(I)))$.

Algorithm 1: Boundary, finding all the maximal elements of an ideal of a Cartesian product of finite chains.

- **Input:** finite chain C_i, $i = 1, 2, \cdots, m$ and an ideal property I on chain-product $V(\triangleq C_1 \times C_2 \times \cdots \times C_m)$
- **Output:** M, the set of all maximal elements of I.
- **Method:**
  - **(1):** $posM := \varnothing$; // posM saves the maximal elements of $pos(I)$
  - **(2):** if $value(\langle 0, 0, \cdots, 0\rangle) \in I$ then
  - **(3):** $get \max(\langle\rangle)$;
  - **(4):** return value(posM);
- **procedure:** getmax(h)
- **parameter:** h. $h \in H$, d(h)-prefix of the position of a value in V, and h-section of $pos(I)$ is nonempty.
- **function:** to obtain all elements in h-section of $M(pos(I))$, and join them into posM.
  - **(1):** $G :=$ the set of all elements, in posM, whose d(h)-prefix are greater than h;
  - **(2):** if $G \neq \varnothing$ then
  - **(3):** $g :=$ the maximum of all (d(h)+1)-th components of vectors in G
  - **(4):** else $g := 0$;
  - **(5):** $t := g + 1$;
  - **(6):** while $t \leq n_{d(h)+1}$ and $value(\langle h, \langle t, 0, \cdots, 0\rangle\rangle) \in I$ do
  - **(7):** $t := t + 1$;
  - **(8):** $e := t - 1$;
  - **(9):** if $d(h) < m - 1$ then
  - **(10):** for $x = e$ downto 0
  - **(11):** getmax($\langle h, \langle x\rangle\rangle$)
  - **(12):** else if $e > g$ or $G = \varnothing$ then
  - **(13):** $posM := posM \cup \{\langle h, \langle e\rangle\rangle\}$;

Mining Quasi-Maximal WRR

A WRR$(A \Rightarrow B)$ in $R_W(X \Rightarrow Y)$ can be expressed uniquely as a $(p + q)-$ dimensional vector of positive real numbers $\langle A(x_1), \cdots, A(x_p), B(y_1), \cdots, B(y_q)\rangle$, in which the former p components generate the antecedent $A : A(x_1)/x_1 + \cdots + A(x_p)/x_p$ the latter q components generate the consequent $B : B(y_1)/y_1 + \cdots + B(y_q)/y_q$. We call $\langle A(x_1), \cdots, A(x_p), B(y_1), \cdots, B(y_q)\rangle$ generate a WRR supported by $(X \Rightarrow Y)$, simply "generate a WRR".

$\forall i \in \{1, \cdots, p\}$, finite chain C_{x_i} is defined as:

$$C_{x_i} = \{D_t(x_i) \mid t \in t(X \cup Y, \text{supp } \mathcal{D})\},$$

in which the partial order is $\geq$, the usual greater than or equal to relation between real numbers. $\forall j \in \{1, \cdots, q\}$, finite chain C_{y_j} is defined as:

$$C_{y_j} = \{D_t(y_i) \mid t \in t(X \cup Y, \text{supp } \mathcal{D})\},$$

in which the partial order is $\leq$, the usual less than or equal to relation between real numbers. That is to say, the finite chain determined by an item in X consists of the different values in rows of transactions in $t(X \cup Y, \mathrm{supp}\,\mathcal{D})$ and sorts its elements in descending order, and the finite chain determined by an item in Y sorts on the contrary. We use $\mathrm{V}(X \Rightarrow Y)$ to denote the chain-product $C_{x_1} \times \cdots \times C_{x_p} \times C_{y_1} \times \cdots \times C_{y_q}$, determined completely by PQTD $\mathcal{D}$ and $\mathrm{BAR}(X \Rightarrow Y)$.

Every element in $\mathrm{V}(X \Rightarrow Y)$ is a $(p+q)-$ dimensional vector of positive real numbers, but which elements can generate a WRR supported by $(X \Rightarrow Y)$?

We consider a property S: v can generate a WRR supported by $(X \Rightarrow Y)$, v is an element in $\mathrm{V}(X \Rightarrow Y)$. By Corollary 35, if $\langle A(x_1), \cdots, A(x_p), B(y_1), \cdots, B(y_q) \rangle$ can generate a WRR supported by $(X \Rightarrow Y)$ and $A_1(x_1) \geq A(x_1), \cdots, A_1(x_p) \geq A(x_p)$, $B_1(y_1) \leq B(y_1), \cdots, B_1(y_q) \leq B(y_q)$ then $\langle A_1(x_1), \cdots, A_1(x_p), B_1(y_1), \cdots, B_1(y_q) \rangle$ can also generate a WRR supported by $(X \Rightarrow Y)$. This shows that S is an ideal property on $\mathrm{V}(X \Rightarrow Y)$. By Algorithm 1 Boundary, we can obtain $M(S)$, the set of all maximal elements of S. For any v in $M(S)$, v can generate a WRR supported by $(X \Rightarrow Y)$, the WRR is called quasi-maximal. The set of all quasi-maximal WRRs supported by $(X \Rightarrow Y)$ is denoted by $\mathrm{Q}_\mathrm{W}(X \Rightarrow Y)$, which is a subset of $\mathrm{R}_\mathrm{W}(X \Rightarrow Y)$ and determined completely by PQTD $\mathcal{D}$ and $\mathrm{BAR}(X \Rightarrow Y)$. Of course, $\mathrm{R}_\mathrm{W}(X \Rightarrow Y)$ is an short form of $\mathrm{R}_\mathrm{W}(\mathcal{D}; ms, mc; X \Rightarrow Y)$, and $\mathrm{Q}_\mathrm{W}(X \Rightarrow Y)$ is an short form of $\mathrm{Q}_\mathrm{W}(\mathcal{D}; ms, mc; X \Rightarrow Y)$. Without special specification, the notations $\mathrm{V}(X \Rightarrow Y)$, S and $\mathrm{Q}_\mathrm{W}(X \Rightarrow Y)$ in this section have the above meaning.

The above idea for finding $\mathrm{Q}_\mathrm{W}(X \Rightarrow Y)$ can be summarized as following algorithm:

Algorithm 2: Finding all quasi-maximal WRRs supported by $(X \Rightarrow Y)$

- **Input:** PQAR $\mathcal{D}$, minimum support threshold ms, minimum confidence thresh-

old mc, and $\mathrm{BAR}(X \Rightarrow Y)$, $X = \{x_1, x_2, \cdots, x_p\}$, $Y = \{y_1, y_2, \cdots, y_q\}$.

- **Output:** $\mathrm{Q}_\mathrm{W}(X \Rightarrow Y)$, the set of all quasi-maximal WRRs supported by $(X \Rightarrow Y)$.

- **Method:**
  - **(1):** Calculating finite chains $C_{x_1}, \cdots, C_{x_p}, C_{y_1}, \cdots, C_{y_q}$;
  - **(2):** By Algorithm 1, to find $M(S)$, the set of all maximal elements of ideal property S on $C_{x_1} \times \cdots \times C_{x_p} \times C_{y_1} \times \cdots \times C_{y_q}$, where S is "v can generate a WRR supported by $(X \Rightarrow Y)$";
  - **(3):** Generating $\mathrm{Q}_\mathrm{W}(X \Rightarrow Y)$ from M (S).

- **Example 68:** Consider the PQTD $\mathcal{D}$ in Table 1. Let ms=0.5, mc=0.75, $X = \{i_1\}$, $Y = \{i_4\}$, then $(X \Rightarrow Y)$ is a BAR. In Algorithm 2, $C_{i_1} = \{2, 1\}$, $C_{i_4} = \{2, 5\}$; $M(S) = \{\langle 1, 2 \rangle\}$, Therefore, $\mathrm{Q}_\mathrm{W}(X \Rightarrow Y) = \{1/i_1 \Rightarrow 2/i_4\}$.

In Algorithm 2, the time-consuming operation is to judge whether the test point $v \triangleq \langle A(x_1), \cdots, A(x_p), B(y_1), \cdots, B(y_q) \rangle$ in $C_{x_1} \times \cdots \times C_{x_p} \times C_{y_1} \times \cdots \times C_{y_q}$ has ideal property S, i.e., to judge $A \Rightarrow B \in \mathrm{R}_\mathrm{W}(X \Rightarrow Y)$. By Proposition 32, we need only verify

$$|t(A \Rightarrow B, \mathcal{D})| \geq (ms \times |T|) \vee (mc \times |t(X, \mathrm{supp}\,\mathcal{D})|).$$

We can use Definition 9 to calculate the number $|t(A \Rightarrow B, \mathcal{D})|$.

Algorithm 3: A matrix algorithm to judge $A \Rightarrow B \in \mathrm{R}_\mathrm{W}(X \Rightarrow Y)$

- **Input:** PQTD $\mathcal{D}$, minimum support threshold ms, minimum confidence threshold mc, BAR $(X \Rightarrow Y)$, $X = \{x_1, x_2, \cdots, x_p\}$, $Y = \{y_1, y_2, \cdots, y_q\}$,

$\langle A(x_1), \cdots, A(x_p), B(y_1), \cdots, \qquad B(y_q) \rangle$
$\in \mathrm{V}(X \Rightarrow Y)$.

- **Function:**
  Judging $A \Rightarrow B \in \mathrm{R}_W(X \Rightarrow Y)$.

- **Method:**
  - **(1):** $|T| :=$ the number of transactions in $\mathcal{D}$
  - **(2):** Scan all the transactions t of $\mathcal{D}$, if there exists element x_i of X such that $D_t(x_i) = 0$, then delete transaction t. $|t(X, \mathrm{supp}\,\mathcal{D})| :=$ the number of left transactions;
  - **(3):** Scan all the transactions t, if there exists element y_j of Y such that $D_t(y_j) = 0$, then delete transaction t (the left transactions are all the transactions in $t(X \cup Y, \mathrm{supp}\,\mathcal{D})$);
  - **(4):** For any transaction t, calculate the matrix $M(D_t(Y)/D_t(X))$:

$$
\begin{pmatrix}
D_t(y_1)/D_t(x_1) & D_t(y_2)/D_t(x_1) & \cdots & D_t(y_q)/D_t(x_1) \\
D_t(y_1)/D_t(x_2) & D_t(y_2)/D_t(x_2) & \cdots & D_t(y_q)/D_t(x_2) \\
\vdots & \vdots & \ddots & \vdots \\
D_t(y_1)/D_t(x_p) & D_t(y_2)/D_t(x_p) & \cdots & D_t(y_q)/D_t(x_p)
\end{pmatrix};
$$

  - **(5):** Calculate matrix $M(B(Y)/A(X))$:

$$
\begin{pmatrix}
B(y_1)/A(x_1) & B(y_2)/A(x_1) & \cdots & B(y_q)/A(x_1) \\
B(y_1)/A(x_2) & B(y_2)/A(x_2) & \cdots & B(y_q)/A(x_2) \\
\vdots & \vdots & \ddots & \vdots \\
B(y_1)/A(x_p) & B(y_2)/A(x_p) & \cdots & B(y_q)/A(x_p)
\end{pmatrix};
$$

  - **(6):** $|t(A \Rightarrow B, \mathcal{D})| := 0$;
  - **(7):** Scan all the transactions t, if the values in matrix $M(D_t(Y)/D_t(X))$ $-M(B(Y)/A(X))$ are all positive, then add 1 to $|t(A \Rightarrow B, \mathcal{D})|$;
  - **(8):** If

$|t(A \Rightarrow B, \mathcal{D})|$
$\geq (ms \times |T|) \vee (mc \times |$
$t(X, \mathrm{supp}\,\mathcal{D})|)$, then
$(A \Rightarrow B) \in \mathrm{R}_W(X \Rightarrow Y)$, else
$(A \Rightarrow B) \notin \mathrm{R}_W(X \Rightarrow Y)$.

The steps (4), (5), (7) can obtain $t(A \Rightarrow B, \mathcal{D})$, because there is the following proposition.

- **Proposition 69:** Under the input conditions of Algorithm 3, $t \in t(A \Rightarrow B, \mathcal{D})$ if and only if $t \in t(X \cup Y, \mathrm{supp}\,\mathcal{D})$ and the values in matrix $M(D_t(Y)/D_t(X))$ $-M(B(Y)/A(X))$ are all positive (now we call the matrix is positive).
  - **Proof:** It is trivial.
- **Remark 70:**
  - **(1):** The steps (1)-(4) in Algorithm 3 are not related to the test point $\langle A(x_1), \cdots, A(x_p), B(y_1), \cdots, B(y_q) \rangle$, therefor can be implemented before the step (2) in Algorithm 2.
  - **(2):** The right hand of inequality $|t(A \Rightarrow B, \mathcal{D})|$ $\geq (ms \times |T|) \vee (mc \times |$ $t(X, \mathrm{supp}\,\mathcal{D})|)$ in step(8) is not related to the test point $\langle A(x_1), \cdots, A(x_p), B(y_1), \cdots, B(y_q) \rangle$, therefore the calculation of its value can be implemented before the step (2) in Algorithm 2.
  - **(3):** By Proposition 29, the maximum element of $\mathrm{V}(X \Rightarrow Y)$ has ideal property S, so the judgment in step (2) of Algorithm 1 can be omitted.

Combining the Algorithms 2 and 3, we can get the complete algorithm to find the set of all quasi-maximal WRRs supported by $(X \Rightarrow Y)$.

Algorithm 4: Finding the set of all quasi-maximal WRRs supported by $(X \Rightarrow Y)$.

- **Input:** PQTD $\mathcal{D}$, minimum support threshold ms, minimum confidence threshold mc, $\text{BAR}(X \Rightarrow Y)$, $X = \{x_1, x_2, \cdots, x_p\}$, $Y = \{y_1, y_2, \cdots, y_q\}$.
- **Output:** $Q_W(X \Rightarrow Y)$, the set of all quasi-maximal WRRs supported by $(X \Rightarrow Y)$
- **Method:**
  - **(1):** $|T| :=$ the number of transactions in $\mathcal{D}$;
  - **(2):** Scan all the transactions t of $\mathcal{D}$, if there exists element x_i of X such that $D_t(x_i) = 0$, then delete transaction t. $|t(X, \text{supp}\,\mathcal{D})| :=$ the number of left transactions;
  - **(3):** $\text{SupCountsLowerBound} := (ms \times |T|) \vee (mc \times |t(X, \text{supp}\,\mathcal{D})|)$;
  - **(4):** Scan all the transactions t, if there exists element y_j of Y such that $D_t(y_j) = 0$, then delete transaction t (the left transactions are all the transactions in $t(X \cup Y, \text{supp}\,\mathcal{D})$);
  - **(5):** For any $x_i \in X(i = 1, 2, \cdots p)$, sort the set $C_{x_i} := \{D_t(x_i) \mid t \in t(X \cup Y, \text{supp}\,\mathcal{D})\}$ as $\{a_0^{(i)}, a_1^{(i)}, \cdots, a_{n_i}^{(i)}\}$, where $a_0^{(i)} > a_1^{(i)} > \cdots > a_{n_i}^{(i)}$ $i = 1, 2, \cdots, p$;
  - **(6):** For any $y_j \in Y(j = 1, 2, \cdots q)$, sort the set $C_{y_j} := \{D_t(y_i) \mid t \in t(X \cup Y, \text{supp}\,\mathcal{D})\}$ as $\{b_0^{(j)}, b_1^{(j)}, \cdots, b_{n_{p+j}}^{(j)}\}$, where $b_0^{(j)} < b_1^{(j)} < \cdots < b_{n_{p+j}}^{(j)}$, $j = 1, 2, \cdots q$ $m := p+q$.
  - **(7):** For any transaction t, calculate the matrix $M(D_t(Y)/D_t(X))$:

$$\begin{pmatrix} D_t(y_1)/D_t(x_1) & D_t(y_2)/D_t(x_1) & \cdots & D_t(y_q)/D_t(x_1) \\ D_t(y_1)/D_t(x_2) & D_t(y_2)/D_t(x_2) & \cdots & D_t(y_q)/D_t(x_2) \\ \vdots & \vdots & \ddots & \vdots \\ D_t(y_1)/D_t(x_p) & D_t(y_2)/D_t(x_p) & \cdots & D_t(y_q)/D_t(x_p) \end{pmatrix};$$

  - **(8):** $\geq SupCountsLowerBound$
  - **(9):** $\text{getmax}(\langle\rangle)$;
  - **(10):** Generating $Q_W(X \Rightarrow Y)$ from value(posM).
- **procedure:** getmax(h)
- **parameter:** *h*. $h \in H$, d(h)-prefix of the position of a value in $V(X \Rightarrow Y)$, and h-section of pos(S) is nonempty.
- **function:** to obtain all elements in h-section of M(*pos(S)*), and join them into *posM*.
  - **(1):** $G :=$ the set of all elements, in posM, whose d(h)-*prefix are greater than h,*
  - **(2):** if $G \neq \varnothing$ then
  - **(3):** $g :=$ the maximum of all (d(h)+1)-*th* components of vectors in G
  - **(4):** else $g := 0$;
  - **(5):** $t := g + 1$;
  - **(6):** while $t \leq n_{d(h)+1}$ and IsWRRPos $(\langle h, \langle t, 0, \cdots, 0\rangle\rangle)$ do
  - **(7):** $t := t + 1$;
  - **(8):** $e := t - 1$;
  - **(9):** if $d(h) < m - 1$ then
  - **(10):** for $x = e$ downto 0
  - **(11):** $\text{getmax}(\langle h, \langle x\rangle\rangle)$
  - **(12):** else if $e > g$ or $G = \varnothing$ then
  - **(13):** $posM := posM \cup \{\langle h, \langle e\rangle\rangle\}$;
- **procedure:** IsWRRPos(w)
- **parameter:** *w*, an element in position lattice $pos(V(X \Rightarrow Y))$, a $(p+q)$-dimensional vector of natural numbers.
- **function:** to judge whether the $(p+q)$-dimensional vector *value(w)* in $V(X \Rightarrow Y)$ can generate a WRR supported by $(X \Rightarrow Y)$.

(1): Define two nonnegative real-valued functions *A*, *B* on *I*. $A(x_i) := a_{w(i)}^{(i)}$ for any $i = 1, 2, \cdots p$; $B(y_j) := b_{w(p+j)}^{(j)}$ for any $j = 1, 2, \cdots q$; The values of A, B on other items are 0;

(2): Calculate matrix $M(B(Y)/A(X))$:

$$\begin{pmatrix} B(y_1)/A(x_1) & B(y_2)/A(x_1) & \cdots & B(y_q)/A(x_1) \\ B(y_1)/A(x_2) & B(y_2)/A(x_2) & \cdots & B(y_q)/A(x_2) \\ \vdots & \vdots & \ddots & \vdots \\ B(y_1)/A(x_p) & B(y_2)/A(x_p) & \cdots & B(y_q)/A(x_p) \end{pmatrix};$$

(3): $| t(A \Rightarrow B, \mathcal{D}) | := 0$;

(4): Scan all the transactions *t, if* $M(D_t(Y)/D_t(X))$ - $M(B(Y)/A(X))$ is positive, then add 1 to $| t(A \Rightarrow B, \mathcal{D}) |$;

(5): if $| t(A \Rightarrow B, \mathcal{D}) | \geq SupCountsLowerBound$ then

(6): return TRUE

(7): else return FALSE

• **Remark 71:** Whether $(X \Rightarrow Y) \in R_b$ or not is only related to the columns corresponding to items in $X \cup Y$. By Definition 12 and Proposition 20(3), we also know that, $(A \Rightarrow B) \in R_w$ or not is only related to the columns corresponding to items in

supp $A \cup$ supp B. According to definition of $Q_W(X \Rightarrow Y)$, it is only related to the columns corresponding to items in $X \cup Y$ So the input PQTD $\mathcal{D}$ in Algorithm 4 can only contain the columns corresponding to items in $X \cup Y$, i.e., the p+q columns $x_1, x_2, \cdots, x_p, y_1, y_2, \cdots, y_q$.

• **Example 72:** Consider the PQTD $\mathcal{D}$ in Table 3. Let $ms = 1/3$, $mc = 2/3$, $X = \{x_1, x_2\}$, $Y = \{y_1\}$, then $(X \Rightarrow Y)$ is a BAR. We use Algorithm 4 to mine $Q_W(X \Rightarrow Y)$, then every variable will change as follows:

$|T| = 5$;

$t(X, \text{supp } \mathcal{D}) = \{t_1, t_2, t_3\}$, $| t(X, \text{supp } \mathcal{D}) | = 3$;

SupCountsLowerBound:=2;

$t(X \cup Y, \text{supp } \mathcal{D}) = \{t_1, t_2, t_3\}$;

$C_{x_1} = \{a_0^{(1)}, a_1^{(1)}, a_2^{(1)}\} = \{3, 2, 1\}, n_1 = 2$,

$C_{x_2} = \{a_0^{(2)}, a_1^{(2)}, a_2^{(2)}\} = \{3, 2, 1\}, n_2 = 2$,

$C_{y_1} = \{a_0^{(3)}\} = \{1\}, n_3 = 0$;

p=2, q=1, m=p+q=3;

$M(D_{t_1}(Y)/D_{t_1}(X)) = \begin{pmatrix} 1 \\ 1/3 \end{pmatrix}$,

$M(D_{t_2}(Y)/D_{t_2}(X)) = \begin{pmatrix} 1/2 \\ 1/2 \end{pmatrix}$,

Table 3. The PQTD in Example 72

	x_1	x_2	y_1	y_2
t_1	1	3	1	1
t_2	2	2	1	0
t_3	3	1	1	3
t_4	0	10	15	10
t_5	2	0	0	2

$$M(D_{t_3}(Y)/D_{t_3}(X)) = \begin{pmatrix} 1/3 \\ 1 \end{pmatrix};$$

$posM := \varnothing$;

getmax($\langle\rangle$)

$h = \langle\rangle$, $G := \varnothing$, $g := 0$;

$t := g + 1 = 1 \leq n_{d(h)+1} = n_1 = 2$ *is TRUE, to judge*

IsWRRPos($\langle 1, 0, 0\rangle$)

$\langle A(x_1), A(x_2), B(y_1)\rangle = \langle 2, 3, 1\rangle$,

$$M(B(Y)/A(X)) = \begin{pmatrix} 1/2 \\ 1/3 \end{pmatrix};$$

$$M(D_{t_1}(Y)/D_{t_1}(X)) - M(B(Y)/A(X)) = \begin{pmatrix} 1 - 1/2 \\ 1/3 - 1/3 \end{pmatrix}$$
is positive;

$$M(D_{t_2}(Y)/D_{t_2}(X)) - M(B(Y)/A(X)) = \begin{pmatrix} 1/2 - 1/2 \\ 1/2 - 1/3 \end{pmatrix}$$
is positive;

$$M(D_{t_3}(Y)/D_{t_3}(X)) - M(B(Y)/A(X)) = \begin{pmatrix} 1/3 - 1/2 \\ 1 - 1/3 \end{pmatrix}$$
is not positive;

$\mid t(A \Rightarrow B, \mathcal{D}) \mid = 2 \geq SupCountsLowerBound$, *into while sentence*

$t := t + 1 = 2 \leq n_{d(h)+1} = n_1 = 2$ *is TRUE, to judge*

IsWRRPos($\langle 2, 0, 0\rangle$) return FALSE, quit while sentence, into sentence (8) in procedure getmax(h)

$e := t - 1 = 1$;

$d(h) = 0 < m - 1 = 2$ is TRUE, into *sentences* (10)-(11) in procedure *getmax(h)*

getmax($\langle 1\rangle$)

$h = \langle 1\rangle, G := \varnothing, g := 0$;

$t := g + 1 = 1 \leq n_{d(h)+1} = n_2 = 2$ *is TRUE, to judge*

IsWRRPos($\langle 1, 1, 0\rangle$) return FALSE, quit while sentence, into sentence (8) in procedure getmax(h)

$e := t - 1 = 0$;

$d(h) = 1 < m - 1 = 2$ is TRUE, into *sentences* (10)-(11) in procedure *getmax(h)*

getmax($\langle 1, 0\rangle$)

$h = \langle 1, 0\rangle, G := \varnothing, g := 0$;

$t := g + 1 = 1 \leq n_{d(h)+1} = n_3 = 0$ is FALSE, into sentence (8) in procedure getmax(h)

$e := t - 1 = 0$;

$d(h) = 2 = m - 1$ is TRUE, into sentence (12). $G := \varnothing$, so

$posM := posM \cup \{\langle h, \langle e\rangle\rangle\} = \{\langle 1, 0, 0\rangle\}$;

getmax($\langle 0\rangle$)

$\vdots$

IsWRRPos($\langle 0, 1, 0\rangle$) *return TRUE,*

IsWRRPos $(\langle 0, 2, 0\rangle)$ *return FALSE,*

$\vdots$

getmax $(\langle 0, 1\rangle)$

$h = \langle 0, 1\rangle, G := \varnothing, g := 0$;

$t := g + 1 = 1 \le n_{d(h)+1} = n_3 = 0$ is FALSE, into sentence (8) in procedure getmax(h)

$e := t - 1 = 0$;

$d(h) = 2 = m - 1$ is TRUE, into sentence (12). $G := \varnothing$, so

$posM := posM \cup \{\langle h, \langle e\rangle\rangle\}$
$= \{\langle 1, 0, 0\rangle, \langle 0, 1, 0\rangle\}$;

$\vdots$

obtain $posM := \{\langle 1, 0, 0\rangle, \langle 0, 1, 0\rangle\}$.

$M(S) = value(posM) = \{\langle 2, 3, 1\rangle, \langle 3, 2, 1\rangle\}$, *therefore*

$$Q_{W}(X \Rightarrow Y) = \{r_1 : (\frac{2}{x_1} + \frac{3}{x_2} \Rightarrow \frac{1}{y_1}),$$

$$r_2 : (\frac{3}{x_1} + \frac{2}{x_2} \Rightarrow \frac{1}{y_1})\}.$$

- **Proposition 73:** The set $Q_{W}(X \Rightarrow Y)$ in Example 72 is a basis of $R_{W}(X \Rightarrow Y)$.
  - **Proof:** Firstly we prove that every rule r in $R_{W}(X \Rightarrow Y)$ can be deduced by r_1 or r_2.

Suppose $r = (A \Rightarrow B)$, then there must be at least two transactions in $t(X \cup Y, \text{supp } D)$ supporting the rule r. Consider the following three cases:

1. If t_1, t_2 support r, then by t_1 supports r we have $1 \ge B(y_1)/A(x_1)$, $1/3 \ge B(y_1)/A(x_2)$, and by t_2 supports r we have $1/2 \ge B(y_1)/A(x_1)$, $1/2 \ge B(y_1)/A(x_2)$. Denote $B(y_1) \triangleq \alpha$, then $A(x_2) \ge 3\alpha$, $A(x_1) \ge 2\alpha$. Therefore

$$r \le (\frac{2\alpha}{x_1} + \frac{3\alpha}{x_2} \Rightarrow \frac{\alpha}{y_1}) = \alpha r_1,$$

i.e., r can be deduced by r_1 .

2. If t_2, t_3 support r, then $1/2 \ge B(y_1)/A(x_2)$ $1/3 \ge B(y_1)/A(x_1)$. Denote $B(y_1) \triangleq \alpha$, then $A(x_2) \ge 2\alpha$, $A(x_1) \ge 3\alpha$. Therefore, $r \le \alpha r_2$, r can be deduced by r_2 .

3. If t_1, t_3 support r, then $r \le B(y_1)r_3$, where

$$r_3 : (\frac{3}{x_1} + \frac{3}{x_2} \Rightarrow \frac{1}{y_1}),$$

However, $r_3 \le r_1$ and $r_3 \le r_2$, so r can be deduced by r_1 and also r_2 .

Secondly, we prove one of r_1 , r_2 can not deduce another. On the contrary, if there exists $\alpha \in (0, +\infty)$ such that $r_1 \le \alpha r_2$, then $2 \ge 3\alpha$,

Figure 1. The visualization of $R_{W}(X \Rightarrow Y)$ *in Example 72*

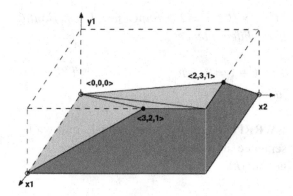

$3 \geq 2\alpha$, $1 \leq \alpha$, which is impossible, so r_2 can not deduce r_1. Similarly r_1 can not deduce r_2.

The above discussion shows that $Q_W(X \Rightarrow Y)$ is a basis of $R_W(X \Rightarrow Y)$.

By Proposition 73, we can obtain the set $R_W(X \Rightarrow Y)$ in Example 72 is that

$$\{(\frac{a_1}{x_1} + \frac{a_2}{x_2} \Rightarrow \frac{b_1}{y_1}) \mid \exists \alpha \in (0, +\infty) \text{ such that}$$
$$(a_1 \geq 2\alpha, a_2 \geq 3\alpha, b_1 \leq \alpha) \text{ or}$$
$$(a_1 \geq 3\alpha, a_2 \geq 2\alpha, b_1 \leq \alpha)\}.$$

The set

$$\{\langle a_1, a_2, b_1 \rangle \mid (\frac{a_1}{x_1} + \frac{a_2}{x_2} \Rightarrow \frac{b_1}{y_1}) \in R_W(X \Rightarrow Y)\}$$

can be visualized as the shaded area in Figure 1 (only the part inside the cube $[0,3] \times [0,3] \times [0,1]$).

Similarly, for the data in Table 2, let *ms*=*mc*=0.8, then $Q_W(\{x_1, x_2\} \Rightarrow \{y_1\})$

$$= \{r_1 : (\frac{1}{x_1} + \frac{2}{x_2} \Rightarrow \frac{3}{y_1}), r_2 : (\frac{2}{x_1} + \frac{4}{x_2} \Rightarrow \frac{4}{y_1}),$$
$$r_3 : (\frac{5}{x_1} + \frac{10}{x_2} \Rightarrow \frac{15}{y_1}), r_4 : (\frac{10}{x_1} + \frac{20}{x_2} \Rightarrow \frac{30}{y_1})\}.$$

We can prove easily that $Q_W(\{x_1, x_2\} \Rightarrow \{y_1\})$ can deduce $R_W(\{x_1, x_2\} \Rightarrow \{y_1\})$. Actually, every rule $r : (A \Rightarrow B)$ in $R_W(\{x_1, x_2\} \Rightarrow \{y_1\})$ can be deduced by r_1. The following segment is a proof:

By Proposition 32, there are at least 4 transactions supporting the rule r. However by Proposition 22(3), t_1, t_2, t_4 either all support r or all not support r, so t_2 must support r. By Proposition 20(3), we know that t_2 supports r is equivalent to r_1 deduces r.

From the above several $Q_W(X \Rightarrow Y)$ examples, we know that it is enough to only mine

a basis of $Q_W(X \Rightarrow Y)$ and we have the following Conjecture.

- **Conjecture 74:** $Q_W(X \Rightarrow Y)$ *can deduce* $R_W(X \Rightarrow Y)$.

Mining Standard Basis

In this subsection, we suppose $X = \{x_1\}$, $Y = \{y_1, y_2, \cdots, y_q\}$. Let $\tilde{C}_{x_1} = \{1\}$, and $\forall j = \{1, \cdots, q\}$,

$$\tilde{C}_{y_j} = \{\frac{D_t(y_j)}{D_t(x_1)} \mid t \in t(X \cup Y, \text{supp } \mathcal{D})\},$$

in which the partial order is $\leq$, the usual less than or equal to relation between real numbers. Let

$$\tilde{V}(X \Rightarrow Y) \triangleq \tilde{C}_{x_1} \times \tilde{C}_{y_1} \times \cdots \times \tilde{C}_{y_q},$$

then the partial order $\leq$ in chain-product $\tilde{V}(X \Rightarrow Y)$ is defined as:

$$\forall \langle 1, b^{(1)}, \cdots, b^{(q)} \rangle, \langle 1, \beta^{(1)}, \cdots, \beta^{(q)} \rangle \in \tilde{V}(X \Rightarrow Y),$$

$$\langle 1, b^{(1)}, \cdots, b^{(q)} \rangle \leq \langle 1, \beta^{(1)}, \cdots, \beta^{(q)} \rangle$$
$$\Leftrightarrow b^{(j)} \leq \beta^{(j)}, \forall j = \{1, \cdots, q\}.$$

The ideal property S on $\tilde{V}(X \Rightarrow Y)$ is defined as:

$\langle 1, \beta^{(1)}, \cdots, \beta^{(q)} \rangle$ has property
$$S \Leftrightarrow (\frac{1}{x_1} \Rightarrow \frac{\beta^{(1)}}{y_1} + \cdots + \frac{\beta^{(q)}}{y_q}) \in R_W(X \Rightarrow Y).$$

When $\langle 1, \beta^{(1)}, \cdots, \beta^{(q)} \rangle \in S$, the WRR $(\frac{1}{x_1} \Rightarrow \frac{\beta^{(1)}}{y_1} + \cdots + \frac{\beta^{(q)}}{y_q})$, denoted by $g(\langle 1, \beta^{(1)}, \cdots,$

$\beta^{(q)}\rangle)$, is called rule generated by $\langle 1, \beta^{(1)}, \cdots, \beta^{(q)} \rangle$

.

- **Proposition 75:** $\langle 1, b_0^{(1)}, \cdots, b_0^{(q)} \rangle \in S$, *where $b_0^{(j)}$ is the minimum element of $\tilde{C}_{y_j}$, $j = 1, \cdots, q$.*

  ○ **Proof:** By the definition of $\tilde{V}(X \Rightarrow Y)$, $\forall t \in t(X \cup Y, \mathrm{supp}\, \mathcal{D})$ $\forall j \in \{1, \cdots, q\}$, we have $\dfrac{D_t(y_j)}{D_t(x_1)} \geq b_0^{(j)}$

  . By Definition 9, t supports $(\dfrac{1}{x_1} \Rightarrow \dfrac{b_0^{(1)}}{y_1} + \cdots + \dfrac{b_0^{(q)}}{y_q})$, so

$$t(\frac{1}{x_1} \Rightarrow \frac{b_0^{(1)}}{y_1} + \cdots + \frac{b_0^{(q)}}{y_q}, \mathcal{D}) = t(X \cup Y, \mathrm{supp}\, \mathcal{D}).$$

Now that $(X \Rightarrow Y)$ is a BAR, therefore

$$| t(\frac{1}{x_1} \Rightarrow \frac{b_0^{(1)}}{y_1} + \cdots + \frac{b_0^{(q)}}{y_q}, \mathcal{D}) | = | t(X \cup Y, \mathrm{supp}\, \mathcal{D}) |$$
$$\geq (ms \times | T |) \vee (mc \times | t(X, \mathrm{supp}\, \mathcal{D}) |),$$

hence $(\dfrac{1}{x_1} \Rightarrow \dfrac{b_0^{(1)}}{y_1} + \cdots + \dfrac{b_0^{(q)}}{y_q}) \in \mathrm{R_W}(X \Rightarrow Y)$, i.e., $\langle 1, b_0^{(1)}, \cdots, b_0^{(q)} \rangle \in S$.

Proposition 75 shows that the ideal S of chain-product $\tilde{V}(X \Rightarrow Y)$ is nonempty, therefore, the set $M(S)$, of all maximal elements of S, is non-empty.

"$(\dfrac{1}{x_1} \Rightarrow \dfrac{b^{(1)}}{y_1} + \cdots + \dfrac{b^{(q)}}{y_q}) \in \mathrm{R_W}(X \Rightarrow Y)$ implies $\langle 1, b^{(1)}, \cdots, b^{(q)} \rangle \in S$" is true when $\forall j = 1, \cdots, q$, $b^j \in \tilde{C}_j$, otherwise the conclusion is not true. However, we have the following conclusion.

- **Proposition 76:** If $(\dfrac{1}{x_1} \Rightarrow \dfrac{b^{(1)}}{y_1} + \cdots + \dfrac{b^{(q)}}{y_q}) \in \mathrm{R_W}(X \Rightarrow Y)$, then there exists $\langle 1, \beta_{m_1}^{(1)}, \cdots, \beta_{m_q}^{(q)} \rangle \in M(S)$ such that $\forall j = \{1, \cdots, q\}$, $b^{(j)} \leq \beta_{m_j}^{(j)}$.

  ○ **Proof:** $\forall j = \{1, \cdots, q\}$, let

$$\beta^{(j)} \triangleq \min\{\frac{D_t(y_j)}{D_t(x_1)} \mid t \in t(\frac{1}{x_1} \Rightarrow \frac{b^{(1)}}{y_1} + \cdots + \frac{b^{(q)}}{y_q}, \mathcal{D})\},$$

then $b^{(j)} \leq \beta^{(j)} \in \tilde{C}_{y_j}$, and $\forall t \in t(\dfrac{1}{x_1} \Rightarrow \dfrac{b^{(1)}}{y_1} + \cdots + \dfrac{b^{(q)}}{y_q}, \mathcal{D})$, $\forall j = \{1, \cdots, q\}$, we have

$$\frac{D_t(y_j)}{D_t(x_1)} \geq \beta^{(j)}$$

so $t \in t(\dfrac{1}{x_1} \Rightarrow \dfrac{b^{(1)}}{y_1} + \cdots + \dfrac{b^{(q)}}{y_q}, \mathcal{D})$, therefore,

$$| t(\frac{1}{x_1} \Rightarrow \frac{b^{(1)}}{y_1} + \cdots + \frac{b^{(q)}}{y_q}, \mathcal{D}) |$$
$$\leq | t(\frac{1}{x_1} \Rightarrow \frac{\beta^{(1)}}{y_1} + \cdots + \frac{\beta^{(q)}}{y_q}, \mathcal{D}) |.$$

By Proposition 32, $(\dfrac{1}{x_1} \Rightarrow \dfrac{\beta^{(1)}}{y_1} + \cdots + \dfrac{\beta^{(q)}}{y_q}) \in \mathrm{R_W}(X \Rightarrow Y)$, hence $\langle 1, \beta^{(1)}, \cdots, \beta^{(q)} \rangle \in S$. S is finite, so there exists $\langle 1, \beta_{m_1}^{(1)}, \cdots, \beta_{m_q}^{(q)} \rangle \in M(S)$ such that $\forall j \in \{1, \cdots, q\}$, $b^{(j)} \leq \beta^{(j)} \leq \beta_{m_j}^{(j)}$.

- **Proposition 77:**

$$g(M(S)) \triangleq \{(\frac{1}{x_1} \Rightarrow \frac{\beta^{(1)}}{y_1} + \cdots + \frac{\beta^{(q)}}{y_q}) \mid$$
$$\langle 1, \beta^{(1)}, \cdots, \beta^{(q)} \rangle \in M(S)\}$$

is the standard basis of $R_W(X \Rightarrow Y)$.

○ **Proof:** Firstly, we prove $g(M(S))$ can deduce $R_W(X \Rightarrow Y)$. Suppose $(A \Rightarrow B) \in R_W(X \Rightarrow Y), \forall j = \{1, \cdots, q\}$, let $b^{(j)} = B(y_j)/A(x_1)$, then

$$(\frac{1}{x_1} \Rightarrow \frac{b^{(1)}}{y_1} + \cdots + \frac{b^{(q)}}{y_q}) \in R_W(X \Rightarrow Y),$$

by Proposition 76, there exists $\langle 1, \beta_{m_1}^{(1)}, \cdots, \beta_{m_q}^{(q)} \rangle \in M(S)$ such that $\forall j = \{1, \cdots, q\}, b^{(j)} \leq \beta_{m_j}^{(j)}$. So

$$(A \Rightarrow B) = A(x_1)(\frac{1}{x_1} \Rightarrow \frac{b^{(1)}}{y_1} + \cdots + \frac{b^{(q)}}{y_q})$$

$$\leq A(x_1)(\frac{1}{x_1} \Rightarrow \frac{\beta_{m_1}^{(1)}}{y_1} + \cdots + \frac{\beta_{m_q}^{(q)}}{y_q}),$$

i.e., $(A \Rightarrow B)$ can be deduced by element $(\frac{1}{x_1} \Rightarrow \frac{\beta_{m_1}^{(1)}}{y_1} + \cdots + \frac{\beta_{m_q}^{(q)}}{y_q})$ of $g(M(S))$.

Secondly, we prove that for any two different rules in $g(M(S))$ one can not deduce another. Let

$$r_1 : (\frac{1}{x_1} \Rightarrow \frac{b^{(1)}}{y_1} + \cdots + \frac{b^{(q)}}{y_q}),$$

$$r_2 : (\frac{1}{x_1} \Rightarrow \frac{\beta^{(1)}}{y_1} + \cdots + \frac{\beta^{(q)}}{y_q}), \in g(M(S))$$ and

$r_1 \neq r_2$. i.e., $\langle 1, b^{(1)}, \cdots, b^{(q)} \rangle, \langle 1, \beta^{(1)}, \cdots, \beta^{(q)} \rangle \in M(S)$ and $\langle 1, b^{(1)}, \cdots, b^{(q)} \rangle \neq \langle 1, \beta^{(1)}, \cdots, \beta^{(q)} \rangle$. If r_1 can deduce r_2, then there exists $\alpha \in (0, +\infty)$ such that

$$(\frac{1}{x_1} \Rightarrow \frac{\beta^{(1)}}{y_1} + \cdots + \frac{\beta^{(q)}}{y_q}) \leq \alpha(\frac{1}{x_1} \Rightarrow \frac{b^{(1)}}{y_1} + \cdots + \frac{b^{(q)}}{y_q})$$

so $1 \geq \alpha$ and $\forall j = \{1, \cdots, q\}, \beta^{(j)} \leq \alpha b^{(j)} \leq b^{(j)}$, therefore $\langle 1, \beta^{(1)}, \cdots, \beta^{(q)} \rangle \leq \langle 1, b^{(1)}, \cdots, b^{(q)} \rangle$, which is contrary to $\langle 1, \beta^{(1)}, \cdots, \beta^{(q)} \rangle \in M(S)$. Hence r_1

can not deduce r_2. Similarly, r_2 can not deduce r_1.

By Proposition 58, we have the following proposition, but we still offer a direct proof.

● **Proposition 78:** $g(M(S))$ is the set of all *standard maximal rules of* $R_W(X \Rightarrow Y)$.

○ **Proof:** Firstly, we prove that every element of $g(M(S))$ is a standard maximal rule, i.e., if $\langle 1, \beta_{m_1}^{(1)}, \cdots, \beta_{m_q}^{(q)} \rangle \in M(S)$, then

$$r_m : (\frac{1}{x_1} \Rightarrow \frac{\beta_{m_1}^{(1)}}{y_1} + \cdots + \frac{\beta_{m_q}^{(q)}}{y_q}) \in M_W(X \Rightarrow Y).$$

Suppose $r : (A \Rightarrow B) \in R_W(X \Rightarrow Y)$ and $r_m < r$, we will prove $r_m = r$. Let $b^{(j)} = B(y_i)/A(x_1)$ then $(\frac{1}{x_1} \Rightarrow \frac{v}{y_1} + \cdots + \frac{v}{y_q}) \in R_W(X \Rightarrow Y).$ By Proposition 76, there exists $\langle 1, \beta^{(1)}, \cdots, \beta^{(q)} \rangle \in S$ such that $\forall j = \{1, \cdots, q\}, b^{(j)} \leq \beta^{(j)}$ so

$$\frac{1}{A(x_1)} r_m \leq \frac{1}{A(x_1)} r = (\frac{1}{x_1} \Rightarrow \frac{b^{(1)}}{y_1} + \cdots + \frac{b^{(q)}}{y_q}) \leq (\frac{1}{x_1} \Rightarrow \frac{\beta^{(1)}}{y_1} + \cdots + \frac{\beta^{(q)}}{y_q}),$$

therefore, $\frac{1}{A(x_1)} \geq 1$ and

$$\beta^{(j)} \geq \frac{1}{A(x_1)} \beta_{m_j}^{(j)} \geq \beta_{m_j}^{(j)}, \forall j = \{1, \cdots, q\}$$

hence $\langle 1, \beta_{m_1}^{(1)}, \cdots, \beta_{m_q}^{(q)} \rangle \leq \langle 1, \beta^{(1)}, \cdots, \beta^{(q)} \rangle$. $\langle 1, \beta_{m_1}^{(1)}, \cdots, \beta_{m_q}^{(q)} \rangle$ is a maximal element of S, so $\langle 1, \beta_{m_1}^{(1)}, \cdots, \beta_{m_q}^{(q)} \rangle = \langle 1, \beta^{(1)}, \cdots, \beta^{(q)} \rangle$. Therefore

$$\frac{1}{A(x_1)}\, r_m \le \frac{1}{A(x_1)}\, r \le (\frac{1}{x_1} \Rightarrow \frac{\beta^{(1)}}{y_1} + \cdots + \frac{\beta^{(q)}}{y_q}) = r_m.$$

By Proposition 36(3), we know $\dfrac{1}{A(x_1)} = 1$, so $r_m = r$.

Secondly, we prove that every standard maximal rule $(\dfrac{1}{x_1} \Rightarrow \dfrac{\beta^{(1)}}{y_1} + \cdots + \dfrac{\beta^{(q)}}{y_q})$ is a element of $g(M(S))$. By Proposition 76, there exists $\langle 1, \beta_{m_1}^{(1)}, \cdots, \beta_{m_q}^{(q)} \rangle \in M(S)$ such that $\forall j = \{1, \cdots, q\}, \beta^{(j)} \le \beta_{m_j}^{(j)}$ so

$$(\frac{1}{x_1} \Rightarrow \frac{\beta^{(1)}}{y_1} + \cdots + \frac{\beta^{(q)}}{y_q}) \le (\frac{1}{x_1} \Rightarrow \frac{\beta_{m_1}^{(1)}}{y_1} + \cdots + \frac{\beta_{m_q}^{(q)}}{y_q}).$$

The former is maximal, so the two rules are equal, i.e., $\forall j = \{1, \cdots, q\}$, $\beta^{(j)} = \beta_{m_j}^{(j)}$, Hence $\langle 1, \beta^{(1)}, \cdots, \beta^{(q)} \rangle = \langle 1, \beta_{m_1}^{(1)}, \cdots, \beta_{m_q}^{(q)} \rangle \in M(S)$.

$g(M(S))$ have finite elements, so the number of standard maximal elements of $\mathrm{R_W}(X \Rightarrow Y)$ is finite, and the number of equivalence classes of $\mathrm{M_W}(X \Rightarrow Y)$ with regard to $\sim_d$ is finite.

By Proposition 22(3), the set of all WRRs in PQTD $\mathcal{D}$ whose every row t is multiplied by α (i.e., D_t changes to αD_t) does not change. For any transaction $t \in t(X \cup Y, \mathrm{supp}\,\mathcal{D})$, t is multiplied by $\dfrac{1}{D_t(x_1)}$, and we denote the changed PQTD as $\mathcal{D}(x_1)$, then

$$\mathrm{R_W}(\mathcal{D}(x_1); ms, mc; X \Rightarrow Y) = \mathrm{R_W}(\mathcal{D}; ms, mc; X \Rightarrow Y). \tag{4.3.1}$$

It is obvious that $g(M(S))$ is actual the set $\mathrm{Q_W}(X \Rightarrow Y)$ in $\mathcal{D}(x_1)$, i.e.,

$$g(M(S)) = \mathrm{Q_W}(\mathcal{D}(x_1); ms, mc; X \Rightarrow Y). \tag{4.3.2}$$

Therefore, by the Algorithm 4, we can easily obtain an algorithm to find $g(M(S))$, and the difference is only that, $p=1$ and inserting the following operation between step (4) and step (5):

- **(4.5):** For any transaction t, the row t is multiplied by $\dfrac{1}{D_t(x_1)}$.

- **Example 79:** Suppose $\mathcal{D}$ is the PQTD in Table 4, ms=mc=0.5, $X = \{x_1\}$, $= \mathrm{R_W}(\mathcal{D}; ms, mc; X \Rightarrow Y)$. then $(X \Rightarrow Y) \in \mathrm{R_b}(\mathcal{D}; ms, mc)$. By Algorithm 4, we can get two elements of $g(M(S))$, i.e., *the two standard maximal rules of* $\mathrm{R_W}(X \Rightarrow Y)$: $(1/x_1 \Rightarrow 0.5/y_1 + 1/y_2)$ and $(1/x_1 \Rightarrow 1/y_1 + 0.5/y_2)$. Therefore, $\mathrm{R_W}(X \Rightarrow Y)$ *is just the set* $\{(\dfrac{a_1}{x_1} \Rightarrow \dfrac{b_1}{y_1} + \dfrac{b_2}{y_2}) \mid \exists \alpha \in (0, +\infty)$ *such that* $(a_1 \ge \alpha, b_1 \le 0.5\alpha, b_2 \le \alpha)$ *or* $(a_1 \ge \alpha, b_1 \le \alpha, b_2 \le 0.5\alpha)\}$. The set

$$\{\langle a_1, b_1, b_2 \rangle \mid (\frac{a_1}{x_1} \Rightarrow \frac{b_1}{y_1} + \frac{b_2}{y_2}) \in \mathrm{R_W}(X \Rightarrow Y)\}$$

can be visualized as the shaded area in Figure 2 (only the part inside the cube $[0,1]^3$).

Table 4. The PQTD in Example 79

	x_1	y_1	y_2
t_1	1	1	1
t_2	1	0.5	1
t_3	1	1	0.5
t_4	1	0.5	0.5

Figure 2. All WRRs in Example 79

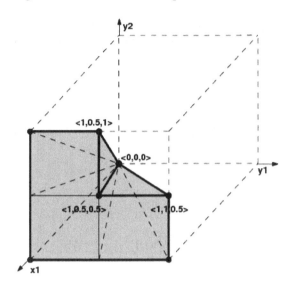

- **Remark 80:** *Proposition 77 shows that* $g(M(S))$ *is the standard basis of* $\mathrm{R}_\mathrm{W}(\mathcal{D}; ms, mc; X \Rightarrow Y)$. *By Equations 4.3.1 and 4.3.2,* $\mathrm{Q}_\mathrm{W}(\mathcal{D}(x_1); ms, mc; X \Rightarrow Y)$ *is the standard basis of* $\mathrm{R}_\mathrm{W}(\mathcal{D}(x_1); ms, mc; X \Rightarrow Y)$. *But we cannot obtain* $\mathrm{Q}_\mathrm{W}(\mathcal{D}; ms, mc; X \Rightarrow Y)$, *the standard basis of* $\mathrm{R}_\mathrm{W}(\mathcal{D}; ms, mc; X \Rightarrow Y)$.

UNCERTAINTY REASONING METHOD BASED ON WRR

Using Fuzzy reasoning method for a reference, we propose two WRR reasoning methods, whose intuitive meaning reflects a practical significance of research on WRR.

- **Proposition 81:** If $(A \Rightarrow B) \in \mathrm{R}_\mathrm{W}$, $F \in [0, +\infty)^I$, $\operatorname{supp} F = \operatorname{supp} A$, then $(F \Rightarrow \operatorname{Inf}(F/A)B) \in \mathrm{R}_\mathrm{W}$.
  - **Proof:** By the conditions given, we have $\operatorname{Inf}(F/A) \in (0, +\infty)$. By

Proposition 33(5), we have $(\operatorname{Inf}(F/A)A \Rightarrow \operatorname{Inf}(F/A)B) \in \mathrm{R}_\mathrm{W}$. $\operatorname{Inf}(F/A)A \subseteq F$, $\operatorname{supp}(\operatorname{Inf}(F/A)A) = \operatorname{supp} A = \operatorname{supp} F$, so by Proposition 34, we have $(F \Rightarrow \operatorname{Inf}(F/A)B) \in \mathrm{R}_\mathrm{W}$.

The Proposition 81 actually gives a reasoning method below:

Reasoning Method (I):

$$
\begin{array}{rl}
\text{rule}: & A \Rightarrow B \\
\text{fact}: & F \\
\hline
\text{conclusion}: & C
\end{array}
$$

where, $A, B, F, C \in [0, +\infty)^I$, For given A, B and F, the conclusion C can be obtained by formula

$$C \triangleq \operatorname{Inf}(F/A)B.$$

i.e., $\forall j \in I$,

$$
C(j) = \begin{cases}
(\underset{i \in \operatorname{supp} A}{\wedge} \dfrac{F(i)}{A(i)})B(j), & j \in \operatorname{supp} B, \\
0, & j \notin \operatorname{supp} B.
\end{cases}
$$

This reasoning method is compatible with MP (i.e., if $F=A$, then $C=B$).

The WRR reasoning method (I) has the intuitive meaning: Given mined WRR $(A \Rightarrow B; ms, mc)$ and the fact "one customer purchases $F(i)$ unit quantity item i for any $i \in \operatorname{supp} A$", then there is $(100 \times mc)\%$ possibility that the customer purchases at least $(\underset{i \in \operatorname{supp} A}{\wedge} \dfrac{F(i)}{A(i)})B(j)$ unit quantity item j for any $j \in \operatorname{supp} B$.

In the following, we use $r(F)$ to denote the conclusion $\text{Inf}(F/A)B$ obtained by reasoning method (I) with rule $r : (A \Rightarrow B)$ and fact F.

- **Proposition 82:** Suppose $r_1, r_2 \in \mathrm{R_W}(X \Rightarrow Y)$, then

  ○ **(1):** $r_2 \leq_d r_1$ if and only if $\forall F \in [0, +\infty)^I$ and $\text{supp} F = X$, we have $r_2(F) \subseteq r_1(F)$;

  ○ **(2):** $r_2 \sim_d r_1$ if and only if $\forall F \in [0, +\infty)^I$ and $\text{supp} F = X$, we have $r_2(F) = r_1(F)$.

  ○ **Proof:** We only prove (1). Suppose $r_k : (A_k \Rightarrow B_k), k = 1, 2$.

  ○ **(necessity):** Suppose $\alpha \in (0, +\infty)$ such that $A_2 \supseteq \alpha A_1, B_2 \subseteq \alpha B_1$. Then $\forall i \in X$ $A_2(i) \geq \alpha A_1(i)$.

  $\text{Inf}(F/A_2) = \bigwedge_{i \in X} \dfrac{F(i)}{A_2(i)} \leq$

  $\bigwedge_{i \in X} \dfrac{F(i)}{\alpha A_1(i)} = \dfrac{1}{\alpha} \text{Inf}(F/A_1)$. So

  $r_2(F) = \text{Inf}(F/A_2)B_2$

  $\subseteq (\dfrac{1}{\alpha} \text{Inf}(F/A_1))$.

  $(\alpha B_1) = r_1(F)$

  ○ **(sufficiency):** Let $F = A_2$, then $B_2 = r_2(F) \subseteq r_1(F) = \text{Inf}(A_2/A_1)B_1$. By Proposition 42, we can obtain $r_2 \leq_d r_1$.

The above reasoning method (I) can be generalized to the following general reasoning method:

Reasoning Method (II):

rule 1 : $A_1 \Rightarrow B_1$

$\vdots$

rule n : $A_n \Rightarrow B_n$

fact : P

———————————————

conclusion : $\qquad Q$

where $A_k, B_k, F, C \in [0, +\infty)^I$
$\text{supp} F = \text{supp} A_k = X, \text{supp} B_k = Y$
$\forall k = 1, \cdots, n$. For given rule $1, \cdots$, rule n and fact F, the conclusion C can be obtained by formula

$$C \triangleq \bigcup_{k=1}^{n} (\text{Inf}(F/A_k)B_k).$$

i.e., $\forall j \in I$,

$$C(j) = \begin{cases} \bigvee_{k=1}^{n} ((\bigwedge_{i \in X} \dfrac{F(i)}{A_k(i)})B_k(j)), & j \in Y, \\ 0, & j \notin Y. \end{cases}$$

The WRR reasoning method (II) has the intuitive meaning: Given mined WRRs $(A_k \Rightarrow B_k; ms, mc), k = 1, \cdots, n$, and the fact "one customer purchases $F(i)$ unit quantity item i for any $i \in X$ ", then there is $(100 \times mc)\%$ possibility that the customer purchases at least $\bigvee_{k=1}^{n} ((\bigwedge_{i \in X} \dfrac{F(i)}{A_k(i)})B_k(j))$ unit quantity item j for any $j \in Y$.

- **Proposition 83:** *Suppose E, M are two nonempty subsets of* $\mathrm{R_W}(X \Rightarrow Y)$, $E \subseteq M$ *and* E *can deduce* M. $F \in [0, +\infty)^I$ *and* $\text{supp} F = X$, *then*

  ○ **(1):** $\bigcup_{r \in M} r(F)$ is the conclusion obtained by reasoning method (II) with rule set M and fact F ;

  ○ **(2):** $\bigcup_{r \in E} r(F) = \bigcup_{r \in M} r(F)$.

  ○ **Proof:** We only prove (2). $\forall r \in M$, there exists $r_1 \in E$ such that $r \leq_d r_1$ By Proposition 82(1), we know $r(F) \subseteq r_1(F)$. So $\bigcup_{r \in M} r(F) \subseteq \bigcup_{r \in E} r(F)$

$$\bigcup_{r \in E} r(F) \subseteq \bigcup_{r \in M} r(F)$$ is obvious, therefore, (2) is true.

○ **Corollary 84:** In reasoning method (II), when the rule set is replaced with its basis, the conclusion is unchanged.

• **Remark 85:** *In reasoning method (I),* $(F \Rightarrow C)$ *is a WRR. But in reasoning method (II),* $(F \Rightarrow C)$ *may not be a WRR. For instance, we consider the PQTD in Table 5. Let* ms=mc= 0.5, $A_1 = A_2 = F = 2/i_1 + 6/i_2$ $B_1 = 7/i_3 + 2/i_4$, $B_2 = 4/i_3 + 5/i_4$, *then premise in reasoning method (II) is established and conclusion* $C = 7/i_3 + 5/i_4$, *but* $(F \Rightarrow C)$ *is not a WRR.*

The uncertainty reasoning method (II) can be applied to reconstructing lost data, forecasting and outlier detection.

APPLICATION OF WRR

Flip Korn's Ratio Rules (Korn et al., 1998) can be applied to data cleaning, forecasting and outlier detection. The following instance reconstructing lost data comes from Wang et al. (2001) using Korn et al.'s (1998) method. Wang et al. (2001) used the ratio rule 1.000:0689:0.147:0.002 mined from Table 6 to guess the values at * in Table 7. The guessed results are shown as the underline data in Table 8. The absolute error between guessed value and raw data is shown as Table 9. Wang

Table 5. The PQTD in Remark 85

	i_1	i_2	i_3	i_4
t_1	1	7	7	2
t_2	2	1	4	5
t_3	2	7	1	8
t_4	1	3	5	5
t_5	1	5	8	2
t_6	2	6	7	5

Table 6. Raw data (adapted from Wang et al., 2001)

Rec #	i_1	i_2	i_3	i_4
1	149.3	4.2	108.1	15.9
2	161.2	4.1	114.8	16.4
3	171.5	3.1	123.2	19.0
4	175.5	3.1	126.9	19.1
5	180.8	1.1	132.1	18.8
6	190.7	2.2	137.7	20.4
7	202.1	2.1	146.0	22.7
8	212.4	5.6	154.1	26.5
9	226.1	5.0	162.3	28.1
10	231.9	5.1	164.3	27.6
11	239.0	0.7	167.6	26.3

Table 7. Lost data (adapted from Wang et al., 2001)

Rec #	i_1	i_2	i_3	i_4
1	*	4.2	108.1	15.9
5	180.8	*	132.1	18.8
7	202.1	2.1	146.0	*
9	226.1	5.0	*	*
11	239.0	0.7	*	26.3

Table 8. The guessed values by Ratio Rules method (adapted from Wang et al., 2001)

Rec #	i_1	i_2	i_3	i_4
1	155.18	4.2	108.1	15.9
5	180.8	0.33	132.1	18.8
7	202.1	2.1	146.0	30.16
9	226.1	5.0	155.38	33.19
11	239.0	0.7	163.38	26.3

Table 9. The absolute error by Ratio Rules method (adapted from Wang et al., 2001)

Rec #	i_1	i_2	i_3	i_4
1	5.88	0	0	0
5	0	0.77	0	0
7	0	0	0	7.46
9	0	0	6.92	5.09
11	0	0	4.22	0

Table 10. The absolute error by column average method (adapted from Wang et al., 2001)

Rec #	i_1	i_2	i_3	i_4
1	45.29	0	0	0
5	0	2.2	0	0
7	0	0	0	0.81
9	0	0	22.56	6.21
11	0	0	27.86	0

et al. (2001) compared Ratio Rule method with column average method in Table 10, the absolute error of two methods shows that the Ratio Rule method is more accurate. The root-mean-square RMS of Ratio Rule method absolute error is 2.04, and the root-mean-square RMS of column average method absolute error is 8.77, where

$$RMS = \sqrt{\frac{1}{11 \times 4} \sum_{i=1}^{11} \sum_{j=1}^{4} (\hat{d}_{ij} - d_{ij})^2},$$

$\hat{d}_{ij}$ is the guessed value and d_{ij} is the raw data.

In the following, taking the above instance, we illustrate the process of reconstructing lost data by WRR method. For example, the value i_3, i_4 of Rec 9 in Table 7 can be reconstructed as following:

1. Let *ms*=*mc*=0.5, now $(\{i_1, i_2\} \Rightarrow \{i_3, i_4\})$ is a BAR in Table 6.
2. Mining a basis of all quasi-maximal WRRs supported by BAR $(\{i_1, i_2\} \Rightarrow \{i_3, i_4\})$.

$161.20 / i_1 + 3.10 / i_2 \Rightarrow 108.10 / i_3 + 16.40 / i_4,$

$161.20 / i_1 + 4.10 / i_2 \Rightarrow 114.80 / i_3 + 16.40 / i_4,$

$171.50 / i_1 + 3.10 / i_2 \Rightarrow 114.80 / i_3 + 16.40 / i_4,$

$171.50 / i_1 + 4.10 / i_2 \Rightarrow 108.10 / i_3 + 18.80 / i_4,$

$171.50 / i_1 + 4.20 / i_2 \Rightarrow 114.80 / i_3 + 18.80 / i_4,$

$171.50 / i_1 + 5.00 / i_2 \Rightarrow 123.20 / i_3 + 16.40 / i_4,$

$175.50 / i_1 + 4.10 / i_2 \Rightarrow 123.20 / i_3 + 16.40 / i_4,$

$175.50 / i_1 + 4.10 / i_2 \Rightarrow 114.80 / i_3 + 19.10 / i_4,$

$175.50 / i_1 + 5.00 / i_2 \Rightarrow 123.20 / i_3 + 19.10 / i_4,$

$180.80 / i_1 + 3.10 / i_2 \Rightarrow 123.20 / i_3 + 18.80 / i_4,$

$180.80 / i_1 + 4.10 / i_2 \Rightarrow 126.90 / i_3 + 19.10 / i_4,$

$190.70 / i_1 + 3.10 / i_2 \Rightarrow 123.20 / i_3 + 19.00 / i_4,$

$190.70 / i_1 + 4.10 / i_2 \Rightarrow 132.10 / i_3 + 20.40 / i_4,$

$190.70 / i_1 + 5.60 / i_2 \Rightarrow 137.70 / i_3 + 19.10 / i_4,$

$202.10 / i_1 + 4.10 / i_2 \Rightarrow 137.70 / i_3 + 20.40 / i_4,$

$212.40 / i_1 + 4.10 / i_2 \Rightarrow 146.00 / i_3 + 20.40 / i_4,$

$212.40 / i_1 + 4.10 / i_2 \Rightarrow 132.10 / i_3 + 22.70 / i_4,$

$212.40 / i_1 + 5.00 / i_2 \Rightarrow 146.00 / i_3 + 22.70 / i_4,$

$$226.10 / i_1 + 4.10 / i_2 \Rightarrow 154.10 / i_3 + 22.70 / i_4,$$

$$226.10 / i_1 + 5.00 / i_2 \Rightarrow 162.30 / i_3 + 22.70 / i_4,$$

$$231.90 / i_1 + 4.10 / i_2 \Rightarrow 162.30 / i_3 + 22.70 / i_4,$$

$$231.90 / i_1 + 5.10 / i_2 \Rightarrow 164.30 / i_3 + 22.70 / i_4,$$

$$239.00 / i_1 + 4.20 / i_2 \Rightarrow 164.30 / i_3 + 22.70 / i_4,$$

$$239.00 / i_1 + 5.00 / i_2 \Rightarrow 167.60 / i_3 + 22.70 / i_4,$$

$$239.00 / i_1 + 5.60 / i_2 \Rightarrow 154.10 / i_3 + 26.30 / i_4,$$

3. Taking the basis rules in Step 2 as premise rules, the given value $F \triangleq 226.10/i_1 + 5.0/i_2$ in Rec 9 as fact in reasoning method (II), we can obtain the conclusion $C = 162.3/i_3 + 24.19/i_4$.

4. The value 162.3, 24.19 of i_3, i_4 in C are taken as the guessed value of i_3, i_4 of Rec 9 in Table 7.

Similarly, we can use the given values of record t in Table 7 to guess the lost values in record t. By comparing the guessed values with raw data,

we know that except the guessed value of i_3 of Rec 11, other guessed values are closer to the raw data. Through analysis, the reason having large difference about i_3 is that the value 0.7 of i_2 has been taken as a fact value to reasoning method.

If we only use the values of i_1, i_4 to guess the value of i_3, the guessed value will be closer to the raw data. Actually, the value 0.7 of i_2 is an outlier. The process how to detect outlier will be described later, here we summarize firstly the process mentioned above of reconstructing lost data by WRR method.

- **Step 0:** For any record t (corresponding a transaction) which has known data (lossless data) and lost data, let X be the set of all items whose corresponding known data on row t are not outliers, and let Y be the set of all items whose corresponding data on row t are lost.
- **Step 1:** Let $ms=mc=0.5$ or smaller than 0.5 to ensure that $(X \Rightarrow Y)$ is a BAR of the original PQTD $\mathcal{D}$.
- **Step 2:** In $\mathcal{D}$, mining a basis of all quasi-maximal WRRs supported by BAR $(X \Rightarrow Y)$ or if the X is a singleton set, mining the standard basis of WRR supported by BAR $(X \Rightarrow Y)$.
- **Step 3:** Taking the basis rules in Step 2 as premise rules, and let the non-outlier and known data of the record t be the fact P. By the WRR uncertainty reasoning method (II), we can get the conclusion C.

Table 11. The guessed values by WRR method

Rec #	i_1	i_2	i_3	i_4
1	143.51	4.2	108.1	15.9
5	180.8	3.08	132.1	18.8
7	202.1	2.1	146.0	12.87
9	226.1	5.0	162.3	24.19
11	239.0	0.7	167.77	26.3

Table 12. The absolute error by WRR method

Rec #	i_1	i_2	i_3	i_4
1	5.79	0	0	0
5	0	1.98	0	0
7	0	0	0	9.83
9	0	0	0	3.91
11	0	0	0.17	0

• **Step 4:** Let the values in conclusion C be the reconstructed values of t on items of Y.

In this paper, we call the above method as *WRR method*. By this WRR method, we can reconstruct the values at * in Table 7. The result is shown in Table 11. The absolute error between guessed value and raw data is shown in Table 12.

From Table 12, we can know that the total guess error RMS of WRR method is 1.84, and it is less than the total guess error of Ratio Rules method, which is 2.04.

• **Remark 86:** In WRR method, *if $X = \{x\}$ $Y = \{y\}$ and $\forall t \in T$, $D_t(x) > 0$, $D_t(y) > 0$,* then by Proposition 77, Proposition 58 and Proposition 18, when ms=mc=0.5, the standard basis which generate from Step 2 only has one rule
$$b_0 = \max\{b \,\|\, \{t \in T$$
$$(1/x \Rightarrow b_0/y), \text{and} \mid D_t(y)/D_t(x) \geq b\} \mid / \mid$$
$$\geq 0.5\},$$
i.e., the maximum slope of line y=bx above which the data points in $P = \{\langle D_t(x),$ $D_t(y)\rangle \mid t \in T\}$ are more than half. If the data points set P can fit on a straight line through the origin, b_0 will be close to the slope of the fitting line. That's the reason to assume ms=mc=0.5 in WRR method.

Experiments show that when the data in PQTD change slightly, the reconstructed data also change slightly. This shows that the WRR method has some continuity.

The above process of reconstructing lost data by WRR method can also be used to forecast the problem such as, if a customer spends $22 on bread and $30 on beer, how much will he/she spend on chocolate?

In WRR method, the reasoning fact F could not be an outlier, then how we detect the outlier? Taking 0.7 of Rec 11 in Table 6 for instance, we explain in the following:

1. Let *ms=mc=0.9*, we can mine a basis of all quasi-maximal WRRs supported by BAR $\{i_1, i_3, i_4\} \Rightarrow \{i_2\}$ in Table 7:

$$180.80/i_1 + 132.10/i_3 + 18.80/i_4 \Rightarrow 1.10/i_2$$

2. Taking $239.0/i_1 + 167.6/i_3 + 26.3/i_4$ as fact, we can get the conclusion $1.40/i_2$ by the reasoning method (II).

By the intuitive meaning of the reasoning method (II), we can know that the possibility that the value of i_2 in Rec 11 is not less than 1.40 is 90%. So we can think 0.7 is an outlier.

The above WRR method that detects 0.7 is an outlier can be used to detect outliers in any PQTD. The threshold *ms, mc* may be greater than or less than 0.9, depending on the different specific issues.

In this paper, we use WRR method to reconstruct lost data. In the method, we take the value in conclusion obtained by the uncertainty reasoning method (II) as the guessed value. In fact, the value in the conclusion is lower bound by the intuitive meaning of the reasoning method (II). We can modify WRR model to guess the upper bound, then take the average of the guessed lower bound and guessed upper bound as the guessed

CONCLUSION

We have proposed a new association relation (called weak ratio rule, simply WRR) between nonnegative real-valued data in transactional database. The WRR problem is a generalization of BAR (Boolean association rule) problem, and WRR can also better (than Flip Korn's ratio rule) describe partially the relationship between nonnegative real-valued data when the data points are not linearly correlated. Through discussing the mathematical model of WRR, we get that every WRR can induce a BAR as its support rule. We present an algorithm for mining an important subset of all WRRs supported by a given BAR. By the reasoning meaning of WRR, we propose a WRR uncertainty reasoning method. The WRR can be applied to reconstructing lost data, forecasting and outlier detection. Our present WRR model can only guess lower bound in pure quantitative transactional database. In the future we will construct further a new WRR model which can also guess upper bound. The research can focus on applying WRR to datasets that also contain categorical data.

ACKNOWLEDGMENT

This work was supported by the National Natural Science Foundation of P. R. China (60875034) and the Henan Innovation Project for University Prominent Research Talents (2007KYCX018)

REFERENCES

Agrawal, R., & Srikant, R. (1994). Fast algorithms for mining association rules in large databases. In *Proceedings of the 20th International Conference on Very Large Data Bases (VLDB '94)*, Santiago, Chile (pp. 487-499).

Ashrafi, M. Z., Taniar, D., & Smith, K. (2004). ODAM: An Optimized Distributed Association Rule Mining Algorithm. *IEEE Distributed Systems Online*, *5*(3), 11–18. doi:10.1109/MDSO.2004.1285877

Ashrafi, M. Z., Taniar, D., & Smith, K. (2007). Redundant association rules reduction techniques. *International Journal of Business Intelligence and Data Mining*, *2*(1), 29–63. doi:10.1504/IJBIDM.2007.012945

Bezrukov, S. L., & Leck, U. (2005). Macaulay posets. *The Electronic Journal of Combinatorics*. Retrieved from http://www.combinatorics.org/Surveys

Burdick, D., Calimlim, M., Flannick, J., Gehrke, J., & Yiu, T. (2005). MAFIA: A maximal frequent itemset algorithm. *IEEE Transactions on Knowledge and Data Engineering*, *17*(11), 1490–1504. doi:10.1109/TKDE.2005.183

Burris, S., & Sankappanavar, H. P. (1981). *A Course in Universal Algebra*. New York, NY: Springer.

Casali, A., Nedjar, S., Cicchetti, R., & Lakhal, L. (2010). Constrained Cube Lattices for Multidimensional Database Mining. *International Journal of Data Warehousing and Mining*, *6*(3), 43–72. doi:10.4018/jdwm.2010070104

Daly, O., & Taniar, D. (2004). Exception Rules Mining Based on Negative Association Rules. In *Proceedings of the International Conference on Computational Science and Its Applications (ICCSA 2004)* (LNCS 3046, pp. 543-552).

Giannikopoulos, P., Varlamis, I., & Eirinaki, M. (2010). Mining Frequent Generalized Patterns for Web Personalization in the Presence of Taxonomies. *International Journal of Data Warehousing and Mining*, *6*(1), 58–76. doi:10.4018/jdwm.2010090804

Gierz, G., Hofmann, K. H., Keimel, K., Lawson, J. D., Mislove, M., & Scott, D. S. (1980). *A Compendium of Continuous Lattices*. New York, NY: Springer.

Gouda, K., & Zaki, M. J. (2005). GenMax: An efficient algorithm for mining maximal frequent itemsets. *Data Mining and Knowledge Discovery*, *11*, 1–20. doi:10.1007/s10618-005-0002-x

Habib, M., & Nourine, L. (1997). Gray codes for the ideals of interval orders. *Journal of Algorithms*, *25*, 52–66. doi:10.1006/jagm.1997.0863

Han, J., & Kamber, M. (2006). *Data Mining: Concepts and Techniques* (2nd ed.). San Francisco, CA: Morgan Kaufmann.

Jiang, B. (2005). *Study on Mining and Reasoning of Weak Ratio Rules*. Unpublished doctoral dissertation, Southwest Jiaotong University, China.

Korn, F., Labrinidis, A., Kotidis, Y., & Faloutsos, C. (1998). Ratio rules: A new paradigm for fast, quantifiable data mining. In *Proceedings of the 24th International Conference on Very Large Data Bases (VLDB)*, New York, NY (pp. 582-593).

Kuok, C. M., Fu, A., & Wong, M. H. (1998). Mining fuzzy association rules in databases. *SIGMOD Record, 27*(1), 41–46. doi:10.1145/273244.273257

Kwok, T., Smith, K. A., Lozano, S., & Taniar, D. (2002). Parallel Fuzzy c-Means Clustering for Large Data Sets. In *Proceedings of the 8th International Euro-Par Conference (Euro-Par 2002)* (LNCS 2400, pp. 365-374).

Loof, K. D., Baets, B. D., & Meyer, H. D. (2007). On the random generation and counting of weak order extensions of a poset with given class cardinalities. *Information Sciences, 177*(1), 220–230. doi:10.1016/j.ins.2006.04.003

Marcus, A., Maletic, J. I., & Lin, K. I. (2001). Ordinal association rules for error identification in data sets. In *Proceedings of the 10th International Conference on Information and Knowledge Management*, Atlanta, GA (pp. 589-591).

Pitteloud, P. (2002). Log-concavity and compressed ideals in certain macaulay posets. *Discrete Mathematics, 254*, 421–432. doi:10.1016/S0012-365X(01)00360-0

Rosen, K. H. (2000). *Handbook of discrete and combinatorial mathematics*. Boca Raton, FL: CRC Press.

Srikant, R., & Agrawal, R. (1996). Mining quantitative association rules in large relational tables. In *Proceedings of the 1996 ACM-SIGMOD International Conference on Management of Data (SIG-MOD '96)*, Montreal, QC, Canada (pp. 1-12).

Stanat, D. F., & McAllister, D. F. (1977). *Discrete Mathematics in Computer Science*. Englewood Cliffs, NJ: Prentice-Hall.

Taniar, D., Rahayu, W., Lee, V., & Daly, O. (2008). Exception rules in association rule mining. *Applied Mathematics and Computation, 205*(2), 735–750. doi:10.1016/j.amc.2008.05.020

Tjioe, H. C., & Taniar, D. (2005). Mining Association Rules in Data Warehouses. *International Journal of Data Warehousing and Mining, 1*(3), 28–62. doi:10.4018/jdwm.2005070103

Tong, Q., Yan, B., & Zhou, Y. (2005). Mining quantitative association rules on overlapped intervals. In *Advanced Data Mining and Applications* (LNCS 3584, pp. 43-50).

Wang, Q., Shi, D., He, B., & Cai, Q. (2001). Research on linear association rules. *Mini-Micro System, 22*(11), 1349–1352.

Yu, G., Shao, S., Luo, B., & Zeng, X. (2009). A Hybrid Method for High-Utility Itemsets Mining in Large High-Dimensional Data. *International Journal of Data Warehousing and Mining, 5*(1), 57–73. doi:10.4018/jdwm.2009010104

Zaki, M. J. (2000). Generating non-redundant association rules. In *Proceedings of the 6th ACM SIGKDD International Conference on Knowledge Discovery and Data Mining* (pp. 34-43). New York, NY: ACM.

This work was previously published in the International Journal of Data Warehousing and Mining, Volume 7, Issue 3, edited by David Taniar, pp. 50-87, copyright 2011 by IGI Publishing (an imprint of IGI Global).

Chapter 11
Decision Rule Extraction for Regularized Multiple Criteria Linear Programming Model

DongHong Sun
Tsinghua University, China

Peng Zhang
Chinese Academy of Sciences, China

Li Liu
University of Technology, Sydney, Australia

Xingquan Zhu
University of Technology, Sydney, Australia

Yong Shi
Chinese Academy of Sciences, China, & University of Nebraska at Omaha, USA

ABSTRACT

Due to the flexibility of multi-criteria optimization, Regularized Multiple Criteria Linear Programming (RMCLP) has received attention in decision support systems. Numerous theoretical and empirical studies have demonstrated that RMCLP is effective and efficient in classifying large scale data sets. However, a possible limitation of RMCLP is poor interpretability and low comprehensibility for end users and experts. This deficiency has limited RMCLP's use in many real-world applications where both accuracy and transparency of decision making are required, such as in Customer Relationship Management (CRM) and Credit Card Portfolio Management. In this paper, the authors present a clustering based rule extraction method to extract explainable and understandable rules from the RMCLP model. Experiments on both synthetic and real world data sets demonstrate that this rule extraction method can effectively extract explicit decision rules from RMCLP with only a small compromise in performance.

INTRODUCTION

With the development of large storage equipment and high performance computing technology, we are now able to collect large volumes of data from different sources. Discovering hidden patterns and useful knowledge from such large volume data to support decision making has become a pressing task for modern intelligent systems.

To meet this requirement, a new discipline called Data Mining (Olson & Shi, 2007; Peng, Kou, Shi, & Chen, 2008) has emerged, in which

DOI: 10.4018/978-1-4666-2148-0.ch011

a number of learning methods are proposed to extract knowledge from large scale databases. Depending on the data characteristics and mining objectives, existing data mining models can be categorized into three types: association rule mining, clustering unlabeled data, and generating prediction models from labeled data (Zhang, Zhu, & Shi, 2008; Zhu, Zhang, Lin, & Shi, 2010; Qin, Zhang, & Zhang, 2010).

In the domain of classification, many effective models have been proposed in recent years, such as the decision tree model (Breiman, Friedman, Olshen, & Stone, 1984), Artificial Neural Networks (ANN) (Aleksander & Morton, 1990), and Support Vector Machines (SVMs) (Vapnik, 1998). According to their differences in utilizing decision logics, these models can be further categorized into two types: transparent models or non-transparent models.

Transparent models provide explicit (transparent) decision logics (such as decision rules or decision trees) from training samples, so that predictions are highly understandable for end users. Transparent decision making is, in fact, required in many business-related applications or medical systems in which decisions must be understandable by domain experts.

The decision logics of non-transparent decision models, such as SVMs, ANNs and others, on the other hand, are like black-box models and are not interpretable by human experts. Although users are able to obtain a prediction, example, they are nevertheless incapable of knowing the logic or the reasons as to why such a prediction is made. Compared to transparent models, which are widely used in human society, non-transparent black-box models are often used in machine society where explanation of the mining results is less important.

A family of Multiple Criteria Mathematical Programming (MCMP) based classification models (Shi, Liu, Yan, & Chen, 2008c) has recently been proposed for data classification.

Shi (2001), Shi, Wise, Lou, and Lin (2001), Shi, Peng, Xu, and Tang (2002), and Kou, Liu, and Peng (2003) proposed the use of Multiple Criteria Linear Programming (MCLP) for credit card fraud detection. Based on the MCLP model, He, Liu, and Shi (2004) and He, Shi, and Xu (2004) further proposed a Fuzzy Multiple Criteria Linear Programming (FMCLP) model and a Multiple Criteria Nonlinear Programming (MCNP) model for credit card analysis.

Kou, Peng, Shi, and Chen (2006c) proposed a Multiple Criteria Quadratic Programming (MCQP) model by adapting the linear objective functions of MCLP to quadratic ones. Kou, Peng, Shi, and Chen (2006a, 2006b) also proposed a multiple groups MCLP model to solve the multiple groups classification problem of MCLP.

Following promising results from MCQP, Kou, Peng, Chen, and Shi (2009) stepped forward and proposed a kernel-based MCQP method which extends MCQP to nonlinear classification problems. Further to this method, Zhang and Tian (2007) proposed a kernelized MCLP by adopting the inner product form of SVM to MCLP, which is a popular method for extending a linear classifier to non-linear one.

Zhang, Zhu, Zhang, and Shi (2010) and Zhang, Zhang, and Shi (2007) proposed a MQLC model for VIP E-mail Analysis. Based on rough set theory, Zhang, Shi, Zhang, and Gao (2008) proposed a rough set-based MCLP model and reported its efficiency on several UCI benchmark datasets.

Shi, Tian, Chen, and Zhang (2007) and Zhang, Tian, Li, Zhang, and Shi (2008) proposed a RMCLP model and compared its accuracy on both synthetic and UCI benchmark datasets with several other multiple criteria programming models, such as MCLP and MCQP, and the well-known SVM model. All these results show that RMCLP is a promising method for classification, and its prediction accuracies are superior to other models on many UCI datasets. For ease of understanding, the family of multiple criteria programming models (Shi, Liu, Yan, & Chen, 2008a, 2008b) is described in Figure 1.

Figure 1. The family of multiple criteria programming models for classification. Fuzzy MCLP, rough MCLP, MCQP and RMCLP models were proposed to enhance the original MCLP model's performance. To solve multi-group classification problems, many multi-group classification models (e.g., multi-group MCLP, multi-group MCQP, and multi-group RMCLP) were proposed. To solve non-linear classification problems, the kernelized MCLP method listed on the left side were proposed.

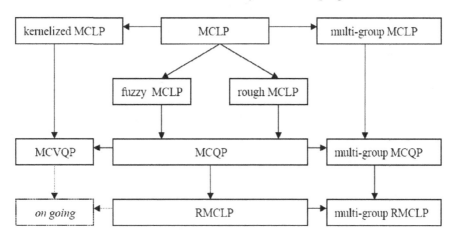

Although many theoretical and empirical studies have demonstrated that RMCLP is an effective model for classification, a major disadvantage of RMCLP is that it merely generates unexplainable black-box models, which prevents its use in many applications where high interpretability for decision making and reasoning is necessary. For example, in credit card portfolio management, RMCLP is able to predict the high-risk customers, but is unable to tell why these customers are assigned high-risk scores.

In this paper, we present a clustering-based rule extraction method to generate decision rules from the black box RCMLP model. Our method can improve the interpretability of the RMCLP model by using explicit and explainable decision rules. To achieve this goal, a clustering algorithm will first be used to generate prototypes (which are the clustering centers) for each group of examples identified by the RMCLP model. Then, hyper cubes (whose edges are parallel to the axes) will be extracted around each prototype. This procedure will be repeated until all the training examples are covered by a hyper cube. Finally, the hyper cubes

will be translated to a set of *if-then* decision rules. Experiments on both synthetic and real world data sets have demonstrate the effectiveness of our rule extraction method.

The rest of this paper is organized as follows. In Section 2, we provide a brief introduction to the RMCLP model. Section 3 presents our clustering-based rule extraction algorithm. Experiments and comparisons are reported in Section 4. Finally, we conclude this paper in Section 5.

REGULARIZED MULTIPLE CRITERIA LINEAR PROGRAMMING (RMCLP) CLASSIFICATION MODEL

In this section, we will introduce the formulation of the RMCLP model. Since the RMCLP model originates from the multiple criteria linear programming (MCLP) model (Shi et al., 2001), we will first introduce the MCLP model.

Assume we have two groups of training examples $A = \{a_i\}_{i=1}^{n}$, each of which has r attributes, the MCLP model tries to find a projection direc-

Figure 2. An illustration of a two-group MCLP classification model. Examples in G_1 are denoted by black dot while in G_2 are denoted by stars. If an example is perfectly classified, then classification boundary will equal to b; otherwise, two relaxed boundaries $b - u^*$ and $b + u^*$ will be used to separate the misclassified examples.

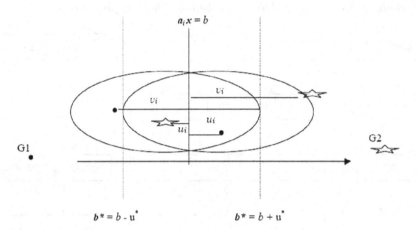

tion x and a boundary b such that all the examples in the first group G_1 and the second group G_2 can be separated as far as possible. To achieve this goal, MCLP first defines an internal measurement vector $u \in R_+^n$ to measure the overlapping degree between boundary b and each training example a_i, and then defines an external measurement vector $v \in R_+^n$ to measure the distance between each training example a_i and the adjusted boundary $b*$ (where $b* = b - u_i$ or $b* = b + u_i$).

The objective of the MCLP model is to minimize the internal measurement $u \in R_+^n$, and meanwhile maximize the external measurement $v \in R_+^n$. By using the weight vectors $d, c \in R_{1*2n}$ to combine the two objectives, the MCLP model can be formulated as follow:

$$\min_{u,v} \quad d^t u - c^t u$$
$$s.t. :$$
$$a_i x - u_i + v_i = b, \ a_i \in G_1$$
$$a_i x - u_i + v_i = b, \ a_i \in G_2$$

(1)

To make Equation 1 much easier to understand, we give an example in Figure 2 for illustration.

The MCLP model is a special linear programming, which always has a solution. Obviously, the feasible set of MCLP is nonempty, as the zero vector is a feasible point. However, when $c \geq 0$, the objective function may not always have a lower bound on the feasible set. To ensure the existence of a solution, RMCLP adds two regularization terms $\frac{1}{2} x^T H x$ and $\frac{1}{2} u^T Q u$ in the objective function of Equation 1, and thus can be formulated as follows:

$$Min_z \frac{1}{2} x^T H x + \frac{1}{2} u^T Q u + d^T u - c^T v$$
$$s.t. :$$
$$a_i x - u_i + v_i = b, \ \forall a_i \in G_1; \qquad (2)$$
$$a_i x + u_i - v_i = b, \ \forall a_i \in G_2;$$
$$u_i, v_i \geq 0.$$

where $z = (x, u, v, b) \in R^{r+2n+1}$, $H \in R^{r*r}$ and $Q \in R^{n*n}$ are symmetric positive definite matrices.

Algorithm 1. Build RMCLP model

Input: The training sample $A = \{a_1, a_2, ..., a_n\}$, training percentage p
Output: RMCLP model
Begin
Step 1. Randomly select $p*|x|$ examples as the training set **TR**, the remaining examples are combined as the testing set **TS**;
Step 2. Choose appropriate parameters of (H, Q, d, c) ;
Step 3. Apply the RMCLP model Equation 2 to compute the optimal solution $x^* = (x_1, x_2, ..., x_n)$ as the projection direction and b as the boundary;
Step 4. if the classification result of Step 3 is unacceptable, choose different values of control parameters (H, Q, d, c) and go back to Step 1;
Step 5. Output $y = sgn(Ax-b)$ as the model.
End

The RMCLP model in Equation 2 is a convex quadratic program. Although the objective function $f(z) := \frac{1}{2}x^T H x + \frac{1}{2}u^T Q u + d^T u - c^T v$ is not a strictly convex function, it always has a solution. Furthermore, the solution of Equation 2 is bounded if H, Q, d, c are chosen wisely.

Assume there are l examples in group G_1, let $I_1 \in R^{l*l}$, $I_2 \in R^{(n-l)*(n-l)}$ be identity matrices,

$$A_1 = \begin{pmatrix} a_1 \\ ... \\ a_l \end{pmatrix}, \qquad A_2 = \begin{pmatrix} a_{l+1} \\ ... \\ a_n \end{pmatrix}, \qquad A = \begin{pmatrix} A_1 \\ A_2 \end{pmatrix},$$

$$E = \begin{pmatrix} -I_1 & \\ & I_2 \end{pmatrix},$$ and $e \in R^n$ be the vector with all elements to be 1. Let $B = (A \quad E - E - e)$, the feasible set of Equation 2 is given by $F = \{z \mid Bz = 0, u \geq 0, v \geq 0\}$.

Because Equation 2 is a convex program with linear constraints, KKT condition is a necessary and sufficient condition for optimality. To show that $f(z)$ is bounded on F, Shi et al. (2007) gives the following two Theorems:

(1) According to the Frank-Wolfe Theorem (Shi et al., 2007), RMCLP always has a solution;
(2) Suppose that $AH^{-1}A^T$ is nonsingular. Let $G = (AH^{-1}A^T)^{-1}$, $\mu = 1 / e^T G e$ and

$$M = \begin{pmatrix} Q + EGE - \mu EGee^T GE & \mu EGee^T GE - EGE \\ -EGE - \mu EGee^T GE & EGE - \mu EGee^T GE \end{pmatrix},$$

$$q = \begin{pmatrix} d \\ -c \end{pmatrix}, y = \begin{pmatrix} u \\ v \end{pmatrix},$$ Equation 2 is equivalent to the linear complementarity problem $My + q \geq 0, y \geq 0, y^T(My + q) = 0$. If Q and H are chosen appropriately (which makes M a positive semi-definite matrix), and vectors c, d satisfy $d + 2Qe > (\mu EGee^T GE - EGE)e > c$, then Equation 2 has a nonempty and bonded solution set. Algorithm 1 lists the detailed procedures on building the RMCLP model.

RULE EXTRACTION METHOD FOR RMCLP

The Framework of the Rule Extraction Algorithm

As we discussed above, many mathematical programming-based classification models (e.g., SVM, ANN, and RMCLP) are black-box models which can only give results without reasons. To overcome this shortcoming, a number of methods have been proposed to open these black-box models to obtain explainable rules. These approaches can be categorized into two types: decompositional method and pedagogical method (Martens, Baesens, Gestelc, & Vanthienena, 2007).

Decompositional method is closely intertwined with the internal structure of models. For example, in 2002, Nunez, Angulo, and Catala proposed a clustering-based rule extraction of SVM models by creating rule-defining regions based on prototype and support vectors. The extracted rules are represented by equation rules and interval rules. In 2005, Fung, Sandilya, and Bharat proposed a non-overlapping rule by constructing hyper cubes with axis-parallel surfaces, which directly extracts rules by using hierarchical learning procedure. For example, after building a SVM model, a rule-extraction algorithm (e.g., C4.5) is again used to extract rules from each generated group (Craven, 1996; Craven & Shavlik, 1996).

In this paper, we present a clustering-based rule extraction method to extract rules from the RMCLP model. The procedure can be described as follows: firstly, a traditional RMCLP model is built and all training examples are classified into one class. In each class, a clustering method (e.g., a K-Means model) will be used to derive several prototype points (which are the cluster centers).

The distance between the prototype points and the classification boundary will then be calculated to decide the length of each edge of the hyper cubes. Next, a series of hyper cubes will be generated with all edges parallel to the axes and one vertex on the classification boundary. Moreover, if not all examples are covered by the hyper cubes, new prototypes will be generated from the remaining uncovered examples and new hyper cubes will be generated until all training examples are covered. Finally, all the hyper cubes will be translated to *if-then* decision rules.

Compared with the original RMCLP model, these decision rules are much easier to understand and explain. For ease of understanding, we list the whole rule extraction procedure in Algorithm 2.

There are two key steps in Algorithm 2, Steps 3.2 and 3.3. In Step 3.2, a distance function $d = Distance(f, P_i)$ will be calculated; while in Step 3.3, a hyper cube H is generated according to the prototype point p and the pre-computed distance d.

Algorithm 2. Extract rules from MCLP models

Input: The data set $A = \{a_1, a_2, ..., a_n\}$, RMCLP model f
Output: Rule Set $\{w\}$
Begin
Step 1. Classify all the examples in A using model f;
Step 2. Define Covered set $C = \Phi$, Uncovered set $U = A$;
Step 3. **While** (*U is not empty*) do
Step 3.1 **For** each group G_i
 Calculate the clustering center $P_i = Kmeans(G_i \cap U)$;
 End for
Step 3.2 Calculate distances between each P_i and boundary $d = Distance(f, P_i)$;
Step 3.3 Draw a new hypercube $H = DrawHC(d, P_i)$;
Step 3.4 **For** all the examples $a_i \in U$,
 If a_i is covered by H
  $U = U \setminus a_i, C = C \cup a_i$;;
 End If
 End For
 End While
Step 4 Translate each hypercube H into rule;
Step 5 Return the rule set $\{w\}$
End

For ease of description, we introduce some notations first. Assume a r-dimensional space, the coordinate of the clustering center p is $p=(p_1, .., p_r)$, and the classification hyper plane is $\sum_{i=1}^{r} a_i x_i = b$ (where x_i is the direction of the hyper plane). For each class, we prefer hyper cubes which cover as many examples as possible. Intuitively, if we pick a point u on the classification boundary and then draw cubes based on both clustering center p and u, then the generated hyper cube will cover the largest area with respect to the current prototype p. The distance from p to the hyper plane can be calculated by Equation 3 as follows:

$$d = \text{Distance}(f, p_i) = \sum_{i=1}^{r} \frac{p_i x_i - b}{\sqrt{x_i^2}} \qquad (3)$$

After computing d, Step 3.3 draws hyper cubes $H=DrawHC(d, P_i)$ by using the prototype point P_i as the central point, and each edge has a length of $\sqrt{2}d$ meanwhile parallel with the axis. By so doing, we can get *if-then* rules which are easy to understand. For example, for a specific example $a_1 \in G_1$, a decision rule can be described in the following form:

$$if(l_1 \leq a_{11} \leq u_1)and(l_2 \leq a_{12} \leq u_2)......and$$
$$(l_r \leq a_{1r} \leq u_r)then\ a_1\ belongs\ to\ class\ 1 \qquad (4)$$

Figure 3 illustrates an example with two dimensions. Examples in G_1 $(a_i \in G_1)$ are covered by hyper cubes with a central point as its clustering center and a vertex on the hyper plane $\sum_{i=1}^{r} a_i x_i = b$.

Time Complexity Analysis

The main computational cost of Algorithm 2 is from Steps 3.1~3.3, where a KMeans clustering model and two distance functions are calculated. Assume there are l iterations of KMeans. In each iteration, there are k clusters. Therefore, the total time complexity of KMeans will be O($lknr$), where n is the number of training examples, r is the number of dimensions.

Figure 3. An illustration of Algorithm 2 which generates hyper cubes from RMCLP models. Based on the RMCLP model's decision boundary (the red line), Algorithm 2 first calculates several clustering centers for each class (e.g., the red circle in Group 1), then it calculates the distance d from the classification boundary to the clustering center (the blue line). After that, it generates a series of hyper cubes. Each hyper cube's edge is parallel to the axes and the length is $\sqrt{2}d$. Finally, the hyper cubes can be easily translated into rules that are explainable and understandable.

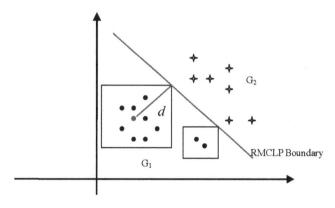

On the other hand, calculating distance d for each clustering center by Equation 3 will take a linear time complexity, so the computational cost of Step 3.2 will be $O(k)$ for k clustering centers. Finally, the time cost of extracting hyper cubes in Step 3.3 will be $O(kr)$ for k clustering centers in r dimensional space. To sum up, the total computational complexity of Algorithm 2 can be denoted by Equation 5,

$$O(lknr) + O(k) + O(kr) = O(lknr) \qquad (5)$$

The above analysis indicates that the hyper cube extracting method in Steps 3.2 and 3.3 is dominated by the KMeans clustering model in Step 3.1. It is in linear time complexity with respect to training example size.

EXPERIMENTS

Experimental Settings

To demonstrate the effectiveness of the proposed rules extraction method, we will test our method on both synthetic and real world data sets. The whole testing system is implemented in a Java environment by integrating WEKA data mining tools (Witten & Frank, 2005). The clustering method used in our experiments is the *simpleK-Means* package in WEKA.

Synthetic Dataset

As shown in Figure 4(a), we generate a 2-dimensional 2-class data set containing 60 examples, with 30 examples for each class. In each class, we use 50% of the examples to train a RMCLP model. That is, 30 training examples in total are used to train the RMCLP model. All examples comply with Gaussian distribution $x \sim N(\mu, \Sigma)$, where μ is mean vector and Σ is covariate matrix. The first group is generated by a mean vector $\mu_1 =$

[1,1] with a covariance matrix $\sum_1 = \begin{pmatrix} 0.1 & 0 \\ 0 & 0.1 \end{pmatrix}$

The second group is generated by a mean vector $\mu_2 = [2,2]$ with a covariance matrix $\Sigma_2 = \Sigma_1$.

Here we only discuss the two-group classification problem. It is not difficult to extend to multiple-group classification applications. It is expected to extract knowledge from the RMCLP model in the form of:

if $(a \leq x1 \leq b, c \leq x2 \leq d)$ then Definition 1 (6)

The result is shown in Figure 4(b); we can observe that for the total of 60 examples, three examples in group 1, and one example in group 2 are misclassified by the RMCLP model. That is to say, the accuracy of RMCLP on this synthetic dataset is 56/60=93.3%. By using our rule extraction algorithm, we can generate nine squares, 4 squares for group 1, and 5 squares for group 2. All the squares can be translated to explainable rules in the form of (6) as follows:

- K_1: If $0.6 \leq x_1 \leq 0.8$ and $2 \leq x_2 \leq 2.8$, then $x \in G_1$.
- K_2: If $1.1 \leq x_1 \leq 1.3$ and $1.8 \leq x_2 \leq 2.1$, then $x \in G_1$.
- K_3: If $0.4 \leq x_1 \leq 1.5$ and $-1 \leq x_2 \leq 1.6$, then $x \in G_1$.
- K_4: If $0.9 \leq x_1 \leq 2.2$ and $-0.8 \leq x_2 \leq 0$, then $x \in G_1$.
- K_5: If $1.2 \leq x_1 \leq 1.6$ and $2.2 \leq x_2 \leq 3.2$, then $x \in G_2$.
- K_6: If $1.4 \leq x_1 \leq 1.6$ and $1.8 \leq x_2 \leq 2.0$, then $x \in G_2$.
- K_7: If $1.7 \leq x_1 \leq 2.8$ and $1.0 \leq x_2 \leq 4.0$, then $x \in G_2$.
- K_8: If $1.9 \leq x_1 \leq 2.0$ and $0.7 \leq x_2 \leq 0.8$, then $x \in G_2$.
- K_9: If $2.1 \leq x_1 \leq 2.4$ and $0.1 \leq x_2 \leq 0.5$, then $x \in G_2$.

Figure 4. (a) The synthetic dataset; (b) Experimental results. The straight line is the RMCLP model's classification boundary, and the squares are hyper cubes generated by using Algorithm 2. All the examples are covered by the squares whose edges are parallel to the axes.

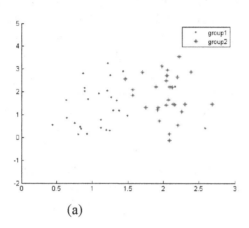

(a)

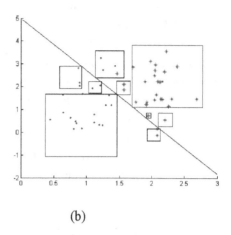

(b)

where k_i $(i=1, .., 9)$ denotes the ith rule. From the results on this synthetic data set, we can observe that by using the proposed rule extraction method, we can not only obtain prediction results from RMCLP, but also comprehensible rule.

Real World VIP E-Mail Dataset

As one of the basic services offered by the Internet, e-mail usage is becoming increasingly widely adopted. Along with constant global network expansion and network technology improvement, people's expectations of an e-mail service are increasingly demanding. E-mail is no longer merely a communication tool for people to share their ideas and information; its wide acceptance and technological advancement has given it the characteristics of a business service (Thomsen & Pedersen, 2009), and it is being commercialized as a technological product.

At the same time, many business and specialized personal users of e-mail want an e-mail account that is safe, reliable, and equipped with a first class customer support service. Therefore, many websites have developed their own user-pays e-mail service to satisfy this market demand.

According to statistics, the Chinese network has advanced so much in the past few years that, by 2005, the total market size of Chinese VIP e-mail services reached 6.4 hundred million RMB. This enormous market demand and market prospect also means increasing competition between the suppliers. How to analyze the pattern of lost customer accounts and decrease the customer loss rate have become a focal point of competition in today's market (Zhang et al., 2007, 2010).

Our partner company's VIP e-mail data are mainly stored in two kinds of repository systems; one is customer databases, the other is log files. They are mainly composed of automated machine recorded customer activity journals and large amount of manually recorded tables; these data are distributed among servers located in different departments of our partnering companies, coving more than 30 kinds of transaction data charts and journal documents, with over 600 attributes.

If we were to directly analysis these data, it would lead to a "course of dimensionality", that is to say, a drastic rise in computational complexity and classification error with data of large dimensions. Hence, the dimensionality of the feature space must be reduced before classification is undertaken. According to the accumulated experience functions, we eventually selected 230 attributes from the original 600 attributes.

Figure 5 displays the procedure of feature selection of the VIP e-mail dataset. We selected a part of the data charts and journal documents from the VIP E-mail System. The left upper part of Figure 5 displays the three logging journal documents and two e-mail transaction journal documents; when the user logs into the pop3 server, the machine will record the user's login into the log file *pop3login*; similarly when the user logs into the smtp server, the machine will record this into the log file *smtplogin*; when the user logs into the e-mail system through http protocol, the machine will record it into the log file *weblogin*; when the user successfully sends an e-mail by smtp protocol, the system will record it into the log file *smtprcptlog*; when receiving a letter, it will be recorded into the log file *mx_rcptlog*.

We extracted 37 attributes from these five log files, that is, 184 attributes in total, to describe user logins and transactions. From the databases, shown in the left lower section of Figure 3, we extracted six features about "customer complaint

about the VIP E-mail Service", 24 features about "customer payment" and 16 features about "customer's personal information" (for example, age, gender, occupation, income, etc.) to form the operational table. Thus, 185 features from log files and 65 features from databases eventually formed the Large Table, and the 230 attributes depicted the features of the customers. The accumulated experience functions used in the feature selection are confidential, and further discussion of them exceeds the range of this paper.

Considering the integrality of the customer records, we eventually extracted two groups from a huge number of data: the current and the lost. 10996 customers, 5498 for each class, were chosen from the dataset. Combining the 10996 SSN with the 230 features, we eventually acquired the Large Table with 5498 current records and 5498 lost records, which became the dataset for data mining.

Table 1 lists the ten-folder cross validation results of the RMCLP model's performance on the VIP E-mail Dataset. The columns "LOST" and "CURRENT" refer to the number of records that were correctly classified as "lost" and "current" respectively. The column "Accuracy" was calcu-

Figure 5. The roadmap of the VIP e-mail dataset

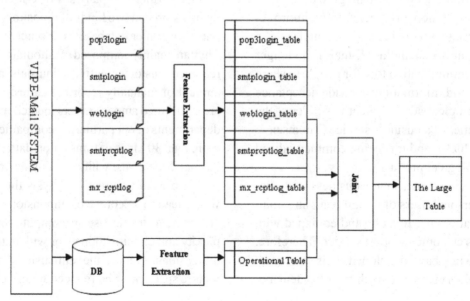

Table 1. Ten folder cross validation on VIP E-mail Dataset

Cross Validation	Training Set (500 Bad data+500 Good data)				Testing Set (4998 Bad data+4998 Good data)			
	LOST	Accuracy	CURRENT	Accuracy	LOST	Accuracy	CURRENT	Accuracy
DataSet 1	444	88.80%	455	91.00%	4048	80.99%	4311	86.25%
DataSet 2	447	89.40%	459	91.80%	4081	81.65%	4355	87.13%
DataSet 3	449	89.80%	465	93.00%	4079	81.61%	4362	87.27%
DataSet 4	440	88.00%	467	93.40%	4006	80.15%	4286	85.75%
DataSet 5	435	87.00%	460	92.00%	4010	80.23%	4420	88.44%
DataSet 6	436	87.20%	460	92.00%	3995	79.93%	4340	86.83%
DataSet 7	445	89.00%	464	92.80%	4008	80.19%	4403	88.10%
DataSet 8	443	88.60%	455	91.00%	4052	81.07%	4292	85.87%
DataSet 9	429	85.80%	457	91.40%	3955	79.13%	4436	88.76%
DataSet 10	440	88.00%	456	91.20%	4087	81.77%	4355	87.13%

lated using correctly classified records divided by the total records in that class. From Table 1, we can observe that the average prediction accuracy of the RMLCP on this data set is 80.67% on the first class and 87.15% on the second class. That is, on the whole 10996 test examples, the average accuracy of RMCLP is 83.91%.

As discussed above, a decision tree is widely used to extract rules from training examples. In the following experiments, we will compare our

method with a decision tree (which is implemented by the WEKA *J48* package).

Table 2 shows the comparison results between our method and the decision tree. By using our rule extraction method, we obtain more than 20 hyper cubes. Due to space limitation, we only list the two most representative rules (i.e., Rule 1 for class "LOST" and Rule 6 for class "CURRENT") in the left side of Table 2. Then we find the corresponding rules from the decision tree

Table 2. Comparisons between RMCLP's rule and decision tree's rule

RMCLP's Rule	Decision Tree's Rule
RULE 1: if 0<= The number of e-mails<= 3 *and* 0<=the number of POP3 login on Tuesday <= 6 *and* 0<=the number of HTTP login <= 1 *and* 0<=Free E-mail Service <= 1 *and* 0<=The percentage of Charge Type 7<= 0.3 *and* 0<=The total Charge Fee<= 45 ... then *class LOST* [0.816]	**RULE 1':** if The number of e-mails <= 1 *and* the number of POP3 login on Tuesday <= 3 *and* number of HTTP login <= 1 *and* Free E-mail Service = 1 *and* The percentage of Charge Type 7 <= 0.25 *and* The total Charge Fee <= 50 ... then *class LOST* [0.746]
RULE 6: if 0<= The number of HTTP Login <= 5 *and* 0<=Free E-mail Service Status <= 1 *and* 0.2<=The percentage of Charge Type 11<= 0.5 *and* 0<=The total Charge Fee<= 4 *and* 0<= The number of e-mails<= 3 *and* 0<=CONTACT_NUMBER<=1 *and* 0<=IDNUM<=1 ... then *class CURRENT* [0.802]	**RULE 6':** if The number of HTTP Login <= 3 *and* Free E-mail Service Status = 0 *and* The percentage of Charge Type 11 > 0.294 *and* The total Charge Fee <= 5 *and* The number of e-mails <= 1 *and* CONTACT_NUMBER = 1 *and* IDNUM = 0 ... then *class CURRENT* [0.739]
Average Accuracy: 80.90%	**Average Accuracy: 74.25%**

(i.e., Rule 1' for class "LOST" and Rule 6' for class "CURRENT"), and list them in the right side of Table 2.

From these results, we can observe that our rule extraction method acquires much more accurate rules than the decision tree method. For example, when comparing Rule 1 with Rule 1', we can safely say that Rule 1 is supported by 81.6% examples in the "LOST" class; by contrast, rules from decision tree only get 74.6% supportive examples. Similarly, when comparing Rule 6 with Rule 6', our method also achieves better support than the decision tree.

At the bottom of Table 2, we list the average accuracy of the two methods. It is obvious that the average accuracy of rules extracted from RMCLP is 80.90%. This is better than the decision tree's accuracy of 74.25%. Moreover, compared to the RMCLP's performance in Table 1 (which equals 83.91%), we can say that the average accuracy of the extracted rules (i.e., 80.90%) suffers only a little loss in performance. Therefore, our rule extraction method from the RMCLP model can effectively extract comprehensible rules from the RMCLP model.

CONCLUSION

Regularized Multiple Criteria Linear Programming (RMCLP) has recently received much attention in relation to complex decision making. However, like many other mathematical programming-based classification models, RMCLP suffers from an inherent disadvantage of poor interpretability and low comprehensibility for end users. This shortcoming prevents RMCLP from being used in many real-world applications where both accuracy and comprehensibility are required, such as in business intelligence, healthcare, or customer relationship management. To overcome this limitation, we present in this paper a clustering-based method to extract decision rules

from RMCLP models. Our method first extracts hyper cubes whose edges are parallel to the axes. All the hyper cubes are then translated to a set of explicit self-explainable rules. Experimental results on both synthetic and real-world datasets demonstrate its effectiveness in acquiring accurate rules from an RMCLP model.

Many interesting works exist for future investigations. For example, the rule extraction model presented in this paper can only be used to extract decision rules from linear classification models. For non-linear models, for example, Kou et al. (2006c, 2009) proposed a MCVQP model with non-linear kernel functions, our method may not be able to achieve satisfactory results. Besides, the hyper cubes generated by our algorithm may heavily overlap with each other, so how to decrease the overlapping degree so that the generated rules are much more concise is another direction for future work.

ACKNOWLEDGMENT

This work was partially supported by the National Natural Science Foundation of China (NSFC #61003167, #60803134, #90812001, #70621001, #70921061), the Chinese Academy of Sciences (Grant for Overseas Collaboration Group), and the Australian Research Council Discovery Project scheme under grant No. DP1093762.

REFERENCES

Aleksander, I., & Morton, H. (1990). *An introduction to neural computing*. London, UK: Chapman and Hall.

Breiman, L., Friedman, J., Olshen, R., & Stone, C. (1984). *Classification and regression trees*. Monterey, CA: Wadsworth & Brooks/Cole Advanced Books & Software.

Craven, M. W. (1996). *Extracting comprehensible models from trained neural networks.* Unpublished doctoral dissertation, University of Wisconsin-Madison, Madison, WI.

Craven, M. W., & Shavlik, J. W. (1996). Extracting tree-structured representations of trained neural networks. In *Proceedings of the Conference on Advances in Neural Information Processing Systems* (pp. 824-830).

Fung, G., Sandilya, S., & Bharat, R. (2005). Rule extraction from linear support vector machines. In *Proceedings of the KDD 2005 Conference* (pp. 32-40).

He, J., Liu, X., & Shi, Y. (2004). Classifications of credit card holder behavior by using fuzzy linear programming. *International Journal of Information Technology and Decision Making, 3*(4), 633–650. doi:10.1142/S021962200400129X

He, J., Shi, Y., & Xu, W. (2004). Classifications of credit cardholder behavior by using multiple criteria non-linear programming. In *Proceedings of the Chinese Academy of Sciences Symposium on Data Mining and Knowledge Management* (pp. 154-163).

Kou, G., Liu, X., & Peng, Y. (2003). Multiple criteria linear programming approach to data mining: Models, algorithm designs and software development. *Optimization Methods and Software, 18*(4), 453–473. doi:10.1080/1055678030001600953

Kou, G., Peng, Y., Chen, Z., & Shi, Y. (2009). Multiple criteria mathematical programming for multi-class classification and application in network intrusion detection. *Information Sciences, 179*(4), 371–381. doi:10.1016/j.ins.2008.10.025

Kou, G., Peng, Y., Shi, Y., & Chen, Z. (2006a). Network intrusion detection by multi-group mathematical programming based classifier. In *Proceedings of the ICDM Workshops, 2006,* 803–807.

Kou, G., Peng, Y., Shi, Y., & Chen, Z. (2006b). Multiclass credit cardholders; behaviors classification methods. In *Proceedings of the International Conference on Computational Science* (pp. 485-492).

Kou, G., Peng, Y., Shi, Y., & Chen, Z. (2006c). A new multi-criteria convex quadratic programming model for credit analysis. In *Proceedings of the International Conference on Computational Science* (pp. 476-484).

Martens, D., Baesens, B., Gestelc, T., & Vanthienena, J. (2007). Comprehensible credit scoring models using rule extraction from support vector machines. *European Journal of Operational Research, 183*(3), 1466–1476. doi:10.1016/j.ejor.2006.04.051

Nunez, H., Angulo, C., & Catala, A. (2002). Rule based learning systems from SVMs. In *Proceedings of the European Symposium on Artificial Neural Networks* (pp. 107-112).

Olson, D., & Shi, Y. (2007). *Introduction to business data mining.* New York, NY: McGraw-Hill/Irwin.

Peng, Y., Kou, G., Shi, Y., & Chen, Z. (2008). A descriptive framework for the field of data mining and knowledge discovery. *International Journal of Information Technology and Decision Making, 7*(4), 639–682. doi:10.1142/S0219622008003204

Qin, Y., Zhang, S., & Zhang, C. (2010). Combining kNN imputation and Bootstrap calibrated: Empirical likelihood for incomplete data analysis. *International Journal of Data Warehousing and Mining, 6*(4), 61–73. doi:10.4018/jdwm.2010100104

Shi, Y. (2001). *Multiple criteria and multiple constraint levels linear programming: Concepts, techniques and applications.* Singapore: World Scientific.

Shi, Y., Liu, R., Yan, N., & Chen, Z. (2008a). A family of optimization based data mining methods. In *Proceedings of the APWeb 2008 Conference* (pp. 26-38).

Shi, Y., Liu, R., Yan, N., & Chen, Z. (2008b). Multiple criteria mathematical programming and data mining. In *Proceedings of the International Conference on Computational Science* (pp. 7-17).

Shi, Y., Liu, R., Yan, N., & Chen, Z. (2008c). A family of optimization based data mining methods. In *Proceedings of the APWeb 2008 Conference* (pp. 26-38).

Shi, Y., Peng, Y., Xu, W., & Tang, X. (2002). Data mining via multiple criteria linear programming: Applications in credit card portfolio management. *International Journal of Information Technology and Decision Making, 1*, 131–151. doi:10.1142/S0219622002000038

Shi, Y., Tian, Y., Chen, X., & Zhang, P. (2007). A regularized multiple criteria linear program for classification. In *Proceedings of the ICDM 2007 Workshops* (pp. 253-258).

Shi, Y., Wise, M., Luo, M., & Lin, Y. (2001). Data mining in credit card portfolio management: a multiple criteria decision making approach. In *Multiple Criteria Decision Making in the New Millennium* (pp. 427-436).

Thomsen, C., & Pedersen, T. (2009). A survey of open source tools for business intelligence. *International Journal of Data Warehousing and Mining, 5*(3), 56–75. doi:10.4018/jdwm.2009070103

Vapnik, V. (1998). *Statistical learning theory.* New York, NY: Wiley.

Witten, I., & Frank, E. (2005). *Data mining: Practical machine learning tools and techniques.* Boston, MA: Morgan Kaufmann.

Zhang, P., Tian, Y., Li, X., Zhang, Z., & Shi, Y. (2008). Select representative samples for regularized multiple-criteria linear programming classification. In *Proceedings of the International Conference on Computational Science* (pp. 436-440).

Zhang, P., Zhang, J., & Shi, Y. (2007). A new multi-criteria quadratic-programming linear classification model for VIP email analysis. In *Proceedings of the International Conference on Computational Science* (pp. 499-502).

Zhang, P., Zhu, X., & Shi, Y. (2008). Categorizing and mining concept drifting data streams. In *Proceedings of the KDD 2008 Conference* (pp. 812-820).

Zhang, P., Zhu, X., Zhang, Z., & Shi, Y. (2010). Multiple criteria programming for VIP Email behavior analysis. *Web Intelligence & Agent Systems, 8*(1), 69–78.

Zhang, Z., Shi, Y., Zhang, P., & Gao, G. (2008). A rough set-based multiple criteria linear programming approach for classification. In *Proceedings of the International Conference on Computational Science* (pp. 476-485).

Zhang, Z., & Tian, Y. (2007). Kernelized multiple criteria linear programming. In *Proceedings of the 19th International Conference on Multiple Criteria Decision Making.*

Zhu, X., Zhang, P., Lin, X., & Shi, Y. (2010). Active learning from stream data using optimal weight classifier ensemble. *IEEE Transactions on System, Man, Cybernetics. Part B, 40*(6), 1607–1621.

This work was previously published in the International Journal of Data Warehousing and Mining, Volume 7, Issue 3, edited by David Taniar, pp. 88-104, copyright 2011 by IGI Publishing (an imprint of IGI Global).

Chapter 12
Incremental Algorithm for Discovering Frequent Subsequences in Multiple Data Streams

Reem Al-Mulla
University of Sharjah, UAE

Zaher Al Aghbari
University of Sharjah, UAE

ABSTRACT

In recent years, new applications emerged that produce data streams, such as stock data and sensor networks. Therefore, finding frequent subsequences, or clusters of subsequences, in data streams is an essential task in data mining. Data streams are continuous in nature, unbounded in size and have a high arrival rate. Due to these characteristics, traditional clustering algorithms fail to effectively find clusters in data streams. Thus, an efficient incremental algorithm is proposed to find frequent subsequences in multiple data streams. The described approach for finding frequent subsequences is by clustering subsequences of a data stream. The proposed algorithm uses a window model to buffer the continuous data streams. Further, it does not recompute the clustering results for the whole data stream at every window, but rather it builds on clustering results of previous windows. The proposed approach also employs a decay value for each discovered cluster to determine when to remove old clusters and retain recent ones. In addition, the proposed algorithm is efficient as it scans the data streams once and it is considered an Any-time algorithm since the frequent subsequences are ready at the end of every window.

DOI: 10.4018/978-1-4666-2148-0.ch012

INTRODUCTION

In recent years, many new applications emerged that generate data streams. Examples of applications that generate data streams are: financial applications, network monitoring, web applications, sensor networks, etc. (Tjioe & Taniar, 2005; Goh & Taniar, 2004). Unlike traditional static databases, data streams are continuous, unbounded in size, and usually with high arrival rate.

The nature of data streams poses some requirements when designing an algorithm to mine them such as finding the frequent subsequences. For example, since data streams are unbounded in size and have high arrival rate, algorithms are allowed only one look at the data. This means that algorithms for data streams may not have the chance to revisit the data twice. To solve this problem a buffer is used to collect the data temporarily for processing. A sliding window model (Zhu & Shasha, 2002) can be used to buffer *n* values of a data stream. Also the algorithm should be incremental, which means that the algorithm does not recompute the results after every window, but rather it only updates and builds on computed results of previous windows.

In this paper, we investigate finding frequent subsequences in multiple data streams. The approach of the proposed algorithm for finding frequent subsequences is by clustering subsequences of a data stream. A subsequence is considered to be frequent if the number of similar subsequences in a cluster is above a threshold value called support. Due to the challenging characteristics of data streams (continuous, unbounded in size, and usually with high arrival rate), the proposed algorithm is incremental, efficient and any-time algorithm. That is at the end of every window, the proposed algorithm does not recompute the clustering results of similar subsequences however it updates the previous clustering results. Therefore it employs a decay value for each discovered cluster to determine when to remove old clusters and retain recent ones. In addition, the proposed algorithm

is efficient as it scans the data streams once and also it is considered an Any-time algorithm since the frequent subsequences are ready at the end of every window.

Finding Frequent subsequences, or clusters of subsequences, can be used in many applications. For example, Network monitoring to discover common usage patterns, exploring common stocks' trend in financial markets, which will lead to good prediction of their future behavior, discovering web click patterns on websites would help website administrators in more efficient buffering and pre-fetching of busy web pages and in the placement of advertisements, and finding the load pattern on busy servers would assist system administrators in placing a more efficient load balancing scheme. Applications like the aforementioned ones and the lack of efficient and incremental algorithms for finding frequent subsequences motivated us to do this work.

Although there are many works on mining frequent itemsets over transactional data streams, little is done on mining frequent subsequences over streaming real-valued data. Also most of the works dealt with single a data stream, while the proposed algorithm deals with multiple data streams. The main contributions of this paper are:

- The proposed algorithm is incremental because clustering results of a current window is built on results of previous windows and also it employs a decay value to remove old frequent subsequences and retain the most recent frequent ones.
- The proposed algorithm is any-time algorithm since the clustering results of frequent subsequences are readily available at the end of every window.
- The proposed algorithm is an exact algorithm since no approximation for the data is used.
- The proposed algorithm is designed to be executed in parallel for multiple data streams.

The rest of this paper is organized as follows. Section 2 discusses the related work. In Section 3, we present some background information and formally define the problem and propose a solution. The proposed algorithm is presented in Section 4. In Section 5, we discuss the results of our experiments and show the feasibility of our approach. Finally, we conclude the paper in Section 6.

RELATED WORK

Finding frequent subsequences in data streams has received the attention of many researchers in the data mining community. One of the early works in designing incremental algorithms for mining frequent itemsets in data streams is the one presented by Manku and Motwani (2002). They introduced the lossy counting algorithm, which produces the frequent itemsets over the entire history of the data stream. The lossy counting algorithm inspired a number of researchers. For example, Li, Lee, and Shan (2004) used the estimation method for the support value in a lossy counting algorithm to produce a single pass algorithm for frequent itemsets mining. Their algorithm uses the prefix tree as a compact data structure for the frequent subsequences. Wong and Fu (2006) dealt with the problem of mining top *K* frequent itemsets by designing an algorithm based on a lossy counting method. Their algorithm would let the user specify the size of the result instead of specifying the support threshold.

Using the prefix tree as a data structure for maintaining the frequent itemsets in transactional data, has attracted many researchers. In Chang and Lee (2003), the authors used the prefix tree with a mechanism that gives less weight for old transactions. Jin and Agrawal (2005) developed a compact data structure for storing the frequent itemsets. This data structure benefited from the

prefix tree which gives a compact representation for the frequent itemsets, and benefited from the hash table which allows the deletion of the itemsets when they no longer needed. Other researchers, such as Mozafari, Thakkar, and Zaniolo (2008), were interested in using the FP-tree as the data structure to maintain the frequent itemsets. The FP-tree is an extension form of the prefix tree.

A graph structure for maintain the frequent itemsets was proposed by Naganthan and Dhanaseelan (2008). Li, Ho, and Lee (2009) proposed an algorithm for mining frequent closed itemsets using transaction sensitive sliding window. In a transaction sensitive sliding window model, the data captured in the window for processing is decided by a completed transaction. Raissi, Poncelet, and Teisseire (2007) were interested in finding the maximal frequent itemsets. Jiang (2006) proposed an algorithm with in-memory data structure for mining closed frequent itemset over data streams. An algorithm for mining the temporal high utility itemsets was introduced by Chu, Tseng, and Liang (2008). In Yu, Chong, Lu, Zhang, and Zhou (2006), the authors used a false-negative approach instead of a false-positive one to reduce the amount of consumed memory.

Lin, Hsueh, and Hwang (2008) claimed that using fix support threshold is not realistic and they developed an algorithm that would allow the user to change the support threshold after evaluating the produced results. Silvestri and Orlando (2007) introduced an algorithm that uses an interpolation method to infer the support of some itemsets that were infrequent in the past time windows, but are frequent in the current one. They used this method because keeping counter for each item would be very costly in term of memory consumption. Chu, Tseng, and Liang (2009) were interested in keeping track of the itemsets that are non-frequent in the current sliding window but may be frequent in the coming ones.

As mining data streams consumes a lot of the computational resources like the CPU capacity and memory, a number of researchers paid attention to this problem. Dang, Ng, Ong and Lee (2007) used load shedding to automatically shed the unprocessed data when an overloaded CPU case is discovered. To save the memory used in mining the frequent itemsets, Li and Lee (2009) proposed a bit-sequence representation for the items.

All the works are interested in finding frequent itemsets where the order of items is not important (Ashrafi, Taniar, & Smith, 2007; Raahemi & Mumtaz, 2010). On the other hand, a number of researchers (Laur, Symphor, Nock, & Poncelet, 2007; Ashrafi, Taniar, & Smith, 2007; Welzker, Zimmermann, & Bauckhage, 2010) focused on the problem of mining sequential subsequence over data streams where the order of items is important. To reduce the number of discovered subsequences, Raissi, Poncelet, and Teisseire (2006) found the maximal sequential subsequences over data streams. Instead of using the support value, the researchers in Barouni-Ebrahimi and Ghorbani (2007) developed a frequency rate equation. If the frequency rate of a sequence is greater than the frequency rate specified by the user, then the sequence is considered to be frequent.

The aforementioned works are dealing with a single stream. Sun, Papadimitriou, and Faloutsos (2006) are interested in finding frequent subsequences over multiple data streams. Otey, Parthasarathy, Wang, and Veloso (2004) designed parallel methods for mining the frequent itemsets for distributed data streams; they considered the communication overhead in their algorithms. Mining sequential subsequences over multiple data streams were studied by Chen, Wu, and Zhu (2005). They incorporated prior knowledge about the data distribution to improve the mining process. Most of the works above dealt with transactional streaming data. However, we propose to find frequent subsequences in multiple streams with continuous data values.

BACKGROUND AND NOTATION

Before formally defining the problem to be solved in this paper and its proposed solution, we briefly present a background on data streams.

Data Streams

A data stream is a collection of ordered items that arrive in a continuous manner, with high arrival rate, and has unbounded size. These characteristics raise many issues when designing algorithms for data streams (Jiang & Gruenwald, 2006). One of these issues is the need for incremental algorithms for mining data streams. Thus, there is no need to recompute the mining result as new data arrives; instead the result should be updated based on the old mining results.

Another issue when processing data streams is the period of the data that is most applicable for the application. This question is answered by choosing the right window model. According to Zhu and Shasha (2002) there are three kinds of window models to use when dealing with data streams. These models are the landmark window model, the damped window model, and the sliding window model. The choice of the window model decides the period of time that the data will be taken from. In the landmark window model, data can be taken from any time point called landmark till the current point. When using the damped window model, the older data is given less weight than the newer one, and thus gradually the effect of older data is decreased. The sliding window model is used when the interest is only in the current data.

The high arrival (incoming) rate of a data stream challenges the resources available to process it, like the CPU, memory, etc. That is the higher the arrival rate of the data, the faster the consumption of memory (Jiang & Gruenwald, 2006). According to Gaber, Krishnaswamy, and Zaslavsky (2003) the high incoming rate problem can be solved through two solutions. First one is the input and output rate adaption. In this solution, the input data stream is adapted to the available resources by selecting subset of it instead of processing it as a whole. Different techniques like sampling, aggregation, and load shedding can be used to select the subset of the stream to be processed. To adapt to the output rate, measurements such as available memory, time, and data rate should be taken into consideration. The second solution is to use approximate algorithms. These algorithms only have one look at the data, and they produce the results with some margin of error.

The nature of data streams makes it necessary to enforce some restrictions when designing data mining algorithms (Bhatnagar, Kaur, & Mignet, 2009; Golfarelli & Rizzi, 2009). Since there is a huge amount of data, some researchers chose to represent the data with summary information. Many techniques are used to summarize the data. These techniques include Wavelets, Discrete Fourier Transform, Piecewise Linear Representation, etc. Since the summarization techniques produce approximations of the original data, the solutions produced by these techniques are approximate ones. Thus, in this paper we propose an exact solution based on the original data.

Notations and Definitions

In this section, we introduce the definitions and notation used in explaining the purposed algorithm for finding frequent subsequences in multiple data streams. A data stream, S, is formally defined as follows:

- **Definition 1:** A data stream, S, is an unbounded sequence of items arriving at fixed interval. $S = s_0, s_1, s_2, \ldots, s_\infty$.
  Each item, s_i of S is a real valued number. The proposed algorithm uses the *Sliding Window* model to buffer the incoming data items of a data stream. When a window is full, the proposed algorithm processes the

items in the window, w, to find the frequent subsequences.

- **Definition 2:** A window, w, is a subset of the stream from time t to $t + w\text{-}1$, where $w = s_t, s_{t+1}, \ldots, s_{t+w-1}$.
  A subsequence is a subset of a data stream within a window. Each subsequence has a length l, which is between a minimum length h and a maximum length m.

- **Definition 3:** A subsequence, s, is a subset of the window of length l, where $h \leq l \leq m$. The proposed algorithm finds the frequent subsequences by means of clustering the subsequences. Two subsequences are placed in the same cluster if they are neighbors in the subsequences space.

- **Definition 4:** A subsequence, s_n, is considered a neighbor of another subsequence $s_{t,l}$ starting at time t and has length l, if the distance between them is $d(s_{t,l}, s_n) \leq \Theta$.
  A subsequence is considered frequent if the number of its neighbors, η, in a cluster is greater or equal to some threshold, τ. Otherwise, the subsequence is considered non-frequent and thus ignored.

- **Definition 5:** A frequent subsequence, FS, is considered frequent in a window if the number of its neighbors, $\eta, \geq \tau$.

Table 1 lists the symbols used in the proposed algorithm.

Problem Definition

In this paper, we address the problem of finding frequent subsequences in multiple data streams. We assume that these data streams are synchronized, that is they have the same arrival rate. A stream has unbounded size, and consists of real numbers that arrive in a specific rate. Formally, given a set of input data streams $\xi = S_1, S_2, \ldots, S_p$ our algorithm finds subsequences that are frequent, (*FSs*), over all data streams.

Table 1. Symbols used in the proposed algorithm

Symbol	Definition
ξ	Set of input streams, $\xi = S_1, S_2, ..., S_p$
S	An input stream, $S_i = s_1, s_2, ..., s_\infty$
$s_{t,l}$	A subsequence starting from time t, having length l
w	window size
h	Minimum subsequence length
m	Maximum subsequence length
η	Number of neighbors of a subsequence, s.
τ	Support threshold for a subsequence to be considered frequent.
r	Arrival rate of the data stream elements
t	Arrival time of the data stream elements
δ	A decay value to decide if a subsequence is frequent for the current window or not.
Θ	A threshold value to decide if a subsequence is a neighbor to another subsequence.

Due the nature of data streams, the proposed algorithms should be:

- Incremental, that is the algorithms computes the current results based on previously computed ones without the need to recompute the result from the whole history of a data stream.
- Efficient, by scanning the data streams only once.
- Any time, that is the results can be readily retrieved after every window without having to recompute it on demand.

Proposed Solution

Finding frequent subsequences, *FSs*, is challenging because of the nature of the data streams. Due to the unbounded nature of the data streams, we employ a sliding window model to retrieve a set of *w* values from each data stream. Then, we find *FSs* by clustering the subsequences of data streams. A subsequence *s* in a window is considered frequent if it has enough number of neighbors ($\eta \geq \tau$). That is if the number of subsequences in a cluster is greater or equal than τ. A subsequence s_i enters

the neighborhood of another subsequence s_j if the distance between the two is less than a threshold, $d(s_i, s_j) < \Theta$. keep the clusters up-to-date, we employ a decay value, δ, with each subsequence, to be able to remove old subsequences. The δ variable makes the algorithm incremental, by only keeping the most recent *FSs*, which are in subsequent windows without the need to recompute *FSs* from the whole history of data streams.

DISCOVERING FREQUENT SUBSEQUENCES

In this paper, we address the problem of finding *FSs* in multiple data streams. We assume that the data streams are synchronized and elements of data streams arrive sequentially at a specified arrival rate.

Algorithms

The main algorithm for finding *FSs* starts when a window becomes full. Thus, our solution consists of two algorithms. The first algorithm, called *BufferDataStreams()* (Algorithm 1), which collects the elements of a data stream, *S*, till the buffer (equivalent to one window, *w*) becomes full (see line 3). When *w* is full, the *FindFrequentSubsequences()* algorithm (Algorithm 2) is called for each stream to process the current window (line 3-5). At the end of *BufferDataStreams()* algorithm, the *List*s of all data streams are added into one global link list, called *Glist*, that contains all the *FSs*. Thus, Algorithm 1 and Algorithm 2 are applied to every data stream.

In this paper we applied the idea of monotonicity property used by the Apriori algorithm (Tan, Steinbach, & Kumar, 2005) on data streams to reduce the number of frequency computation of subsequences. That is, the algorithm omits the frequency computation of subsequences that have non-frequent subsets. This leads to less invocation to the Euclidean distance function, and as a result less execution time. Figure 1 shows the effect of

Algorithm 1. BufferDataStreams

```
Input: S, w
Output: List contains the frequent subsequences
while ( elements of Sᵢ is still arriving) do
        Store the arriving element in the buffer
 if (buffer size = w) then
 List = FindFrequentSubsequence()
            end if
end while
```

applying the monotonicity property in our algorithm. If subsequence $s_{t,\,lmin}$ is frequent, then $s_{t,\,lmin+1}$ could be either frequent or not frequent. If we found that $s_{t,\,lmin+1}$ is not frequent, then all its superset subsequences are not frequent and thus are not processed.

The approach we are using to find the *FSs* is a clustering approach, so while we are explaining the FFS algorithm (Algorithm 2), we may use the terms frequent subsequence and cluster interchangeably. A cluster is a frequent subsequence with its neighbors. The first subsequence arriving into the cluster is considered the representative of the cluster. The algorithm begins by setting the number of neighbors, η, for every subsequence to 0, so that the value of η of every subsequence is not affected by the results of the previous window (lines 1-3). The algorithm starts extracting the subsequences of length *l*, where $h \leq l \leq m$, from the buffer. Every subsequence has a minimum length *h* and a maximum length *m*. We discuss how these lengths are determined later in this section. Then, the FFS algorithm checks the subsets of every subsequence $s_{t,l}$, if a subset is frequent, it finds the subsequence in the list of frequent subsequences, *List*, that has the minimum distance with $s_{t,l}$. Non-frequent subsequences are ignored. The minimum Euclidean distance is stored in $s_{t,lMin}$ (line 6-7). Only non-trivial matches (Keogh & Lin, 2005) are considered.

Figure 1. Applying the monotonicity property in our algorithm

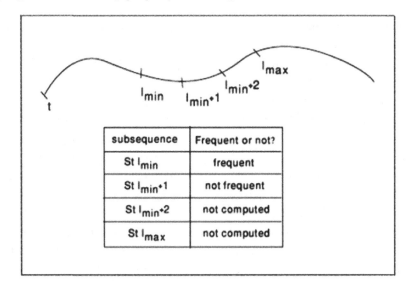

subsequence	Frequent or not?
St l_{min}	frequent
St l_{min+1}	not frequent
St l_{min+2}	not computed
St l_{max}	not computed

Figure 2. Example of trivial matches of a subsequence. Bold-line bounded subsequence has a trivial match with two thin-line bounded subsequences at both ends

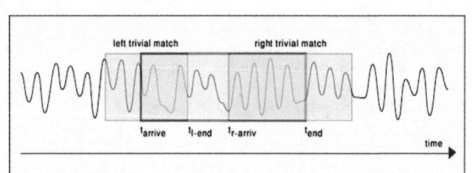

- **Definition 6, A Trivial Match:** A trivial match of a subsequence $s_{t,l}$ of time t_{arrive} and length l, is the one that overlaps with it.

Figure 2 gives an example of trivial matches of a subsequence. A subsequence under consideration is bounded by a bold-line rectangle. Two overlapping subsequences are bounded by thin-line rectangles (one on the left and another on the right). Both of these overlapping subsequences are considered trivial matches of the bold-line subsequence

The FSS algorithm, line 8 checks if the $s_{t,lMin}$ distance from $s_{t,l}$ is less than the threshold, Θ; if so, it then checks if the extracted subsequence is a trivial match with the last neighbor of the subsequence in the $s_{t,lMin}$ cluster (line 9). If the last neighbor subsequence, LN, of the subsequence $s_{t,lMin}$, and the new subsequence, $s_{t,l}$, makes a trivial match, then choose the one with the smaller distance from $s_{t,lMin}$ (lines 10-11). Otherwise $s_{t,l}$ is placed in the $s_{t,lMin}$ cluster and η of this cluster is incremented by one (lines 14-15). If the $s_{t,lMin}$ distance from $s_{t,l}$ is not less than Θ, $s_{t,l}$ starts a new cluster (line 18).

The number of neighbors η of every subsequence of length l in *List* is checked, before moving to the subsequences with larger lengths to apply the monotonicity property. That is if η of the subsequence $s_{t,l}$ is less than the minimum number of neighbors, $\eta < \tau$, then this subse-

quence is considered non-frequent in the current w and thus the algorithm decrements the decay value δ of the cluster, or *FS*, (lines 22-24). If δ of a subsequence reaches -1, this means that the subsequence is becoming non-frequent for the current window (this cluster, or subsequence, has decayed and thus considered non-frequent in the current window), and it is removed from *List* (lines 25-26). Otherwise if $\eta \geq \tau$, δ of a subsequence is incremented, which means that the subsequence is frequent for the current window (line 29). We used JAVA threads to execute the FFS algorithm in parallel for each stream.

We explain some of the parameters affecting the number of produced frequent subsequences. These parameters are the threshold value Θ, the support value τ, the decay value δ, and the subsequence length, l.

The Threshold Value (Θ)

Choosing the threshold value, which decides if a subsequence is a neighbor to another subsequence, has a great impact on the produced *FSs*. A very small threshold value may result in too many *false negatives*. On the other hand, a very large Θ may result in too many *false positives*. The threshold used to decide if a subsequence is in the neighborhood of another subsequence is equal to (derived from the Euclidean distance). This means that under the Euclidean distance, for

Algorithm 2. FindFrequentSubsequence (FFS)

Input: The current window buffer, *List* contains the frequent subsequences computed from the previous window, and threshold value Θ to decide if a subsequence is a neighbor to another subsequence.

Output: *List* contains the frequent subsequences for the current window

for every($s_{t,l}$ in *List*) **do**

 Set the frequency count (*fc*) of every subsequence in the *list* to 0

end for

for every (*l* from *h* to *m*) **do**

    for every (*t* from1 to *w*) **do**

       If ($s_{t,l-1}$ is frequent) **then**

           $s_{t,lMin}$ = findMinimumDistance($s_{t,l}$, *List*)

               //trivial matches not considered

        if ($d(s_{t,lMin}$, $s_{t,l}$) <= Θ) **then**

           If ($s_{t,lMin}$ last neighbor, *LN*, is trivial match of $s_{t,l}$) **then**

               if ($d(s_{t,lMin}$, $s_{t,l}$) < $d(s_{t,lMin}$, *LN*)) **then**

                   Replace *LN* with $s_{t,l}$ in $s_{t,lMin}$ cluster

               end if

           else

               $s_{t,l}$ belongs to $s_{t,lMin}$ cluster

               Increment η of $s_{t,lMin}$ of the current *w*

           end if

        else

           $s_{t,l}$ is a new cluster

        end if

       end if

    end for

    for every(subsequence of length *l* in *List*) **do**

      if (η < τ) **then**

          decrement the δ of the cluster

          if (δ == -1) **then**

             Remove $s_{t,l}$ from *List*

          end if

      else

          Increment the δ of the cluster

      end if

    end for

end for

a subsequence of length *l*, the maximum difference allowed between the values of two correspondence elements in neighboring subsequencs is equal to C, where *C* is a user defined parameter. Thus, Θ is computed in terms of *l* and *C* as explained above.

The Support Threshold (τ)

The support threshold, which is a user defined parameter, decides whether a subsequence has enough number of neighbors to be considered frequent in the current window.

The Decay Value (δ)

Because the data is coming in a streaming fashion, we need to check if a cluster, or *FS*, is still frequent in each window. The δ decides whether a subsequence is frequent in the current window or not. If number of neighbors, $\eta \geq \tau$, then δ is increased by 1. Otherwise the δ is decreased by 1. When δ reaches -1 the subsequence is removed from the list of frequent subsequences. This δ parameter makes the algorithm incremental, by only keeping the most recent *FSs*, which are in subsequent windows without the need to recompute *FSs* from the whole history of data streams.

Figure 3 presents an example to show the affect of δ. Assuming τ is set to 3, a) At the beginning of the algorithm, three subsequences *s1*, *s2* and *s3* forming three clusters were found and their decay values is initialized to, $\delta = 0$. b) After finding 3, 3 and 1 neighbors for *s1, s2* and *s3*, respectively, the algorithm updates $\delta.s1=1$, and $\delta.s2=1$ since they are frequent ($\tau \geq 3$) in this window and so,

$\delta.s3=-1$ since it is not frequent and thus removed. c) *s1* has no new neighbors, therefore the value of δ is decreased by 1, while *s2* has three new neighbors and thus its δ is increased by 1. d) *s1*, has only one new neighbor in this window, so it is considered not frequent and its δ is decreased to -1 and thus removed. Since s2 has no neighbors in this window, its δ value is decreased by 1. e) Again *s2* has no new neighbors, so its δ is decreased by 1 to be 0, but this cluster will remain in the next window (window 5), because its δ didn't reach -1 yet.

- **Definition 7, Frequent Subsequence:** A subsequence is called frequent in a window, if δ is greater than zero, $\delta \geq 0$.

In Section 3.2 we defined a frequent subsequence as the one that has enough neighbors. However in definition 7 we redefine the frequent subsequence in relation with the decay value. The two definitions are not contradicting, but rather they complement each other. A subsequence will not reach a decay value greater than 0 unless it had enough number of neighbors in at least one window. If in the next windows it didn't have enough number of neighbors but δ didn't reach -1, then it will be kept in the *List* of *FSs*.

Figure 3. The affect of δ. a) three subsequences s1, s2, and s3 are found, b) s1 and s2 are frequent and s3 is not frequent and thus removed, c) s1 is not frequent and s2 remains frequent, d) s1 and s2 are not frequent in this window and their δ is decremented; δof s1 reaches -1, thus removed, e) s2 is not frequent and its δ is decremented

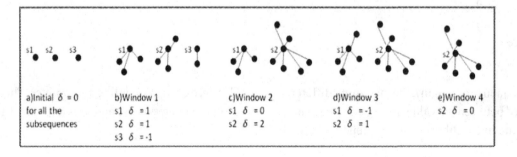

The Subsequence Length (l)

h is the minimum subsequence length, and we left it as a parameter to be specified by the user. m is the maximum subsequence length and it is equal to $w / (\tau + 1)$. This formula is derived from the requirement of our algorithm that for a subsequence to be frequent in a window of size w it should have at least τ neighbors. So to make sure that all the subsequences of length m have enough number of neighbors in a window of size w we restricted the maximum subsequence length to the above formula.

Data Structure

One of the important issues in designing the algorithm is the choice of the data structure. In the first stage, each stream submits the *FSs* results to a linked list. So, each stream has its own local list *List*. Each subsequence in *List* has linked list of neighbors. After each window the *List*s are submitted to a global linked list *GList*. The subsequences in the global list are sorted in ascending order based on time.

Our choice for the data structure was a linked list for both stages: local lists and global lists. This choice is justified because there are a lot of insertion and deletion to these lists during and after each window. Furthermore, the size of the results is not known in advance. Thus, for these reasons we chose a linked list structure to store the *FSs*.

Sliding Window Model

In Section 3.1, we discussed the window models used in data streams mining algorithm. One of the window models is the sliding window model which we are using in our algorithm. The sliding window model gives preference to the most recent data. But, as our algorithm is incremental, the *FSs* results of the current window are built on results of previous windows. The window size, *uw*, is a user parameter, however the FFS algorithm uses a buffer of size w. We extend the size of the window specified by the user to $w = uw+(m-1)$. That is the buffer of *window*$_i$ should includes the *uw* elements of *window*$_i$ plus *m-1* elements from *window*$_{i+1}$ before the buffer of *window*$_i$ is processed by the FFS algorithm. These *m-1* extra elements will make sure that the last element in *window*$_i$ has subsequences of all possible lengths.

Figure 4 shows the time in which the result of *window*$_i$ is reported. Our algorithm is designed to be efficient enough to report the result of *window*$_i$ before the next window gets all its elements. This is because data streams are continuous in nature and thus the proposed algorithms try to avoid the drop of new elements in the next window if they arrive before the *window*$_i$ has not been completely processed. Thus, one of the goals of the proposed algorithms is to efficiently process online data streams to find *FSs*.

Figure 4. The results are reported before getting all the elements for the next buffer

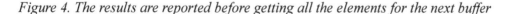
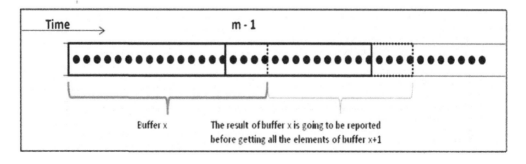

Complexity Analysis

The algorithm starts by passing through every subsequence in *List* to initialize its η to zero, so this operation is performed in $O(L)$ where L is the *List* size. The subsequences are extracted from the window of size w starting from the subsequences with minimum length h to the subsequences with maximum length m. Thus, the number of possible extracted subsequences is $(m-h+1)*w$. Each extracted subsequence is then compared to the subsequences in the *List* to find the closest one, that is the one with the minimum Euclidean distance, and each subsequence requires $O(m*L)$ to compute the distance (Actually it takes l instead of m, and l varies from h to m, but as we consider the worst case, we assumed that all the subsequences have the maximum length m). Before extracting larger subsequences, every subsequence of length l is checked for its frequency for the current window (Algorithm 2, line 28-38). This operation requires $O(L*(m-h+1))$. The aforementioned operations are the main tasks performed on the extracted subsequences. There are some other operations that take constant time per extracted subsequence. We ignored these operations in the computation of the complexity.

Therefore, the complexity of the algorithm is: $O(L)+O(((m-h+1)*(w))*(m*L))) + O(L*(m-h+1)) = O(((m-h+1)*(w))*(m*L))$. Considering the worst length of subsequence, that is when $h = 1$, the complexity is $O(m^2wL)$.

EXPERIMENTAL RESULTS

To evaluate the performance of the proposed algorithm, we conducted a set of experiments. In these experiments, we evaluate the purity of clustering, and the effect of the data arrival rate r (data incoming rate) on the performance under different parameters. By evaluating r, we are measuring the speed performance of the system.

We implemented the dataset generator, and the algorithms in JAVA, JDK 6. We run the experiments on a PC running Windows XP, Intel Core 2 CPU 2GHz, and 2GB of RAM.

Description of the Dataset

To evaluate the proposed algorithms, we developed a data generator that produces multiple data streams. Each stream consists of real numbers. These numbers are generated based on some prototypes. A prototype is created by selecting random numbers falling in the range [A, B]. The prototypes can overlap if the overlapping-value $\alpha > 0\%$. Figure 5 explains the effect of α in the generation of the prototypes. In Figure 5, all the points falling in the range [A, B], and the range [C, D], are represented on a line. In case 1, where $\alpha = 0\%$, there is no overlap of values between the two ranges. In the second case, $\alpha = 30\%$, which means that 30% of the range of values [A, B] is shared with 30% of the range of values [C, D]. The data streams of a cluster, which is represented by

Figure 5. Case 1 there is no overlapping between the prototypes. Case 2 there is overlapping of about 30% between the prototypes

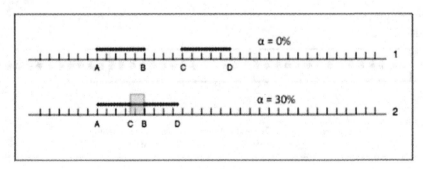

a prototype, are generated by tweaking the values of the prototype by adding a random number in the range of $[0..v]$, where v is a parameter to simulate the density of clusters.

Evaluating FFS Algorithm

We performed two sets of experiments to evaluate the performance of FFS algorithm. The first set of experiments focuses on evaluating the effect of two parameters on the purity of clustering. These two parameters are the overlap value α, which is the overlap between the generated values of the data streams in a cluster, and density C of a cluster, which is the amount of change allowed between the corresponding values of a cluster's members, The second set of experiments evaluates the effect of the arrival rate on the performance of the algorithm under different parameters.

Clustering Purity

We compute the purity of the clusters produced under different parameters. The purity of the clustering algorithm is a supervised measure for validating the clusters (Tan, Steinbach, & Kumar, 2005). We compute the purity of a cluster as follows:

$$purity\,of\,cluster(A) = \frac{\#\,correct\,neighbors\,of\,cluster\,A}{Total\,\,\#\,neighbors\,for\,all\,clusters}$$

Thus, the purity of a cluster is computed as the number of correct neighbors of the cluster divided by the total number of neighbors in all clusters. However, the purity of clustering the subsequences in a window, w, is the sum of the purities of the clusters that exist in the window. If there are k clusters in w, the purity of clustering of in w is computed as follows:

$$purity\,of\,clustering\,w = \sum_{i=1}^{k} purity\,of\,cluster(i)$$

To compute the purity of clustering a stream of subsequences over n windows, the purity would be the average of purities of clustering the n windows.

$$purity\,of\,a\,stream = \frac{1}{n}\sum_{i=1}^{n} purity\,of\,clustering\,w_i$$

In our experiments, the purity results are the average of running 100 streams under the same parameters and for each stream we computed the average of running 5 windows.

From the above formula it can be seen that the purity of a cluster is affected by how many subsequences are assigned to the wrong clusters.

Purity vs. Overlap Value α Between Clusters

In this experiment, we evaluated the effect of the overlap value α between clusters on the purity, while fixing the other parameters as follows: w to 120, $\tau = 3$, $C = 4$ and the number of clusters $= 4$. From Figure 6 we notice that the larger the value of α, the less the purity we achieve, which agrees with our expectation. This is because an overlap between clusters causes some member subsequences of different clusters to have similar values. Thus, these overlaps result in assignments of the subsequences to the wrong clusters. That is the number of false positives and true negatives increase in the produced clusters.

Purity vs. Cluster Density C

Figure 7 shows the effect of the cluster density C, which is the amount of change allowed between the corresponding values of the members of a cluster, on the purity. While computing the purity vs. C, we fixed the other parameters as follows: w to 120, $\tau = 3$, $\alpha = 60\%$ and the number of clusters $= 4$. As the value of C increases the purity decreases. This is due to the fact that increasing C makes the cluster sparser and thus allows some far subsequences,

Figure 6. The effect of the overlap value α between clusters on the purity of clustering

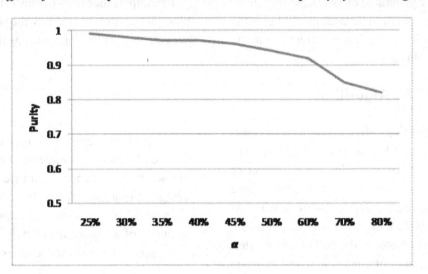

which are not necessarily members of the current cluster, to join the cluster. These far subsequences may belong to other clusters.

Performance Experiments

The next sets of experiments are conducted to evaluate the speed performance of the FFS algorithm. To evaluate the speed performance we measure the value of arrival rate r that our algorithm can cope with under different parameters. In other words, we are measuring to what speed extent of the data incoming rate the proposed algorithm can cope with under different parameters. The value of r is affected by the amount of time needed to process a window and produce *FSs*.

If a new window is ready to be processed while the FFS algorithm is still processing the previous one the new window will be dropped, which causes a loss of data. The processing time is affected by the number of subsequences needed to be processed. In turn, the number of subsequences to be processed is affected by window size w, number of prototypes, the support threshold τ and the minimum subsequence length h. Also, we compared the performance of two versions of the FFS algorithm: one using the Euclidean

distance and the other using the Uniform Scaling (US) distance (Yankov, Keogh, Medina, Chiu, & Zordan, 2007). In these experiments, the Y-axis is the arrival rate; higher values means slower incoming rate of element per msec.

Arrival Rate vs. Window Size

In this experiment we evaluate the effect of the window size w on the arrival rate r, while fixing the other parameters as follows: $\alpha = 50\%$, $\tau = 3$, $C = 1.5$ and the number of prototypes = 4. We notice from Figure 8 that the larger the size of the window, the more time required processing the window and thus the slower the required r. This is to avoid any drop of new data. Furthermore, the larger the size of the window, the larger the number of subsequences needed to be processed.

Arrival Rate vs. Number of Prototypes

The number of the prototypes represents the distribution of the data. This means that, as the number of the prototypes decreases, then over a fixed w, the number of subsequences that belong to the same prototype in w increases, and vice versa.

Figure 7. The effect of cluster density C on the purity of clustering

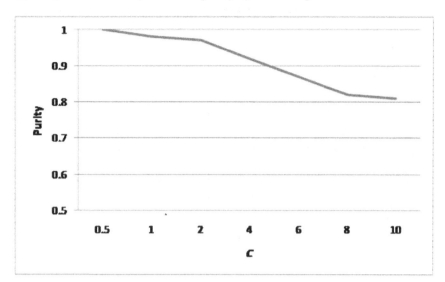

Thus, decreasing the number of prototypes would result in forming clusters with more member subsequences and thus more frequent subsequences to be found. In this experiment we measure r for different values of the number of prototypes (Figure 9), while fixing other parameters as follows: $\alpha = 50\%$, $\tau = 3$, $C = 1.5$ and $w = 120$. We compare the performance of the FFS algorithm when applying the monotonicity property and when not using it. When using the monotonicity property, as the number of prototypes increases, the number of FSs decreases. In addition, the use of the monotonicity property avoids processing the non-frequent subsequences, which results in reduction of the time required to process the window. In contrast, without using monotonicity property, r that the FSS algorithm can cope with increases when the number of prototypes increases.

Figure 8. The effect of window size on the arrival rate

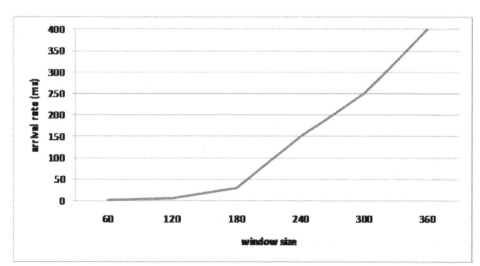

Figure 9. The effect of the number of prototypes on the arrival rate. It compare two versions of the proposed algorithm: one when using the monotonicity property and the other without using it

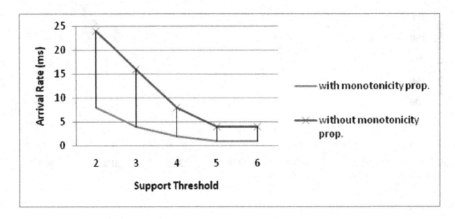

This shows that using the monotonicity property allows the FFS algorithm to cope with faster arrival rates of streaming data.

Arrival Rate vs. Support Threshold

In this experiment we evaluate the effect of the support threshold τ on the arrival rate r, while fixing the other parameters $\alpha = 50\%$, $C = 1.5$, $w = 120$ and the number of prototype = 4. These experiments are conducted on two versions of the FFS algorithm: one using the monotonicity property and the other one without using the monotonicity property. Figure 10 shows that the general trend of both version of the FFS algorithm is that as τ increases, the proposed algorithm can cope with faster arrival rates. Again this is because the smaller τ we have, the more subsequences will satisfy the threshold condition and thus the larger number of subsequences to be processed. We notice from Figure 10 that using the monotonicity property makes FFS algorithm perform faster as the num-

Figure 10. The effect of the support threshold on the arrival rate on two version of the FFS algorithm (with and without using monotonicity property)

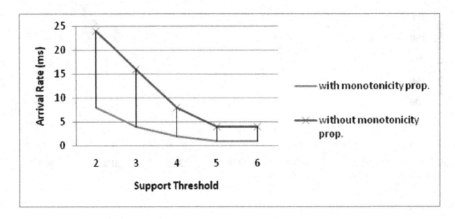

Figure 11. The effect of the minimum subsequence length on the arrival rate

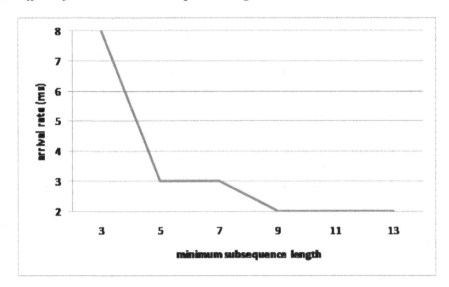

ber of processed subsequences becomes less due to the pruning process of monotonicity property.

Arrival Rate vs. Minimum Subsequence Length

For a fixed size of w, the maximum subsequence length *m* is fixed and depends on *w* (see Sec-

tion 4.1). We conducted a set of experiments to evaluate the effect of varying the size of minimum subsequence length *h* on the arrival rate, while fixing $\alpha = 50\%$, $C = 1.5$, $w = 120$, $\tau = 3$ and the number of prototype = 4. Figure 11 shows that as *h* increases, *r* that the algorithm can cope with becomes faster. Since the number of subsequences that are extracted from a window is equal to $m-h+1$,

Figure 12. A comparison between two versions of the algorithm (using Euclidean distance vs. Uniform Scaling distance) on the effect of support threshold on arrival rate

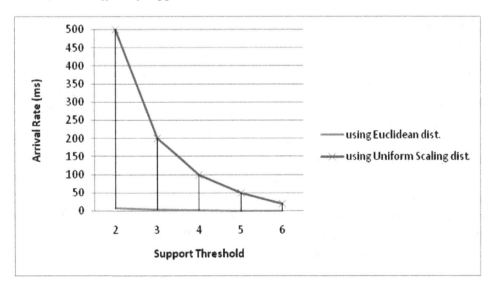

it is obvious that as h increases the number of subsequences to be processed decreases. As a result, it is expected that the required r is faster.

Euclidean Distance vs. Uniform Scaling Distance

The arrival rate r that the FFS algorithm can cope with is calculated for different values of the support threshold τ, while fixing $\alpha = 50\%$, $C = 1.5$, $w = 120$, $\tau = 3$, $h = 3$, and the number of prototype $= 4$. Figure 12 shows the results of a comparison between the performances of two versions of the FFS algorithm: one that uses the Euclidean distance that finds the distance between two subsequences with similar lengths, with another version that uses the Uniform Scaling, US, distance (Yankov, Keogh, Medina, Chiu, & Zordan, 2007). The US distance finds the distance between two subsequences with variable lengths. The results shows that the general trend is that when τ is decreased the FFS algorithm can cope with slower r. However, in the US version as τ decreases, the r that the algorithm can handle degrades quickly (becomes very slow), which means that the US version is not suitable for fast data streams.

CONCLUSION

We presented the FFS algorithm, which is incremental, any-time and exact algorithm, to find *FSs* in multiple data streams. The FFS algorithm benefits from the use of the monotonicity property to reduce the number of processed subsequences. By this property, subsequences, which have non-frequent subsets, are not considered frequent and thus ignored during the process of finding *FSs*. The FFS algorithm employs a decay value to timeout and removes older subsequences as they are considered non-frequent subsequences in the current window. In addition, the FFS algorithm is any-time algorithm as *FSs* are readily available at

the end of every window of the data stream and it is considered an exact algorithm since it works on the original data (no approximation).

We conducted extensive experiments to evaluate the FFS algorithm and show its feasibility. We evaluated the purity of clustering subsequences under different parameters. We noticed that the distribution of the data and the value of threshold have an impact on the purity of the clusters. We evaluated the arrival rate that the algorithm can handle under different parameters. We experimented with two versions of our proposed FFS algorithm, one with using monotonicity property, and one without using it. The one with using monotonicity property showed its performance superiority over the other one. Also we test our algorithm under two distance measures, the Euclidean distance and the Uniform Scaling distance and showed that the Euclidean distance version could handle faster arrival rates of data streams and thus more suitable for online applications.

REFERENCES

Ashrafi, M. Z., Taniar, D., & Smith, K. A. (2007). Redundant association rules reduction techniques. *International Journal of Business Intelligence and Data Mining*, 2(1), 29–63. doi:10.1504/IJBIDM.2007.012945

Barouni-Ebrahimi, M., & Ghorbani, A. A. (2007). An online frequency rate based algorithm for mining frequent sequences in evolving data streams. In *Proceedings of International Conference on Information Technology and Management* (pp. 56-63).

Bhatnagar, V., Kaur, S., & Mignet, L. (2009). A parameterized framework for clustering streams. *International Journal of Data Warehousing and Mining*, 5(1), 36–56. doi:10.4018/jdwm.2009010103

Chang, J. H., & Lee, W. S. (2003). Finding recent frequent itemsets adaptively over online data streams. In *Proceedings of the Ninth ACM SIGKDD International Conference on Knowledge Discovery and Data Mining* (pp. 487-492).

Chen, G., Wu, X., & Zhu, X. (2005). Sequential pattern mining in multiple streams. In *Proceedings of the Fifth IEEE International Conference on Data Mining* (pp. 585-588).

Chu, C. J., Tseng, V. S., & Liang, T. (2008). An efficient algorithm for mining temporal high utility itemsets from data streams. *Journal of Systems and Software*, *81*(7), 1105–1117. doi:10.1016/j.jss.2007.07.026

Chu, C. J., Tseng, V. S., & Liang, T. (2009). Efficient mining of temporal emerging itemsets from data streams. *Expert Systems with Applications: An International Journal*, *36*(1), 885–893. doi:10.1016/j.eswa.2007.10.040

Dang, X. H., Ng, W. K., Ong, K. L., & Lee, V. C. S. (2007). Discovering frequent sets from data streams with CPU constraint. In *Proceedings of the Sixth Australasian Conference on Data Mining and Analytics* (pp. 121-128).

Gaber, M. M., Krishnaswamy, S., & Zaslavsky, A. (2003). *Adaptive mining techniques for data streams using algorithm output granularity.* Paper presented at the Australasian Data Mining Workshop.

Goh, J. Y., & Taniar, D. (2004). Mobile data mining by location dependencies. In Z. Rong Yang, H. Yin, & R. M. Everson (Eds.), *Proceedings of the 5th International Conference on Intelligent Data Engineering and Automated Learning* (LNCS 3177, pp. 225-231).

Golfarelli, M., & Rizzi, S. (2009). A survey on temporal data warehousing. *International Journal of Data Warehousing and Mining*, *5*(1), 1–17. doi:10.4018/jdwm.2009010101

Jiang, N. (2006). CFI-Stream: Mining closed frequent itemsets in data streams. In *Proceedings of the 12th ACM SIGKDD International Conference on Knowledge Discovery and Data Mining* (pp. 592-597).

Jiang, N., & Gruenwald, L. (2006). Research issues in data stream association rule mining. *SIGMOD Record*, *35*(1), 14–19. doi:10.1145/1121995.1121998

Jin, R., & Agrawal, G. (2005). An algorithm for in-core frequent itemset mining on streaming data. In *Proceedings of the Fifth IEEE International Conference on Data Mining* (pp. 210-217).

Keogh, E., & Lin, J. (2005). Clustering of time-series subsequences is meaningless: implications for previous and future research. *Knowledge and Information Systems*, *8*(2), 154–177. doi:10.1007/s10115-004-0172-7

Laur, P. A., Symphor, J. E., Nock, R., & Poncelet, P. (2007). Statistical supports for mining sequential patterns and improving the incremental update process on data *streams*. *Intelligent Data Analysis*, *11*(1), 29–47.

Li, H. F., Ho, C. C., & Lee, S. Y. (2009). Incremental updates of closed frequent itemsets over continuous data streams. *Expert Systems with Applications: An International Journal*, *36*(2), 2451–2458. doi:10.1016/j.eswa.2007.12.054

Li, H. F., & Lee, S. Y. (2009). Mining frequent itemsets over data streams using efficient window sliding techniques. *Expert Systems with Applications: An International Journal*, *36*(2), 1466–1477. doi:10.1016/j.eswa.2007.11.061

Li, H. F., Lee, S. Y., & Shan, M. K. (2004). An efficient algorithm for mining frequent itemsets over the entire history of data streams. In *Proceedings of the 1st International Workshop on Knowledge Discovery in Data Streams*.

Lin, M. Y., Hsueh, S. C., & Hwang, S. K. (2008). Interactive mining of frequent itemsets over arbitrary time intervals in a data stream. In *Proceedings of the Nineteenth Conference on Australasian Database* (pp. 15-21).

Manku, G. S., & Motwani, R. (2002). Approximate frequency counts over data streams. In *Proceedings of the 28th International Conference on Very Large Data Bases* (pp. 346-357).

Mozafari, B., Thakkar, H., & Zaniolo, C. (2008). Verifying and mining frequent patterns from large windows over data streams. In *Proceedings of the IEEE 24th International Conference on Data Engineering* (pp. 179-188).

Naganthan, E. R., & Dhanaseelan, F. R. (2007). Efficient graph structure for the mining of frequent itemsets from data streams. *International Journal of Computer Science and Engineering Systems*, *1*(4), 283–290.

Otey, M. E., Parthasarathy, S., Wang, C., & Veloso, A. (2004). Parallel and distributed methods for incremental frequent itemset mining. *IEEE Transactions on Systems, Man, and Cybernetics. Part B, Cybernetics*, *34*(5), 2439–2450. doi:10.1109/TSMCB.2004.836887

Raahemi, B., & Mumtaz, A. (2010). Classification of peer-to-peer traffic using a two-stage window-based classifier with fast decision tree and IP layer attributes. *International Journal of Data Warehousing and Mining*, *6*(3), 28–42. doi:10.4018/jdwm.2010070103

Raissi, C., Poncelet, P., & Teisseire, M. (2006). SPEED: Mining maximal sequential patterns over data streams. In *Proceedings of the 3rd IEEE International Conference on Intelligent Systems* (pp. 546-552).

Raissi, C., Poncelet, P., & Teisseire, M. (2007). Towards a new approach for mining frequent itemsets on data stream. *Journal of Intelligent Information Systems*, *28*(1), 23–36. doi:10.1007/s10844-006-0002-3

Silvestri, C., & Orlando, S. (2007). Approximate mining of frequent patterns on streams. *Intelligent Data Analysis*, *11*(1), 49–73.

Sun, J., Papadimitriou, S., & Faloutsos, C. (2006). Distributed pattern discovery in multiple streams. In *Proceedings of the Pacific-Asia Conference on Knowledge Discovery and Data Mining* (pp. 713-718).

Tan, P. N., Steinbach, M., & Kumar, V. (2005). *Introduction to data mining*. Reading, MA: Addison-Wesley.

Taniar, D., Rahayu, Lee, W., & Daly, O. (2008). Exception rules in association rule mining. *Applied Mathematics and Computation*, *205*(2), 735–750. doi:10.1016/j.amc.2008.05.020

Tjioe, H. C., & Taniar, D. (2005). Mining association rules in data warehouses. *International Journal of Data Warehousing and Mining*, *1*(3), 28–62. doi:10.4018/jdwm.2005070103

Welzker, R., Zimmermann, C., & Bauckhage, C. (2010). Detecting trends in social bookmarking systems: A del.icio.us endeavor. *International Journal on Data Warehousing and Mining*, *6*(1), 38-57.

Wong, R. C., & Fu, A. W. (2006). Mining top-K frequent itemsets from data streams. *Data Mining and Knowledge Discovery*, *13*(2), 193–217. doi:10.1007/s10618-006-0042-x

Yankov, D., Keogh, E., Medina, J., Chiu, B., & Zordan, V. (2007). Detecting time series motifs under uniform scaling. In *Proceedings of the 13th ACM SIGKDD International Conference on Knowledge Discovery and Data Mining* (pp. 844-853).

Yu, J. X., Chong, Z., Lu, H., Zhang, Z., & Zhou, A. (2006). A false negative approach to mining frequent itemsets from high speed transactional data streams. *Information Sciences*, *176*(14), 1986–2015. doi:10.1016/j.ins.2005.11.003

Zhu, Y., & Shasha, D. (2002). StatStream: Statistical monitoring of thousands of data streams in real time. In *Proceedings of the 28th International Conference on Very Large Data Bases* (pp. 358-369).

This work was previously published in the International Journal of Data Warehousing and Mining, Volume 7, Issue 4, edited by David Taniar, pp. 1-20, copyright 2011 by IGI Publishing (an imprint of IGI Global).

Chapter 13
HYBRIDJOIN for Near–Real–Time Data Warehousing

M. Asif Naeem
The University of Auckland, New Zealand

Gillian Dobbie
The University of Auckland, New Zealand

Gerald Weber
The University of Auckland, New Zealand

ABSTRACT

An important component of near-real-time data warehouses is the near-real-time integration layer. One important element in near-real-time data integration is the join of a continuous input data stream with a disk-based relation. For high-throughput streams, stream-based algorithms, such as Mesh Join (MESHJOIN), can be used. However, in MESHJOIN the performance of the algorithm is inversely proportional to the size of disk-based relation. The Index Nested Loop Join (INLJ) can be set up so that it processes stream input, and can deal with intermittences in the update stream but it has low throughput. This paper introduces a robust stream-based join algorithm called Hybrid Join (HYBRIDJOIN), which combines the two approaches. A theoretical result shows that HYBRIDJOIN is asymptotically as fast as the fastest of both algorithms. The authors present performance measurements of the implementation. In experiments using synthetic data based on a Zipfian distribution, HYBRIDJOIN performs significantly better for typical parameters of the Zipfian distribution, and in general performs in accordance with the theoretical model while the other two algorithms are unacceptably slow under different settings.

INTRODUCTION

Near-real-time data warehousing exploits the concepts of data freshness in traditional static data repositories in order to meet the required decision support capabilities. The tools and techniques for promoting these concepts are rapidly evolving (Thomsen & Pedersen, 2009; Golfarelli & Rizzi, 2009a, 2009b; Vassiliadis, 2009). Most data warehouses have already switched from a full refresh (Gupta & Mumick, 1999; Zhang & Rundensteiner, 2002; Zhuge, García-Molina,

DOI: 10.4018/978-1-4666-2148-0.ch013

Hammer, & Widom, 1995) to an incremental refresh policy (Labio & Garcia-Molina, 1996; Labio, Wiener, Garcia-Molina, & Gorelik, 2000; Labio, Yang, Cui, Garcia-Molina, & Widom, 2000). Furthermore, the batch-oriented, incremental refresh approach is moving towards a continuous, incremental refresh approach (Thiele, Fischer, & Lehner, 2007; Karakasidis, Vassiliadis, & Pitora, 2005; Nguyen, 2003).

With regards to terminology, data warehousing approaches that follow such a best-effort data freshness approach have various names. Frequently used terms are zero-latency, active, real-time or near-real-time data warehouses. The term near-real-time is the most descriptive in a context where there could be confusion with real-time control systems, but for the sake of brevity, we will mostly use the term real-time in this paper where no such confusion is possible.

One important research area in the field of data warehousing is data transformation, since the updates coming from the data sources are often not in the format required for the data warehouse. For real-time data warehousing a continuous transformation from a source to target format is required, so the task becomes more challenging.

In the ETL (Extract-Transform-Load) layer, a number of transformations are performed such as the detection of duplicate tuples, identification of newly inserted tuples, and the enriching of updates with values from the master data. Enrichment in particular can often be expressed as a join between the update stream and the master data (Naeem, Dobbie, & Weber, 2008). One important example of enrichment is a key transformation. Normally the key used in the data source is different from that in the data warehouse and therefore needs to be replaced. This transformation can be obtained by implementing a join operation between the update tuples and a lookup table. The lookup table contains the mapping between the source keys and the warehouse keys. Figure 1 shows a graphical interpretation of such a transformation. The attributes with column name *id* in both data

sources DS_1 and DS_2 contain the source data keys and the attribute with name *warehouse key* in the lookup table contains the warehouse key value corresponding to these data source keys. Before loading each transaction into the data warehouse each source key is replaced by the warehouse key with the help of a join operator.

In traditional data warehousing the update tuples are buffered in memory and joined when resources become available (Wilschut & Apers, 1991; Shapiro, 1986). Whereas, in real-time data warehousing these update tuples are joined immediately when they are generated in the data sources. One important factor related to the join is that both inputs of the join come from different sources with different arrival rates. The input from the data sources is in the form of an update stream which is fast, while the access rate of the lookup table is comparatively slow due to disk I/O cost.

A novel stream-based equijoin algorithm, MESHJOIN (Polyzotis, Skiadopoulos, Vassiliadis, Simitsis, & Frantzell, 2007; Neoklis Polyzotis, Skiadopoulos, Vassiliadis, Simitsis, & Frantzell, 2008) is in principle a hash join, where the stream serves as the build input and the disk-based relation serves as the probe input. The main contribution is a staggered execution of the hash table build and an optimization of the disk buffer for the disk-based relation.

The algorithm successfully joins the continuous data stream of updates with the slow access rate disk-based relation. However, we have identified two issues that have to be addressed. Firstly, the throughput of MESHJOIN is inversely proportional to the size of the disk-based master data table. Secondly, the algorithm cannot deal with an intermittent update stream efficiently. An intermittent stream is a stream that is dropping to a rate close to zero tuples per unit of time for periods of time. A detailed explanation of these issues is provided in Section 3.

The Index Nested Loop Join (INLJ) (Ramakrishnan, 1999) is traditionally considered for non-stream data, but it can easily be set up so

Figure 1. An example of stream-based join

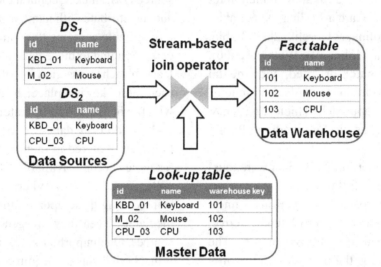

that it joins a continuous data stream with a disk-based relation, which is capable of dealing with intermittent data streams. However, every index has to be considered non-clustered with respect to the stream data. This is because stream data arrive in the order that the updates are performed. The natural assumption is e.g., that purchases are random. INLJ is known to be inefficient for non-clustered index access. The disk I/O cost cannot be amortized over multiple tuples of the stream and eventually produces a low service rate.

Based on these observations, we propose a stream-based join, called Hybrid Join (HYBRIDJOIN, http://www.cs.auckland.ac.nz/research/groups/serg/hybridjoin/). The key difference between HYBRIDJOIN and MESHJOIN is that HYBRIDJOIN does not read the entire disk relation sequentially but instead accesses it using an index. This can reduce the disk I/O cost by guaranteeing that every partition read from the disk-based relation is at least used for one stream tuple, while in MESHJOIN there is no guarantee. To amortize the disk read over many stream tuples, the algorithm performs the join of a disk partition with all stream tuples currently in memory. This approach guarantees that HYBRIDJOIN is never asymptotically slower than MESHJOIN. In addition, in HYBRIDJOIN, unlike MESHJOIN, the disk load is not synchronised with stream input providing better service rates for intermittent streams.

The rest of this paper is structured as follows. The related work is presented in Section 2. Section 3 describes our observations with regard to the current approach. In Section 4 we present the architecture, algorithm, theoretical analysis, cost model, and tuning of our proposed HYBRIDJOIN. The design and implementation of a benchmark for testing HYBRIDJOIN is described in Section 5. The experimental study is discussed in Section 6 and finally Section 7 concludes the paper.

RELATED WORK

In real-time data warehousing, updates occurring at the source need to be processed in an online fashion. This real-time processing of the update stream introduces the interesting challenges related to throughput for join algorithms. Some techniques have been introduced already to process join queries over continuous streaming data (Golab & Özsu, 2003; Babu & Widom, 2001; Hammad, Aref, & Elmagarmid, 2008; Palma, Akbarinia,

Pacitti, & Valduriez, 2009; Kim & Park, 2005; Nguyen, Brezany, Tjoa, & Weippl, 2005). In this section we will outline the well known work that has already been done in this area with a particular focus on those which are closely related to our problem domain.

The non-blocking symmetric hash join (SHJ) (Wilschut & Apers, 1990, 1991) promotes the proprietary hash join algorithm by generating the join output in a pipeline. In the symmetric hash join there is a separate hash table for each input relation. When the tuple of one input arrives it probes the hash table of the other input, generates a result and stores it in its own hash table. SHJ can produce a result before reading either input relation entirely, however, the algorithm keeps both the hash tables, required for each input, in memory.

The Double Pipelined Hash Join (DPHJ) (Ives, Florescu, Friedman, Levy, & Weld, 1999) with a two stage join algorithm is an extension of SHJ. The XJoin algorithm (Urhan & Franklin, 2000) is another extension of SHJ. Hash-Merge Join (HMJ) (Mokbel, Lu, & Aref, 2004) which is also based on symmetric join algorithm, uses push technology and consists of two phases, hashing and merging.

Early Hash Join (EHJ) (Lawrence, 2005) is a further extension of XJoin. EHJ introduces a new biased flushing policy that flushes the partitions of the largest input first. EHJ also simplifies the strategies to determine the duplicate tuples, based on cardinality and therefore no timestamps are required for arrival and departure of input tuples. However, because EHJ is based on pull technology, a reading policy is required for inputs.

Mesh Join (MESHJOIN) (Polyzotis et al., 2007; Neoklis et al., 2008), is designed especially for joining a continuous stream with a disk-based relation for active data warehousing. Although it is an adaptive approach, there are some issues related to the strategy for accessing the disk-based relation.

Most recently a partition-based approach (Chakraborty & Singh, 2009) was introduced that focuses on minimizing the disk overhead in

the MESHJOIN algorithm. However, a switch operator is introduced to switch between the Index Nested Loop Join (INLJ) and MESHJOIN. This switching mode depends on a threshold value for stream tuples in the input buffer. The key component is a wait buffer that holds only join attribute values and maintains them in separate slots with respect to the partitions of the disk-based relation. Each disk invocation takes place when either the number of attribute values in any slot of the wait buffer crosses the predefined threshold value or when the whole wait buffer becomes full. We observe that the join attribute values waiting in the slots of the wait buffer, which are not frequent in the input stream, need to wait longer than in the original MESHJOIN algorithm, because the slot does not reach the threshold limit. In addition the author focuses on the analysis of the stream buffer in terms of back log tuples and the delay time rather than analysing the algorithm performance in terms of service rate. Because the author does not provide code for his implementation, we are unable to test this approach in practice.

PRELIMINARIES: MESHJOIN

In this section we summarize the constraints on the MESHJOIN and INLJ algorithms. At the end of the section we outline the observations that we focus on in this paper.

MESHJOIN was designed to support streaming updates over persistent data in the field of real-time data warehousing. The algorithm reads the disk-based relation sequentially in partitions. Once the last partition is read, it again starts from the first partition. The algorithm contains a buffer, called the disk buffer, to store each disk partition in memory one at a time. The algorithm uses a hash table to store the stream tuples, while the key attribute for each tuple is stored in the queue. All partitions in the queue are equal in size. The total number of partitions is equal to the number of partitions on the disk while the size of each partition on the disk is equal to the size of the disk buffer. There is a stream buffer of negligible size that is used to hold the fast stream if required.

In each iteration the algorithm reads one disk partition into the disk buffer and loads a chunk of stream tuples into the hash table while also placing their key attributes in the queue. After loading the disk partition into memory it joins each tuple from that partition with matching stream tuples in the hash table. Before the next iteration the oldest stream tuples are removed from the hash table with their key attribute values from the queue. All chunks of the stream in the queue are advanced by one step. In the next iteration the algorithm replaces the current disk partition with the next one, loads a chunk of new stream tuples into the hash table and places their key attributes values in the queue, and repeats the above procedure.

The crux of the algorithm is that the total number of partitions in the stream queue must be equal to the total number of partitions on the disk and that number can be determined by dividing the size of the disk-based relation R by the size of the disk buffer b (i.e., $k=N_R/b$). This constraint ensures that a stream tuple that is loaded into memory is matched against the entire disk relation before it expires.

An overview of MESHJOIN is presented in Figure 2 where we consider only three partitions in the queue, with the same number of partitions on disk. At any time t, for example when disk partition p_3 is in memory the status of the stream tuples in memory can be explained. In the queue w_1 tuples have already joined with disk partition p_1 and p_2 and therefore after joining with partition p_3 they will be dropped out of memory. While tuples w_2 have joined with partition p_2 only and therefore, after joining with partition p_3 they will advance one step in the queue. Finally, tuples w_3 have not joined with any disk partition and they will also advance one step in the queue after joining with partition p_3. Once the algorithm completes the cycle of R, it again starts loading sequentially from the first partition.

Figure 2. Example of MESHJOIN when disk partition p_3 is in memory

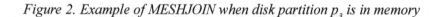
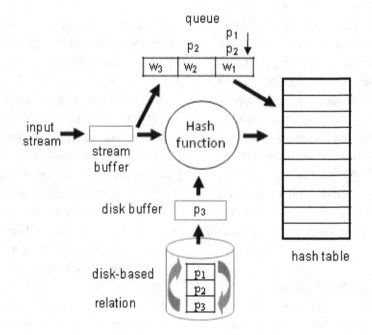

The MESHJOIN algorithm successfully amortizes the fast arrival rate of the incoming stream by executing the join of disk partitions with a large number of stream tuples. However there are still some further issues that exist in the algorithm. Firstly due to the sequential access of *R*, the algorithm reads the unused or less used partitions of *R* into memory with equal frequency, which increases the *processing time* for every stream tuple in the queue due to extra disk I/O. *Processing time* is the time that every stream tuple spends in the join window from loading to matching without including any delay due to the low arrival rate of the stream. The average *processing time* in the case of MESHJOIN can be estimated using the given formula.

Average *processing time* (secs) = $\frac{1}{2}$ (*seek time* + *processing time*) for the whole of *R*

To determine the access rate of disk partitions of *R* we performed an experiment using a benchmark that is based on Zipf's Law to model commercial applications (Knuth, 1998; Anderson, 2006), the detail is available in Section 5. In this experiment we assumed that *R* is sorted in ascending order with respect to the join attribute value and we measure the rate of use for the pages at different locations of *R*. From the results shown in Figure 3 it can be seen that the rate of page use decreases towards the end of *R*. The MESHJOIN algorithm does not consider this factor and reads all disk pages with the same frequency.

Secondly, MESHJOIN cannot deal with bursty input streams effectively. In MESHJOIN a disk invocation occurs when the number of tuples in the stream buffer is equal to or greater than the stream input size *w*. In the case of intermittent or low arrival rate (λ) of the input stream, the tuples already in the queue need to wait longer due to

Figure 3. Measured rate of page use at different locations of R while the size of total R is 16000 pages

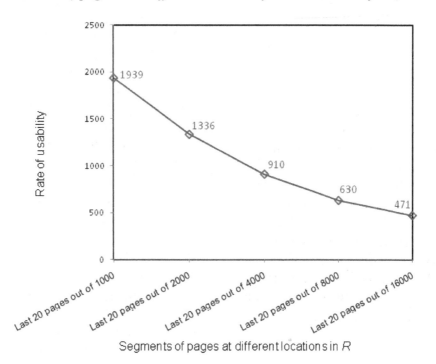

disk invocation delay. This *waiting time* negatively affects the performance. The average waiting time can be calculated using the given formula.

$$\text{Average } waitingtime \text{ (secs)} = \frac{w}{\check{e}}$$

Index Nested Loop Join (INLJ) is another join operator that can be used to join an input stream S with the disk-based relation R, using an index on the joint attributes. In INLJ for each iteration, the algorithm reads one tuple from S and accesses R randomly with the help of the index. Although in this approach both of the issues presented in MESHJOIN can be handled, the access of R for each tuple of S makes the disk I/O cost dominant. This factor affects the ability of the algorithm to cope with the fast arrival stream of updates and eventually decreases the performance significantly.

In summary, the problems that we consider in this paper are: (a) the minimization of the processing time and waiting time for the stream tuples by accessing the disk-based relation efficiently, (b) dealing with bursty stream effectively.

HYBRIDJOIN

In previous section we highlighted observations related to the MESHJOIN and INLJ algorithms. As a solution to the stated problems we propose a stream-based join algorithm called Hybrid Join (HYBRIDJOIN). In HYBRIDJOIN we address two major aims which are not supported in MESH-JOIN: (a) efficient access of disk-based relation R by loading only the useful part of R into memory, (b) dealing with bursty streams effectively. This section describes the data structures, pseudo-code and run time analysis of HYBRIDJOIN. We also present the cost model that is used for estimating the cost of our algorithm, and for tuning the algorithm.

Data Structures and Architecture

The data structures that HYBRIDJOIN uses are shown in Figure 4. Like in MESHJOIN key components of HYBRIDJOIN are disk buffer, hash table, queue and stream buffer. The disk-based relation R and stream S are the inputs. Contrary to MESHJOIN in HYBRIDJOIN we assume that R contains the unique values of join attribute and has an index on it. We also assume that the values of join attribute are sorted. The disk partition of size v_p from relation R is loaded into the disk buffer in memory. The queue is used to store the value of the join attribute and each node in the queue also contains the addresses of its one step neighbour nodes. Unlike the queue in MESH-JOIN we implement an extra feature of random deletion in our HYBRIDJOIN queue by using a doubly-linked-list.

The hash table is an important component that stores the stream tuples and the addresses of the nodes in the queue corresponding to the tuples. The key benefit of this is when the disk partition is loaded into memory using the join attribute value from the queue as an index, instead of only matching one tuple as in INLJ; the algorithm matches the disk partition with all the matching tuples in the queue. This helps to amortize the expensive disk I/O cost over fast arrival stream. In the case where there is a match, the algorithm generates that tuple as an output and deletes it from the hash table along with the corresponding node from the queue while the unmatched tuples in the queue are dealt with in a similar way to the MESHJOIN strategy. The role of the stream buffer is just to hold the fast stream if necessary.

To deal with the intermittencies in the stream, for each iteration the algorithm checks the status of the stream buffer. In the case where no stream tuples are available in the stream buffer the al-

Figure 4. Data structures used in HYBRIDJOIN

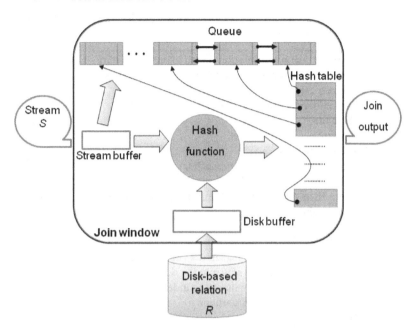

gorithm will not stop but continues its working until the hash table becomes empty. However, the queue keeps on shrinking continuously and will become empty when all tuples in the hash table are joined. On the other hand when tuples arrive from the stream, the queue again starts growing.

In MESHJOIN every disk input is bound to the stream input while in HYBRIDJOIN we remove this constraint by making each disk invocation independent from the stream input.

Algorithm

Once the memory is distributed among the join components HYBRIDJOIN starts its execution according to the procedure defined in Figure 5. Initially since the hash table is empty, h_S is assigned to stream input size w where h_S is the total number of slots in the hash table H (line 1). The algorithm consists of two loops: one is called the outer loop while the other one is called the inner loop. The outer loop which is an endless loop is used to read the stream input into the hash table (line 2), while the inner loop is used to probe the hash table (line 9). In each outer loop iteration, the algorithm examines the availability of stream tuples in the stream buffer. If the required number of stream tuples available, the algorithm reads w tuples of the stream and loads those into the hash table while placing their join attribute values in the queue. Once the stream input is read the algorithm resets the value of w to 0 (line 3-6). The algorithm then reads the oldest value of a join attribute from the queue and loads a disk partition p into the disk buffer, using that join attribute value as an index (line 7, 8). After loading the disk partition into memory the inner loop starts and for each iteration of the inner loop the algorithm reads one disk tuple from the disk buffer and probes the hash table. In the case of a match, the algorithm generates the join output. Since the hash table is multi-hash-map, there can be more than one match against one disk tuple. After generating the join output the algorithm deletes all matched tuples from the hash table along with the corresponding nodes from the queue. Finally, the algorithm increments w with the number of vacated slots in the hash table (line 9-15).

Figure 5. Pseudo-code for HYBRIDJOIN

HYBRIDJOIN algorithm

Input: A disk based relation R with an index on join attribute and a stream of updates S

Output: Stream $R \bowtie S$

Parameters: w tuples of S and a partition p of R

Method:

1. $w \leftarrow h_S$
2. **While** (*true*)
3.   **If** (*available stream tuples $\geq w$*)
4.   **Read** w tuples from stream buffer and load them into H while adding their join attribute values in Q
5. $w \leftarrow 0$
6.   **EndIf**
7.   **Read** the oldest join attribute value from Q
8.   **Load** a partition p of R into the disk buffer using that join attribute value as an index
9.   **For** each tuple r in partition p
10.   **If** $r \in H$
11.   **Output** $r \bowtie H$
12.   **Delete** all matched tuples from H and the corresponding nodes from Q
13. $w \leftarrow w +$ number of matching tuples found in H
14.   **EndIf**
15.   **EndFor**
16. **EndWhile**

Asymptotic Runtime Analysis

We compare the asymptotic runtime of HYBRIDJOIN with that of MESHJOIN and INLJ. As a unit of measurement we use the time needed to process a stream chunk. The time needed to process a single tuple is the inverse of the service rate, which is the number of tuples processed in a time interval. The unit of measurement used here has the advantage, that "smaller is better" in accordance with common usage in asymptotic analysis of algorithms. Every stream section can be viewed as a binary sequence, and by viewing this binary sequence as a natural number, we can apply asymptotic complexity classes to functions on stream sections as binary numbers. Note therefore that the following theorems do not use functions on input lengths, but on binary numbers representing stream sections. We denote the time needed to process stream section s as MEJ(s) for MESHJOIN, as INLJ(s) for index nested loop join, and as HYJ(s) for HYBRIDJOIN. The resulting theorems imply analogous asymptotic behavior on input length, but are stronger than statements on input length. We assume that the setup for HYBRIDJOIN and for MESHJOIN is such that they have the same number h_S of stream tuples in the hash table - and in the queue accordingly.

Comparison with MESHJOIN

- **Theorem 1:** HYJ(s) = O(MEJ(s)).
- **Proof:** To prove the theorem, we have to prove that HYBRIDJOIN performs no worse than MESHJOIN. The cost of MESHJOIN is dominated by the num-

ber of accesses to R. For asymptotic run-time, random access of disk partitions is as fast as sequential access (seek time is a constant factor). For MESHJOIN with its cyclic access pattern for R, every partition of R is accessed exactly once after every h_S stream tuples. We have to show that for HYBRIDJOIN no partition is accessed more frequently. For that we look at an arbitrary partition p of R at the time it is accessed by HYBRIDJOIN. The stream tuple at the front of the queue has some position i in the stream. There are h_S stream tuples currently in the hash table, and the first tuple of the stream that is not yet read into the hash table has position $i+h_S$ in the stream. All stream tuples in the hash table are joined against the disk-based master data tuples on p, and all matching tuples are removed from the queue. We now have to determine the earliest time that p could be loaded again by HYBRIDJOIN. For p to be loaded again, a stream tuple must be at the front of the queue, and has to match a master data tuple on p. The first stream tuple that can do so is the aforementioned stream tuple with position $i+h_S$, because all earlier stream tuples that match data on p have been deleted from the queue. This proves the theorem.

Comparison with INLJ

- **Theorem 2:** $HYJ(s) = O(INLJ(s))$.
- **Proof:** INLJ performs a constant number of disk accesses per stream tuple. For the theorem it suffices to prove that HYBRIDJOIN performs no more than a constant number of disk accesses per stream tuple as well. We consider first those stream tuples that remain in the queue until they reach the front of the queue. For each of these tuples, HYBRIDJOIN loads a part of R and hence

makes a constant number of disk accesses. For all other stream tuples, no separate disk access is made. This proves the theorem.

The theorems show that except for a single constant factor c, HYBRIDJOIN performs on each individual input at least as well as any of the two other algorithms. The maximum factor is determined by the ratio of continuous disk access time versus random disk access time for different disk portions. This is a free parameter of the cost model. In practice it depends on the technical parameters of the disk used, particularly the seek time, and on the choice of the disk portions that are loaded in one step. In our setup the factor is smaller than 2 for Theorem 1 and smaller than 5 for Theorem 2, i.e., even in the worst case, HYBRIDJOIN would be at most 2 times slower than MESHJOIN and at most 5 times slower than index nested loop join.

Cost Model

In this section we derive the general formulas to calculate the cost of our proposed HYBRIDJOIN. Since it is important to compare our cost model with the cost model presented for MESHJOIN in Neoklis et al. (2008) we use the same notation where possible and also calculate the cost in terms of memory and processing time. Equation 1 describes the total memory used to implement the algorithm (excluding the stream buffer). Equation 3 calculates the processing cost for w tuples while the average size for w can be calculated using Equation 2. The service rate can be calculated using Equation 4. The symbols used in the equations are specified in Table 1.

Memory Cost

In HYBRIDJOIN, the largest portion of the total memory is used for the hash table H while a comparatively smaller amount is used for the disk buffer. The queue size is linear to the hash

Table 1. Notations used for cost estimation of HYBRIDJOIN

Parameter name	Symbol
Total allocated memory (bytes)	M
Stream arrival rate (tuples/sec)	λ
Service rate (processed tuples/sec)	μ
Average stream input size (tuples)	w
Stream tuple size (bytes)	v_S
Size of disk buffer (bytes)	v_P
Size of disk tuple (bytes)	v_R
Size of disk buffer (tuples)	d
Memory weight for hash table	α
Memory weight for queue	$(1-\alpha)$
Size of hash table (tuples)	h_S
Size of disk-based relation R (tuples)	R_t
Exponent value for benchmark	e
Cost to read one disk partition into disk buffer (nanosecs)	$c_{I/O}(v_P)$
Cost to probe one disk tuple into hash table (nanosecs)	c_H
Cost to generate output for one tuple (nano sec)	c_O
Cost to delete one tuple from hash and queue (nanosecs)	c_E
Cost to read one tuples into stream buffer (nanosecs)	c_S
Cost to add one tuples into hash and queue (nanosecs)	c_A
Cost for one loop iteration of HYBRIDJOIN (sec)	c_{loop}

table size, but considerably smaller. We can easily calculate the size for each of them separately.

- Memory for the disk buffer (bytes) = v_P.
- Memory for the hash (bytes) = $á(M - v_P)$.
- Memory for the queue (bytes) = $(1 - á)(M - v_P)$.

The total memory used by HYBRIDJOIN can be determined by aggregating all the above.

$$M = v_P + á\left(M - v_P\right) + \left(1 - á\right)(M - v_P) \quad (1)$$

We are not including the memory reserved for the stream buffer because it is negligible (0.05 MB was sufficient in all our experiments).

Processing Cost

In this section we calculate the processing cost for HYBRIDJOIN. To calculate the processing cost it is necessary to calculate the average stream input size, w, first.

- **Calculate average stream input size w:** In HYBRIDJOIN the average stream input size w depends on the following four parameters.
  - Size of hash table h_S
  - Size of disk buffer d
  - Size of disk-based relation R_t
  - The exponent value for benchmark e

In our experiments w is directly proportional to the size of the hash table h_S and the size of the disk buffer d, and is inversely proportional to the size of disk-based relation R_t. The fourth parameter represents the exponent value for Zipfian distribution, explained in Section 5, and by using an exponent value of 1 we approximately model the 80/20 Rule (Anderson, 2006) for market sales. Therefore, the formula for w is:

$$w \propto \frac{h_S \times d \times e}{R_t}$$

$$w = k \frac{h_S \times d}{R_t} \qquad (2)$$

where k is a constant influenced by system parameters. We obtained the value of k from measurements, in our setup it is 1.36.

On the basis of w we can calculate the processing cost for one step of the iteration. In order to calculate the cost for one loop iteration the major components are:

- Cost to read one disk partition = $c_{I/O}(v_P)$.
- Cost to probe one disk partition into the hash table = $\frac{v_P}{v_R} c_H$.
- Cost to generate the output for w matching tuples = $w.c_O$.
- Cost to delete w tuples from the hash table and the queue = $w.c_E$.
- Cost to read w tuples from stream S = $w.c_S$.
- Cost to append w tuples into the hash table and the queue = $w.c_A$.

By aggregation, the total cost for one loop iteration is:

$$c_{loop} = 10^{-9}[c_{I/O}(v_P) + \frac{v_P}{v_R} c_H + w.c_O + w.c_E + w.c_S + w.c_A]$$

$$(3)$$

Since in c_{loop} seconds, the algorithm processes w tuples of stream S, the service rate μ can be calculated by dividing w by the cost for one loop iteration.

$$\mu = \frac{w}{c_{loop}} \qquad (4)$$

Tuning

Tuning of the join components is important to make efficient use of available resources. In HYBRIDJOIN the disk buffer is the key component to tune to amortize the disk I/O cost on fast input data streams. From Equation 4 the service rate depends on w and the cost c_{loop} which is required to process these w tuples. In HYBRIDJOIN for a particular setting (M=50MB) assuming the size of R and the exponent value for Zipfian distribution are fixed (R_t = 2 million and e =1), from Equation 2 w then depends on the size of hash table and the size of disk buffer. Furthermore the size of hash table is also dependent on the size of the disk buffer as shown in Equation 1. Therefore, using Equations 2, 3 and 4 the service rate μ can be specified as a function of v_P and the value for v_P at which the service rate is maximum can be determined by applying standard calculus rules.

Figure 6 shows the relationship between the I/O cost and service rate as measured in experiments. From Figure 6 it can be observed that in the beginning, for a small disk buffer size, the service rate is also small because there are fewer matching tuples in the queue. However, the service rate increases with an increase in the size of the disk buffer due to more matching tuples in the queue. After reaching a particular value of the disk buffer size the trend changes and performance decreases with further increments in the size of the disk buffer. The plausible reason behind this decrease is the rapid increase in the disk I/O cost and the decrease in memory size for the hash table.

Figure 6. Tuning of disk buffer

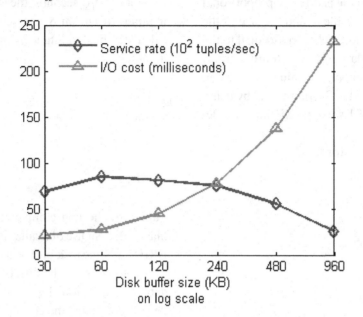

TESTS WITH LOCALITY OF DISK ACCESS

Crucial to the HYBRIDJOIN performance is the distribution of master data keys in the stream. If the distribution is uniform, then HYBRIDJOIN may perform worse than MESHJOIN, but by a constant factor, in line with the theoretical analysis. Note however, that HYBRIDJOIN still has the advantage of being efficient for intermittent streams, while the original MESHJOIN would pause with intermittent streams, and leave tuples unprocessed for an open-ended period.

It is also obvious that HYBRIDJOIN has advantages if R contains unmatched data, for example if there are old product records that are currently very rarely accessed, that are clustered in R. HYBRIDJOIN would not access these areas of R, while MESHJOIN accesses the whole of R.

More interestingly, however, is whether HYBRIDJOIN can also benefit from more general locality. Therefore the question arises whether we can demonstrate a natural distribution where HYBRIDJOIN measurably improves over the uniform distribution, because of locality.

Common non-uniform distributions are Zipfian distributions, which exhibit a power law similar to Zipf's law (Knuth, 1998). Zipfian distributions are discussed as a plausible model for sales (Anderson, 2006), where some products are sold frequently while most are sold rarely. The distribution generated using Zipf's law with an exponent 1 is close to the 80/20 Rule (Anderson, 2006) i.e., 80% of the sales are from 20% of the products.

We designed a generator for synthetic data that follows a Zipfian distribution. The generated benchmark is based on two characteristics: (a) the frequency of selling each product and it approximately models the 80/20 Rule, (b) the flow of sales transactions and it is a self-similar. By using the generated benchmark we demonstrate that HYBRIDJOIN performance improves when locality is considered, and that HYBRIDJOIN outperforms MESHJOIN.

In order to simplify the model, we assume that the product keys are sorted in the master data table according to their frequency in the stream. This is a simplifying assumption that would not automatically hold in typical warehouse catalogues, but it does provide a plausible locality behavior and makes the degree of locality very transparent.

EXPERIMENTS

We performed an experimental evaluation of HYBRIDJOIN, using synthetic datasets. In this section we describe the environment of our experiments and analyze the results that we obtained using different scenarios.

Experimental Setup

In order to implement the prototypes of existing MESHJOIN, Index Nested Loop Join (INLJ) and our proposed HYBRIDJOIN algorithms we used the following hardware and data specifications.

- **Hardware Specifications:** We carried out our experimentation on a Pentium-IV 2X2.13GHz machine with 3G main and 160G disk memory under WindowsXP. We implemented the experiment in Java using the Eclipse IDE 3.3.1.1. We also used built-in plugins, provided by Apache, and *nanoTime()*, provided by the Java API, to measure the memory and *processing time* respectively.
- **Data Specifications:** We analyzed the performance of each of the algorithms using synthetic data. The relation R is stored on disk using MySQL 5.0 database, while the bursty type of stream data is generated at run time using our own generator. Both the algorithms read master data from the database. In transformation, join is normally performed between the primary key of the lookup table and the foreign key in the stream tuple and therefore our HYBRIDJOIN supports join for one-to-many relationships and it can be extended for many-to-many relationships easily. In order to implement the join for one-to-many relationships it needs to store multiple values in the hash table against one key value. However the hash table provided by the Java API does not support this feature

therefore, we used Multi-Hash-Map, provided by Apache, as the hash table in our experiments. The detailed specification of the data set that we used for analysis is shown in Table 2.

We compare the performance of HYBRIDJOIN with MESHJOIN and INLJ while varying total allocated memory M, the size of relation R on disk, the value of the exponent for the Zipfian distribution, and the stream arrival rate λ. The other parameters such as the size of disk buffer, size of stream buffer, size of each disk tuple, size of each stream tuple, and the size of each node in the queue are considered fixed. The stream dataset we used to evaluate HYBRIDJOIN is based on Zipf's law and has two important characteristics, bursty and self-similarity (for details, see the Appendix). We test the performance of all the algorithms by varying the Zipfian exponent value from 0 to 1.

- **Measurement Strategy:** The performance or service rate of the join is measured by

Table 2. Data specifications

Parameter	Value
Memory	
Total allocated memory M	50MB to 250MB
Exponent	
Zipfian exponent value	0 to 1
Disk-based data	
Size of disk-based relation R	0.5 million to 8 million tuples
Size of each disk tuple	120 bytes
Stream data	
Size each stream tuple	20 bytes
Size of each nodes in queue	12 bytes
Stream arrival rate λ	125 to 2000 tuples/sec
Benchmark	
Based on	Zipf's law
Characteristics	Bursty and self-similar

calculating the maximum number of tuples processed in a unit second. In each experiment the algorithm runs for one hour and we start our measurements after 20 minutes and continue it for 20 minutes. For more accuracy we take three readings for each specification and then calculate confidence intervals for every result by considering 95% accuracy. Moreover, during the execution of the algorithm it is assumed that no other application is running in parallel.

Experimental Results

We conducted two kinds of evaluation. In Section 6.2.1 we compare the performance of all three approaches, while in Section 6.2.2 we validate the cost by comparing it with the predicted cost.

Performance Comparison

As the source code for MESHJOIN is not openly available, we implemented the MESHJOIN algorithm ourselves. In our experiments we compare the performance in two different ways. First, we compare HYBRIDJOIN with MESHJOIN with respect to the time, both *processing time* and *waiting time*. Second, we compare the performance in terms of service rate with other two algorithms.

- **Performance comparisons with respect to time:** To test the performance with respect to time we conduct two different experiments. The experiment, shown in Figure 7(a), presents the comparisons with respect to *processing time* on a log scale, while Figure 7(b) depicts the comparisons with respect to the *waiting time*. The terms *processing time* and *waiting time* have already been defined in Section 3. According to Figure 7(a) the *processing time* in the case of HYBRIDJOIN is significantly smaller than that of MESHJOIN. The reason behind this is the different strategy to

access R. The MESHJOIN algorithm accesses all disk partitions with the same frequency without considering the rate of use of each partition on the disk. In HYBRIDJOIN an index based approach is implemented that never reads unused disk partitions of R. In this experiment we do not reflect the *processing time* for INLJ because it is constant even when the size of R changes.

In the experiment shown in Figure 7(b) we compare the time that each algorithm waits (except Index Nested Loop Join). In the case of INLJ, since the algorithm works at tuple level, the algorithm does not need to wait but this delay then appears in the form of stream backlog that occurs due to a faster incoming stream rate than the processing rate. Also this delay (*waiting time*) increases with an increase in the stream arrival rate.

In the other two approaches the *waiting time* in MESHJOIN is greater than in HYBRIDJOIN. In HYBRIDJOIN since there is no constraint to match each stream tuple with the whole of R, each disk invocation is not synchronized with the stream input. However, for stream arrival rates less than 150 tuples/sec, the *waiting time* in HYBRIDJOIN is greater than that in INLJ. A plausible reason for this is the greater I/O cost in the case of HYBRIDJOIN when the size of the input stream is assumed to be equal in both algorithms.

- **Performance comparisons with respect to service rate:** In this category of our experiments we compare the performance of HYBRIDJOIN in terms of the service rate with the other two join algorithms by varying different parameters such as the total memory budget, the size of R, and the value of Zipfian exponent. In the experiment shown in Figure 7(c) we assume the total allocated memory for the join is fixed while the size of R varies exponentially. From Figure 7(c) it can be observed

Figure 7. Performance evaluation

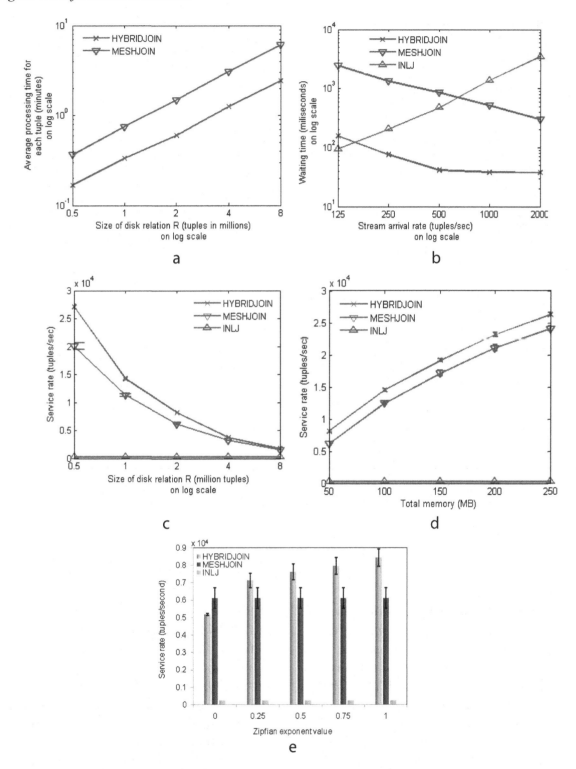

Figure 8. Cost validation

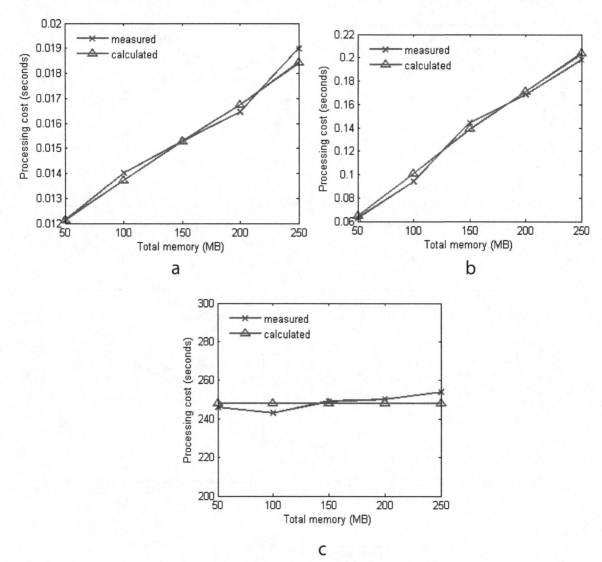

that for all sizes of *R*, the performance of HYBRIDJOIN is significantly better compared with the other join approaches. In our second experiment of this category we analyse the performance of HYBRIDJOIN using different memory budgets, while the size of *R* is fixed (2 million tuples). Figure 7(d) depicts the comparisons of all three approaches. From Figure 7(d) it is clear that for all memory budgets the performance of HYBRIDJOIN is better as compared to the other two algorithms.

Finally, we evaluate the performance of HYBRIDJOIN by varying the skew in input stream *S*. To vary the skew, we vary the value of the Zipfian exponent *e*. In our experiments we allow it to range from 0 to 1. At 0 the input stream *S* is uniform and the skew increases as *e* increases. Figure 7(e) presents the results of our experiment. It is clear from Figure 7(e) that under all values of *e* except 0, HYBRIDJOIN performs considerably better than MESHJOIN and INLJ. Also this improvement increases with an increase in *e*. The plausible reason for this better performance in the case of HYBRIDJOIN is that the algorithm does not read unused parts of R into memory and it saves unnecessary I/O cost. Moreover, when e increases the input stream S gets more skewed and consequently, the I/O cost decreases due to an increase in the size of the unused part of R. However, when e is equal to 0, HYBRIDJOIN performs worse than MESHJOIN but it is only worse by a constant factor.

Cost Validation

In this experiment we validate the cost model for all three approaches by comparing the predicted cost with the measured cost. Figure 8 presents the comparisons of both costs. In Figure 8 it is demonstrated that the predicted cost closely resembles the measured cost in every approach which validates the accuracy of our cost model.

CONCLUSION AND FUTURE WORK

In the context of real-time data warehousing a join operator is required to perform a continuous join between the fast stream and the disk-based relation within limited resources. In this paper we investigated two available stream-based join algorithms and presented a robust join algorithm, HYBRIDJOIN.

Our main objectives in HYBRIDJOIN are: (a) to minimize the stay of every stream tuple in the join window by improving the efficiency of the access to the disk-based relation, (b) to deal with the bursty data streams. We developed a cost model and tuning methodology in order to achieve the maximum performance within the limited resources. We designed our own benchmark to test our approach according to current market economics. To validate our arguments we implemented a prototype of HYBRIDJOIN that demonstrates a significant improvement in service rate under limited memory. We also provide the implementations.

In order to further improve the performance of HYBRIDJOIN, we will extend the implementation of the proposed join algorithm by dynamically ordering the disk-based relation with respect to access frequency.

REFERENCES

Anderson, C. (2006). *The long tail: Why the future of business is selling less of more* (pp. 130–135). New York, NY: Hyperion.

Babu, S., & Widom, J. (2001). Continuous queries over data streams. *SIGMOD Record, 30*(3), 109–120. doi:10.1145/603867.603884

Chakraborty, A., & Singh, A. (2009). A partition-based approach to support streaming updates over persistent data in an active data warehouse. In *Proceedings of the IEEE International Symposium on Parallel & Distributed Processing* (pp. 1-11).

Golab, L., & Özsu, M. T. (2003). Processing sliding window multi-joins in continuous queries over data streams. In *Proceedings of the 29th International Conference on Very Large Data Bases*, Berlin, Germany (pp. 500-511).

Golfarelli, M., & Rizzi, S. (2009a). A survey on temporal data warehousing. *International Journal of Data Warehousing and Mining, 5*(1), 1–17. doi:10.4018/jdwm.2009010101

Golfarelli, M., & Rizzi, S. (2009b). What-if simulation modeling in business intelligence. *International Journal of Data Warehousing and Mining, 5*(4), 24–43. doi:10.4018/jdwm.2009080702

Gupta, A., & Mumick, I. S. (1999). *Maintenance of materialized views: Problems, techniques, and applications (Vol. 18)*. Cambridge, MA: MIT Press.

Hammad, M. A., Aref, W. G., & Elmagarmid, A. K. (2008). Query processing of multi-way stream window joins. *Very Large Data Bases Journal, 17*(3), 469–488. doi:10.1007/s00778-006-0017-y

Ives, Z. G., Florescu, D., Friedman, M., Levy, A., & Weld, D. S. (1999). An adaptive query execution system for data integration. *SIGMOD Record*, *28*(2), 299–310. doi:10.1145/304181.304209

Karakasidis, A., Vassiliadis, P., & Pitoura, E. (2005). ETL queues for active data warehousing. In *Proceedings of the 2nd International Workshop on Information Quality in Information Systems*, Baltimore, MD (pp. 28-39).

Kim, J., & Park, S. (2005). Periodic streaming data reduction using flexible adjustment of time section size. *International Journal of Data Warehousing and Mining*, *1*(1), 37–56. doi:10.4018/jdwm.2005010102

Knuth, D. E. (1998). *The art of computer programming* (*Vol. 3*, pp. 400–401). Reading, MA: Addison-Wesley.

Labio, W., & Garcia-Molina, H. (1996). Efficient snapshot differential algorithms for data warehousing. In *Proceedings of the 22nd International Conference on Very Large Data Bases*, San Francisco, CA (pp. 63-74.)

Labio, W., Wiener, J. L., Garcia-Molina, H., & Gorelik, V. (2000). Efficient resumption of interrupted warehouse loads. *SIGMOD Record*, *29*(2), 46–57. doi:10.1145/335191.335379

Labio, W., Yang, J., Cui, Y., Garcia-Molina, H., & Widom, J. (2000). Performance issues in incremental warehouse maintenance. In *Proceedings of the 26th International Conference on Very Large Data Bases*, San Francisco, CA (pp. 461-472).

Lawrence, R. (2005). Early hash join: A configurable algorithm for the efficient and early production of join results. In *Proceedings of the 31st International Conference on Very Large Data Bases*, Trondheim, Norway (pp. 841-852).

Mokbel, M. F., Lu, M., & Aref, W. G. (2004). Hash-merge join: A non-blocking join algorithm for producing fast and early join results. In *Proceedings of the 20th International Conference on Data Engineering*, Washington, DC (pp. 251-263).

Naeem, M. A., Dobbie, G., & Weber, G. (2008). An event-based near real-time data integration architecture. In *Proceedings of the 12th Enterprise Distributed Object Computing Conference Workshops*, Washington, DC (pp. 401-404).

Nguyen, T. M. (2003). Zero-latency data warehousing for heterogeneous data sources and continuous data streams. In *Proceedings of the Fifth International Conference on Information Integration and Web-based Applications Services*, Jakarta, Indonesia (pp. 55-64).

Nguyen, T. M., Brezany, P., Tjoa, A. M., & Weippl, E. (2005). Toward a grid-based zero-latency data warehousing implementation for continuous data streams processing. *International Journal of Data Warehousing and Mining*, *1*(4), 22–55. doi:10.4018/jdwm.2005100102

Palma, W., Akbarinia, R., Pacitti, E., & Valduriez, P. (2009). DHTJoin: Processing continuous join queries using DHT networks. *Distributed and Parallel Databases*, *26*(2-3), 291–317. doi:10.1007/s10619-009-7054-7

Polyzotis, N., Skiadopoulos, S., Vassiliadis, P., Simitsis, A., & Frantzell, N. (2008). Meshing streaming updates with persistent data in an active data warehouse. *IEEE Transactions on Knowledge and Data Engineering*, *20*(7), 976–991. doi:10.1109/TKDE.2008.27

Polyzotis, N., Skiadopoulos, S., Vassiliadis, P., Simitsis, A., & Frantzell, N. E. (2007). Supporting streaming updates in an active data warehouse. In *Proceedings of the 23rd International Conference on Data Engineering*, Istanbul, Turkey (pp. 476-485).

Ramakrishnan, R. (1999). *Database management systems* (2nd ed., pp. 337–339). New York, NY: McGraw-Hill.

Shapiro, L. D. (1986). Join processing in database systems with large main memories. *ACM Transactions on Database Systems*, *11*(3), 239–264. doi:10.1145/6314.6315

Thiele, M., Fischer, U., & Lehner, W. (2007). Partition-based workload scheduling in living data warehouse environments. In *Proceedings of the ACM Tenth International Workshop on Data Warehousing and OLAP*, Lisbon, Portugal (pp. 57-64).

Thomsen, C., & Pedersen, T. B. (2009). A survey of open source tools for business intelligence. *International Journal of Data Warehousing and Mining, 5*(3), 56–75. doi:10.4018/jdwm.2009070103

Urhan, T., & Franklin, M. (2000). XJoin: A reactively-scheduled pipelined join operator. *A Quarterly Bulletin of the Computer Society of the IEEE Technical Committee on Data Engineering, 23*(27).

Vassiliadis, P. (2009). A survey of extract–transform–load technology. *International Journal of Data Warehousing and Mining, 5*(3), 1–27. doi:10.4018/jdwm.2009070101

Wilschut, A. N., & Apers, P. M. G. (1990). Pipelining in query execution. In *Proceedings of the International Conference on Databases, Parallel Architectures and their Applications*, Miami Beach, FL (p. 562).

Wilschut, A. N., & Apers, P. M. G. (1991). Dataflow query execution in a parallel main-memory environment. In *Proceedings of the First International Conference on Parallel and Distributed Information Systems*, Miami, FL (pp. 68-77).

Zhang, X., & Rundensteiner, E. A. (2002). Integrating the maintenance and synchronization of data warehouses using a cooperative framework. *Information Systems, 27*(4), 219–243. doi:10.1016/S0306-4379(01)00049-7

Zhuge, Y., García-Molina, H., Hammer, J., & Widom, J. (1995). View maintenance in a warehousing environment. In *Proceedings of the ACM SIGMOD International Conference on Management of Data*, San Jose, CA (pp. 316-327).

APPENDIX

BENCHMARK

In order to demonstrate the behavior of the algorithm with a bursty stream, we implemented a stream generator that produces stream tuples with a timing that is self-similar.

This bursty generation of tuples models a flow of sales transactions which depends upon fluctuations over several time periods, such as market hours, weekly rhythms and seasons.

The pseudo-code for the generation of our benchmark is shown in Figure 9. In Figure 9 *STREAM-GENERATOR* is the main procedure while *GETDISTRIBUTIONVALUE* and *SWAPSTATUS* are the sub-procedures that are called from the main procedure. According to the main procedure a number of virtual stream objects (in our case 10), each representing the same distribution value obtained from the *GETDISTRIBUTIONVALUE* procedure, are inserted into a priority queue, which always keeps sorting these objects into ascending order (line 5 to 7). Once all the virtual stream objects are inserted into the priority queue the top most stream object is taken out (line 8). To generate an infinite stream a loop is executed (line 9 to 18). In each iteration of the loop, the algorithm waits for a while (depending on the value of variable *oneStep*) and then checks whether the current time is greater than the time when that particular object was inserted. If the condition is true the algorithm dequeues the next object from the priority queue and calls the *SWAPSTATUS* procedure (line 11 to 14). The *SWAPSTATUS* procedure enqueues the current dequeued stream object by updating its time interval and bandwidth (line 19 to 27). Once the value of the variable *totalCurrentBandwidth* is updated, the main procedure generates the final stream tuple values as an output using the procedure *GETDISTRIBUTIONVALUE* line (15 to 17). For each call to procedure *GETDISTRIBUTIONVALUE*, it returns the random value by implementing Zipf's law with exponent value equal to 1 (line 28 to 31).

The experimental representation of our benchmark is shown in Figure 10 and Figure 11, while the environment in which the experiments are conducted is described in Section 6.1. As described earlier in this section, our benchmark is based on two characteristics; one is the frequency of selling each product while the other is the flow of these sales transactions. Figure 10 validates the first characteristic about real market sales. In Figure 10 the x-axis represents the variety of products while the y-axis represents the sales. Therefore, from Figure 10 it can be observed that only a limited number of products (20%) are sold frequently while the rest of the products are rarely sold.

Our proposed HYBRIDJOIN is fully adapted to such kinds of data in which only a small portion of R is accessed again and again while the rest of R is accessed rarely.

Figure 11 represents the flow of transactions, which is the second characteristic of our benchmark. From Figure 11 it is clear that the flow of transactions varies with time and is bursty rather than appearing at a regular rate.

Figure 9. Pseudo-code for benchmark

Procedure STREAMGENERATOR

---

1. *totalCurrentBandwidth* ← 0
2. *timeInChosenUnit* ← o
3. *on* ← *false*
4. *d* ← GETDISTRIBUTIONVALUE( )
5. **For** *i=1* to *N*
6.   *PriorityQueue.enqueue(d,bandwidth=*
     Math.power(2,i),timeInChosenUnit=currentTime( ))
7. **EndFor**
8. *current* ← *PriorityQueue.dequeue( )*
9. **While** (*true*)
10.   Wait(*oneStep*)
11.   **If** (*currentTime( ) > current.timeInChosenUnit*)
12.   *current* ← *PriorityQueue.dequeue( )*
13.   SWAPSTATUS(*current*)
14.   **EndIf**
15.   **For** *j=1* to *totalCurrentBandwidth*
16.   **Output** GETDISTRIBUTIONVALUE( )
17.   **EndFor**
18. **EndWhile**

Procedure SWAPSTATUS (*current*)

---

19. *timeInChosenUnit* ← *(current.timeInChosenUnit +*
    getNextRandom() × oneStep × current.bandwidth)
20. **If** (*on*)
21.   *totalCurrentBandwidth* ← *totalCurrentBandwidth –*
                   current.bandwidth
22.   *on* ← *false*
23. **Else**
24.   *totalCurrentBandwidth* ← *totalCurrentBandwidth +*
                   current.bandwidth
25.   *on* ← *true*
26. **EndIf**
27. *PriorityQueue.enqueue(current)*

Procedure GETDISTRIBUTIONVALUE

---

28. $sumOfFrequency \leftarrow \int \frac{1}{x} dx_{atx-max} - \int \frac{1}{x} dx_{atx-min}$

29. *random* ← *getNextRandom()*
30. *distributionValue* ← *inverseIntegralOf (random* x
             $sumOfFrequency + \int \frac{1}{x} dx_{atx-min})$
31. **return** ⌊*distributionValue*⌋

Figure 10. A skewed distribution based on Zipf's law using exponent value is equal to 1

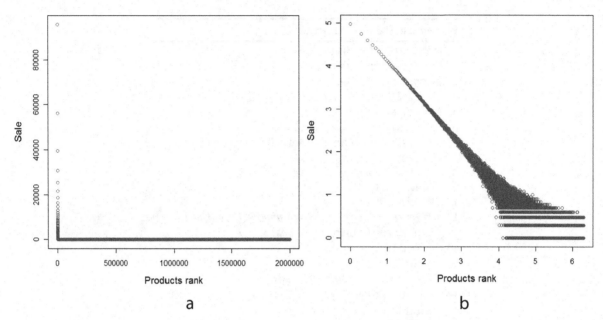

a   b

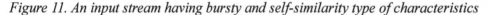

Figure 11. An input stream having bursty and self-similarity type of characteristics

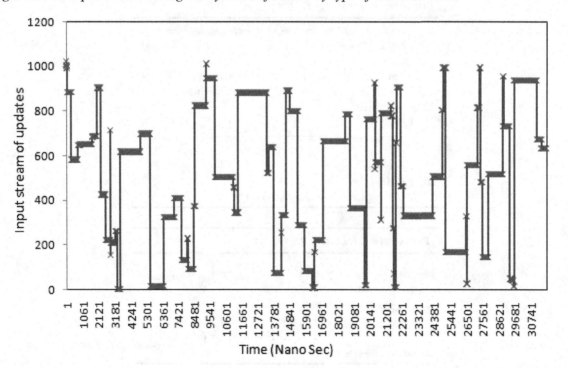

This work was previously published in the International Journal of Data Warehousing and Mining, Volume 7, Issue 4, edited by David Taniar, pp. 21-42, copyright 2011 by IGI Publishing (an imprint of IGI Global).

Chapter 14
Data Field for Hierarchical Clustering

Shuliang Wang
The University of Pittsburgh, USA & Wuhan University, China

Deyi Li
Tsinghua University, China

Wenyan Gan
Nanjing University of Science and Technology, China

Deren Li
Wuhan University, China

ABSTRACT

In this paper, data field is proposed to group data objects via simulating their mutual interactions and opposite movements for hierarchical clustering. Enlightened by the field in physical space, data field to simulate nuclear field is presented to illuminate the interaction between objects in data space. In the data field, the self-organized process of equipotential lines on many data objects discovers their hierarchical clustering-characteristics. During the clustering process, a random sample is first generated to optimize the impact factor. The masses of data objects are then estimated to select core data object with nonzero masses. Taking the core data objects as the initial clusters, the clusters are iteratively merged hierarchy by hierarchy with good performance. The results of a case study show that the data field is capable of hierarchical clustering on objects varying size, shape or granularity without user-specified parameters, as well as considering the object features inside the clusters and removing the outliers from noisy data. The comparisons illustrate that the data field clustering performs better than K-means, BIRCH, CURE, and CHAMELEON.

INTRODUCTION

The rapid advance in massive data acquisition, transmission and storage results in the growth of vast computerized datasets at unprecedented rates. These datasets come from various sectors, e.g., business, education, government, scientific community, Internet, or one of many readily available off-line and online data sources in the form of text, graphic, image, video, audio, animation, hyperlinks, markups, and so on (Li, Zhang, & Wang, 2006; Bhatnagar, Kaur, & Mignet, 2009). Moreover, they are continuously increasing and amassed in both attribute depth and scope of in-

DOI: 10.4018/978-1-4666-2148-0.ch014

stances every time. Although many decisions are made on large datasets, the huge amounts of the computerized datasets have far exceeded human ability to completely interpret (Li et al., 2006). In order to understand and make full use of these data repositories when making decisions, it is necessary to develop some technique for uncovering the physical nature inside such huge datasets.

Clustering is one of the techniques to discover a segmentation rule from these data repositories. It assigns a set of objects into clusters (subsets) by virtue of their observations so that objects are similar to one another within the same cluster and are dissimilar to the objects in other clusters (Murtagh, 1983; Grabmeier & Rudolph, 2002; Xu & Wunsch, 2005; Li, Wang, & Li, 2006; Malik et al., 2010). It is an unsupervised technique without the knowledge what causes the grouping and how many groups exist (Song, Hu, & Yoo, 2009; Engle & Gangopadhyay, 2010; Silla & Freitas, 2011). The arbitrary shaped clustering was further treated (Wan, Wang, & Su, 2010). Clustering may be implemented on hierarchy, partition, density, grid, constraint, subspace and so on (Sander et al., 1998; Kwok et al., 2002; Grabmeier & Rudolph, 2002; Parsons, Haque, & Liu, 2004; Zhang et al., 2008; Horng et al., 2011).

Hierarchy-Based Clustering

Hierarchy-based clustering finds successive clusters using previously established clusters (Murtagh, 1983). It uncovers a nested sequence of clusters with a single, all-inclusive cluster at the top and single-point clusters at the bottom. In the sequence, each cluster is nested into the next cluster (Guha, Rastogi, & Shim, 1998). Hierarchical clustering algorithms are either agglomerative or divisive. Agglomerative algorithms start with each element as a disjoint set of clusters and merge them into successively larger clusters (Sembiring, Zain, & Embong, 2010). Divisive algorithms begin with the whole set and proceed to divide it

into successively smaller clusters (Malik et al., 2010). One of the simplest methods is K-means that take each point belonging to a given data set and associate it to the nearest centroid after each cluster is defined with a centroid on the basis of a sample (MacQueen, 1967). But its cluster assumption of hyper-ellipsoidal and similar sizes prevented from uncovering the clusters that vary in size or concave shapes. When the amount of input data was large, the algorithms further broke down due to their non-linear time complexity and huge input costs. BIRCH (Balanced Iterative Reducing and Clustering using Hierarchies) was proposed to remedy this problem (Zhang, Ramakrishnman, & Linvy, 1996). In pre-clustering phase to reduce input size, dense regions of points were represented by compact summaries, and using the centroids of summaries as cluster seeds, each data point was assigned to the summarized cluster with the closest seed in labeling phase. Only using the centroid to redistribute the data, if the clusters did not have uniform sizes and shapes, a number of points in the bigger cluster were labeled as belonging to the smaller cluster since they were closer to the centroid of the smaller cluster. To alleviate their shortcomings, CURE (Clustering Using Representatives) was presented to adopt a middle ground between the all data extremes and the centroid-based approaches. Drawing a random sample from the database to shrink the representative points toward the centroid, CURE could group the clusters of arbitrary shapes and sizes, even avoid some problems associated with outliers (Guha, Rastogi, & Shim, 1998). Ignoring the information about the aggregate interconnectivity of items in two clusters, it failed to account for special characteristics of individual clusters. Accounting for both interconnectivity and closeness in identifying the most similar pair of clusters, CHAMELEON was given to yields accurate results for highly variable clusters using dynamic modeling (George, Han, & Kumar, 1999). However, CHAMELEON was not suitable to group large volume of data (Li, Wang, & Xu, 2008). Some clustering algorithms were further hybridized, for example, CHAMELEON based on clustering feature tree (CBCFT) hybridizing BIRCH with CHAMELEON (Li, Wang, & Xu, 2008). Hierarchical clustering was also implemented together with other methods, for example, Bayesian hierarchical clustering on evaluating marginal likelihoods of a probabilistic model (Heller & Ghahramani, 2005), support vector machine (Horng et al., 2011), fuzzy clustering with comprehensive evaluation (Wang & Wang, 2007).

Although they got the resulting clusters in some cases, existing algorithms reveal some disadvantage of hierarchical clustering at different levels with different cluster granularities. Most algorithms look for clusters to fit some static model but cannot take full advantage of the nature of individual clusters. The model sometimes cannot adequately capture the clusters' characteristics. Partially neglecting either the aggregate interconnectivity of items in two clusters, or the similarity closeness of items across two clusters, the wrong pair of clusters is easily selected as they are merged. Even some algorithms break down if the data include the clusters of diverse shapes, densities, and sizes. Usually, a user is obliged to specify the agglomerative or divisive conditions. If the user sets inappropriate model parameters, the data may be clustered incorrectly in a chainable sequence. Once the termination threshold has been determined, a cluster cannot be cancelled that some mistakes may result in clusters with low accuracy. Besides the obvious spherical bias, the algorithmic complexity is at least $O(n^2)$. Such algorithms as BIRCH, CURE, and CHAMELEON improved the clustering accuracy, but they still depended on the suitable parameter given by the users (MacQueen, 1967; Murtagh, 1983; Grabmeier & Rudolph, 2002; Xu & Wunsch, 2005; Li, Wang, & Li, 2006; Malik et al., 2010). When the amount of dataset is larger and data objects have many dimensional attributes, it becomes much more difficult for a user to give the algorithmic parameters, even it is impracticable. The outliers are also ignored to process effectively. Thus, it is necessary to discover novel algorithms for clustering large data sets.

From Physical Field to Data Field

Anaxagoras, a Greek philosopher, thought physical nature was "a portion of everything in everything." Visible or invisible particles are mutually interacted. Sometimes, the interaction is untouched between physical particles. Michael Faraday first put forward the field concept to describe such the interaction. He believed that the untouched interaction between physical particles had to be performed via a transforming media that was the field. In order to visually portray an electronic field configuration, he further introduced the concept of electronic field line, drawing a vector of proper length and direction at every point of space. Each field line has a starting point and an ending point, which originates at the source and terminates at the sink. In a charge–free-region, every field line is continuous that originates a positive charge and terminates on a negative charge, and they do not intersect. In space, a particle makes a field, and a field acts on another particle (Giachetta, Mangiarotti, & Sardanashvily, 2009).

In physical space, interacted-particles lead to various fields. Due to the interacting particles, the field can be either classical field or quantum field. According to the interacting range, the field may be long-range or short-range. As interacting range increases, the strength of the long-range field slowly diminishes to the point of being undetectable, e.g., gravitational field, electromagnetic fields, while the strength of the short-range field rapidly attenuates to zero, e.g., nuclear field (Blatt, 1986). Based on the interacting transformation, the field is often classified as scalar field, vector field, tensor field, and spinor field. At each point, scalar field's values are given by a single variable on quantitative difference, vector field is specified by attaching a vector with magnitude and direction, tensor field is specified by a tensor, and spinor field is for quantum field theory. The vector field may be with sources or without sources. A vector field with constant zero divergence is a field without sources, e.g., magnetic field, otherwise it is a field with sources, e.g., electrostatic field. In basic physics, the vector field is often studied on the field with sources, such as Newton's law of universal gravitation and Coulomb's law. When it is put in the field with sources, an arbitrary particle feels a force with strength (Giachetta, Mangiarotti, & Sardanashvily, 2009). Moreover, according to the values of field quantity whether changes over time at each point, the field with sources can be further grouped into time-varying field and stable active field. The stable field with sources is also known as a potential field.

The field strength is often represented by using the potential. In the field, the potential difference between an arbitrary point and another referenced point is a determinate value on a unit particle. The physical potential means the work performed by a field force when a unit particle is moved from an arbitrary point to another referenced point in the field. It is a scalar quantity of the amount of energy transferred by the force acting through a distance. The energy is the capacity to do the work, and the potential energy refers to the ability of a system to do work by virtue of its position or internal structure (Blatt, 1986). The distribution of the potential field corresponds to the distribution of the potential energy determined by the relative position between interacted particles. Specifying the potential value at a point in space requires such parameters as object mass or electrical charge, distance between a point and its field source, while it is independent of the direction of distance vector. The strength of the field is visualized via the equipotential that refers to a region in space where every point in it is at the same potential.

In physics, it is a fact that the vacuum is free of matter but not free of field. Modern physics even think that the field is one of the basic forms of particle existence, for example, mechanical field, nuclear field, gravitational field, thermal field, electromagnetic field, and crystal field. With the development of field theory, the field is abstracted as a mathematical concept to depict the distribution rule of a physical quantity or mathematical function in space (Landau & Lifshitz, 1980). The potential function is often simply seen as a monotonic function of spatial location, having nothing to do with the existence of the particle. That is, there exists a field of the physical quantity or mathematical function in a space if every point in the space has an exact value from the physical quantity or mathematical function.

Inspiration from Physical Field

Data space is an exact branch of physical space. In the data space, all objects are mutually interacted via data too. From a generic physical space to an exact data space, the physical nature of the relationship between the objects is identical to that of the interaction between the particles. If the object described with data is taken as a particle with mass, then data field can be derived from physical field.

Enlightened by the field in physical space, the field is introduced to illuminate the interaction between objects in data space. In the data space, all objects are mutually interacted via data. An object described with data is treated as a particle with mass. The data refer to the attributes of the object as determined from observation, while the mass is the physical quantity of matter as determined from its weight or from Newton's second law of motion. Surrounding the object, there is a virtual field simulating the physical field around particles. Each objet has its own field. Given a task, the field gives a virtual media to show the mutual interaction between objects without touching each other. An object transforms its field to other objects, and it also receives all the fields from those. According to their contributions to the given task, the field strength of each object is different, which uncovers different interaction. By using such the interaction, objects may be self-organized under the given data and task. Some patterns that are previously unknown, potentially useful and ultimately understood may be further extracted from datasets.

In this paper, data field is proposed to characterize the interaction between objects for extracting the interested patterns, inspired by the ideology of physical field. In an internal field of a force without any external forces, two objects are oppositely moved because of their mutual attraction. When they meet each other or the distance between them is small enough, the objects are merged into a new object whose momentum is the sum of two objects' ones under the law of momentum conservation. If the velocity is the same, the mass of the merged object is the sum of two objects' ones. In the data field that describes the interactions among the objects, data objects are grouped into clusters by simulating their opposite movements. During the process of iterative amalgamation at different levels, a structure of hierarchical clusters comes into being.

In the rest of this paper, the definition and functions of data field are presented, which is followed by the clustering algorithms with data fields. The case study is examined and finally, the conclusion is drawn.

DATA FIELDS

Data field is to depict the interaction between objects associated to each data point of the whole space, simulating the methodology of physical field. Its field function mathematically models how the data strengths on a given task are diffused from the universe of sample to the universe of population when interacting between objects. In the universe of discourse, all objects with sampled data not only radiate their data strengths but also receive the data strengths from others. According to the given task and the physical nature of objects from data distribution, the field function may be derived from physical field. All the equipotential lines depict the interesting topological relationships among the objects, which visually indicate the interacted characteristics of objects.

Fundamental Definitions

Definition 1: In data space $\Omega \subseteq R^P$, let dataset $D = \{x_1, x_2, ..., x_n\}$ denote a P-dimensional independent random sample, where $x_i = (x_{i1}, x_{i2}, ..., x_{iP})^T$ with $i = 1, 2, ..., n$. Each data object x_i is taken as a particle with mass m_i. x_i radiates its data energy and is also influenced by others simultaneously. Surrounding x_i, a virtual field is derived from the corresponding physical field. Such the virtual field is called data field.

In the context of the definition, there exit a data field only if the necessary conditions are characterized, i.e., short-range, with source and temporal behavior.

1. Data field is a short-range field. For an arbitrary point in the data space Ω, all the fields from different objects are overlapped to get a superposed field. If there are two points, x_1 with enough data samples, and x_2 with less or no data samples, it is obvious that the summarized strength of data field at the point x_1 must be stronger than that of x_2. That is, the range of data field is so short that its magnitude decreases rapidly to 0 as the distance increases. The rapid attenuation may reduce the affect from noisy data or outlier data. The effect of the superposed field may further highlight the clustering characteristics of the objects in close proximity within data-intensive areas. The potential value of an arbitrary point in space does not reply on the direction from the object so that data field is isotropic and spherical symmetry. The interaction between two faraway objects can be ignored.

2. Data field is a field with sources. The divergence is to measure the magnitude of a vector field at a given point, in terms of a signed scalar. If it is positive, it is called a source. If it is negative, it is called a sink. If it is zero in a domain, there is no source or sink, and it is called solenoidal (Landau & Lifshitz, 1980). Data field is smooth everywhere away from the original source. And the outward flux of a vector field through a closed surface is equal to the volume integral of the divergence on the region inside the surface.

3. Data field has temporal behavior. The data on objects are static independent of time. For the stable field with sources independent of time in space, there exists a scalar potential function $\varphi(x)$ corresponding to the vector field function $\vec{F}(x)$ that describes the intensity function. Both functions can be interconnected with differential operator (Giachetta, Mangiarotti, & Sardanashvily, 2009), $\vec{F}(x) = \nabla\phi(x)$.

Mathematical Model

The distribution law of data field can be mathematically described with scalar potential function and vector strength function. In a data space $\Omega \subseteq R^p$, a data object x_i brings about a virtual field with the mass m_i. If there exists an arbitrary point $x = (x_1, x_2, \ldots, x_p)^T$ in Ω, the scalar potential function of data field on x_i is defined as Equation 1.

$$\phi(x_i) = m_i \times K\left(\frac{\|x - x_i\|}{\sigma}\right) \tag{1}$$

where $m_i \left(m_i \geq 0, \sum_{i=1}^{n} m_i = 1 \right)$ is treated as the mass of data object x_i, and it represents the strength of data field from x_i. $K(x)$ that satisfies $\int K(x)dx = 1, \int xK(x)dx = 0$ is the unit poten-

tial function to express the law that x_i always radiates its data energy in the same way in its data field. $\|x\text{-}x_i\|$ is the distance between data object x_i and the point x in the field. $\sigma \in (0, +\infty)$ is an impact factor that controls the interacted distance between objects. In fact, the potential function reflects the density of data distribution. It can be proved that there is only a normalized constant between the potential function and its probabilistic density function if $\int_{\Omega} K(x)dx = M < +\infty$ (Giachetta, Mangiarotti, & Sardanashvily, 2009).

Obviously, each data object x_i in D has its own data field in the data space Ω. All the data fields will be superposed on the point x. In other words, any data object is affected by all the other objects in the data space. So the potential value of the arbitrary point x in the data fields on D in Ω is defined as

$$\phi(x) = \sum_{i=1}^{n} m_i \times K\left(\frac{\|x - x_i\|}{\sigma}\right) \tag{2}$$

Because the gradient of a potential function is the strength function of the corresponding force field, the data field vector at x is

$$\vec{F}(x) = \nabla\phi(x) = \sum_{i=1}^{n}\left[(x_i - x) \times m_i \times K\left(\frac{\|x - x_i\|}{\sigma}\right) \right] \tag{3}$$

Simulating Nuclear Field

Selecting the function format may have to consider such conditions as the nature inside data characteristics, the feature of data radiation, the standard to determine the field-strength, the application domain of the data field and so on (Li, Wang, & Li, 2006). In the context of physical nature of data, data field has to be short-range, with source and temporal behavior. Because scalar operation is simpler, more intuitive than vector operation, the following criteria is recommended on selecting the potential function of the data field that the potential $\varphi(x)$ of an arbitrary data object x_i at an arbitrary position x should satisfy three conditions: [1] $\varphi(x)$ is a continuous, smooth, and finite function that is defined in Ω, [2] $\varphi(x)$ is isotropic, and [3] $\varphi(x)$ is a monotonically decreasing function on the distance between x_i and x. $\varphi(x)$ is maximum when the distance is 0, while $\varphi(x)$ approaches 0 when the distance tends to infinity. Generally speaking, a function that matches the above three criteria can define the potential function of data field.

It is known that a nucleon generates a centralized force field in an atomic nucleus. In space, the nuclear force acts radially toward or away from the source of the force field, and the potential of the nuclear field decreases rapidly to 0. Thus, a potential function of data field is studied to simulate nuclear field. There are three methods to compute the potential value of a point in the nuclear field, Gaussian potential, Square-well potential, and Exponential potential. Because Gaussian distribution is ubiquitous and Gaussian function matches the physical nature of data field, Gaussian potential is selected to depict the scalar potential of data field. At the arbitrary point $x \in \Omega$, the scalar potential and vector strength of the data field from data object x_i is Equation 4 and 5. And the scalar potentials and vector strengths of the data fields from all data objects in dataset D is Equation 6 and 7.

$$\phi(x_i) = m_i \times e^{-\left(\frac{\|x-x_i\|}{\sigma}\right)^2} \tag{4}$$

$$\vec{F}(x_i) = \nabla\phi(x_i) = (x_i - x) \times m_i \times e^{-\left(\frac{\|x-x_i\|}{\sigma}\right)^2} \tag{5}$$

$$\phi(x) = \sum_{i=1}^{n}\left[m_i \times e^{-\left(\frac{\|x-x_i\|}{\sigma}\right)^2} \right] \tag{6}$$

$$\vec{F}(x) = \nabla\phi(x) = \sum_{i=1}^{n}\left[(x_i - x) \times m_i \times e^{-\left(\frac{\|x-x_i\|}{\sigma}\right)^2} \right] \tag{7}$$

Field Lines and Equipotential Lines

A field line is a line with arrowhead and length. The line arrowhead indicates the direction, and the line length indicates the field strength. A series of field lines visually portray the field of a data object. The density of the field lines further shows the field strength. The field of the source is the strongest. With the distance $\|x\text{-}x_i\|$ leaving from the field source, the bigger the distance grows, the weaker the field becomes. The same is with the field line, i.e., leaving from data object, the length of the field lines become short, and the density gets scarce. With Equation 5, Figure 1 is the data field from a single data object ($m=1$, $\sigma=1$).

In Figure 1, Figure 1(a) is the field function, and Figure 1(b) is its data field vector in two-dimensional space. Figure 1(a) presents the rule of the field function changing along with the distance $\|x\text{-}x_i\|$. When approximately $\|x\text{-}x_i\|>2.121\sigma$, the field function rapidly decreases to 0, which gives a short-range field. When approximately $\|x\text{-}x_i\|=0.705\sigma$, the field function may be the strongest. Figure 1(b) also visualizes such the rules by using the data field lines. All the data field lines centralize the data object. When approaching the source, the length of the field lines becomes long and the density gets thick. Their distribution shows that the data field is a distribution of spherical symmetry.

Equipotential lines come into being if the points with the same potential value are lined together. The equipotential lines are mathematical entities that describe the spherical circles at a distance $\|x\text{-}x_i\|$ on which the field has a constant value, as contour lines on a map tracing lines of equal altitude. They always cross the field lines at right angles to each other, without direction at all. The potential difference compares the potential from

Figure 1. Data field from a single data object (m=1, σ =1)

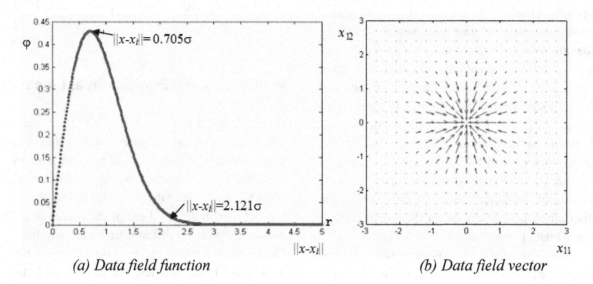

(a) Data field function   *(b) Data field vector*

one equipotential line to the next. In the context of equal data masses, the area distributed with intensive data will have a bigger potential value when the potential functions are superposed. On the position with the biggest potential value, the data objects are the most intensive. In a multi-dimensional space, the equipotential lines are extended to the equipotential surfaces for the field becomes a set of nested spheres with the

center of the coordinate of data object, and the radius is $\|x-x_i\|$. Every topology of equipotential lines containing data objects actually corresponds to a cluster with relatively dense data distribution. The nested structure composed of different equipotential line may be treated as the clustering partitions at different density levels.

With Equation 4, 5, 6, and 7, Figure 2 shows the distribution of field lines and equipotential

Figure 2. The distribution of field lines and equipotential lines on data objects in two-dimensional space

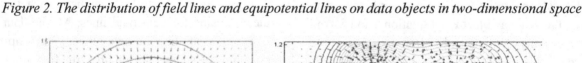

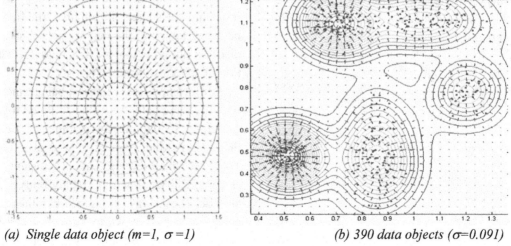

(a) Single data object (m=1, σ =1)   *(b) 390 data objects (σ=0.091)*

lines on data objects in two-dimensional space. In Figure 2, Figure 2(a) is those from a single data object ($m=1$, $\sigma=1$), and Figure 2(b) is those from 390 data objects ($\sigma=0.091$). Figure 2(a) shows that the equipotential lines are always perpendicular to the field lines associated with the data field. Seen from Figure 2(b), all data objects in the field are centralized surrounding 5 positions under the forces from data objects. The field lines always point to 5 positions with local maximum potentials in the data field, and 390 data objects can be self-organized in the data field level by level.

In Figure 3, 5 positions are marked, i.e., A, B, C, D, and E (Figure 3(a)), and the self-organized process discovers the hierarchical clustering-characteristics of data objects with the field level by level (Figure 3(b)). Under a set of suitable potential values, the corresponding set of equipotential lines show the clustering feature of data objects via taking different data-intensive areas as the centers. When the potential is 0.0678 at level 1, all data objects are self-grouped into five clusters A, B, C, D, and E. With the decreasing of the potential, the clusters that are in close proximity are merged. Cluster A and cluster B form the same lineage AB at level 2. Cluster D

and cluster E are amalgamated as cluster DE at level 3. When the potential is 0.0085 at level 5, all clusters join the generalized cluster ABCDE (Figure 3(a)). During the process from the five clusters A, B, C, D, and E at bottom level 1 to the generalized cluster ABCDE at top level 5, a clustering spectrum automatically comes into being (Figure 3(b)). In other words, the center in the data-intensive area has the potential maximum. From the local maximums to the final global maximum, 5 positions are further self-organized cluster by cluster.

Impact Factor

The impact factor controls the interacted distance between data objects. Its value has a great impact on the spatial distribution of data field. The effectiveness of the impact factor is from various sources, for examples, radiation brightness, radiation gene, data amount, distance between the neighbor equipotential lines, grid density of Descartes coordinate, and so on. They all make their contributions to the data field. As a result, the distribution of potential value is determined by impact factor and different potential function has

Figure 3. The self-organized characteristics of 390 data objects in the field level by level ($\sigma=0.091$)

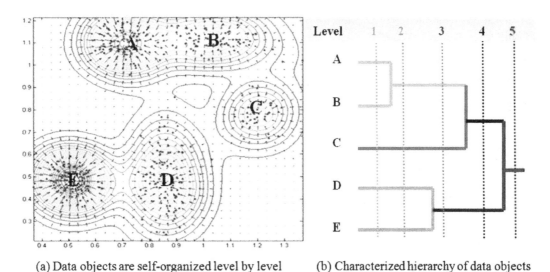

(a) Data objects are self-organized level by level　　(b) Characterized hierarchy of data objects

Figure 4. Equipotential distributions of data field from 5 objects with different σ

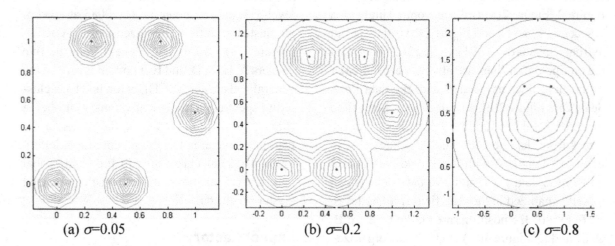

(a) σ=0.05   (b) σ=0.2   (c) σ=0.8

much smaller influence on the estimation. Take an example in two-dimensional space, Figure 4 shows the equipotential distributions of data field from 5 data objects with the same mass when σ becomes different.

When σ is very small (Figure 4(a)), the interaction distance between two data objects is very short. $\varphi(x)$ is equivalent to the superposition of n peak functions, each center of which is the data

object. The potential value around every data object is very small. Extremely, there is no interaction between two objects, and the potential value is $1/n$ at the position of data object. Otherwise, when σ is very big (Figure 4(c)), data objects are interacted strongly. $\varphi(x)$ is equivalent to the superposition of n basic functions that change slowly with big width. The potential value around every data object is very big. Extremely, the po-

Figure 5. The optimal selection of impact factor on 400 data objects

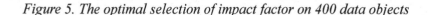

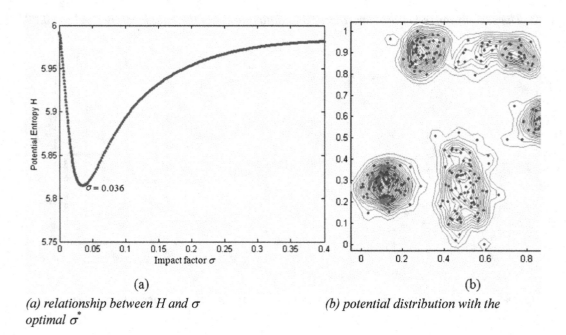

(a)   (b)

(a) relationship between H and σ optimal σ*   *(b) potential distribution with the*

tential value is approximate 1 at the position of data object. When the integral of unit potential function is finite, there is a normalized constant between the potential function and the probability intensity function at most (Giachetta, Mangiarotti, & Sardanashvily, 2009). Seen from the abovementioned two extreme conditions, the potential distribution of data field may not uncover the required rule on inherent data characteristics. Thus, the selection of impact fact σ does portray the inherent distribution of data objects (Figure 4(b)).

CLUSTERING ALGORITHMS WITH DATA FIELDS

In the data field that describes the interactions among the objects, data objects are grouped into clusters by simulating their mutual interactions and opposite movements. In data space $\Omega \subseteq R^p$, there are n data objects in dataset $D=\{x_1, x_2, ..., x_n\}$, the population of which is n. Sampling capacity is n_{sample}. The number of core objects is n_{core}. During the process of clustering with data field, a random sample $D_{sample} \subset D$ is first generated to optimize the impact factor. With the optimized impact factor, the masses of data objects are estimated. The data objects with nonzero masses are selected into the set of core object $D_{core}=\{x_i^* \in D | m_i^* > 0, i=1, 2, ..., n\} \subseteq D$. Taking the core data objects as the initial clusters H_0, the clusters are iteratively merged via simulating the mutual interactions and opposite movements among the core data objects hierarchy by hierarchy. The hierarchical clusters are finally resulted $\{H_1, H_2, ..., H_k\}$ with good performance.

Optimizing Impact Factor

Entropy is introduced to measure the uncertainty of potential distribution. The entropy is a measure of system uncertainty associated with random variables (Shannon, 1948). The bigger the entropy is,

the bigger the uncertainty is. In the data field from data objects $x_1, x_2, ..., x_n$, if the potential value on the position of one data object is equal to that of the other data object, the uncertainty of original data distribution is the biggest, i.e., the entropy is the biggest. Otherwise, if the potential values on the positions of data objects are extremely asymmetric, the uncertainty is the smallest, i.e., the entropy is the smallest. Suppose that Ψ_1, Ψ_2, ..., Ψ_n are the potential values of objects $x_1, x_2, ..., x_n$ the potential entropy is defined as Equation 8 under the Shannon entropy (Shannon, 1948).

$$H = -\sum_{i=1}^{n} \frac{\Psi_i}{Z} \log(\frac{\Psi_i}{Z}) \tag{8}$$

where, $Z = \sum_{i=1}^{n} \Psi_i$, $0 \leq H \leq \log(n)$. The entropy is the biggest when $H=\log(n) \Leftrightarrow \Psi_1=\Psi_2=...=\Psi_n$. That is, the potential value on the position of one data object is equal to that of the other data object, and the uncertainty of original data distribution is the biggest (Figure 5).

Figure 5(a) is the relationship curve between potential entropy H and impact factor σ. When σ trends to 0, H approaches the maxima log(400). When σ increases from 0 to ∞, H first decreases. The minimum H is got when σ is optimized most. Corresponding to the minimum of potential entropy with the most optimized σ^*, the distribution of the equipotential lines in the data field is shown in Figure 5(b). Figure 5(b) indicates that the distribution of data field matches the distribution of original data very much. With the continuous increase of σ, H then increases up to the maxima again (Figure 5(a)).

In essence, the optimal of impact factor σ is a nonlinear function with a single variable, i.e., minimize the potential entropy, $\min H(\sigma)$. To solve such questions, there exist many algorithms, e.g., simple heuristics, random search method, simulated annealing. Here a golden section method is proposed under simple heuristics that the search interval containing the minimum point is continuously decreased by selecting heuristics point and comparing function vales until the function minimum is reached to meet the demanded precision. The algorithm is followed.

- **Algorithm**: Optimize the impact factor σ.
- **Input**: dataset $D=\{x_1, x_2, ..., x_n\}$
- **Output**: optimized σ^*
- Process

$$a = \frac{\sqrt{2}}{3} \min_{i \neq j} \|x_i - x_j\|,$$

  ○ Let $b \frac{\sqrt{2}}{3} \max_{i \neq j} \|x_i - x_j\|,$, set the

$$\gamma = \frac{\sqrt{5}-1}{2}$$

  demanded precision ε,
  ○ Let σ_l=a+(1-γ)(b-a), σ_r=a+γ(b-a)
  ○ Compute H_l=$H(\sigma_l)$, and H_r=$H(\sigma_r)$
  ○ While |b-a|> ε, do{
    ■ If $H_l < H_r$ then {let b=σ_r, σ_r=σ_l, H_r=H_l, compute σ_l=a+(1-γ)(b-a), and H_l=$H(\sigma_l)$}
    ■ Else {let a=σ_l, σ_l=σ_r, H_l=H_r, compute σ_r=a+γ(b-a), and H_r=$H(\sigma_r)$}
  ○ } End while
  ○ If $H_l < H_r$ then { σ=σ_l }
    ■ Else { σ =σ_r}
  ○ Return σ^*=σ.

Suppose that the iterative times is t, and the time complexity to compute the potential entropy H is $O(n^2)$ every iteration. The total time complexity of the algorithms is $O(t \cdot n^2)$. If n is very big, then the algorithm is performed very slowly. When it is applied, the time cost can be decreased by random sampling with a sample capacity $n_{sample} << n$. Because random sampling may lose the distribution information of original data, the sample capacity n_{sample} should remain the inherent structure of the original data distribution as far as possible to ensure the effectiveness of parameter optimization. It was proved that in sampling-based clustering algorithms, the results accurately identify the clustering characteristics of the original data if the sampling rate is no less than a threshold. That is, the sample dataset maintains the distribution characteristics of the original data. When n is large, the sampling rate of 2.5% can usually lead to quite accurate clustering results (Guha, 1998). So if the dataset to be processed is large, the random sampling method with the sampling rate of no less than 5% can improve the performance of optimization algorithms. However, if σ is optimized too much, the clustering may be vulnerable to the impact of noise or outlier data. In practical application, σ is usually chosen to be slightly larger than its optimal value, i.e., $\sigma = c \times \sigma^*$ ($1 < c \leq 2$). For example, the impact factor $\sigma = c \times \sigma^* = 0.091$ (c=1.618) in Figure 3 after optimization.

Estimating Masses

The objective to estimate the mass of each data object in data field is to get a small number of core objects with nonzero mass as different objects make different contributions to data field in Ω. The small number of the data objects is called a core data object of the original object.

Definition 2: In Ω, $D=\{x_1, x_2, ..., x_n\}$, if $D_{core} \subseteq D, D_{core}=\{x_i^* \in D | m_i^* > 0, i=1, 2, ..., n\}$, then D_{core} is called the core dataset of dataset D. At an arbitrary position $x \in \Omega$, the scalar potentials and vector strengths of the data fields on dataset D is simplified as Equation 9 and 10 on D_{core}.

$$\phi(x) = \phi_{D_{core}}(x) = \sum_{x_i^* \in D_{core}} \left(m_i^* \times e^{-\left(\frac{\|x-x_i^*\|}{\sigma}\right)^2} \right) \quad (9)$$

$$\vec{F}(x) = \nabla \phi_{D_{core}}(x) = \sum_{x_i^* \in D_{core}} \left((x_i^* - x) \times m_i^* \times e^{-\left(\frac{\|x-x_i^*\|}{\sigma}\right)^2} \right)$$
$$(10)$$

Usually, the potential distribution is unknown. Because there is only a normalized constant between the potential function and its probabilistic density function (Giachetta, Mangiarotti, & Sardanashvily, 2009), if the overall distribution is known, the masses of data objects may be estimated via minimizing a certain error criterion between the potential function $\varphi(x)$ and the overall distribution of a density function. In Equation 2, if the masses of data objects are not asked for being equal to each other, the masses, $m_1, m_2, ..., m_n$ may be taken as a set of functions of positions $x_1, x_2,$ $..., x_n$, which are n samples from P-dimensional continuous population with the overall density $p(x)$. When σ is constant, the objective function is to minimize the integral square error criterion.

$$\min J = \frac{\min}{\{m_i\}} \int_\Omega \left(\frac{\phi(x)}{\left(\sqrt{\pi}\sigma\right)^d} - p(x) \right)^2 dx = \frac{\min}{\{m_i\}}$$

$$\int_\Omega \left(\frac{\phi^2(x)}{\left(\sqrt{\pi}\sigma\right)^{2d}} - \frac{2\phi(x)p(x)}{\left(\sqrt{\pi}\sigma\right)^d} + p^2(x) \right) dx$$

Obviously, $\int_\Omega p^2(x)dx$ has nothing with the masses $m_1, m_2, ..., m_n$. Thus the above objective function is simplified.

$$\min J = \frac{\min}{\{m_i\}} \left(\int_\Omega \frac{\phi^2(x)}{2\left(\sqrt{\pi}\sigma\right)^d} dx - \int_\Omega \phi(x)p(x)dx \right)$$

Because $\int_\Omega \phi(x)p(x)dx$ is the mathematical expectation of $\varphi(x)$, which can be approximated with the average of $x_1, x_2, ..., x_n$, the Equation is

further simplified as Equation 11. Put Equation 6 into Equation 11 to get Equation 12.

$$\min J = \frac{\min}{\{m_i\}} \left(\frac{1}{2\left(\sqrt{\pi}\sigma\right)^d} \int_\Omega \phi^2(x)dx - \frac{1}{n}\sum_{j=1}^n \phi(x_j) \right) \tag{11}$$

It is a problem on constrained quadratic programming that satisfies linear constraints $m_i \geq 0, \sum_{i=1}^n m_i = 1$ (i=1, 2,..., n). There exist many algorithms to resolve the problem in Equation 12. It may firstly be resolved with conjugate gradient method via simplifying into a problem of unconstrained nonlinear optimization problem. This method has linear convergence rate, but the optimized results depend on the selection of initial points. Independent of the selection of initial points, Sequential Minimal Optimization (SMO) is more robust (Schölkop et al., 2010). Because its time complexity is $O(n^2)$, random sampling with the sample size $n_{sample} \ll n$, is used to improve the time cost to simplify and estimate the object mass when the population n of dataset is large. In order to ensure the effectiveness of sampling methods, the minimum sampling rate is usually recommended not less than 2.5% (Guha, 1998). When the problem is resolved, a set of optimal resolution is got to estimate the mass $m_1, m_2, ...,$ m_n.

The necessary and sufficient condition to get the minimum of objective function Equation 12 is Equation 13. Put Equation 13 into Equation 12 to get Equation 14

Box 1. Equation 12

$$\min J = \frac{\min}{\{m_i\}} \left(\frac{1}{2\left(\sqrt{2}\sigma\right)^d} \sum_{i=1}^n \sum_{j=1}^n m_i \times m_j \times e^{-\left(\frac{\|x_i - x_j\|}{\sqrt{2}\sigma}\right)^2} - \frac{1}{n}\sum_{i=1}^n \sum_{j=1}^n m_i \times e^{-\left(\frac{\|x_i - x_j\|}{\sigma}\right)^2} \right)$$		(12)

$$\frac{\partial J}{\partial m_i}\Bigg|_{i=1,2,\ldots,n} = \frac{1}{\left(\sqrt{2}\right)^d}\sum_{j=1}^{n} m_j \times e^{-\left(\frac{\|x_i - x_j\|}{\sqrt{2}\sigma}\right)^2} -$$

$$\frac{1}{n}\sum_{j=1}^{n} e^{-\left(\frac{\|x_i - x_j\|}{\sigma}\right)^2} = 0 \tag{13}$$

$$\min J = \frac{1}{2\left(\sqrt{2}\sigma\right)^d}\sum_{i=1}^{n}\sum_{j=1}^{n} m_i \times m_j \times e^{-\left(\frac{\|x_i - x_j\|}{\sqrt{2}\sigma}\right)^2} \tag{14}$$

That is, minimize the objective function is equivalent to maximize $\sum_{i=1}^{n}\sum_{j=1}^{n} m_i \times m_j \times e^{-\left(\frac{\|x_i - x_j\|}{\sqrt{2}\sigma}\right)^2}$. For $\sum_{i=1}^{n} m_i = 1$, maximize $\sum_{i=1}^{n}\sum_{j=1}^{n} m_i \times m_j \times e^{-\left(\frac{\|x_i - x_j\|}{\sqrt{2}\sigma}\right)^2}$ may be implemented by assigning bigger masses to a small number of neighbor objects. That is, the resulting optimization of the objective function is that a small number of data objects in intensive areas have bigger masses while most of the far apart objects have less mass or even the mass is zero. For example, simplify and estimate the masses of 1200 data objects (Figure 6). In Figure

6(a), 71 data objects with nonzero masses are all marked with red circles. They are located in relatively dense areas of data distribution, and the number is far smaller than the number of data points in the original data set. Figure 6(b) is the equipotential lines in the data field of original data objects. Figure 6(c) is the equipotential lines in the data field of simplified data objects. Comparing Figure 6(b) with Figure 6(c), it is obvious that both of them have very similar distribution of potential function in data field. Figure 6 indicates that the data field from original dataset can be well approached by using the data field from a small number of its simplified core dataset. The performance of clustering algorithms will be significantly improved if the dimensionality of the feature space is reduced greatly, as the number of discovered clusters directly depends on the number of initial items (Malik et al., 2010).

Figure 6 further uncovers that the spatial distribution of data field mainly depends on the interactions of the core dataset with bigger masses, while most of the other objects actually do not contribute to the formation of data field because their masses are too small. It is well known that large data collections often suffer from huge amount, while 1200 data objects rapidly decreased

Figure 6. Comparing original data objects with its core data objects (marked with red circles) after simplification and estimation (σ = 0.078) (a) simplification and estimation of the masses of data objects in data field (b) equipotential lines in the data field of original dataset (c) equipotential lines in the data field of simplified core dataset

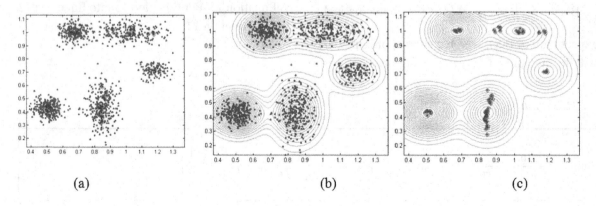

(a) (b) (c)

to its 71 core objects without changing the distribution characteristics of original dataset in Figure 6. Thus the simplified core dataset also provide a new alternative to compress massive dataset.

Initially Partitioning

In Ω, the distribution of data field mainly depends on the interactions of a small number of data objects with larger masses, while most of the other objects actually do not contribute to the formation of data field. The fact may be used to initially partition the original datasets for clustering. Each core object is taken as a clustering representative, and all objects attracted to the same core object are taken as a cluster. Based on the core objects, original objects may be clustered such that the data objects absorbed by a core object within a cluster are more similar to each other than data objects attracted by other core objects in different clusters.

Definition 3: In $\Omega \subseteq R^p$, given $D_{core} \subseteq D$, $D_{core} = \{x_i^* \in D | m_i^* > 0, i=1, 2, ..., n\}$, if $\exists C \subseteq D$, $\forall x_0 \in C$, there is a subset $\{x_0, x_1, x_2, ..., x_k\} \subseteq \Omega$, $\|x_j - x_i^*\| < 0.705 \sigma m_i^*$, x_j is in the gradient direction of $x_{j-1} (0 < j < k < n)$. C is a cluster with the representative of x_i^*.

Taking the core objects with nonzero masses as the cluster center, clustering centralizing the core objects groups other data objects into clusters by simulating their oppositely moving trend in the data field. To effectively remove the outlier of noise data, the maximum distance from each object $x \in D$ to the core object set D_{core} is computed. If there is no core objects within 3σ range of neighboring x location, i.e., $\max\limits_{x^* \in Dcore} \|x^* - x\| > 3\sigma$, such object x is removed as an outlier. Other non-noise data objects are amalgamated to the corresponding core objects separately by using the mountain climb method guided by the data field direction (Li, Wang, & Li, 2006). When data objects are initially partitioned, the initial clusters can be hierarchically

merged by interactively simulating the mutual interaction among core objects.

Iteration Clustering

Given D_{core}, clustering with the interaction among core objects essentially finds out the possible cluster amalgamation by interactively simulating the movement of each core object in the temporal interval $[t, t+\Delta t]$. Suppose that there is a core object $x_i^* \in D_{core}$ $(i=1, 2, ..., n)$ at time t. The mass is $m_i^*(t) > 0$ and the location vector is $x_i^*(t)$. When there is no external force, the force of object in the data field is computed via Equation 15. Due to Newton's second law of motion, the instantaneous acceleration vector of $x_i^*(t)$ is Equation 16.

$$\vec{F}^{(t)}\left(x_i^*\right) = m_i^*(t) \cdot$$
$$\left(\sum_{x_j^* \in D_{core}}^{n} \left[m_j^*(t) \cdot (x_j^*(t) - x_i^*(t)) e^{-\left(\frac{\left\|x_j^*(t) - x_i^*(t)\right\|}{\sigma}\right)^2} \right]\right) \quad (15)$$

$$\vec{a}^{(t)}\left(x_i^*\right) = \frac{\vec{F}^{(t)}\left(x_i^*\right)}{m_i^*(t)} =$$
$$\left(\sum_{x_j^* \in D_{core}}^{n} \left[m_j^*(t) \cdot (x_j^*(t) - x_i^*(t)) e^{-\left(\frac{\left\|x_j^*(t) - x_i^*(t)\right\|}{\sigma}\right)^2} \right]\right) \quad (16)$$

If Δt is small enough, each core object x_i^* moves approximately with uniform variable motion in $[t, t+\Delta t]$. Let the speed vector of x_i^* be $v^{(t)}(x_i^*)$ at time t, the location vector and speed vector of x_i^* at time $t+\Delta t$ are approximately Equation 17

$$x_i^*(t + \Delta t) = x_i^*(t) + v^{(t)}(x_i^*) \cdot \Delta t + \frac{1}{2} a^{(t)}(x_i^*) \cdot \Delta t^2$$
$$v^{(t+\Delta t)}(x_i^*) = v^{(t)}(x_i^*) + a^{(t)}(x_i^*) \cdot \Delta t$$
$$\quad (17)$$

When they meet or their distance is $\|x_j - x_i^*\| < 0.705\sigma(m_i^*(t) + m_j^*(t))$, two core objects are merged into a new core object x_{new}^*. Under the law of conservation momentum, the mass, position, and speed are computed via Equation 18.

$$m_{new}^*(t) = m_i^*(t) + m_j^*(t)$$

$$x_{new}^*(t) = \frac{m_i^*(t) \cdot x_i^*(t) + m_j^*(t) \cdot x_j^*(t)}{m_i^*(t) + m_j^*(t)}$$

$$v^{(t)}(x_{new}^*) = \frac{m_i^*(t) \cdot v^{(t)}(x_i^*) + m_j^*(t) \cdot v^{(t)}(x_j^*)}{m_i^*(t) + m_j^*(t)} \tag{18}$$

The iterative algorithms are performed recursively until all core objects are aggregated to a single object or the terminated conditions given by a user is satisfied.

With the decreasing number of remaining objects during the dynamic clustering, the mass of core objects becomes larger and larger while the inertia to maintain the movement trends of the initial moment get stronger and stronger, which may result in the algorithms cannot converge. In order to ensure the final convergence, the speed vector is set to zero at the initial moment. The location vector is simplified.

$$x_i^*(t + \Delta t) = x_i^*(t) + \frac{1}{2} a^{(t)}(x_i^*) \cdot \Delta t^2 \tag{19}$$

Equation 19 indicates that the location vector of core objects at time $t + \Delta t$ depends on the location $x_i^*(t)$, acceleration vector and the iteration interval Δt. Before iteration is implemented, compute the current minimum distance among core objects and maximum acceleration, Equation 20. Then Δt can be got adaptively under core objects, Equation 21.

$$d_{min} = \min_{i \neq j} \left\| x_i^*(t) - x_j^*(t) \right\|,$$

$$a_{max} = \max_i \left\| a^{(t)}(x_i^*) \right\| \tag{20}$$

$$\Delta t = \frac{1}{f}\left(\sqrt{\frac{2 d_{min}}{a_{max}}} \right) \tag{21}$$

where, f is the time resolution. In this paper, $f = 100$.

Algorithms and Performance

- **Algorithms**: Hierarchical clustering with data field.
- **Input**: $D = \{x_1, x_2, ..., x_n\}$, impact factor σ.
- **Output**: Hierarchical clusters $\{H_0, H_1, ..., H_k\}$
- Process
  - Generate a random sample $D_{sample} \subset D$ to optimize the impact factor to get the optimized σ^*;
  - Estimate the masses $m_1, m_2, ..., m_n$ of data objects $x_1, x_2, ..., x_n$.
  - Select the core data objects $x_i^*(m_i^* > 0, i = 1, 2, ..., n)$.
  - Get the initial clusters H_0 by taking the core data objects as the beginning centers.
  - Iteratively merge the initial clusters via simulating the mutual interactions and opposite movements among the core data objects hierarchy by hierarchy
  - Get and output the resulting hierarchical clusters $\{H_1, H_2, ..., H_k\}$.

Look at the algorithmic performance. Sept(2) estimate the masses of objects by solving the problem on constrained quadratic programming in Equation 12. The time complexity of Sequential Minimal Optimization (Schölkop et al., 2010) is $O(n_{sample}^2)$, with randomly sampling size $n_{sample} \ll n$. All data objects whose masses are nonzero are allocated to the core objects Sept(3).. Based on Step(3), the initial clusters H_0 comes into being in Step(4). If the number of the core objects is n_{core}, the average time complexity is $O(n_{core} (n$

$-n_{core}$)). In Step(5), the average time complexity of iteratively merging clusters is $O(n_{core}^2)$. To sum up, the total time complexity is $O(n_{sample}^2 + n_{core}(n - n_{core}) + n_{core}^2) \approx O(n)$. In order to ensure the clustering effectiveness, the sampling capacity of n_{sample} should preserve the original characteristics of the data distribution as far as possible. When the population n of dataset is large, the minimum sampling rate is usually recommended not less than 2.5% (Guha, 1998).

CASE STUDY

The data set (Guha, Rastogi, & Shim, 1998) contains 10,000 points in two dimensions that form five clusters with different geometric shapes, proximity and varying densities, along with significant noise and special artifacts. 8,000 data points are stochastically sampled from 10,000 points, the remained 2,000 ones are for test. To illustrate the concept of data field and its application in hierarchical clustering, data field's performance is compared against that of K-means (MacQueen, 1967), BIRCH (Zhang, Ramakrishnman, & Linvy, 1996), CURE (Guha, Rastogi, & Shim, 1998), and CHAMELEON (George, Han, & Kumar, 1999). All are implemented with Matlab 7 software on a personal computer (Intel Core 4G CPU, 1G memory). To denote different clusters, points in different clusters are represented using a different color. As a result, points that belong to the same cluster use the same color. They are all shown in Figure 7.

Data Field Results

Data field has better clustering quality and diminishes the contribution of noisy data more effectively without the threshold specified by a user (Figure 7(b)). In the data field that describes the interactions among the objects, data objects are grouped into clusters by simulating their mutual interactions and opposite movements. Every topology of equipotential lines containing data objects actually corresponds to a cluster with relatively dense data distribution. The nested structure composed of different equipotential line is treated as the clustering partitions at different density levels. Although the clusters with different geometric shapes, proximity and varying densities, along with significant noise and special artifacts, data field correctly identifies the genuine five clusters, a big green circle, a small green circle, a small pink circle, a small red ellipse plus a line, and a small light-blue ellipse.

The clusters correspond to the earliest iteration at which data field identifies the genuine clusters and places each in a single cluster. Moreover, the outliers are really removed by using 3σ range of neighboring $\max_{x^* \in Dcore} \|x^* - x\| > 3\sigma$, only non-noise data objects are amalgamated to the corresponding core objects separately. Furthermore, the parameters are extracted from the data set, and a user is not forced to specify them anymore. Such the extracted parameters not only depend on the data set objectively, but also avoid the subjective difference specified by different users, which practically improves the accuracy of clustering result.

Results of Other Methods

K-means assume that clusters are hyper-ellipsoidal and of similar sizes. They attempts to break a data set into K clusters such that the partition optimizes a given criterion. But the algorithms failed to find clusters that vary in size concave shapes (Figure 7(c)). They are unable to find the right clusters for the data set (Figure 7(a)). It is the worst that the data points in the big circle cluster are grouped into three partitions wrongly, and two small circle clusters are merged in the same cluster. The noisy data are amalgamated into their neighboring clusters separately.

BIRCH is only suitable to find clusters with spherical shape because clustering feature is

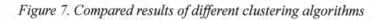

Figure 7. Compared results of different clustering algorithms

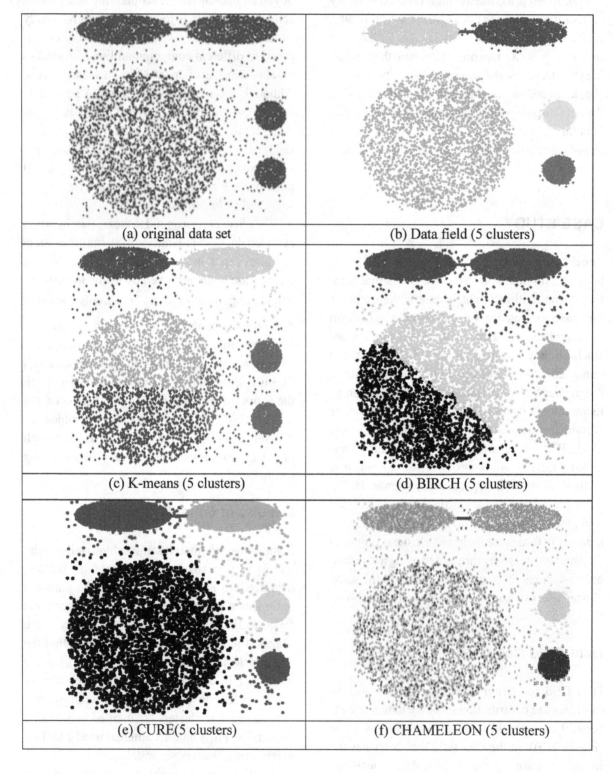

defined through radius, as shown in Figure 7(d). The results get (Figure 7(d)) better than K-means (Figure 7(c)). However, BIRCH's merging scheme still makes multiple mistakes for the data set (Figure 7(a)). The data points in the big circle are wrongly partitioned into two clusters. Two small circle clusters are put together in a cluster. The noisy data are merged in different clusters due to their distance to the corresponding clusters.

CURE measures the similarity between two clusters by the similarity of the closest pair of points belonging to different clusters. Select ten representative points and $\alpha=0.3$, it is able to correctly find the clustering structure of data distribution (Figure 7(e)), and contain as five clusters as those discovered by data field (Figure 7(b)). The data points in the big circle cluster are not wrongly partitioned, and two small circle clusters are differencing from each other. Compared to BIRCH, CURE becomes much better for the data set (Figure 7(a)). But it cannot effectively handle noisy data, all of which have been allocated to the nearest cluster.

Chameleon ($\alpha=2.0$) groups the data points into 5 clusters using a nearest-neighbor graph. Though the result is better than CURE, the outliers are still merged into the nearest cluster. The parameter should be specified by the user.

Comparison and Extensibility

To sum up, different clustering solutions contain different clusters. Data field performs better than K-means, BIRCH, CURE, and CHAMELEON because the latter's neglect the features inside the clusters. And they fail to detect and remove the outliers from noisy data. If the cluster number is not constrained to five, much worse clustering may be resulted. The noisy data are only allocated to the nearest cluster. K-means and BIRCH are considerably worse than data field for there is obvious spherical bias in their solutions. Without user-specified parameters, data field for hierarchical clustering is able to identify the non-spherical cluster with any size and density.

Figure 8. The extensibility of data field for hierarchical clustering

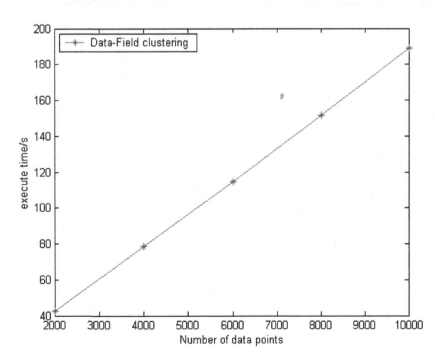

Data field not only outperforms the existing algorithms but also scales well for large databases without sacrificing clustering quality. With the remained 2,000 data points for test, the extensibility of data field for hierarchical clustering is further shown in Figure 8.

In Figure 8, it is an approximate linear relationship between the time to perform the algorithms and the volume of data set. That is, the proposed data field is not sensitive to noisy data for hierarchical clustering.

CONCLUSION

Hierarchical clustering is one of the clustering techniques to group and understand massive dataset. Enlightened by the field in physical space, data field in this paper was proposed that data objects were grouped into clusters by simulating their mutual interactions and opposite movements, in spite of the clusters with different geometric shapes, proximity, varying densities and noise. As the potential of the nuclear field decreases rapidly to 0, data field was studied to simulate nuclear field. In the field, the self-organized process of equipotential lines on many data objects discovered their hierarchical clustering-characteristics with approximate linear performance. Optimizing the impact factor was to control the interacted distance between data objects, and the mass estimation was to select core data object with nonzero masses for initial clusters. The clustering results were achieved by iteratively merging the core data objects hierarchy by hierarchy. A case study illustrated data field could consider the object features inside the clusters, remove the outliers from noisy data, and without user-specified parameters performed better than K-means, BIRCH, CURE, and CHAMELEON.

At present, the rapid advance in massive dataset results in the growth of vast computerized datasets at unprecedented rates. Data field gives a novel method for unsupervised clustering under hierarchical demands. It is a valuable alternative to make use of dataset.

ACKNOWLEDGMENT

Thanks to Professor Kevin P.CHEN for his proof-reading and great help. This paper is supported by National 973 of China under Grant No.2007CB310804, and the National Science Foundation of China under Grant No. 60743001.

REFERENCES

Bhatnagar, V., Kaur, S., & Mignet, L. (2009). A parameterized framework for clustering streams. *International Journal of Data Warehousing and Mining*, 5(1), 36–56. doi:10.4018/jdwm.2009010103

Blatt, F. J. (1986). *Principles of physics* (2nd ed.). Boston, MA: Allyn and Bacon.

Engle, K., & Gangopadhyay, A. (2010). An efficient method for discretizing continuous attributes. *International Journal of Data Warehousing and Mining*, 6(2), 1–21. doi:10.4018/jdwm.2010040101

George, K., Han, E. H., & Kumar, V. (1999). CHAMELEON: A hierarchical clustering algorithm using dynamic modeling. *IEEE Computer*, 27(3), 329–341.

Giachetta, G., Mangiarotti, L., & Sardanashvily, G. (2009). *Advanced classical field theory*. Singapore: World Scientific. doi:10.1142/9789812838964

Grabmeier, J., & Rudolph, A. (2002). Techniques of cluster algorithms in data mining. *Data Mining and Knowledge Discovery*, 6, 303–360. doi:10.1023/A:1016308404627

Guha, S., Rastogi, R., & Shim, K. (1998). CURE: An efficient clustering algorithm for large databases. In *Proceedings of the ACM SIGMOD International Conference on Management of Data* (pp.73-84). New York, NY: ACM Press.

Heller, K. A., & Ghahramani, Z. (2005). Bayesian hierarchical clustering. In *Proceedings of the 22nd International Conference on Machine Learning* (pp. 297-304). New York, NY: ACM Press.

Horng, S. J., Su, M. Y., Chen, Y. H., Kao, T. W., Chen, R. J., Lai, J. L., & Perkasa, C. D. (2011). A novel intrusion detection system based on hierarchical clustering and support vector machines. *Expert Systems with Applications, 38*(1), 306–313. doi:10.1016/j.eswa.2010.06.066

Kim, S., Shephard, N., & Chib, S. (1998). Stochastic volatility: Likelihood inference and comparison with ARCH model. *The Review of Economic Studies, 65*, 361–393. doi:10.1111/1467-937X.00050

Kwok, T., Smith, K. A., Sebastián, L., & Taniar, D. (2002). Parallel fuzzy c-means clustering for large data sets. In B. Monien & R. Feldmann (Eds.), *Proceedings of the 8th International Euro-Par Conference* (LNCS, 2400, pp. 365-374).

Labini, F. S. (2008). *Gravitational clustering: An overview* (Tech. Rep. No. arXiv 0806.2560). Retrieved from http://arxiv.org/abs/0806.2560

Lam, K. M., & Yan, H. (1995). Locating and extracting the eye in human face images. *Pattern Recognition, 29*, 771–779.

Li, D. R., Wang, S. L., & Li, D. Y. (2006). *Spatial data mining theories and applications* (pp. 171–177). Beijing, China: Science Press.

Li, J., Wang, K., & Xu, L. (2008). Chameleon based on clustering feature tree and its application in customer segmentation. *Annals of Operations Research, 168*(1), 225–245. doi:10.1007/s10479-008-0368-4

Li, X., Zhang, S. C., & Wang, S. L. (2006). Advances in data mining applications. *International Journal of Data Warehousing and Mining, 2*(3), i–iii.

MacQueen, J. (1967). Some methods for classification and analysis of multivariate observations. In *Proceedings of the Fifth Berkeley Symposium on Mathematical Statistics and Probability*, Berkeley, CA (Vol. 1, pp. 281-297).

Malik, H. H., Kender, J. R., Fradkin, D., & Moerchen, F. (2010). Hierarchical document clustering using local patterns. *Data Mining and Knowledge Discovery, 21*, 153–185. doi:10.1007/s10618-010-0172-z

Murtagh, F. (1983). A survey of recent advances in hierarchical clustering algorithms. *The Computer Journal, 26*(4), 354–359.

Parsons, L., Haque, E., & Liu, H. (2004). Subspace clustering for high dimensional data: A review. *SIGKDD Explorations, 6*(1), 90–105. doi:10.1145/1007730.1007731

Sander, J., Ester, M., Kriegel, H. P., & Xu, X. W. (1998). Density-based clustering in spatial databases: The algorithm GDBSCAN and its applications. *Data Mining and Knowledge Discovery, 2*, 169–194. doi:10.1023/A:1009745219419

Schölkop, B., Platt, J. C., Shawe-Taylor, J., Smola, A. J., & Williamson, R. C. (2001). Estimating the support of a high-dimensional distribution. *Neural Computation, 13*(7), 1443–1471. doi:10.1162/089976601750264965

Sembiring, R. W., Zain, J. M., & Embong, A. (2010). A comparative agglomerative hierarchical clustering method to cluster implemented course. *Journal of Computing, 2*(12), 1–6.

Shannon, C. E. (1948). A mathematical theory of communication. *The Bell System Technical Journal, 27*, 379–423, 623–656.

Silla, C. N. Jr, & Freitas, A. A. (2011). A survey of hierarchical classification across different application domains. *Data Mining and Knowledge Discovery, 22,* 31–72. doi:10.1007/s10618-010-0175-9

Song, M., Hu, X. H., Yoo, I., & Koppel, E. (2009). A dynamic and semantically-aware technique for document clustering in biomedical literature. *International Journal of Data Warehousing and Mining, 5*(4), 44–57. doi:10.4018/jdwm.2009080703

Wan, R. X., Wang, L. X., & Su, X. K. (2010). ASCCN: Arbitrary shaped clustering method with compatible nucleoids. *International Journal of Data Warehousing and Mining, 6*(4), 1–15. doi:10.4018/jdwm.2010100101

Wang, S. L., & Wang, X. Z. (2007). A fuzzy comprehensive clustering method. In R. Alhajj, H. Gao, X. Li, J. Li, & O. R. Zaïane (Eds.), *Proceedings of the Third International Conference on Advanced Data Mining and Applications* (LNCS 4632, pp. 488-499).

Xu, R., & Wunsch, D. (2005). Survey of clustering algorithms. *IEEE Transactions on Neural Networks, 16*(3), 645–678. doi:10.1109/TNN.2005.845141

Zhang, T., Ramakrishnman, R., & Linvy, M. (1996). BIRCH: An efficient method for very large databases. In *Proceedings of ACM SIGMOD International Conference on Management of Data* (pp.103-114). New York, NY: ACM Press.

Zhang, X. D., Jing, L. P., Hu, X. H., Ng, M., Xia, J. L., & Zhou, X. H. (2008). Medical document clustering using ontology-based term similarity measures. *International Journal of Data Warehousing and Mining, 4*(1), 62–73. doi:10.4018/jdwm.2008010104

Zhao, Y., & Karypis, G. (2005). Hierarchical clustering algorithms for document datasets. *Data Mining and Knowledge Discovery, 10*(2), 141–168. doi:10.1007/s10618-005-0361-3

This work was previously published in the International Journal of Data Warehousing and Mining, Volume 7, Issue 4, edited by David Taniar, pp. 43-63, copyright 2011 by IGI Publishing (an imprint of IGI Global).

Chapter 15
Preserving Privacy in Time Series Data Mining

Ye Zhu
Cleveland State University, USA

Yongjian Fu
Cleveland State University, USA

Huirong Fu
Oakland University, USA

ABSTRACT

Time series data mining poses new challenges to privacy. Through extensive experiments, the authors find that existing privacy-preserving techniques such as aggregation and adding random noise are insufficient due to privacy attacks such as data flow separation attack. This paper also presents a general model for publishing and mining time series data and its privacy issues. Based on the model, a spectrum of privacy preserving methods is proposed. For each method, effects on classification accuracy, aggregation error, and privacy leak are studied. Experiments are conducted to evaluate the performance of the methods. The results show that the methods can effectively preserve privacy without losing much classification accuracy and within a specified limit of aggregation error.

INTRODUCTION

Privacy has been identified as an important issue in data mining. The challenge is to enable data miners to discover knowledge from data, while protecting data privacy. On one hand, data miners want to find interesting global patterns. On the other hand, data providers do not want to reveal the identity of individual data. This leads to the study of privacy-preserving data mining (Agrawal & Srikant, 2000).

Two common approaches in privacy-preserving data mining are data perturbation and data partitioning. In data perturbation, the original data is modified by adding noise, aggregating, transforming, obscuring, and so on. Privacy is preserved by mining the modified data instead of the original data. In data partitioning, data is split

DOI: 10.4018/978-1-4666-2148-0.ch015

among multiple parties, who securely compute interesting patterns without sharing data.

However, privacy issues in time series data mining go beyond data identity. In time series data mining, characteristics in time series can be regarded as private information. The characteristics can be trend, peak and trough in time domain or periodicity in frequency domain. For example, a company's sales data may show periodicity which can be used by competitors to infer promotion periods. Certainly, the company does not want to share such data. Moreover, existing approaches to preserve privacy in data mining may not protect privacy in time series data mining. In particular, aggregation and naively adding noise to time series data are prone to privacy attacks.

In this paper, we study privacy issues in time series data mining. The objective of this research is to identify effective privacy-preserving methods for time series data mining. We first present a model for publishing and mining time series data and then discuss potential attacks on privacy. As a counter measure to privacy threat, we propose to add noise into original data to preserve privacy. The effects of noise on preserving privacy and on data mining performance are studied. The data mining task in our study is classification and its performance is measured by classification accuracy.

We propose a spectrum of methods for adding noise. For each method, we first explain the intuition behind the idea and then present its algorithm. The methods are implemented and evaluated in terms of their impacts on privacy preservation, classification accuracy, and aggregation error in experiments. Our experiments show that these methods can preserve privacy without seriously sacrificing classification accuracy or increasing aggregation error.

The contributions of our paper are: (a) We identify privacy issues in time series data mining and propose a general model for protecting privacy in time series data mining. (b) We propose a set of methods for preserving privacy by adding noise. Their performance is evaluated

against real data sets. (c) We analyze the effect of noise on preserving privacy and the impact on data mining performance for striking a balance between the two.

The rest of the paper is organized as follows. In Section 2, we discuss related work in privacy preserving and time series data mining. A general model for publishing and mining time series data is proposed in Section 3, along with discussion on its privacy concerns. Methods for preserving privacy by adding noise are proposed in Section 4. The effects of noise on privacy preserving, classification accuracy, and aggregation error are studied in Section 5. Related issues are discussed in Section 6. Section 7 concludes the study and gives a few future research directions.

RELATED WORK

Privacy Preserving Data Mining

To preserve privacy in data mining, researchers have proposed many approaches which can be categorized into two main groups: data perturbation and data partitioning.

In data perturbation approaches, data is modified by adding noise, aggregation, suppression, transformation, and so on. Data mining is performed on modified data instead of original data to preserve privacy. Random noise is added to preserve privacy in decision tree construction (Agrawal & Srikant, 2000) and association rules (Evfimievski, Srikant, Agrawal, & Gehrke, 2002). The effects of random noise on privacy preserving and data mining performance are studied in (Du & Zhan, 2003), as well effective approaches to randomization (Huang, Du, & Chen, 2005; Zhu & Liu, 2004). Generalization is proposed to achieve *k*-anonymity where each record is identical to at least *k-1* other records in the data set (Bayardo & Agrawal, 2005; LeFevre, DeWitt, & Ramakrishnan, 2006; Iyengar, 2002). Anonymization for classification is studied in Fung and Wang (2007).

A privacy-preserving protocol for computing aggregation queries using randomized algorithms is proposed in She, Want, Fu, and Yabo (2008).

In data partitioning approaches, data is distributed among multiple parties. To preserve privacy, the parties do not share their data, but cooperate to find global patterns. In most cases, secure multi-party computation (Du & Atallah, 2001; Yildizli, Pedersen, Saygin, Savas, & Levi, 2011) is employed and many use encryptions too. Secure multi-party computation has been introduced for building decision tree (Lindell & Pinkas, 2000), mining association rules (Vaidya & Clifton, 2002; Kantarcioglu & Clifton, 2004), clustering with k-means (Vaidya & Clifton, 2003; Jagannathan & Wright, 2005), and learning Bayesian network structures (Wright & Yang, 2004).

These existing approaches to privacy preserving data mining are not sufficient to preserve privacy of time series data. Data perturbation approaches may not protect the privacy of time series data, since data sources can be separated apart from each other and from noises by Blind Source Separation as we discuss in Section 3. In data partitioning approaches, secure multi-party computation is too computational expensive for time series data because of the high dimension of such data. Moreover, secure multi-party computation requires collaboration among data providers, which is not always the case. In our model, we do not require collaboration among data providers. As we point out in Section 1, time series data poses new challenges to privacy preservation. This will be further explained when we present our model in Section 3.

Time Series Data Mining

Because time series data is usually large and noisy, direct application of data mining algorithms on raw data is time-consuming and unreliable. Therefore research in time series data mining mostly focuses on data preprocessing techniques, such as transformation, indexing, feature extraction, and feature reduction (Agrawal, Faloutsos, & Swami, 1993; Faloutsos, Ranganathan, & Manolopoulos, 1994; Agrawal, Lin, Sawhney, & Shim, 1995; Mörchen & Ultsch, 2005; Bagnall & Janacek, 2004; Cole, Shasha, & Zhao, 2005; Mielikinen, Terzi, & Tsaparas, 2006; Golfarelli, & Rizzi, 2009). Research has also been done to improve related techniques such as representation and similarity metric (Berndt & Clifford, 1994; Keogh & Pazzani, 1998; Keogh, Chakrabarti, Mehrotra, & Pazzani, 2001; Keogh & Pazzani, 2000; Liabotis, Theodoulidis, & Saraaee, 2006). The data mining tasks studied by researchers include subsequence matching (Agrawal et al., 1993, 1995; Faloutsos et al., 1994; Keogh & Smyth, 1997; Ge & Smyth, 2000), classification (Geurts, 2001), clustering (Keogh & Lin, 2005), frequent pattern mining (Patel, Keogh, Lin, & Lonardi, 2002), temporal relation patterns mining (Amo, Junior, & Giacometti, 2008), and association rule mining (Das, Lin, Mannila, Renganathan, & Smyth, 1998).

It is clear that most research in time series data mining does not address privacy issues, let alone time series privacy issues.

Privacy in Time Series Data Mining

Recently, some researchers have studied specifically the topic of privacy in time series data.

A privacy preserving algorithm for mining frequent patterns in time series data has been proposed by Costa da Silva and Klusch (2007). A frequent pattern is a subsequence which occurs frequently in a time series. The algorithm uses encryption and secure multiparty computing to ensure the privacy of individual party.

Privacy of time series data has been studied by Papadimitriou et al. (2007). They argue that time series data has unique characteristics in terms of privacy. In order to preserve privacy, they propose two perturbation methods based on Fourier and wavelet transformations. It is shown that white noise perturbation does not preserve privacy while the proposed methods are effective.

We agree with these researchers that time series data poses new challenges to privacy in data publishing and data mining. Unlike previous research on this topic, we present a general model for privacy preserving in time series data publishing and mining. We propose to add noise to preserve privacy instead of secure multiparty computing as proposed in Costa da Silva and Klusch (2007). Another difference is that our data mining problem is classification rather than frequent patterns in Costa da Silva and Klusch (2007). Like Papadimitriou et al. (2007), we propose to add noise for privacy preservation. Unlike Papadimitriou et al. (2007), our privacy problem is constrained with classification accuracy and aggregation error which are beyond the scope of Papadimitriou et al. (2007). As we will see in Section 3, classification accuracy and aggregation error make privacy preservation more complex.

TIME SERIES DATA PUBLISHING AND MINING SYSTEM

In this section we first present a real-world model of time series Data Publishing and Mining System (DPMS). We then analyze the weakness of the DPMS in preserving privacy of time series data providers, that motivates us to propose new approaches to preserve privacy in a DPMS.

System Model

A DPMS consists of data providers and research companies. A data provider is a data source which generates time series data. In a DPMS, data providers are willing to share data with trusted research companies. Research companies in a DPMS have the following two functions:

- **Publishing Data:** Research companies aggregate data from different data providers according to different criteria and then publish aggregate data through public announcement such as web sites or paid reports such as consumer reports.
- **Providing Data Mining Solutions:** Research companies can generate data mining models from time series data that they collect from data providers. The generated models can be shared with data providers or other data miners. Since these models are created from global or industry-wide data, they are generally more accurate and reliable than models created from individual provider's data. One incentive for data providers to share data with research companies is to obtain these models.

An example of DPMS is shown in Figure 1 which consists of two auto manufacturers as data providers, and a set of research companies which publish aggregate sales data the two manufacturers according to various criteria.

The performance of a DPMS is measured by the following three criteria. Data providers and research companies have conflicting objectives based on these criteria.

- **Aggregation Error:** Research companies want to minimizing aggregate errors. At least, they want to guarantee aggregate data is within certain error limit.
- **Privacy of Data Providers:** To protect privacy, data providers may add noise to their time series data before sharing the data with research companies. Data providers desire to add as much noise as possible. But to guarantee the accuracy of aggregate data, research companies will limit the amount of noise that can be added by data providers.
- **Data Mining Performance:** Research company will generate data mining models from noisy time series data provided by various providers. Performance of these

Figure 1. An example of DPMS

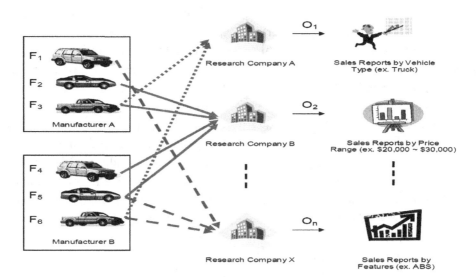

models depends on the noise added by data providers. In this paper, we consider classification of time series data and the performance metric is classification accuracy.

In a DPMS, we assume data providers can trust research companies. Therefore, the privacy of data providers should be protected from outside adversaries, not from research companies. We present the threat model in Section 3.

It is clear from the model that aggregating and publishing data is one of the main tasks of research companies in a DPMS. Aggregation also serves as a means to preserve data providers' privacy by mixing individual time series data and thus preventing direct access to individual time series data by adversaries. However, aggregation itself is incapable of protecting privacy as shown in Section 3.

Threat Model

In this paper we assume adversaries are external to a DPMS. More specifically, adversaries have the following capabilities:

- Adversaries can obtain aggregate data from research companies for a small amount of fee or for free.
- Adversaries cannot obtain data contributed by data providers because of lack of trust with data providers. This assumption excludes the possibility of a data provider being a privacy attacker. We do not study the case of compromised data provider in this paper. But obviously privacy will be a more serious problem if an adversary, being a provider of original data, can know part of original data aggregated by research companies.
- Adversaries can obtain data aggregated according to different criteria.
- Research companies have various data providers as their data sources and research companies do not want to disclose the composition of data sources.

The goal of adversaries is to obtain as much information as possible about data providers through various privacy attacks.

Privacy in a DPMS

A DPMS must protect privacy of data providers from external adversaries. Otherwise, external adversaries can recover individual time series from data providers by applying blind source separation algorithm to aggregate time series data.

Blind Source Separation: Blind source separation is a methodology in statistical signal processing to recover unobserved "source" signals from a set of observed mixtures of the signals. The separation is called "blind" to emphasize that the source signals are not observed and that the mixture is a black box to the observer. While no knowledge is available about the mixture, in many cases it can be safely assumed that source signals are independent. In its simplest form (Cardoso, 1998), the blind source separation model assumes n independent signals $F = F_1(t), ..., F_n(t)$ and n observations of mixture $O = O_1(t), ..., O_n(t)$ where t is the time and $Oi(t) = \sum_{j=1}^{n} a_{ij}F_j(t)$, $i = 1, ..., n$. The parameters a_{ij} are mixing coefficients. The goal of blind source separation is to reconstruct the source signals F using only the observed data O, with the assumption of independence among the signals in F. A very nice introduction to the statistical principles behind blind source separation is given in (Cardoso, 1998). The common methods employed in blind source separation are minimization of mutual information (Comon, 1994), maximization of nongaussianity (Hyvärinen, 1999), and maximization of likelihood (Gaeta & Lacoume, 1990).

Data Flow Separation as a Blind Source Separation Problem: For an attacker who is interested in sensitive information contained in individual data flow, it will be very helpful to separate the individual data flows based on the aggregate data flows. Because the separation of the data flows enables the recovery of the data flows and the patterns in the separated data flows, such as periodicities in the frequency domain and trend,

peak, and trough in the time domain, can be used for further attacks such as the frequency matching attack (Zhu & Fu, 2007).

The data flow separation can be formulated as a blind source separation problem. For example, in Figure 1, the attacker can get aggregate data flows O_1 from Research Company A, O_2 from Research Company B, etc. The attacker's objective is to recover the time series F_i of each individual data flow. Note that an individual data flow may appear in multiple aggregate flows, e.g., in Figure 1, F_3 is contained in both aggregate flows O_1 and O_2, i.e., $O_1 = F_3 + F_6$, $O_2 = F_2 + F_3 + F_4 + F_5$.

In general, with l observations $O_1, ..., O_l$, and m individual data flows $F1, ..., Fm$, we can rewrite the problem in vector-matrix notation,

$$\begin{pmatrix} O_1 \\ O_2 \\ \vdots \\ O_l \end{pmatrix} = A_{l \times m} \begin{pmatrix} F_1 \\ F_2 \\ \vdots \\ F_m \end{pmatrix} \qquad (1)$$

where $\mathbf{A}_{l \times m}$ is called the mixing matrix in blind source separation problems.

Data flow separation can be achieved using blind source separation techniques. The individual data flows are independent from each other since the individual data flows are from different sources. Given the observations $O_1, ..., O_l$, blind source separation techniques can be used to estimate the independent individual flows $F_1, ..., F_m$ by maximizing the independence among the estimated individual data flows.

A simple example of data flow separation is shown in Figure 2. In this simple experiment, four time series of stock prices are mixed into four aggregate flows. Figure 2(a) and Figure 2(b) show the actual data flows and separated data flows from the aggregate flows. We can observe for data flows 1, 2, and 3, the separated data flows are flipped, scaled and lifted versions of the corresponding actual data flows. We can also observe

Figure 2. Example of data flow separation

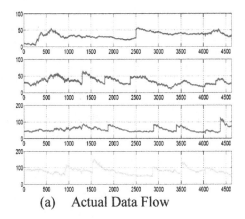

(a)   Actual Data Flow

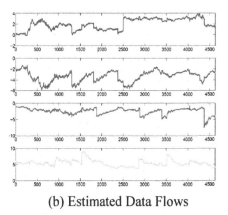

(b) Estimated Data Flows

the resemblance between the separated flow and the actual flow for data flow 4.

In the rest of the paper, our measure of privacy is defined on the base of correlation for two reasons: (a) Correlation is a widely adopted statistics metrics to measure similarity/ dependency. Since as introduced in Section 1, potentially any characteristics in time series can be regarded as private information, correlation as a general metric to measure resemblance serves well for our purpose. (b) Correlation will not change if the separated data flow of interest is a lifted and scaled version of an actual data flow.

Figure 3 shows the performance of data flow separation in terms of the correlation metric for the simple example. Correlation value between separated data flows and corresponding actual data flows are shown in the figure. We can observe that separated data flows are highly resembling the actual data flows. In other words, most of characteristics of time series are still kept in the separated data flows.

Figure 3. Performance of data flow separation on a small example

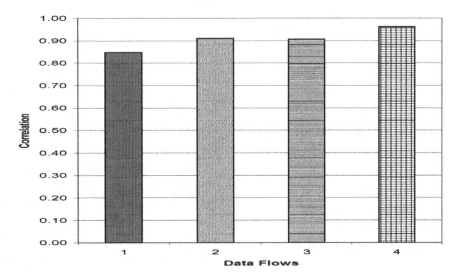

We did extensive experiments on data flow separation attack (Zhu & Fu, 2007). Our experiments demonstrated that data flow separation attack was very effective to find original flows from aggregate flows. Aggregation was ineffective for privacy protection under data flow separation attack.

Preserving Privacy in a DPMS: Existing privacy preserving techniques are inadequate or inapplicable in a DPMS. First, data partitioning approaches using secure multiparty computing are useful for protecting data providers' privacy from each other and from research companies, but not applicable for protecting data providers' privacy from external adversaries. The latter is the focus of this paper.

Second, data perturbation approaches such as aggregation and adding noise are ineffective if naively employed, as explained in the previous section. Besides, these approaches do not consider aggregation error which is one of the three criteria of a DPMS.

In Section 4, we present methods that add noise to protect privacy while limiting aggregation errors. Moreover, unlike previous random noise approaches, our methods are specific for time series data.

Definitions

We define the basic concepts used in the rest of the paper.

Definition: A data flow F is a time series $F=[f_1, f_2, ..., f_n]$ where f_i, $i = 1, ..., n$, is a data point in the flow.

When the context is clear, we use flow and point for data flow and data point, respectively.

How much privacy of a flow F is leaked by a compromised flow $\hat{F}$ is decided by their resemblance. Correlation has proven to be a good resemblance measure for time series data.

Definition: Given an original flow F and a compromised flow $\hat{F}$, the privacy leak between

F and $\hat{F}$ is defined as the correlation between them:

$$pl) = \text{corr}(F, \hat{F})$$

where *corr* is the linear or Pearson correlation.

The greater correlation between F and $\hat{F}$ implies that the more information about F is learned by $\hat{F}$, and therefore the higher privacy leak.

Based on the definition of privacy leak for individual flows, we can define privacy leak for a set of flows.

Definition: The privacy leak between a set of original flows, $\mathbf{F} = \{\hat{F}_1, \hat{F}_2, ..., \hat{F}_n\}$, and set of compromised flows, $\hat{\mathbf{F}} = \{\hat{F}_1, \hat{F}_2, ..., \hat{F}_n\}$, is defined as

$$pl(\mathbf{F}, \hat{\mathbf{F}}) = \frac{\sum_{i=1}^{n}(\max_{j=1}^{n} pl(F_i, \hat{F}_j))}{n}$$

METHODS FOR PRESERVING PRIVACY

As presented in Section 3, aggregation alone cannot protect privacy in a DPMS. We propose to add noise to original time series data to preserve privacy. However, noise will adversely affect classification accuracy and aggregation error. In this section, we discuss various approaches to add noise and their effects on privacy leak, classification accuracy, and aggregation error. Our objective is to identify effective approaches to add noise that can preserve privacy with minimal effect on classification accuracy and aggregation error.

Since data flow separation attacks employ blind source separation techniques which are based on the independence among original data flows, the countermeasure to flow separation attack should add noise to increase dependence among noised data flows. According to dependence change caused by noise, we classify the approaches to preserve privacy into three categories: naive approaches, guided approaches, and optimal approach. In naïve approaches, data providers add noise independently. In guided approaches, research companies send guidance to data providers on how to add noise so that noised data flows from different data providers are more dependent than original data flows. In optimal approach, data providers are willing to let research companies decide how to add noise to maximize the dependence among noised data flows.

We first give two naive approaches to add noise in Section 4. They are simple methods that do not consider dependence among flows. In the second part of Section 4, we propose three methods for adding noise which try to increase the dependence among sources. The intuition is that by increasing dependence among flows, it will be harder to separate aggregate flows and therefore improve privacy preservation.

Naive Approaches

The first naive approach, random, adds noise to each point in a flow independent of other points in the flow and to each flow independent of other flows. The second naive approach, *same_noise*, is to add the exact same noise to every flow.

These naive approaches, though simple, are ineffective in protecting privacy. Less dependent flows lead to easier separation and higher privacy breach. For random, since the noise is independent, they will decrease the dependence among flows. For *same_noise*, adding the same noise to all flows is similar to translate all flows so the relative distance among data flows does not change and it can increase dependence among data flows. Intuitively *same_noise* is a good candidate for privacy preserving. But the noise commonly contained in all the noised data flows can be treated by blind source separation algorithm as another source data flow. Therefore *same_noise* can not inherently increase dependence among flows to be aggregated by research companies.

Guided Approaches

There are two objectives for adding noise and any method should try to meet both objectives, which are usually conflicting with each other. First, to increase dependence among flows, we would like to add noise that is dependent. Increasing dependence among flows makes separation harder and privacy leak lower. Second, adding noise should not significantly affect classification accuracy and aggregation error.

To achieve the first objective, we propose to use segments, instead of individual points as units for adding noise. A segment is a subsequence of a flow. Every flow is broken into a set of non-overlapping segments. All segments have the same size, i.e., the number of points. Similar noise is added to all points in a segment.

To achieve the second objective, a threshold is introduced for noise. The threshold limits the maximum level of noise that may be added. The noise threshold is represented as a percentage of a point's value. For example, a noise threshold of 10% lets us change a point whose value is 10, to between 9 and 11.

Based on these two objectives, three methods for adding noise are proposed to balance privacy preservation and accuracies. In our discussion, we assume a time series can be separated into segments of equal size. It is straightforward to deal with the case when the last segment has a smaller size.

The first method, independent, adds the same level of noise to the points in each segment, i.e., a percentage of a point's value is computed as noise and added to its value. Each series independently adds its noise. The algorithm for independent is given in Algorithm 1. It is obvious that the naive approach random is a special case of independent, when the segment length is 1.

The second method, conform, is similar to independent that noise levels are measured as a percentage of a point's value. The difference is that in conform, for each segment; all series add the same level of noise. In other words, the *i*th

333

segment of all series adds the same level of noise. The algorithm for conform is given in Algorithm 2.

The third method, smooth, tries to introduce dependence by smoothing flows. In each segment, the mean value of the segment is calculated. For each point in the segment, if the difference between its value and the mean is within noise threshold, it is replaced by the mean. Otherwise, it is unchanged. The algorithm for smooth is given in Algorithm 3.

Optimal Approach

In both naive approaches and guided approaches, because data providers control their noise addition, the dependence among noised data flows cannot be maximized. In this section, we assume data providers are willing to let research companies decide noise addition. All data providers will share the original data flows with research companies. With the knowledge of all data flows, a research company can possibly maximize the dependence among noised data flows to protect privacy or select optimal way of adding noise to balance privacy protection and accuracies.

The optimal approach can be formulated as a nonlinear programming (NLP) problem.

The cost function of the NLP problem is

$$\max_{\{N_1, N_2, ..., N_n\}} \left[\begin{matrix} Dep(F_1 + N_1, F_2 + N_2, ..., F_n + N_n) + \\ \Pr ecision(F_1 + N_1, F_2 + N_2, ..., F_n + N_n) \end{matrix} \right] \quad (2)$$

where F_i is the ith original data flow and N_i is the noise vector added to the F_i. We use function $Dep(F_1, F_2, ..., F_n)$ to denote the total dependence of every pair in data flows $F_1, F_2, ..., F_n$. The dependence among the data flows decides the performance of data flow separation, i.e., the privacy protection. The function $\Pr ecision(F_1, F_2, ..., F_n)$ represents the percentage of flows which are in the same class as their closest neighboring flow. In other words, it is the

accuracy by the classification algorithm k nearest neighbors ($k = 1$) which is used in our experiments.

The constraint of the NLP problem is

$$\forall i, j \; \frac{\left| O_j^i - O_j'^i \right|}{O_j^i} \leq T \quad (3)$$

where T denotes the noise threshold. We use O_j^i and $O_j'^i$ to denote the jth data point in ith flow aggregated from original data flows and noised flows respectively. Please note that the linear combinations to form aggregate flows O_i and O_i' are the same.

PERFORMANCE EVALUATION

To evaluate the effectiveness of methods proposed in Section 4, we conduct a set of experiments using the UCR Time Series Classification/Clustering data collection (Keogh, Xi, Wei, & Ratanamahatana, 2006). The collection consists of 20 time series data sets each of which has a training set and a test set. The data sets are of various sizes and the time series are of various lengths. Unless stated otherwise, our experiments are conducted using all 20 data sets and the results are averaged across all data sets.

In general, time series data to be published is positive, for example, sales data and stock data. So we focus on positive data flows in this paper[1]. Therefore, without loss of generality, we add twice the absolute value of the minimum value to all data points for each data set. This does not affect the correlation and distance among the flows.

In each experiment, noise is added to the training set. To distinguish the two versions of the training data, we call the original flow and training set clean flow and clean set, and the other noised flow and noised set respectively. Each experiment consists of two steps and we repeat experiments with random noise to minimize randomness in experiment results.

Algorithm 1. Independent: add random noise to segments in flows independently

Input: D : a data flow set

      T : a noise threshold {Maximum level of noise allowed}

      W : a segment size

Output: A perturbed data set, $D' = D +$ random noise

1: **for** each flow F in D **do**

2: break F into a set of segments of size W

3: $s_i \Leftarrow$ segment i of F

4: r = random(); {a random number in [-1,1]}

5: **for** each segment s_i **do**

6: **for** each point $p \in s_i$ **do**

7: $F'(p) \Leftarrow F(p) * (1 + r * T)$

          #We use *F(p)* and *F'(p)* to denote the *p*th data point in Flow *F* and *F'* #respectively. Flow *F'* is a flow in the perturbed

          data set D'.

8: **end for**

9: **end for**

10: **end for**

Algorithm 2. Conform: add the same level of noise to all flows

Input: D : a data flow set

      T : a noise threshold

      W : a segment size

Output: A perturbed data set, $D' = D +$ random noise

1: n = length of flows in (D) $/W$ {# of segments}

2: **for** i = 1 to n **do**

3: r = random(); {a random number in [-1,1]}

4: **for** each flow F in D **do**

5: $s_i \Leftarrow$ segment i of F

6: **for** each point $p \in s_i$ **do**

7: $F'(p) \Leftarrow F(p) * (1 + r * T)$

          #We use *F(p)* and *F'(p)* to denote the *p*th data point in Flow *F* and *F'* #respectively. Flow *F'* is a flow in the perturbed

data set D'.

8: **end for**

9: **end for**

10: **end for**

In the first step of a experiment, the test set is classified using kNN (k Nearest Neighbors) to find out classification accuracy. In our experiments, k is set to 1 and Euclidean distance is used. For every flow in test set, the kNN finds its closest neighbor in the noised set, and if they are from the same class, the test set flow is corrected classified. The classification accuracy is the percentage of flows in the test set that are correctly classified.

Algorithm 3. Smooth: replace individual points by segment mean

Input: D : a time series data set

   T : a noise threshold

   W : a segment size

Output: A smoothed data set, $D^{'}$

1: **for** each flow F in D **do**

2: break F into a set of segments of size W

3: $s_i \Leftarrow$ segment i of F

4: **for** each segment si **do**

5: $m = \text{mean}(s_i)$;

6: **for** each point $p \in s_i$ **do**

7: **if** $| F(p) - m |/ F(p) \le T$ **then**

8: $F'(p) \Leftarrow m$

9: **else**

10: $F'(p) = F(p)$

   #We use $F(p)$ and $F'(p)$ to denote the pth data point in Flow F and F' #respectively. Flow F' is a flow in the perturbed data set $D^{'}$.

11: **end if**

12: **end for**

13: **end for**

14: **end for**

In the second step of a experiment, 10 noised flows are selected randomly. The selected noised flows and their corresponding clean flows are used to compute privacy leak and aggregation error. The noised flows are aggregated and their aggregates are compared to aggregates from the clean flows to calculate aggregation error. Next, the aggregate flows are separated using the data flow separation attack mentioned in Section 3. The separated flows are compared to the clean flows to find privacy leaks. For comparison, we also aggregate the clean flows, then separate the aggregate flows and calculate the privacy leak of separated flows.

Performance Metrics

The performance metrics include classification accuracy, aggregation error, and privacy leak.

The classification accuracy measures the percentage of flows in test set that are correctly classified by kNN using the noised set. It is defined as follows:

$$acc = cl / N \qquad (4)$$

where cl is the number of flows in test set correctly classified by kNN and N is the total number of flows in test set.

The aggregation error measures the difference between aggregate noised flows and aggregate clean flows. Given a set of clean flows, $F_1, F_2, ..., F_n$, their corresponding noised flows, $F'_1, F'_2, ..., F'_n$, and an aggregate function *agg*, let O and O' be aggregate flows from clean flows and noised flows, respectively, i.e., $O = agg\left(F_1, F_2, ..., F_n\right)$ and $O' = agg\left(F'_1, F'_2, ..., F'_n\right)$. Aggregation error $err\left(O, O'\right)$ is defined as follows:

$$err(O,O') = \left(\sum_{i=1}^{L} \frac{\left| O'_i - O_i \right|}{O_i} \right) / L \qquad (5)$$

where O_i and O'_i are the *ith* point of O and O' respectively, and L is the length of the flows.

As we mentioned, 10 noised flows are selected for aggregate in each run of each experiment, which generates 10 aggregate flows. The aggregation error is averaged over all aggregate flows.

To measure the effects on privacy preservation, we calculate privacy leak between separated flows and noised flows, and between separated flows and clean flows, to evaluate how much privacy is added by noise and how much privacy is added by aggregation.

For comparison, we also use clean flows as sources and calculate privacy preservation by aggregation only.

Given a set of noised flow $\mathbf{F'} = \{F'_1, F'_2, ..., F'_n\}$, and their clean counterparts, $\mathbf{F} = \{F_1, F_2, ..., F_n\}$, we measure the privacy leaks before and after adding noise. That is, privacy leaks of separated flows from clean ag-

gregate flows $PLC = pl\left(\hat{F}, F\right)$, and the privacy leaks of separated flows from noised aggregate flows $PLN = pl(\hat{F}', F)$. The definition of $pl(\hat{F}, F)$ is given in Definition 3 in Section 3.

The notations are summarized in Table 1.

Table 2 lists the two parameters used in naive and guided approaches and their default values.

Naive Approaches

We first look at the performance of naive approaches.

Figure 4 shows the privacy leaks before and after applying random to individual data set, i.e., *PLN* and *PLC* respectively. We sort the data sets according to their average correlation among flows. From Figure 4, we can see that for data sets with small to medium average correlation, random reduces little privacy leak.

An interesting discovery is that for data sets with large correlation, random actually increases privacy leak. This can be explained as follows. Two factors have to be considered when evaluating effects of noise on privacy leak. The first factor is the difference between clean flows and noised flows. The second factor is the dependence among noised flows. Adding noise increases the first factor and thus reduces privacy leak. On the other hand, noise decreases the second factor and thus making flow separation easier and privacy leak higher. These two factors cancel out each other. For a data set with high average correlation, adding even little noise can greatly change dependence among noised flows. As a consequence,

Table 1. Notations

System	Desription
F	a clean flow
F'	a noised flow
$\hat{f}$	a separated flow from an aggregate flow
$\mathbf{F}$	a set of flows
acc	Classification accuracy
err	Aggregation error
$pl\ F\ \hat{F})$	Privacy leak between $\hat{F}$ and F
PLN	Privacy leak after noise
PLC	Privacy leak before noise

Table 2. Parameters

Parameter	Description	Default Value
T	noise threshold	10%
W	segment size	8

Figure 4. Privacy leak using random

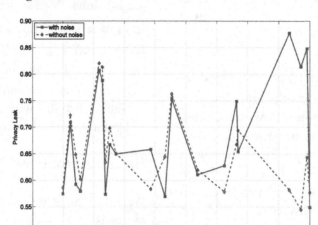

the second factor outweighs the first factor in random which causes privacy leak to increase.

To evaluate *same_noise*, we randomly select a flow and add a percentage of it to all flows. The percentage is specified by a parameter, *noise ratio*. Figure 5 shows the effects of *noise ratio* on classification accuracy, aggregation error, and privacy leak.

It is obvious from Figure 5 that *same noise* has little effect on privacy leak. Moreover, it greatly reduces classification accuracy. Finally, the aggregation error increases linearly with *noise ratio* which makes *same noise* very sensitive to noise.

To sum up, Figures 4 and 5 clearly demonstrate that naive approaches are insufficient to preserve privacy. Moreover, *same noise* significantly reduces classification accuracy and increases aggregation error.

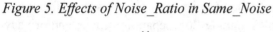

Figure 5. Effects of Noise_Ratio in Same_Noise

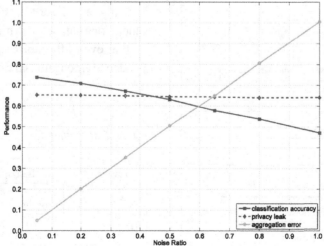

Figure 6. Classification accuracy for various noise thresholds

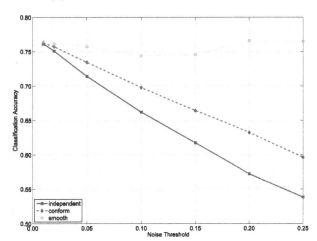

Guided Approaches

The three segment-based methods for adding noise, independent, conform, and smooth, are compared with respect to different noise thresholds and segment sizes.

Effects of Noise Threshold: Figure 6 shows the classification accuracy for the three methods. It is observed smooth is insensitive to noise threshold while in conform, and more in independent, clas-

sification accuracy reduces significantly as noise threshold increases.

This means we can add more noise in smooth without hurting classification accuracy.

Figure 7 shows the aggregation error for various noise thresholds. In independent and conform, aggregation error grows linearly as noise threshold increases, and it grows faster in conform than in independent. This is understandable since independent allows each flow to select their noise

Figure 7. Aggregation error for various noise thresholds

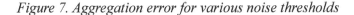

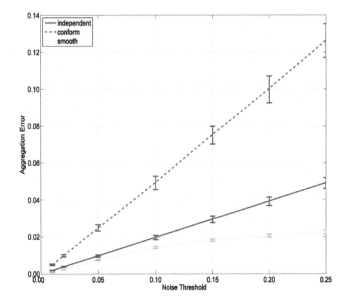

Figure 8. Privacy leak for various noise thresholds

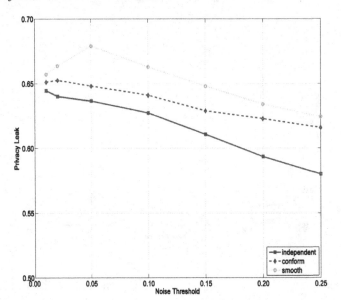

independently and the noise can be from $-T$ to T. The noises may cancel out when flows are aggregated. Again, smooth is insensitive to noise threshold and outperforms the other two methods.

In Figure 8, privacy leak for various noise thresholds is compared. As expected, privacy leak decreases as noise threshold increases for all three methods. Here, independent beats conform, which in turn beats smooth.

Effects of Segment Size: In this section, the effects of segment size are evaluated.

Figure 9 shows classification accuracy for various segment sizes. In general, as segment size increases, classification accuracy decreases for all three methods. The smooth method is the best, followed by conform, and finally independent.

For independent and conform, initially, when segment size increases, noise causes a larger seg-

Figure 9. Classification accuracy

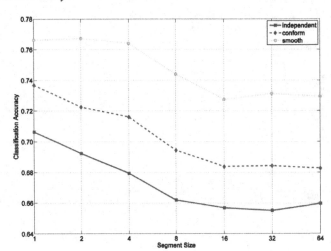

Figure 10. Aggregation error for various segment sizes

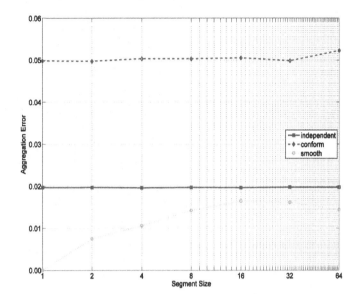

ment to change in one direction. This increases randomness of kNN since nearest neighbors become unpredictable, which decreases its classification accuracy.

For smooth, when segment size increases, more data points can be smoothed if the data points are independent and identically Gaussian distributed.

As shown in Figure 10, the aggregation error is insensitive to segment size for independent and conform. This is because noise level is independent of segment size. For smooth, as segment size increases, aggregation error increases. When segment size increases, the segment mean differs more from most points which increases aggrega-

Figure 11. Privacy leak PL_{NN}

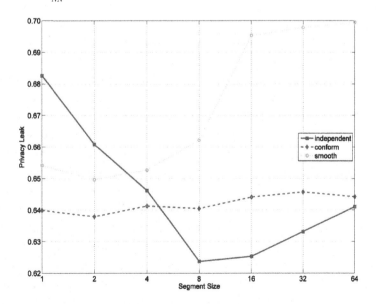

Figure 12. Comparison between optimal approach and guided approaches

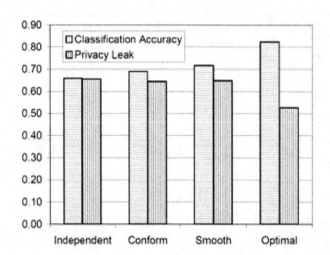

tion error. However, it should be pointed out that smooth is still the best among three.

Figure 11 shows privacy leak for various segment size. We can observe that initially when segment size increases from 1, the privacy leak decreases because of dependence increase caused by segmentation. Segmentation can bring same periodicity to all the data flows. But when segment size increases, less periods can exist in time series, i.e., less dependence.

Optimal Approach

Figure 12 shows the comparison between the optimal approach and the guided approaches. We use simulated annealing algorithm to solve the NLP problem defined in Section 4. We can observe that the optimal approach can achieve highest classification accuracy and lowest privacy leak among all approaches. The aggregation error is comparable for all approaches.

DISCUSSION

Most results in the previous section are averaged over all time series datasets (Keogh et al., 2006). The dataset are very diverse in terms of number of classes, length of time series, size of dataset, classification accuracy, and dependence among different time series. In general, for datasets with longer time series and lower dependence among time series, the performance of the proposed approaches to protect privacy is better because data flow separation attacks are more effective on these datasets without noise addition.

In this paper, we focus on absolute noise threshold. In other words, the noise threshold is defined for each data elements in aggregate data flows. So a low threshold like 10% gives very little room to increase the dependence among noised data flows. If a threshold averaged for more than one data elements is acceptable, the proposed approaches will be more effective.

In our model, we assume the data providers are semi-honest, i.e., they do not provide false data to intentionally mislead research companies, but they may use whatever available information to their advantage. If a data provider is malicious, it may provide false data to uncover other data provider's data, just like other adversaries. In this case, the research company may need extra caution in publishing data mining models. It should also try to detect malicious data provider, for example, through data validation and analysis. It is an interesting topic for future work.

For the optimal approach, equal weights are given to both dependence and precision. In practice, research companies can adjust the weights to trade off between data mining accuracy and privacy protection.

CONCLUSION

In this paper, we have identified privacy issues in time series data mining and presented a general model to protect privacy in time series data mining. We have also proposed a spectrum of methods to preserve privacy and evaluated their performance using real datasets. Our experiments show that these methods can preserve privacy without seriously sacrificing classification accuracy or increasing aggregation error. We have also analyzed the effect of noise on privacy preservation, aggregation error, and classification accuracy.

A possible extension of our research is to adapt other privacy preserving techniques such as transformation for time series data. For example, time series data may be transformed by discrete Fourier transformation and insignificant coefficients may be dropped to protect privacy.

A very interesting problem is privacy in frequency domain and its relationship with privacy in time domain. It will be interesting to investigate if the proposed approaches for preserving privacy in time domain also work for preserving privacy in frequency domain.

Classification is chosen as the data mining task in our paper. One obvious direction for future work is other data mining tasks, such as clustering and prediction.

ACKNOWLEDGMENT

We thank Professor Keogh for the data sets used in our experiments.

REFERENCES

Agrawal, R., Faloutsos, C., & Swami, A. N. (1993). Efficient similarity search in sequence databases. In *Proceedings of the 4th International Conference on Foundations of Data Organization and Algorithms* (pp. 69-84).

Agrawal, R., Lin, K.-I., Sawhney, H. S., & Shim, K. (1995). Fast similarity search in the presence of noise, scaling, and translation in time-series databases. In *Proceedings of the 21st International Conference on Very Large Data Bases* (pp. 490-501).

Agrawal, R., & Srikant, R. (2000). Privacy-preserving data mining. In *Proceedings of the ACM SIGMOD International Conference on Management of Data* (pp. 439-450). New York, NY: ACM Press.

Amo, S., Junior, W., & Giacometti, A. (2008). MILPRIT*: A constraint-based algorithm for mining temporal relational patterns. *International Journal of Data Warehousing and Mining, 4*(4), 42–61. doi:10.4018/jdwm.2008100103

Bagnall, A. J., & Janacek, G. J. (2004). Clustering time series from arma models with clipped data. In *Proceedings of the Tenth ACM SIGKDD International Conference on Knowledge Discovery and Data Mining* (pp. 49-58). New York, NY: ACM Press.

Bayardo, R. J., & Agrawal, R. (2005). Data privacy through optimal k-anonymization. In *Proceedings of the 21st International Conference on Data Engineering* (pp. 217-228). Washington, DC: IEEE Computer Society.

Berndt, D., & Clifford, J. (1994). Using dynamic time warping to find patterns in time series. In *Proceedings of the AAAI Workshop on Knowledge Discovery in Databases.*

Cardoso, J. (1998). Blind signal separation: Statistical principles. *Proceedings of the IEEE*, *9*(10), 2009–2025. doi:10.1109/5.720250

Cole, R., Shasha, D., & Zhao, X. (2005). Fast window correlations over uncooperative time series. In *Proceedings of the Eleventh ACM SIGKDD International Conference on Knowledge Discovery in Data Mining* (pp. 743-749). New York, NY: ACM Press.

Comon, P. (1994). Independent component analysis, a new concept? *Signal Processing*, *36*(3), 287–314. doi:10.1016/0165-1684(94)90029-9

Costa da Silva, J. C., & Klusch, M. (2007). Privacy-preserving discovery of frequent patterns in time series. In P. Perner (Ed.), *Proceedings of the 7ᵗʰ Industrial Conference on Data Mining* (LNCS 4597, pp. 318-328).

Das, G., Lin, K.-I., Mannila, H., Renganathan, G., & Smyth, P. (1998). Rule discovery from time series. In *Proceedings of the ACM SIGKDD International Conference on Knowledge Discovery and Data Mining* (pp. 16-22). New York, NY: ACM Press.

Du, W., & Atallah, M. J. (2001, September 10-13). Secure multi-party computation problems and their applications: A review and open problems. In *Proceedings of the New Security Paradigms Workshop*, Cloudcroft, NM (pp. 13-22).

Du, W., & Zhan, Z. (2003). Using randomized response techniques for privacy-preserving data mining. In *Proceedings of the Ninth ACM SIGKDD International Conference on Knowledge Discovery and Data Mining* (pp. 505-510). New York, NY: ACM Press.

Evfimievski, A. V., Srikant, R., Agrawal, R., & Gehrke, J. (2002). Privacy preserving mining of association rules. In *Proceedings of the ACM SIGKDD International Conference on Knowledge Discovery and Data Mining* (pp. 217-228). New York, NY: ACM Press.

Faloutsos, C., Ranganathan, M., & Manolopoulos, Y. (1994). Fast subsequence matching in timeseries databases. In *Proceedings of the ACM SIGMOD International Conference on Management of Data* (pp. 419-429). New York, NY: ACM Press.

Fung, B. C. M., & Wang, K. (2007). Anonymizing classification data for privacy preservation. *IEEE Transactions on Knowledge and Data Engineering*, *19*(5), 711–725. doi:10.1109/TKDE.2007.1015

Gaeta, M., & Lacoume, J.-L. (1990). Source separation without prior knowledge: The maximum likelihood solution. In *Proceedings of the European Signal Processing Conference* (pp. 621-624).

Ge, X., & Smyth, P. (2000). Deformable Markov model templates for time-series pattern matching. In *Proceedings of the Sixth ACM SIGKDD International Conference on Knowledge Discovery and Data Mining* (pp. 81-90). New York, NY: ACM Press.

Geurts, P. (2001). Pattern extraction for time series classification. In L. De Raedt & A. Siebes (Eds.), *Proceedings of the 5th European Conference on Principles of Data Mining and Knowledge Discovery* (LNCS 2168, pp. 115-127).

Golfarelli, M., & Rizzi, S. (2009). A survey on temporal data warehousing. *International Journal of Data Warehousing and Mining*, *5*(1), 1–17. doi:10.4018/jdwm.2009010101

Huang, Z., Du, W., & Chen, B. (2005). Deriving private information from randomized data. In *Proceedings of the ACM SIGMOD International Conference on Management of Data* (pp. 37-48). New York, NY: ACM Press.

Hyvärinen, A. (1999). Fast and robust fixed-point algorithms for independent component analysis. *IEEE Transactions on Neural Networks*, *10*(3), 626–634. doi:10.1109/72.761722

Iyengar, V. S. (2002). Transforming data to satisfy privacy constraints. In *Proceedings of the Eighth ACM SIGKDD International Conference on Knowledge Discovery and Data Mining* (pp. 279-288). New York, NY: ACM Press.

Jagannathan, G., & Wright, R. N. (2005). Privacy-preserving distributed k-means clustering over arbitrarily partitioned data. In *Proceedings of the Eleventh ACM SIGKDD International Conference on Knowledge Discovery in Data Mining* (pp. 593-599). New York, NY: ACM Press.

Kantarcioglu, M., & Clifton, C. (2004). Privacy-preserving distributed mining of association rules on horizontally partitioned data. *IEEE Transactions on Knowledge and Data Engineering, 16*(9). doi:10.1109/TKDE.2004.45

Keogh, E. J., Chakrabarti, K., Mehrotra, S., & Pazzani, M. J. (2001). Locally adaptive dimensionality reduction for indexing large time series databases. In *Proceedings of the ACM SIGMOD Conference on Management of Data* (pp. 151-162). New York, NY: ACM Press.

Keogh, E. J., & Lin, J. (2005). Clustering of time-series subsequences is meaningless: Implications for previous and future research. *Knowledge and Information Systems, 8*(2), 154–177. doi:10.1007/s10115-004-0172-7

Keogh, E. J., & Pazzani, M. J. (1998). An enhanced representation of time series which allows fast and accurate classification, clustering and relevance feedback. In *Proceedings of the ACM SIGKDD International Conference on Knowledge Discovery in Data Mining* (pp. 239-243). New York, NY: ACM Press.

Keogh, E. J., & Pazzani, M. J. (2000). Scaling up dynamic time warping for data mining applications. In *Proceedings of the ACM SIGKDD International Conference on Knowledge Discovery in Data Mining* (pp. 285-289). New York, NY: ACM Press.

Keogh, E. J., & Smyth, P. (1997). A probabilistic approach to fast pattern matching in time series databases. In *Proceedings of the ACM SIGKDD International Conference on Knowledge Discovery in Data Mining* (pp. 24-30). New York, NY: ACM Press.

Keogh, E. J., Xi, X., Wei, L., & Ratanamahatana, C. A. (2006). *The UCR time series classification/clustering homepage.* Retrieved from http://www.cs.ucr.edu/~eamonn/time_series_data/

LeFevre, K., DeWitt, D. J., & Ramakrishnan, R. (2006). Workload-aware anonymization. In *Proceedings of the 12th ACM SIGKDD International Conference on Knowledge Discovery and Data Mining* (pp. 277-286). New York, NY: ACM Press.

Liabotis, I., Theodoulidis, B., & Saraaee, M. (2006). Improving similarity search in time series using wavelets. *International Journal of Data Warehousing and Mining, 2*(2), 55–81. doi:10.4018/jdwm.2006040103

Lindell, Y., & Pinkas, B. (2000). Privacy preserving data mining. In *Journal of Cryptology, 15*(3), 36–54.

Mielikäinen, T., Terzi, E., & Tsaparas, P. (2006). Aggregating time partitions. In *Proceedings of the ACM SIGKDD International Conference on Knowledge Discovery in Data Mining* (pp. 347-356). New York, NY: ACM Press.

Mörchen, F., & Ultsch, A. (2005). Optimizing time series discretization for knowledge discovery. In *Proceedings of the ACM SIGKDD International Conference on Knowledge Discovery in Data Mining* (pp. 660-665). New York, NY: ACM Press.

Papadimitriou, S., Li, F., Kollios, G., & Yu, P. S. (2007). Time series compressibility and privacy. In *Proceedings of the 33rd International Conference on Very Large Data Bases* (pp. 459-470).

Patel, P., Keogh, E. J., Lin, J., & Lonardi, S. (2002). Mining motifs in massive time series databases. In *Proceedings of the IEEE International Conference on Data Mining* (pp. 370-377). Washington, DC: IEEE Computer Society.

She, R., Want, K., Fu, A., & Yabo, X. (2008). Computing join aggregates over private tables. *International Journal of Data Warehousing and Mining, 4*(4), 22–41. doi:10.4018/jdwm.2008100102

Vaidya, J., & Clifton, C. (2002). Privacy preserving association rule mining in vertically partitioned data. In *Proceedings of the ACM SIGKDD International Conference on Knowledge Discovery in Data Mining* (pp. 639-644). New York, NY: ACM Press.

Vaidya, J., & Clifton, C. (2003). Privacy-preserving k-means clustering over vertically partitioned data. In *Proceedings of the ACM SIGKDD International Conference on Knowledge Discovery in Data Mining* (pp. 206-215). New York, NY: ACM Press.

Wright, R. N., & Yang, Z. (2004). Privacy-preserving Bayesian network structure computation on distributed heterogeneous data. In *Proceedings of the ACM SIGKDD International Conference on Knowledge Discovery in Data Mining* (pp. 713-718). New York, NY: ACM Press.

Yildizli, C., Pedersen, T., Saygin, Y., Savas, E., & Levi, L. (2011). Distributed privacy preserving clustering via homomorphic secret sharing and its application to (vertically) partitioned spatio-temporal data. *International Journal of Data Warehousing and Mining, 7*(1), 46–66. doi:10.4018/jdwm.2011010103

Zhu, Y., & Fu, Y. (2007). *On privacy in time series data mining* (Tech. Rep. No. CSU-ECE-TR-07-02). Cleveland, OH: Cleveland State University.

Zhu, Y., & Liu, L. (2004). Optimal randomization for privacy preserving data mining. In *Proceedings of the ACM SIGKDD International Conference on Knowledge Discovery in Data Mining* (pp. 761-766). New York, NY: ACM Press.

This work was previously published in the International Journal of Data Warehousing and Mining, Volume 7, Issue 4, edited by David Taniar, pp. 64-85, copyright 2011 by IGI Publishing (an imprint of IGI Global).

Compilation of References

Abiteboul, S., Hull, R., & Vianu, V. (1995). *Foundations of Databases*. Reading, MA: Addison-Wesley.

Abul, O., Bonchi, F., & Nanni, M. (2008). Never walk alone: Uncertainty for anonymity in Moving objects databases. In *Proceedings of the IEEE International Conference on Data Engineering* (pp. 376-385). Washington, DC: IEEE Computer Society.

Adam, N. R., Janeja, V. P., & Atluri, V. (2004). Neighborhood based detection of anomalies in high dimensional spatio-temporal sensor datasets. In *Proceedings of the 2004 ACM Symposium on Applied Computing*.

Adomavicius, G., & Tuzhilin, A. (2005). Toward the next generation of recommender systems: A survey of the state-of-the-art and possible extensions. *IEEE Transactions on Knowledge and Data Engineering, 17*(6), 734–749. doi:10.1109/TKDE.2005.99

Agarwal, S., Agrawal, R., Deshpande, P., Gupta, A., Naughton, J., Ramakrishnan, R., et al. (1996). On the computation of multidimensional aggregates. In *Proceedings of VLDB* (pp. 506–521).

Aggarwal, C. C., & Yu, P. S. (Eds.). (2008). *Privacy-Preserving Data Mining*. New York: Springer.

Agrawal, R., & Srikant, R. (1994). Fast algorithms for mining association rules in large databases. In J. B. Bocca, M. Jarke, & C. Zaniolo (Eds.), *Proceedings of the 20th International Conference on Very Large Data Bases* (pp. 487-499). San Francisco, CA: Morgan Kaufmann Publishers.

Agrawal, R., & Srikant, R. (1995). Mining Sequential Patterns. In *Proceedings of the 11th International Conference on Data Engineering,* Taipei, Taiwan (pp. 3-14).

Agrawal, R., & Srikant, R. (2000). Privacy-preserving data mining. In *Proceedings of the ACM SIGMOD International Conference on Management of Data* (pp. 439-450). New York, NY: ACM Press.

Agrawal, R., Faloutsos, C., & Swami, A. N. (1993). Efficient similarity search in sequence databases. In *Proceedings of the 4th International Conference on Foundations of Data Organization and Algorithms* (pp. 69-84).

Agrawal, R., Imielinski, T., & Swami, A. N. (1993). Mining association rules between sets of items in large databases. In P. Buneman & S. Jajodia (Eds.), *Proceedings of the 1993 ACM SIGMOD International Conference on Management of Data* (pp. 207-216). New York, NY: ACM.

Agrawal, R., Lin, K.-I., Sawhney, H. S., & Shim, K. (1995). Fast similarity search in the presence of noise, scaling, and translation in time-series databases. In *Proceedings of the 21st International Conference on Very Large Data Bases* (pp. 490-501).

Agrawal, S., Chaudhuri, S., & Narasayya, V. (2000). Automated Selection of Materialized Views and Indexes for SQL Databases. In *Proceedings of the 26th International Conference on Very Large Databases,* Cairo, Egypt (pp. 496-505).

Agrawal, S., Chaudhuri, S., Kollar, L., Marathe, A., Narasayya, V., & Syamala, M. (2004). Database Tuning Advisor for Microsoft SQL Server 2005. In *Proceedings of the 30th VLDB Conference,* Toronto, ON, Canada (pp. 1110- 1121).

Agrawal, S., Narasayya, V., & Yang, B. (2004). Integrating Vertical and Horizontal Partitioning into Automated Physical Database Design. In *Proceedings of the SIGMOD 2004 Conference,* Paris, France (pp. 359-370).

Agrawal, R., & Srikant, R. (2000). Privacy-preserving data mining. *SIGMOD Record*, *29*(2), 439–450. doi:10.1145/335191.335438

Ahmad, A., & Dey, L. (2007). A k-mean clustering algorithm for mixed numeric and categorical data. *Data & Knowledge Engineering*, *63*(2), 503–527. doi:10.1016/j.datak.2007.03.016

Ahmed, M., Agrawal, V., & Sundararaghavan, P. (2007). Statistical Sampling to Instantiate Materialized View Selection Problems in Data Warehouses. *International Journal of Data Warehousing and Mining*, *3*(1), 1–28. doi:10.4018/jdwm.2007010101

Aleksander, I., & Morton, H. (1990). *An introduction to neural computing*. London, UK: Chapman and Hall.

Amo, S., Junior, W., & Giacometti, A. (2008). MILPRIT*: A constraint-based algorithm for mining temporal relational patterns. *International Journal of Data Warehousing and Mining*, *4*(4), 42–61. doi:10.4018/jdwm.2008100103

Anderson, C. (2006). *The long tail: Why the future of business is selling less of more* (pp. 130–135). New York, NY: Hyperion.

Andrienko, G., & Andrienko, N. (2008). Spatio-temporal aggregation for visual analysis of movements. In *Proceedings of IEEE Symposium on Visual Analytics Science and Technology* (pp. 51–58). Washington, DC: IEEE Computer Society Press.

Andrienko, G., Andrienko, N., & Wrobel, S. (2007). Visual Analytics Tools for Analysis of Movement Data. *ACM SIGKDD Explorations*, *9*(2), 28–46. doi:10.1145/1345448.1345455

Andrienko, N., & Andrienko, G. (2007). Designing visual analytics methods for massive collections of movement data. *Cartographica*, *42*(2), 117–138.

Antonie, M.-L., & Zaiane, O. R. (2002). Text document categorization by term association. In *Proceedings of the 2002 IEEE International Conference on Data Mining (ICDM '02)* (pp. 19-26). Washington, DC: IEEE Computer Society.

Aouiche, K., Jouve, P. E., & Darmont, J. (2006). Clustering-Based Materialized View Selection in Data Warehouses. In *Proceedings of the ADBIS '06 Conference* (LNCS 4152, pp. 81-95).

Aouiche, K., & Darmont, J. (2009). Data mining-based materialized view and index selection in data warehouses. *Journal of Intelligent Information Systems*, *32*(1), 65–93. doi:10.1007/s10844-009-0080-0

Asgharzadeh Talebi, Z., Chirkova, R., Fathi, Y., & Stallmann, M. (2008). Exact and Inexact Methods for Selecting Views and Indexes for OLAP Performance Improvement. In *Proceedings of the EDBT '08 Conference* (pp. 311-322).

Ashrafi, M. Z., Taniar, D., & Smith, K. A. (2004). ODAM: An Optimized Distributed Association Rule Mining Algorithm. *IEEE Distributed Systems Online*, *5*(3).

Ashrafi, M. Z., Taniar, D., & Smith, K. (2004). ODAM: An Optimized Distributed Association Rule Mining Algorithm. *IEEE Distributed Systems Online*, *5*(3), 11–18. doi:10.1109/MDSO.2004.1285877

Ashrafi, M. Z., Taniar, D., & Smith, K. A. (2007). Redundant association rules reduction techniques. *International Journal of Business Intelligence and Data Mining*, *2*(1), 29–63. doi:10.1504/IJBIDM.2007.012945

Asuncion, A., & Newman, D. (2007). *UCI machine learning repository*. Retrieved from http://www.ics.uci.edu/~mlearn/MLRepository.html

Au, W. H., & Chan, K. C. C. (1999). FARM: A Data Mining System for Discovering Fuzzy Association Rules. In *Proceedings of the 8th IEEE International Conference on Fuzzy Systems*, Seoul, Korea (pp. 1217-1222).

Babu, S., & Widom, J. (2001). Continuous queries over data streams. *SIGMOD Record*, *30*(3), 109–120. doi:10.1145/603867.603884

Baglioni, M., de Macedo, J., Renso, C., Trasarti, R., & Wachowicz, M. (2009). Towards semantic interpretation of movement behaviour. In *Proceedings of the 12th AGILE International Conference on Geographic Information Science*. Berlin: Springer.

Bagnall, A. J., & Janacek, G. J. (2004). Clustering time series from arma models with clipped data. In *Proceedings of the Tenth ACM SIGKDD International Conference on Knowledge Discovery and Data Mining* (pp. 49-58). New York, NY: ACM Press.

Balestre, M., Von Pinho, R. G., Souza, J. C., & Lima, J. L. (2008). Comparison of maize similarity and dissimilarity genetic coefficients based on microsatellite markers. *Genetics and Molecular Research, 7*(3), 695–705. doi:10.4238/vol7-3gmr458

Baralis, E., Paraboschi, S., & Teniente, E. (1997). Materialized View Selection in a Multidimensional Database. In *Proceedings of the 23rd VLDB Conference,* Athens, Greece (pp. 156-165).

Baroni-Urbani, C., & Buser, M. W. (1976). Similarity of binary data. *Systematic Zoology, 25*(3), 251–259. doi:10.2307/2412493

Barouni-Ebrahimi, M., & Ghorbani, A. A. (2007). An online frequency rate based algorithm for mining frequent sequences in evolving data streams. In *Proceedings of International Conference on Information Technology and Management* (pp. 56-63).

Bayardo, R. J., & Agrawal, R. (2005). Data privacy through optimal k-anonymization. In *Proceedings of the 21st International Conference on Data Engineering* (pp. 217-228). Washington, DC: IEEE Computer Society.

Beizer, B. (1990). *Software Testing Techniques*. New York, NY: Van Nostrand Reinhold.

Bellatreche, L., Giacometti, A., Marcel, P., Mouloudi, H., & Laurent, D. (2005). A personalization framework for OLAP queries. In *Proceedings of the 8th ACM International Workshop on Data Warehousing and OLAP* (pp. 9–18). New York, NY: ACM.

Bellatreche, L., Boukhalfa, K., Richard, P., & Woameno, K. Y. (2009). Referential Horizontal Partitioning Selection Problem in Data Warehouses: Hardness Study and Selection Algorithms. *International Journal of Data Warehousing and Mining, 5*(4), 1–23. doi:10.4018/jdwm.2009080701

Ben-Or, M., Goldwasser, S., & Wigderson, A. (1998). Completeness theorems for non-cryptographic fault-tolerant distributed computation. In *STOC '88: Proceedings of the Twentieth Annual ACM Symposium on Theory of Computing* (pp. 1–10). New York: ACM.

Berndt, D., & Clifford, J. (1994). Using dynamic time warping to find patterns in time series. In *Proceedings of the AAAI Workshop on Knowledge Discovery in Databases.*

Berzal, F., Blanco, I., Sánchez, D., & Vila, M. A. (2002). Measuring the accuracy and interest of association rules: A new framework. *Intelligent Data Analysis, 6*(3), 221–235.

Bethencourt, J. (2010). *Paillier library.* Retrieved from http://acsc.cs.utexas.edu/libpaillier/

Bezrukov, S. L., & Leck, U. (2005). Macaulay posets. *The Electronic Journal of Combinatorics.* Retrieved from http://www.combinatorics.org/Surveys

Bhatnagar, V., Kaur, S., & Mignet, L. (2009). A parameterized framework for clustering streams. *International Journal of Data Warehousing and Mining, 5*(1), 36–56. doi:10.4018/jdwm.2009010103

BiPM. (2009). *Data warehouse testing and implementation.* Retrieved from http://www.bipminstitute.com/data-warehouse

Blatt, F. J. (1986). *Principles of physics* (2nd ed.). Boston, MA: Allyn and Bacon.

Bodon, F. (2003). A Fast Apriori Implementation. In *Proceedings of the 1st IEEE ICDM Workshop on Frequent Itemset Mining Implementations (FIMI2003),* Melbourne, FL. Retrieved from http://www.ceur-ws.org/vol-90/

Bonifati, A., Cattaneo, F., Ceri, S., Fuggetta, A., & Paraboschi, S. (2001). Designing data marts for data warehouses. *ACM Transactions on Software Engineering and Methodology, 10*(4), 452–483. doi:10.1145/384189.384190

Bookstein, A., Klein, S. T., & Raita, T. (1998). Clumping properties of content-bearing words. *Journal of the American Society for Information Science American Society for Information Science, 49*(2), 102–114.

Boyce, R. L., & Ellison, P. C. (2001). Choosing the best similarity index when performing fuzzy set ordination on binary data. *Journal of Vegetation Science, 12*, 711–720. doi:10.2307/3236912

Brahmkshatriya, K. (2007). *Data warehouse testing.* Retrieved from http://www.stickyminds.com

Breiman, L., Friedman, J., Olshen, R., & Stone, C. (1984). *Classification and regression trees.* Monterey, CA: Wadsworth & Brooks/Cole Advanced Books & Software.

Bruckner, R., List, B., & Schiefer, J. (2001). Developing requirements for data warehouse systems with use cases. In *Proceedings of the Americas Conference on Information Systems* (pp. 329–335).

Burdick, D., Calimlim, M., Flannick, J., Gehrke, J., & Yiu, T. (2005). MAFIA: A maximal frequent itemset algorithm. *IEEE Transactions on Knowledge and Data Engineering, 17*(11), 1490–1504. doi:10.1109/TKDE.2005.183

Burris, S., & Sankappanavar, H. P. (1981). *A Course in Universal Algebra.* New York, NY: Springer.

Cai, C. H., Fu, A. W. C., Cheng, C. H., & Kwong, W. W. (1998). Mining association rules with weighted items. In *Proceedings of the 1998 International Symposium on Database Engineering & Applications (IDEAS '98)* (pp. 6877). Washington, DC: IEEE Computer Society.

Calders, T., Lakshmanan, L. V. S., & Paredaens, J. (2006). Expressive power of an algebra for data mining. *ACM Transactions on Database Systems, 31*(4), 1169–1214. doi:10.1145/1189769.1189770

Cardoso, J. (1998). Blind signal separation: Statistical principles. *Proceedings of the IEEE, 9*(10), 2009–2025. doi:10.1109/5.720250

Cariou, V., Cubillé, J., Derquenne, C., Goutier, S., Guisnel, F., & Klajnmic, H. (2007). Built-in indicators to automatically detect interesting cells in a cube. In *Proceedings of the 9th International Conference on Data Warehousing and Knowledge Discovery* (LNCS 4654, pp. 123–134).

Cariou, V., Cubillé, J., Derquenne, C., Goutier, S., Guisnel, F., & Klajnmic, H. (2008). Built-in indicators to discover interesting drill paths in a cube. In *Proceedings of the 10th International Conference on Data Warehousing and Knowledge Discovery* (LNCS 5182, pp. 33–44).

Carrio, J. A., Pinto, F. R., Simas, C., Nunes, S., Sousa, N. G., & Frazão, N. (2005). Assessment of band-based similarity coefficients for automatic type and subtype classification of microbial isolates analyzed by pulsed-field gel electrophoresis. *Journal of Clinical Microbiology, 43*(11), 5483–5490. doi:10.1128/JCM.43.11.5483-5490.2005

Casali, A., Nedjar, S., Cicchetti, R., & Lakhal, L. (2010). Constrained Cube Lattices for Multidimensional Database Mining. *International Journal of Data Warehousing and Mining, 6*(3), 43–72. doi:10.4018/jdwm.2010070104

Cha, S-H., Tappert, C., & Yoon, S. (2006). Enhancing binary feature vector similarity measures. *Journal of Pattern Recognition Research*, 63-77.

Chakraborty, A., & Singh, A. (2009). A partition-based approach to support streaming updates over persistent data in an active data warehouse. In *Proceedings of the IEEE International Symposium on Parallel & Distributed Processing* (pp. 1-11).

Chang, J. H., & Lee, W. S. (2003). Finding recent frequent itemsets adaptively over online data streams. In *Proceedings of the Ninth ACM SIGKDD International Conference on Knowledge Discovery and Data Mining* (pp. 487-492).

Chatzopoulou, G., Eirinaki, M., & Polyzotis, N. (2009). Query recommendations for interactive database exploration. In *Proceedings of the 21st International Conference on Scientific and Statistical Database Management* (LNCS 5566, pp. 3–18).

Chaudhuri, S., & Narasayya, V. (1997). An Efficient, Cost-Driven Index Selection Tool for Microsoft SQL Server. In *Proceedings of the 23rd VLDB Conference, Athens, Greece* (pp. 146-155).

Chen, G., Wu, X., & Zhu, X. (2005). Sequential pattern mining in multiple streams. In *Proceedings of the Fifth IEEE International Conference on Data Mining* (pp. 585-588).

Chen, L., Wenny Rahayu, J., & Taniar, D. (2010). Towards Near Real-Time Data Warehousing. In *Proceedings of the AINA 2010 Conference* (pp. 1150-1157).

Chen, X., & Wu, Y.-F. (2006). Personalized knowledge discovery, mining novel association rules from text. In *Proceedings of the 6th SIAM International Conference on Data Mining* (pp. 589-597). Bethesda, MD: Society of Industrial and Applied Mathematics.

Chen, G., & Wei, Q. (2002). Fuzzy Association Rules and the Extended Mining Algorithms. *Information Sciences*, *147*(1-4), 201–228. doi:10.1016/S0020-0255(02)00264-5

Choi, C. H., Xu Yu, J., & Lu, H. (2003). Dynamic Materialized View Management Based on Predicates. In *Proceedings of the APWeb 2003 Conference* (LNCS 2642, pp. 583-594).

Choi, W., Kwon, D., & Lee, S. (2006). Spatio-temporal data warehouses using an adaptive cell-based approach. *DKE*, *59*(1), 189–207. doi:10.1016/j.datak.2005.08.001

Chu, C. J., Tseng, V. S., & Liang, T. (2008). An efficient algorithm for mining temporal high utility itemsets from data streams. *Journal of Systems and Software*, *81*(7), 1105–1117. doi:10.1016/j.jss.2007.07.026

Chu, C. J., Tseng, V. S., & Liang, T. (2009). Efficient mining of temporal emerging itemsets from data streams. *Expert Systems with Applications: An International Journal*, *36*(1), 885–893. doi:10.1016/j.eswa.2007.10.040

Clementine. (2010). *Statistical analysis software SPSS Clementine*. Retrieved April 20, 2010, from http://www.spss.com/clementine/

Clifton, C., Kantarcioglu, M., Vaidya, J., Lin, X., & Zhu, M. Y. (2002). Tools for privacy preserving distributed data mining. *SIGKDD Explorations*, *4*(2), 28–34. doi:10.1145/772862.772867

Coenen, F. P., Leng, P., & Ahmed, S. (2004). Data Structures for Association Rule Mining: T-trees and P-trees. *IEEE Transactions on Data and Knowledge Engineering*, *16*(6), 774–778. doi:10.1109/TKDE.2004.8

Coenen, F., Goulbourne, G., & Leng, P. (2004). Tree structures for mining association rules. *Data Mining and Knowledge Discovery*, *8*(1), 25–51. doi:10.1023/B:DAMI.0000005257.93780.3b

Cohen, E., Datar, M., Fujiwara, S., Gionis, A., Indyk, P., & Motwani, R. (2001). Finding interesting association rules without support pruning. *IEEE Transactions on Knowledge and Data Engineering*, *13*, 64–78. doi:10.1109/69.908981

Cole, R., Shasha, D., & Zhao, X. (2005). Fast window correlations over uncooperative time series. In *Proceedings of the Eleventh ACM SIGKDD International Conference on Knowledge Discovery in Data Mining* (pp. 743-749). New York, NY: ACM Press.

Comon, P. (1994). Independent component analysis, a new concept? *Signal Processing*, *36*(3), 287–314. doi:10.1016/0165-1684(94)90029-9

Cooper, R., & Arbuckle, S. (2002). *How to thoroughly test a data warehouse*. Paper presented at the STAREAST Conference, Orlando, FL.

Costa da Silva, J. C., & Klusch, M. (2007). Privacy-preserving discovery of frequent patterns in time series. In P. Perner (Ed.), *Proceedings of the 7th Industrial Conference on Data Mining* (LNCS 4597, pp. 318-328).

Craven, M. W. (1996). *Extracting comprehensible models from trained neural networks*. Unpublished doctoral dissertation, University of Wisconsin-Madison, Madison, WI.

Craven, M. W., & Shavlik, J. W. (1996). Extracting tree-structured representations of trained neural networks. In *Proceedings of the Conference on Advances in Neural Information Processing Systems* (pp. 824-830).

da Silva Meyer, A., Franco Garcia, A. A., Pereira de Souza, A., & Lopes de Souza, C. Jr. (2004). Comparison of similarity coefficients used for cluster analysis with dominant markers in maize (zea mays l). *Genetics and Molecular Biology*, *27*(1), 83–91.

Dalirsefat, S., da Silva Meyer, A., & Mirhosein, S. Z. (2009). Comparison of similarity coefficients used for cluster analysis with amplified fragment length polymorphism markers in the silkworm, bombyx mori. *Journal of Insect Science*, *9*, Retrieved from http://www.insect-science.org/9.71/. doi:10.1673/031.009.7101

Daly, O., & Taniar, D. (2004). Exception Rules Mining Based on Negative Association Rules. In *Proceedings of the International Conference on Computational Science and Its Applications (ICCSA 2004)* (LNCS 3046, pp. 543-552).

Daneshpour, N., & Abdollahzadeh Barfourosh, A. (2008). *View Selection Algorithms to Build Data Warehouse* (Tech. Rep. No. CE/ TR.DS/ 86/ 01). Tehran, Iran: AIS Lab, IT & Computer Engineering Department, Amirkabir University of Technology. Retrieved from http://ceit.aut. ac.ir/~daneshpour/Publications.htm

Daneshpour, N., & Abdollahzadeh Barfourosh, A. (in press). A Solution to View Management to Build a Data Warehouse. *Amirkabir Journal of Science and Technology.*

Dang, X. H., Ng, W. K., Ong, K. L., & Lee, V. C. S. (2007). Discovering frequent sets from data streams with CPU constraint. In *Proceedings of the Sixth Australasian Conference on Data Mining and Analytics* (pp. 121-128).

Das, G., Lin, K.-I., Mannila, H., Renganathan, G., & Smyth, P. (1998). Rule discovery from time series. In *Proceedings of the ACM SIGKDD International Conference on Knowledge Discovery and Data Mining* (pp. 16-22). New York, NY: ACM Press.

De Raedt, L., & Nijssen, S. (2006). IQL: A proposal for an inductive query language. In *Proceedings of the 5th International Workshop Knowledge Discovery in Inductive Databases (KDID 2006)* (pp. 189-207).

Dehne, F., Eavis, T., & Rau-Chaplin, A. (2008). RCUBE: Parallel Multi-Dimensional ROLAP Indexing. *International Journal of Data Warehousing and Mining, 4*(3), 1–14. doi:10.4018/jdwm.2008070101

Delgado, M., Marin, M., Martín-Bautista, M. J., Sánchez, D., & Vila, M. A. (2003). Mining Fuzzy Association Rules: An Overview. In *Proceedings of the BISC International Workshop on Soft Computing for Internet and Bioinformatics* (pp. 351-373).

Delgado, M., Marin, N., Sánchez, D., & Vila, M. A. (2003). Fuzzy association rules: general model and applications. *IEEE Transactions on Fuzzy Systems, 11*(2), 214–225. doi:10.1109/TFUZZ.2003.809896

Delgado, M., Sánchez, D., Martín-Bautista, M. J., & Vila, M. A. (2001). Mining association rules with improved semantics in medical databases. *Artificial Intelligence in Medicine, 21*(1-3), 241–245. doi:10.1016/S0933-3657(00)00092-0

Delgado, M., Sánchez, D., & Vila, M. A. (2002). Acquisition of fuzzy association rules from medical data. In Barro, S., & Marin, R. (Eds.), *Fuzzy Logic in Medicine* (pp. 286–310).

Doganay, M. C., Pedersen, T. B., Saygin, Y., Sava s , E., & Levi, A. (2008). Distributed privacy preserving k-means clustering with additive secret sharing. In F. Fotouhi, L. Xiong, & T. M. Truta (Eds.), *PAIS '08: Proceedings of the 2008 International Workshop on Privacy and Anonymity in Information Society* (pp. 3–11). New York: ACM.

Dong, L., & Tjortjis, C. (2003). Experiences of Using a Quantitative Approach for Mining Association Rules. In *Proceedings of the IDEAL 2003 Conference* (LNCS 2690, pp. 693-700).

Downey, D., Dumais, S. T., Liebling, D. J., & Horvitz, E. (2008). Understanding the relationship between searchers' queries and information goals. In *Proceedings of the 17th ACM Conference on Information and Knowledge Management* (pp. 449–458). New York, NY: ACM.

Drecki, I., & Forer, P. (2000). *Tourism in New Zealand - international visitors on the move (a1 cartographic plate)*. Lincoln, NE: Tourism, Recreation Research and Education Centre, Lincoln University.

Du, W., & Atallah, M. J. (2001, September 10-13). Secure multi-party computation problems and their applications: A review and open problems. In *Proceedings of the New Security Paradigms Workshop*, Cloudcroft, NM (pp. 13-22).

Du, W., & Zhan, Z. (2003). Using randomized response techniques for privacy-preserving data mining. In *Proceedings of the Ninth ACM SIGKDD International Conference on Knowledge Discovery and Data Mining* (pp. 505-510). New York, NY: ACM Press.

Dubois, D., Hüllermeier, E., & Prade, H. (2006). A Systematic Approach to the Assessment of Fuzzy Association Rules. *Data Mining and Knowledge Discovery, 13*(2), 167–192. doi:10.1007/s10618-005-0032-4

Dykes, J. A., & Mountain, D. M. (2003). Seeking structure in records of spatio-temporal behavior: visualization issues. *Computational Statistics & Data Analysis, 43*(4), 581–603. doi:10.1016/S0167-9473(02)00294-3

El-Helw, A., Ilyas, I. F., & Zuzarte, C. (2009). StatAdvisor: Recommending Statistical Views. In *Proceedings of the VLDB '09 Conference* (pp. 1306-1317).

Engle, K., & Gangopadhyay, A. (2010). An efficient method for discretizing continuous attributes. *International Journal of Data Warehousing and Mining, 6*(2), 1–21. doi:10.4018/jdwm.2010040101

Evans, D. A., & Lefferts, R. G. (1995). CLARIT-TREC experiments. In *Proceedings of the 2nd Text Retrieval Conference* (pp. 385-395). Elmsford, NY: Pergamon Press.

Evfimievski, A. V., Srikant, R., Agrawal, R., & Gehrke, J. (2002). Privacy preserving mining of association rules. In *Proceedings of the ACM SIGKDD International Conference on Knowledge Discovery and Data Mining* (pp. 217-228). New York, NY: ACM Press.

Faloutsos, C., Korn, F., Labrinidis, A., Labrinidis, R., Kotidis, Y., Perkovic, D., & Kaplunovich, A. (1997). *Quantifiable data mining using principal component analysis* (Tech. Rep. No. CS-TR-3754). College Park, MD: Institute for Systems Research, University of Maryland.

Faloutsos, C., Ranganathan, M., & Manolopoulos, Y. (1994). Fast subsequence matching in timeseries databases. In *Proceedings of the ACM SIGMOD International Conference on Management of Data* (pp. 419-429). New York, NY: ACM Press.

Fayyad, U. M., Piatetsky-Shapiro, G., & Smyth, P. (1996). From Data Mining to Knowledge Discovery: An Overview. In *Advances in Knowledge Discovery & Data Mining* (pp. 1–34). Cambridge, MA: MIT Press.

Feldman, R., & Hirsh, H. (1996). Mining associations in text in the presence of background knowledge. In *Proceedings of the 2nd International Conference on Knowledge Discovery and Data Mining (KDD-96)* (pp. 343-346). Menlo Park, CA: AAAI Press.

Fernández-Medina, E., Trujillo, J., Villarroel, R., & Piattini, M. (2007). Developing secure data warehouses with a UML extension. *Information Systems, 32*(6), 826–856. doi:10.1016/j.is.2006.07.003

Fischlin, M. (2001). A cost-effective pay-per-multiplication comparison method for millionaires. In D. Naccache (Ed.), *CT-RSA 2001: Topics in Cryptology -The Cryptographers' Track at RSA Conference* (LNCS 2010, pp. 457–471).

Flajolet, P., & Martin, G. (1985). Probabilistic counting algorithms for data base applications. *Journal of Computer and System Sciences, 31*(2), 182–209. doi:10.1016/0022-0000(85)90041-8

Forer, P., & Huisman, O. (2000). Information, Place and Cyberspace: Issues in Accessibility. In *Time and Sequencing: Substitution at the Physical/Virtual Interface* (pp. 73–90). Berlin: Springer Verlag.

Frappier, M., Matwin, S., & Mili, A. (1994). *Software metrics for predicting maintainability*. Longueuil, QC, Canada: Canadian Space Agency.

Fredrikson, A., North, C., Plaisant, C., & Shneiderman, B. (1999). Temporal, geographical and categorical aggregations viewed through coordinated displays: a case study with highway incident data. In *Proceedings of the Workshop on New Paradigms in Information Visualization and Manipulation* (pp. 26–34).

Freitas, A. A. (1998). On Objective Measures of Rule Surprisingness. In *Proceedings of the 2nd European Symposium on Principle of Data Mining and Knowledge Discovery (PKDD-98)* (LNAI 1510, pp. 1-9).

Fromonnd, E., Goethals, B., Prado, A., Blockeel, H., & Calders, T. (2008). Mining views: Database views for data mining. In *Proceedings of the 24th IEEE International Conference on Data Engineering* (pp.1608-1611). Washington, DC: IEEE Computer Society.

Fung, G., Sandilya, S., & Bharat, R. (2005). Rule extraction from linear support vector machines. In *Proceedings of the KDD 2005 Conference* (pp. 32-40).

Fung, B. C. M., & Wang, K. (2007). Anonymizing classification data for privacy preservation. *IEEE Transactions on Knowledge and Data Engineering, 19*(5), 711–725. doi:10.1109/TKDE.2007.1015

Gaber, M. M., Krishnaswamy, S., & Zaslavsky, A. (2003). *Adaptive mining techniques for data streams using algorithm output granularity*. Paper presented at the Australasian Data Mining Workshop.

Gaeta, M., & Lacoume, J.-L. (1990). Source separation without prior knowledge: The maximum likelihood solution. In *Proceedings of the European Signal Processing Conference* (pp. 621-624).

Ge, X., & Smyth, P. (2000). Deformable Markov model templates for time-series pattern matching. In *Proceedings of the Sixth ACM SIGKDD International Conference on Knowledge Discovery and Data Mining* (pp. 81-90). New York, NY: ACM Press.

George, K., Han, E. H., & Kumar, V. (1999). CHAMELEON: A hierarchical clustering algorithm using dynamic modeling. *IEEE Computer, 27*(3), 329–341.

Geurts, P. (2001). Pattern extraction for time series classification. In L. De Raedt & A. Siebes (Eds.), *Proceedings of the 5th European Conference on Principles of Data Mining and Knowledge Discovery* (LNCS 2168, pp. 115-127).

Giachetta, G., Mangiarotti, L., & Sardanashvily, G. (2009). *Advanced classical field theory*. Singapore: World Scientific. doi:10.1142/9789812838964

Giacometti, A., Marcel, P., & Negre, E. (2008). A framework for recommending OLAP queries. In *Proceedings of the 11th ACM International Workshop on Data Warehousing and OLAP* (pp. 73–80). New York, NY: ACM.

Giacometti, A., Marcel, P., & Negre, E. (2009). Recommending multidimensional queries. In *Proceedings of the 11th International Conference on Data Warehousing and Knowledge Discovery* (LNCS 5691, pp. 453–466).

Giacometti, A., Marcel, P., & Negre, E. (2009). Query recommendation for OLAP discovery driven analysis. In *Proceedings of the 12th ACM International Workshop on Data Warehousing and OLAP* (pp. 81–88). New York, NY: ACM.

Giannikopoulos, P., Varlamis, I., & Eirinaki, M. (2010). Mining Frequent Generalized Patterns for Web Personalization in the Presence of Taxonomies. *International Journal of Data Warehousing and Mining, 6*(1), 58–76. doi:10.4018/jdwm.2010090804

Giannotti, F., Nanni, M., Pinelli, F., & Pedreschi, D. (2007). Trajectory pattern mining. In *Proceedings of ACM SIGKDD* (pp. 330-339). New York: ACM.

Giannotti, F., & Pedreschi, D. (2008). *Mobility, Data Mining, and Privacy*. Berlin: Springer-Verlag. doi:10.1007/978-3-540-75177-9

Gierz, G., Hofmann, K. H., Keimel, K., Lawson, J. D., Mislove, M., & Scott, D. S. (1980). *A Compendium of Continuous Lattices*. New York, NY: Springer.

Giorgini, P., Rizzi, S., & Garzetti, M. (2008). GRAnD: A goal-oriented approach to requirement analysis in data warehouses. *Decision Support Systems, 5*(1), 4–21. doi:10.1016/j.dss.2006.12.001

Goh, J. Y., & Taniar, D. (2004). Mobile data mining by location dependencies. In Z. Rong Yang, H. Yin, & R. M. Everson (Eds.), *Proceedings of the 5th International Conference on Intelligent Data Engineering and Automated Learning* (LNCS 3177, pp. 225-231).

Golab, L., & Özsu, M. T. (2003). Processing sliding window multi-joins in continuous queries over data streams. In *Proceedings of the 29th International Conference on Very Large Data Bases*, Berlin, Germany (pp. 500-511).

Golfarelli, M., & Rizzi, S. (2009). Expressing OLAP preferences. In *Proceedings of the 22th International Conference on Scientific and Statistical Database Management* (LNCS 5566, pp. 83–91).

Golfarelli, M., Maio, D., & Rizzi, S. (1998). The dimensional fact model: A conceptual model for data warehouses. *International Journal of Cooperative Information Systems, 7*(2-3), 215–247. doi:10.1142/S0218843098000118

Golfarelli, M., & Rizzi, S. (2009). A survey on temporal data warehousing. *International Journal of Data Warehousing and Mining, 5*(1), 1–17. doi:10.4018/jdwm.2009010101

Golfarelli, M., & Rizzi, S. (2009). *Data warehouse design: Modern principles and methodologies*. New York, NY: McGraw-Hill.

Golfarelli, M., & Rizzi, S. (2009). A survey on temporal data warehousing. *International Journal of Data Warehousing and Mining, 5*(1), 1–17. doi:10.4018/jdwm.2009010101

Golfarelli, M., & Rizzi, S. (2009). What-if simulation modeling in business intelligence. *International Journal of Data Warehousing and Mining, 5*(4), 24–43. doi:10.4018/jdwm.2009080702

Gómez, L., Kuijpers, B., Moelans, B., & Vaisman, A. (2009). A survey on spatio-temporal data warehousing. *International Journal of Data Warehousing and Mining*, *5*(3), 28–55.

Gong, A., & Zhao, W. (2008). Clustering-based Dynamic Materialized View Selection Algorithm. In *Proceedings of the 5th IEEE International Conference on Fuzzy Systems & Knowledge Discovery* (pp. 391-395).

Gouda, K., & Zaki, M. J. (2005). GenMax: An efficient algorithm for mining maximal frequent itemsets. *Data Mining and Knowledge Discovery*, *11*, 1–20. doi:10.1007/s10618-005-0002-x

Gou, G., Xu Yu, J., & Lu, H. (2006). A* Search: An Efficient and Flexible Approach to Materialized View Selection. *IEEE Transactions on Systems, Man and Cybernetics. Part C, Applications and Reviews*, *36*(3), 411–425. doi:10.1109/TSMCC.2004.843248

Grabmeier, J., & Rudolph, A. (2002). Techniques of cluster algorithms in data mining. *Data Mining and Knowledge Discovery*, *6*, 303–360. doi:10.1023/A:1016308404627

Gray, J., Chaudhuri, S., Bosworth, A., Layman, A., Reichart, D., & Venkatrao, M. (1997). Data cube: A relational aggregation operator generalizing group-by, cross-tab and sub-totals. *Data Mining and Knowledge Discovery*, *1*(1), 29–54. doi:10.1023/A:1009726021843

Guha, S., Rastogi, R., & Shim, K. (1998). CURE: An efficient clustering algorithm for large databases. In *Proceedings of the ACM SIGMOD International Conference on Management of Data* (pp.73-84). New York, NY: ACM Press.

Guha, S., Rastogi, R., & Shim, K. (2000). Rock: A robust clustering algorithm for categorical attributes. In *Proceedings of the 15th International Conference on Data Engineering*.

Guo, D. (2007). Visual Analytics of Spatial Interaction Patterns for Pandemic Decision Support. *International Journal of Geographical Information Science*, *21*(8), 859–877. doi:10.1080/13658810701349037

Gupta, H. (1997). Selection of Views to Materialize in a Data Warehouse. In *Proceedings of the International Conference on Database Theory*, Delphi, Greece (pp. 98-112).

Gupta, H., Harinarayan, V., Rajaraman, A., & Ullman, J. (1997). Index Selection for OLAP. In *Proceedings of the ICDE Conference*, Birmingham, UK (pp. 208-219).

Gupta, A., & Mumick, I. S. (1999). *Maintenance of materialized views: Problems, techniques, and applications* (*Vol. 18*). Cambridge, MA: MIT Press.

Gupta, H., & Mumick, I. S. (2005). Selection of Views to Materialize in a Data Warehouse. *IEEE Transactions on Knowledge and Data Engineering*, *17*(1), 24–43. doi:10.1109/TKDE.2005.16

Gyenesei, A. (2001). A Fuzzy Approach for Mining Quantitative Association Rules. *Acta Cybernetica*, *15*(2), 305–320.

Habib, M., & Nourine, L. (1997). Gray codes for the ideals of interval orders. *Journal of Algorithms*, *25*, 52–66. doi:10.1006/jagm.1997.0863

Haertzen, D. (2009). *Testing the data warehouse.* Retrieved from http://www.lnfogoal.com

Hammad, M. A., Aref, W. G., & Elmagarmid, A. K. (2008). Query processing of multi-way stream window joins. *Very Large Data Bases Journal*, *17*(3), 469–488. doi:10.1007/s00778-006-0017-y

Han, J., Pei, J., Mortazavi-Asl, B., Chen, Q., Dayal, U., & Hsu, M.-C. (2000). FreeSpan: Frequent pattern-projected sequential pattern mining. In *Proceedings of the 2000 ACM SIGKDD International Conference on Knowledge Discovery in Databases (KDD'00)*, Boston, MA (pp. 355-359).

Han, J., Stefanovic, N., & Kopersky, K. (1998). Selective materialization: An efficient method for spatial data cube construction. In *Proceedings of PAKDD* (pp. 144–158).

Han, J., & Kamber, M. (2006). *Data mining Concepts and Techniques*. San Francisco, CA: Morgan Kaufmann.

Han, J., & Kamber, M. (2006). *Data Mining: Concepts and Techniques* (2nd ed.). San Francisco, CA: Morgan Kaufmann.

Hanusse, N., Maabout, S., & Tofan, R. (2009). A view selection algorithm with performance guarantee. In *Proceedings of the EDBT 2009 Conference* (pp. 946-957).

Haranczyk, M., & Holliday, J. (2008). Comparison of similarity coefficients for clustering and compound selection. *Journal of Chemical Information and Modeling, 48*(3), 498–508. doi:10.1021/ci700413a

Harinarayan, V., Rajaraman, A., & Ullman, J. D. (1996). Implementing Data Cubes Efficiently. In *Proceedings of the SIGMOD'96 Conference,* Montreal, QC, Canada (pp. 205-216).

He, J., Shi, Y., & Xu, W. (2004). Classifications of credit cardholder behavior by using multiple criteria non-linear programming. In *Proceedings of the Chinese Academy of Sciences Symposium on Data Mining and Knowledge Management* (pp. 154-163).

He, J., Liu, X., & Shi, Y. (2004). Classifications of credit card holder behavior by using fuzzy linear programming. *International Journal of Information Technology and Decision Making, 3*(4), 633–650. doi:10.1142/S021962200400129X

Heller, K. A., & Ghahramani, Z. (2005). Bayesian hierarchical clustering. In *Proceedings of the 22nd International Conference on Machine Learning* (pp. 297-304). New York, NY: ACM Press.

Herzog, P. (2010). *Open Source Security Testing Methodology Manual.* Retrieved from http://www.isecom.org/osstmm/

Holmes, G., Pfahringer, B., Reutemann, P., Witten, I. H., Hall, M., & Frank, E. (2009). The Weka data mining software. *SIGKDD Explorations, 11*(1).

Holt, J. D., & Chung, S. M. (2001). Multipass algorithms for mining association rules in text databases. *Knowledge and Information Systems, 3*(2), 168–183. doi:10.1007/PL00011664

Horng, S. J., Su, M. Y., Chen, Y. H., Kao, T. W., Chen, R. J., Lai, J. L., & Perkasa, C. D. (2011). A novel intrusion detection system based on hierarchical clustering and support vector machines. *Expert Systems with Applications, 38*(1), 306–313. doi:10.1016/j.eswa.2010.06.066

Huang, Z., Du, W., & Chen, B. (2005). Deriving private information from randomized data. In *Proceedings of the ACM SIGMOD International Conference on Management of Data* (pp. 37-48). New York, NY: ACM Press.

Hung, M. C., Huang, M. L., Yang, D. L., & Hsueh, N. L. (2007). Efficient approaches for materialized views selection in a data warehouse. *Information Sciences, 177,* 1333–1348. doi:10.1016/j.ins.2006.09.007

Hyvärinen, A. (1999). Fast and robust fixed-point algorithms for independent component analysis. *IEEE Transactions on Neural Networks, 10*(3), 626–634. doi:10.1109/72.761722

Imielinski, T., & Mannila, H. (1996). A data base perspective on knowledge discovery. *Communications of the ACM, 39,* 58–64. doi:10.1145/240455.240472

Ives, Z. G., Florescu, D., Friedman, M., Levy, A., & Weld, D. S. (1999). An adaptive query execution system for data integration. *SIGMOD Record, 28*(2), 299–310. doi:10.1145/304181.304209

Iyengar, V. S. (2002). Transforming data to satisfy privacy constraints. In *Proceedings of the Eighth ACM SIGKDD International Conference on Knowledge Discovery and Data Mining* (pp. 279-288). New York, NY: ACM Press.

Jackson, D. A., Somers, K. M., & Harvey, H. H. (1989). Similarity coefficients: Measures of co-occurrence and association or simply measures of occurrence? *American Naturalist, 133*(3), 436–453. doi:10.1086/284927

Jagannathan, G., & Wright, R. N. (2005). Privacy-preserving distributed k-means clustering over arbitrarily partitioned data. In *Proceedings of the Eleventh ACM SIGKDD International Conference on Knowledge Discovery in Data Mining* (pp. 593-599). New York, NY: ACM Press.

Janeja, V. P., Adam, N., Atluri, V., & Vaidya, J. (2010). Spatial neighborhood based anomaly detection in sensor datasets. *Data Mining and Knowledge Discovery, 20*(2), 221–258. doi:10.1007/s10618-009-0147-0

Jerbi, H., Ravat, F., Teste, O., & Zurfluh, G. (2009). Preference-based recommendations for olap analysis. In *Proceedings of the 11th International Conference on Data Warehousing and Knowledge Discovery* (LNCS 5691, pp. 467–478).

Jiang, B. (2005). *Study on Mining and Reasoning of Weak Ratio Rules.* Unpublished doctoral dissertation, Southwest Jiaotong University, China.

Jiang, H., Zhao, Y., Yang, C., & Dong, X. (2008). Mining both positive and negative weighted association rules with multiple minimum supports. In *Proceedings of the International Conference on Computer Science and Software Engineering* (pp. 407-410). Washington, DC: IEEE Computer Society.

Jiang, N. (2006). CFI-Stream: Mining closed frequent itemsets in data streams. In *Proceedings of the 12th ACM SIGKDD International Conference on Knowledge Discovery and Data Mining* (pp. 592-597).

Jiang, N., & Gruenwald, L. (2006). Research issues in data stream association rule mining. *SIGMOD Record*, *35*(1), 14–19. doi:10.1145/1121995.1121998

Jian, W., & Ming, L. X. (2008). An effective mining algorithm for weighted association rules in communication networks. *Journal of Computers*, *3*(4), 20–27.

Jin, R., & Agrawal, G. (2005). An algorithm for in-core frequent itemset mining on streaming data. In *Proceedings of the Fifth IEEE International Conference on Data Mining* (pp. 210-217).

Jing, L.-P., Huang, H.-K., & Shi, H.-B. (2002). Improved feature selection approach TF-IDF in text mining. In *Proceedings of the 2002 Conference on Machine Learning and Cybernetics* (pp. 944-946). Washington, DC: IEEE Computer Society.

Johnson, T., Lakshmanan, L. V. S., & Ng, R. T. (2000). The 3W Model and Algebra for Unified Data Mining. In *Proceedings of the Very Large Data Base Conference* (pp. 21-32). San Francisco: Morgan Kaufmann Publishers.

Kalnis, P., Mamoulis, N., & Papadias, D. (2002). View Selection Using Randomized Search. *Data & Knowledge Engineering*, *42*, 89–111. doi:10.1016/S0169-023X(02)00045-9

Kantarcioglu, M., & Clifton, C. (2004). Privacy-preserving distributed mining of association rules on horizontally partitioned data. *IEEE Transactions on Knowledge and Data Engineering*, *16*(9), 1026–1037. doi:10.1109/TKDE.2004.45

Karabatis, G., Chen, Z., Janeja, V. P., Lobo, T., Advani, M., Lindvall, M., & Feldmann, R. L. (2009). Using semantic networks and context in search for relevant software engineering artifacts. *Journal of Data Semantics*.

Karakasidis, A., Vassiliadis, P., & Pitoura, E. (2005). ETL queues for active data warehousing. In *Proceedings of the 2nd International Workshop on Information Quality in Information Systems*, Baltimore, MD (pp. 28-39).

Katic, N., Quirchmayr, G., Schiefer, J., Stolba, M., & Tjoa, A. M. (1998). A prototype model for data warehouse security based on metadata. In *Proceedings of the DEXA Workshop* (pp. 300–308).

Kaya, S. V. (2007). *Toolbox for Privacy Preserving Data Mining.* Unpublished master's thesis, Sabanci University, Istanbul, Turkey.

Kaya, S. V., Pedersen, T. B., Savas, E., & Saygin, Y. (2007). Efficient privacy preserving distributed clustering based on secret sharing. In *PAKDD 2007 International Workshops: Emerging Technologies in Knowledge Discovery and Data Mining* (LNCS 4819, pp. 280–291).

Keogh, E. J., & Pazzani, M. J. (1998). An enhanced representation of time series which allows fast and accurate classification, clustering and relevance feedback. In *Proceedings of the ACM SIGKDD International Conference on Knowledge Discovery in Data Mining* (pp. 239-243). New York, NY: ACM Press.

Keogh, E. J., & Pazzani, M. J. (2000). Scaling up dynamic time warping for data mining applications. In *Proceedings of the ACM SIGKDD International Conference on Knowledge Discovery in Data Mining* (pp. 285-289). New York, NY: ACM Press.

Keogh, E. J., & Smyth, P. (1997). A probabilistic approach to fast pattern matching in time series databases. In *Proceedings of the ACM SIGKDD International Conference on Knowledge Discovery in Data Mining* (pp. 24-30). New York, NY: ACM Press.

Keogh, E. J., Chakrabarti, K., Mehrotra, S., & Pazzani, M. J. (2001). Locally adaptive dimensionality reduction for indexing large time series databases. In *Proceedings of the ACM SIGMOD Conference on Management of Data* (pp. 151-162). New York, NY: ACM Press.

Keogh, E. J., Xi, X., Wei, L., & Ratanamahatana, C. A. (2006). *The UCR time series classification/ clustering homepage.* Retrieved from http://www.cs.ucr.edu/~eamonn/time_series_data/

Keogh, E., & Lin, J. (2005). Clustering of time-series subsequences is meaningless: implications for previous and future research. *Knowledge and Information Systems*, *8*(2), 154–177. doi:10.1007/s10115-004-0172-7

Khabbaz, M., Kianmehr, K., Al-Shalalfa, M., & Alhajj, R. (2008). Effectiveness of Fuzzy Classifier Rules in Capturing Correlations between Genes. *International Journal of Data Warehousing and Mining*, *4*(4), 62–83. doi:10.4018/jdwm.2008100104

Khan, M. S., Muyeba, M., & Coenen, F. (2008). Mining Fuzzy Association Rules from Composite Items. In *Proceedings of the IFIP International Conference on Artificial Intelligence (IFIP-AI 2008)*, Milan, Italy (pp. 67-76).

Khan, M. S., Muyeba, M., Tjortjis, C., & Coenen, F. (2006). An effective Fuzzy Healthy Association Rule Mining Algorithm (FHARM). In *Proceedings of the 7th Annual Workshop on Computational Intelligence* (p. 14).

Khoussainova, N., Balazinska, M., Gatterbauer, W., Kwon, Y., & Suciu, D. (2009). A case for a collaborative query management system. In *Proceedings of 4th Biennial Conference on Innovative Data Systems Research*. Retrieved from http:// www.cidrdb.org

Kim, W., Banerjee, J., Chou, H., Garza, J., & Woelk, D. (1987). Composite object support in an object-oriented database system. In *Proceedings of the OOPSLA'87 Conference*, Orlando, FL (pp. 118-125).

Kimball, R., Ross, M., Thornthwaite, W., Mundy, J., & Becker, B. (2008). *The Data Warehouse Lifecycle Toolkit, 2nd Edition: Practical Techniques for Building Data Warehouse and Intellingent Business Systems*. New York: John Wiley & Sons.

Kimball, R., & Caserta, J. (2004). *The Data Warehouse ETL Toolkit*. New York, NY: John Wiley & Sons.

Kim, J., & Park, S. (2005). Periodic streaming data reduction using flexible adjustment of time section size. *International Journal of Data Warehousing and Mining*, *1*(1), 37–56. doi:10.4018/jdwm.2005010102

Kim, S., Shephard, N., & Chib, S. (1998). Stochastic volatility: Likelihood inference and comparison with ARCH model. *The Review of Economic Studies*, *65*, 361–393. doi:10.1111/1467-937X.00050

Kim, W., Bertino, E., & Garza, J. (1989). Composite objects revisited. *SIGMOD Record*, *18*(2), 337–347. doi:10.1145/66926.66958

Knuth, D. E. (1998). *The art of computer programming* (Vol. 3, pp. 400–401). Reading, MA: Addison-Wesley.

Koh, Y. S., & Rountree, N. (2005). Finding sporadic rules using apriori-inverse. In T. B. Ho, D. Cheung, & H. Liu (Eds.), *Advances in Knowledge Discovery and Data Mining* (LNCS 3518, pp. 97-106).

Koh, Y. S., Pears, R., & Yeap, W. (2010). Valency based weighted association rule mining. In M. Zaki, J. Yu, B. Ravindran, & V. Pudi (Eds.), *Advances in Knowledge Discovery and Data Mining* (LNCS 6118, pp. 274-285).

Koh, Y. S., Rountree, N., & O'Keefe, R. A. (2006). Finding Non-Coincidental Sporadic Rules Using Apriori-Inverse. *International Journal of Data Warehousing and Mining*, *2*(2), 38–54. doi:10.4018/jdwm.2006040102

Korn, F., Labrinidis, A., Kotidis, Y., & Faloutsos, C. (1998). Ratio rules: A new paradigm for fast, quantifiable data mining. In *Proceedings of the 24th International Conference on Very Large Data Bases (VLDB)*, New York, NY (pp. 582-593).

Kosman, E., & Leonard, K. J. (2005). Similarity coefficients for molecular markers in studies of genetic relationships between individuals for haploid, diploid, and polyploid species. *Molecular Ecology*, *14*, 415–424. doi:10.1111/j.1365-294X.2005.02416.x

Kotidis, Y., & Roussopoulos, N. (1999). DynaMat: A Dynamic View Management System for Data Warehouses. In *Proceedings of the SIGMOD'99 Conference*, Philadelphia, PA (pp. 371-382).

Kotidis, Y., & Roussopoulos, N. (2001). A Case for Dynamic View Management. *ACM Transactions on Database Systems*, *26*(4), 388–423. doi:10.1145/503099.503100

Kou, G., Peng, Y., Shi, Y., & Chen, Z. (2006). Multiclass credit cardholders; behaviors classification methods. In *Proceedings of the International Conference on Computational Science* (pp. 485-492).

Kou, G., Peng, Y., Shi, Y., & Chen, Z. (2006). A new multi-criteria convex quadratic programming model for credit analysis. In *Proceedings of the International Conference on Computational Science* (pp. 476-484).

Kou, G., Liu, X., & Peng, Y. (2003). Multiple criteria linear programming approach to data mining: Models, algorithm designs and software development. *Optimization Methods and Software*, *18*(4), 453–473. doi:10.108 0/10556780310001600953

Kou, G., Peng, Y., Chen, Z., & Shi, Y. (2009). Multiple criteria mathematical programming for multi-class classification and application in network intrusion detection. *Information Sciences*, *179*(4), 371–381. doi:10.1016/j. ins.2008.10.025

Kou, G., Peng, Y., Shi, Y., & Chen, Z. (2006). Network intrusion detection by multi-group mathematical programming based classifier. In *Proceedings of the ICDM Workshops*, *2006*, 803–807.

Kuok, C. M., Fu, A., & Wong, M. H. (1998). Mining fuzzy association rules in databases. *SIGMOD Record*, *27*(1), 41–46. doi:10.1145/273244.273257

Kwok, T., Smith, K. A., Lozano, S., & Taniar, D. (2002). Parallel Fuzzy c-Means Clustering for Large Data Sets. In *Proceedings of the 8th International Euro-Par Conference (Euro-Par 2002)* (LNCS 2400, pp. 365-374).

Labini, F. S. (2008). *Gravitational clustering: An overview* (Tech. Rep. No. arXiv 0806.2560). Retrieved from http:// arxiv.org/abs/0806.2560

Labio, W., & Garcia-Molina, H. (1996). Efficient snapshot differential algorithms for data warehousing. In *Proceedings of the 22nd International Conference on Very Large Data Bases*, San Francisco, CA (pp. 63-74.)

Labio, W., Yang, J., Cui, Y., Garcia-Molina, H., & Widom, J. (2000). Performance issues in incremental warehouse maintenance. In *Proceedings of the 26th International Conference on Very Large Data Bases*, San Francisco, CA (pp. 461-472).

Labio, W., Wiener, J. L., Garcia-Molina, H., & Gorelik, V. (2000). Efficient resumption of interrupted warehouse loads. *SIGMOD Record*, *29*(2), 46–57. doi:10.1145/335191.335379

Lakshmanan, L., Pei, J., & Zhao, Y. (2003). QC-Trees: An efficient summary structure for semantic OLAP. In *Proceedings of the 2003 ACM International Conference on Management of Data* (pp. 64–75). New York, NY: ACM.

Lam, K. M., & Yan, H. (1995). Locating and extracting the eye in human face images. *Pattern Recognition*, *29*, 771–779.

Laur, S., Lipmaa, H., & Mielikäinen, T. (2006). Cryptographically private support vector machines. In *KDD '06: Proceedings of the 12th ACM SIGKDD International Conference on Knowledge Discovery and Data Mining* (pp. 618–624). New York: ACM.

Laur, P. A., Symphor, J. E., Nock, R., & Poncelet, P. (2007). Statistical supports for mining sequential patterns and improving the incremental update process on data streams. *Intelligent Data Analysis*, *11*(1), 29–47.

Lawrence, R. (2005). Early hash join: A configurable algorithm for the efficient and early production of join results. In *Proceedings of the 31st International Conference on Very Large Data Bases*, Trondheim, Norway (pp. 841-852).

Lawrence, M., & Rau-Chaplin, A. (2008). Dynamic View Selection for OLAP. *International Journal of Data Warehousing and Mining*, *4*(1), 47–61. doi:10.4018/ jdwm.2008010103

Lechtenbörger, J., & Vossen, G. (2003). Multidimensional normal forms for data warehouse design. *Information Systems*, *28*(5), 415–434. doi:10.1016/S0306-4379(02)00024-8

Le, D. X. T., Wenny Rahayu, J., & Taniar, D. (2007). A high performance integrated web data warehousing. *Cluster Computing*, *10*(1), 95–109. doi:10.1007/s10586-007-0008-9

LeFevre, K., DeWitt, D. J., & Ramakrishnan, R. (2006). Workload-aware anonymization. In *Proceedings of the 12th ACM SIGKDD International Conference on Knowledge Discovery and Data Mining* (pp. 277-286). New York, NY: ACM Press.

Lehner, W., Albrecht, J., & Wedekind, H. (1998). Normal forms for multidimensional databases. In *Proceedings of the Scientific and Statistical Database Management Conference,* Capri, Italy (pp. 63–72).

Lewis, D. M. (2008). *Using similarity coefficients to identify synonymous routers.*

Lewis, D. M., & Janeja, V. P. (2009). An evaluative comparison of similarity coefficients for binary valued data. In *Proceedings of ACM SIGMOD: Undergraduate Research Competition*.

Li, H. F., Lee, S. Y., & Shan, M. K. (2004). An efficient algorithm for mining frequent itemsets over the entire history of data streams. In *Proceedings of the 1st International Workshop on Knowledge Discovery in Data Streams*.

Liabotis, I., Theodoulidis, B., & Saraaee, M. (2006). Improving similarity search in time series using wavelets. *International Journal of Data Warehousing and Mining*, 2(2), 55–81. doi:10.4018/jdwm.2006040103

Li, D. R., Wang, S. L., & Li, D. Y. (2006). *Spatial data mining theories and applications* (pp. 171–177). Beijing, China: Science Press.

Li, H. F., Ho, C. C., & Lee, S. Y. (2009). Incremental updates of closed frequent itemsets over continuous data streams. *Expert Systems with Applications: An International Journal*, 36(2), 2451–2458. doi:10.1016/j.eswa.2007.12.054

Li, H. F., & Lee, S. Y. (2009). Mining frequent itemsets over data streams using efficient window sliding techniques. *Expert Systems with Applications: An International Journal*, 36(2), 1466–1477. doi:10.1016/j.eswa.2007.11.061

Li, J., Wang, K., & Xu, L. (2008). Chameleon based on clustering feature tree and its application in customer segmentation. *Annals of Operations Research*, 168(1), 225–245. doi:10.1007/s10479-008-0368-4

Lin, M. Y., Hsueh, S. C., & Hwang, S. K. (2008). Interactive mining of frequent itemsets over arbitrary time intervals in a data stream. In *Proceedings of the Nineteenth Conference on Australasian Database* (pp. 15-21).

Lindell, Y., & Pinkas, B. (2000). Privacy preserving data mining. In *Journal of Cryptology*, 15(3), 36–54.

Lindvall, M., Feldmann, R. L., Karabatis, G., Chen, Z., & Janeja, V. P. (2009). Searching for relevant software change artifacts using semantic networks. In *Proceedings of the Symposium on Applied Computing* (pp. 496-500).

Lin, W. Y., & Kuo, I. C. (2004). A Genetic Selection Algorithm for OLAP Data Cubes. *Knowledge and Information Systems*, 6, 83–102. doi:10.1007/s10115-003-0093-x

Liu, B., Dai, Y., Li, X., Lee, W. S., & Yu, P. S. (2003). Building text classifiers using positive and unlabeled examples. In *Proceedings of the 3rd IEEE International Conference on Data Mining (ICDM '03)* (pp. 179-186). Washington, DC: IEEE Computer Society.

Liu, B., Hsu, W., & Ma, Y. (1999). Mining association rules with multiple minimum supports. In *Proceedings of the 5th ACM SIGKDD International Conference on Knowledge Discovery and Data Mining* (pp. 337-341). New York, NY: ACM.

Liu, K., Kargupta, H., & Ryan, J. (2006). Random projection-based multiplicative data perturbation for privacy preserving distributed data mining. *IEEE Transactions on Knowledge and Data Engineering*, 18(1), 92–106. doi:10.1109/TKDE.2006.14

Liu, Y. C., Hsu, P. Y., Sheen, G. J., Ku, S., & Chang, K. W. (2008). Simultaneous determination of view selection and update policy with stochastic query and response time constraints. *Information Sciences*, 178, 3491–3509. doi:10.1016/j.ins.2008.05.021

Li, X., Zhang, S. C., & Wang, S. L. (2006). Advances in data mining applications. *International Journal of Data Warehousing and Mining*, 2(3), i–iii.

Loof, K. D., Baets, B. D., & Meyer, H. D. (2007). On the random generation and counting of weak order extensions of a poset with given class cardinalities. *Information Sciences*, 177(1), 220–230. doi:10.1016/j.ins.2006.04.003

Lopes, A., Pinho, R., Paulovich, F., & Minghim, R. (2007). Visual text mining using association rules. *Computers & Graphics*, 31(3), 316–326. doi:10.1016/j.cag.2007.01.023

MacQueen, J. (1967). Some methods for classification and analysis of multivariate observations. In *Proceedings of the Fifth Berkeley Symposium on Mathematical Statistics and Probability*, Berkeley, CA (Vol. 1, pp. 281-297).

Mahboudi, H., Aouiche, K., & Darmon, J. (2006). Materialized View Selection by Query Clustering in XML Data Warehouses. In *Proceedings of the 4th International Multi-Conference on Computer Science and Information Technology (CSIT 2006)*, Amman, Jordan (Vol. 2, pp. 68-77).

Malik, H. H., Kender, J. R., Fradkin, D., & Moerchen, F. (2010). Hierarchical document clustering using local patterns. *Data Mining and Knowledge Discovery, 21*, 153–185. doi:10.1007/s10618-010-0172-z

Manco, G., Giannotti, F., Kujpers, B., Raffaeta, A., Baglioni, M., & Renso, C. (2008). Querying and reasoning for spatio-temporal data mining. In *Mobility, Data Mining, and Privacy: Geographic Knowledge Discovery*. Berlin: Springer-Verlag. doi:10.1007/978-3-540-75177-9_13

Manku, G. S., & Motwani, R. (2002). Approximate frequency counts over data streams. In *Proceedings of the 28th International Conference on Very Large Data Bases* (pp. 346-357).

Marcus, A., Maletic, J. I., & Lin, K. I. (2001). Ordinal association rules for error identification in data sets. In *Proceedings of the 10th International Conference on Information and Knowledge Management*, Atlanta, GA (pp. 589-591).

Marketos, G., Frentzos, E., Ntoutsi, I., Pelekis, N., Raffaetà, A., & Theodoridis, Y. (2008). Building real world trajectory warehouses. In *Proceedings of 7th International ACM Workshop on Data Engineering for Wireless and Mobile Access* (pp. 8–15).

Martens, D., Baesens, B., Gestelc, T., & Vanthienena, J. (2007). Comprehensible credit scoring models using rule extraction from support vector machines. *European Journal of Operational Research, 183*(3), 1466–1476. doi:10.1016/j.ejor.2006.04.051

Maurer, D., Wenny Rahayu, J., Rusu, L. I., & Taniar, D. (2009). A Right-Time Refresh for XML Data Warehouses. In *Proceedings of the DASFAA 2009 Conference* (pp. 745-749).

McCall, J., Richards, P., & Walters, G. (1977). *Factors in software quality* (Tech. Rep. No. AD-A049-014, 015, 055). Springfield, VA: NTIS.

Microsoft. (2008). *Multidimensional expressions (MDX) reference*. Retrieved September 23, 2010, from http://msdn.microsoft.com/ en-us/library/ms145506.aspx

Mielikäinen, T., Terzi, E., & Tsaparas, P. (2006). Aggregating time partitions. In *Proceedings of the ACM SIGKDD International Conference on Knowledge Discovery in Data Mining* (pp. 347-356). New York, NY: ACM Press.

Mokbel, M. F., Lu, M., & Aref, W. G. (2004). Hash-merge join: A non-blocking join algorithm for producing fast and early join results. In *Proceedings of the 20th International Conference on Data Engineering*, Washington, DC (pp. 251-263).

Mookerjea, A., & Malisetty, P. (2008). *Best practices in data warehouse testing*. Paper presented at the Test 2008 Conference, New Delhi, India.

Mörchen, F., & Ultsch, A. (2005). Optimizing time series discretization for knowledge discovery. In *Proceedings of the ACM SIGKDD International Conference on Knowledge Discovery in Data Mining* (pp. 660-665). New York, NY: ACM Press.

Moura Duarte, J., Bosco dos Santos, J., & Cunha Melo, L. (1999). Comparison of similarity coefficients based on rapd markers in the common bean. *Genetics and Molecular Biology, 22*(3), 427–432.

Mozafari, B., Thakkar, H., & Zaniolo, C. (2008). Verifying and mining frequent patterns from large windows over data streams. In *Proceedings of the IEEE 24th International Conference on Data Engineering* (pp. 179-188).

Murguia, M., & Villasenor, J. L. (2003). Estimating the effect of the similarity coefficient and the cluster algorithm on biogeographic classifications. *Annales Botanici Fennici, 40*, 415–421.

Murtagh, F. (1983). A survey of recent advances in hierarchical clustering algorithms. *The Computer Journal, 26*(4), 354–359.

Muyeba, M., Sulaiman Khan, M., Malik, Z., & Tjortjis, C. (2006). Towards Healthy Association Rule Mining (HARM), A Fuzzy Quantitative Approach. In *Proceedings of the IDEAL '06 Conference* (LNCS 4224, pp. 1014-1022).

Nadeau, T. P., & Teorey, T. J. (2002). Achieving Scalability in OLAP Materialized View Selection. In *Proceedings of the DOLAP '02 Conference*, McLean, VA (pp. 28-34).

Naeem, M. A., Dobbie, G., & Weber, G. (2008). An event-based near real-time data integration architecture. In *Proceedings of the 12th Enterprise Distributed Object Computing Conference Workshops*, Washington, DC (pp. 401-404).

Naganthan, E. R., & Dhanaseelan, F. R. (2007). Efficient graph structure for the mining of frequent itemsets from data streams. *International Journal of Computer Science and Engineering Systems, 1*(4), 283–290.

Nanni, M., Abul, O., & Bonchi, F. (2010). *Anonymization of moving objects data bases by clustering and perturbation.*

Nanni, M., & Pedreschi, D. (2006). Time-focused clustering of trajectories of moving objects. *Journal of Intelligent Information Systems, 27*(3), 267–289. doi:10.1007/s10844-006-9953-7

Nergiz, N. E., Atzori, M., & Saygin, Y. (2008). Towards trajectory anonymization: a generalization-based approach. In *Proceedings of the Workshop on Security and Privacy in GIS and LBS - SPRINGL 2008* (pp. 52-61). New York: ACM.

Nguyen, T. M. (2003). Zero-latency data warehousing for heterogeneous data sources and continuous data streams. In *Proceedings of the Fifth International Conference on Information Integration and Web-based Applications Services*, Jakarta, Indonesia (pp. 55-64).

Nguyen, T. M., Brezany, P., Tjoa, A. M., & Weippl, E. (2005). Toward a grid-based zero-latency data warehousing implementation for continuous data streams processing. *International Journal of Data Warehousing and Mining, 1*(4), 22–55. doi:10.4018/jdwm.2005100102

Nunez, H., Angulo, C., & Catala, A. (2002). Rule based learning systems from SVMs. In *Proceedings of the European Symposium on Artificial Neural Networks* (pp. 107-112).

Octotelematics. (2010). *Octo Telematics Italia.* Retrieved April 20, 2010, from http://www.octotelematics.it/

Olson, D., & Shi, Y. (2007). *Introduction to business data mining.* New York, NY: McGraw-Hill/Irwin.

Oracle Semantic Technologies. (2010). *Oracle Database Semantic Technologies.* Retrieved April 20, 2010, from http://www.oracle.com/technology/tech/semantic_technologies

Oracle Spatial. (2010). *Oracle Spatial e Oracle Locator.* Retrieved April 20, 2010, from http://www.oracle.com/lang/it/database/spatial.html

Ordonez, C., & Chen, Z. (2009). Evaluating statistical tests on OLAP cubes to compare degree of disease. *IEEE Transactions on Information Technology in Biomedicine, 13*(5), 756–765. doi:10.1109/TITB.2008.926989

Ordonez, C., & García-García, J. (2008). Referential integrity quality metrics. *Decision Support Systems, 44*(2), 495–508. doi:10.1016/j.dss.2007.06.004

Orlando, S., Orsini, R., Raffaetà, A., Roncato, A., & Silvestri, C. (2007). Trajectory Data Warehouses: Design and Implementation Issues. *Journal of Computing Science and Engineering, 1*(2), 240–261.

Ortale, R., Ritacco, E., Pelekis, N., Trasarti, R., Costa, G., Giannotti, F., et al. (2008). The DAEDALUS Framework: Progressive Querying and Mining of Movement Data. In *Proceedings of the ACM SIGSPATIAL International Conference on Advances in Geographic Information Systems (ACM GIS 2008).*

Otey, M. E., Parthasarathy, S., Wang, C., & Veloso, A. (2004). Parallel and distributed methods for incremental frequent itemset mining. *IEEE Transactions on Systems, Man, and Cybernetics. Part B, Cybernetics, 34*(5), 2439–2450. doi:10.1109/TSMCB.2004.836887

Paetz, J. (2002). A Note on Core Regions of Membership Functions. In *Proceedings of the EUNITE 2002 Conference*, Albufeira, Portugal (pp. 167-173).

Palma, W., Akbarinia, R., Pacitti, E., & Valduriez, P. (2009). DHTJoin: Processing continuous join queries using DHT networks. *Distributed and Parallel Databases, 26*(2-3), 291–317. doi:10.1007/s10619-009-7054-7

Papadimitriou, S., Li, F., Kollios, G., & Yu, P. S. (2007). Time series compressibility and privacy. In *Proceedings of the 33rd International Conference on Very Large Data Bases* (pp. 459-470).

Papastefanatos, G., Vassiliadis, P., Simitsis, A., & Vassiliou, Y. (2007). What-if analysis for data warehouse evolution. In *Proceedings of the DaWaK Conference*, Regensburg, Germany (pp. 23–33).

Papastefanatos, G., Vassiliadis, P., Simitsis, A., & Vassiliou, Y. (2008). Design metrics for data warehouse evolution. In *Proceedings of the ER Conference* (pp. 440–454).

Parikh, N., & Sundaresan, N. (2008). Inferring semantic query relations from collective user behavior. In *Proceedings of the 17ᵗʰ ACM Conference on Information and Knowledge Management* (pp. 349–358). New York, NY: ACM.

Parsons, L., Haque, E., & Liu, H. (2004). Subspace clustering for high dimensional data: A review. *SIGKDD Explorations, 6*(1), 90–105. doi:10.1145/1007730.1007731

Patel, P., Keogh, E. J., Lin, J., & Lonardi, S. (2002). Mining motifs in massive time series databases. In *Proceedings of the IEEE International Conference on Data Mining* (pp. 370-377). Washington, DC: IEEE Computer Society.

Pei, J., Han, J., Mortazavi-Asl, B., Pinto, H., Chen, Q., Dayal, U., & Hsu, M.-C. (2001). PrefixSpan: Mining sequential patterns efficiently by prefix-projected pattern growth. In *Proceedings of the International Conference on Data Engineering (ICDE'01),* Heidelberg, Germany (pp. 215-224).

Pei, J., Han, J., Mortazavi-Asl, B., Wang, J., Pinto, H., & Chen, Q. (2004). Mining sequential patterns by pattern-growth: The prefixspan approach. *IEEE Transactions on Knowledge and Data Engineering, 16*, 1424–1440. doi:10.1109/TKDE.2004.77

Pelekis, N., & Theodoridis, Y. (2006). Boosting location-based services with a moving object database engine. In *Proceedings of the Fifth ACM International Workshop on Data Engineering for Wireless and Mobile Access, MOBIDE 2006* (pp. 3-10). New York: ACM.

Pelekis, N., Frentzos, E., Giatrakos, N., & Theodoridis, Y. (2008). HERMES: aggregative LBS via a trajectory DB engine. In *Proceedings of the ACM SIGMOD International Conference on Management of Data* (pp. 1255–1258). New York: ACM.

Pelekis, N., Theodoridis, Y., Vosinakis, S., & Panayiotopoulos, T. (2006). Hermes – a framework for location-based data management. In *Proceedings of EDBT* (pp. 1130–1134).

Peng, Y., Kou, G., Shi, Y., & Chen, Z. (2008). A descriptive framework for the field of data mining and knowledge discovery. *International Journal of Information Technology and Decision Making, 7*(4), 639–682. doi:10.1142/S0219622008003204

Pentaho. (2009). *Mondrian open source OLAP engine.* Retrieved September 23, 2010, from http:// mondrian. pentaho.org/

Pfoser, D., Jensen, C. S., & Theodoridis, Y. (2000). Novel Approaches in Query Processing for Moving Object Trajectories. In *Proceedings of VLDB* (pp. 395–406).

Phan, T., & Li, W. S. (2008). Dynamic Materialization of Query Views for Data Warehouse Workloads. In *Proceedings of the ICDE 2008 Conference* (pp. 436-445). Washington, DC: IEEE Computer Society.

Pitteloud, P. (2002). Log-concavity and compressed ideals in certain macaulay posets. *Discrete Mathematics, 254,* 421–432. doi:10.1016/S0012-365X(01)00360-0

Polyzotis, N., Skiadopoulos, S., Vassiliadis, P., Simitsis, A., & Frantzell, N. E. (2007). Supporting streaming updates in an active data warehouse. In *Proceedings of the 23rd International Conference on Data Engineering,* Istanbul, Turkey (pp. 476-485).

Polyzotis, N., Skiadopoulos, S., Vassiliadis, P., Simitsis, A., & Frantzell, N. (2008). Meshing streaming updates with persistent data in an active data warehouse. *IEEE Transactions on Knowledge and Data Engineering, 20*(7), 976–991. doi:10.1109/TKDE.2008.27

Pressman, R. (2005). *Software Engineering: A practitioner's approach.* New York, NY: McGraw-Hill.

Priebe, T., & Pernul, G. (2001). A pragmatic approach to conceptual modeling of OLAP security. In *Proceedings of the ER Conference* (pp. 311–324).

Qin, Y., Zhang, S., & Zhang, C. (2010). Combining kNN imputation and Bootstrap calibrated: Empirical likelihood for incomplete data analysis. *International Journal of Data Warehousing and Mining, 6*(4), 61–73. doi:10.4018/jdwm.2010100104

Qu, S., Wang, S., & Zou, Y. (2008). Improvement of text feature selection method based on TF-IDF. In *Proceedings of the 2008 International Seminar on Future Information Technology and Management Engineering (FITME '08)* (pp. 79-81). Washington, DC: IEEE Computer Society.

Raahemi, B., & Mumtaz, A. (2010). Classification of peer-to-peer traffic using a two-stage window-based classifier with fast decision tree and IP layer attributes. *International Journal of Data Warehousing and Mining, 6*(3), 28–42. doi:10.4018/jdwm.2010070103

Raissi, C., Poncelet, P., & Teisseire, M. (2006). SPEED: Mining maximal sequential patterns over data streams. In *Proceedings of the 3rd IEEE International Conference on Intelligent Systems* (pp. 546-552).

Raissi, C., Poncelet, P., & Teisseire, M. (2007). Towards a new approach for mining frequent itemsets on data stream. *Journal of Intelligent Information Systems, 28*(1), 23–36. doi:10.1007/s10844-006-0002-3

Ramachandran, K., Shah, B., & Raghavan, V. (2005). *Access Pattern-Based Dynamin Pre-fetching of Views in an OLAP System.* Paper presented at the International Conference on Enterprise Information Systems.

Ramakrishnan, R. (1999). *Database management systems* (2nd ed., pp. 337–339). New York, NY: McGraw-Hill.

Ravat, F., Teste, O., Tournier, R., & Zurfluh, G. (2008). Algebraic and Graphic Languages for OLAP Manipulations. *International Journal of Data Warehousing and Mining, 4*(1), 17–46. doi:10.4018/jdwm.2008010102

Ritchie, D. S. (2010). *Students hit hard as swine flu clobbers schools.* Retrieved October 20, 2010, from http://www.times-age.co.nz/local/news/students-hit-hard-as-swine-flu-clobbers-schools/3918707/

Romero, O., & Abelló, A. (2009). A Survey of Multidimensional Modeling Methodologies. *International Journal of Data Warehousing and Mining, 5*(2), 1–23. doi:10.4018/jdwm.2009040101

Rosen, K. H. (2000). *Handbook of discrete and combinatorial mathematics.* Boca Raton, FL: CRC Press.

Roychowdhury, S., & Pedrycz, W. (2001). A survey of defuzzification strategies. *International Journal of Intelligent Systems, 16*(6), 679–695. doi:10.1002/int.1030

Russell, S., & Norvig, P. (2003). *Artificial Intelligence: A Modern Approach* (2nd ed.). Upper Saddle River, NJ: Prentice Hall.

Rusu, L. I., Wenny Rahayu, J., & Taniar, D. (2006). Warehousing Dynamic XML Documents. In *Proceedings of the DaWaK 2006 Conference* (pp. 175-184).

Rusu, L. I., Wenny Rahayu, J., & Taniar, D. (2005). A Methodology for Building XML Data Warehouses. *International Journal of Data Warehousing and Mining, 1*(2), 23–48. doi:10.4018/jdwm.2005040102

Rusu, L. I., Wenny Rahayu, J., & Taniar, D. (2009). Partitioning methods for multi-version XML data warehouses. *Distributed and Parallel Databases, 25*(1-2), 47–69. doi:10.1007/s10619-009-7034-y

Sánchez, D. (1999). *Acquisition of Relationships between Attributes in Relational Databases.* Unpublished doctoral dissertation, Department of Computer Science and Artificial Intelligence, University of Granada.

Sander, T., Young, A., & Yung, M. (1999). Non-interactive cryptocomputing for NC[1]. In *FOCS '99: Proceedings of the 40th Annual Symposium on Foundations of Computer Science* (pp. 554). Washington, DC: IEEE Computer Society.

Sander, J., Ester, M., Kriegel, H. P., & Xu, X. W. (1998). Density-based clustering in spatial databases: The algorithm GDBSCAN and its applications. *Data Mining and Knowledge Discovery, 2*, 169–194. doi:10.1023/A:1009745219419

Sanjay, R., Ranka, S., & Tsur, S. (1997). *Weighted association rules, Model and algorithm.* Retrieved from http://citeseer.ist.psu.edu/185924.html

Sapia, C. (1999). On modeling and predicting query behaviour in OLAP systems. In *Proceedings of the International Workshop on Design and Management of Data Warehouses* (pp. 2.1–2.10). CEUR-WS.org.

Sapia, C. (2000). Promise: Predicting query behavior to enable predictive caching strategies for OLAP systems. In *Proceedings of the International Conference on Data Warehousing and Knowledge Discovery* (LNCS 1874, pp. 224–233).

Sarawagi, S. (1999). Explaining differences in multidimensional aggregates. In *Proceedings of the 25th International Conference on Very Large Data Bases* (pp. 42–53). San Francisco, CA: Morgan Kaufmann.

Sarawagi, S. (2009). *I3: Intelligent, interactive inspection of cubes*. Retrieved September 23, 2010, from http://www.cse.iitb.ac.in/ ~sunita/icube/

Sarawagi, S., Agrawal, R., & Megiddo, N. (1998). Discovery-driven exploration of OLAP data cubes. In *Proceedings of the 6th International Conference on Extending Database Technology* (LNCS 1377, pp. 168–182).

Sathe, G., & Sarawagi, S. (2001). Intelligent rollups in multidimensional OLAP data. In *Proceedings of the 27th International Conference on Very Large Data Bases* (pp. 531–540). San Francisco, CA: Morgan Kaufmann.

Schölkop, B., Platt, J. C., Shawe-Taylor, J., Smola, A. J., & Williamson, R. C. (2001). Estimating the support of a high-dimensional distribution. *Neural Computation, 13*(7), 1443–1471. doi:10.1162/089976601750264965

Sembiring, R. W., Zain, J. M., & Embong, A. (2010). A comparative agglomerative hierarchical clustering method to cluster implemented course. *Journal of Computing, 2*(12), 1–6.

Serrano, M., Calero, C., & Piattini, M. (2003). Experimental validation of multidimensional data models metrics. In *Proceedings of the HICSS Conference* (p. 327).

Serrano, M., Trujillo, J., Calero, C., & Piattini, M. (2007). Metrics for data warehouse conceptual models understandability. *Information and Software Technology, 49*(8), 851–870. doi:10.1016/j.infsof.2006.09.008

Shah, B., Ramachandran, K., & Raghavan, V. (2006). A Hybrid Approach for Data Warehouse View Selection. *International Journal of Data Warehousing and Mining, 2*(2), 1–37. doi:10.4018/jdwm.2006040101

Shamir, A. (1979). How to share a secret. *Communications of the ACM, 22*(11), 612–613. doi:10.1145/359168.359176

Shannon, C. E. (1948). A mathematical theory of communication. *The Bell System Technical Journal, 27*, 379–423, 623–656.

Shapiro, L. D. (1986). Join processing in database systems with large main memories. *ACM Transactions on Database Systems, 11*(3), 239–264. doi:10.1145/6314.6315

Shepard, D. (1968). A two-dimensional interpolation function for irregularly-spaced data. In *Proceedings of the 1968 23rd ACM National Conference* (pp. 517-524). New York, NY: ACM.

She, R., Want, K., Fu, A., & Yabo, X. (2008). Computing join aggregates over private tables. *International Journal of Data Warehousing and Mining, 4*(4), 22–41. doi:10.4018/jdwm.2008100102

Shi, Y., Liu, R., Yan, N., & Chen, Z. (2008). A family of optimization based data mining methods. In *Proceedings of the APWeb 2008 Conference* (pp. 26-38).

Shi, Y., Liu, R., Yan, N., & Chen, Z. (2008). Multiple criteria mathematical programming and data mining. In *Proceedings of the International Conference on Computational Science* (pp. 7-17).

Shi, Y., Tian, Y., Chen, X., & Zhang, P. (2007). A regularized multiple criteria linear program for classification. In *Proceedings of the ICDM 2007 Workshops* (pp. 253-258).

Shi, Y., Wise, M., Luo, M., & Lin, Y. (2001). Data mining in credit card portfolio management: a multiple criteria decision making approach. In *Multiple Criteria Decision Making in the New Millennium* (pp. 427-436).

Shi, Y. (2001). *Multiple criteria and multiple constraint levels linear programming: Concepts, techniques and applications*. Singapore: World Scientific.

Shi, Y., Peng, Y., Xu, W., & Tang, X. (2002). Data mining via multiple criteria linear programming: Applications in credit card portfolio management. *International Journal of Information Technology and Decision Making, 1*, 131–151. doi:10.1142/S0219622002000038

Shukla, A., Deshpande, P. M., & Naughton, J. F. (1998). Materialized View Selection for Multidimensional Datasets. In *Proceedings of the 24th VLDB Conference,* New York, NY (pp. 488-499).

Silberschatz, A., & Tuzhilin, A. (1995). On subjective measures of interestingness in knowledge discovery. In U. Fayyad & R. Uthurusamy (Eds.), *Proceedings of the 1st ACM SIGKDD International Conference on Knowledge Discovery and Data Mining (KDD-1995)* (pp. 275-281). Cambridge, MA: AAAI/MIT Press.

Silla, C. N. Jr, & Freitas, A. A. (2011). A survey of hierarchical classification across different application domains. *Data Mining and Knowledge Discovery, 22,* 31–72. doi:10.1007/s10618-010-0175-9

Silverstein, C., Brin, S., & Motwani, R. (1998). Beyond market baskets: Generalizing association rules to dependence rules. *Data Mining and Knowledge Discovery, 2,* 39–68. doi:10.1023/A:1009713703947

Silvestri, C., & Orlando, S. (2007). Approximate mining of frequent patterns on streams. *Intelligent Data Analysis, 11*(1), 49–73.

Sommerville, I. (2004). *Software Engineering.* Upper Saddle River, NJ: Pearson Education.

Song, M., Hu, X. H., Yoo, I., & Koppel, E. (2009). A dynamic and semantically-aware technique for document clustering in biomedical literature. *International Journal of Data Warehousing and Mining, 5*(4), 44–57. doi:10.4018/jdwm.2009080703

Spiliopoulou, M., Srivastava, J., Kohavi, R., & Masand, B. M. (2000). Web mining for e-commerce. *SIGKDD Explorations, 2*(2), 106–107.

Srikant, R., & Agrawal, R. (1996). Mining quantitative association rules in large relational tables. In *Proceedings of the 1996 ACM-SIGMOD International Conference on Management of Data (SIG-MOD '96),* Montreal, QC, Canada (pp. 1-12).

Srikant, R., & Agrawal, R. (1996). Mining sequential patterns: Generalizations and performance improvements. In *Proceedings of the 5ᵗʰ International Conference on Extending Database Technology (EDBT '96),* Avignon, France (pp. 3-17).

Srikant, R., & Agrawal, R. (1996). Mining quantitative association rules in large relational tables. *SIGMOD Record, 25*(2), 1–12. doi:10.1145/235968.233311

Stanat, D. F., & McAllister, D. F. (1977). *Discrete Mathematics in Computer Science.* Englewood Cliffs, NJ: Prentice-Hall.

Stefanidis, K., Drosou, M., & Pitoura, E. (2009). « You may also like » results in relational databases. In *Proceedings of the 3rd International Workshop on Personalized Access, Profile Management and Context Awareness in Databases* (pp. 37–42). New York, NY: ACM.

Sun, J., Papadimitriou, S., & Faloutsos, C. (2006). Distributed pattern discovery in multiple streams. In *Proceedings of the Pacific-Asia Conference on Knowledge Discovery and Data Mining* (pp. 713-718).

Sun, K., & Bai, F. (2008). Mining weighted association rules without preassigned weights. *IEEE Transactions on Knowledge and Data Engineering, 20*(4), 489–495. doi:10.1109/TKDE.2007.190723

Taniar, D., Rahayu, Lee, W., & Daly, O. (2008). Exception rules in association rule mining. *Applied Mathematics and Computation, 205*(2), 735–750. doi:10.1016/j.amc.2008.05.020

Taniar, D., Leung, C. H. C., Wenny Rahayu, J., & Goel, S. (2008). *High Performance Parallel Database Processing and Grid Databases.* New York, NY: John Wiley & Sons. doi:10.1002/9780470391365

Taniar, D., Rahayu, W., Lee, V. C. S., & Daly, O. (2008). Exception rules in association rule mining. *Applied Mathematics and Computation, 205*(2), 735–750. doi:10.1016/j.amc.2008.05.020

Taniar, D., & Wenny Rahayu, J. (2002). A Taxonomy of Indexing Schemes for Parallel Database Systems. *Distributed and Parallel Databases, 12*(1), 73–106. doi:10.1023/A:1015682215394

Taniar, D., & Wenny Rahayu, J. (2002). Parallel database sorting. *Information Science, 146*(1-4), 171–219. doi:10.1016/S0020-0255(02)00196-2

Taniar, D., & Wenny Rahayu, J. (2002). Parallel group-by query processing in a cluster architecture. *International Journal of Computer Systems: Science and Engineering, 17*(1), 23–39.

Taniar, D., & Wenny Rahayu, J. (2002). Parallel sort-merge object-oriented collection join algorithms. *International Journal of Computer Systems: Science and Engineering, 17*(3), 145–158.

Taniar, D., & Wenny Rahayu, J. (2004). Global parallel index for multi-processors database systems. *Information Science, 165*(1-2), 103–127. doi:10.1016/j.ins.2003.09.019

Tan, P.-N., Steinbach, M., & Kumar, V. (2006). *Introduction to Data Mining.* Upper Saddle River, NJ: Pearson.

Tanuska, P., Verschelde, W., & Kopcek, M. (2008). The proposal of data warehouse test scenario. In *Proceedings of the ECUMICT Conference*, Gent, Belgium.

Tao, F., Murtagh, F., & Farid, M. (2003). Weighted association rule mining using weighted support and significance framework. In *Proceedings of the 9th ACM SIGKDD International Conference on Knowledge Discovery and Data Mining* (pp. 661-666). New York, NY: ACM.

Tao, Y., & Papadias, D. (2005). Historical spatio-temporal aggregation. *Proceedings of ACM TOIS, 23*, 61–102.

Tao, Y., Kollios, G., Considine, J., Li, F., & Papadias, D. (2004). Spatio-temporal aggregation using sketches. In *Proceedings of ICDE* (pp. 214–225).

Thiele, M., Fischer, U., & Lehner, W. (2007). Partition-based workload scheduling in living data warehouse environments. In *Proceedings of the ACM Tenth International Workshop on Data Warehousing and OLAP*, Lisbon, Portugal (pp. 57-64).

Thomas, J., & Cook, K. (2005). *Illuminating the Path: The Research and development Agenda for Visual Analytics*. Washington, DC: IEEE Computer Society.

Thomsen, C., & Pedersen, T. (2009). A survey of open source tools for business intelligence. *International Journal of Data Warehousing and Mining, 5*(3), 56–75. doi:10.4018/jdwm.2009070103

Tjioe, H. C., & Taniar, D. (2005). Mining Association Rules in Data Warehouses. *International Journal of Data Warehousing and Mining, 1*(3), 28–62. doi:10.4018/jdwm.2005070103

Tobler, W. (1987). Experiments in migration mapping by computer. *The American Cartographer, 14*(2), 155–163. doi:10.1559/152304087783875273

Tong, Q., Yan, B., & Zhou, Y. (2005). Mining quantitative association rules on overlapped intervals. In *Advanced Data Mining and Applications* (LNCS 3584, pp. 43-50).

Tzanis, G., & Berberidis, C. (2007). Mining for Mutually Exclusive Items in Transaction Databases. *International Journal of Data Warehousing and Mining, 3*(3), 45–59. doi:10.4018/jdwm.2007070104

Urhan, T., & Franklin, M. (2000). XJoin: A reactively-scheduled pipelined join operator. *A Quarterly Bulletin of the Computer Society of the IEEE Technical Committee on Data Engineering, 23*(27).

Vaidya, J., & Clifton, C. (2002). Privacy preserving association rule mining in vertically partitioned data. In *Proceedings of the ACM SIGKDD International Conference on Knowledge Discovery in Data Mining* (pp. 639-644). New York, NY: ACM Press.

Vaidya, J., & Clifton, C. (2003). Privacy-preserving k-means clustering over vertically partitioned data. In *KDD '03: Proceedings of the ninth ACM SIGKDD International Conference on Knowledge Discovery and Data Mining* (pp. 206–215). New York: ACM.

Vaisman, A., & Zimányi, E. (2009). What is spatio-temporal data warehousing? In *Proceedings of the 11th International Conference on Data Warehousing and Knowledge Discovery* (pp. 9–23). Berlin: Springer-Verlag.

Valluri, S. R., Vadapalli, S., & Karlapalem, K. (2002). View Relevance Driven Materialized View Selection in Data Warehousing Environment. In *Proceedings of the ADC2002 Conference* (Vol. 5, pp. 187-196).

Van Bergenhenegouwen, A. (2008). *Data warehouse testing*. Retrieved from http://www.ti.kviv.be

Vapnik, V. (1998). *Statistical learning theory*. New York, NY: Wiley.

Vassiliadis, P., Bouzeghoub, M., & Quix, C. (1999). Towards quality-oriented data warehouse usage and evolution. In *Proceedings of the CAiSE Conference*, Heidelberg, Germany.

Vassiliadis, P. (2009). A survey of extract–transform–load technology. *International Journal of Data Warehousing and Mining, 5*(3), 1–27. doi:10.4018/jdwm.2009070101

Vijayan, J. (2007, September 18). House committee chair wants info on cancelled DHS data-mining programs. *Computer World*.

Voters leave Australia hanging. (2010). Retrieved October 20, 2010, from http://www.abc.net.au/news/stories/2010/08/21/2989767.htm

Wang, K., Liu, J. N., & Ma, W. (2006). Mining the Most Reliable Association Rules with Composite Items. In *Proceedings of the 6th IEEE International Conference on Data Mining Workshops* (pp. 749-754).

Wang, S. L., & Wang, X. Z. (2007). A fuzzy comprehensive clustering method. In R. Alhajj, H. Gao, X. Li, J. Li, & O. R. Zaïane (Eds.), *Proceedings of the Third International Conference on Advanced Data Mining and Applications* (LNCS 4632, pp. 488-499).

Wang, W., Yang, J., & Yu, P. S. (2000). Efficient mining of weighted association rules (WAR). In *Proceedings of the 6th ACM SIGKDD International Conference on Knowledge Discovery and Data Mining (KDD '00)* (pp. 270-274). New York, NY: ACM.

Wang, Q., Shi, D., He, B., & Cai, Q. (2001). Research on linear association rules. *Mini-Micro System, 22*(11), 1349–1352.

Wan, R. X., Wang, L. X., & Su, X. K. (2010). ASCCN: Arbitrary shaped clustering method with compatible nucleoids. *International Journal of Data Warehousing and Mining, 6*(4), 1–15. doi:10.4018/jdwm.2010100101

Warrens, M. J. (2008). Bounds of resemblance measures for binary (presence/absence) variables. *Journal of Classification, 25*, 195–208. doi:10.1007/s00357-008-9024-6

Welzker, R., Zimmermann, C., & Bauckhage, C. (2010). Detecting trends in social bookmarking systems: A del.icio.us endeavor. *International Journal on Data Warehousing and Mining, 6*(1), 38-57.

Wilschut, A. N., & Apers, P. M. G. (1990). Pipelining in query execution. In *Proceedings of the International Conference on Databases, Parallel Architectures and their Applications*, Miami Beach, FL (p. 562).

Wilschut, A. N., & Apers, P. M. G. (1991). Dataflow query execution in a parallel main-memory environment. In *Proceedings of the First International Conference on Parallel and Distributed Information Systems*, Miami, FL (pp. 68-77).

Witten, I., & Frank, E. (2005). *Data mining: Practical machine learning tools and techniques*. Boston, MA: Morgan Kaufmann.

Wong, P. C., Whitney, P., & Thomas, J. (1999). Visualizing association rules for text mining. In *Proceedings of the IEEE Symposium on Information Visualization* (pp. 120-123). Washington, DC: IEEE Computer Society.

Wong, R. C., & Fu, A. W. (2006). Mining top-K frequent itemsets from data streams. *Data Mining and Knowledge Discovery, 13*(2), 193–217. doi:10.1007/s10618-006-0042-x

Wright, R. N., & Yang, Z. (2004). Privacy-preserving Bayesian network structure computation on distributed heterogeneous data. In *Proceedings of the ACM SIGKDD International Conference on Knowledge Discovery in Data Mining* (pp. 713-718). New York, NY: ACM Press.

Wu, S.-T., Li, Y., Xu, Y., Pham, B., & Chen, P. (2004). Automatic pattern-taxonomy extraction for web mining. In *Proceedings of the 2004 IEEE/WIC/ACM International Conference on Web Intelligence (WI '04)* (pp. 242-248). Washington, DC: IEEE Computer Society.

Xu, W., Theodoratos, D., & Zuzarte, C. (2007). A Dynamic View Materialization Scheme for Sequences of Query & Update Statements. In *Proceedings of the DaWaK 2007 Conference* (LNCS 4654, pp. 55-65).

Xu, R., & Wunsch, D. (2005). Survey of clustering algorithms. *IEEE Transactions on Neural Networks, 16*(3), 645–678. doi:10.1109/TNN.2005.845141

Yan, L., & Li, C. (2006). Incorporating pageview weight into an association-rule-based web recommendation system. In A. Sattar & B. H. Kang (Eds.), *Proceedings of the Australian Conference on Artificial Intelligence* (LNCS 4304, pp. 577-586).

Yang, Y., Claramunt, C., Aufaure, M., & Zhang, W. (2010). User-Centric Similarity and Proximity Measures for Spatial Personalization. *International Journal of Data Warehousing and Mining, 6*(2), 59–78. doi:10.4018/jdwm.2010040104

Yankov, D., Keogh, E., Medina, J., Chiu, B., & Zordan, V. (2007). Detecting time series motifs under uniform scaling. In *Proceedings of the 13th ACM SIGKDD International Conference on Knowledge Discovery and Data Mining* (pp. 844-853).

Yao, A. C. (1982). Protocols for secure computations. In *Proceedings of the 23rd Annual IEEE Symposium on Foundations of Computer Science* (pp. 160–164). Washington, DC: IEEE Computer Society.

Ye, X., & Keane, J. A. (1997). Mining composite items in association rules. In *Proceedings of the 1997 IEEE International Conference on Systems, Man, and Cybernetics (SMC 1997)*, Orlando, FL (pp. 1367-1372).

Yildizli, C., Pedersen, T., Saygin, Y., Savas, E., & Levi, L. (2011). Distributed privacy preserving clustering via homomorphic secret sharing and its application to (vertically) partitioned spatio-temporal data. *International Journal of Data Warehousing and Mining, 7*(1), 46–66. doi:10.4018/jdwm.2011010103

Yin, Y., & Yasuda, K. (2005). Similarity coefficient methods applied to the cell formation problem: a comparative investigation. *Computers & Industrial Engineering, 48*, 471–489. doi:10.1016/j.cie.2003.01.001

Yu, G., Shao, S., Luo, B., & Zeng, X. (2009). A Hybrid Method for High-Utility Itemsets Mining in Large High-Dimensional Data. *International Journal of Data Warehousing and Mining, 5*(1), 57–73. doi:10.4018/jdwm.2009010104

Yu, H., Han, J., & Chang, K. C.-C. (2004). PEBL Web page classification without negative examples. *IEEE Transactions on Knowledge and Data Engineering, 16*(1), 70–81. doi:10.1109/TKDE.2004.1264823

Yu, J. X., Chong, Z., Lu, H., Zhang, Z., & Zhou, A. (2006). A false negative approach to mining frequent itemsets from high speed transactional data streams. *Information Sciences, 176*(14), 1986–2015. doi:10.1016/j.ins.2005.11.003

Zaki, M. J. (2000). Generating non-redundant association rules. In *Proceedings of the 6th ACM SIGKDD International Conference on Knowledge Discovery and Data Mining* (pp. 34-43). New York, NY: ACM.

Zaki, M. (2001). SPADE: An efficient algorithm for mining frequent sequences. *Machine Learning, 40*, 31–60. doi:10.1023/A:1007652502315

Zhang, P., Tian, Y., Li, X., Zhang, Z., & Shi, Y. (2008). Select representative samples for regularized multiple-criteria linear programming classification. In *Proceedings of the International Conference on Computational Science* (pp. 436-440).

Zhang, P., Zhang, J., & Shi, Y. (2007). A new multi-criteria quadratic-programming linear classification model for VIP email analysis. In *Proceedings of the International Conference on Computational Science* (pp. 499-502).

Zhang, P., Zhu, X., & Shi, Y. (2008). Categorizing and mining concept drifting data streams. In *Proceedings of the KDD 2008 Conference* (pp. 812-820).

Zhang, T., Ramakrishnman, R., & Linvy, M. (1996). BIRCH: An efficient method for very large databases. In *Proceedings of ACM SIGMOD International Conference on Management of Data* (pp.103-114). New York, NY: ACM Press.

Zhang, Z., & Tian, Y. (2007). Kernelized multiple criteria linear programming. In *Proceedings of the 19th International Conference on Multiple Criteria Decision Making*.

Zhang, Z., Shi, Y., Zhang, P., & Gao, G. (2008). A rough set-based multiple criteria linear programming approach for classification. In *Proceedings of the International Conference on Computational Science* (pp. 476-485).

Zhang, C., Yang, J., & Kalapalem, K. (2003). Dynamic Materialized View Selection in Data Warehouse Environment. *Informatica, 27*(1), 451–460.

Zhang, P., Zhu, X., Zhang, Z., & Shi, Y. (2010). Multiple criteria programming for VIP Email behavior analysis. *Web Intelligence & Agent Systems, 8*(1), 69–78.

Zhang, X. D., Jing, L. P., Hu, X. H., Ng, M., Xia, J. L., & Zhou, X. H. (2008). Medical document clustering using ontology-based term similarity measures. *International Journal of Data Warehousing and Mining, 4*(1), 62–73. doi:10.4018/jdwm.2008010104

Zhang, X., & Rundensteiner, E. A. (2002). Integrating the maintenance and synchronization of data warehouses using a cooperative framework. *Information Systems, 27*(4), 219–243. doi:10.1016/S0306-4379(01)00049-7

Zhao, Y., Jiang, H., Geng, R., & Dong, X. (2009). Mining weighted negative association rules based on correlation from infrequent items. In *Proceedings of the International Conference on Advanced Computer Control* (pp. 270-273). Washington, DC: IEEE Computer Society.

Zhao, Y., & Karypis, G. (2005). Hierarchical clustering algorithms for document datasets. *Data Mining and Knowledge Discovery*, *10*(2), 141–168. doi:10.1007/s10618-005-0361-3

Zhu, Y., & Fu, Y. (2007). *On privacy in time series data mining* (Tech. Rep. No. CSU-ECE-TR-07-02). Cleveland, OH: Cleveland State University.

Zhu, Y., & Liu, L. (2004). Optimal randomization for privacy preserving data mining. In *Proceedings of the ACM SIGKDD International Conference on Knowledge Discovery in Data Mining* (pp. 761-766). New York, NY: ACM Press.

Zhu, Y., & Shasha, D. (2002). StatStream: Statistical monitoring of thousands of data streams in real time. In *Proceedings of the 28th International Conference on Very Large Data Bases* (pp. 358-369).

Zhuge, Y., García-Molina, H., Hammer, J., & Widom, J. (1995). View maintenance in a warehousing environment. In *Proceedings of the ACM SIGMOD International Conference on Management of Data*, San Jose, CA (pp. 316-327).

Zhu, X., Zhang, P., Lin, X., & Shi, Y. (2010). Active learning from stream data using optimal weight classifier ensemble. *IEEE Transactions on System, Man, Cybernetics. Part B*, *40*(6), 1607–1621.

About the Contributors

Zaher Al Aghbari received his B.Sc degree from the Florida Institute of Technology, Melbourne, USA, in 1987, and the M.Sc. and Ph.D. degrees in computer science from Kyushu University, Fukuoka, Japan, in 1998 and 2001, respectively. He was with at the Department of Intelligent Systems, Kyushu University, Japan, from 2001 to 2003. From 2003 to 2008, he was with the Computer Science Department, University of Sharjah, UAE. Since 2008 he has been the Chairperson for the Department of Computer Science, University of Sharjah, UAE. His research interests include multimedia databases, data mining, multidimensional indexing, distributed indexing, data streams management, image/video semantic representation and classification, and Arabic handwritten text retrieval.

Reem Al-Mulla received her B.Sc degree in Computer Science from the University of Sharjah, UAE, in 2004, and the M.Sc. degree in Computer Science from University of Sharjah, UAE, in 2010. She has been working as a lecturer in the Department of Computer Science, University of Sharjah, since 2010. Her research interests include databases, data mining and data stream management.

Gennady and Natalia Andrienko received their Master degrees in Computer Science from Kiev State University in 1986 and 1985 and PhD. equivalents in Computer Science from Moscow State University in 1992 and 1993, respectively. They undertook research on knowledge-based systems at the Institute for Mathematics of Moldavian Academy of Sciences (Kishinev, Moldova), then at the Institute for Mathematical Problems of Biology of Russian Academy of Sciences (Pushchino Research Center, Russia). Since 1997, Natalia Andrienko and Gennady Andrienko have research positions at GMD, now Fraunhofer Institute for Intelligent Analysis and Information Systems (IAIS). Since 2007, they are lead scientists of the institute responsible for the visual analytics research. They are co-authors of the monograph 'Exploratory Analysis of Spatial and Temporal Data' (published in December 2005 by Springer), 45 peer-reviewed journal papers, 20 + book chapters and 100 + papers in conference proceedings. They have been involved in numerous international research projects. Their research interests include geovisualisation, information visualisation with a focus on spatial and temporal data, visual analytics, interactive knowledge discovery and data mining, spatial decision support and optimisation. Since 2007, Gennady Andrienko is chairing the ICA Commission on GeoVisualization. He co-organized several scientific events on visual analytics, geovisualisation and visual data mining, and co-edited several special issues of journals and proceedings volumes.

Ahmad Abdollahzadeh Barfourosh is a professor in the Computer Engineering and Information Technology faculty of Amirkabir University of Technology, Tehran, Iran. He received his B.S. degree in accounting from Tehran University, in 1975. He received his M.Sc. degree in computer science from West Coast University, Los Angeles, California, USA, in 1980. He also received his PhD in computer science from University of Bristol, England, in 1990. Dr. Abdollahzadeh served as a visiting professor in department of Computer Science of Maryland University at College Park, USA and Orsay University in Paris, France from 2000-2002. He is an author of a book named "An Introduction to Distributed Artificial Intelligence" that has been published in 2006. His research interests include information retrieval, artificial intelligence techniques, distributed artificial intelligence (DAI), automated negotiation, expert systems, natural language processing (NLP), decision support systems (DSS), business intelligence (BI), data warehousing, data mining and software engineering. His web site can be accessed at http://ceit.aut. ac.ir/islab/Peoples/CE-Dr_abdollahzadeh.html.

Frans Coenen has a general background in AI, and has been working in the field of data mining and Knowledge Discovery in Data (KDD) for the last twelve years. He is particularly interested in: Social Network Mining; Trend Mining; the mining of non-standard data sets such as Graph, Image and document collections; and the practical application of data mining in its many forms. Current applications include the classification of retina image and MRI scan data, and the discovery of trends in cattle movement data. He has some 200 refereed publications on KDD and AI related research, and has been on the programme committees for many KDD events. Frans Coenen is currently a senior lecturer within the Department of Computer Science at the University of Liverpool where he is the director of studies for the department's on-line MSc programmes.

Negin Daneshpour is an assistant professor in the Electrical & Computer Engineering faculty of Shahid Rajaee Teacher Training University, Tehran, Iran. She received her BS degree in computer engineering-hardware from the department of electronics and computer engineering at Shahid Beheshti University, Iran where she graduated summa cum laude in 1999. She received the MS degree and PhD in computer engineering-software from the Department of Computer Engineering and Information Technology at Amirkabir University of Technology, Iran in 2002 and 2010 respectively. Her research interests focuses on data warehousing, specifically, view selection to build data warehouse; data mining; and software engineering. Her web site can be accessed at http://ceit.aut.ac.ir/~daneshpour/.

Li Deren, scientist in photogrammetry and remote sensing, dual membership of both the Chinese Academy of Sciences and the Chinese Academy of Engineering, member of the Euro-Asia International Academy of Science, Professor and PhD supervisor of Wuhan University, Vice-President of the Chinese Society of Geodesy, Photogrmmetry and Cartography, Chairman of the Academic Commission of Wuhan University and the National Laboratory for Information Engineering in Surveying, Mapping and Remote Sensing (LIESMARS). He has concentrated on the research and education in spatial information science and technology represented by remote sensing (RS), global positioning system (GPS) and geographic information system (GIS). His majors are the analytic and digital photogrammetry, remote sensing, mathematical morphology and its application in spatial databases, theories of object-oriented GIS and spatial data mining in GIS as well as mobile mapping systems, etc. Prof. Deren Li served as Comm. III and Comm. VI president of ISPRS in 1988-1992 and 1992-1996, worked for CEOS in 2002-2004 and president of Asia GIS Association in 2003-2006. He got Dr.h.c. from ETH in 2008. In 2010 he has been elected ISPRS fellow.

Gillian Dobbie is a Professor in the Department of Computer Science at The University of Auckland, New Zealand. She received a Ph.D. from the University of Melbourne, an M.Tech.(Hons) and B.Tech.(Hons) in Computer Science from Massey University. She has lectured at Massey University, the University of Melbourne, and Victoria University of Wellington, and held visiting research positions at Griffith University and the National University of Singapore. Her research interests include formal foundations for databases, object oriented databases, semi-structured databases, logic and databases, data warehousing, data mining, access control, e-commerce and data modeling. She has published over 100 international refereed journal and conference papers. More information is available at http://www.cs.auckland.ac.nz/people/profile.php?id=gdob002.

Elias Frentzos, received his Diploma in Civil Engineering and MSc in Geoinformatics, both from NTUA. He also holds a PhD from the Department of Informatics of the University of Piraeus where he is currently a Postdoc researcher, scholar of the Greek State's Scholarships Foundation. He has published more than 20 papers in scientific journals and conferences such as IEEE TKDE, ACM SIGMOD and IEEE ICDE. He has participated in several national and European research projects, and also involved in the development of several commercial GIS-related applications and projects. His research interests include spatial and spatiotemporal databases, location-based services and geographical information systems.

Huirong Fu, Ph.D. is an associate professor at Oakland University, MI, USA. She has been working as an assistant professor at North Dakota State University and as a post-doctoral research associate at Rice University before joining Oakland University. Dr. Fu has been actively conducting research in the area of information security. Her primary research interests are in information assurance and security, networks, Internet data centers, and multimedia system and services.

Yongjian Fu is an Associate Professor in the Electrical and Computer Engineering Department at Cleveland State University, Ohio, USA. He got his Ph.D. in computing science from Simon Fraser University, Canada. His main research interests are data mining and software engineering. Specifically, he is interested in applying data mining techniques in various software engineering activities, from development to testing.

Wenyan Gan, Ph.D., is an associate professor in Nanjing University of Science and Technology in China. Her research interests include data field, complex network, and data mining.

Arnaud Giacometti is Professor of computer science at the Université François Rabelais Tours (France) since 1995, where he is heading the Computer Science Department (since 2006). Since 2009, he is also vice-president for international affairs of University of Tours. His research interests include data mining in relational databases, development of inductive databases, multi-dimensional databases and OLAP, user preference modelling and query personnalisation and recommendation in databases. Arnaud Giacometti received his PhD in Computer Science from Ecole Nationale Suprieure des Tlcommunications of Paris (ENST) in 1989. He has more than 30 publications in referred conferences and journals.

Fosca Giannotti is a senior researcher at the Information Science and Technology Institute of the National Research Council at Pisa, Italy. Her current research interests include data mining query languages, knowledge discovery support environment spatio- temporal data mining, and privacy preserving data mining. In the last two years she started to investigate the interactions among data mining and social network analysis. Thanks to such interest she spent one year visiting (2009-2010) at Barabasi Lab at the Centre of Complex Network of Northeastern University in Boston. She has been the coordinator of various European and National research projects. From 2004 to 2009 she coordinates the FP6- IST project GeoPKDD: Geographic Privacy-aware Knowledge Discovery and Delivery. From 2005 to 2009 she served as project coordinator (Data Mining and Semantic Web) of department ICT of CNR. She has taught classes on databases and data mining at universities in Italy and abroad. She is the author of more than one hundred publications and served in the scientific committee of main Data Mining conferences. In 2004 she co-chaired the European conference on Machine Learning and Knowledge Discovery in Data Bases ECML/PKDD 2004. She is the program co-chair of ICDM 2008, the IEEE Int. Conf. on Data Mining.

Nikos Giatrakos is a PhD Candidate at the Department of Informatics, University of Piraeus (Greece), supervised by Assoc. Professor Yannis Theodoridis. He received his Bachelor of Science degree (2006) in Informatics from the University of Piraeus and his Master of Science degree (2008) in Information Systems from the Athens University of Economics and Business (Greece). He has coauthored 5 conference papers including ACM SIGMOD and IEEE ICDE. His research interests include distributed mining on data streams, mining spatiotemporal streaming data and trajectory warehousing.

Matteo Golfarelli received his PhD for his work on autonomous agents in 1998. Since 2005 he is Associate Professor, teaching Information Systems, Database Systems, and Data Mining. He has published about 70 papers in refereed journals and international conferences in the fields of pattern recognition, mobile robotics, multi-agent systems, and business intelligence that is now his main research field, and he is co-author of a book on data warehouse design. He is co-chair of the MiproBIS Conference and member of the editorial board of the Int. Jour. of Data Mining, Modeling, and Management and of the Int. Jour. of Knowledge-Based Organizations. His current research interests include distributed and semantic data warehouse systems, what-if analysis, and Business Performance Monitoring.

Chong Han was born in Henan Province, China on June, 1985. He received his M. S. degree in major of Computer Science from Henan University, Kaifeng, China in 2010. Now he is a Ph. D. student of Nanjing University of Posts and Telecommunications, China. His research field covers data mining and knowledge discovery.

Xiaohua Hu is currently an associate professor and the founding director of the data mining and bioinformatics lab at the College of Information Science and Technology. He is also an adjunct professor of Henan University. He is the now also serving as the IEEE Computer Society Bioinformatics and Biomedicine Steering Committee Chair. Xiaohua is a scientist, teacher and entrepreneur. He joined Drexel University in 2002, founded the International Journal of Data Mining and Bioinformatics (SCI indexed) in 2006, International Journal of Granular Computing, Rough Sets and Intelligent Systems in 2008. Earlier, he worked as a research scientist in the world-leading R&D centers such as Nortel

Research Center, GTE labs and HP Labs. In 2001, he founded the DMW Software in Silicon Valley, California. His research ideas have been integrated into many commercial products and applications. He has published more than 190 peer-reviewed papers in various journals and conference proceedings.

Vandana Janeja received her PhD and M.B.A in Information technology from Rutgers Business School, Rutgers University in 2007, M.S in Computer Science from the New Jersey Institute of Technology (NJIT) in 2001 and M.S. in Computer Management from Devi Ahilya Vishwa Vidhyalaya, India in 1999. She is currently an Assistant Professor at the Information Systems department at University of Maryland, Baltimore County (UMBC), USA. She also worked as a Research Associate at CIMIC, Rutgers University. Her general area of research is Data Mining with a focus on anomaly detection in traditional and spatial data. She has published in various refereed conferences such as ACM SIGKDD, SIAM Data Mining, IEEE ICDM, National Conference on Digital Government Research, IEEE ISI and journals such as IEEE TKDE, DMKD and IDA. She has served in the program committees of various international conferences, and has also been a reviewer for the leading academic journals and conferences in her field.

Baoqing Jiang was born in Henan Province, China, on November 26, 1964. He received the B. S. degree in Foundation Mathematics from Henan University in 1984, M. S. degree in fuzzy mathematics from Southwest Jiaotong University in 1989, and Ph. D. degree from the School of Information Science & Technology, Southwest Jiaotong University in 2006. He went to department of computer science of Peking university as a visiting scholar from September 1997 to June 1999. He is currently a professor of School of Compute and Information Engineering at Henan University, China. His research interests include Data Mining, Fuzzy logic, and Uncertainty reasoning. He is a member of ACM.

Muhammad Sulaiman Khan has recently joined University of Liverpool, Department of Computer Science, as a Research Associate and working on a project Innovative Manufacturing of complex Ti sheet components. He received his first MSc in Computing from The University of Lahore in 2001, his second MSc in Distributed Systems from Liverpool Hope University in 2006 and a PhD in Computing from the University of Liverpool in 2010 (PhD title: Extending Association Rule Mining). Dr. M. S. Khan has several years of teaching, research and development experience in academia as well as in the industry. He has authored over 15 papers, including conference papers, a book chapter and journal articles. His main areas of research interests include, but are not limited to, Intelligent Systems, Performance of Data Mining Algorithms, Temporal Patterns, Fuzzy Logic (as applied to Data Mining), Pervasive Computing and their applications to medical and industrial data.

Yun Sing Koh is currently a postdoctoral researcher in the Knowledge Management Group at the Department of Computer Science, University of Auckland. She obtained her PhD in Computer Science in University of Otago, New Zealand. From 2007- 2010 she worked as a lecturer at the School of Computing and Mathematical Sciences, Auckland University of Technology. Her current research interests include data mining, machine learning, and information retrieval.

Luca Leonardi is a Ph.D student at the Department of Computer Science of University Ca' Foscari - Venezia (Italy), supervised by prof. Alessandra Raffaetà. In 2006 he got a Bachelor Degree in Computer Science at University Ca' Foscari - Venezia. In 2008 he took his Master Degree in Computer Science at the same university. His research interests include mining spatio-temporal data, trajectory warehousing and visual OLAP analysis.

Albert Levi received B.S., M.S. and Ph.D. degrees in Computer Engineering from Bogazici University, Istanbul, Turkey, in 1991, 1993 and 1999, respectively. He served as a visiting faculty member in the Department of Electrical and Computer Engineering, Oregon State University, OR, between 1999 and 2002. He was also a postdoctoral research associate in the Information Security Lab of the same department. Since 2002, Dr. Levi is a faculty member of Computer Science and Engineering in Sabanci University, Faculty of Engineering and Natural Sciences, Istanbul, Turkey and co-director of the Cryptography and Information Security Group (CISec) at Sabanci University. He has been promoted to associate professor in January 2008. His research interests include computer and network security with emphasis on mobile and wireless system security, public key infrastructures (PKI), privacy, and application layer security protocols. Dr. Levi has served in the program committees of various international conferences. He also served as general chair of SecureComm 2008, technical program co-chair of NTMS 2009, and publicity chair of GameSec 2010. He is editorial board member of The Computer Journal published by Oxford University Press.

David M. Lewis earned a degree in Information Systems Management from the University of Maryland, Baltimore County in 2009 and is currently pursuing a Masters in the same field at Carnegie Mellon University. Between semesters, he has interned in New York City and Silicon Valley. David is currently interested in exploring the applicability of data mining to social media.

Deyi Li, Ph.D., is the founder of cloud model. He is now a professor in Tsinghua University in China, a membership of Chinese Academy of Engineering and a membership of Eurosian Academy of Science. His research interests include networked data mining, artificial intelligence with uncertainty, cloud computing, and cognitive physics. For his contribution, he was awarded many international and national prizes or awards, e.g. the Premium Award by IEE Headquarters, the IFAC World Congress Outstanding Paper Award, National Science and Technology Progress Award and so on.

Meng Liang was born in Henan Province, China. He is a M. S. student of School of Computer and Information Engineering, Henan University, Kaifeng, Henan Province, China. His research field is data mining.

Li Liu has been a Senior Research Assistant in the Centre for Quantum Computation & Intelligent Systems at University of Technology, Sydney (UTS) since 2006. She had been the Research Assistant at UTS from 2002 to 2005 and the Associate Lecturer at Deakin University from 1999 to 2002. She obtained the degree of the Master of Computer Studies in 1998 at the University of New England. Her research interests are databases and data mining. She had published 20 refereed papers in international and national conferences.

Patrick Marcel is assistant professor at the Computer Science Department and the Computer Science Laboratory of Université François Rabelais Tours, since 1999. He received is PhD from INSA Lyon in 1998. He has more than 25 publications in referred conferences and journals. He has been reviewer for several conferences. His research interests include database query languages, On-Line Analytical Processing, Knowledge Discovery in Databases, query personalization and recommendation in databases.

Gerasimos Marketos is a post-doctoral researcher at InfoLab, University of Piraeus (UniPi), Greece. Born in 1981, he received his Bachelor of Science degree (2003) and Ph.D. (2009) in Informatics from University of Piraeus and his Master of Science degree (2004) in Information Systems Engineering from University of Manchester Institute of Science and Technology (UMIST), UK. He has participated in several national and European research projects in the area of data management and data analytics. His research interests include mobility data warehousing and mining, spatiotemporal and scientific databases. He is member of BCS.

Maybin Muyeba received the BSc in Mathematics from University of Zambia, an MSc degree from Hull University, and a PhD in Computing from University of Manchester Institute of Science and Technology in 2001. He joined the University of Bradford as a lecturer in Computing in 2001 and then worked as Software engineer in industry for 2 years. In 2003, he was appointed as senior lecturer in Liverpool, and now works for Manchester Metropolitan University. He has authored over 20 papers, including conferences and journals, and is a program committee member and reviewer of several conferences. His current research interests include fuzzy data mining, mathematical modeling, intelligent systems and their applications to bio and financial data.

M. Asif Naeem is in the final year of his PhD at The University of Auckland, New Zealand. His research topic is "Efficient Joins to Process Stream Data". His supervisors are Prof. Gillian Dobbie and Dr. Gerald Weber. Before that he received the Master from Balochistan University of Information Technology and Management Science, Pakistan in 2006. His Master's thesis title was "Web Structure Mining in Hidden Web Data". Apart from research; Asif has about six years of teaching experience in Public Sector University of Pakistan. His research interests include online stream processing, data management and integration, business intelligence, and web mining. More information is available at http://www.cs.auckland.ac.nz/research/groups/kmg/asif.html.

Mirco Nanni holds a PhD in Computer Science obtained at the University of Pisa in 2001. He is currently a KDDLab researcher at ISTI-CNR. His current research interests are mainly focused on models and algorithms for spatio temporal data mining, and in particular: methods for trajectory clustering; trajectory patterns extraction; modelling of interaction among moving objects and trajectory classification based on interaction patterns. Moreover, his research covered other areas, such as spatio-temporal data anonymity techniques, workflow mining and data mining in business intelligence applications. He was co-chair of the IEEE Workshop on Spatio-Temporal Data Mining (STDM 2007), and served as PC member for several conferences in the data mining, data base and artificial intelligence area, such as ICDM, KDD, PKDD, SIAM DM, VLDB and PODS, as well as reviewer for several journals in the same fields.

Elsa Negre received her PhD for her work on collaborative exploration of datacubes in 2009 from Université François Rabelais Tours (France). Currently, she has a postdoctoral position at the Laboratoire de Recherche sur l'Information Multimédia (Multimedia Information Research Laboratory) of the Université du Québec en Outaouais (Canada). Her research interests are multidimensional databases, data warehousing, OLAP, knowledge discovery in databases, recommendations and personalization. She is the author of articles and papers in national and international conferences on these subjects.

Salvatore Orlando (Laurea/MSc. (summa cum laude,1985) and PhD (1991) in Computer Science, University of Pisa) has been an associate professor of Computer Science at Ca' Foscari University of Venice since August 2000. His research interests include the design of scalable algorithms for various data mining and knowledge discovery problems, distributed and P2P systems for information retrieval, parallel/distributed systems and programming environments. He published over 100 papers in international journals and conference/workshop proceedings. He co-chaired conferences (EuroPVM/MPI, SASO), conference tracks, and workshops. He served on the program committees of international conferences, among which the premier conferences on data mining run by ACM, IEEE, SIAM (KDD, ICDM, SDM), and many others, such as ECML/PKDD, Europar, INFOSCALE, CCGRid, SASO.

Russel Pears (PhD, Cardiff University UK) is a Senior Lecturer and Programme Leader of the Doctoral Programme at the School of Computing and Mathematical Sciences at the Auckland University of Technology, New Zealand. His current research interests are in mining high speed data streams, mining weighted association rules, financial time series modelling and prediction.

Thomas B. Pedersen received his M.S. (2002) and Ph.D. (2006) degrees in Computer Science from the University of Aarhus, Denmark. From 2006 to 2008 he was a postdoctoral fellow at Sabanci University, where he is now a visiting faculty member. His main research interests are cryptographic protocols, security, and privacy.

Dino Pedreschi is a full professor at the Dipartimento di Informatica of the University of Pisa. He has been a visiting scientist and professor at the University of Texas at Austin (1989/90), at CWI Amsterdam (1993) and at UCLA (1995), Northeastern University (2010). His current research interests are in mobility data mining, spatio-temporal data mining, and in privacy-preserving data mining. Recently he received a Google research award for his work on data anonymity. He is spending is sabbatical (209-2010) at Barabasi Lab, Northeastern University in Boston. During this period he is investigating on synergies among data mining and network analysis. He has taught classes on programming languages, databases and data mining in universities in Italy and abroad. He has published more than one hundred articles. He is a member of the program committee of the main international conferences on data mining and database and co-editor several data mining journals. He has been a co-chair of ECML/PKDD 2004, the international conference on Machine Learning and Knowledge Discovery in Databases. He served as the coordinator of the undergraduate studies in Computer Science at the University of Pisa, and as a vice-rector of the same university, with responsibility in teaching affairs. He has been the National coordinator of the project "GeoPKDD.it", Geographic Privacy-aware Knowledge Discovery and Delivery.

Nikos Pelekis is a lecturer at the Department of Statistics and Insurance Science, University of Piraeus. Born in 1975, he received his B.Sc. degree from the Computer Science Department of the University of Crete (1998). He has subsequently joined the Department of Computation in the University of Manchester (former UMIST) to pursue his M.Sc. in Information Systems Engineering (1999) and his Ph.D. in Moving Object Databases (2002). He has been working for almost ten years in the field of data management and data mining. He has co-authored more than 40 research papers and book chapters and he is a reviewer in many international journals and conferences. His research interests include knowledge discovery, data mining, machine learning and spatiotemporal databases.

Alessandra Raffaetà is an assistant professor in the Department of Computer Science of the University Ca' Foscari of Venezia (Italy). She graduated in Computer Science (summa cum laude) in 1994 and she took a PhD in Computer Science in 2000 from the University of Pisa. Her research interests include Data warehouses, GISs, spatio-temporal reasoning, design and formal semantics of programming languages and constraint logic programming. She participated to several national and international research projects and she has published over 40 papers on international journals and conferences. She was co-chair of the workshop Complex Reasoning on Geographical Data (2001) and she was member of the program committee of several international workshops.

David Reid is a Senior Lecturer in the Department of Computer Science at Liverpool Hope University. Having attained his Ph.D. in 1995, researching in the fields of intelligent agent systems and adapted hypertext systems, Dr Reid joined a newly formed group at Liverpool University dedicated to developing and promoting innovative technological solutions for local businesses. After implementing the first electronic 'shopping mall' in the U.K., Dr Reid spent eight years providing technical leadership on many Internet and Intranet projects. These projects usually involved exploiting newly emergent technology. Dr Reid's current research interests are derived from experience gained in both his academic and industrial background; these include distributed, grid and cloud computing, bio-inspired computing, membrane computing, spiking neural networks, evolvable hardware, ultra low power embedded systems and intelligent green computing.

Chiara Renso holds a PhD and M.Sc. degree in Computer Science from University of Pisa (1992, 1997). She is currently a KDDLab member and permanent researcher at ISTI Institute of CNR, Italy. Her research interests are related to spatio-temporal reasoning, data mining query languages, and ontologies. She has been involved in GeoPKDD Project (http://www.geopkdd.eu). She is author of more than 40 publications and has been reviewer for several data mining conferences. She has been co-chair of the ICLP Workshop on Complex Reasoning on Geographical Data (2001) and Spatial, Temporal, and Spatio-temporal Data Mining (SSTDM'08) in conjunction IEEE ICDM 2008. She also served as Local Organizer Chair for IEEE International Conference on Data Mining 2008. She has been co-chair of the First and the Second International Workshop on Semantic Aspects of Data Mining (2008 and 2009) in conjunction with IEEE ICDM conference. She is co-editor for the special issue of KAIS journal (Knowledge And Information System edited by Springer) on Context-aware data mining.

Stefano Rizzi received his PhD in 1996 from the University of Bologna, Italy. Since 2005 he is Full Professor at the University of Bologna, where he is the head of the Data Warehousing Laboratory and teaches Business Intelligence and Software Engineering. He has published about 100 papers in refereed journals and international conferences mainly in the fields of data warehousing, pattern recognition, and mobile robotics, and a research book on data warehouse design. He joined several research projects on the above areas and has been involved in the PANDA thematic network of the European Union concerning pattern-base management systems. He is member of the steering committee of DOLAP. His current research interests include data warehouse design and business intelligence, in particular multidimensional modeling, OLAP preferences, and what-if analysis.

Alessandro Roncato is an assistant professor in the Department of Computer Science of the University Ca' Foscari of Venezia (Italy). He graduated (summa cum laude) in Computer Science in 1989, from the University of Udine, and he took a PhD in Computer Science from the University of Pisa in 1995. His main research interests include distributed computing, spatio-temporal Data Warehouses and data mining. He is currently working on the implementation of a data warehouse for trajectories of moving objects and on the design of adequate visual OLAP operations.

Erkay Savas received the BS (1990) and MS (1994) degrees in electrical engineering from the Electronics and Communications Engineering Department at Istanbul Technical University. He completed the Ph.D. degree in the Department of Electrical and Computer Engineering (ECE) at Oregon State University in June 2000. He had worked for various companies and research institutions before he joined Sabanci University as an assistant professor in 2002. He is the director of the Cryptography and Information Security Group (CISec) of Sabanci University. His research interests include cryptography, data and communication security, privacy in biometrics, trusted computing, security and privacy in data mining applications, embedded systems security, and distributed systems. He is a member of IEEE, ACM, the IEEE Computer Society, and the International Association of Cryptologic Research (IACR).

Yucel Saygin is a faculty member at Sabanci University, Faculty of Engineering and Natural Sciences in Turkey. He received his B.S. and M.S. degrees from the Department of Computer Engineering at Bilkent University in 1994, and 1996 respectively. His main research interests include data mining, and application of data mining technology to database management systems. He has done extensive research on privacy preserving data mining in specific which were published in international journals and conferences. He is the coordinator of the EU project MODAP (Mobility, Data Mining, and Privacy).

Yong Shi received the Ph.D. degree in management science from the University of Kansas, USA. He is the Executive Deputy Director of the Fictitious Economy and Data Science (FEDS) Research Center, Chinese Academy of Sciences, Beijing, China. Since 1999, he has been the Charles W. and Margre H. Durham Distinguished Professor of information technology with the College of Information Science and Technology, Peter Kiewit Institute, University of Nebraska, Omaha, NE. He has published more than 15 books, over 150 papers in various journals, and numerous conferences/proceedings papers. He is the Editor-in-Chief of the *International Journal of Information Technology and Decision Making* and a member of Editorial Board for a number of academic journals. He has consulted or worked on business projects for a number of international companies in data mining and knowledge management. His research interests include business intelligence, data mining, and multiple criteria decision making. Dr.

Shi has received a number of distinguished awards including the Georg Cantor Award of the International Society on Multiple Criteria Decision Making in 2009, the Outstanding Young Scientist Award, the National Natural Science Foundation of China in 2001, and the Speaker of Distinguished Visitors Program (DVP) for 1997–2000 from the IEEE Computer Society.

Claudio Silvestri received the Laurea cum laude in Computer Science from the University Ca' Foscari Venezia (Italy), and the Ph.D. in Computer Science from the same University. He is currently a Research Fellow at Istituto di Scienza e Tecnologie dell'Informazione – Consiglio Nazionale delle Ricerche, and was formely a Research Fellow at the Universities of Milan and Venice. He has partecipated several Italian and European research projects in the area of mobility data management and analytics. His research focuses on security and privacy in mobile computing, spatio-temporal data warehouses, and data mining algorithms.

Jingjing Song was born in Henan Province, China on February 12, 1980. She received her M. S. degree from Henan University, Kaifeng, China in 2007. Now she is a Lecturer of Web and Information Center, Qingyuan Polytechnic, Qingyuan, Guangdong Province, China. Her research field is data mining.

Arnaud Soulet is assistant professor in computer science at Computer Science Laboratory of University François Rabelais Tours since 2007. He received his PhD in 2006 from the University of Caen, France. His research interests include On-Line Analytical Processing, data mining and machine learning.

DongHong Sun received the Ph.D. degree in computer science. She is currently an Assistant Professor with the Network Research Center of Tsinghua University, Beijing, China. Her research interests include information filtering, network and information security.

Hissam Tawfik is an Associate Professor of Computer Science at Liverpool Hope University (UK). Hissam holds an MSc and PhD in Computer Engineering from UMIST (University of Manchester), and an established research track in the areas of Biologically Inspired Systems, User-centred E-Health and Applied Modelling and Simulation. Dr. Tawfik is the leader of the Intelligent and Distributed Systems (IDS) Group at Liverpool Hope University serves on various editorial boards and review committees for International journals and conferences and is a Conference Chair and Organiser of the International Conference Series on Developments in eSystems Engineering DESE.

Roberto Trasarti holds a M.Sc. degree in Computer Science from University of Pisa (2006). He started the PhD in Computer Science at the School for Graduate Studies "Galileo Galilei", University of Pisa in November 2006 and he is currently a KDDLab member at ISTI Institute of CNR, Italy. His research interests are related to spatio-temporal data mining, reasoning, data mining query languages. He has been involved in GeoPKDD Project (http://www.geopkdd.eu). He is author and reviewer in some of the major data mining conferences.

Shuliang Wang, Ph.D., is a professor in Wuhan University in China, and a visiting professor in the University of Pittsburgh in USA. His research interests include spatial data mining, software engineering, and service science. For his innovatory study of view-angle of spatial data mining, he was awarded one of the best national thesis.

Gerald Weber is Senior Lecturer in the Department of Computer Science at The University of Auckland. He joined The University of Auckland in 2003. Gerald holds a PhD from the FU Berlin. He is information director of the Proceedings of the VLDB Endowment, and he has been program chair of several conferences. He is co-author of the book "Form-Oriented Analysis", and of over 40 peer-reviewed publications. His research interests include Databases and Data Models, Human-Computer Interaction and Theory of Computation.

Qing Wei was born in Henan Province, China, on November 21, 1977. He received his M. S. degree in major from Henan University, Kaifeng, China in 2006. Now he is a Lecturer of School of Computer and Information Engineering, Henan University of Economics and Law, Zhengzhou, China. His research fields include data mining and streaming media.

Can Yildizli is currently an M.S. student in Computer Science program at Sabanci University. He received his B.S. degree in 2009 in Computer Science from Sabanci University. He works in the field of computer security. His research interests include information security, malicious software, reverse engineering cryptography and covert channels.

Peng Zhang received the Ph.D. degree in computer science from the Graduate University of the Chinese Academy of Sciences, Beijing, China, in 2009. He is currently an Assistant Professor with the Institute of Computing Technology, Chinese Academy of Sciences, Beijing, China. His research interests include data stream mining, information filtering, and information security.

Xingquan Zhu received the Ph.D. degree in computer science from Fudan University, Shanghai, China, in 2001. His research mainly focuses on data mining, machine learning, and multimedia systems. Since 2000, he has published more than 100 referred journal and conference proceeding papers. Dr. Zhu has been an Associate Editor of the IEEE Trans. on Knowledge and Data Engineering (TKDE) since 2009 and is a Program Committee Co-chair for the 9th International Conference on Machine Learning and Applications (ICMLA 2010).

Ye Zhu received the PhD degree from the Electrical and Computer Engineering Department at Texas A&M University. He was a research assistant in the NetCamo research group during the graduate study. He is currently an assistant professor in the Department of Electrical and Computer Engineering at Cleveland State University. His current research interests include privacy-perserving data mining, network security, and traffic engineering.

Index